Canada First, Not Canada Alone

Canada First, Not Canada Alone

A History of Canadian Foreign Policy

ADAM CHAPNICK AND ASA McKERCHER

OXFORD
UNIVERSITY PRESS

Oxford University Press is a department of the University of Oxford.
It furthers the University's objective of excellence in research, scholarship,
and education by publishing worldwide. Oxford is a registered trade mark of
Oxford University Press in the UK and in certain other countries.

Published in the United States of America by Oxford University Press
198 Madison Avenue, New York, NY 10016, United States of America.

© Oxford University Press 2024

All rights reserved. No part of this publication may be reproduced,
stored in a retrieval system, or transmitted, in any form or by any means,
without the prior permission in writing of Oxford University Press,
or as expressly permitted by law, by license, or under terms agreed with
the appropriate reprographics rights organization. Inquiries concerning
reproduction outside the scope of the above should be sent to
the Rights Department, Oxford University Press, at the address above.

You must not circulate this work in any other form
and you must impose this same condition on any acquirer

Library of Congress Cataloging-in-Publication Data
Names: Chapnick, Adam, 1976– author. | McKercher, Asa, author.
Title: Canada first, not Canada alone : a history of Canadian foreign
policy / Adam Chapnick and Asa McKercher.
Other titles: History of Canadian foreign policy
Description: New York, NY : Oxford University Press, [2024] | Includes
bibliographical references and index.
Identifiers: LCCN 2024013760 | ISBN 9780197653715 (paperback ; acid-free paper) |
ISBN 9780197653739 (epub)
Subjects: LCSH: Canada—Foreign relations—1945–
Classification: LCC F1034.2 .C45 2024 | DDC 327.71—dc23/eng/20240621
LC record available at https://lccn.loc.gov/2024013760

DOI: 10.1093/oso/9780197653715.001.0001

Printed in Canada by Marquis

To Elva McGaughey, Mike Gendron, and Norman Hillmer

Contents

Acknowledgments	ix
Introduction	1
1. Ideas and Antecedents	9
2. William Lyon Mackenzie King and the Evolution of Canada's Global Posture, 1935–1948	35
Case Studies	45
3. Louis St Laurent and the Expansion of the Canadian Foreign Policy Realm, 1948–1957	59
Case Studies	67
4. John Diefenbaker and the Politics of Foreign Policy Decision Making, 1957–1963	84
Case Studies	91
5. Lester B. Pearson and the Domestic Implications of Canadian Foreign Policy, 1963–1968	106
Case Studies	111
6. Pierre Elliott Trudeau and the Re-Imagination of "Canada First," 1968–1984	124
Case Studies	134
7. Brian Mulroney and the Transformation of Canadian International Affairs, 1984–1993	151
Case Studies	158
8. Jean Chrétien, Frugality, and Boldness, 1993–2001	173
Case Studies	182
9. Jean Chrétien, Paul Martin, and the Aftermath of 9/11, 2001–2006	198
Case Studies	205
10. Stephen Harper's Conservative Values on the World Stage, 2006–2015	220
Case Studies	228

viii CONTENTS

11. Justin Trudeau and an Increasingly Dangerous World, 2015–   243
    Case Studies   250

    Conclusion: Canada First in the Future   267

Endnotes   273
Index   325

Acknowledgments

Our friend and colleague Matthew Hayday introduced us to what was then a new series at Oxford University Press Canada and encouraged us to write this book. Elizabeth Ferguson and then Mariah Fleetham were involved editorially as we began to research and write. When the book moved to Oxford's USA office, Susan Ferber kindly took over editorial responsibility, and her keen eye made our prose infinitely stronger. Oxford's production team, including Nathalie Jasper, Saraswathi Ethiraju, Susan Bindernagel, and Heather Macdougall has been a pleasure to work with.

Clint Barker, Agradip Dutta, Isaac Lo, Elizabeth McNeely, and Alexandra Southgate provided outstanding research assistance. David Webster and the late Greg Donaghy read parts of the manuscript and provided us access to their own unpublished research. Global Affairs Canada's Colleen Durkee and Janice Cavell tracked down some hard-to-find statistics. Catherine Boucher, Kerry Buck, Holly King, and Marie Legault helped identify practitioners who could speak to their personal foreign policy experiences. The staff in the Canadian Forces College's Information Resource Centre, especially Alexandra Gabauer, MacKenzie Gott, and Cathy Murphy, were their usual, reliable selves.

The academic/practitioner Canadian foreign policy community is small but incredibly generous and supportive. Lloyd Axworthy, Donald Barry, David Black, Raymond Blake, Mike Blanchfield, Robert Bothwell, Duane Bratt, Jill Campbell-Miller, Mike Carroll, John Cochrane, Laura Dawson, Mark Eaton, John English, Robin Gendron, Richard Goette, Mary Halloran, Kathryn Harrison, Peter Henshaw, Norman Hillmer, Joseph Jockel, Thomas Juneau, Brendan Kelly, Veronica Kitchen, Bohdan Kordan, Adam Lajeunesse, Andrea Lane, Sheryl Lightfoot, Joanne Lostracco, Laura Macdonald, Daniel MacFarlane, Laura Madokoro, Michaek Manulak, Don Munton, Kim Richard Nossal, Galen Perras, Krenare Recaj, Gaëlle Rivard-Piché, Colin Robertson, Tim Sayle, Nassisse Solomon, Matthew Willis, and Paul Wilson all provided feedback on parts of the manuscript. We could not have completed it without them. Eight anonymous peer reviewers also read three early chapters and six read the whole manuscript. We are grateful for their detailed comments and suggestions.

We also thank our families for their patience and support.

This book is dedicated to our greatest teachers: Elva McGaughey, Mike Gendron, and Norman Hillmer.

Introduction

What was Canada to do: step up or slink away? On 3 October 1935, under the direction of fascist leader Benito Mussolini, the Italian military invaded Abyssinia (Ethiopia). Italy, Abyssinia, and Canada were all members of the League of Nations, an international security organization formed in the aftermath of the First World War that prohibited such aggression. The future of collective security was at stake. The League had to respond, and all of its representatives in Geneva wrote home for advice. Canada's top foreign policy official, O.D. Skelton, instructed the Canadian delegation to abstain on any resolution declaring Italy an aggressor unless Prime Minister R.B. Bennett himself indicated otherwise. Canada was in the midst of a federal election, and Skelton thought it unwise to commit any future government to actions that might have concrete political, economic, or military consequences. The Canadians in Geneva were furious. They had already condemned Mussolini's disregard for international peace and security. The entire Assembly, save for a few Italian client states, was going to declare Italy an aggressor.[1] Canada would be left isolated and humiliated. Much to Skelton's chagrin, they used a personal connection to reach Bennett directly and received permission to use their best judgment at the upcoming meetings. When it was his turn to speak, Canada's advisory officer Walter Riddell condemned the invasion and volunteered to join a subcommittee considering economic sanctions.[2]

William Lyon Mackenzie King's Liberals defeated the Bennett Conservatives in the election of 14 October. At the first Cabinet discussion of the situation in Africa the following week, King's senior minister from Quebec, Ernest Lapointe, threatened to resign if Ottawa ever agreed to military sanctions against Italy. "No interest in Ethiopia, of any nature whatsoever, is worth the life of a single Canadian citizen," he had said earlier.[3] King instructed Riddell to explain that Canada remained "prepared to cooperate fully" with its fellow League members so as not to compromise the delegation's stated position, but to make no further commitments.[4] Yet Riddell continued to advocate aggressive sanctions. Not doing so, he rationalized, would mean weakening the sanctions regime, and his government had pledged to maintain its previous stance.[5]

The reprimand from Ottawa was swift: "You must of course realize that you are acting for the Government of Canada and not for any other government, delegation or committee," King wrote. "You should not take action on any

Canada First, Not Canada Alone: A History of Canadian Foreign Policy. Adam Chapnick and Asa McKercher, Oxford University Press. © Oxford University Press 2024. DOI: 10.1093/oso/9780197653715.003.0001

question of importance such as those recently considered without definite and positive instructions."[6] King hoped that Riddell's initiative would be forgotten. Instead, "the Canadian proposal" drew extensive international coverage. Media reports at home were at best lukewarm but downright hostile in Quebec. By the end of November, Lapointe, as well as King, deemed the situation intolerable. The government had never conceived of nor supported the politically unpopular policy with which it was being so publicly credited. A 2 December press release disavowed responsibility for Riddell's initiative and accused the public servant of acting independently of his government.[7]

A week later, British and French League representatives conceded much of Abyssinia to Mussolini. In July 1936, the League abandoned the sanctions regime. By then, Italy's invasion was complete, and the Nazi government in Germany had launched a similar occupation of the Rhineland, a blatant violation of the peace agreement enacted at the end of the First World War. The international situation appeared increasingly fraught.

King represented Canada personally at the next League Assembly, emphasizing his country's faith in the organization's principles but also its unwillingness to commit to collective security in practice. "I believe that Canada's first duty to the league [sic] and to the British empire, with respect to all the great issues that come up," he later told the House of Commons, "is, if possible, to keep this country united."[8] In his memoirs, the former diplomat and Prime Minister Lester Pearson was less certain. "My own view," he wrote, "is the failure in 1935 of the members of the League of Nations, including Canada, to stand up to a single aggressor, had much to do with the world war in 1939."[9]

The extent of Canada's obligation to contribute to the maintenance of international peace and security is one of the key themes in this book. In 1935, King argued that, even in questions of foreign policy, "our own domestic situation must be considered first."[10] The Second World War altered Canada's circumstances. Before King retired in 1948, Ottawa had completed a mutual defence agreement with the United States, become a founding member of the United Nations (UN), and was in the final stages of helping establish the North Atlantic Treaty Organization (NATO). "Canada first, not Canada alone" was how one of the leading diplomats of the early postwar period explained it.[11] According to Assistant Undersecretary of State for External Affairs John Holmes, Canada had national interests that could no longer be preserved and advanced through a policy that was detached from the goings-on around the world. "Free and friendly collaboration, based upon a due regard for the rights and the responsibility of others," benefited both the state and its people.[12]

Holmes's view persists. Canada is a sovereign state within an international system legitimized, however imperfectly, by the League of Nations' successor organization, the UN. Although non-state actors can influence the global

Figure I.1 "After you my dear Alphonse—" *Vancouver Sun*, 4 December 1935. On 3 October 1935, League of Nations member Italy brazenly attacked fellow League member Ethiopia (sometimes known as Abyssinia). Initially, and much to the chagrin of Undersecretary of State for External Affairs O.D. Skelton, the Canadian delegation to the League in Geneva condemned the attack. But when the Mackenzie King–led Liberals replaced R.B. Bennett's Conservatives in government, Canada's League representatives were ordered to be more cautious. Diplomat Walter Riddell pushed ahead anyway. When King learned that a sanctions proposal had become associated with Canadian leadership, he was furious and issued a press release disavowing Riddell's action. This editorial cartoon, published two days after the press release, refers to a situation in which two individuals are too polite to go first. Fittingly, in this instance, a lack of leadership in Geneva ultimately caused the sanctions regime to fail. Italy soon conquered much of Ethiopia.

agenda, efforts to mitigate climate change, to end massive violations of human rights, and to promote disarmament, among other initiatives discussed in this book, still rely on the leadership and co-operation of states and their governments. Cross-border problems like pandemics and money laundering are also easiest to manage when states cooperate. Successful activists, civil society organizations, and other transnational groups often gear their strategies toward shaping state behaviour.

4　CANADA FIRST, NOT CANADA ALONE

To survive and flourish, Canada needs policies that keep the state and its people secure within a stable international system, economically prosperous, politically autonomous, and united at home. A good international reputation is less vital, but still helpful.[13] Ottawa's pursuit of these national interests on the world stage, its practice of foreign policy, is shaped by a series of enduring features.[14] The first is geography, including its physical, human, and geopolitical elements. Canada stretches over nearly ten million square kilometres, making it the second-largest country in the world. It has the longest coastline in the world (243,000 kilometres) and is surrounded by water (or ice) to the north, east, and west. To the south is a nearly 6400-kilometre border with the United States. Natural resources are plentiful, but they are not distributed evenly across the land. The combination of the country's large size and its low population density makes a reliance on foreign trade inevitable. As one writer put it: "Canada is built on the assumption that other people can and will buy [its] staple products."[15] Geography makes the United States an obvious customer but, to avoid utter dependence, Ottawa must also nurture broader global relationships.

The diversity of Canada's relatively small population facilitates such connections. Hundreds of Indigenous nations have lived on the land since time immemorial. British and French settlers, speaking different languages and practising different religions, arrived in the 1500s and 1600s. Since then, immigration has largely continued unabated, with the number and diversity of sending countries gradually increasing. Today, Canadians speak over 200 languages at home, as well as when they connect with their extended families and broader networks around the world. Such a diverse population and worldwide linkages make active engagement internationally a necessity.

Since the Second World War, the United States has been Canada's primary geopolitical ally, making it all but impossible for Canadian governments to separate national and continental security.[16] Fortunately, Canada's long-standing liberal-democratic tradition leaves it with much in common with its southern neighbour. Canadians and Americans have used force in conflicts ranging from world wars, to regional hostilities, to peacekeeping operations. The history of negotiation and compromise that has shaped the evolution of their relationship has informed the Canadian penchant for mediation on the world stage.

The division of powers and responsibilities between the central government and the provinces is also critical to Canada's global posture. In the late nineteenth and early twentieth centuries, British Columbians' overtly and aggressively racist attitudes toward immigration risked compromising Ottawa's relationships within the British Empire. Throughout the two world wars, Quebecers diverged sharply from other Canadians in their rejection of compulsory military service, or conscription, overseas. More recently, provincial and regional priorities in Alberta and elsewhere have informed the federal approach to international trade and environmental reform. The provinces themselves often seek to develop their own links abroad, sometimes raising concerns in Ottawa.

Taken together, Canada's demography, geography, liberal democratic traditions, and federal system limit the state's capacity for long-term strategic foreign policy planning.[17] In 2003, a collection of historians, political scientists, and policy practitioners explained it well: "Especially for the smaller powers, the conduct of foreign policy is to some extent unavoidably reactive. For those that are securely placed and richly endowed, like Canada, the messes they confront are usually not of their own making, and the pressures they face are largely beyond their control."[18] It is not that Ottawa can never exert global leadership—there are notable examples to the contrary—but such efforts are exceptional.

Canadian foreign policy has always been an exercise in balancing competing practical, idealistic, and political priorities. How can Ottawa promote freer trade while trying to protect Canadian businesses from foreign competition? How can it justify the provision of humanitarian aid to faraway countries in the face of unacceptable levels of poverty at home? How can it demonstrate global leadership without compromising national interests that could be more easily preserved through diplomatic subtlety and moderation? To answer these questions, foreign policy decision makers view the world through a variety of political lenses: global, continental, national, governmental, and bureaucratic.[19] Today, they consider issues like race, religion, gender, and Indigeneity as critical factors in an evolving strategic landscape.[20] They negotiate and they compromise, doing what is necessary to maintain credibility at home and overseas. As John Holmes often said, diplomacy inevitably involves "the recognition of contradiction and the acceptance of paradox."[21]

This book begins by presenting a series of controversial statements about the history and practice of British North America's, and then Canada's, foreign relations from the eighteenth century through to 1935. In doing so, it introduces sub-themes that resonate throughout the rest of the text. The ten chronological chapters that follow are divided, roughly, by the governments of individual prime ministers. As leaders, prime ministers have a unique responsibility for foreign policy.[22] The chapters focus on case studies—presenting particular decisions faced by Canada's political leadership at specific moments in time—while taking into account the internal and external factors that shaped their thinking. In addition to laying out these competing factors, the chapters examine the implications of Canadian action, and inaction, domestically and abroad. They consider not just the elements that shaped Ottawa's international posture, but also those that were consciously—and subconsciously—silenced, excluded, and ignored. A "Beyond the Book" section at the end of each chapter offers the beginnings of an additional case to be further explored through the recommended readings. The case studies are supplemented by primary source evidence on the book's website.

6 CANADA FIRST, NOT CANADA ALONE

Canadian foreign policy is complex, messy, and rarely fully satisfying. Decision makers act without the benefit of hindsight, frequently under political pressure and short time frames.[23] When they fail, the consequences of their actions are obvious. Their successes can be harder to measure, leading some to view the practice of diplomacy as elitist, exclusive, and ineffective. At times it might be, but that does not detract from its importance to Canada's viability as an independent, prosperous country. The story of Canada's statecraft that follows therefore deserves our attention and understanding.

Readings

The first comprehensive account of the Ethiopian crisis is Walter Alexander Riddell's memoir *World Security by Conference* (Toronto: Ryerson Press, 1947). Lester Pearson's memoirs portray the situation similarly: Lester B. Pearson, *Mike: The Memoirs of the Right Honourable Lester B. Pearson*, vol. 1, *1897–1948* (Toronto: University of Toronto Press, 1972). The most thorough analyses are Robert Bothwell and John English, "'Dirty work at the crossroads': New perspectives on the Riddell incident," *Historical Papers* 7, no. 1 (1972): 263–85, https://doi.org/10.7202/030752ar; Brock Millman, "Canada, Sanctions, and the Abyssinian Crisis of 1935," *Historical Journal* 40, no. 1 (1997): 143–68, https://doi.org/10.1017/S0018246X96006887; and Roy MacLaren, *Mackenzie King in the Age of the Dictators: Canada's Imperial and Foreign Policies* (Montreal: McGill-Queen's University Press, 2019), 82–152. For a view from Quebec, see John MacFarlane, *Ernest Lapointe and Quebec's Influence on Canadian Foreign Policy* (Toronto: University of Toronto Press, 1999), and Lita-Rose Betcherman, *Ernest Lapointe, Mackenzie King's Great Quebec Lieutenant* (Toronto: University of Toronto Press, 2002). On Skelton, see Norman Hillmer, *O.D. Skelton: A Portrait of Canadian Ambition* (Toronto: University of Toronto Press, 2015) and Hillmer, *O.D. Skelton: The Work of the World* (Montreal: McGill-Queen's University Press, 2013).

Previous Canadian foreign policy overviews include, from the perspective of political science, R.A. MacKay and E.B. Rogers, *Canada Looks Abroad* (London: Oxford University Press, 1938); F.R. Scott, *Canada Today: A Study of the National Interest and National Policy* (London: Oxford University Press, 1938); James Eayrs, *The Art of the Possible: Government and Foreign Policy in Canada* (Toronto: University of Toronto Press, 1961); R. Barry Farrell, *The Making of Canadian Foreign Policy* (Scarborough: Prentice Hall, 1969); Andrew F. Cooper, *Canadian Foreign Policy: Old Habits and New Directions* (Scarborough: Prentice Hall, 1997); Kim Richard Nossal, Stéphane Roussel, and Stéphane Paquin, *The Politics of Canadian Foreign Policy*, 4th ed.

(Kingston: McGill-Queen's University Press, 2015); and Nossal, Roussel, and Paquin, *Politique internationale et défense au Canada et au Québec, deuxième edition enriche et mis à jour*. (Montreal: Les Presses de l'Université de Montréal, 2023). For the multilateral context, see Tom Keating, *Canada and World Order: The Multilateralist Tradition in Canadian Foreign Policy*, 3rd ed. (Don Mills: Oxford University Press, 2013). From an international relations theory point of view, see John Kirton, *Canada in a Changing World* (Toronto: Thomson Nelson, 2007). From the point of view of strategic decision-making, see Brian W. Tomlin, Norman Hillmer, and Fen Osler Hampson, *Canada's International Policies: Agendas, Alternatives, and Politics* (Don Mills: Oxford University Press, 2008). For a public administration lens, see H. Gordon Skilling, *Canadian Representation Abroad: From Agency to Embassy* (Toronto: Ryerson Press, 1945); John Hilliker, *Canada's Department of External Affairs*, vol. 1, *The Early Years, 1909–1946* (Montreal: McGill-Queen's University Press, 1990); Hilliker and Donald Barry, *Canada's Department of External Affairs*, vol. 2, *Coming of Age, 1946–1968* (Montreal: McGill-Queen's University Press, 1995); and Hilliker, Mary Halloran, and Greg Donaghy, *Canada's Department of External Affairs*, vol. 3, *Innovation and Adaptation, 1968–1984* (Toronto: University of Toronto Press, 2017). Narrative histories include G.P. de T. Glazebrook, *A History of Canadian External Relations* (London: Oxford University Press, 1950); C.P. Stacey, *Canada and the Age of Conflict*, 2 vols. (Toronto: University of Toronto Press, 1977, 1981); Robert Bothwell, *Alliance and Illusion: Canada and the World, 1945–84* (Vancouver: University of British Columbia Press, 2007); Norman Hillmer and J.L. Granatstein, *Empire to Umpire: Canada and the World into the 21st Century*, 2nd ed. (Toronto: Nelson Canada, 2007); Asa McKercher, *Canada and the World since 1867* (London: Bloomsbury, 2019); and Patrice Dutil, ed., *Statesmen, Strategists, and Diplomats: Canada's Prime Ministers and the Making of Foreign Policy* (Vancouver: UBC Press, 2023). The only previous collection of historical case studies is Don Munton and John Kirton, *Canadian Foreign Policy: Selected Cases* (Scarborough: Prentice Hall, 1992).

The most comprehensive bibliography of the field of Canadian foreign policy that draws equally from the scholarship of history and political science is Adam Chapnick and Jean-Christophe Boucher, "Canadian foreign policy," in Sandy Maisel, ed., *Oxford Bibliographies in Political Science* (New York: Oxford University Press, 2021), https://doi.org/10.1093/OBO/9780199756223-0175. David Carment and Brandon Jamieson, "Canadian foreign policy," in Patrick James, ed., *Oxford Bibliographies in International Relations* (New York: Oxford University Press, 2020), https://doi.org/10.1093/OBO/9780199743292-0280 focuses almost exclusively on the latter. An earlier attempt to bring historians and political scientists together to support the teaching of Canadian foreign policy is Brian Bow and Adam Chapnick,

8 CANADA FIRST, NOT CANADA ALONE

"Teaching Canada-US relations: Three great debates," *International Journal* 71, no. 2 (2016): 291–312, https://doi.org/10.1177/0020702016641710. Asa McKercher and Philip van Huizen provide a historiographical overview of debates over new directions in the history of Canada in the world in their introduction to *Undiplomatic History: Rethinking Canada in the World* (Montreal: McGill-Queen's University Press, 2019). Students interested in more critical approaches to the study of Canadian foreign policy should consult Karen Dubinsky, Sean Mills, and Scott Rutherford, *Canada and the Third World: Overlapping Histories* (Toronto: University of Toronto Press, 2016). Finally, historians and political scientists offer the most recent state of the field analyses in Brian Bow and Andrea Lane, eds., *Canadian Foreign Policy: Reflections on a Field in Transition* (Vancouver: UBC Press, 2020).

Official and semi-official Canadian foreign policy statements include Louis St Laurent, *The Foundations of Canadian Policy in World Affairs* (Toronto: University of Toronto Press, 1947); Lester B. Pearson, *Words & Occasions* (Toronto: University of Toronto Press, 1970), 67–76; Canada, Department of External Affairs, *Foreign Policy for Canadians* (Ottawa: DEA, 1970), https://gac.canadiana.ca/view/ooe.b1603784E/1; *Competitiveness and Security: Directions for Canada's International Relations* (Ottawa: Minister of Supply and Services Canada, 1985), https://gac.canadiana.ca/view/ooe.b1955366E/1; *Canada in the World* (Ottawa: Public Works and Government Services Canada, 1995), https://gac.canadiana.ca/view/ooe.b2644952E/1; *A Role of Pride and Influence in the World*, 5 vols. (Ottawa: Department of Foreign Affairs and International Trade, 2005), https://gac.canadiana.ca/view/ooe.b3735102E/1; and Address by Minister Freeland on Canada's foreign policy priorities, 6 June 2017, https://www.canada.ca/en/global-affairs/news/2017/06/address_by_ministerfreelandoncanadasforeign-policypriorities.html. There was also an unspectacular "dialogue on foreign policy" in 2003: Department of Foreign Affairs and International Trade, *A Dialogue on Foreign Policy* (Minister of Foreign Affairs, 2003), https://publications.gc.ca/Collection/E2-481-2002E.pdf.

1

Ideas and Antecedents

Introduction

There is no obvious starting point to the history of Canadian diplomatic engagement in the world. Although elements of today's Canada existed well before Confederation in 1867, at the time, there was no Canadian state. Indigenous peoples in what became Canada certainly conducted nation-to-nation diplomacy, but they did so outside of any formalized system of international order. Nor did Confederation make Canada an independent actor on the world stage. Indeed, some might argue that Canada was not fully independent until it acquired the right to amend its own constitution in 1982. This book begins with the Seven Years' War (1756–63), because its ramifications have shaped Canada's foreign policy posture ever since.

Borders are critical to the study of Canadian Foreign Policy

By the mid-eighteenth century, France and Britain had established colonies along the eastern half of North America, dispossessing the Indigenous peoples who had lived on the land since time immemorial. The French claimed much of the territory north of the Great Lakes and St Lawrence River and west of the Mississippi River. They formed alliances with Indigenous fur traders to maintain control of what became known as New France. The British population was focused in what is now Nova Scotia and Newfoundland as well as across the eastern seaboard of the present-day United States, where colonists used slave labour to establish lucrative cash crops. As the land-hungry settlers looked to move further westward in the summer of 1754, a series of skirmishes ballooned into full-blown war.

After a difficult start, the British mounted a major naval campaign and invaded New France. In September 1759, British forces under General James Wolfe captured the colonial capital of Quebec. The following spring, the French surrendered Montreal and, with it, their hopes of a military victory in North America. The 1763 Treaty of Paris saw the French exchange New France for several captured Caribbean colonies.[1] French-speaking Catholic settlers were left largely on their own. Their loyalty to France was shattered.

Canada First, Not Canada Alone: A History of Canadian Foreign Policy. Adam Chapnick and Asa McKercher, Oxford University Press. © Oxford University Press 2024. DOI: 10.1093/oso/9780197653715.003.0002

Within months of the end of the war, a coalition of Indigenous nations and former French allies in the Great Lakes region led by the Odawa leader Obwandiyag (Pontiac) took up arms against the British.[2] Ultimately, London sought a political solution. King George III's Royal Proclamation of 1763 established a border along the Appalachian Mountains separating Britain's North American colonies from a so-called Indian Reserve, a huge expanse of territory in the centre of North America. (The Hudson's Bay Company's territory of Rupert's Land was explicitly exempted.) The proclamation forbade settlement within the reserve without special permission and mandated that Indigenous land sales be transacted through the Crown. The goal was to ensure that further colonial expansion was orderly. British authorities would conclude treaties with Indigenous peoples to pave the way for settlement. The proclamation served as "the foundation of Britain's treaty-making policy."[3] It also recognized the sovereignty of the Indigenous peoples in the region and has since formed the basis of Indigenous land claims.

National unity—traditionally considered a bedrock principle of an effective Canadian foreign policy—is a loaded term

Many North American settlers took offence at limitations on their capacity to expand the frontier inherent in the Royal Proclamation and refused to abide by its provisions. British efforts to assimilate Quebec's Catholic, French-speaking *Canadien* majority were similarly unsuccessful. When the government in London implemented a series of taxes upon the peoples of North America unilaterally (allegedly to offset the debts incurred on their behalf during the Seven Years' War), violent anti-colonial protests broke out across the continent. In 1774, in response to the growing threat of armed insurrection, the British Parliament passed the Quebec Act. The act revoked the provision of the Royal Proclamation of 1763 calling for the assimilation of Quebec's French-speaking majority, guaranteed its Catholic population freedom of worship, and reinstated French regime property rights and civil law. In an effort to prevent colonists from illegally settling on reserve land, the act also expanded the borders of Quebec to include much of the territory reserved for Indigenous peoples. When it came to conflict management in British North America, London chose what has since become known as national unity (consciously defined without reference to Indigenous peoples) over assimilation. That unity would frame the parameters of Canadian foreign policy decision making for over two centuries.

The United States is central to Canada's foreign policy history

The Quebec Act was a sensible recognition by the British government of the French presence in North America, but it did not satisfy everyone. Opponents of British rule in what is now the United States cited the legislation among a series of intolerable actions by colonial authorities and called for revolution. On 4 July 1776, representatives of the thirteen American colonies declared their independence. Though they had successfully repelled an American invasion of Quebec in 1775–6, the British failed to defeat the rebels in battle. The 1783 Treaty of Paris brought a temporary end to the hostilities and legitimized the now independent United States of America. Nonetheless, tensions remained. The British continued to occupy forts that lay within US territory, and commercial disputes persisted. What came to be known as Jay's Treaty (1794–5) offered a diplomatic solution. The British pulled back their garrisons and both Washington and London allowed merchants unrestricted access across the new border between the United States and British North America (BNA).

Fifteen years later, the implications of renewed Anglo-French conflict in Europe reignited the conflict in North America. After the Royal Navy imposed a maritime blockade on French ships, London pressured the neutral Americans to abide by the restrictions. American merchants and politicians were furious, and ongoing British support of Indigenous leaders (such as the Shawnee chief Tecumseh) who resisted American westward settlement all but compelled Washington to respond. In June 1812, the Americans were at war against Britain once again. After two-and-a-half years of fighting, with neither side appearing capable of a decisive victory, domestic pressure grew to end the conflict. A peace agreement, the Treaty of Ghent, was signed in Belgium on 24 December 1814. The treaty made no provision for the protection of the sovereignty of Britain's Indigenous allies who were, for all intents and purposes, abandoned once the Crown no longer appeared to need them.

The peaceful resolution of the conflict led to further diplomatic negotiations. In 1817, London and Washington concluded the Rush-Bagot Treaty, one of the most successful arms limitation agreements in history. The treaty restricted the number of warships permitted on the Great Lakes. The following year, the Convention of 1818 marked the 49th parallel as the border between the United States and BNA from the Lake of the Woods to the Rockies. The agreement cut through Indigenous nations and divided traditional territory in two. The 1842 Webster-Ashburton Treaty settled a longstanding quarrel over the Maine-New Brunswick boundary. The Oregon Treaty of 1846 extended the existing border

12 CANADA FIRST, NOT CANADA ALONE

along the 49th parallel to the Pacific Ocean.[4] The idea of an undefended border between Canada and the United States was born in these peaceful settlements.

Independence in Canadian foreign policy has always been relative

The British never felt fully secure in North America. Between the signing of the Convention of 1818 and the completion of the Webster-Ashburton Treaty, they built major fortifications at Halifax, Quebec City, and Kingston and constructed the Rideau Canal to move troops and supplies in the case of a future conflict with the United States. Such fear was not without merit: during the 1837–8 rebellions in Upper and Lower Canada, rebel forces found succour from American sympathizers, some of whom even took up arms in support of their northern neighbours' revolutionary cause. There had also been a war scare over the Oregon boundary in 1846. Concern about an American invasion northward was also a central element of the push behind Canadian Confederation in 1867. The union of the colonies of New Brunswick, Nova Scotia, and the Province of Canada (present-day Quebec and Ontario) took place under the shadow of the US Civil War and tensions it created between Britain and the United States. Although domestic factors certainly motivated the so-called Fathers of Confederation (women were systemically excluded from strategic decision-making processes), international pressures also played a role.

The US Civil War (1861–5), fought between the Union in the North and the rebel Confederacy in the South, saw more than half a million Americans die in battle and from disease. Thousands of Canadians also participated, with most volunteering for the Union. Many shared the Northern goal of abolishing slavery; others were drawn by the promise of adventure, or at least employment. Backers of the Confederacy typically maintained that a divided United States represented less of a threat to British North America. Certainly, that was Britain's position, and several incidents of British support for the rebels reignited tensions between London and Washington. The Union government was particularly upset that British shipyards were constructing warships for the South. Confederate spies and saboteurs operated openly in Toronto and Montreal, which were used as bases for raids across the BNA–US border.[5] In a sign of anger, Washington announced in 1864 that it would abrogate a trade agreement with Britain that had granted its North American colonies privileged access to the US market. When the Reciprocity Treaty officially ended in 1866, the colonies faced an economic crisis.

Their defences were also at risk. In 1865, after the North claimed victory in the Civil War, certain members of Congress voiced a desire to turn the Union army northward. British officials had little interest in fighting on behalf of the North American settlers; part of the imperial government's support for Confederation was a desire to see BNA take responsibility for its own defence. While the threat of an actual attack by US forces may have been exaggerated, a real danger was posed by a transnational revolutionary organization operating in North America and the British Isles. Members of the Fenian Brotherhood were committed to securing Irish independence.[6] In 1866, hundreds of Fenians planned to seize the colonies and ransom them to London in exchange for Ireland's freedom. Their incursions were repelled by colonial militia and British soldiers, but the fear they generated increased popular support for Confederation.[7]

The external factors of trade and defence led Canada's founders to set aside their partisan disagreements, however temporarily. In creating what became the Dominion of Canada, they took each other "not by the hand but rather by the throat,"[8] as historian Ged Martin memorably put it. The country formed on 1 July 1867 could conduct trade and commerce and oversee its own defence; otherwise, external dealings were handled by Britain in the interests of ensuring the unity of the Empire. Indeed, the British North America Act made a passing reference to foreign affairs. "The Parliament and Government of Canada," read Section 132, "shall have all powers necessary or proper for performing the Obligations of Canada or of any Province thereof, as Part of the British Empire, towards Foreign Countries arising under Treaties between the Empire and such Foreign Countries."[9]

Abroad, Canada was represented via British diplomatic posts. British officials negotiated and signed agreements on Ottawa's behalf. Matters of peace and war were decided in London. Since many Canadians considered themselves British and took pride in their imperial membership, this situation suited them. "Gradually a different colonial system is being developed," Canada's first prime minister, Sir John A. Macdonald, explained, "and it will become, year by year, less a case of dependence on our part and of overruling protection on the part of the Mother Country, and more a case of a healthy and cordial alliance. Instead of looking upon us as a newly independent colony, England will have in us a friendly nation—a subordinate but still a powerful people—to stand by her in North America in peace or in war."[10]

The flaws in this arrangement quickly became apparent. In 1871, British and American representatives met to resolve outstanding issues in North America stemming from the US Civil War. The resultant Treaty of Washington did not address Canada's specific concerns, such as a renewed reciprocity agreement or compensation for the damages caused by the Fenians. Worse, the British gave Americans fishing rights in Canadian waters. As a member of the British delegation, Macdonald delivered little for his country. At one point during the talks, he remarked to a colleague that his fellow British negotiators "seem to have only one thing on their minds—that is, to go home to England with a treaty in their pockets, settling everything, no matter at what cost to Canada."[11]

Figure 1.1 The British High Commissioners for the Treaty of Washington. After the American Civil War ended in 1865, the United States and Great Britain launched a joint commission in Washington to resolve disputes that had arisen between them during the conflict. The Americans were most concerned with damage to Northern ships caused by British-built Southern ones like the *Alabama*. The British, and the Canadians, sought compensation for illegal fishing in Canadian waters as well as the illegal raids launched into Canada by the Irish Republican Brotherhood (the Fenians). This photo includes the six British representatives to the negotiations, among whom (third from the left) was Canadian Prime Minister Sir John A. Macdonald. Although the British accepted virtually all of the Americans' terms, Macdonald's presence marked a first, preliminary step toward greater Canadian independence in international affairs. (Standing to Macdonald's left is Lord Tenterden and to his right is Montague Bernard. Seated, from left to right, are Sir Stafford Northcote, Earl de Grey & Ripon, and Sir Edward Thornton.) ©Library and Archives Canada. Reproduced with the permission of Library and Archives Canada. Library and Archives Canada/Duncan Cameron Fonds/PA_113742.

Canada has its own colonial history

Canadians had further reasons to be upset. When Washington purchased Alaska from Russia in 1867, a number of Americans, including US Secretary of State William Seward, spoke openly of annexing British Columbia (BC) in order to link their new property with the rest of the country.[12] Concern over annexation was part of the push for BC to join Canada in 1871 and drove the Dominion's own expansion across the western prairies.[13] As Prime Minister Macdonald put it: "if Englishmen do not go there, Yankees will."[14]

Westward expansion forcibly displaced Indigenous peoples of the region. In 1869, Ottawa set about purchasing Rupert's Land and the North Western Territory (what is today most of Canada between BC and Ontario) from the Hudson's Bay Company. The move alarmed the Métis—descendants of Indigenous peoples and European fur traders—particularly around the Red River settlement (in present-day Winnipeg). The Métis government, led by Louis Riel, prevented Canadian officials from entering the territory and pressed Canada to respect its land and cultural rights. Although Ottawa dispatched military forces, negotiations proved successful: in 1870, the province of Manitoba was born.

Canada continued to expand westward by negotiating treaties with the Indigenous nations of the prairies. The Numbered Treaties were, in effect, Canada's first diplomatic agreements. To compel Indigenous peoples to relocate to the land reserved for them under these treaties, the Canadian government employed a policy of starvation, withholding emergency rations until forced migrations were complete.[15] What's more, as Ottawa negotiated the treaties, surveyors from Canada and the United States set about physically demarcating the western Canada–US border along the 49th parallel, ultimately preventing Indigenous peoples from roaming across the vast prairie expanse as they had previously.[16] The Indian Act of 1876 consolidated previous legislation that had transformed Indigenous peoples across Canada into colonial subjects lacking many rights and freedoms.

Diplomacy is not for amateurs

Annexation was not the only Canadian concern brought to the fore by the US purchase of Alaska. The border between Alaska and what became Canada had been set out in the Anglo-Russian Treaty of St Petersburg of 1825. Since the negotiators never visited the land in question, many of the treaty's specific provisions over the location of the boundary line were ambiguous. At the time, the border was of little importance since few, other than the local First Nations, lived nearby. That changed with the discovery of gold in the Klondike region of the present-day Yukon Territory. In 1896, tens of thousands of prospectors, mainly Americans, travelled to the Yukon to seek their fortunes. They accessed the territory primarily through the American ports of Dyea and Skagway in the Alaska Panhandle and therefore paid US, rather than Canadian, customs duties as they passed through. Canadians soon objected to their own lack of maritime

16   CANADA FIRST, NOT CANADA ALONE

access and loss of potential revenue. Some even attempted to claim much of the Panhandle for Canada.

The Canadian claim was weak. Ottawa had made no previous complaints or objections to the establishment of Dyea or Skagway. Several Canadian maps—including one hanging in the Parliament Buildings—depicted the boundary line as consistent with the American claim. A Joint High Commission, made up of British, American, and Canadian authorities, had considered the issue in 1898–9, but failed to reach a consensus. When Prime Minister Wilfrid Laurier pressed Canada's claim, US President Theodore Roosevelt dispatched troops to the disputed region.[17] With tensions rising, the British proposed to take the issue to a tribunal.

The tribunal was composed of three Americans, two Canadians, and one Briton. Although the commissioners were meant to be impartial jurists, Roosevelt's appointments included his Secretary of War Elihu Root and Senator Henry Cabot Lodge, who had once called for Canada's annexation. The tribunal ruled 4–2 in favour of the bulk of the American claim. The British commissioner sided with the Americans.[18]

The Canadians felt betrayed. Laurier lamented in the House of Commons "that so long as Canada remains a dependency of the British crown the present powers that we have are not sufficient for the maintenance of our rights." Privately, he understood, as Macdonald had in 1871, that "the Empire's interest and the Empire's policy were in most cases Great Britain's interest and Great Britain's policy."[19] The dispute underscored the lack of a government department in Canada capable of and responsible for handling such matters, as well as the inadequate keeping of records, including maps.[20] Sir Joseph Pope, who had prepared the Canadian claim, complained of having to "make bricks without straw."[21] Pope would later call for a proper archive and a central registry for important papers, the genesis of Canada's Department of External Affairs.

Canada's development as a foreign policy actor was ad hoc, cautious, and evolutionary

The desire to establish an independent foreign service did not come easily to Canadians. In 1882, Sir John A. Macdonald had claimed that doing so would mean being "cast upon our own resources" and result in the "ruin of Canada."[22] At the time, the governor general—a British appointee—formed a link between Ottawa and various ministries and departments in London as well as British diplomatic posts in other countries. The prime minister represented Canada at a series of colonial, and then imperial, conferences that were precursors to Commonwealth Heads of Government Meetings.

But the Canadian prime minister could not be everywhere at all times, and Canada had interests abroad. In 1869, Macdonald appointed a personal representative in London to promote trade and immigration. In 1880, he sent Alexander Galt, a former finance minister, to London as high commissioner. Even though Britain refused to grant Galt diplomatic status (and Canada's governor general read Galt's official correspondence), Macdonald maintained that the high commission was "a very important step towards asserting the importance of the Dominion of Canada as a portion of Her Majesty's Empire."[23]

In 1882, the Quebec provincial government sent Senator Hector Fabre to Paris to promote the province as a destination for trade and immigration. Ottawa responded by having Fabre represent the federal government as well, largely on immigration, trade, and cultural issues. Like the high commission in London, the Paris commission had official sanction but lacked diplomatic status.[24] In 1885, Nova Scotia opened a trade and immigration office in London. New Brunswick followed two years later. By the early 1900s, most provinces were represented in the imperial capital.

Trade promotion was one area where Canada could take initiative. Macdonald oversaw the use of quasi-official commercial agents to promote trade mainly in Europe and the Caribbean. In 1893, High Commissioner Sir Charles Tupper negotiated a trade agreement with France. The treaty was signed on Canada's behalf by the British ambassador in Paris. The following year, Minister of Trade and Commerce Mackenzie Bowell welcomed delegates from nearly a dozen British colonies to Ottawa to discuss issues of common concern, such as mail and telegraphic communication. The delegates agreed to a trade treaty, but it was rejected by London. "To give the Colonies the power of negotiated Treaties for themselves without reference to Her Majesty's Government," wrote the colonial secretary, "would be to give them an international status as separate and Sovereign States, and would be equivalent to breaking up the Empire."[25] That same year, the Department of Trade and Commerce established its first permanent trade mission in Sydney, Australia. Canadian trade offices soon dotted Europe, the Caribbean, and East Asia.

Canadian officials conducted their own diplomatic negotiations under the careful watch of British representatives. Several transnational environmental issues arose, for example, out of Canada's geographic position next to the United States. Between 1908 and 1916, Canada and the United States engaged in "conservation diplomacy," negotiating and concluding three comprehensive wildlife protection agreements: the Inland Fisheries Treaty (1908), the North Pacific Fur Seal Convention (1911), and the Migratory Bird Treaty (1916). They also agreed to the Boundary Waters Treaty (1909), which created the International Joint Commission (IJC)—a permanent body devoted to resolving issues arising from the shared lakes and rivers that stretched across North America.[26] In all of these instances, although the negotiations had been officially carried out by British and US representatives, Canadian members of the British delegations conducted the bulk of the talks, and the agreements were concluded between

18   CANADA FIRST, NOT CANADA ALONE

the United States and Canada, with Britain countersigning. Membership on the IJC was confined to Canadians and Americans.

The fundamental reason for a new government department responsible for external developments was less about Canadian independence than efficiency. Indeed, British officials supported Ottawa's initiative. British embassy officials in Washington complained that three-quarters of their workload involved Canadian issues.[27] Although Prime Minister Laurier had complained about the need for greater autonomy, when he ultimately argued for a Department of External Affairs (DEA) before the House of Commons, he proposed merely "an improvement in the administration of that class of public affairs which related to matters other than those purely of internal concern."[28]

The DEA was not a department of foreign affairs, which would have implied that Britain and other parts of the empire were foreign countries rather than parts of the same imperial entity. It became instead, in the words of James Bryce, the British ambassador in Washington, "a sort of foreign office."[29] Headquartered above a barber shop several blocks from Parliament Hill, the department served as a repository and clearing house of correspondence with Britain's government and with other governments via British diplomatic posts. At its inception, the new department was headed by an independent minister, the Secretary of State for External Affairs Charles Murphy. It had no staff posted abroad. In 1912, the Conservative government of Robert Borden placed the external affairs portfolio under the purview of the prime minister. This centralization and personalization of international policy lasted until 1946.

Canada's foreign policy realm has always extended beyond the North Atlantic

In the nearly five decades between Confederation and the outbreak of the First World War, successive Canadian governments encouraged immigration. Canada desperately needed consumers, industrial workers, prairie farmers, and labourers in the resource sector. Securing new Canadians (then still legally recognized as British subjects) proved difficult. Migrants preferred the relatively warmer climates of Australia and the western United States. In the 1870s and 1880s, as the Canadian economy struggled, more people left the country than arrived as immigrants.[30] The situation was reversed in 1896, when the Laurier Liberals implemented a mass immigration policy to the "Last Best West," offering free farmland to those who qualified. Just 17,000 immigrants had come to Canada in 1896; in 1913 more than 400,000 newcomers arrived.[31]

Not all immigrants were welcome. While encouraging the migration of white, Christian Americans, Britons, and northern Europeans, Ottawa restricted migrants from the Caribbean, India, and East Asia, and it barred Black Americans from coming north. In part, this attitude was based on economic fears. Labour unions, for instance, opposed Asian migration on the grounds that it would depress wages and deprive white workers of jobs.[32] Indeed, when Sir John A. Macdonald's government set out to build the transcontinental railroad in the 1880s, it imported roughly 15,000 Chinese labourers, who were paid a fraction of what a white worker would have earned. "At present it is simply a question of alternatives," Macdonald explained to the House of Commons in 1882. "Either you must have this labor or you cannot have the railway." In that same speech, he added that his government did not foresee the Chinese "becoming permanent settlers" in Canada. "I believe they would not be a wholesome element for this country. I believe it is an alien race in every sense, that would not and could not be expected to assimilate with our Arian population."[33] In 1885, as the railroad neared completion, Macdonald's government introduced the Chinese Head Tax, an exorbitant levy on would-be Chinese immigrants. The fee increased over time, and legal immigration from China plummeted.

Ottawa's efforts to ensure a "white Canada forever"—the title of a popular song—reflected attitudes prevalent among Canadians and shared by people in other English-speaking countries, especially the United States.[34] Canadian and American officials soon established some of the first border and immigration controls in North America, aimed at barring non-white immigrants.[35]

In the late 1890s and early 1900s, the British Columbia provincial government passed its own series of laws blocking Asian migrants and preventing non-whites from working in certain professions. But immigration was a federal prerogative, and each iteration of the legislation implicated a British ally (Japan), so the Laurier government disallowed it.[36] The Liberals sought economic inroads in Asia. As the prime minister remarked to an aide, it was not possible to "kick the Jap and expect to trade with him at the same time."[37] In 1906, Ottawa acceded to the 1894 Anglo-Japanese Treaty of Commerce and Navigation, which required the Canadian government to protect the lives and property of Japanese nationals and to allow Japanese citizens to enter and reside in Canada.

In a move echoing outbreaks of anti-Asian violence in nearby Washington State, the people of British Columbia revolted. In 1907, hundreds of white demonstrators, led by members of the Asiatic Exclusion League, marched through Vancouver's Chinatown, smashing storefronts and homes and damaging property. The mob then descended on the city's Japanese section, where they were ultimately stopped by local residents.

The riot raised questions about whether Canada could ensure the safety of Japanese nationals as required under the terms of the Anglo-Japanese Treaty,

20 CANADA FIRST, NOT CANADA ALONE

but Ottawa's concern was with future migrants.[38] Since Canada was legally unable to conduct its own negotiations with a foreign government, Laurier dispatched Rodolphe Lemieux, the minister of labour, and Sir Joseph Pope, a senior civil servant, on an informal mission to Japan to seek a reduction in immigration. Ottawa only requested the assistance of Britain's ambassador in Tokyo after Lemieux and Pope were en route. The two Canadians eventually secured a promise from Hayashi Tadasu, Japan's foreign minister, to voluntarily restrict the number of immigrants to Canada to 400 annually.[39] In selling the Hayashi-Lemieux Agreement, or "Gentlemen's Agreement," to fellow MPs, Lemieux explained that it was difficult to bar Japanese immigration altogether. "Can we consistently ask the Ally and friend of Great Britain to brand themselves before the whole world, as an inferior race—which they are not? They are, on the contrary, the rising power in the Far East," he explained.[40] Ratified by the Canadian Parliament in 1908, the agreement showcased the confluence of domestic and imperial interests on Canada's dealings with the world and the connections between immigration policy and foreign policy.

Canadian foreign policy has always been political

The 1911 federal election marked a high point in the early history of the politicization of Canadian external relations. Free trade with the United States was the central issue, although Canada's defence commitment to the British empire also played a role. The election hinged on questions of loyalty and identity, with the opposition Conservatives led by Robert Borden insinuating that Laurier's Liberal government was guilty of treason.

Free trade negotiations between Canada and the United States were nothing new in 1911. After Confederation, Prime Minister John A. Macdonald sought and failed to re-establish the 1854 Reciprocity Treaty. The Liberal government of Alexander Mackenzie (1873–8) reached an agreement with the administration of US President Ulysses S. Grant, but it failed to pass the US Senate. In light of that failure, in the 1878 federal election, the Conservatives campaigned on the promise of protectionism. "You cannot get anything by kissing the feet of the people of the United States," Macdonald claimed.[41] The message of latent anti-Americanism was received well. The Conservatives won a majority. In 1879, the Macdonald government introduced the National Policy. Meant to protect Canadian industry from foreign competition, the policy imposed stiff tariffs on American (and British) imports. The tariffs did not please everyone. Canadians in the expanding west soon became resentful of the high cost of Canadian-made farm equipment. To evade the tariff barriers, US and British investors poured money into the development of Canadian branch plants and subsidiary businesses. Ontario and Quebec boomed, but the Maritimes—which lacked the same industrial base—did not. Seeking to capitalize on opposition in western and eastern Canada, in 1891 the Liberals pledged to abandon the National Policy in favour of unrestricted reciprocity with the United States. Macdonald once again painted the Liberals as sellouts to US interests and swept to victory.[42] When the Liberals finally formed a government in 1896, reciprocity had been dropped from their platform.

Ironically, it was under Laurier that the National Policy paid its greatest dividends. "The nineteenth century was the century of the United States," the prime minister boasted in 1904. "I think we can claim that it is Canada that shall fill the twentieth century."[43] Sensing that Canadian industry could finally compete with US firms and hoping to placate voters in the booming western provinces, the Laurier government agreed to free trade talks with the William Howard Taft administration in 1910.

A reciprocity agreement reached in 1911 sailed through the US Congress. The speed at which the Americans embraced it raised suspicions in Canada. When Speaker of the House James "Champ" Clark boasted: "I hope to see the day when the American flag will float over every square foot of the British North American possessions clear to the North Pole," he seemed to confirm those fears.[44] Canadian nationalists and imperialists protested, as did self-interested figures such as the so-called Toronto Eighteen, a group of wealthy Liberal industrialists. Although he personally supported reciprocity, Conservative leader Robert Borden rallied opposition to free trade. "Reciprocity means Annexation," declared the Montreal Women's Anti-Reciprocity League. The Toronto *World* asked: "Which will it be? Borden and King George, or Laurier and Taft?"[45] Canada's Governor General Lord Grey observed that "feeling in Montreal and Toronto against the Agreement could hardly be stronger if the United States troops had already invaded our territory."[46] Borden's Tories (another name for Conservatives) won a majority, though the Liberals dominated in the pro-reciprocity west, where anti-American and pro-imperial sentiments carried less weight with a diverse population of migrants from continental Europe.

War, and its aftermath, can be a foreign policy catalyst

Three years into Robert Borden's government, Canada found itself in a conflict that would leave tens of thousands of its newly trained military personnel dead or wounded. A host of factors led to the Great War, including imperial rivalries and secret pacts among Europe's great powers, rampant militarism, and nationalism that fuelled public support for conflict. The assassination of Austrian

22 CANADA FIRST, NOT CANADA ALONE

Archduke Franz Ferdinand in July 1914 provided the final spark. Although Canadians were geographically distant from the conflict, "'Rule Britannia' and 'God Save the King' filled the air," and "Union Jacks appeared in windows and storefronts" in Toronto following Britain's declaration of war against Germany in August 1914.[47] Legally, as a member of the Empire, Canada was immediately at war, but Ottawa defined the extent of its contribution. For the fiercely pro-Empire Borden, there was little doubt that Canada should dispatch ground troops. By October, 31,000 men comprising the First Canadian Division had left for Europe, with tens of thousands more volunteers flooding into recruitment centres.

Borden had promised that only volunteers would serve in the Great War, so initially both Laurier and the leading Quebec nationalist Henri Bourassa supported the war effort. Noting that France was fighting alongside Britain, Laurier even proclaimed that French Canadians "had a double duty to perform."[48] By 1917, the situation had changed. With heavy casualties and a sharp contraction in the number of volunteers, the Canadian Expeditionary Force was operating beyond its capacity. In May, Borden introduced a controversial bill to implement conscription. Laurier condemned it, but many Liberals joined Borden's Conservatives in a Union government. When the Liberal-dominated Senate refused to pass the conscription bill, Borden took the issue to voters. The December 1917 election was the most divisive in Canada's history. To ensure victory, the Borden government passed two pieces of legislation: one gave women relatives of soldiers a vote—the first time they could cast a ballot federally—but stripped the vote from recent migrants from Germany and Austria-Hungary. The other enfranchised all Canadian soldiers, regardless of their period of residency in Canada, and allowed the governing Union party to assign their votes to particular constituencies.[49] Borden's Unionists won a majority, but the introduction of conscription the following year triggered violent riots in Quebec and protests from farmers whose promised exemptions were cancelled. These conflicts belied the myth of war as a nation-building experience.

Overall, wartime developments enhanced Canada's ability to advance its own interests abroad.[50] By late 1916, frustrated with the British military leadership, which he blamed for the unnecessary loss of Canadian lives, Borden prepared to press for a more independent Canadian voice in the world. At his insistence, Loring Christie, the Department of External Affairs' legal advisor, prepared a report on "The political relations of Canada and the Empire as they will be developed out of the war."[51] In response to complaints from Borden and the other Dominion prime ministers, British Prime Minister David Lloyd George included them in a new, consultative Imperial War Cabinet. The group convened twice, in 1917 and 1918, and provided Borden and the Australian, South African, and New Zealand prime ministers with a forum to press their concerns.

Alongside these meetings, Lloyd George hosted two Imperial War Conferences. At the first, in April 1917, Borden and South African Prime Minister Jan Smuts secured the passage of Imperial War Conference Resolution IX, which called for a postwar negotiation to confirm "full recognition of the Dominions as autonomous nations of an Imperial commonwealth" with "a right...to an adequate voice in foreign policy and in foreign relations."[52] The development recognized the Dominions' wartime commitments and their newfound status as Britain's equals. "I conceive," Borden announced after returning to Canada, "that the battle for Canadian liberty and autonomy is being fought to-day on the plains of France and of Belgium."[53]

Even though no such meeting was held, the Dominion leaders remained committed to asserting a measure of autonomy as recompense for the blood and treasure spilt in defence of Britain. As Borden told Lloyd George in 1918: "the idea of nationhood has developed wonderfully of late in my own Dominion: I believe the same is true of all the Dominions."[54] At a discussion at a December 1918 Imperial War Cabinet meeting on British representation at planned peace talks in Paris, Lloyd George expressed his preference that one member of the British delegation represent the Empire in its entirety. Borden and Australia's Billy Hughes objected. At the Paris Peace Conference of 1919, all of the Dominions were represented formally as part of the British Empire Delegation.

Canadian autonomy advanced as a result of the Paris negotiations. Canada signed (as part of the British Empire) the Treaty of Versailles, which brought an end to the war with Germany. Canada and the other Dominions also won the right to sit on the newly created League of Nations and International Labour Organization independently of Britain. In Loring Christie's view, Canada was now "in some degree an international person,"[55] even though it officially remained part of the British Empire.

The state does not hold a monopoly on Canadian engagement in the global realm

The First World War raised a central question about what it meant to be Canadian. For decades prior to the war, a leading strain of nationalism had defined the Canadian identity in British and Protestant terms, excluding Catholics, French Canadians, Indigenous peoples, and various ethnic and racial minorities. With the start of the war, many of those who faced discrimination volunteered for military service to demonstrate their loyalty and earn a place in the body politic. For Irish Catholics, serving in uniform did result in increased acceptance, but others struggled.[56] Canadian military leaders initially viewed the conflict as a "white man's war" and banned Black, Asian, and Indigenous participation.[57] Only in December 1915, as the volunteer pool

Figure 1.2 "Signs of the times" *Halifax Herald*, 3 August 1918. Even though the British North America Act (1867) recognized Canada as a "Dominion," on 4 August 1914 Britain declared war against Germany on behalf of the entire Empire. For the next two years, the Conservative government of Sir Robert Borden did not object strongly to London's dictation of wartime strategy, but London's increasing disregard for Canada's military and economic contributions prompted the prime minister to demand a greater voice in imperial decision making. By 3 August 1918, when this editorial cartoon was published, Borden had a seat on the Imperial War Cabinet and had attended two Imperial War Conferences as a full participant. British Prime Minister Sir Lloyd George had even promised that, after the war, London would recognize Canada as a nation. The cartoon depicts John Bull—meant to personify the United Kingdom—as recognizing Canada's evolution from colony to dominion to nation. The Canada–UK relationship, the blank space at the bottom of the sign suggests, remained a work in progress.

IDEAS AND ANTECEDENTS 25

began to dry up, were they permitted to join. Collectively on a per capita basis, Indigenous soldiers comprised the largest demographic group of military personnel in Canada. At least 4000 Indigenous men volunteered, roughly 35 per cent of the eligible population, compared to 30 per cent of military-aged Canadians.[58]

Indigenous peoples' reasons for participating in the war varied. Some sought acceptance by Canadians. Others felt obligated to honour their nations' centuries-old alliances with the British. Still other groups refused to send volunteers, objecting to participation in a conflict fought on behalf of an oppressive colonial government. Just as the battle of Vimy Ridge symbolized nascent nationalism among some Canadians who chafed at British rule, the upheavals of the First World War stoked nationalist sentiments around the world, and many colonial peoples demanded independence.[59] Such hopes were further kindled by US President Woodrow Wilson, who had called for self-determination for various ethnic minorities in Europe.[60] For the Haudenosaunee of the Grand River Territory in southern Ontario, the League of Nations offered the possibility of international recognition of their sovereignty, still not acknowledged by the Government of Canada. In turn, League membership could provide them with a platform to draw attention to the federal government's effort to impose its own governance structure in place of the traditional hereditary council.

The problem facing the Six Nations of Grand River Territory was that many foreigners viewed them as colonial subjects rather than as citizens of their own sovereign state. In 1921, Deskaheh (Levi General), spokesperson for the Grand River Territory's hereditary council, attempted to meet with King George V in London, but he was turned away by British officials who told him to deal with Ottawa. Three years later, he took the Haudenosaunee's case to the League of Nations. Deskaheh asserted that the Six Nations "are, and have been for many centuries, organized and self-governing peoples, respectively, within domains of their own, and united in the oldest League of Nations, the League of the Iroquois," and therefore deserving of independent membership in the league. As evidence of the Six Nations' sovereign status he presented centuries-old treaties signed by the Haudenosaunee and the Netherlands, France, Britain, and the United States.[61] Given the three-century-old treaty of alliance between the Haudenosaunee and the Dutch crown, the Netherlands presented Deskaheh's petition to address the organization, which won support from the Persian, Panamanian, Estonian, and Irish delegations. Britain, Canada, and the United States successfully lobbied these countries to withdraw their backing, and the League's secretariat rejected the petition.[62] It would be decades before the international community would take the concept of self-determination for Indigenous peoples seriously.[63]

The idea of putting "Canada first" by turning away from the rest of the international community has a long history

While Ottawa was lobbying against international recognition of Haudenosaunee sovereignty, it was busy asserting its own autonomy. In the wake of the economic and social strains caused by the Great War, such advocacy was initially meant to relieve Canada of global responsibilities. Upon returning from Europe in 1919, Winnipeg journalist J.W. Dafoe reflected that he was "more than ever glad to live in North America separated from Europe by the Atlantic Ocean and from Asia by the Pacific Ocean."[64] At the Paris peace talks in 1919, Prime Minister Borden opposed Article X of the proposed League of Nations Covenant—the key collective security provision—because it committed members to come to one another's defence in case of aggression. At the inaugural meeting of the League in 1920, Newton Rowell, the Canadian representative, told the gathered delegates that "it was European policy, European statesmanship, European ambition, that drenched this world in blood and from which we are still suffering and will suffer for generations."[65] Ottawa soon embarked on an unsuccessful three-year campaign to amend Article X to allow individual countries to decide how they would enforce collective security.[66]

In some quarters there was also growing distaste for being dragged into British imperial entanglements. In 1922, the new Liberal prime minister, William Lyon Mackenzie King, deflected British requests to contribute troops to a possible conflict with Turkey over the Mediterranean port of Chanak. Tired of war, Canadians saw little at stake for them there. The British government had assumed that Canada would follow London's lead. Britain, King feared, was playing an "imperial game," seeking to "test out centralization vs. autonomy as regards European wars." In a position he adhered to throughout the international crises of the 1930s, the prime minister resolved that "no contingent will go without parliament being summoned."[67]

The idea that Parliament—MPs and, through them, voters—would determine Canadian policy in matters of peace and war was an assertion of Canadian autonomy. Although he valued Canada's connection to the Empire, King believed that Canada should be able to chart its own course if its interests differed from Britain's. At the 1923 Imperial Conference, he successfully led Dominion opposition to a common imperial foreign policy. In effect, the conference concluded that Dominions could make their own decisions in foreign affairs.[68] That same year, in a test of Canadian autonomy, Ottawa and Washington negotiated a treaty overseeing the halibut fishery. Canada's signature on the treaty independent of Britain marked an important assertion of a Canadian right to conduct its own international affairs.[69]

In 1926, an inter-imperial relations committee chaired by Arthur Balfour, a senior British minister, reported that the United Kingdom and the Dominions were "autonomous Communities within the British Empire, equal in status, in no way subordinate to one another in any aspect of their domestic or external affairs, though united by a common allegiance to the Crown, and freely associated as members of the British Commonwealth of Nations." The following year Canada was elected to the League of Nations Council, the organization's executive body, and Canada opened its first diplomatic mission, a legation in Washington.[70] Missions followed in Paris in 1928 and in Tokyo in 1929. Britain responded in kind, opening its first high commission in Ottawa in 1928.

At the 1930 Imperial Conference, Dominion prime ministers demanded that the principle of equality be translated into legislative practice. Canada was represented not by King, whose Liberals had been voted out of office, but by R.B. Bennett, who represented the traditionally pro-empire Conservatives. London accepted the recommendation, and in 1931, the Statute of Westminster officially granted the Dominions legal freedom from Britain except in areas where they chose to remain subordinate.

Canada is particularly vulnerable to international economic upheaval

At the time, most Canadians hardly noticed because their country was in the throes of the Great Depression. The global financial and industrial crisis began in 1929 with a sudden and combined drop in commodity prices, consumer demand, and available credit. A sharp retraction in international trade sparked by American protectionism made the situation worse.[71] For Canada, a state that relied on foreign investment and exports of commodities like lumber, wheat, fish, and ore, the situation was dire. Factories, mines, and lumber camps closed, throwing tens of thousands of unskilled labourers out of work.[72]

Throughout the July 1930 federal election campaign, Bennett promised an external tariff program that would "blast a way through all our difficulties."[73] Increased trade with Britain and the British Empire was one of his goals; another was freer trade with the United States. By late 1935 Ottawa and Washington had reached a tentative agreement to lower duties on a range of products. The deal was ultimately signed after the Conservatives had been replaced.

Economic insecurity tends to foster political radicalism at home and abroad

Beyond boosting trade, Bennett believed that fixing the economy required a balanced federal budget and sound finances. Welfare money, he contended,

28 CANADA FIRST, NOT CANADA ALONE

would be wasted by the poor on "candy and beer."[74] Other forms of intervention risked creating "a government soviet in character."[75] Worse, "organizations in foreign lands desiring to destroy our institutions"[76]—that is, the Communist Party, backed by the Soviet Union—were sowing dissent. Bennett's concern with the growing communist threat at home extended to antagonism toward Joseph Stalin's totalitarian regime in Moscow.[77] King had cut official relations with the Communist government in 1927 after revelations of Soviet spying in Britain. Bennett adhered to this stance.[78] He embargoed imports from the Soviet Union in 1931 after the Soviets depressed prices of important Canadian exports by dumping wheat and lumber on the international markets.

For Bennett, communism's growing popularity—the result of record unemployment and the wider crisis of capitalism—and clashes between radicals and government authorities, such as the violent 1931 coal strike in Estevan, Saskatchewan, threatened Canada's future. The severe conditions created by the Depression stirred up considerable political and ideological ferment. The Co-operative Commonwealth Federation, or CCF (the precursor to the present-day New Democratic Party), was formed in 1932 through the merger of farmer and labour groups bent on overturning the existing economic order. The party's 1933 Regina Manifesto called for the nationalization of all industry and for public ownership and management of the Canadian economy. In Alberta, the right-wing Social Credit Party took power in 1935 under William Aberhart, a populist radio preacher opposed to press freedoms, federal interference, and international Jewish financiers whom he held responsible for the Depression. In Ontario and Quebec, populist governments came to power on slates opposed to communism, elitism, and Ottawa. Together, ideology and populism heightened clashes between the federal and provincial governments.

The national unrest reflected the rise of extremist movements globally. The depression drove support for the Nazis in Germany, eventually bringing them to power. Nazi Germany, imperialist Japan, and fascist Italy challenged the tenuous international order by seeking to redraw borders in Europe, Asia, and Africa through threat and force. The Japanese invasion of Manchuria in 1931 sparked a crisis at the League of Nations. Canada's delegation was among the many disinclined to punish this act of aggression against China. Indeed, some Canadians even backed Japan, believing that its forces were bringing order to the region.[79] Many Canadians showed similar ambivalence to the rise of Nazism. Some, including Mackenzie King, viewed Adolf Hitler's regime favourably in its early years and felt that Germany had been unduly punished for its role in the First World War.[80] Even if they opposed the rise of fascism in principle, few Canadians relished the thought of another war in Europe.

The role of non-governmental and civil society organizations in shaping foreign policy is subtle, but noteworthy

There was, however, a small group with a growing interest in the world beyond Canada's borders. They met through organizations like the League of Nations Society, the Canadian Institute of International Affairs, the Canadian Association for Adult Education, the Women's International League for Peace and Freedom (WILPF), the Institute of Economic and International Relations, the League for Social Reconstruction, and the Canadian Youth Congress. Many of them were part of the international peace movement.[81] Women played a prominent part in these groups, taking the stand that as mothers they wanted to avoid their sons being sent off to another war. White Canadian women had gained the right to vote in 1918 and wanted to bring their newfound political power to bear. Typical in this regard was Agnes Macphail, the first woman MP, who was a member of both WILPF and the League of Nations Society. "Blessed are we who live in the North American continent," she wrote after touring Europe in 1929, "and because of our happy position we owe leadership to the world."[82]

The idea that Canada had a role to play in the world's councils may have gained prominence in some segments of Canadian civil society, but foreign policymakers remained cautious. Bennett opposed a DEA proposal to expand Canada's overseas diplomatic presence to Argentina, Belgium, Brazil, China, Cuba, Mexico, Norway, and Poland. As for wider issues of international security, his view was "What can one man do who represents only ten and a half million people?"[83] Better to let the British Empire take the lead.

Conclusion

The importance of Great Britain to Canada's foreign policy history is undeniable. In the century following the Seven Years' War, British negotiators and British interests drove what became Canada's foreign policy posture. Confederation, the 1867 act that created the framework for an ultimately independent Canadian state, resulted as much from London's desire to rid itself of colonial obligations as from a national insistence on greater autonomy. At no point during this period was it common to think of "Canada first."

Even when Ottawa came to recognize the limits to which London was willing to promote Canada's national interests, the desire for complete independence was circumspect. Canadian governments sought a degree of international recognition, but not the responsibility that might entail. Nonetheless, Canada projected a degree of chauvinistic self-assuredness globally during these early

30 CANADA FIRST, NOT CANADA ALONE

years. The state's British sensibilities implied a superiority to American culture, and only certain immigrants were welcomed into the nation. Yet, closer economic relations with the United States and a larger population were critical to national prosperity, leaving both Canada–US relations and Canadian immigration policy vulnerable to gross politicization.

In the early twentieth century, the Government of Canada gradually extended its global reach. The Great War accelerated the trend toward increased autonomy even as the leadership in Ottawa aggressively prevented Indigenous nations from doing the same. By 1935, Canada had the legal and constitutional prerogatives necessary to act boldly in world affairs, even if Ottawa remained hesitant to do so.

To position Canada first in 1935 meant many things: a preference for negotiation as an approach to conflict management; a reluctance to commit to European entanglements; an effort to maximize economic prosperity through international trade; an abrogation of Indigenous rights; a campaign for immigrants of similar cultural and religious backgrounds; a recognition of the benefits derived from a stable Anglo-American relationship; an understanding of the need to manage provincial interventions in the international realm; and a desire to be recognized as an independent global actor. Apart from the period of the First World War, national defence was hardly a priority. The prime minister was, by definition, the secretary of state for external affairs. Individual members of Parliament, let alone the average Canadian, had no direct role in foreign policy even if a select few were becoming more curious, while missionaries in Asia and Africa, graduate students in the United States and the United Kingdom, and successive waves of immigrants from Northern and Western Europe indicated that some Canadians understood that there was a world beyond Canada's borders.

Readings

International Relations in British North America

Important aspects of the immediate post–Seven Years' War period in British North America are analyzed in Phillip Buckner and John G. Reid, *Revisiting 1759: The Conquest of Canada in Historical Perspective* (Toronto: University of Toronto Press, 2012) and David Dixon, *Never Come to Peace Again: Pontiac's Uprising and the Fate of the British Empire in North America* (Norman: University of Oklahoma Press, 2005). Alan Taylor has authored two essential studies of eastern North America between the American Revolution and the War of 1812: *The Divided Ground: Indians, Settlers, and the Northern Borderland of the American Revolution* (New York: Alfred A. Knopf, 2006) and *The Civil War of 1812: American Citizens, British Subjects, Irish Rebels, & Indian Allies*

(New York: Alfred A. Knopf, 2010). Aspects of "Canadian"–American relations are explored in Jane Errington's *The Lion, the Eagle, and Upper Canada: A Developing Colonial Ideology*, 2nd ed. (Montreal: McGill-Queen's University Press, 2012); Francis M. Carroll, *A Good and Wise Measure: The Search for the Canadian-American Boundary, 1783–1842* (Toronto: University of Toronto Press, 2001); and Robin Winks, *The Civil War Years: Canada and the United States*, 2nd ed. (Montreal: McGill-Queen's University Press, 1998).

Confederation and Canadian Politics

Although more than half a century old, P.B. Waite's *Life and Times of Confederation: Politics, Newspapers, and the Union of British North America* (Toronto: University of Toronto Press, 1962) is an essential introduction to Canadian Confederation. A more recent treatment is Christopher Moore's *1867: How the Fathers Made a Deal* (Toronto: McClelland & Stewart, 1997). Various aspects of Confederation are explored in two collections of essays: Jacqueline Krikorian, Marcel Martel, and Adrian Shubert, *Globalizing Confederation: Canada and the World in 1867* (Toronto: University of Toronto Press, 2017) and Daniel Heidt, *Reconsidering Confederation: Canada's Founding Debates 1864–1999* (Calgary: University of Calgary Press, 2018). For a sense of political life in early Canada, readers should consult Christopher Pennington, *The Destiny of Canada: Macdonald, Laurier, and the Election of 1891* (Toronto: Penguin, 2011); Patrice Dutil and David MacKenzie, *Canada 1911: The Decisive Election That Shaped the Country* (Toronto: Dundurn Press, 2011); and Patrice Dutil and David MacKenzie, *Embattled Nation: Canada's Wartime Election of 1917* (Toronto: Dundurn Press, 2017).

Canada and Indigenous Peoples

Canada's relationship with Indigenous peoples is a subject that has only begun to receive considerable attention. J.R. Miller has produced two important general introductions: *Skyscrapers Hide the Heavens: A History of Native-Newcomer Relations in Canada*, 4th ed. (Toronto: University of Toronto Press, 2018) and *Compact, Contract, Covenant: Aboriginal Treaty Making in Canada* (Toronto: University of Toronto Press, 2009). On the impact of Canada's westward expansion, see Jean Teillet, *The North-West Is Our Mother: The Story of Louis Riel's People, the Métis Nation* (Toronto: Patrick Crean Editions, 2019); Sarah Carter, *Lost Harvests: Prairie Indian Reserve Farmers and Government Policy* (Montreal: McGill-Queen's University Press,

32 CANADA FIRST, NOT CANADA ALONE

1990); and James Daschuk, *Clearing the Plains: Disease, Politics of Starvation, and the Loss of Aboriginal Life* (Winnipeg: University of Manitoba Press, 2013). Canada's shameful experience with Indian Residential Schools is the subject of John S. Milloy's *A National Crime: The Canadian Government and the Residential School System, 1870 to 1986* (Winnipeg: University of Manitoba Press, 1999).

Immigration and Identity

The standard work on Canadian immigration history is Ninette Kelley and Michael Trebilcock, *The Making of the Mosaic: A History of Canadian Immigration Policy*, 2nd ed. (Toronto: University of Toronto Press, 2010). Important works that examine immigration restrictions include Patricia Roy, *A White Man's Province: British Columbia Politicians and Chinese and Japanese Immigrants, 1858–1914* (Vancouver: UBC Press, 1989), and Julie Gilmour, *Trouble on Main Street: Mackenzie King, Reason, Race and the 1907 Vancouver Riots* (Toronto: Penguin, 2014). Migration is a major focus of a wider literature that explores Canada's place within the so-called British World. See Katie Pickles, *Female Imperialism and National Identity: Imperial Order Daughters of the Empire* (Manchester: Manchester University Press, 2002); Phillip Buckner and R. Douglas Francis, *Canada and the British World: Culture, Migration, and Identity* (Vancouver: UBC Press, 2006); and Lisa Chilton, *Agents of Empire: British Female Migration to Canada and Australia, 1860s–1930* (Toronto: University of Toronto Press, 2007). The classic study of Canadian views on the British empire is Carl Berger, *The Sense of Power: Studies in the Ideas of Canadian Imperialism, 1867–1914*, 2nd ed. (Toronto: University of Toronto Press, 2013). Finally, French Canadians' views on imperialism are the subject of Serge Courville's *Rêves d'empire: le Québec et le rêve colonial* (Ottawa: University of Ottawa Press, 2000), and Sylvie Lacombe's *La rencontre de deux peuple élus: Comparison des ambitions nationale et impérial au Canada entre 1896 et 1920* (Quebec: Les Presses de l'Université Laval, 2002).

Canada and the First World War

Broad overviews of Canada's Great War experience include the valuable collection of essays in David MacKenzie, *Canada and the First World War*, 2nd ed. (Toronto: University of Toronto Press, 2018) and Tim Cook's two-volume history, *At the Sharp End: Canadians Fighting the Great War, 1914–1916*

(Toronto: Penguin, 2007) and *Shock Troops: Canadians Fighting the Great War, 1917–1918* (Toronto: Penguin, 2009), as well as Cook and J.L. Granatstein, eds., *Canada 1919: A Nation Shaped by War* (Vancouver: UBC Press, 2020). Vimy Ridge and the wider mythmaking around this battle have their own history, with important works including Geoffrey Hayes, Andrew Iarocci, and Mike Bechthold, *Vimy Ridge: A Canadian Reassessment* (Waterloo: Wilfrid Laurier University Press, 2007); Ian McKay and Jamie Swift, *The Vimy Trap* (Toronto: Between the Lines, 2016); and Tim Cook, *Vimy: The Battle and the Legend* (Toronto: Penguin, 2017). Other aspects of the war are explored in Timothy Winegard's *For King and Kanata: Canadian Indians and the First World War* (Winnipeg: University of Manitoba Press, 2012); Geoff Keelan's *Duty to Dissent: Henri Bourassa and the First World War* (Vancouver: UBC Press, 2019); and Sarah Glassford and Amy Shaw's collection, *A Sisterhood of Suffering and Service: Women and Girls of Canada and Newfoundland during the First World War* (Vancouver: UBC Press, 2012).

Interwar International Security

On interwar international security, see Zara Steiner, *The Lights that Failed: European International History, 1919–1933* (Oxford: Oxford University Press, 2005); Zara Steiner, *The Triumph of the Dark: European International History, 1933–1939* (Oxford: Oxford University Press, 2011); Patricia Clavin, *Securing the World Economy: The Reinvention of the League of Nations, 1920–1946* (Oxford: Oxford University Press, 2013); Susan Pedersen, *The Guardians: The League of Nations and the Crisis of Empire* (New York: Oxford University Press, 2015); and Cecelia Lynch, *Beyond Appeasement: Interpreting Interwar Peace Movements in World Politics* (Ithaca: Cornell University Press, 1999).

Canadian External Affairs

The evolution of Canada's early foreign policy is explored in C.P. Stacey's *Canada and the Age of Conflict,* vol. 1: *1867–1921* (Toronto: University of Toronto Press, 1984). Two official histories examine the founding and development of Canada's two key ministries: O. Mary Hill, *Canada's Salesman to the World: The Department of Trade and Commerce, 1892–1939* (Montreal: McGill-Queen's University Press, 1977) and John Hilliker, *Canada's Department of External Affairs: The Early Years, 1909–1946* (Montreal: McGill-Queen's University Press, 1990). On the 1920s and 1930s, see Stacey, *Canada in the Age of Conflict,* vol. 2: *1921–1948, The Mackenzie King Era* (Toronto: University of

34 CANADA FIRST, NOT CANADA ALONE

Toronto Press, 1981). For primary source documents, see Alex I. Inglis, ed., *Documents on Canadian External Relations*, vol. 5, *1931–1935* (Ottawa: Information Canada, 1973) and Norman Hillmer, *O.D. Skelton: The Work of the World* (Montreal: McGill-Queen's University Press, 2013). On Canada–US relations, see Gordon T. Stewart, *The American Response to Canada since 1776* (East Lansing: Michigan State University Press, 1992). For a history of Canadian trade policy, there is Michael Hart, *A Trading Nation: Canadian Trade Policy from Colonialism to Globalization* (Vancouver: UBC Press, 2002). Key figures in the early development of Canadian external relations have received biographical treatments. See Robert Bothwell, *Loring Christie: The Failure of Bureaucratic Imperialism* (New York: Garland Publishing, 1988); John MacFarlane, *Ernest Lapointe and Quebec's Influence on Canadian Foreign Policy* (Toronto: University of Toronto Press, 1999); Norman Hillmer, *O.D. Skelton: A Portrait of Canadian Ambition* (Toronto: University of Toronto Press, 2015); J.L. Granatstein, *A Man of Influence: Norman A. Robertson and Canadian Statecraft, 1929–1968* (Toronto: Deneau Publishers, 1981); and P.B. Waite, *In Search of R.B. Bennett* (Montreal: McGill-Queen's University Press, 2012).

2

William Lyon Mackenzie King and the Evolution of Canada's Global Posture, 1935–1948

Ethiopia's Aftermath

In spite of King's unwillingness to oppose Italy aggressively at the League of Nations, he lamented "the real danger" posed by "Fascism vs. Communism, Capital vs. Labour" and class warfare across Europe and North America.[1] At home, the National Unity Party of Canada (NUP), a coalition of fascist parties modelled on Adolf Hitler's Nazi Party and led by Adrien Arcand, the self-proclaimed Canadian führer, loudly and often violently opposed immigration and modern life.[2]

While Ottawa made little effort to save Jewish refugees subjected to the Nazis' increasingly violent attacks, some Canadians urged a more receptive attitude, just as some warned against the rise of fascism overseas. In 1936, conservative members of the Spanish military sought to overthrow that country's left-wing government, plunging Spain into civil war. Germany and Italy backed the rebels. The Soviet Union supported the republicans. The Canadian government and the other democracies steered clear of the conflict, but in July 1937, a group of largely left-wing Canadians formed the Mackenzie-Papineau Brigade, named for two nineteenth-century revolutionaries. Roughly 1700 "Mac-Paps" went to Spain to fight, ultimately unsuccessfully, the fascist forces. Canadian officials' fears that the returning paramilitaries would foment a communist revolution were unfounded. Indeed, when the Mac-Paps returned in 1939, the country stood on the brink of war with Germany.[3]

Viewed in retrospect, Canada's entry into the Second World War seems almost certain. At the time, there were doubts. King saw considerable good in the Nazis' economic policies.[4] In spite of calls for Canada to boycott the 1936 Olympic Games in Berlin, his Trade Minister William Euler travelled there to conclude an agreement with Hitler's government.[5] In a sign that Ottawa had no compunction about dealings with totalitarian regimes across the political spectrum, that same year King lifted the embargo on the Soviet Union.

Canada First, Not Canada Alone: A History of Canadian Foreign Policy. Adam Chapnick and Asa McKercher,
Oxford University Press. © Oxford University Press 2024. DOI: 10.1093/oso/9780197653715.003.0003

36 CANADA FIRST, NOT CANADA ALONE

King himself travelled to Germany in June 1937 after an Imperial Conference in London. When British officials pressed for a common approach to confronting Nazi aggression, King had insisted on Canada's autonomy. Worried about a possible war, he seized the chance to carry a message of peace to Hitler. During a lengthy chat, the German leader assured the prime minister that his international policy would be benign. "My sizing up of the man as I sat and talked with him," King recorded, "was that he is really one who truly loves his fellow-men, and his country, and would make any sacrifice for their good."[6] He conveyed to skeptical British officials that Hitler had no desire for war.

A month after King's return from Germany, Japanese forces attacked China. Canada had a legation in Tokyo, but official interest in the region was limited. "British interests in China," King asserted, "will not be a sufficient ground for our participation in a war in the Orient."[7] Peace organizations, the League of Nations Society, labour unions, church groups, and opposition politicians urged sanctions on Japan. J.S. Woodsworth, leader of the social-democratic Canadian Commonwealth Federation, spoke for many concerned Canadians when he declared that, by trading with the Japanese regime, Canada was complicit in "assisting an aggressor nation to kill men, women and children in China."[8] As with the Abyssinian crisis, King judged that sanctions on Japan were a path to armed conflict. Canada, he believed, had a special duty "to spike the guns of those who want boycott's (*sic*) & sanctions, leading to war."[9] Since the Liberal government refused to act, individuals, especially among Canada's small Chinese community, boycotted Japanese goods themselves.

A North American Country in a North Atlantic Triangle

King's pursuit of peace reflected his deeply held sense that crises abroad were none of Ottawa's business. Rather, in October 1935, three days after becoming prime minister, and in recognition of the United States having displaced Great Britain as Ottawa's largest trading partner, King divulged to an American official his desire to bring the two North American neighbours "closer in every way, political as well as economic."[10] One of his first acts in office was to sign a limited free trade agreement with the Roosevelt administration. Originally negotiated by Bennett's government, this trade pact dated 11 November, Remembrance Day, seemed particularly symbolic: while Canada and the United States were cementing peaceful relations, the great powers of Europe and Asia were fomenting war. The notion that Canadians and Americans had worked out a constructive relationship—despite the obvious power imbalance between the two countries—appealed to many North Americans, including Department of External Affairs (DEA) Undersecretary O.D. Skelton. No isolationist—he wanted Canada to establish diplomatic relations with countries in Latin America and Europe—Skelton put great stock in interchange between the two North American neighbours.[11]

Canada's isolationism from conflict was tested when Nazi Germany annexed Austria in March 1938. In May, Hitler demanded that the Sudetenland, the western portion of Czechoslovakia home to ethnic Germans, be ceded to Germany. When the Czechoslovakian government refused, a war among Europe's great powers seemed imminent. Despite his opposition to involvement in British conflicts, King affirmed that it was "a self-evident national duty, if Britain entered the war, that Canada should regard herself as part of the British Empire," adding the caveat that Canada would be free to define the extent of its participation.[12] Still, King's response indicated the limits of Canada's autonomy while ties to Britain remained strong. As the humorist Stephen Leacock wrote, "If you were to ask any Canadian, 'Do you have to go to war if England does?' he'd answer at once 'Oh, no.' If you then said, 'would you go to war if England does?' he'd answer 'Oh, yes.' And if you asked, 'Why?' he would say, reflectively, 'Well, you see, we'd have to.'"[13] Hostilities were avoided when, in September, British Prime Minister Neville Chamberlain and French Premier Édouard Daladier conceded the Sudetenland to Hitler in Munich.

Meanwhile, American, British, and Canadian diplomats had been working on a series of interlocking trade agreements. The arrangement was finalized in November amid hopes that the treaties would show the fascist powers that the so-called North Atlantic Triangle countries were united in common purpose.[14] The North Atlantic Triangle idea was rooted in the notion that Canada was at once British and North American. Some Canadians even took it to mean that Canada had a special role to play in interpreting London to Washington and vice versa. Americans and Britons seldom needed Canada to play this role and never saw Canadians as equal partners.[15] In an August 1938 speech in Kingston, Ontario, President Roosevelt affirmed that Canada, while "part of the sisterhood of the British Empire," could count on the assurance that the United States would "not stand idly by if domination of Canadian soil [was] threatened by any other empire."[16] The well-meaning statement underscored the possibility that Canada could lose its newly won autonomy from Britain to the United States. Although King and Roosevelt were friendly, the prime minister was mindful that a change in leadership in Washington "might lead to vassalage so far as our Dominion was concerned."[17] Two years earlier, Roosevelt had announced that if the United States were at war with Japan and if Washington perceived a national threat through British Columbia, American forces would be deployed. Alarmed by this potential violation of Canadian sovereignty, in 1937 King had begun to re-arm Canada's military.[18]

Off to War at Britain's Side

In March 1939, Hitler broke the Munich agreement by seizing the remainder of Czechoslovakia. Britain and France responded with a guarantee to defend Poland, the Nazi leader's next target. In the House of Commons, King described Europe as a "continent that cannot run itself." Even so, in the event of "an aggressor launching an attack on Britain, with bombers raining death on London," Canadians would intervene.[19] When Hitler precipitated such a conflict by invading Poland in September, King recognized his responsibility "of bringing the Canadian nation into war for freedom 'at Britain's side.'"[20] In line with his long-standing view that Parliament would determine whether Canada would join a war, King recalled Canadian parliamentarians from summer recess and announced his government's intent to declare war in the speech from the throne. Apart from J.S. Woodsworth, a committed pacifist, Canada's MPs—including those from Quebec—voted confidence in the government as it prepared for war on 10 September, a week after London had joined France in the battle against Germany. The delay was symbolically important. As King later boasted, "The Canadian people entered this war of their own free will."[21] Skelton was less sure. "The first casualty in this war," he wrote privately, "has been Canada's claim to independent control of her own destinies. In spite of a quarter century of proclamation and achievement of equality and independent status, we have thus far been relegated to the role of a Crown colony."[22]

King's initial wartime policy emphasized limited liability. To avoid a repeat of the terrible losses on the Western Front in the First World War, Canada would focus on its navy and air force. Both services could be used to defend Canadian territory, a selling point with Quebecers. In December 1939, Ottawa launched the British Commonwealth Air Training Plan, which eventually saw over 130,000 Allied pilots and aircrew train in Canadian airspace. Limited liability was a reasonable response given the minimal fighting in Western Europe in late 1939 and early 1940. With the opposition Conservatives nonetheless demanding a more aggressive policy, King put his position to voters. The March 1940 federal election saw the Liberals increase both their share of the vote and their majority in the House of Commons.

Within weeks of the election, the so-called Phony War ended. German forces swiftly advanced across Western Europe, conquering Denmark, Norway, the Low Countries, and France. Following the French surrender in June, Britain stood alone in Europe. In response, the Canadian government promulgated the National Resources Mobilization Act, transforming Canada into the second-most important ally in the war against Germany. Conscription for home defence freed up soldiers for overseas deployment, while federal control of industrial production accelerated the wartime economy.

Despite Washington's official neutrality, the Canadian and US militaries began secret staff talks in July 1940. Roosevelt and King met at Ogdensburg, New York, the following month to announce the formation of a Permanent Joint Board on Defence "to consider in the broad sense the defence of the north half of the western hemisphere."[23] The Ogdensburg Agreement was just a press release, but it marked the beginning of the Canada–US alliance.[24]

Ogdensburg and its economic complement, the Hyde Park Declaration of 1941, were products of the easy rapport between the two leaders.[25] The King-Roosevelt relationship became even more critical after the Japanese attack on the Pearl Harbor naval base drew the United States into the war in December 1941. To support the war effort against Japan and to resupply the Soviet Union by air, the US military constructed a variety of infrastructure projects across Canada's North: an oil pipeline, airfields, weather stations, and the Alaska Highway. Concerned with preserving sovereignty, the King government eventually assumed the costs of much of the northern infrastructure and ensured that ownership was transferred to Canada.[26]

The Functional Principle

The danger of losing sovereign control over parts of the North reflected Canada's lesser stature among its allies. Although Ottawa contributed billions of dollars in agricultural and industrial production, offered billions more in financial support, and put one in ten Canadians in uniform, Canada never ranked among the great powers. During the Allied conferences at Casablanca, Teheran, and Yalta, Churchill, Roosevelt, and Soviet leader Joseph Stalin made the major decisions. Even when King was present, as he was at two Anglo-American conferences in Quebec City in 1943 and 1944, he confined his role—as he freely admitted—"to that of the General Manager of the Chateau Frontenac," the conference hotel.[27] Having spent his career avoiding controversial foreign policy issues, and knowing little about military affairs, King did not wish to become embroiled in grand strategy.

In contrast, King and his officials bristled when Canada's economic interests or contributions were overlooked by the larger powers. Canadian diplomats, led by the minister-counsellor in Washington, Hume Wrong, argued that Canada "should have a voice in the conduct of the war proportional to its contribution to the general war effort."[28] They invoked this "functional principle" to justify national representation on the Combined Food Board and the Combined Production and Resources Board, two committees central to the Allies' economic and industrial war effort. This principle meant that, as a major

Figure 2.1 *Maclean's Magazine*, 15 August 1940. Germany's military successes in the early stages of the Second World War forced Canada to reconsider its defence posture. In July 1940, the Canadian Forces entered secret negotiations with their American counterparts. By 15 August, when *Maclean's Magazine* released this editorial cartoon of Uncle Sam tied to a Mountie in what a appears to be a three-legged race, the two sides were days away from one of the most transformational Canada–US accords of the century. The Ogdensburg Agreement, announced on 18 August, established a Permanent Joint Board on Defence to coordinate Canadian and American actions on continental security. The permanency of the board symbolized a shift in the understanding of Canada's strategic realm. The Commonwealth country had become a North American nation. Reaction to the agreement was mixed. A majority recognized the inevitability of closer Canadian–American defence and security co-operation. Some lamented the lessening of Canada's traditional British ties.

Figure 2.2 President Franklin D. Roosevelt, Rt Hon. W.L. Mackenzie King, and Rt Hon. Winston Churchill at the Citadel during the Quadrant Conference, August 1943. In August 1943, Prime Minister William Lyon Mackenzie King hosted President Roosevelt and Prime Minister Churchill in Quebec City to discuss military strategy in the Second World War. Although King made a point of being photographed in between the two leaders (Roosevelt is to King's left and Churchill to his right), the Canadian was not involved in their operational planning meetings. The arrangement suited King's purpose. He did not want, nor would he be permitted, responsibility for the Allies' military strategy, but he was adamant that he and Canada receive public recognition of their wartime contributions. The two Allied leaders returned to Quebec for a second conference in September 1944. National Film Board of Canada. Photothèque/Library and Archives Canada/C-031186.

producer of food and armaments, Canada ultimately forced its way onto the two economic committees.

The functional principle appealed to Canadian diplomats who relished a more active course in the world than King. Still, functionalism had limits. Despite Canada's significant military commitment—perhaps most apparent when Canadian troops captured one of the five Normandy beaches on D-Day, 6 June 1944—decisions guiding the Western Allies' military strategy were made by senior US and British officers on the Combined Chiefs of Staff (CCOS). When Ottawa pushed for a presence on the committee, General Maurice Pope was made a semi-official observer. Pope could access papers produced by the CCOS, but when it came to the committee's work, he admitted, Canadians "were merely bystanders."[29] Canada was accorded greater status on the Manhattan Project, the Anglo-American effort to build an atomic bomb. At British insistence, and largely because of Canada's stores of uranium, Ottawa became a junior partner, meaning that King and other senior officials were privy to information about the secret program and Canadian scientists took part in the research. On 16 July 1945, the first atomic weapon was tested in the New Mexico desert. On 6 August, the Americans dropped an atomic bomb on Hiroshima, Japan, followed by another on Nagasaki. The Japanese surrendered on 15 August. With Nazi Germany having given up on 8 May, the Allied victory was complete.

Although Canada possessed the scientific knowhow and economic capacity to build its own nuclear weapons, policymakers in Ottawa judged that there was no military need to take this step. Developing the bomb would have placed Canada among the top tier of powers, but Canadian officials had no aspiration for great power status. As one of the architects of Canada's civilian nuclear program reflected in 1953, Canada was "the only country in the world with sizeable atomic energy establishments where no bombs are being made, and where all the thinking and planning is focussed on peacetime aspects."[30]

War as a Catalyst

During and after the war, Canada's diplomatic presence expanded to meet its growing interests. Ottawa appointed high commissioners to Australia, Ireland, New Zealand, and South Africa. With Latin America increasingly vital as a source of trade and war supplies, Canadian missions were established in Brazil and Argentina (1940), Chile (1941), Mexico and Peru (1944), and Cuba (1945). Major allies, the Soviet Union and China, were accommodated in 1942. Following the liberation of Europe, Canadian diplomats returned to Belgium, the Netherlands, and France, and new posts were opened in Norway and Greece. In 1943, Canada's mission in Washington was upgraded to an embassy. The hectic pace of wartime activity and diplomatic expansion led the DEA to hire women employees for administrative tasks. In fact, several women were already serving in quasi-diplomatic roles—including Elizabeth MacCallum, the department's sole expert on the Middle East—but women were not formally admitted to the foreign service until 1947.[31]

Domestically, extensive wartime production brought about through partnerships between government and private enterprise ended the Depression. Where there were no companies to fill orders for munitions or armaments,

Ottawa created its own firms. To fill the need for industrial manpower, private firms and the federal government turned to women. During the war, the number of women in the workforce grew from 638,000 to over 1,000,000. An additional 50,000 women served in non-combat roles in the military. The flood of women into the industrial workforce and uniform marked more the desperation of total war than mainstream societal endorsement of female empowerment.[32] Following the Allied victory, many of these women lost their jobs.

By the conflict's end, Canada's gross domestic product had doubled to $11 billion. Flush with cash, King's government introduced a range of social welfare programs, including Unemployment Insurance (1941), Universal Family Allowances (1944), and generous benefits for most veterans. (Indigenous peoples who served received less support.) These programs, one writer quipped, were "the price that Liberalism is willing to pay in order to prevent socialism,"[33] a demand for greater state control over the economy growing louder across the Western world. The Canadian measures proved popular enough with voters that the Liberals retained a majority in the 1945 federal election.

Even with investments in the economy and the building of a rudimentary social safety net, Ottawa was able to cancel wartime loans to Britain valued at $2 billion and to give London another $1.25 billion in 1946 to support reconstruction efforts.[34] These developments were both a testament to ongoing Canadian sentiment for Britain and a sign of Canada's growing economic clout.

The power shift was important. In 1943, *The Economist*, the British newspaper, opined that Canada had "made a category for herself all of her own. Relative to her resources her effort is second to none. In absolute terms the distance which separates Canada from the Great Powers is less than that between her own achievements and that of any other of the smaller powers."[35] "The evidence of Canada's new position in the world is unmistakable," wrote academic Lionel Gelber in the American periodical *Foreign Affairs* in 1946. "Henceforth in world politics she must figure as a Middle Power."[36] The concept of the middle power came to signify the perceived role that Canadian diplomats played in the world, as negotiators—"honest brokers" became the preferred term—embroiled in the midst of international disputes. There was some truth to this notion, but the "middle power myth" ultimately became a self-aggrandizing aspect of Canada's international identity that overstated the country's influence and importance.[37]

In 1945, under King, prudence prevailed in Ottawa. At the San Francisco Conference, where delegates from 50 states established the United Nations Organization (UN), Canadian diplomats pursued a cautious line. While a group of middle powers led by Australia sought to limit great power domination of the world organization, Canada's delegates supported the decision to grant the five permanent members of what came to be known as the Security

44 CANADA FIRST, NOT CANADA ALONE

Council (the United States, United Kingdom, France, China, and the Union of Soviet Socialist Republics [USSR]) vetoes over the council's resolutions. Norman Robertson, the DEA's undersecretary, explained to fellow San Francisco delegates that it was "better to take the organization we can get" than no organization at all.[38] This prudent position upset other middle and minor powers, who punished Canada by rejecting its candidacy for the Security Council in 1946.[39]

The Onset of the Cold War

In much of Canada there were high hopes for the UN and for the possibility of the effective enforcement of collective security. A vote ratifying membership in the organization passed the House of Commons unanimously, and the United Nations Association—created out of the defunct League of Nations Society—soon counted thousands of members across the country.[40] Those hopes foundered in the face of the Cold War. In late 1946, with the Soviet Union setting up puppet governments across eastern Europe, Lester Pearson, the DEA's new undersecretary, lamented that the world organization was not, and was "not likely to be for many years, in a position to preserve the peace and punish the big aggressor." Although convinced of the need "to work for a strong United Nations," he warned that Western statespeople "should not make the mistake we made with Hitler" by ignoring Soviet aggression.[41]

Canadian officials could not help but view Russian actions in Europe through a negative lens. In September 1945 Igor Gouzenko, a cipher clerk at the Soviet embassy in Ottawa, had defected, bringing with him evidence of a Soviet espionage operation involving Canadian and British officials. Twenty-one suspects in the plot were arrested and tried in secret; eleven of them were jailed.[42] By early 1948, following the Soviet-backed communist take-over of governments in Poland, Romania, and Czechoslovakia, tensions between the West and the Soviet Union at the UN had worsened to the point that Canada, the United States, and Western European countries created a collective security pact, the North Atlantic Treaty Organization (NATO). For defenders of this alliance, such as Louis St Laurent, secretary of state for external affairs in 1946 and King's successor as prime minister in 1948, it was essential to "avoid the fatal repetition of the history of the pre-war years when the Nazi aggressor picked off its victims one by one. Such a process does not end at the Atlantic."[43] Banding together with like-minded countries was a means of avoiding this fate and testified to a newfound Canadian interest in collective security.

Case Studies

The following three cases span a remarkable evolution in the history of Canadian foreign policy and understandings of what it means for the federal government to put Canada first. The opening case, Ottawa's decision to turn away Jewish refugees fleeing Nazi Germany in 1939, contrasts with the second, the Canadian government's successful navigation of its position as the smallest of three state-members of the North Atlantic Triangle. The final, postwar, case demonstrates that, rather than shirking international obligations, the Canadian government sought to expand the reach and scope of the North Atlantic Treaty with mixed success. The Beyond the Book case emphasizes the pragmatism that predominated government officials' approaches to international conflict management during the early Cold War period.

The Voyage of the MS *St Louis*, 1939

> To what extent must the Canadian government respond to international humanitarian crises?

Between 1933 and 1939, approximately 800,000 Jews attempted to flee Nazi Germany. Less than half of them were successful. Following the passage of the Nuremburg Laws in 1935, Jews had their citizenship revoked; they became, for all intents and purposes, enemies of the German state. They found little welcome elsewhere. As a future president of Israel said at the time, "The world seemed to be divided into two parts—those places where the Jews could not live, and those where they could not enter."[44] Six million of Europe's Jews would ultimately perish during the Holocaust between 1939 and 1945.

Canada's response to this humanitarian crisis took place under what some have called "the blackest cloud in Canadian immigration history."[45] While the Great Depression undoubtedly played a role in successive federal governments' decisions to restrict immigration, Jews, Blacks, and immigrants of Asian descent were less welcome than people from Great Britain, the United States, and Christians from northern and central Europe.[46] The problem with Jews, according to Frederick Blair, the powerful director (deputy minister equivalent) of the immigration branch of the Department of Mines and Resources from 1936 to 1944, was that they were unassimilable. Most preferred to live and work in the cities, while Ottawa sought farmers who were less likely to compete for jobs with unemployed urban Canadians and disrupt the national social fabric.[47]

46 CANADA FIRST, NOT CANADA ALONE

Blair's anti-Semitism was tolerated, if not condoned, by Mackenzie King's Liberal government. Thomas Crerar, the minister of mines and resources, had virtually no interest in the immigration file. King's diary entry from 29 March 1938 is revealing:

> My own feeling is that nothing is to be gained by creating an internal problem in an effort to meet an international one....We must...seek to keep this part of the Continent free from unrest and from too great an intermixture of foreign strains of blood....I fear we would have riots if we agreed to a policy that admitted numbers of Jews. Also we would add to the difficulties between the Provinces and the Dominion.[48]

By provinces, King primarily meant Quebec. Although Jews faced restrictions on where they could work, attend school, and buy property throughout Canada, Quebec's fiercely Catholic population was particularly anti-Semitic. At one point, the St Jean Baptiste Society gathered nearly 128,000 signatures on a petition protesting "all immigration, especially Jewish immigration."[49] With his Liberal government reliant on Quebec voters, King was responsive to this view. In July 1938, Franklin Roosevelt organized a conference in Evian, France, to coordinate a response to the growing European refugee crisis; Ottawa instructed its representative to make no commitments. Instead, the Canadian government increased the capital requirements for prospective immigrants to the point that almost no Jews, having been stripped of their possessions by the Nazis, could qualify.

Events forced King to rethink Canada's lacklustre response. On 9 November 1938, Jews in Germany and its recently incorporated territories were deliberately terrorized in a series of Nazi atrocities that came to be known as *Kristallnacht*. Businesses and synagogues were destroyed and individual Jews beaten, arrested, and killed under the direction of the German government.[50] A few days later, upon his return from a funeral for the wife of one of Canada's three Jewish members of Parliament, King wrote in his diary: "I feel Canada must do her part in admitting some of the Jewish refugees. It is going to be difficult politically, and I may not be able to get the Cabinet to consent, but will fight for it as right and just, and Christian."[51]

His commitment collapsed in the face of concerted opposition from his Quebec ministers. When the Canadian Jewish Congress pleaded with Ottawa to accept 10,000 refugees over five years, with a guarantee that its members would personally cover any related costs, King refused. Efforts by Crerar, who felt guilty about his previous inaction, met the same fate. The government's position was made easier in mid-December when the Conservative party leader, R.J. Manion, gave a controversial speech in Quebec City. According to the *Globe and Mail*, King's main political competition opposed the admission of any Jewish refugees so long as the national unemployment rate remained uncomfortably high. Although Manion later conceded privately that his comments had been misrepresented as more extreme than he had intended, he never retracted them publicly.[52]

The end result, six months later, was virtually inevitable. On 13 May 1939, over 900 passengers, nearly all Jewish refugees, departed Hamburg aboard the Motorschiff *St Louis* (or MS *St Louis*) headed for Havana, Cuba. Prior to purchasing their non-refundable tickets, the passengers had secured landing permits from the Cuban government. They intended to remain on the island until they gained entry into the United States. A week before their departure, the Cuban government voided their visas. With nowhere to turn, the refugees boarded the ship and hoped for the best.[53]

After being denied entry to Havana, the *St Louis* spent a week docked while the American Jewish Joint Distribution Committee negotiated with Cuba's government and neighbouring Latin American countries. A request for mercy from Washington went unanswered. In desperation, the ship headed toward Florida, where the US Coast Guard ensured that it never got close enough to shore to tempt desperate passengers to jump overboard and seek asylum. Canada appeared to be the refugees' final hope. The Canadian Jewish Congress arranged for a group of prominent citizens to plead with King to show mercy. The prime minister was in Washington, so he left the decision to his Cabinet. The acting prime minister, Quebec's Ernest Lapointe, turned to Frederick Blair for a recommendation. His response was blunt and unflinching: the refugees were not Canada's problem. "The line must be drawn somewhere,"[54] Blair is said to have argued.

On 6 June, the *St Louis* turned back for Germany. Frantic European diplomatic maneuvering offered the refugees temporary respite in Britain, France, Belgium, and the Netherlands. When the latter three countries fell to the Nazis within the year, their Jewish refugees were once more in mortal danger. Two hundred and fifty-four of the *St. Louis*'s passengers died in the Holocaust. Despite the grave humanitarian crisis, Canada accepted 4000 Jewish refugees during the entirety of the war, the worst record in the developed world.[55] Nonetheless, under King's leadership, the Liberals were re-elected with majorities in 1940 and 1945.

In 1997, an interdenominational Christian group, Watchmen for the Nations, initiated a campaign to convince the Canadian government to acknowledge its anti-Semitism with particular reference to the *St Louis* tragedy. In 2000, a reunion of the voyage's survivors was held in Ottawa. Representatives from Canadian churches, including Baptist minister Doug Blair, great-nephew of the former director of immigration, offered institutional and personal apologies. In

48 CANADA FIRST, NOT CANADA ALONE

2011, the Canadian Jewish Congress commissioned a memorial in Halifax, the "Wheel of Conscience," inspired by the plight of the refugees.[56] Prime Minister Justin Trudeau formally apologized in November 2018 in the House of Commons to families of the passengers of the *St Louis* for Ottawa's conduct.[57] Nonetheless, anti-Semitism in Canada persists.

Not all Canadians approved of their governments' actions in 1939, nor did the entirety of the public service.[58] *Saturday Night* magazine and writers for the *Winnipeg Free Press* frequently objected.[59] Individual public servants, select media outlets, and civil society were no match against an empowered and vociferous director of immigration whose racist views complemented a cautious prime minister's effort to maintain what he called national unity. To King, threats to that unity, as indicated by the positions of his senior Cabinet ministers, posed grave danger to Canada's strategic interests. No international humanitarian disaster was worth the risk of undermining the viability of his government.

The Hyde Park Declaration, 1941

What can Canada do when its interests are compromised by powerful allies?

On the whole, Canada benefits from having friends in high places. Prior to the Second World War, its Commonwealth ties to the United Kingdom and its close relations with the United States typically reinforced its efforts to advance the national interest. But when London faced possible defeat in 1940, Washington responded in a manner that risked undermining Canada's economic prospects. The actions of King's Liberal government illustrate both the benefits and the drawbacks of Canada's place in the North Atlantic Triangle.[60]

Shortly after the outbreak of the Second World War, the fall of France to German invasion, the nearly catastrophic loss of the British Expeditionary Force at Dunkirk, and a significant loss of wartime supplies produced a series of shocks to the UK economy. The British Purchasing Mission in the United States was able to take over France's remaining American contracts to prevent them from falling into Nazi hands, but London was unable to fund a proper defence of the European continent. Within months, Winston Churchill's government had depleted its supply of US currency.[61] In January 1941, the Roosevelt Administration introduced the Lend-Lease Act, which enabled Washington to provide London with the equivalent of a $7 billion line of credit toward military goods. Neither side expected the money to be paid back.

The implications for Canada were dire. With France defeated and the United States not yet formally involved in the war, Ottawa had become London's most significant ally against German aggression. Canadians had willingly supplied the British war machine with as much materiél as they could ship, but doing so meant drawing down Canada's reserves of US currency to pay for American parts and components. Ottawa had traditionally balanced its trade surplus with London against its deficit with Washington. However, the combination of Lend Lease and changes to currency exchange laws in response to the war threatened to end British spending in Canada altogether. Why buy Canadian when America was offering similar products for free? Without sales to Britain, Ottawa would quickly deplete its US dollar reserves and compromise its own industrial production. Accepting Lend Lease was not an option—American conditions for doing so, which included the divestment of all of Canada's US assets, would have compromised Ottawa's long-term financial position.[62] Canada needed another way to restore its reserve of US dollars.

King regarded the outcome of the Canadian response, the Hyde Park Declaration, as "a triumph of personal diplomacy."[63] The reality was more complex. A combination of Canadian public servants and Cabinet ministers ultimately devised a two-tier approach to solving the balance of payments crisis without undermining Canada's long-term negotiating position in Washington. First, America would allow the costs of US component parts purchased by Canadian industry for use in production to support the British military effort to be charged to London's Lend-Lease account. Second, America would offset Canadian investments in the United States by agreeing to purchase at least $200–$300 million in defence materiél from Canada every year. The latter idea was pitched to Roosevelt's Treasury Secretary Henry Morgenthau Jr by King's Minister for Munitions and Supply C.D. Howe as a kind of "barter."[64] It was clever, even if Robert Borden's government had reached a similar arrangement with Washington near the end of the First World War.[65]

On 21 March, Canada's Deputy Minister of Finance Clifford Clark suggested to the Cabinet War Committee that only a personal conversation between King and Roosevelt could finalize the agreement. In mid-April, Howe and Clark laid the groundwork for King's visit with US Secretary of State Cordell Hull and Morgenthau. The prime minister was briefed by Howe's staff and provided with a press release, drafted by Clark and his team, for Roosevelt to sign. King then boarded a train for the Roosevelt family home in Hyde Park.

The meeting could not have been more successful. As King later noted in his diary, "I confess that I was never more surprised in my life than when he accepted the statement as a whole without a word, unless it was when he told me to give it out myself to the press when I got to the [train] station."[66] Roosevelt agreed that America would cover the cost of Canadian purchases in the United

50 CANADA FIRST, NOT CANADA ALONE

States intended for export to Britain under Lend-Lease and to annual purchases of at least $200 million to $300 million in Canadian war supplies. King was asked for nothing in return.[67] Howe created a new Crown corporation, War Supplies Limited, to facilitate sales. Canada's shortage of US dollars ended almost immediately. A Joint Economic Committee was formed two months later in part to prevent the problem from recurring.[68]

No doubt King's excellent relationship with Roosevelt contributed to this grand success, as did the president's general sympathy for Canada's situation.[69] But the work of the two men's Cabinets also mattered. So did preparatory negotiations led by the Canadian public service, especially within the departments of Finance, External Affairs, and Munitions and Supply. The agreement was also easy for Washington to make. Given the extent of US investment in Canada, the collapse of the Canadian manufacturing industry posed a risk to America's economic health. Even $300 million represented less than 5 per cent of Washington's commitment to Lend-Lease. The declaration did not require additional approval from Congress, and it provided the US military with immediate access to much needed armaments.[70]

When King briefed Parliament on the agreement on 28 April, he characterized the Hyde Park Declaration as "more than an extension of the Ogdensburg Agreement for hemispheric defence. It is also a joint agreement between Canada and the United States for aid to Britain."[71] Strategically, it was also "a common plan of the economic defence of the western hemisphere."[72] Through it, Canada and the United States were "laying the enduring foundations of a new world order, an order based on international understanding, on mutual aid, on friendship and good will."[73] That final phrase was telling: good relations between the two leaders were critical to overcoming the unintended consequences of great power unilateralism. But they were not enough on their own. Canada would have to cultivate relations across Washington and beyond on a continuous basis to preserve its otherwise privileged position in the North Atlantic Triangle.

The Debate over Article 2 of the North Atlantic Treaty, 1947–1949

What role can, or should, idealism play in Canadian foreign policy?

Long-time Canadian diplomat Escott Reid called his memoir on the history of the founding of the North Atlantic Treaty Organization (NATO) *Time of Fear and Hope*.[74] The fear, explained Lester Pearson, was of Soviet aggression, "a fear intensified by the failure of every effort to bring about a more friendly and co-operative relationship with Moscow, both at the United Nations and in the

Four Power machinery set up after the war to plan the peace settlement."[75] The hope was that a new regional security arrangement, complementary to but outside of the United Nations, might unify the West and strengthen its capacity to resist and deter. Reid, an assistant undersecretary; Pearson, his immediate superior; and their minister, Louis St Laurent, began to express this idea publicly toward the end of 1947.[76]

The British, led by Foreign Secretary Ernest Bevin, were thinking similarly. In March 1948, Belgium, France, Luxembourg, the Netherlands, and the United Kingdom signed the Treaty of Brussels and formed the Western Union. The new organization was meant in part to feed into a broader North Atlantic security alliance to include Canada and the United States. British and Canadian diplomats joined their colleagues in Washington for a series of secret "Security Conversations" a few days later. The Canadian contribution to what ultimately became the 12-country North Atlantic Treaty Organization on 4 April 1949 was unspectacular. Canada's negotiators were competent and respected, but their critical goal—the inclusion of the United States in a multilateral defence agreement—was uncontroversial. Nevertheless, NATO histories reference the North Atlantic Treaty's second, "Canadian" or "general welfare," article:

> The Parties will contribute toward the further development of peaceful and friendly international relations by strengthening their free institutions, by bringing about a better understanding of the principles upon which these institutions are founded, and by promoting conditions of stability and well-being. They will seek to eliminate conflict in their international economic policies and will encourage economic collaboration between any or all of them.[77]

With a number of Western diplomats, most notably Secretary of State Dean Acheson, opposed to this language, Article 2 might have been excluded from the final text were it not for Ottawa's persistence.

Ironically, even the Canadians doubted its value. The disagreement centred on two complementary issues: the purpose of the alliance and the best diplomatic strategy to achieve it. Some officials, with Reid most prominent among them, were more ambitious and aggressive. Those who preferred a bare-bones agreement led by Canada's ambassador to the United States, Hume Wrong, were diplomatic pragmatists. In early 1948, Canada's Western European partners were ambivalent on the idea of a new international institution, the British were opposed, and Washington's views were inconsistent. A simple agreement, Wrong argued, was most easily achievable.[78]

Proponents of a comprehensive institution believed that a military alliance was insufficient. Norman Robertson, high commissioner in London,

52   CANADA FIRST, NOT CANADA ALONE

maintained that greater North Atlantic unity would facilitate the diversification of Canadian trade, an important consideration given increasing economic reliance on the United States. Pearson worried that "an alliance founded on the fear of aggression [could] disappear," were that fear ever removed. Communities were the glue that kept alliances together.[79] King, who accepted the initial British request to negotiate a North Atlantic treaty before retiring, believed that political and cultural integration enabled military co-operation. Louis St Laurent—first as King's foreign minister and then as prime minister himself—agreed, but also recognized the political benefits of a less exclusively military alliance on the campaign trail in Quebec and in ridings where the social democratic Co-operative Commonwealth Federation was strong.[80]

The community seekers disagreed among themselves over tactics.[81] Robertson hesitated to put forth any idea that might be deemed far-fetched by Canada's negotiating partners. Pearson foresaw the development of a North Atlantic community in evolutionary terms. King preferred that the great powers drive the treaty negotiations, with Canada providing support only when called upon. All three might have disputed Wrong's interpretation of the purpose of NATO, but they understood his caution and heeded his warning in June 1948 that pushing for more than a "simple general article which would cover economic collaboration and set up some sort of consultative organ or organs...[could] wreck the whole project."[82]

In a letter to Pearson, Wrong contended: "There is a profound difference between setting one's sights high and taking the line that if you can't get what you want you won't take half a loaf."[83] Wrong and Robertson outranked Reid and, in normal circumstances, that might have been enough for their views to prevail. But the year-long negotiations did not take place in normal times. In January 1948, King had announced his intent to resign as prime minister. Pearson, formerly the undersecretary of state for external affairs, joined the government as St Laurent's replacement. Pearson himself was not replaced on a permanent basis for half a year, meaning that Assistant Undersecretary Reid became Wrong's acting superior for a significant portion of the North Atlantic discussions.[84]

The Canadian delegation therefore pressed the inclusion of what became the treaty's second article unevenly. Pearson mentioned it only in passing during the first, secret, talks with London and Washington in March 1948. As Reid's influence increased, the Canadians pushed harder during broader consultations between July and September. That autumn the Europeans adopted the British, minimalist, view of the alliance, prompting Reid to urge the Canadian delegation to fight back. Wrong did, reluctantly, albeit successfully, until Acheson took over as secretary of state in early 1949. Acheson was not convinced that the community idea would be acceptable to the US Congress, where many members were already skeptical of joining a peacetime military alliance. The Europeans quickly backed off, and Ottawa was left alone in advocating a more comprehensive agreement. By then, however, St Laurent was firmly established as prime minister, and Pearson had taken command of the department. Together, they decided to press the issue. Ottawa lobbied the European capitals; St Laurent spoke with the new US president, Harry Truman; and Wrong made one final, successful effort to convince Acheson, his friend, to change his mind.[85]

The treaty article that emerged was, paradoxically, both an utter failure and a veritable success. Despite Pearson and others' efforts, it was never institutionalized. NATO ultimately formalized a series of military committees, but it never created similar economic, social, or cultural ones.[86] Yet the existence of an article that proclaimed the regional organization to be more than just a military operation retained diplomatic value. As one analyst has noted, "Article 2 later became the principal authority for the improvement of political consultation in the alliance, an objective that took on ever more importance as the Cold War intensified. The smaller allies had an interest in enforcing club rules, and Article 2 helped to serve the purpose."[87]

Conclusion

William Lyon Mackenzie King's departure from Canada's political scene was as deliberate as his approach to international diplomacy. In 1946, when his preferred successor, Louis St Laurent, mused about returning to the private sector, King reluctantly made him foreign minister. When the longest-serving Canadian prime minister announced his plan to retire sixteen months later, the Liberals chose St Laurent as his replacement. St Laurent took over as prime minister in November 1948.

King's departure coincided with an evolving understanding of how to maximize Canadian interests on the world stage. His governments had hesitated before engaging abroad. Only an existential threat to the security of the British Empire, or the wider Western world, merited more than passive support for international commitments that always risked dividing the country at home. Jewish refugees fleeing the Nazis in 1939 did not meet his litmus test.

By the middle of the Second World War, many Canadians had begun to think of their country as part of an international community, membership in which outweighed its drawbacks. Such popular sentiment, welcomed by the DEA under the leadership of Norman Robertson, all but obligated King to open up Canadian foreign policy, however prudently. Under St Laurent, the commitment to multilateralism as a basis for advancing the national interest

54 CANADA FIRST, NOT CANADA ALONE

was normalized. Certainly, Canada continued to look out for its own needs. Doing so, however, increasingly meant active participation in the governance and management of the world order, whether through NATO or other global arrangements.

Readings

The international history of the 1930s and 1940s is vast. On the descent to war in the 1930s, Zara Steiner's opus is essential: *The Triumph of the Dark: European International History, 1933–1939* (Oxford: Oxford University Press, 2011). For a thorough look at Anglo-American relations, see B.J.C. McKercher, *Transition of Power: Britain's Loss of Global Pre-eminence to the United States, 1930–1945* (Cambridge: Cambridge University Press, 1999). The essential studies of the Roosevelt administration's foreign policy remain: Robert Dallek, *Franklin D. Roosevelt and American Foreign Policy, 1932–1945* (New York: Oxford University Press, 1979) and Warren F. Kimball, *The Juggler: Franklin Roosevelt as Wartime Statesman* (Princeton: Princeton University Press, 1994). Key studies of international history in relation to the early Cold War include David Reynolds, *From World War to Cold War: Churchill, Roosevelt, and the International History of the 1940s* (Oxford: Oxford University Press, 2006); Wilson D. Miscamble, *From Roosevelt to Truman: Potsdam, Hiroshima, and the Cold War* (Cambridge: Cambridge University Press, 2007); and the essays in Melvyn P. Leffler and Odd Arne Westad, *The Cambridge History of the Cold War: Volume 1, Origins* (Cambridge: Cambridge University Press, 2010).

The standard examination of Canadian foreign policy during the late King era is C.P. Stacey, *Canada in the Age of Conflict*, vol. 2: *1921–1948, The Mackenzie King Record* (Toronto: University of Toronto Press, 1981). For recent critical analyses, see Roy MacLaren, *Mackenzie King in the Age of the Dictators: Canada's Imperial and Foreign Policies* (Montreal: McGill-Queen's University Press, 2019) and Robert Teigrob, *Four Days in Hitler's Germany: Mackenzie King's Mission to Avert a Second World War* (Toronto: University of Toronto Press, 2019). Teigrob also authored a critical examination of Canadian foreign policy at the onset of the Cold War: *Warming Up to the Cold War: Canada and the United States' Coalition of the Willing, from Hiroshima to Korea* (Toronto: University of Toronto Press, 2009). Other key histories of King's wartime years include Iain Johnston-White, *The British Commonwealth and Victory in the Second World War* (London: Palgrave, 2016), and Galen Roger Perras, *Franklin Roosevelt and the Origins of the Canadian-American Security Alliance, 1933–1945* (Westport: Praeger, 1998). J.L. Granatstein has also authored an important text covering Canada's place amid the Anglo-American transition of power: *How Britain's Weakness Forced Canada into the Arms of the United States* (Toronto: University of Toronto Press, 1989). In addition to C.P. Stacey, *Mackenzie King and the Atlantic Triangle* (Toronto: University of Toronto Press, 1976) and Ian M. Drummond and Norman Hillmer, *Negotiating Freer Trade: The United Kingdom, the United States, Canada, and the Trade Agreements of 1938* (Waterloo: Wilfrid Laurier University Press, 1989), there are several chapters on the North Atlantic Triangle under King in B.J.C. McKercher and Lawrence Aronsen, eds., *The North Atlantic Triangle in a Changing World* (Toronto: University of Toronto Press, 1996). Justin Massie makes the case for transforming the triangle to include France in his "North Atlantic Quadrangle: Mackenzie King's lasting imprint on Canada's international security policy," *London Journal of Canadian Studies* 24, no. 5 (2008–9): 85–105. On Canada's war effort as viewed from Ottawa, see J.L. Granatstein, *Canada's War: The Politics of the Mackenzie King Government, 1939–1945* (Toronto: Oxford University Press, 1975), and Tim Cook, *Warlords: Borden, Mackenzie King, and Canada's World Wars* (Toronto: Penguin, 2012).

The best article on the voyage of the MS *St Louis* remains Irving Abella and Harold Troper, " 'The line must be drawn somewhere': Canada and Jewish refugees, 1933–9," *Canadian Historical Review* 60, no. 2 (1979): 178–209, https://doi.org/10.3138/CHR-060-02-04. That essay forms much of the first two chapters of their book *None Is Too Many: Canada and the Jews of Europe, 1933–1948* (Toronto: Lester & Orpen Dennys, 1982). For a popular account, see Gordon Thomas and Max Morgan Witts, *Voyage of the Damned* (New York: Stein and Day, 1974). A broader summary of Canadian refugee policy during this period can be found in Gerald E. Dirks, *Canada's Refugee Policy: Indifference or Opportunism?* (Montreal: McGill-Queen's University Press, 1977), 44–71. Broader histories of Canadian immigration policy include Valerie Knowles, *Strangers at Our Gates: Canadian Immigration and Immigration Policy, 1540–2015*, 4th ed. (Toronto: Dundurn Press, 2016) and Ninette Kelley and Michael Trebilcock, *The Making of the Mosaic: A History of Canadian Immigration Policy*, 2nd ed. (Toronto: University of Toronto Press, 2010). On immigration more generally, see the open access *Canadian Immigration History Syllabus* at https://ecampusontario.pressbooks.pub/immigrationsyllabus/. For a look at Canadian attitudes toward German persecution of Jews, see Amanda Grzyb, "From Kristallnacht to the MS *St Louis* tragedy: Canadian press coverage of Nazi persecution of the Jews and the Jewish refugee crisis, September 1938 to August 1939," in L. Ruth Klein, ed., *Nazi Germany, Canadian Responses: Confronting Antisemitism in the Shadow of War* (Montreal: McGill-Queen's University Press, 2012), 78–113. On recent reconciliation efforts, see Robin Long Mullins, "The SS St. Louis and the importance of reconciliation," *Peace and Conflict: Journal of Peace Psychology* 19, no. 4 (2013): 393–8, https://doi.

org/10.1037/a0034610. On the impact of the Holocaust on Canada's Jewish community, see Franklin Bialystok, *Delayed Impact: The Holocaust and the Canadian Jewish Community* (Montreal: McGill-Queen's University Press, 2000).

For a summary of Canadian economic contributions to the evolving world order during this period, see Kathleen Britt Rasmussen, "Canada and the reconstruction of the international economy, 1941–1947," (University of Toronto, PhD thesis, 2001), and Francine McKenzie, *Redefining the Bonds of Commonwealth, 1939–1948: The Politics of Preference* (New York: Palgrave Macmillan, 2002). The best overview of the Hyde Park case is J.L. Granatstein and R.D. Cuff, "The Hyde Park Declaration 1941: Origins and significance," *Canadian Historical Review* 55, no. 1 (1974): 59–80, https://doi.org/10.3138/CHR-055-01-03. The declaration itself is reproduced on pages 79–80. See also J.W. Pickersgill, *The Mackenzie King Record*, vol. 1, *1939–1944* (Toronto: University of Toronto Press, 1960), 186–204. Even more extensive primary source evidence can be found in David R. Murray, ed., *Documents on Canadian External Relations*, vol. 8, *1939–1941*, part 2 (Ottawa: Minister of Supply and Services Canada, 1976), 277–351. For C.D. Howe's role, see Robert Bothwell and William Kilbourn, *C.D. Howe: A Biography* (Toronto: McClelland and Stewart, 1979). On the impact of Clifford Clark and the Department of Finance more broadly, see Robert B. Bryce, *Canada and the Cost of World War II: The International Operations of Canada's Department of Finance, 1939–1947* (Montreal: McGill-Queen's University Press, 2005). Galen Roger Perras considers the issue through an American lens in his *Franklin Roosevelt and the Origins of the Canadian-American Security Alliance, 1933–1945* (Westport: Praeger, 1998).

The best source on the history of Canada's position on NATO's Article 2 and its implications is John C. Milloy, *The North Atlantic Treaty Organization 1948–1957: Community of Alliance?* (Montreal: McGill-Queen's University Press, 2006). Escott Reid's "Canada and the creation of the North Atlantic alliance, 1948–1949," in Michael G. Fry, ed., *Freedom and Change: Essays in Honour of Lester B. Pearson* (Toronto: McClelland and Stewart, 1975), 106–35 is a good summary of the argument he makes in his longer *Time of Fear and Hope: The Making of the North Atlantic Treaty 1947–1949* (Toronto: McClelland and Stewart, 1977). For primary source evidence, see the relevant volumes of the *Documents on Canadian External Relations* and *Foreign Relations of the United States* series, which can be found online at https://www.international.gc.ca/gac-amc/history-histoire/external-relations_relations-exterieures.aspx?lang=eng and https://history.state.gov/historicaldocuments/truman, respectively. The best history of NATO is Timothy Andrews Sayle, *Enduring Alliance: A History of NATO and the Postwar Global Order* (Ithaca: Cornell University Press, 2019).

Beyond the Book

Granting the Great Powers a Veto in the United Nations Organization, 1945

In April 1945, representatives of 50 countries gathered in San Francisco, California, to open the United Nations Conference on International Organization. Their goal was to transform a series of proposals developed by the United States, the United Kingdom, the Union of Soviet Socialist Republics, and China (the Dumbarton Oaks proposals, 1944) into a full-fledged collective security organization. At Dumbarton Oaks, and again in February 1945 at Yalta, it had been made clear that there would be no United Nations if the great powers were not given the right to veto resolutions of the Security Council. Naturally, the smaller states, Canada among them, objected. How could an organization that pledged to promote the equality of its state-members include a provision that was so deliberately unequal? The representatives from Australia and New Zealand were particularly aghast. At San Francisco, Australia's foreign minister, Herbert Evatt, introduced a motion to restrict the veto power. On 16 June, that motion came to a vote. Canada's decision on whether to support Evatt and his smaller power colleagues would be critical to the outcome.

Questions

1. What are Canada's interests in this case?
2. How should Canada vote on the Australian amendment?
3. Should the Canadian delegation advocate on this issue or merely vote when the time comes?

Readings

Among the key sources on this case are Adam Chapnick, *The Middle Power Project: Canada and the Founding of the United Nations* (Vancouver: UBC Press, 2005), chapter 10, especially 134–8; J.L. Granatstein, *A Man of Influence: Norman A. Robertson and Canadian Statecraft, 1929–1968* (Toronto: Deneau Publishers, 1981), 143–55; Hector Mackenzie, "'Writing marginal notes on the pages of history': Escott Reid and the founding of the United Nations, 1945–46," in Greg Donaghy and Stéphane Roussel, eds., *Escott Reid: Diplomat and Scholar* (Montreal: McGill-Queen's University Press, 2004), 23–43, especially

23–32; James Eayrs, *In Defence of Canada*, vol. 3, *Peacemaking and Deterrence* (Toronto: University of Toronto Press, 1972), 152–61; and John W. Holmes, *The Shaping of Peace: Canada and the Search for World Order, 1943–1957*, vol. 1 (Toronto: University of Toronto Press, 1979), 229–57. International sources include Ruth B. Russell, *A History of the United Nations Charter* (Washington, DC: Brookings Institution, 1958), especially 735–41; and Neville Meaney, "Dr HV Evatt and the United Nations: The problem of collective security and liberal internationalism," in James Cotton and David Lee, eds., *Australia and the United Nations* (Canberra: Longueville Books, 2012), 34–47. For primary source evidence, see John F. Hilliker, ed., *Documents on Canadian External Relations*, vol. 11, *1944–1945*, pt 2 (Ottawa: Supply and Services Canada, 1990), 784–93; *Foreign Relations of the United States: Diplomatic Papers, 1945, General: The United Nations*, vol. 1 (Washington, DC: United States Government Printing Office, 1967), especially chapters 5 and 6, https://history.state.gov/historicaldocuments/frus1945v01; and United Nations, *Documents of the United Nations Conference on International Organization, San Francisco, 1945*, vol. 11 (London: United Nations Information Organization, 1945), especially 675–806, https://digitallibrary.un.org/record/1300969/files/UNIO-Volume-11-E-F.pdf.

3

Louis St Laurent and the Expansion of the Canadian Foreign Policy Realm, 1948–1957

The Golden Age

The period from roughly 1948 to 1957 has often been characterized as the golden age of Canadian foreign policy. George Ignatieff, a leading diplomat of the era, recalled that, with Louis St Laurent as prime minister and Lester Pearson as secretary of state for external affairs, "there was a sense of mission in our foreign policy, a conviction that, as a middle-sized power with a good deal of economic clout and international prestige, Canada had both an obligation and the ability to act as an architect of peaceful solutions to intractable problems."[1] Like the middle power conception, the golden age has had a potent hold on Canadian imaginations. However, more than a period of revolution, the era was the product of a unique set of temporary circumstances. Canada's relative position of power and importance increased largely because of the wartime devastation of Europe and Asia. At home, policy was guided by a cohesive and capable foreign service whose members, having lived through depression and war, largely shared the same internationalist outlook, as well as the same gender, ethnicity, first language, and religion.[2]

More foreign policy was made under St Laurent's leadership than during the King years. Missions were established in Pakistan (1949), Ceylon (1952), Indonesia (1953), Israel and Egypt (1954), Lebanon (1955), and Malaysia and Ghana (1957). In addition to NATO, Ottawa supported a range of new international organizations: the International Bank for Reconstruction and Development, the International Civil Aviation Organization (based in Montreal), the International Court of Justice, the International Monetary Fund, and the World Health Organization.[3] Some of these organizations were linked to the United Nations—including the UN Relief and Rehabilitation Administration and the UN Technical Assistance Administration[4]—where Canada occupied a seat on the Security Council in 1948–9.[5] The expansion of the Canadian foreign service saw the inclusion of increasing numbers of women within the Department of External Affairs. Although a ban on married women remained

Canada First, Not Canada Alone: A History of Canadian Foreign Policy. Adam Chapnick and Asa McKercher, Oxford University Press. © Oxford University Press 2024. DOI: 10.1093/oso/9780197653715.003.0004

60 CANADA FIRST, NOT CANADA ALONE

in effect until 1971, in 1954 Elizabeth MacCallum became chargé d'affaires in Beirut. Marion Macpherson was named to the International Commission for Supervision and Control in Vietnam. Margaret Meagher served as counsellor at Canada House in London from 1953 to 1957 and later as Canada's first woman ambassador to Israel.[6]

Ottawa's support for internationalist institutions and principles had limits. In 1948, Canadian diplomats looked askance at the adoption of the Universal Declaration of Human Rights (UDHR). Although John Humphrey, a Canadian lawyer, authored much of the document, he contributed as a private citizen. As he later lamented, "the international promotion of human rights had no priority in Canadian foreign policy."[7] Canada's treatment of Indigenous peoples and its racist immigration policy caused St Laurent to fear that the UDHR could become "a source of embarrassment." Eventually, to avoid being placed in the "undesirable minority" of states opposing the declaration—largely members of the Soviet bloc——Canada supported the document.[8] A 1951 revision to the Indian Act implemented a handful of progressive changes at home, including the legalization of traditional cultural practices, but Status Indians remained, in effect, colonial subjects and were not granted the right to vote until 1960. Although Ottawa implemented a huge post-war boost in immigration, the country's immigration laws allowed in only a small quota of non-white immigrants.[9] The initial post-war human rights revolution had its limits.

Canada, Korea, and the Cold War

At minimum, policymakers during the St Laurent years aimed to meet Canada's collective security commitments. This newfound internationalist spirit was reflected not only in support for NATO—including the November 1951 deployment of an infantry brigade and 12 fighter squadrons to Western Europe—but also the dispatch of military units to Korea. Official Canadian involvement in Korea began in 1948, when Ottawa sent observers to the UN Temporary Commission on Korea (UNTCOK). The commission had been formed to oversee elections in the divided peninsula, occupied in the north by the Soviet Union and in the south by the United States. Participation in UNTCOK had split the Canadian Cabinet, with St Laurent and other internationalist-minded ministers pushing against King's isolationism. When St Laurent threatened to resign, King relented.[10]

The UNTCOK experience was difficult. The Canadian delegates opposed US efforts to hold separate elections in South Korea when the Soviets blocked UNTCOK's involvement in the North.[11] Such problems were emblematic of the sclerosis taking hold in the UN as the Cold War unfolded. UNTCOK did nothing to stop the tensions on the peninsula. On 25 June 1950, North Korean forces, backed by the Soviet Union and Communist China, invaded the South.

The outbreak of the Korean War followed two developments that had transformed the Cold War: the Soviet test of a nuclear bomb in August 1949 and the communist victory in China's civil war that October. The former raised the possibility of a Soviet nuclear attack; the latter seemingly made containing communism a global task. Two days after the North Korean invasion, the UN Security Council authorized member states to intervene. Although the Soviet Union could have vetoed the resolution, its representative was boycotting the council to protest the West's refusal to allow communists from Beijing to take over the seat still held by the defeated Nationalists ensconced in Formosa (Taiwan). The UN had inadvertently invoked collective security. Lester Pearson publicly praised President Harry Truman's administration for leading the international response "with admirable dispatch and decisiveness."[12] Privately, he told his fellow Cabinet members that effective US action in Korea "would be helpful generally in the cold war" by showcasing American will to confront communist aggression.[13] After all, it was US power that undergirded the Western alliance.[14]

Canada's initial support for the war included token naval vessels meant more to showcase the multilateral nature of the UN operation than to genuinely augment the primarily American forces based in Japan. Over the summer of 1950, under pressure from Washington to contribute more fulsomely, Canadian officials considered dispatching ground troops. In making the public case for such a move, Pearson recalled the failures of the League of Nations. With the UN intervention in Korea, he declared, "collective security has been shown to mean something."[15] In August 1950, Ottawa appealed for volunteers to form an infantry brigade. This effort, Pearson reminded St Laurent, "underlines the fact that from now on we fight only as a result of UN decisions, and with other UN members."[16] The Canadian brigade first saw action in February 1951, by which point the war had reached a stalemate.[17] In contrast to the world wars, for many Canadians the conflict seemed distant. Still, the military buildup was expensive. Between 1949 and 1954, annual defence spending increased from $361 million to $1.9 billion, the latter representing 7.6% of GDP.[18] The defence budgets of Canada's NATO allies grew similarly.

The End of "Easy and Automatic" Relations with the United States

Diplomatically, the Korean War exposed divisions between Ottawa and Washington. The American-led military offensive launched in September 1950 succeeded in liberating the South and pushing the communist forces back into

62 CANADA FIRST, NOT CANADA ALONE

the North. Rather than considering the intervention a success, the United States rejected the advice of fellow UN members and in October brazenly sent troops to the China–North Korea border, provoking Chinese communist forces to enter the war. As the fighting turned against the United Nations, senior US officers contemplated deploying nuclear weapons. Pearson cautioned the White House that the atomic bomb was more than "just another weapon." Its use, particularly against civilian targets, would damage US prestige and harm the cohesion of the Western alliance.[19] As the situation escalated, Canadian diplomats urged their American counterparts to pursue negotiations with the communist powers and encouraged an Indian effort to broker a ceasefire agreement.[20]

In March 1951, Pearson publicly voiced Ottawa's concerns once more. Taking aim at General Douglas MacArthur, the overbearing American commander of UN forces, he called it "unwise, indeed...dangerous, for the generals to intervene in international policy matters as it would be for the diplomats to try to lay down military strategy."[21] When Truman fired MacArthur for insubordination several days later, some commentators erroneously blamed Pearson.[22] In April 1951, Pearson outlined further dissatisfaction with the fallout over Korea, urging that efforts be taken to ensure that "the United Nations remains the instrument of collective policy of all of its members...and does not become too much an instrument of any one country." In a turn of phrase that made headlines, he stated, "the days of relatively easy and automatic political relations with our neighbour are, I think, over."[23] The Korean Armistice was finally reached on 27 July 1953. Canadian hesitancy in the face of American unilateralism persisted.

Despite such concerns, Ottawa remained mindful of the importance of Canada's alliance with the United States. After the communist victory in China's civil war, Washington refused to recognize the new regime in Beijing. Although other Western powers followed America's lead, the British did not. In early 1950, Ottawa looked as if it would adopt London's position. As diplomat Chester Ronning counselled, it would be better to "have a seat inside the bamboo curtain rather than trying to peer in from the outside."[24] But the pressure to show solidarity with the United States was too great. Canada supported a US-backed UN resolution condemning the Chinese as aggressors during the Korean War. Beijing responded by expelling Ronning from China, and Ottawa backed away from recognition.[25] "As time went on," Ronning later admitted, "Canada's hesitation was due more to American influence than any other single factor."[26] Even so, Canadian policymakers were hardly pleased by US brinkmanship during a military standoff over disputed islands between mainland China and Taiwan. As Pearson remarked to John Foster Dulles, the hawkish American secretary of state, there was a real danger of actions by the superpowers "converting small wars into world wars."[27]

The possibility of a crisis in some far-flung locale escalating to the point of a nuclear exchange between the United States and the Soviet Union was a worst-case scenario for Canadian policymakers. Military and civilian officials understood Canada lay between two nuclear-armed superpowers. Hence, they supported the American strategy of deterrence: to prevent a Soviet-American conflict, both sides had to believe that the other would be willing to respond to an attack with overwhelming force. This threat would deter any conflict from occurring. Canadian military forces assigned to NATO in Europe were part of an allied effort to deter Soviet aggression. Meanwhile, to bolster the American nuclear arsenal, the St Laurent government agreed to co-operate with the US military in fortifying North America. "Obviously everything that is done in Canada to strengthen the defence against air attack," Defence Minister Brooke Claxton affirmed in November 1953, "is done not only for the defence of Canada but, at least equally important, for the defence of targets in the United States."[28] In addition to new fighter aircraft to intercept Soviet bombers and new airfields, Ottawa committed to building several lines of radar stations across Canada's far North. The Soviet test of a thermonuclear weapon in August 1953 only compounded the importance of an effective continental defence network.

Fears of a nuclear attack on Canada were evident throughout the 1950s. As early as August 1945, the editors of a leading Canadian newsmagazine had worried that there was "no guarantee that what happened this week in Hiroshima may not happen at some remote date to Montreal or Edmonton."[29] In response, the federal government rolled out a civil defence program, including new fall-out shelters and duck-and-cover drills for schoolchildren.[30] Cold War fears extended to the hunt for spies and subversives, an extension of the Red Scare mania that poisoned domestic politics in the United States. Hundreds of Canadian civil servants and military personnel were demoted or fired—many were LGBTQ+—on the pretence that they were susceptible to blackmail in an age when gay sex was illegal.[31] Congressional hearings in the United States also snared several Canadians, most notably E. Herbert Norman, Canadian ambassador in Cairo, who was so shaken by accusations that he was a communist spy that he leapt to his death off the rooftop of the Swedish Embassy.[32] This paranoia about communist subversion cast a dark cloud over the economic prosperity that characterized post-war Canada.

Although the St Laurent government was firmly committed to the ideological struggle against communism and to the military effort to deter the Soviets, it continued to pursue diplomatic means to lessen Cold War tension. That task was made easier after Joseph Stalin's death in March 1953. In 1954, Ottawa re-appointed an ambassador to Moscow and in October 1955 Pearson became the first NATO foreign minister to visit the USSR.[33] Upon his return, Pearson told

US President Dwight Eisenhower "that he thought something pretty important was happening in Russia, something which might present us with opportunities which we should exploit."[34] In February 1956, Canada and the Soviet Union concluded a bilateral trade agreement and announced a series of cultural exchanges.

The Impact of Decolonization

Just as important as the Cold War to Canadian foreign policy during the St Laurent years was the overlapping issue of decolonization. The late 1940s witnessed the increasing collapse of formal European imperialism. Decolonization of India in 1946 and Palestine in 1948 exposed religious and racial fault lines that generated their own messy conflicts, a common development in many newly decolonized states. In other cases—the French in Indochina and Algeria, the British in Malaya and Kenya—European powers relinquished control reluctantly and often after mounting stiff resistance to anti-colonial forces. When Newfoundland joined Canada as the tenth province in 1949, its peaceful separation from Britain was an exception to the violent contested processes that transformed much of the globe in the two decades following the Second World War.[35] As decolonization proceeded apace, Canadian policymakers had little interest in helping their Western European allies prop up fading empires. Even so, Ottawa was careful not to upset its allies by backing independence movements or tolerating international condemnation of the imperial powers.[36]

Decolonization and, with it, the creation of dozens of new countries necessitated a further expansion of Canadian ties abroad, particularly in Asia. "Canada," Pearson noted in 1950, "had a general interest as a world power, and a special interest as a Pacific power" in involving itself in Asian affairs.[37] Indeed, in 1954 St Laurent became the first sitting Canadian prime minister to travel to Asia, a tour that opened his eyes to the interests and demands of people in what was then called the Third World—the bloc of countries that stood apart from the Cold War.[38] That same year, Canadian officials reluctantly agreed to help enforce the Geneva Accords that concluded fighting between France and anti-colonial forces in Indochina. Representing the West alongside neutral India and communist Poland, Canada deployed observers to the International Commission for Supervision and Control (ICSC) to monitor the ceasefire.

Considering its size and influence, maintaining and strengthening ties with India was critical. Ottawa backed India's entry into the Commonwealth and promoted a solution to allow that country to remain in the organization even as it became a republic rather than a constitutional monarchy. In a sign of high hopes for warm relations, in 1956 Canada's government-owned nuclear agency began selling India nuclear technology and uranium, which the Indians would later use to build a nuclear bomb.[39] Canada also sought to forge links with countries such as Indonesia and Pakistan. When the leaders of 29 newly independent states met at Bandung, Indonesia, in 1955 to form a loose bloc committed to non-alignment in the Cold War and the promotion of Arab, Asian, and African interests in international fora, Ottawa was the only Western government to send formal greetings to the gathered delegates.[40]

One means of outreach was the Colombo Plan, a development program launched in 1950 that saw donor countries such as Canada, Britain, Australia, and the United States fund development projects in Asian countries, including in many former British colonies. Ottawa's outlays to the Colombo Plan marked an important shift in Canadian thinking. As Canada's first foreign aid program, it involved spending Canadian tax dollars in non-Western states. In a letter to Finance Minister Douglas Abbott, whose department was skeptical of the idea of such assistance, Pearson emphasized that newly independent states "need external financial assistance if they are to have a chance of making some improvement in the appallingly low standard of living of their people and so of sheltering them from the attractions of Communist propaganda."[41] Along with a desire to help alleviate poverty, Canadian policymakers supported development assistance to win hearts and minds in the unfolding Cold War.

The Suez Crisis and the End of the Liberals

Issues surrounding decolonization led to the eruption of the Suez Crisis in November 1956. Newly independent countries protested Anglo-French collusion in an Israeli attack on Egypt, viewing this as a throwback to European gunboat imperialism. "Any effort to use force," Pearson had predicted in July, "would in all likelihood result in an appeal by Egypt to the UN. That would be bringing the UN into the matter with a vengeance, and by the wrong party."[42] That the UN might be used against Canada's European allies reflected the increasing representation of non-Western states in the organization. Canada was partly responsible for this development. In 1955, Canadian diplomats had used their considerable skill and Canada's considerable reputation to broker an agreement for 16 new members to join the UN.[43] As a result, the Western powers no longer held a clear majority in the General Assembly. In November 1956, Britain and France faced international condemnation for their actions, and Canadian policymakers scrambled to protect their allies.

To many Canadians, the Liberal government's actions during the Suez Crisis looked like a betrayal of Britain and France. During a special session of the House of Commons, Howard Green, the Progressive Conservative opposition's

Figure 3.1 Les Callan, "Needs some expert steering," *Vancouver Herald*, 15 September 1955. Although this political cartoon was published in 1955, it would have been equally relevant at any point during Louis St Laurent's time as Canadian prime minister. In 1950, as much of the international community recognized the People's Republic of China, Washington urged Ottawa to wait, which it did. In 1955, the Canadian government helped resolve a US–USSR dispute that threatened to interrupt the evolution of the United Nations into a genuinely universal organization. The following year, Foreign Minister Lester Pearson mediated among competing US, UK, and UN constituencies to resolve a British, French, and Israeli attack on Egypt that pitted Canada's NATO allies against one another. In each case, Canadian diplomatic acuity, not to mention a willingness to listen and compromise, was critical. Fortunately, Canadians of the period generally recognized and respected the expertise of their diplomatic corps. Up through the time of the publication of this cartoon, the domestic political implications of these foreign policy challenges were negligible.

LOUIS ST LAURENT AND THE EXPANSION OF THE CANADIAN 67

external affairs critic, took aim at Pearson and St Laurent: "The man on the street in Canada is asking today, and has asked ever since the Canadian Government took such action, why Canada took the lead in the attack on her friends." In response to Green's charges that the Liberals had taken their orders during the Suez Crisis from Washington, Pearson emphasized that "it is bad to be a chore boy of the United States. It is equally bad to be a colonial chore boy running around shouting 'Ready, aye, ready'."[44] In part, Tory criticisms were a reaction to several domestic moves by the Liberals that seemed to cut imperial ties to Britain: the introduction of Canadian citizenship (1946); the replacement of the British Judicial Committee of the Privy Council as the final court of appeal for Canadians with the Supreme Court of Canada (1949); and the appointment of the first Canadian-born governor general (1952).[45]

Such criticism proved potent with voters, as did accusations that the Liberals had grown too close to the Americans, especially in economic matters. In 1956, the Liberals and Progressive Conservatives had clashed in the House of Commons over the government's effort to seek approval for the construction of the TransCanada Pipeline to carry natural gas from Alberta to central Canada. Since investment in the pipeline was primarily American, the Tories charged that the move was a sellout to "Texas buccaneers."[46] Although the bill passed and the pipeline was built, the incident showcased a growing anti-American nationalist sentiment in Canada. The Suez Crisis would be remembered as the capstone of golden age Canadian foreign policy—a reputation cemented by Pearson's 1957 Nobel Peace Prize—but at the time, the controversial incident illustrated the difficulty policymakers face in operationalizing what it means to place Canada first.

Case Studies

The cases for this chapter are drawn from three themes critical to Canada's international posture: development, defence, and diplomacy. The first considers Ottawa's attitude toward the first comprehensive international commitment to development assistance in the Global South: the Colombo Plan. It highlights the multilateral nature of Canadian diplomacy during this period of decolonization as well as the cautious approach that officials typically advised when it came to potentially costly global engagement. The second case explores Canadian–American defence challenges during the early Cold War. Although departmental officials recognized the need for a distant early warning (DEW) line across the Arctic as a means of detecting and deterring a Soviet attack, Ottawa understood defence in more political terms and sought to maintain Canada's position as an independent global actor. The final case represents high

68 CANADA FIRST, NOT CANADA ALONE

and low points in Canada's diplomatic history. Lester Pearson was deserving of the Nobel Peace Prize for his role in establishing the United Nations Emergency Force in the Middle East during the Suez Crisis. At the same time, the failure of the West to respond meaningfully to Soviet aggression in Hungary demonstrated the limitations of Cold War diplomacy. The Beyond the Book case explores Canadian relations with Latin America in the early 1950s. Ottawa's hesitancy to attend a meeting of the Organization of American States in the spring of 1954 sharply contrasts with its engagement in global affairs elsewhere around the world.

The Launch of the Colombo Plan for Cooperative Economic Development in South and Southeast Asia, 1950–1951

What role can and should international development assistance play in Canadian foreign policy?

Canada's involvement in international development assistance originated in the Second World War. Ottawa contributed $154 million, along with technical advice and other unofficial means of support, to the United Nations Relief and Rehabilitation Administration for its work rebuilding liberated countries.[47] When Canada joined the United Nations in 1945, it committed to promoting economic and social progress around the world. Four years later, the St Laurent government allocated $850,000 to the newly formed UN Expanded Program of Technical Assistance. It did so reluctantly, only after having conceded internally that alleviating global poverty was consistent with the national interest.[48]

Two international developments transformed the initial Canadian commitment into a critical element of foreign policy. The Cold War offered the newly decolonized countries of Asia and Africa starkly different political models for their economic development. Although the Soviets were geographically distant, for the independent or quickly decolonizing South and Southeast Asian states, the newly victorious communists in China were not. Western colonial powers and their North American allies feared that poverty would turn the countries of Asia and Africa toward communism out of desperation. Efforts to improve living standards in the Global South were therefore, in one scholar's words, "an instrument of containment."[49]

Ottawa channelled much of its initial aid not through the United Nations but through an institution created at a series of Commonwealth conferences. Britain's post-war economic struggles explain why. During the Second World War, London had obtained military supplies from its colonies, especially India, on credit. When the war ended, the Indians began to draw down the debt, leaving a fragile British economy vulnerable. A Western aid program was a means of relieving pressure on the British pound while integrating the newly decolonized Commonwealth countries into the liberal democratic realm.[50]

The process began at an October 1948 conference of Commonwealth prime ministers at which members committed to periodic meetings of the senior leadership. Nine months later, the Commonwealth finance ministers gathered in London to consider the economic challenges facing the newly independent members of the organization. Their talks led to a call for concurrent meetings of foreign ministers and economic advisors to discuss the political atmosphere in Asia.[51] That conference took place in Colombo, Ceylon (now Sri Lanka), in January 1950. The foreign ministers discussed the impact of the fall of China on global politics. Lower-level officials sought solutions to the pending economic crisis in the sterling area.

On 9 January, Canada's Secretary of State for External Affairs Lester Pearson offered his Commonwealth peers prepared remarks about the need to contain Soviet expansion. Militarily, that meant combatting Russian imperialism through NATO. Socially, it meant deterring the spread of communism by promoting sustainable economic development across the Global South.[52] Three days later, representatives from Australia, New Zealand, and Ceylon transformed what Pearson had assumed was a conversation among colleagues into a public call for action. Together, the foreign ministers and their economic officials produced a declaration of intent to formalize a development program for Asia and Southeast Asia. The conference recommended that a consultative committee to work out detailed plans in Australia in May.

Pearson liked the idea, but Ottawa resisted. The Canadian government preferred to launch such initiatives through the broader multilateral framework of the United Nations and doubted that sufficient funds could be raised without American involvement. Cabinet members also objected to transferring tax dollars to India and Pakistan while both countries were increasing their defence spending in anticipation of war. Asserting that the North American economies had grown without foreign assistance, some Canadians believed that aid was not the solution to what was ailing the Global South. Finally, they worried that resuscitating the pound might compromise Canadian trade interests across the sterling area—the group of countries that pegged their exchange rates to the British pound rather than the US dollar.[53]

Pearson announced that Canada would attend the conference in Sydney before an interdepartmental committee established to review his report on the Colombo conference had even met. Nonetheless, his efforts to convince his Cabinet colleagues of the value of Canadian attendance were only moderately successful. Ottawa's instructions to its delegation are revealing:

70 CANADA FIRST, NOT CANADA ALONE

The Delegation should carefully avoid at this stage committing the Canadian Government in any way, either directly or by inference, to extending financial assistance to the countries of South and South-East Asia. It should be stressed that the Canadian Government cannot even consider this question until the *basic elements of the problem* have been carefully *examined*, until the possibilities of self-help, *maximum utilization of local resources*, and mutual aid among the under-developed countries themselves have been thoroughly explored and until producers have been suggested to ensure that whatever financial aid may be available will be put to effective use....

The Delegation should...also look with scepticism at overly grandiose schemes of development.[54]

At Sydney, the delegates rejected an Australian call for a new, formal Commonwealth aid organization and accepted instead an Indian proposal that financial support would be provided on a bilateral basis in response to specific requests by members of the Global South. Partnership proposals would have to be detailed, backed by a statement of each country's national economic vision and the estimated dollar value of the aid needed to fulfil it.[55] A further meeting in London in September was planned to finalize initial commitments from Canada and its allies.

During the four months between the meetings, the attack of communist North Korea on the nationalist South created a sense of urgency among the Western delegates. On 12 June, Ottawa grudgingly agreed to commit $400,000 to the Commonwealth project while also setting aside $750,000 for UN development assistance initiatives. At the London conference, Canadian official Douglas LePan played a leading role in drafting a six-year, $2.8 billion economic development program, ultimately called the Colombo Plan for Cooperative Economic Development in Asia and Southeast Asia, effective 1 July 1951. The size of the plan was based on the list of projects to which donors might contribute produced by countries from the Global South. The bilateral partnerships would be coordinated and supervised by a small bureau in Colombo.[56]

Whether Ottawa would increase its initial commitment remained unclear. In October, the Cabinet, led by St Laurent, initially balked at a British suggestion that Canada contribute nearly $50 million per year (a 10 per cent share of the overall plan). Two months later, Pearson wrote the prime minister personally, suggesting a $25 million annual commitment, with only the first year guaranteed. This was approved in early February 1951.[57] The United States joined the plan shortly thereafter. Over time, Canada's contributions increased, albeit cautiously. Aid as an altruistic endeavour soon became part of the national foreign policy lexicon.[58] As it did, Canadians' understanding of the purpose of development assistance transformed from a program intended to promote economic growth and help recipients help themselves emerge from poverty into a form of charity almost entirely decoupled from the national interest.

The Establishment of the Distant Early Warning (DEW) Line, 1953–1957

How does defence policy fit within Canada's foreign policy framework?

Since a critical duty of leaders of liberal-democratic states is to preserve the safety and security of their citizens, the defence portfolio should be important to the Canadian government. Yet, throughout Canada's history, only one minister of national defence has ever become prime minister. Defence policy, in Canadian terms, has typically been, at most, a subset of foreign policy. More often, it has been shaped by a variety of competing interests only tangentially related to traditional conceptions of national security. The early history of continental air defence in the Canadian North illustrates this quandary.

North American military planners' assessment of the global security environment changed significantly after the Soviet Union acquired nuclear weapons in 1949. Canada and the United States were strategically vulnerable to aerial attack, and the radioactive fallout that would inevitably accompany it, from over the North Pole. There was never any serious question about whether Canadian and American efforts to defend the continent would be co-operative. In 1947, both governments reaffirmed their bilateral defence relationship and established joint weather stations in the Canadian Arctic. The stations were staffed equally by representatives from the Canadian Meteorological Service and the United States Weather Bureau.[59] In 1951, when Washington sought to extend its early warning radar network into Canada, Ottawa's response was positive. Indeed, when the Canadian government contemplated what came to be known as the Pinetree Line—a series of 33 radar sites that stretched from Vancouver Island to Newfoundland—its most significant concerns were with how American military operations in Canada might affect perceptions of Canadian sovereignty.[60] Since the stations were equipped to detect approaching enemy aircraft and arrange for their interception, there was a risk that American troops could be seen as defending the interests of the United States using Canadian resources on Canadian soil. Arrangements for Ottawa to pay one-third of the cost of the line's construction, to operate 15 of the sites itself, and to limit the presence of US personnel were therefore critical.[61]

American defence experts soon declared the Pinetree Line insufficient in light of rapid advances in aircraft technology. In 1952, analysts from the Massachusetts Institute of Technology's Lincoln Laboratory Summer Study Group, which included two Canadians, recommended extending the radar network farther north. A Distant Early Warning Line was viable along the 70th parallel and could be complemented by a backup line, known initially as the McGill Fence, along the 55th.[62] The idea was not so much to intercept Soviet bombers as to deter them from northern approaches in the first place. If the

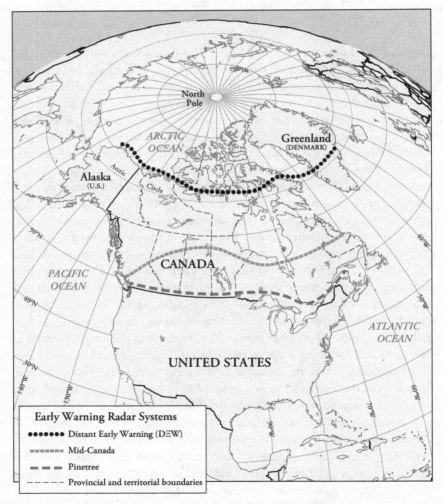

Figure 3.2 Map of Canada–US Early Warning Radar Systems. Nunavut became its own territory separate from the Northwest Territories in 1999.

LOUIS ST LAURENT AND THE EXPANSION OF THE CANADIAN   73

West was aware of the attacks before they took place, it could threaten overwhelming counterstrikes.[63] The best the Soviets could hope for in such circumstances was what was later called mutually assured destruction (MAD).

Once the US administration committed to the DEW Line, Canadian opposition was all but impossible. Nonetheless, Ottawa's response indicates that Canada was hardly a pawn of the American security sector. Canadian officials had initially rejected proposals for northern radar lines as too costly. With defence already making up half of all government spending, and the economy fragile in 1953, Ottawa could not afford to pay for even half of the new line.[64] The obvious alternative—allowing the United States to build and staff the line alone—risked making the Canadian military "merely an appendage of the U.S. military in matters of continental defense."[65] Canadian industry would lose out not just on the project's construction, but also on access to anticipated emergent communications technologies. The public would question how the St Laurent government could commit billions of dollars to forces in Europe and then rely on Americans for their defence. Later, some Canadians challenged the project's military viability.[66]

The political solution to these challenges was more about managing domestic perceptions than the communist threat. The St Laurent government declared that it would fund the McGill Fence, to be known as the Mid-Canada Line, in its entirety. The investment was presented publicly as part of a comprehensive, three-pronged, joint Canadian–American response to the growing Soviet aerial threat. The cost of the Pinetree Line was shared by both countries: Canada would cover the Mid-Canada Line, and the United States would pay for the (more costly) DEW Line.[67]

Construction would be governed by a comprehensive bilateral agreement that affirmed Canadian sovereignty. Ottawa insisted on input on the selection of the locations of all 63 radar and communication centres. American engineers would supply records of all of their planning materials to Canadian authorities upon request. The electronic equipment used onsite would be Canadian by default. Canadian contractors would be treated equally in procurement competitions and, in all projects, preference would be given to Canadian workers. Canadian laws would apply throughout the building process, with particular attention to protecting the hunting, fishing, and land rights of the resident Indigenous peoples.[68]

Canada and the United States reached an agreement to build the DEW Line in September 1954, which St Laurent's Cabinet and US President Dwight Eisenhower officially approved two months later.[69] Construction began in the spring of 1955. American workers were initially criticized for failing to respect Canadian rules and regulations, but once the system became operational in 1957 and the contractors departed, the situation improved. In 1959, Ottawa

74 CANADA FIRST, NOT CANADA ALONE

stationed air force officers at every radar site to reaffirm Canadian sovereignty.[70] The DEW Line was incorporated into a new North Warning System in 1985.

Between 1957 and 1985, the collection of Doppler radars and northern radar stations, staffed by Canadian and American military and civilian personnel, including some Indigenous people, served as a Cold War military deterrent, and supported the recovery of civilian aircraft in distress.[71] The increased accessibility of the North also resulted in the discovery of natural resources and created new agendas for scientific research. While some of those efforts came at the expense of the natural environment and the Indigenous population, the consequential physical presence of so many more Canadians in the North reaffirmed the sovereignty that critics had worried about decades earlier. Although the DEW Line's purpose in the eyes of the security sector was to defend against a Soviet threat, politically, Canadian defence policy aimed to defend Canada's reputation as a sovereign country, preserve employment opportunities in the North, and promote scientific and technological research.

The Suez Crisis and the Hungarian Revolution, 1956

What does it mean to be a middle power at the United Nations?

What is a middle power? One author who studied Canada's role during the Suez crisis explains it as "a country not so large that it was threatening nor so small that it could be easily dismissed."[72] In his memoirs, Lester Pearson explained: "We had as much influence on developments there as any power, I think it is fair to say, apart from the Permanent Members of the Security Council."[73] This case explores the strengths and limitations of Canada's diplomatic posture. During the UN negotiations to separate the warring British, French, and Israelis from the Egyptians in 1956, Hungary—a Soviet satellite— was undergoing a violent revolution that might also have benefited from a UN intervention. Even though Ottawa raised significant concerns about the European upheaval, as one diplomat from the period recalls, "there was no disposition to regard Canada as an acceptable mediator."[74]

The Suez Crisis began in July 1956 when Egyptian president Gamal Abdel Nasser nationalized the Compagnie Universelle du Canal Maritime de Suez. The Egyptian firm, whose shares were controlled by British and French interests, had been operating the waterway that connected the Mediterranean and Red Seas since 1869. Given the canal's importance as a link between Europe and Asia, nationalization threatened the future of British and French trade with the East. When the efforts of London and Paris to choke the Egyptian economy and thereby compel Nasser to reconsider failed, the leadership in both countries contemplated regime change. The issue reached the UN Security Council in September.

Britain and France negotiated half-heartedly. By mid-October, they had secretly plotted with Israel—embroiled in a simmering border conflict with Egypt—to remove Nasser by force. The Israelis would invade Egypt, ostensibly in light of ongoing cross-border raids. London and Paris would demand that both sides retreat from the canal. Once Nasser refused, they would intervene. In spite of Washington's insistence that the dispute be settled diplomatically, the Europeans assumed that the Eisenhower administration would ultimately support NATO allies. On 29 October, Israel attacked. The following day, at the Security Council, the United States and the Soviet Union separately demanded that the Israelis withdraw. Following their plan, the British and French vetoed the resolutions and issued an ultimatum: if Israel and Egypt did not leave the canal region within twelve hours, Anglo-French forces would impose order. The move came as a shock to officials in Washington and Ottawa. On 31 October, British Prime Minister Anthony Eden announced that his country had no choice but to mobilize.[75]

Eden's announcement coincided with a heated meeting of the Soviet Politburo. Calls for political reform in Hungary had begun on 23 October, soon after Moscow had responded sympathetically to similar demonstrations in Poland. When the Soviet-backed Hungarian leader, Ernö Gerö, declared that he would not accept the protestors' demands, the situation turned violent. At Gerö's request, Soviet forces arrived in Budapest on the 24th. On the 30th, after what appeared to be a transition to a more reformist administration, the Soviets announced plans to withdraw, but the Politburo rejected the plan the next day. On 1 November, just as the British and French air forces began bombing the Sinai, 75,000 Soviet troops returned to Hungary unexpectedly. In response, the newly appointed Prime Minister Imre Nagy pleaded with the UN Security Council for protection.[76]

Canada was not serving on the council at the time. Ottawa's engagement in the Middle East was limited and its relations with Hungary were even less significant. Nevertheless, both crises implicated Canadian national interests. The Middle East crisis pitted Canada's most significant NATO allies against one another. The governments of India, Pakistan, and Ceylon were disgusted by what they deemed renewed British imperialism and threatened to leave the Commonwealth. Britain and France's unilateral actions jeopardized the integrity of the United Nations. The UN's credibility was also at stake in Hungary. Failure to prevent Soviet aggression risked undermining the Western position in the Cold War. Finally, the Hungarian revolution had created a refugee crisis in neighbouring Austria to which Ottawa felt an international obligation.

76   CANADA FIRST, NOT CANADA ALONE

The Government of Canada put the full weight of its diplomatic apparatus behind efforts to resolve the Suez Crisis. Pearson and his officials had functioning relationships and access to the highest levels of decision making in all of the relevant state capitals. Canada's reputation in New York was unmatched, and many at the UN were looking to Pearson for answers.[77] Indeed, the Canadian foreign minister had more support to negotiate a solution in New York than he did at home, where some Conservatives demanded complete allegiance to Prime Minister Eden.

Ottawa's position was more nuanced than the opposition let on. Canada's interests were best served by a solution that enabled its British and French allies to depart Egypt with their reputations intact. A UN-led effort to stabilize the region was also critical, as was a plan to establish the conditions for long-term peace in the Middle East that could be tolerated, if not supported, by the recently decolonized Commonwealth members, the United States, and the Soviet Union. When the debate over Suez was moved to the UN General Assembly in the aftermath of the British and French Security Council vetoes, Pearson abstained on an American resolution condemning the invasion. After the vote, he expressed regret that the US proposal did not specify a way ahead. Pearson suggested that perhaps the UN secretary-general could organize a military force to separate the combatants until a negotiated settlement was achieved. Canada would be willing to contribute to any such peacekeeping body.[78] Washington supported the idea immediately. It was acceptable to India, so long as the British and French were excluded from participating. London and Paris relented once they realized that they lacked the economic means to complete the invasion of Egypt without US assistance.[79] Thanks in large part to further Canadian diplomatic prowess, the United Nations Emergency Force was announced within a week, just in time to prevent the Soviet Union from intervening on Egypt's behalf.

Ottawa's reaction to the Hungarian Revolution was initially less assertive. With Washington unwilling to respond militarily, and nearly the entire diplomatic establishment preoccupied with Suez, the St Laurent government limited itself to verbal condemnation of the Soviet intervention. Canada's high commissioner to India, Escott Reid, urged his department to engage New Delhi, whose leadership had initially condoned Moscow's activities, but Pearson refused. Canada needed India's support for its Suez peacekeeping initiative and could not risk alienating Prime Minister Jawaharlal Nehru. Ottawa's position did not waver when the Soviets attacked Hungary on 4 November.[80] Only after the revolution had been crushed did the St Laurent government turn its attention to Eastern Europe. Nearly 200,000 Hungarians had fled the country and needed refuge. Canada accepted nearly 37,000 of them, easily the most in the West.[81]

LOUIS ST LAURENT AND THE EXPANSION OF THE CANADIAN 77

When Escott Reid looked back on the twin challenges of the autumn of 1956, he wrote: "A price was paid for Pearson's spectacular success at the U.N. in helping to resolve the crisis over Suez. He and his associates in the Canadian delegation in the U.N. had to spend so much time and energy and thought on the Suez crisis that they had little left over for the crisis in Hungary."[82] In his memoirs, Pearson described the Soviet intervention in Hungary as the most "brutal and grim betrayal of a people" that he had ever seen. "If I had not been so deeply involved in Suez," he added, "I would have been much tempted to see if we could get a resolution to have a UN Assembly Committee fly straight to Budapest with the UN flag and some men in UN uniforms. This was an emotional reaction. It was a most exhausting time with these two things present in mind and heart."[83]

While it was not the first UN military operation, the United Nations Emergency Force established the principles that would guide peacekeeping operations through to the 1990s and launched Canada's reputation as a peacekeeping country.[84] The Canadian effort demonstrated a level of middle power leadership at the UN that was virtually unprecedented. But Canada's virtual impotence in Hungary, on account of both its limited physical diplomatic capacity and its powerlessness in the face of Soviet aggression, made it clear that secondary players in international relations had to pick their battles carefully. Leadership was possible, but such possibilities were finite and came at a cost.

Conclusion

Louis St Laurent's resignation as Canadian prime minister shortly after the 10 June 1957 election marked the end of 22 consecutive years of Liberal (majority) rule. Under his leadership, ties with the United States had increased—too much, in the eyes of some—while relations with Britain had cooled. The Department of External Affairs, led by a former deputy minister, dominated policymaking in Ottawa, leading some to wonder whether the links between the public service and the Liberal Party had grown too close. Canada had taken small steps to reach out to the Global South and to promote human rights through the Colombo Plan, but those steps were hardly bold.

Ottawa did assert unequivocal support for the United Nations and related post-war international institutions of global governance. The St Laurent government was the first to fully operationalize the idea that pursuing Canada's interests in global affairs meant actively and consistently engaging other like-minded states rather than just hoping that international problems would resolve themselves. Relationships begat influence and influence enabled

78 CANADA FIRST, NOT CANADA ALONE

Canada to monitor and attempt to minimize the implications of great power over-reach.

Readings

The overlap between the Cold War and decolonization is explored in Odd Arne Westad, *The Global Cold War: Third World Interventions and the Making of Our Times* (Cambridge: Cambridge University Press, 2006) and in Robert J. McMahon, *The Cold War in the Third World* (New York: Oxford University Press, 2013). On decolonization and the Third World more broadly, see Vijay Prashad, *The Darker Nations: A People's History of the Third World* (New York: The New Press, 2007) and Jan C. Jansen and Jürgen Osterhammel, *Decolonization: A Short History* (Princeton: Princeton University Press, 2017).

General histories of the Canadian foreign policy in the "golden age" include John W. Holmes, *The Shaping of Peace: Canada and the Search for World Order, 1943–1957*, 2 volumes (Toronto: University of Toronto Press, 1979 and 1982); Robert Bothwell, *Alliance and Illusion: Canada and the World, 1945–1984* (Vancouver: UBC Press, 2007); and Robert Teigrob, *Warming Up to the Cold War: Canada and the United States' Coalition of the Willing, from Hiroshima to Korea* (Toronto: University of Toronto Press, 2009). For the golden age debate, see Andrew Cohen, *While Canada Slept: How We Lost Our Place in the World* (Toronto: McClelland & Stewart, 2003); Adam Chapnick, "The golden age: A Canadian foreign policy paradox," *International Journal* 64, no. 1 (2008/2009): 205–21, https://doi.org/10.1177/002070200906400118; and Hector Mackenzie, "Golden decade(s)? Reappraising Canada's international relations in the 1940s and 1950s," *British Journal of Canadian Studies* 23, no. 2 (2010): 179–206, https://doi.org/10.3828/bjcs.2010.10.

There is no single source on Canada's contribution to the launch of the Colombo Plan. Daniel Oakman's *Facing Asia: A History of the Colombo Plan* (Canberra: Pandanus Books, 2004) views the negotiations through an explicitly Australian lens. A broader international focus can be found in Shigeru Akita, Gerold Krozewski, and Shoichi Watanabe, eds., *The Transformation of the International Order of Asia: Decolonization, the Cold War, and the Colombo Plan* (London: Routledge, 2014). Two PhD theses are particularly helpful: Jill Campbell-Miller, "The mind of modernity: Canadian bilateral foreign assistance to India, 1950–60" (University of Waterloo, PhD dissertation, 2014), and Ademola Adeleke, "Ties without strings? The Colombo Plan and the geopolitics of international aid, 1950–1980" (University of Toronto, PhD dissertation, 1996), as is David McGee and Rian Manson, "Canada, communism, and the Colombo Plan," in Nina Mollers and Bryan Dewalt, eds., *Objects in Motion:*

Globalizing Technology (Washington, DC: Smithsonian Institution Scholarly Press, 2016), 40–64. The best collection of contemporary historical scholarship on Canada and international assistance is Greg Donaghy and David Webster, eds., *A Samaritan State Revisited: Historical Perspectives on Canadian Foreign Aid* (Calgary: University of Calgary Press, 2019). Previous work by authors included in that collection, especially Campbell-Miller, Webster, and Ryan Touhey, is also valuable. Primary source evidence can be found in volumes 16 and 17 of the *Documents on Canadian External Relations* series, https://www.international.gc.ca/gac-amc/history-histoire/external-relations_relations-exterieures.aspx?lang=eng. Canadian memoirs include Lester B. Pearson, *The Memoirs of the Right Honourable Lester B. Pearson*, vol. 2, *1948–1957*, edited by John A. Munro and Alex I. Inglis (Toronto: University of Toronto Press, 1973) and Douglas LePan, *Bright Glass of Memory: A Set of Four Memoirs* (Toronto: McGraw-Hill Ryerson Limited, 1979), 145–226. On the plan's impact, see Canada, Department of External Affairs, *Canada and the Colombo Plan, 1951–1961* (Ottawa: Queen's Printer, 1961), http://gac.canadiana.ca/view/ooe.b1603607E.

The most comprehensive, albeit somewhat dated, introduction to research about the DEW Line is P. Whitney Lackenbauer, Matthew J. Farish, and Jennifer Arthur-Lackenbauer, "The Distant Early Warning (DEW) Line: A Bibliography and Documentary Resource List," paper prepared for the Arctic Institute of North America (2005), http://pubs.aina.ucalgary.ca/aina/DEWLineBib.pdf. The best single source for this case is Alexander W.G. Herd, "A practicable project: Canada, the United States, and the construction of the DEW Line," in P. Whitney Lackenbauer, ed., *Canadian Artic Sovereignty and Security: Historical Perspectives* (Calgary: Centre for Military and Strategic Studies, 2011), 171–200. Joseph Jockel's *No Boundaries Upstairs: Canada, the United States, and the Origins of North American Air Defence, 1945–1958* (Vancouver: UBC Press, 1987), is also excellent. Three valuable more recent contributions are Adam Lajeunesse, "The Distant Early Warning Line and the Canadian battle for public perception," *Canadian Military Journal* 8, no. 2 (2007): 51–9, http://www.journal.forces.gc.ca/vo8/no2/lajeunes-eng.asp; Alexander W.G. Herd, "A 'Common Appreciation': Eisenhower, Canada, and Continental Air Defense, 1953–1954," *Journal of Cold War Studies* 13, no. 3 (2011): 4–26, http://dx.doi.org/10.1162/JCWS_a_00140; and Matthew Trudgen, "Coping with fallout: The influence of radioactive fallout on Canadian decision-making on the Distant Early Warning (DEW) Line," *International Journal* 70, no. 2 (2015): 232–49, https://doi.org/10.1177/0020702015573521. The only full-length work dedicated exclusively to the DEW Line during this period, albeit from a distinctly US perspective, is James Louis Isemann, "To detect, to deter, to defend: The Distant Early Warning (DEW) Line and early Cold War defense policy"

80 CANADA FIRST, NOT CANADA ALONE

(Kansas State University, PhD dissertation, 2009). The *Documents on Canadian External Relations* series' volumes 19–21 (1953–55) provide hundreds of pages of primary source evidence at https://www.international.gc.ca/gac-amc/history-histoire/external-relations_relations-exterieures.aspx?lang=eng. On wider issues surrounding Cold War–era projects in Canada's North, see P. Whitney Lackenbauer and Matthew Farrish, "The Cold War on Canadian soil: Militarizing a northern environment," *Environmental History* 12, no. 4 (2007): 920–50, https://doi.org/10.1093/envhis/12.4.920.

The Suez case was inspired by a brief, provocative article by David A. Lenarcic, "Remembering history: The Suez Crisis and the Hungarian Revolution of 1956 from a Canadian perspective," *Canadian Defence Quarterly* 26, no. 1 (1996): 26–31. The literature on the Canadian contribution to the Suez crisis is outstanding. See, among others, Antony Anderson, *The Diplomat: Lester Pearson and the Suez Crisis* (Fredericton: Goose Lane, 2015); Michael K. Carroll, *Pearson's Peacekeepers: Canada and the United Nations Emergency Force, 1956–67* (Vancouver: UBC Press, 2009); and Michael G. Fry, "Canada, The North Atlantic Triangle, and the United Nations" in Wm. Roger Louis and Roger Owen, eds., *Suez 1956: The Crisis and Its Consequences* (Oxford: Oxford University Press, 1989), 285–316. Anderson's website www.suezcrisis.ca is also helpful. On Canada and peacekeeping, see Norman Hillmer, "Peacekeeping: The inevitability of Canada's role," in Michael A. Hennessy and B.J.C. McKercher, eds., *War in the Twentieth Century: Reflections at Century's End* (Westport, CT: Praeger, 2003), 145–65; Colin McCullough, *Creating Canada's Peacekeeping Past* (Vancouver: UBC Press, 2016); and Michael K. Carroll, "Pragmatic peacekeeping: The Pearson years," in Asa McKercher and Galen Roger Perras, eds., *Mike's World: Lester B. Pearson and Canadian External Affairs* (Vancouver: UBC Press, 2017, 48–69). The Canadian literature on the Hungarian Revolution is sparse. See Escott Reid, *Hungary and Suez 1956: A View from New Delhi* (Oakville: Mosaic Press, 1986) and Greg Donaghy, "'An unselfish interest'? Canada and the Hungarian revolution, 1954–57," in Christopher Adam, Tibor Egervari, Leslie Laczko, and Judy Young, eds., *The 1956 Hungarian Revolution: Hungarian and Canadian Perspectives* (Ottawa: University of Ottawa Press, 2010), 256–74. Ottawa's response to the Hungarian refugee crisis is covered in Gerald E. Dirks, *Canada's Refugee Policy: Indifference or Opportunism?* (Montreal: McGill-Queen's University Press, 1977) and Andrew Thompson and Stephanie Bangarth, "Transnational Christian charity: The Canadian Council of Churches, World Council of Churches, and the Hungarian Refugee Crisis, 1956–1957," *American Review of Canadian Studies* 38, no. 3 (2008): 295–316, https://doi.org/10.3138/chr.2019-0023. Comparative international scholarship includes John C. Campbell, "The Soviet Union, the United States, and the twin crises of Hungary and Suez," in W. Roger Louis and Roger Owen, eds., *Suez 1956: The Crisis and its Consequences*

(Oxford: Clarendon Press, [1989] 2003), 233–53 and Peter C. Boyle, "The Hungarian Revolution and the Suez Crisis," *History* 90, no. 4 (2005): 550–65, https://doi.org/10.1111/j.1468-229X.2005.00350.x. For primary source evidence on the Suez Crisis, see Greg Donaghy, ed., *Documents on Canadian External Relations*, vol. 22, *1956–1957*, part I (Ottawa: Public Works and Government Services Canada, 2001), 131–506, documents 74–302, https://epe.lac-bac.gc.ca/100/206/301/faitc-aecic/history/2013-05-03/www.international.gc.ca/department/history-histoire/dcer/1956/menu-en.asp. On Hungary, see Greg Donaghy, ed., *Documents on Canadian External Relations*, vol. 23, *1956–1957*, part II (Ottawa: Public Works and Government Services Canada, 2002), 749–828, documents 452–506, https://epe.lac-bac.gc.ca/100/206/301/faitc-aecic/history/2013-05-03/www.international.gc.ca/department/history-histoire/dcer/1957/menu-en.asp.

Key biographies of leading Canadian politicians of this period include Dale C. Thomson, *Louis St. Laurent: Canadian* (New York: St. Martin's Press, 1968); Robert Bothwell and William Kilbourn, *C.D. Howe: A Biography* (Toronto: McClelland & Stewart, 1979); David J. Bercuson, *True Patriot: The Life of Brooke Claxton 1898–1960* (Toronto: University of Toronto Press, 1993); and John English, *The Worldly Years: The Life of Lester Pearson*, Vol. 2 (Toronto: Knopf, 1992). Pearson's legacy in foreign policy is also explored in Asa McKercher and Galen Roger Perras, eds., *Mike's World: Lester B. Pearson and Canadian External Affairs* (Vancouver: UBC Press, 2017).

Golden age diplomats have produced a wealth of memoirs: Maurice Pope, *Soldiers and Politicians: The Memoirs of Lt-General Maurice Pope* (Toronto: University of Toronto Press, 1962); A.D.P. Heeney, *The Things that are Caesar's* (Toronto: University of Toronto Press, 1972); Kenneth P. Kirkwood: *The Diplomat at Table: A Social and Anecdotal History through the Looking-Glass* (Metuchen: Scarecrow Press, 1974); Charles Ritchie, *Diplomatic Passport: More Undiplomatic Diaries, 1946–1962* (Toronto: Macmillan, 1981); George Ignatieff, *The Making of a Peacemonger: The Memoirs of George Ignatieff* (Toronto: University of Toronto Press, 1985); Arthur Andrew, *The Rise and Fall of a Middle Power: Canadian Diplomacy from King to Mulroney* (Toronto: James Lorimer, 1993); J.C. Gordon Brown, *Blazes Along a Diplomatic Trail: A Memoir of Four Posts in the Canadian Foreign Service* (Victoria: Trafford, 2000). Escott Reid was a prolific advocate of the golden age—and his role in it: *Envoy to Nehru* (Oxford: Oxford University Press, 1981); *Radical Mandarin: The Memoirs of Escott Reid* (Toronto: University of Toronto Press, 1989). On Reid, see the essays in Greg Donaghy and Stéphane Roussel, eds., *Escott Reid: Diplomat and Scholar* (Montreal: McGill-Queen's University Press, 2004). For a look at women foreign service officers, see Margaret Weiers, *Envoys Extraordinary: Women of the Canadian Foreign Service* (Toronto: Dundurn Press, 1995).

82 CANADA FIRST, NOT CANADA ALONE

On Canada and the newly decolonized world, see Robin S. Gendron, *Towards a Francophone Community: Canada's Relations with France and French Africa, 1945–1968* (Montreal: McGill-Queen's University Press, 2006); David Webster, *Fire and the Full Moon: Canada and Indonesia in a Decolonizing World* (Vancouver: UBC Press, 2009); and Ryan Touhey, *Conflicting Visions: Canada and India in the Cold War World, 1946–76* (Vancouver: UBC Press, 2015).

On the Red Scare in Canada, see Gary Marcuse and Reg Whitaker, *Cold War Canada: The Making of a National Insecurity State, 1945–1957* (Toronto: University of Toronto Press, 1996); Richard Cavell, ed., *Love, Hate, and Fear: Canada in the Cold War* (Toronto: University of Toronto Press, 2004); and Gary Kinsman and Patrizia Gentile, *The Canadian War on Queers: National Security as Sexual Regulation* (Vancouver: UBC Press, 2009). For two contrasting views on E. Herbert Norman's guilt, see Peyton V. Lyon, "The loyalties of E. Herbert Norman," *Labour/Le Travail* 28 (1991): 219–59, https://www.lltjournal.ca/index.php/llt/article/view/4818 and James Barros, *No Sense of Evil: Espionage, the Case of Herbert Norman* (Toronto: Deneau, 1986).

For contrasting views on Canada's response to the Korean War, see Denis Stairs, *The Diplomacy of Constraint: Canada, the Korean War, and the United States* (Toronto: University of Toronto Press, 1974) and Robert Prince, "The limits of constraint: Canadian-American relations and the Korean War, 1950–1," *Journal of Canadian Studies* 27, no. 4 (1992–93): 129–52, https://doi.org/10.3138/jcs.27.4.129. Greg Donaghy has provided two more recent analyses: "Pacific diplomacy: Canadian statecraft and the Korean War, 1950–53," in Rick Guisso and Yong-Sik Yoo, eds., *Canada and Korea: Perspectives 2000* (Toronto: University of Toronto Press, 2002), 81–100 and "Blessed are the peacemakers: Canada, the United Nations, and the search for a Korean armistice, 1952–53," *War & Society* 30, no. 2 (2011): 134–46, https://doi.org/10.1179/204243411X13026863176583. John Price explores Canadian policy in the wider Asian Cold War in *Orienting Canada: Race, Empire, and the Transpacific* (Vancouver: UBC Press, 2011).

Beyond the Book

Attending the Tenth Inter-American Conference of the Organization of American States (OAS) as an Observer, 1952–1954

In September 1952, representatives from the United States began inquiring as to whether the Canadian government might consider sending a representative to the upcoming Inter-American conference of the Organization of American States. Since Canada was not a member of the OAS, the delegation would be granted observer status. Originally set for September 1953, the conference was postponed until the following spring. The prospective invitation launched a 15-month debate within the Department of External Affairs. Some members believed that Canada had profoundly neglected its interests in Latin America. Others worried that acceptance of observer status would inevitably lead to an invitation to join the OAS, which would put Canada in the position of having to pick sides between the United States and the Latin Americans on a regular basis. To them, the solution to any meeting invitation was to ignore it for as long as possible.

Questions

1. What are Canada's interests in this case?
2. If an invitation to attend the conference is received, should Canada accept it?
3. Should relations with the countries of Latin America be a significant Canadian foreign policy priority?

Readings

Scholarship on Canada's relations with Latin America is sparse, but primary source evidence is helpful. See the 1952 and 1953 volumes of the *Documents on Canadian External Relations Series*, http://epe.lac-bac.gc.ca/100/206/301/faitc-aecic/history/2013-05-03/www.international.gc.ca/department/history-histoire/dcer/browse-en.asp. In the 1952 volume, documents 1040–51 are most valuable. In the 1953 volume, see documents 1090–98. This case is mentioned briefly in Peter McKenna, *Canada and the OAS* (Ottawa: Carleton University Press, 1995), 75–6. John Holmes offers another brief summary in *The Shaping of Peace: Canada and the Search for World Order*, vol. 2, *1943–1957* (Toronto: University of Toronto Press, 1982), 287–9. For context, see also Douglas G. Anglin, "United States opposition to Canadian membership in the Pan American Union: A Canadian view," *International Organization* 15, no. 1 (1961): 1–20, https://doi.org/10.1017/S0020818300024541 and Donat Pharand, "Canada and the OAS: The vacant chair revisited," *Revue générale de droit* 17, no. 3 (1986): 429–54, https://doi.org/10.7202/1059251ar.

4

John Diefenbaker and the Politics of Foreign Policy Decision Making, 1957–1963

Prime Minister John Diefenbaker

The Progressive Conservatives' election victory in June 1957 was a political earthquake. During the campaign, Tory leader John Diefenbaker had charged the Liberals with a host of sins, most notably the sellout of Canadian economic interests to the United States and the betrayal of Britain during the Suez crisis. Thanks in part to Diefenbaker's impassioned campaign persona, the strategy proved effective, but it raised the spectre that the consensus around Canada's post-war foreign policy was fracturing.

American diplomats took this development in stride. Following an early meeting with the new prime minster, the US ambassador in Ottawa reported to Washington that there would be "no change in the fundamentals of Canadian foreign policy."[1] The Tories were equally committed to the anti-communist cause as well as to international organizations, such as the United Nations and the Commonwealth. Ottawa almost immediately agreed to bid for a seat on the UN Security Council, where Canada served its second term from 1958 to 1959. Ottawa also maintained the Canadian troop presence in the UN peacekeeping mission in the Sinai. Although Diefenbaker, a small-town Saskatchewan lawyer, lacked the international connections and cachet of Louis St Laurent or Lester Pearson, he had been a Member of Parliament since 1940 and was a significant force within his party. Nonetheless, when it came to foreign affairs, many observers dismissed him as a populist, less concerned with policy than with its domestic ramifications. As one diplomatic advisor later reflected, "for those who wanted a creative, resourceful role for Canada in the world, Diefenbaker was not the answer."[2]

Like R.B. Bennett in the 1930s, Diefenbaker and many of his new ministers were distrustful of the public service, which they viewed as aligned with the long-governing Liberals. In the case of the Department of External Affairs, the situation was not helped by Pearson's deep personal connections across the department. The new prime minister's initial dismissal of Canada's diplomatic

---

Canada First, Not Canada Alone: A History of Canadian Foreign Policy. Adam Chapnick and Asa McKercher,
Oxford University Press. © Oxford University Press 2024. DOI: 10.1093/oso/9780197653715.003.0005

corps as "Pearsonalities" was "understandable," admitted longtime diplomat Arthur Andrew, "but Diefenbaker was given to oversimplification."[3] Regardless of their personal sympathies, the overwhelming majority of public servants were prepared to serve any political master with utmost loyalty.

Diefenbaker acted as his own secretary of state for external affairs (SSEA) for three months, a decision that created headaches for the new government. In September 1957 he finally appointed Sidney Smith, the president of the University of Toronto, as SSEA. When Smith died of a stroke in early 1959, Howard Green, a long-time Tory MP, succeeded him.[4] Meanwhile, a liaison position was created to coordinate the flow of documents between the DEA and the prime minister.[5] Even so, Diefenbaker's suspicions of the foreign service grew when Pearson was awarded the 1957 Nobel Peace Prize and, soon after, succeeded St Laurent as Liberal leader.

The Expansion of Canada's Foreign Policy Realm

If Pearson had the international reputation that Diefenbaker lacked, the reverse was true when it came to political skill. In 1957, the Tories had won only a minority government, and many observers expected a quick return to Liberal rule. Instead, an ill-advised Liberal confidence motion in the House of Commons in early 1958 ultimately led to a snap election call that produced a Progressive Conservative government commanding the largest majority in Canadian history. Secure in his position, Diefenbaker embarked on a month-long world tour across Western Europe, India, Pakistan, Ceylon, Malaya, Australia, and New Zealand in autumn 1958. The outreach effort signalled the government's desire to strengthen links with Europe and the broader Commonwealth, especially with newly independent states in the Global South.[6] To this end, the Cabinet established the External Aid Office, Canada's first stand-alone international assistance agency. Spending on foreign aid, both bilaterally and through multilateral channels, increased, and the geographic scope of Canadian aid expanded to encompass French Africa and the Caribbean. In 1961, the Canadian University Service Overseas (CUSO) began sending Canadian post-secondary students out to aid projects in the Global South.[7] The Diefenbaker government also established missions in the dozens of new countries in Africa, Asia, the Middle East, and Latin America.

The expansion of Canadian links abroad was part of an effort to attract trade and investment. By the 1950s, Canada had become economically reliant on the United States, and during his campaign Diefenbaker had pledged to redress the situation. Within days of becoming prime minister, he travelled to a Commonwealth leaders' summit in London, where he announced his intention of shifting 15 per cent of Canada's trade from the United States to the United Kingdom. The bold announcement was made independently of Canada's business community and without any real policy behind it. The "quest for the Holy Grail," senior Canadian officials admitted cheekily to their British counterparts, "was well organised and far more hopeful in comparison."[8] Still, Diefenbaker held out hope of reducing Canada's economic dependence on the United States. To that end, he visited Mexico in 1960—making him the first sitting prime minister to travel to Latin America—and Japan in 1961, a trip that led to the formation of a bilateral Cabinet-level committee to promote Canadian–Japanese economic ties.

The search for new trade links coincided with recovery from the devastation of the Second World War throughout much of Asia and Western Europe. In 1957, several European countries, led by France and West Germany, formed the European Economic Community (EEC), or Common Market, an organization promoting continental economic integration and protected by an external tariff. The move heralded the creation of a significant regional trade bloc.

Commonwealth Relations

In 1961, British Prime Minister Harold Macmillan announced that the United Kingdom would seek entry into the EEC. Initially, Macmillan had hoped to strengthen economic ties with the Commonwealth. Following the fizzling out of Diefenbaker's trade-diversion proposal, the British had even proposed a Canada–UK free trade pact. After Diefenbaker rejected the terms as too favourable to Britain, Macmillan concluded that his country's economic future lay with Europe. Entry into the Common Market would mean Britain's adoption of the EEC's tariff, a move that threatened to further shrink Canada–UK trade. Worried that this would deepen Canadian reliance on the United States, Diefenbaker demanded that London give special consideration to the Commonwealth. At several meetings with British officials he led the charge against Britain's entry into the EEC, providing ammunition to Macmillan's domestic opponents. Anglo-Canadian relations worsened significantly. A confrontation with his Canadian counterpart at a 1962 summit of Commonwealth leaders led Macmillan to condemn Diefenbaker as "very crooked," "self-centred," and convinced "that the only test of any question is the political advantage of himself and his party."[9] Diefenbaker's cautious support for human rights in discussions of South Africa's status within the multi-racial Commonwealth further angered Macmillan.

Confronting South African apartheid was a sign of human rights' increasing importance in international affairs. In siding with non-white Commonwealth members against South Africa, Diefenbaker had taken a stand against racism. Yet, as he was well aware, Canada's own conduct was hardly spotless. Canadian treatment of Indigenous peoples, one journalist contended, was sufficient grounds for "kicking Canada out of the Commonwealth."[10] As a result, the Conservative government enfranchised Indigenous people and passed a Bill of Rights in 1960. These measures, Diefenbaker explained, were important because "wherever discrimination exists in the world there you have a seed-bed for Communism."[11] Cold War competition provided an impetus to domestic reform, but the prime minister was also motivated by his long-time advocacy of civil liberties. To further burnish Canada's record, in 1962, the Diefenbaker government eliminated racist provisions in Canadian immigration policy. Minister of Citizenship and Immigration Ellen Fairclough, Canada's first woman Cabinet minister, presented the move as a "golden opportunity" to demonstrate a Canadian commitment to human rights to people in newly independent countries.[12] Symbolically, the move was important, though in practice, immigration officials continued to impose discriminatory provisions. A more substantial change to immigration policy came in 1967.

Canada, as a predominantly white country, could at times be poorly postured to interact with newly independent states. In 1960, for instance, Ottawa was asked to contribute to a UN peacekeeping mission in Congo, where a multi-sided civil war had broken out shortly after the country's independence from Belgium. With the Americans and Soviets backing opposing sides, the situation could have sparked a full-blown superpower crisis. When asked whether white Canadian troops would be able to help, Undersecretary of State for External Affairs (USSEA) Norman Robertson hesitated, citing the difficulty of persuading "the Congolese masses that the United Nations force was not another form of white domination." With this consideration in mind, Canadian troops participated in a supporting role, though over the course of the four-year mission several tense interactions occurred between Canadian peacekeepers and the local population.[13] In a world divided by race, it mattered that Canada was a Western country, allied to former imperial powers like France, Belgium, and Britain.

Canada, the United States, and the Cold War

If Anglo-Canadian relations during the Diefenbaker period were bad, Canada–US relations were abysmal, though not at first. In spite of his nationalist rhetoric about the dangers posed by economic reliance on the United States, Diefenbaker believed in a strong political and military alliance between the two neighbours. One of his first acts in office was to conclude an agreement creating the North American Air Defence Command (NORAD). Another marker of

88 CANADA FIRST, NOT CANADA ALONE

close bilateral ties was the opening of the St Lawrence Seaway in 1959. These positive developments occurred under the watch of US President Dwight Eisenhower, who put great stock in building a personal relationship with Diefenbaker.[14] Although personal relations mattered, thorny policy differences, such as Canada's sale of wheat to famine-plagued communist China over US objections and a worrying climate of public opinion, festered. Chatting with the Canadian ambassador to Washington, Arnold Heeney, in August 1960, Diefenbaker confided that "anti-American sentiment was now worse than at any time in his lifetime."[15]

Canadians' ill feeling toward the United States in 1960 was a reaction to a worsening Cold War climate. In May, a summit meeting between Western powers and the Soviet Union collapsed after Soviet forces shot down an American spy plane. Closer to home, a revolution in Cuba toppled a US-backed dictatorship, sparking tension between the United States and the revolutionary government headed by Fidel Castro. Over the summer and autumn, Washington and Havana engaged in tit-for-tat provocations: after Cuba's nationalization of American oil refineries that had refused to process Soviet oil, the US government ended purchases of Cuban sugar; Havana then nationalized all American companies in Cuba, causing Washington to impose an export embargo on trade to the island. Despite pressure from the Eisenhower administration, the Diefenbaker government refused to follow suit. To Ottawa, economic sanctions on non-military goods were unhelpful. For many Canadian nationalists, Canada–Cuba trade became an important symbol of defiance of the United States.

Nonetheless, Ottawa backed Washington in the wider Cold War struggle. At the UN General Assembly in September 1960, Diefenbaker delivered a blistering attack on the Soviet Union over its repression in Eastern Europe. The speech earned Canada's prime minister applause from fellow Western leaders and protests from communist delegates; he later called it "my most important single statement on Canadian external relations."[16]

Canada's military support for the Western cause was even more controversial. In February 1959, Diefenbaker cancelled the CF-105 Avro Arrow, a costly, Canadian-made, state-of-the-art fighter meant to intercept incoming Soviet bombers. In its place, Ottawa procured the American Boeing CIM-10 BOMARC, an anti-aircraft missile meant to be outfitted with a nuclear warhead. Canada's military soon acquired several other nuclear-capable weapons systems for deployment by Canadian forces in Europe. Although his government took possession of these various weapons, Diefenbaker pushed back against pressure to receive the nuclear warheads.

One important influence on Diefenbaker was growing anti-nuclear sentiment within Canada. Beginning in the late 1950s, as the American and Soviet nuclear arsenals grew and as both superpowers developed missiles capable of delivering terrifyingly quick attacks, proponents of nuclear disarmament began to coalesce in the United States, Canada, and Britain. Canadian anti-nuclear activists formed several groups, including the Combined Universities Campaign for Nuclear Disarmament, the Canadian Committee for the Control of Radiation Hazards, and the Voice of Women.[17] Disarmament advocates existed within the Canadian government, too, most notably Howard Green, a First World War veteran deeply fearful of a nuclear conflict. Under Green's watch, Canada expanded its involvement in international arms control efforts.[18] In Green's view, Ottawa could hardly counsel nuclear disarmament while deploying atomic weaponry.[19]

The nuclear issue was one of many thorny topics that John F. Kennedy confronted after becoming US president in January 1961. His visit to Ottawa that May was partly overshadowed by the disastrous Bay of Pigs operation a month earlier, when US-backed anti-communist Cubans invaded Cuba but failed to topple Castro's government. The ill-judged attack undermined Kennedy's efforts to encourage Diefenbaker to join the Organization of American States, just as Latin America seemed to be emerging as a new front in the Cold War.

Other hotspots during the Kennedy presidency included Berlin, site of a standoff between Western and Soviet forces in the summer and autumn of 1961, and Vietnam, where the Americans began to rapidly increase their military assistance. It was Cuba, however, where the most dangerous crisis of the Cold War occurred in October 1962. The Cuban missile crisis brought the question of whether Canada should adopt nuclear weapons to the fore, in turn precipitating a confrontation between the Kennedy administration and the Diefenbaker government. That clash almost produced a Cabinet revolt led by advocates of a Canadian nuclear role. It ultimately caused the fall of the Tory government in a non-confidence vote in the House of Commons and a raucous election that saw Lester Pearson's Liberals claim victory. "The government is out," Charles Ritchie, Canada's ambassador in Washington, wrote in his diary. "Diefenbaker is gone....I consider his disappearance a deliverance; there should be prayers of thanksgiving in the churches. And these sentiments do not come from a Liberal."[20]

Diefenbaker and his time in office have traditionally been dismissed as a brief interregnum between long periods of Liberal rule, even if recent assessments have offered a more nuanced portrait of Canadian foreign policy under "the Chief."[21] Some of the criticisms levelled at Diefenbaker over his indecisiveness with policymaking or pettiness with other world leaders ring true. Yet how best to advance Canadian national interests was rarely clear-cut in the Diefenbaker era. Asian and European recovery from the

Figure 4.1 "Now let's see the Opposition attack that!" *Montreal Gazette*, 7 December 1960.

Canadian Prime Minister John Diefenbaker was a staunch Cold Warrior, but he hesitated to arm the Canadian Forces with nuclear weapons. The Department of External Affairs was promoting nuclear disarmament at the United Nations; if Ottawa were to become a nuclear power, it would compromise its own diplomats' credibility in New York and Geneva. Diefenbaker never fully trusted the United States, and Washington wanted to store some of its own weapons in Canada.

JOHN DIEFENBAKER AND THE POLITICS OF FOREIGN POLICY 91

wartime economic devastation and the emergence of post-colonial states led to a diffusion of power away from the West. And with the development of nuclear missiles, Canada was becoming less important to US security. These shifts continued to play out in the 1960s, a decade of upheaval at home and abroad.

Case Studies

The cases for this chapter draw from the fields of public administration, human rights, and diplomatic practice. The first case examines the implications of a series of questionable personnel management decisions on the Diefenbaker government's decision to join NORAD. Sometimes, it suggests, effective strategic decision making means more than just choosing the best policy option. The second case discusses human rights with particular reference to Commonwealth members' responses to the apartheid regime in South Africa. How the Government of Canada promotes and defends values that resonate with the majority of Canadians without compromising the country's immediate political and economic interests is an ever-present concern in contemporary foreign policy history. The third case illustrates why diplomats so often prefer to negotiate in secret. The Diefenbaker government's management of its nuclear commitments to the United States might have been easier had both sides kept their disputes private. How to balance the public's, and the opposition's, right to be informed with the need for delicacy in diplomatic negotiations is another ever-present foreign policy challenge. The Beyond the Book case considers the Diefenbaker government's conduct during the Cuban Missile Crisis, an incident that brought the world the closest it would come to a global nuclear confrontation during the Cold War.

A growing anti-nuclear movement within Canadian civil society, not to mention among some members of the Progressive Conservative Cabinet, had also convinced Diefenbaker that national opposition to nuclear weapons was greater than the polls were indicating. The prime minister's solution, as depicted in this political cartoon, was to borrow from predecessor William Lyon Mackenzie King's attitude toward imposing conscription during the Second World War. "Nuclear weapons if necessary but not necessarily nuclear weapons" meant to imply that Diefenbaker was on everyone's side. It pleased no one. Instead, the opposition Liberals supported the acquisition of nuclear weapons and defeated Diefenbaker's Conservatives in the 1963 election.

92 CANADA FIRST, NOT CANADA ALONE

The Establishment of the North American Air (now Aerospace) Defence Command (NORAD), 1957–1958

> What is lost when a Canadian prime minister serves as their own secretary of state for external affairs?

When John Diefenbaker was first elected to the House of Commons in 1940, the custom was for the prime minister to concurrently hold the portfolio of foreign minister. The post-war era was more complex, and in 1946 William Lyon Mackenzie King turned external affairs over to Louis St Laurent. So, when Diefenbaker opted to serve as acting secretary of state for external affairs, it seemed to be a reversion to past practice. Ultimately, his failure to grasp the human resource dynamics of his supplementary portfolio during the establishment of NORAD illustrates why this dual position was no longer tenable.

In 1953, in the face of an increasing Soviet airborne threat, US General Omar Bradley, the outgoing chairman of the Joint Chiefs of Staff, suggested that the post-war defence of North America would be well served by a joint continental air command.[22] Even though a Canadian study concluded similarly the following year, for a time, the idea stagnated.[23] Defence officials in both countries recognized Ottawa's political sensitivities to American military engagement on Canadian soil.[24]

On 11 May 1956, Canada and the United States established an ad hoc military study group to explore the implications of a joint command. That December, the group recommended that Canadian and US Air Forces responsible for continental defence be integrated into a joint headquarters under the leadership of a US commander and a Canadian deputy. The structure would be binational: the commander would "be responsible to the Chiefs of Staff of both countries. His mission [w]ould be the air defence of Canada, the Continental United States, and Alaska."[25] In emergencies, the two countries' forces would respond as an integrated whole. The Joint Chiefs of Staff and their Canadian military colleagues both approved in February 1957.

In Canada, the Department of External Affairs supported the recommendation, but also called for a mandatory consultation process should a US commander seek to issue peacetime operational orders on Canadian soil.[26] Sensing controversy, the St Laurent government chose to defer a final decision on the joint command until after the June election, thus leaving the issue to the Progressive Conservatives.[27]

Once the new Cabinet was sworn in, General Charles Foulkes, the chairman of the Canadian Chiefs of Staff Committee, called on his new defence minister and former military colleague, General George Pearkes, to confirm the agreement. To Foulkes, the new government's approval for NORAD was a formality.[28]

Pearkes and Diefenbaker appear to have agreed with his recommendation in principle. Foulkes therefore prepared a briefing note for the Cabinet Defence Committee, but he did not share it with representatives from External Affairs. Presumably, as acting secretary of state for external affairs, Diefenbaker could have received input from his own department, which would have representatives at the committee meeting.

However, Diefenbaker had not yet formed the Cabinet Defence Committee. The USSEA, Jules Léger, learned of the government's intent to accept the military study group's report on 24 July but was not aware that it was final.[29] On 27 July, Diefenbaker conveyed Canada's position to the visiting US Secretary of State John Foster Dulles. A briefing from External Affairs noting the potential political implications of enabling an American commander to have operational control over Canadian forces on Canadian soil during peacetime does not appear to have registered.[30] Cabinet passed an order-in-council to appoint a deputy commander in chief to the new organization on 31 July. A joint Canada–US press release was issued the following day.

On 2 August, the Acting Undersecretary of State for External Affairs John Holmes warned the deputy minister of national defence that the DEA still had concerns about NORAD's political implications, particularly given the lack of exchange of diplomatic notes.[31] Holmes's letter was passed to Foulkes, who responded furiously. Further delays "would have been placing in question the authority of the Secretary of Defense of the United States to set up a joint command with Canada."[32] Neither Foulkes, nor Pearkes, nor Diefenbaker appear to have anticipated that Lester Pearson, leader of the Liberal opposition, who had been privy to the earlier NORAD discussions as minister in the St Laurent government, would seize on the lack of diplomatic consultation to politicize the approval process. In the House of Commons that fall, Pearson accused the government of allowing itself to be bullied into the agreement by over-eager defence advisors. Diefenbaker's inexperience had risked abdicating control over the defence of Canada to the US military. H. Basil Robinson, a senior diplomat acting as a liaison between Diefenbaker and External Affairs, later noted that "Pearson's criticisms...touched a political nerve."[33] The Progressive Conservative government struggled to defend itself in Parliament. After diplomatic notes were finally exchanged on 12 May 1958, the heated debate in the House of Commons resumed.[34] What should have been a simple agreement caused the new government considerable embarrassment.

Some blame General Foulkes for minimizing the political implications of the agreement to his minister. Others criticize Diefenbaker and his government for their poor parliamentary performance.[35] In his memoirs, the prime minister disparaged his public servants: "The point is, and this is especially so because I was Secretary of State from External Affairs, that, had the Department of

94 CANADA FIRST, NOT CANADA ALONE

External Affairs had any useful suggestions to make on NORAD either before the decision was taken or before it was announced on 1 August, there was every opportunity for them to do so. What is more, it was their clear duty to do so. None did so."[36]

None of these perspectives account for the personal and personnel challenges that preoccupied the DEA at the time. In the summer and fall of 1957, Léger was away from the office repeatedly, tending to two critically ill parents. The associate undersecretary was in Egypt as a temporary replacement for a colleague, Herbert Norman, who had just taken his own life. John Holmes had been close with the Norman family, had just lost his father, and was overwhelmed by the additional responsibilities that came with the job of acting undersecretary at a time when Diefenbaker was refusing to fill the department's numerous vacancies. Holmes also lacked experience on the defence file. Paul Tremblay, who had the necessary expertise, was briefed too late to help.[37] A capable foreign minister, free from the responsibilities of running the country and managing a new and untested government, might have recognized the severity of the disarray. They also might have been more personally aggressive in asserting the department's views.

Regardless of who or what was to blame, the struggles of the Diefenbaker government in defending NORAD in the House of Commons were proof that, in 1950s Canada, the development and implementation of Canadian foreign policy had to be more than just a part-time job.

South Africa's Withdrawal from the Commonwealth 1960–1961

How and when does a friendly state's violation of its own citizens' civil rights transform from a Canadian foreign policy concern to be monitored to a Canadian foreign policy problem requiring action?

In January 1960, the Canadian Labour Congress called on Prime Minister John Diefenbaker to support an international campaign to disassociate South Africa from the Commonwealth. Although Diefenbaker disapproved strongly of the apartheid regime, he gave the idea of expulsion "short shrift."[38] Nonetheless, just over a year later, Canada played an active role in convincing Pretoria to leave the organization voluntarily. This case examines how and why the Canadian prime minister changed tactics.

Canada and South Africa's Commonwealth ties are long standing. The two countries fought together in both world wars and shared a commitment to the anti-communist cause in the Cold War.[39] Trade between them was imbalanced—Canada's exports vastly exceeded its imports—and significant more for its contribution to the maintenance of the sterling bloc than for its impact on either country's prosperity. South Africa's relationship with the Commonwealth began to sour after the National Party's victory in the 1948 election. The new government intensified a policy of strict racial segregation, known as apartheid, that privileged the minority white population politically and economically.

Ottawa's response to the institutionalization of race-based discrimination in South Africa was subdued. As a rule, Commonwealth members did not inter-fere in one another's domestic affairs. International law, embodied in the UN Charter, also did not permit sovereign states to interfere internally in another country. No Western country wanted to create a precedent that might enable the Soviets to intervene in the affairs of Europe's colonial empires. The brutality of the South African regime was also not yet fully evident, and advice from the Department of External Affairs indicated that radical opposition to apartheid would cause Pretoria to shield itself from international influence. Maintaining a civil dialogue with the South African government within the Commonwealth and the United Nations offered Canada the best chance to effect change.[40]

In 1957, Ghana, Malaya, and Ceylon joined the United Nations. They also assumed independent positions in the Commonwealth, depriving the United Kingdom and the so-called old white Dominions—Canada, South Africa, Australia, and New Zealand—of their long-standing majority within the organ-ization. At the same time, the Progressive Conservatives came to power in Canada led by a prime minister with a reputation as "an evangelical civil rights crusader."[41] Although Diefenbaker had been the first parliamentarian to criti-cize apartheid in the House of Commons, his government moved relatively cautiously. At the United Nations, Ottawa condemned racism but did not single out South Africa.

Over the next three years, domestic political opposition, the non-governmental community, and members of the media increasingly demanded action.[42] Parliament passed Diefenbaker's proposed Bill of Rights, legislation to grant Indigenous peoples the franchise proceeded, and the Progressive Conservatives moved to eliminate racial restrictions in Canadian immigration policy. Together, these actions insulated the prime minister from charges of hypocrisy in advocating respect for human rights in South Africa.[43] Finally, Robert Bryce, secretary to the Cabinet and a staunch opponent of apartheid, took personal responsibility for advising the prime minister while they were abroad, overriding the DEA and the Progressive Conservative Party's more conservative approach to managing Pretoria.[44]

The United Nations called 1960 the Year of Africa as 17 newly decolonized countries joined the organization. When they co-operated with Asian and Latin American delegations, the anti-colonialist states held an overwhelming balance

96 CANADA FIRST, NOT CANADA ALONE

of power in the UN General Assembly. Furthermore, Nigeria's admission to the Commonwealth gave the new members a majority there, and Prime Minister Abubakar Tafawa Balewa called for South Africa's withdrawal. Even Britain's Prime Minister Harold Macmillan, long a supporter of keeping Pretoria engaged, was losing patience. At a speech in Cape Town, he explained: "As a fellow member of the Commonwealth it is our earnest desire to give South Africa our support and encouragement, but I hope you won't mind my saying frankly that there are some aspects of your policies which make it impossible for us to do this without being false to our own deep convictions about the political destinies of free men to which in our own territories we are trying to give effect."[45]

In March 1960, South African police opened fire on protestors outside a police station in Sharpeville. Nearly 70 people were killed and 250 were wounded. Less than three weeks later, Norman Phillips, a Canadian journalist working for the *Toronto Daily Star*, was arrested for reporting on police behaviour. The Diefenbaker government demanded Phillips's release. He was freed three days later. The Phillips affair made the situation in South Africa real to Canadians at home in a way that Sharpeville had not.[46]

Still, Diefenbaker approached the May 1960 Conference of Commonwealth Prime Ministers hesitantly. In his memoirs, he recalls that he continued to believe that "as long as channels of communication between South Africa and the other governments of the Commonwealth were maintained, there would be hope that even yet an improved situation might be achieved."[47] The conference proved that the old Dominions had no desire to force Pretoria out so long as they perceived even the faintest possibility of reform. The African members were less tolerant but had not yet reached their tipping point. The National Party's decision to hold a whites-only referendum on transforming the country into a republic introduced a complication. By convention, if a Commonwealth member changed its form of government, it had to reapply for membership.[48] South African Foreign Minister Eric Louw argued that readmission should be automatic, but the conference attendees, Diefenbaker included, insisted otherwise.[49]

The Canadian prime minister still believed Pretoria could reform. In his memoirs, Diefenbaker explained: "I realized my past statements on South Africa racial policy, taken together with the passing of the Canadian Bill of Rights, had created a general expectation that I would either advocate or support a move to expel South Africa from the Commonwealth. But South Africa's outstanding record in two world wars and her historical connection with the Commonwealth made it impossible for me conscientiously to assume the responsibility to vote for her expulsion without a further opportunity being given her government to change its racial policies."[50] When Malaya, Ghana, and Nigeria imposed economic sanctions on the apartheid regime, the Canadian government refused to follow suit. Meanwhile, South African Prime

Minister Hendrik Verwoerd pushed on with his referendum. He won it narrowly, making a final Commonwealth confrontation inevitable.

Diefenbaker arrived at the March 1961 Conference of Commonwealth Prime Ministers still uncertain about how he would position his country.[51] The Department of External Affairs continued to explore ways to condemn apartheid without expelling South Africa, but the organization's Asian and African members' patience had been exhausted. Without a firm condemnation, Bryce warned the prime minister, their future in the Commonwealth was unclear. In the end, an intervention from India's Prime Minister Jawaharlal Nehru made Diefenbaker's decision easier. Once Nehru announced that the Commonwealth could not survive without an unequivocal condemnation of racial discrimination by all of its members, the Canadian leader no longer had to worry about being the public face of South Africa's disassociation.[52] He became the only white leader to support India's position, making clear that Pretoria could not count on Canada's support for readmission to the Commonwealth without changes to its domestic policy. After Verwoerd's efforts to distance his country from the Commonwealth communiqué failed, he announced that South Africa was withdrawing its application for readmission.[53]

Diefenbaker was widely praised for his willingness to speak out against racial discrimination at a time when the rest of his white Commonwealth allies were more hesitant. In retrospect, his effort to promote human rights was hardly Herculean and little changed as a result.[54] Canadian arms sales to South Africa continued, as did Ottawa's general disinterest in broad-based economic sanctions against the apartheid regime. The South African problem—caused by a combination of domestic and international pressure, the influence of prominent policy advisers, the prime minister's own personal inclinations, not to mention the African regime's brutal atrocities—ultimately compelled Diefenbaker to act, but the triumph of Canadian national interests persisted.

Negotiations to Acquire Nuclear Weapons, 1957–1963

Why is the diplomatic process so secretive?

On 30 September 1962, Canada's ambassador to the United States, Charles Ritchie, vented in his diary:

> The Canadian government has certainly made it abundantly plain that we are against nuclear weapons as one is against sin, and this moral attitude is shared by the most sophisticated...and the least so among Canadians....This policy might not be rational, but it is very Canadian. This is a deep policy difference

98 CANADA FIRST, NOT CANADA ALONE

between us and the United States. At any rate, so long as the present government lasts, (a) we will not fill the Bomarc gap [Ottawa had agreed to acquire but then refused to accept Bomarc anti-aircraft missiles fitted with nuclear warheads]; (b) we don't want nuclear arms for the RCAF [Royal Canadian Air Force] overseas; (c) we will not store nuclear weapons; (d) we are against the resumption by the United States of nuclear tests. The United States wants all four of these from us. They are exasperated by our attitude, but so far they are holding their hand. It remains to be seen how long they will resist the temptation to bring pressure upon us of a kind that might bring a change in government.[55]

Six months later, John Diefenbaker's Progressive Conservative government collapsed, and some observers blamed the United States for its downfall.[56] Examining the two governments' disagreement over nuclear weapons, this case highlights what can happen when states negotiate in public rather than behind closed doors.

In the aftermath of the Second World War, the Canadian government made a conscious decision not to develop a nuclear arsenal. Just a decade later, global tensions caused by the Cold War forced Ottawa to reconsider.[57] In May 1957, NATO members committed to the American doctrine of massive retaliation: any Soviet attack would be met with a disproportionate response so aggressive as to deter even the thought of such a move in the first place. The decision all but guaranteed that Canada's most significant military alliance would adopt a nuclear posture and all but forced Canada to go along.[58] That those weapons were not so-called strategic ones, capable of levelling cities, but rather tactical ones that were merely far more destructive versions of typical conventional weaponry, was immaterial to the controversy that followed.

Negotiations with the United States—the only possible nuclear supplier at the time—focused on three issues: acquiring weapons for the Canadian armed forces at home; granting the United States Air Force (USAF) permission to store nuclear weapons in Canada; and arming Canada's NATO forces in Europe.[59] The Diefenbaker government initially recognized the need to nuclearize and acquired various weapons systems at considerable cost. However, the prime minister delayed the acceptance of the nuclear warheads that would make these weapons fully functional, and he was adamant that the negotiations to acquire the warheads from the Americans take place in secret. He feared (wrongly, according to the polls) that a majority of Canadians would object to their country becoming a nuclear power. He mistrusted the USAF, specifically that it would adhere to any military co-operation agreement on Canadian soil. And he was concerned that announcing his government's intent to acquire nuclear weapons would undermine the DEA's anti-proliferation efforts at the UN.[60]

John F. Kennedy knew that secrecy was key to any Canadian commitment; nonetheless, his patience for Diefenbaker's notorious cautiousness had limits. After three years of inconclusive negotiations that had begun under Kennedy's predecessor, Dwight Eisenhower, a report of the allegedly confidential talks surfaced in *Newsweek* magazine in September 1961.[61] Kennedy could have denied the rumours, but he chose not to. Perhaps this additional public pressure would do what his visit to Ottawa four months earlier could not. It was an unfortunate decision, with Diefenbaker growing ever more distrustful of his American counterpart.[62]

For a time, it appeared that the October 1962 Cuban missile crisis might rescue the endlessly stalled talks. The presence of Soviet missiles off the coast of the United States impressed on many Canadians the vulnerability of their geostrategic position. Bilateral talks resumed within a week of the resolution of the missile crisis. However, the negotiations bogged down. Diefenbaker— now leading a minority Parliament—proved unwilling to commit. American frustration grew.

At a press conference in Ottawa on 3 January 1963, NATO's outgoing commander, American General Lauris Norstad, announced that "Canada would not be fulfilling its obligations to NATO unless nuclear weapons were provided."[63] Norstad reiterated his concerns in Washington later that week.[64] His comments left Diefenbaker "apoplectic."[65] Then, on 12 January, the leader of the Liberal opposition, Lester Pearson, added his voice to the controversy by reversing his party's long-standing nuclear policy. Polling data, internal lobbying by Liberal defence experts, and a recognition that Canada had indeed reneged on its commitments to NATO and NORAD led Pearson to pledge that, if elected, he would immediately complete the negotiations to equip Canadian troops with nuclear arms. Once they had been acquired, Pearson also promised to begin the process of removing them from Canadian soil. At any other time, the new Liberal policy would have been seen as bizarre, if not irresponsible. In the context of five years of Conservative indecision, it was the best approach on offer.[66]

Two weeks later, following sharp debates within his Cabinet and mounting public pressure for clarity on the issue, Diefenbaker attempted to explain his government's position in the House of Commons.[67] His speech revealed details of what had been top-secret negotiations with the Americans. The White House was furious. Not only had the prime minister violated the confidentiality of the discussions, he had also left the Canadian public with a misleading impression of their progress. Five days later, the State Department took the momentous step of issuing a press release that rejected Diefenbaker's claims that the negotiations

100   CANADA FIRST, NOT CANADA ALONE

were anything but a disaster and declared that "the Canadian government had not yet proposed any arrangement sufficiently practical to contribute effectively to North American defence."[68] Amid the resulting uproar, several Cabinet ministers favouring the adoption of nuclear weapons resigned, and the Conservative government fell on a vote of non-confidence shortly thereafter. After a bruising election, Lester Pearson was sworn in as prime minister in a minority Parliament on 22 April 1963 and quickly completed the negotiations to acquire nuclear weapons. Nuclear weapons remained on Canadian soil until 1984.

Conclusion

Politics dominated the foreign policy of the Diefenbaker era in a way it had not during previous governments. Some might blame Diefenbaker's populism; others might look to a national media increasingly willing to be critical of the government.[69] Still more might attribute the change to Canada's decreasing importance in the global commons: partisanship is more likely to emerge when the stakes are lower. Regardless, when the Progressive Conservatives were faced with a series of challenging foreign policy decisions between 1957 and 1963—whether on relations with the United States, human rights, or nuclear weapons—their calculus of how to ensure that they positioned Canada first was more complicated than in previous eras.

Certainly, John Diefenbaker could have handled foreign policy more effectively. His personnel decisions were at times questionable; his communication with the public was uneven; and his hesitancy to make binding commitments was frustrating. Nonetheless, it is worth recognizing the paradox that Canadian foreign policy practitioners often face. Diplomacy is more straightforward when the stakes are higher and the national interest is clear. The Diefenbaker era was hardly Canada's shining moment in world affairs. Relations with Washington and London in particular suffered, and efforts to promote international development and human rights abroad were uneven. In the end, the prime minister and his Cabinet were responsible for only some of the failures.

Readings

The Diefenbaker years overlapped with some of the tensest years of the Cold War. For histories of US foreign policy in this period, see William Hitchcock's *The Age of Eisenhower: America and the World in the 1950s* (New York: Simon & Schuster, 2018); Lawrence Freedman's *Kennedy's Wars: Berlin, Cuba, Laos, and Vietnam* (New York: Oxford University Press, 2000); and the essays in Diane Kunz, ed., *The Diplomacy of the Crucial Decade: American Foreign Relations*

During the 1960s (New York: Columbia University Press, 1994). Aleksandr Fursenko and Timothy Naftali have authored two vital studies utilizing sources from Soviet archives: *"One Hell of a Gamble": Khrushchev, Castro, and Kennedy, 1958–1964* (New York: W.W. Norton, 1997) and *Khrushchev's Cold War: The Inside Story of an American Adversary* (New York: W.W. Norton, 2007). For an important look at transatlantic relations, see Jeffrey Glen Giauque's *Grand Designs and Visions of Unity: The Atlantic Powers and the Reorganization of Western Europe, 1955–1963* (Chapel Hill: University of North Carolina Press, 2002). Francis J. Gavin explores the nuclear weapons revolution in *Nuclear Statecraft: History and Strategy in America's Atomic Age* (Ithaca: Cornell University Press, 2012). Key sources on the intersection of decolonization and the Cold War are Odd Arne Westad's *The Global Cold War* (Cambridge: Cambridge University Press, 2005) and Lise Namikas's *Battleground Africa: Cold War in the Congo, 1960–1965* (Palo Alto: Stanford University Press, 2015). On the role of race and international history in the post-war world, see Vijay Prashad's *The Darker Nations: A People's History of the Third World* (New York: The New Press, 2007) and Adom Getachew's *Worldmaking After Empire: The Rise and Fall of Self-Determination* (Princeton: Princeton University Press, 2019).

John Diefenbaker had barely stepped down as prime minister when the battle over his legacy began. In 1963, journalist Peter C. Newman published *Renegade in Power: The Diefenbaker Years* (Toronto: McClelland & Stewart, 1963), the first authoritative look at the Progressive Conservative government's six years in office. More recent and nuanced examinations of Diefenbaker's time in office include Denis Smith's phenomenal biography *Rogue Tory: The Life and Legend of John G. Diefenbaker* (Toronto: Macfarlane Walter & Ross, 1995) and the essays in Donald C. Story and R. Bruce Shepard, eds., *The Diefenbaker Legacy: Politics, Law and Society Since 1957* (Regina: Canadian Plains Research Centre, 1998). Journalist Peter Stursberg compiled two volumes of interviews with key players in the Diefenbaker years: *Diefenbaker: Leadership Gained, 1956–62* (Toronto: University of Toronto Press, 1975) and *Diefenbaker: Leadership Lost, 1962–1967* (Toronto: University of Toronto Press, 1976).

Joseph T. Jockel is the most authoritative source on NORAD. See his *No Boundaries Upstairs: Canada, the United States and the Origins of North American Air Defence, 1945–1958* (Vancouver: UBC Press, 1987) and *Canada in NORAD, 1957–2007: A History* (Montreal: McGill-Queen's University Press, 2007). Jon B. McLin's *Canada's Changing Defence Policy, 1957–1963: The Problems of a Middle Power in Alliance* (Baltimore: Johns Hopkins Press, 1967) is also helpful, as is Brad Gladman, "Continental air defence: Threat perception and response," *Technical Memorandum* 2012-257 (Ottawa: Defence R&D Canada—CORA, November 2012). For a revisionist interpretation, see Patricia I. McMahon, *Essence of Indecision: Diefenbaker's Nuclear Policy, 1957–1963* (Montreal: McGill-Queen's University Press, 2009). H. Basil Robinson's quasi-memoir *Diefenbaker's*

102 CANADA FIRST, NOT CANADA ALONE

World: A Populist in Foreign Affairs (Toronto: University of Toronto Press, 1989) is more balanced than John G. Diefenbaker's *One Canada: Memoirs of the Right Honourable John G. Diefenbaker*, vol. 3, *The Tumultuous Years 1962–1967* (Toronto: Macmillan, 1977), chapter 2, but both are helpful. An extensive array of primary source evidence can be found in Greg Donaghy, ed., *Documents on Canadian External Relations*, vol. 23, *1956–1957*, pt. 2, (Ottawa: Minister of Public Works and Government Services, 2002), documents #13–51, http://epe.lac-bac. gc.ca/100/206/301/faitc-aecic/history/2013-05-03/www.international.gc.ca/ department/history-histoire/dcer/1957/menu-en.asp and Michael D. Stevenson, ed., *DCER*, vol. 25, *1957–1958*, pt. 2 (Ottawa: Minister of Public Works and Government Services, 2004), documents #10–105, https://gac.canadiana.ca/ view/ooe.b2217569F_025/79.

Brian Douglas Tennyson's *Canadian Relations with South Africa: A Diplomatic History* (Washington, DC: University Press of America, 1982) is the most comprehensive history of the Canada–South Africa relationship through the 1960s. Peter Henshaw's "Canada and the 'South African disputes' at the United Nations, 1946–1961," *Canadian Journal of African Studies* 33, no. 1 (1999): 1–52, https://doi.org/10.1080/00083968.1999.10751154 is noteworthy for its more sympathetic view of Diefenbaker's conduct and Canada's capacity for influence. Daniel Manulak's "Blood brothers: Moral emotion, the Afro-Asian-Canadian bloc, and South Africa's expulsion from the Commonwealth, 1960–1," *Canadian Historical Review* 103, no. 2 (2022): 252–76 is more moderate. Linda Freeman's *The Ambiguous Champion: Canada and South Africa in the Trudeau and Mulroney Years* (Toronto: University of Toronto Press, 1997) devotes its first chapter to the period covered by this case. Articles that deal with the case specifically include Frank Hayes, "South Africa's departure from the Commonwealth, 1960–1961," *International History Review* 2, no. 3 (1980): 451–84, https://doi.org/10.1080/07075332.1980.9640222 and J.R.T. Wood, "The roles of Diefenbaker, Macmillan, and Verwoerd in the withdrawal of South Africa from the Commonwealth," *Journal of Contemporary African Studies* 6, nos. 1–2 (1987): 152–79, https://doi.org/10.1080/02589008708729471. Ronald Hyam's "The parting of ways: Britain and South Africa's departure from the Commonwealth, 1951–61," *Journal of Imperial and Commonwealth History* 26, no. 2 (1998): 157–75, https://doi.org/10.1080/03086539808583030 emphasizes Pretoria's agency. Asa McKercher's "Sound and fury: Diefenbaker, human rights, and Canadian foreign policy," *Canadian Historical Review* 97, no. 2 (2016): 165–94, https://doi.org/10.3138/chr.3241 adds context. Robinson's *Diefenbaker's World* provides an insider's perspective. Diefenbaker's own account can be found in his *One Canada: Memoirs of the Right Honourable John G. Diefenbaker*, vol. 2, *The Years of Achievement, 1957–1962* (Toronto: Macmillan, 1976). Extensive primary evidence is available in Janice Cavell, ed., *Documents on Canadian External Relations*, vol. 27, *1960*

(Ottawa: Minister of Public Works and Government Services, 2007), 719–66, docs 356–84, http://epe.lac-bac.gc.ca/100/206/301/faitc-aecic/history/2013-05-03/www.international.gc.ca/department/history-histoire/dcer/details-en.asp@intRefid=12842 and Cavell, *Documents on Canadian External Relations*, vol. 28, *1961* (Ottawa: Minister of Public Works and Government Services, 2009), 773–816, docs 459–83, https://gac.canadiana.ca/view/ooe.b2217569F_028/849.

The best single source on the Canada and nuclear weapons case is Michael D. Stevenson, "'Tossing a match into dry hay': Nuclear weapons and the crisis in U.S.-Canadian relations, 1962–1963," *Journal of Cold War Studies* 16, no. 4 (2014): 5–34, https://doi.org/10.1162/JCWS_a_00514. On the military side, see Isabel Campbell, "The defence dilemma, 1957–1963: Reconsidering the strategic, technological, and operational contexts," in Janice Cavell and Ryan M. Touhey, eds., *Reassessing the Rogue Tory: Canadian Foreign Relations in the Diefenbaker Era* (Vancouver: UBC Press, 2018), 123–42; Sean Maloney, "The missing essential part emergency provision of nuclear weapons for RCAF Air Defence Command, 1961–1964," *Canadian Military History*, 23, no. 1 (2015): Article 3: 33–70, http://scholars.wlu.ca/cmh/vol23/iss1/3; and Andrew Richter, *Avoiding Armageddon: Canadian Military Strategy and Nuclear Weapons 1950–1963* (Vancouver: UBC Press, 2002). On the policy side, see McMahon, *Essence of Indecision* and Asa McKercher, *Camelot and Canada: Canadian-American Relations in the Kennedy Era* (New York: Oxford University Press, 2016). For a broader view, see Mark Andrew Eaton, "Canadians, nuclear weapons, and the Cold War security dilemma" (University of Western Ontario, PhD thesis, 2007). For primary evidence, see Janice Cavell, ed., *Documents on Canadian External Relations*, vol. 29, *1962–1963*, documents #210–52, https://gac.canadiana.ca/view/ooe.b2217569F_029/437.

Beyond the Book

Responding to the White House's Decision to Move American NORAD Forces to Defence Condition (DEFCON) 3 without Consulting Ottawa during the Cuban Missile Crisis, 1962

On 16 October 1962, US President John F. Kennedy learned that the Soviet Union had begun to deploy missiles into Cuba, less than 200 kilometres off the coast of the United States. Washington deliberated in secret for nearly a week before determining how to respond. During that period, Canada was not consulted. On 22 October, Kennedy elected to institute a naval quarantine of the island and issue an ultimatum demanding that Moscow remove the missiles. Prime Minister Diefenbaker was shown photographic evidence of the missile sites and was

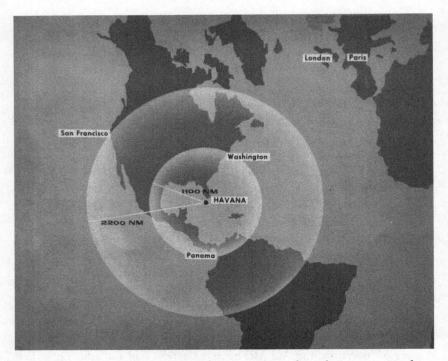

Figure 4.2 Briefing Board #13: Map of Western Hemisphere showing ranges of 1100 and 2200 nautical miles, 6 February 1963. This map depicts the short distance between Cuba and the United States and the capacity of missiles stored in Cuba to reach targets not far from Canada. United States Department of Defense. Department of Defense Cuban Missile Crisis Briefing Materials/John F. Kennedy Presidential Library/DODCMCBM-002-004.

briefed of the president's plan two hours before he addressed the American people on national television. That same day, the US military increased its wartime readiness level to DEFCON 3 and requested that the Canada's NORAD forces do the same. The request ignored NORAD's protocol, which stipulates that the countries would consult with one another before changing their readiness levels.

Questions

1. What are Canada's interests in this case?
2. Should the Canadian government immediately agree to the American request?
3. How, if at all, should Ottawa deal with the breach in protocol?

Readings

The background for this case is covered well in Robert Reford, *Canada and Three Crises* (Toronto: Canadian Institute of International Affairs, 1968), 147–217, especially 149–68. Peyton Lyon is highly critical of Diefenbaker's conduct in *Canada in World Affairs, 1961–1963* (Toronto: Oxford University Press, 1968), 27–64. Jocelyn Ghent-Mallet and Don Munton are much more forgiving in "Confronting Kennedy and the missiles in Cuba 1962," in Don Munton and John Kirton, eds., *Canadian Foreign Policy: Selected Cases* (Scarborough: Prentice Hall, 1992), 78–100. The most recent analysis, which draws from more extensive primary source evidence, is Asa McKercher, "A 'half-hearted response'?: Canada and the Cuban Missile Crisis, 1962," *International History Review* 33, no. 2 (2011): 335–52, https://doi.org/10.1080/07075332.2011.555450. See also Brad Gladman and Peter Archambault, "Advice and indecision: Canada and the Cuban missile crisis," *Canadian Military History* 23, no. 1 (2014): 11–32, https://scholars.wlu.ca/cmh/vol23/iss1/2/ and Patricia I. McMahon, *Essence of Indecision: Diefenbaker's Nuclear Policy, 1957–1963* (Montreal: McGill-Queen's University Press, 2009), 146–70. There is a vast literature on the Cuban missile crisis, but for an introduction, see Don Munton and David A. Welch, *The Cuban Missile Crisis: A Concise History* (New York: Oxford University Press, 2007).

5

Lester B. Pearson and the Domestic Implications of Canadian Foreign Policy, 1963–1968

Prime Minister Lester B. Pearson

Although foreign affairs was the focus of considerable attention during the 1963 federal election, Lester B. Pearson's Liberals won power by emphasizing the need to address a host of domestic issues. Under the slogan "Sixty Days of Decision," the Liberal minority government promised swift action on national unity, a sluggish economy, and several social welfare initiatives. Addressing them took longer than 60 days, and throughout Pearson's five years as prime minister the Liberals faced setbacks and scandals. The conventional wisdom was that Pearson bore much of the blame. As one of his contemporaries quipped, "God made him a statesman, but not a politician."[1] The prime minister, born in 1897, seemed outmoded in what journalist Peter C. Newman called "the age of moonflights, mass marches and mod."[2]

Pearson may not have inspired youthful devotion, but with parliamentary support from the New Democratic Party, his government achieved numerous successes. The Liberals introduced the Canada Pension Plan and the Guaranteed Income Supplement to assist seniors, the Canada Assistance Plan to help those in poverty, and a Canada Student Loans program that made post-secondary education accessible to increasing numbers of Canadians. The capstone was a national health insurance program.[3] In addition, Pearson's government made it easier to access divorce, abortion, and contraception and placed a moratorium on capital punishment.[4] The Liberals also convened a Royal Commission on the Status of Women, whose findings would later lead to greater gender equality. Perhaps the Pearson government's most significant achievement was implementing a new immigration policy that removed restrictions explicitly barring non-white migrants. The resulting points system and the opening of immigration offices across the Global South permanently changed the face of Canada.[5]

Canada First, Not Canada Alone: A History of Canadian Foreign Policy. Adam Chapnick and Asa McKercher,
Oxford University Press. © Oxford University Press 2024. DOI: 10.1093/oso/9780197653715.003.0006

Canada and Quebec: The International Dimension

Expanding the social safety net and advancing human rights proved relatively easy in comparison to the more intractable problem of growing Québécois nationalism. In December 1962, then–opposition leader Pearson had declared that Canada was in the midst of a "serious crisis of national unity" and called for a "true partnership" between English and French Canadians.[6] His statement reflected the mounting consensus that, as it neared the centennial of Confederation in 1967, Canada was in trouble. In Quebec, revulsion against decades of corruption by Premier Maurice Duplessis—ending with his death in 1959—and a more deeply rooted sense that francophones were both the victims of anglophone exploitation and second-class citizens in their own province exploded into an upsurge of nationalism. Under the slogan *Maîtres chez nous*—masters in our own house—the provincial government of Jean Lesage nationalized and consolidated the province's hydroelectric utilities, using the newly created Hydro-Québec to fund economic and public policy initiatives. *Maîtres chez nous* became the *cri de coeur* for a broader effort to assert French language rights, establish provincially directed secular social programs, and, for some, achieve Quebec's independence.

Pearson's efforts to grapple with Quebec's Quiet Revolution included doubling the number of francophone Cabinet members and recruiting several leading Quebec intellectuals to serve as MPs. His government established the Royal Commission on Bilingualism and Biculturalism, whose report would lead to Canada becoming officially bilingual. Ottawa also sought to counter Quebec officials' attempts to assert the province's international personality and win recognition from other countries.

The international dimension was important, for French President Charles de Gaulle actively nurtured Québécois nationalism. Visiting Montreal in 1967, he infamously declared "Vive le Québec libre!" and won wild approval from his audience and the ire of Canadian federalists. Pearson acidly noted that tens of thousands of Canadians had died defending France in two world wars.[7] The damage was done, however. In the wake of de Gaulle's speech, Quebec separatism blossomed. The former general's intervention in Montreal was in keeping with his assertions of French power against what he perceived as the dominance of "Anglo-Saxon" countries—the United States, Britain, and Canada. The previous year, he had taken France out of NATO's military command structure, ordered allied troops off French soil, and shuttered NATO headquarters in Paris. This move signalled growing cracks in the Cold War consensus that had bound Western countries together.

Nationalism and Foreign Policy

Canada had no de Gaulle, but during the 1960s growing numbers of Canadians—particularly among the maturing baby boom generation—were increasingly ill at ease with NATO membership and the state of postwar Canada–US relations. Much of this concern lay on the political left, but some conservatives were also critical. Philosopher George Grant captured the zeitgeist in his 1965 polemic *Lament for a Nation: The Defeat of Canadian Nationalism*.[8] Grant's view that successive Liberal governments going back to William Lyon Mackenzie King had transformed Canada into a satellite of the United States was particularly appealing to leftists who protested racial segregation in the Deep South and the war in Vietnam. In this climate, nationalists called for Canada to assert its cultural sovereignty. Some also advocated withdrawal from Canada's military alliances and neutrality in the Cold War.[9] The Pearson government brushed aside such demands, renewing the NORAD agreement in 1967 and maintaining Canadian forces in Europe.

Nationalists had a greater impact on economic matters. Here, their champion was Pearson's friend and confidant, Walter Gordon, a wealthy businessperson who had helped rebuild the Liberal Party and chaired the Royal Commission on Canada's Economic Prospects.[10] The commission warned of Canada's growing reliance on the United States as an export market and source of investment, as well as of increasing American ownership of Canadian businesses. When the Liberals took power in 1963, Pearson appointed Gordon finance minister. His first budget included a tax on foreign takeovers of national firms. Meant to spur Canadian ownership, the move was rightly seen by US investors as targeting them. Following protests from the Kennedy administration and, critically, a plunge in the stock market, Gordon withdrew the measure.[11]

The showdown over the Gordon budget indicated that, although John Diefenbaker was gone, difficulties in the Canada–US relationship persisted. One sign of progress involved the Columbia River, which stretches from British Columbia down into the United States. In the late 1950s, state and provincial governments had plans to exploit the waterway for hydro power and to manage any possible flooding. Negotiations to reconcile these competing positions had been ongoing for several decades. In 1961, the Diefenbaker government rushed through a bilateral treaty, but British Columbia's Premier W.A.C. Bennett objected both to the terms of the treaty and to what he saw as the federal government's intervention into provincial affairs. Pearson raised the issue with Kennedy, proposing terms that appealed to Bennett. Canada–US and Ottawa–Victoria negotiations produced an agreement in January 1964.[12]

The following year, Ottawa and Washington agreed to the Automotive Products Trade Agreement. The "Auto Pact" integrated the Canadian and US automobile industries and avoided a trade war over Canadian tariffs on American automotive imports. As George Ball, the American undersecretary of state, told a Toronto audience, it was a sign that the two countries were learning to "live together rationally on a single continent."[13]

Although nationalists worried that the Auto Pact further linked the neighbours' economies, the agreement benefited Canada's automotive industry. To secure its passage, President Lyndon B. Johnson had to reassure domestic critics in Congress that the negotiations had not compromised US economic interests.[14] Johnson's lobbying efforts on Canada's behalf came amid a confrontation with Pearson over the latter's comments about the course of the American war in Vietnam. The US president, a politician par excellence, recognized that Pearson faced domestic political demands for him to stand up to the US intervention. Anti-war activists, Johnson told a confidant, had Canada's prime minister "dodging and ducking."[15] Both sides were committed to not letting personal disagreements damage bilateral relations. As historian Greg Donaghy put it, for all their squabbling, in the 1960s, Canadians and Americans remained "tolerant allies."[16]

Peace Movement and Vietnam

Johnson recognized that the anti-war movement was a potent force in Canada. Pearson's decision to acquire nuclear warheads from the Americans had depressed Canada's nuclear disarmament movement, but their fortunes revived with the Vietnam War, and activists' focus shifted accordingly. Alongside demands for a US withdrawal from Southeast Asia, the increasingly vocal coalition of university students, leftists, and pacifists called on the Canadian government to end arms sales to the American military. Pearson's failure to act led the peace movement to charge Ottawa with "complicity" in Washington's war, further evidence of Canada's alleged colonial status.[17] Although the Liberals failed to stop military exports—the 1958 Defence Production Sharing Agreement that had integrated the North American defence industry proved lucrative for Canada—Pearson and Secretary of State for External Affairs Paul Martin authorized several secret diplomatic missions to lay the groundwork for a ceasefire.[18] The failure of these initiatives lay with Washington and Hanoi, not Ottawa.

For opponents of the Vietnam War, Pearson's lack of action belied his reputation as a peacemaker. Yet beyond the conflict in Southeast Asia, the prime minister undertook a number of initiatives to promote the multilateralism that was becoming synonymous with the label "Pearsonian internationalism." In 1964, Ottawa convened an international conference aimed at establishing a permanent UN peacekeeping force. It also sought to secure stable UN funding for peacekeepers, an initiative quashed by the Soviet Union. Canadian soldiers participated in ongoing and new peacekeeping missions, including a major operation in Cyprus, where local fighting threatened to spark a conflict between NATO allies Greece and Turkey.[19] However, there was disillusion around peacekeeping and the UN more broadly. In 1967, Egypt's government expelled the UN Emergency Force (UNEF), the force created by Pearson during the Suez Crisis. Occupying a non-permanent seat on the UN Security Council, Canada had sought to save UNEF and resented UN Secretary General U Thant's failure to intervene. When tensions between Israel and its Arab neighbours erupted in the Six-Day War, Canadian delegates in New York helped broker a ceasefire. For officials in Ottawa, UNEF's demise and the resulting conflict were an indictment of the United Nations.[20]

Beyond the UN, between 1963 and 1968, Canada's foreign aid budget more than tripled from $69.5 million to $253.2 million.[21] Ottawa also developed stronger relations with new Commonwealth members from Africa and the Caribbean. Both developments underscored the effects of decolonization which, by the 1960s, had resulted in the collapse of most formal European imperialism.

The Decline of the British Connection

What of Canada's own imperial legacy? Even in the 1960s, many Canadians strongly valued the British connection. Pearson, for one, had grown up in an era when Canada was firmly part of Britain's empire, had fought for that empire in the First World War, had been educated at Oxford, and had served as a diplomat in London at the outset of the Second World War. Nonetheless, as prime minister, he promoted a new civic nationalism that could appeal to francophone Quebecers, to the many new Canadians who had emigrated from continental Europe and other parts of the world, and to younger Canadians for whom the British Empire was a thing of the past.[22] In 1964, Pearson declared that it was "time now for Canadians to unfurl a flag that is truly distinctive and truly national in character."[23] Traditionalists disagreed. A bruising political fight ensued. Ultimately, those hoping to retain the Red Ensign (bearing the British Union Jack) lost, and the red-and-white Maple Leaf was adopted. Although Pearson retained hopes of abandoning the British monarchy in favour of a distinctly Canadian head of state, the divisiveness of the flag debate convinced him to abandon the idea.[24]

Pearson's promotion of civic nationalism reached its apogee at the 1967 Universal and International Exposition in Montreal. Held during the centenary of Canada's Confederation and attended by 53 million visitors, Expo '67 was a blockbuster affair. For many Canadians, the festivities were a point of pride, showing, as Pearson boasted, that "no longer is our national costume a union jacket worn with star striped trousers!"[25] This boisterous assertion typified the excitement of what journalist Pierre Berton later ominously referred to as "the last good year."[26] By the time Expo '67 closed in October, Pearson had just six months left before his retirement from four decades of public service, a career that spanned an era of great change for Canada and the world.

Case Studies

The cases for this chapter demonstrate the extensive links between domestic and foreign policy in Canada. The first examines the impact of Canada's federal structure on how foreign policy is conceived and implemented. Although it focuses on Quebec's efforts to establish an international personality, other provinces have asserted themselves similarly. Ottawa's response to Quebec in 1965—which emphasized minimizing direct confrontation and defending its jurisdiction by denying the government in Quebec City legal precedents that might be leveraged for increased independence at some later point—was questioned at the time and still is. Nonetheless, the Pearson government's management appears to have dampened calls for separation at that time.

The second case demonstrates that public opinion is measured by more than just polling data. As a prime minister whose party held a minority of seats in the House of Commons, Lester Pearson was particularly sensitive to the opinion of domestic constituencies—in this case left-leaning Canadians—whose votes he needed to expand Liberal Party support. These voters were staunchly opposed to the American war in Vietnam. Even though the majority of Canadians disagreed, as did officials in the Department of External Affairs, Pearson almost had to be sympathetic to calls for Canada to speak out against American aggression.

The Beyond the Book case adds a cultural lens to Canadian foreign (and foreign trade) policy considerations. In the 1960s, American art, drama, and literature dominated the Canadian cultural landscape. Successive governments in Ottawa struggled to respond in a manner that allowed Canadian artists to flourish without compromising relations with Canada's most important ally and trading partner. The case focuses on two leading American magazines, *Time* and *Reader's Digest*, whose success in Canada threatened the future of the Canadian magazine industry.

The Promulgation of the Gérin-Lajoie Doctrine, 1965

What role should Canada's provincial governments play in the development and implementation of Canadian foreign policy?

The British North America Act (1867) established the basis of Canadian federalism—or two-level government. Since section 91 gave the federal level in Ottawa exclusive responsibility for national defence, and section 132 provided it with "all Powers necessary or proper for performing the Obligations of Canada or of any Province thereof, as Part of the British Empire, towards Foreign Countries, arising under Treaties between the Empire and such Foreign Countries," there was initially no debate over who was responsible for foreign policy.[27]

By the early 1960s, as the global decolonization movement inspired "an awakening of self-consciousness" among Quebecers, that consensus was called into question.[28] Writing off the scattered French-speaking communities across Canada, provincial officials in Quebec City concluded that strengthening Quebec provincially was the best way to ensure the survival and prosperity of francophone culture in North America.[29] Such thinking resulted in Quebec's Quiet Revolution.

In 1961, the former federal Liberal Cabinet minister and now Quebec Premier Jean Lesage opened the Maison générale du Québec à Paris in an effort to increase his province's ties to France and thereby affirm its independent foreign policy bona fides. By the time Lesage's former Cabinet colleague Lester Pearson became prime minister two years later, the Quebec state was actively seeking confrontation with Ottawa.[30] As Pearson recalled in his memoirs, the Liberals recognized the challenge that the Quiet Revolution and Quebec's international aspirations posed to the unity of Canada immediately: "if Canada were to be a strong, independent, and distinct state on this continent, we had to do everything in our power to extend French culture and the French language throughout Canada."[31] Foreign policy also had a role to play.[32] Closer relations with France and a more determined effort to recognize the French presence at home would reassure Quebecers that Canada's international realm extended beyond the North Atlantic Triangle.

Pearson's initial efforts to reach out to Paris were disastrous. Ottawa failed to prevent Trans-Canada Airlines from choosing American-made aircraft over those of a French competitor. When President Charles de Gaulle asked that Ottawa's policy of selling uranium to the United States and the United Kingdom without conditions be extended to France, Pearson refused.[33] These decisions left de Gaulle—already sympathetic to Québécois nationalism[34]—determined to sow division between Ottawa and Quebec City.[35]

The domestic angle to the federal strategy was more effective. In 1964, Pearson appointed Marcel Cadieux undersecretary of state for external affairs. Only the second francophone to hold the position, Cadieux was also a staunch federalist with a background in international law. Working under the supervision of Secretary of State for External Affairs Paul Martin, Cadieux was tasked with preserving the unity and integrity of Canada's international personality.

The greatest challenge to that personality was posed by another lawyer, Quebec's Minister of Education Paul Gérin-Lajoie. Gérin-Lajoie foresaw two extensions of his province's identity on the world stage. One was through nation-to-nation relations with France; the other was via control of Canada's educational assistance program in French Africa. He justified what Ottawa considered to be intrusions into areas of federal jurisdiction through a combination of legal and moral arguments. The BNA Act's articles 92 and 93 placed education within exclusive provincial jurisdiction. That exclusivity, Gérin-Lajoie maintained, was unlimited: "provincial responsibility at home was provincial responsibility abroad."[36] Since a 1937 ruling of the Judicial Committee of the Privy Council had established that Ottawa "could not implement an international treaty in a field of provincial jurisdiction without the concurrence of the province,"[37] it made little sense for Quebec to be excluded from international educational arrangements. While Gérin-Lajoie conceded that the federal government might represent Canadians as a whole, he maintained that his government was the only one in Canada to represent a majority of francophones. Quebec City therefore required a special place in Canada's foreign policy architecture—for example, as the manager of the Canadian educational assistance program in French Africa—and the right to conclude international treaties within its areas of jurisdiction.[38]

In February 1965, the government of Quebec concluded an educational entente with France. On 12 April 1965, Gérin-Lajoie officially introduced his doctrine during a speech to Montreal's consular corps. Shortly thereafter, Quebec City launched negotiations with Paris for a bilateral cultural exchange program.[39]

The Canadian government's response was technocratic. As Pearson recalls: "Within the authority of the Canadian government over all international agreements, Quebec or any other province could make arrangements with foreign countries; but to make independent arrangements...went beyond the bounds of acceptability."[40] In November 1965, Ottawa used a hastily negotiated Franco-Canadian Cultural Agreement (known colloquially as an *accord cadre*, or umbrella agreement), under which all franco-provincial agreements would be subsumed, to undermine the legal implications of an allegedly independent cultural entente with Paris that Quebec City was about to complete. To Pearson, Martin, and Cadieux, it was not the substance, but "the form of Quebec's

114   CANADA FIRST, NOT CANADA ALONE

international activities [that] mattered most in international and constitutional law."[41] As Canadian foreign policymakers were all too aware, Canada had asserted its own autonomy from Britain through piecemeal agreements and actions. After a series of failed negotiations with Quebec's Ministry of Education, Ottawa convinced the Tunisian government to reject an independent Quebec City proposal for a bilateral technical assistance program.[42] In May 1967, it concluded a cultural accord with Belgium, once more forcing the Quebec provincial government under the umbrella of a federal agreement.[43]

Quebec nationalists were hardly deterred. In the aftermath of Ottawa's *accord cadre* with France, direct relations with Paris expanded dramatically. A new France-Quebec Permanent Commission on Cooperation (*une commission mixte*) resulted in scholarships to support Quebec students in France, chairs of Quebec civilization at French universities, and other bilateral mechanisms for collaboration.[44] According to one former provincial official, Quebec "was now poised...to consult with Paris as if it were a virtually sovereign state and, thanks to French support, be bidden to international gatherings on the same basis as the other nations of the world."[45]

Did the federal government respond appropriately? The evidence is mixed. Some criticized the Department of External Affairs for its overly legalistic approach.[46] Ottawa was unable to prevent de Gaulle from raising Quebec City's global profile and undermining national unity. The Lesage government and its successors undeniably influenced the formulation and implementation of Canadian foreign policy.[47] But Pearson wanted French-Canadian interests to play a larger role in Canada's external relations, and Ottawa retained exclusive authority over the negotiation and ratification of binding international agreements. Federalism no doubt shapes Canadian global affairs. The province of Quebec still sees the Gérin-Lajoie doctrine as the foundation of its paradiplomatic posture, and Ottawa continues to reject the thinking behind it.

Prime Minister Lester Pearson's Speech at Temple University, 1965

> How might the Canadian government best express misgivings
> about US foreign policy?

No matter how much they have in common, from time to time, allies inevitably disagree. Not long after the minority Liberal government of Lester Pearson took power in 1963, Washington's increasingly unpopular war in Vietnam tested the Canada–US relationship at the highest levels.

When the Second World War ended, the communist Vietminh declared independence of the French colony of Indochina (Vietnam, Laos, and

Cambodia). France reasserted its colonial control, and a war between the Vietminh and French forces ensued. The United States responded with financial and military support to its NATO ally, but, in 1954, the Vietminh claimed victory. The French colony was partitioned into North and South Vietnam, Laos, and Cambodia, and a series of International Commissions on Supervision and Control (ICSCs) were established to encourage de-escalation along the new countries' borders. Volunteered by the British, Canada reluctantly agreed to serve on all three commissions on behalf of the West.

Ottawa was often skeptical of US strategy and tactics in Vietnam, where American money, arms, and eventually soldiers poured into the non-communist South after a communist insurgency—backed by the North—had begun. Canadian–American differences approached a tipping point in February 1965.[48] After communist guerillas targeted a US air base along a critical military logistics corridor in Pleiku, US President Lyndon Johnson ordered a series of air strikes against guerrilla positions. Within weeks, a large force of Marines was deployed to South Vietnam, inaugurating a substantial commitment of ground troops. At the time, US public opinion was still on Johnson's side.[49]

Most Canadians were similarly sympathetic. Experience on the ICSCs instilled profound anti-communist sentiment among the diplomatic corps.[50] It also served as a buffer against American requests for direct Canadian military assistance. As Prime Minister Pearson explained to his Cabinet, "Canada could not consider participating in any military or para-military fashion [because doing so] would conflict with her [ICSC] responsibilities."[51] The differences between Canada's diplomats and its politicians reflected the shaky state of Canadian public opinion. While a silent majority sided with the US, opponents on the political left, among university professors, and in the media objected vociferously.[52] Some of these critics came from some of the very groups (youth and intellectuals) that the Liberals hoped to attract in order to secure a majority government in the next election. Some were members of Pearson's family and close friends.[53]

Daily media reports detailing the extent of the bombings heightened political tensions in Ottawa. Pearson personally disapproved of the military escalation and in May 1964 warned Johnson privately that such a move would be poorly perceived internationally.[54] But he also knew how sensitive the White House was to criticism when American lives and prestige were at risk. Shortly after Pleiku, the Canadian prime minister explained his thinking: "our official doubts about certain U.S. foreign policies should be expressed in private," he said. "It does not mean that we must always remain silent if there is strong disagreement on matters of great moment or principle. Not at all.... But we must never do this merely for the purpose of rousing a chauvinistic cheer at home."[55] Canada cautiously backed an Indian proposal for an international peace conference and Pearson even hinted at his country's increasing discomfort with US policy at a speech in New York City on 5 March.[56]

The latter speech came just days after Washington launched Operation Rolling Thunder, an extensive and controversial bombing campaign against the North. On 27 March, Pearson met with Undersecretary of State for External Affairs Marcel Cadieux. The prime minister was scheduled to speak at Temple University in Philadelphia on 2 April. He asked for a text that would recommend development assistance for Southeast Asia and "find a pretext for peace talks."[57] As Cadieux later reflected in his diary: "It seemed to me that a temporary halt in military operations would have the effect, on the whole, of embarrassing the Americans' enemies and facilitating the mobilization of their friends."[58] Pearson thought that advocating a bombing pause might satisfy the anti-war constituency he was courting in Canada without overly antagonizing Washington. At the time, President Johnson was in the midst of encouraging Congress to support a Canada–US automotive agreement.[59]

While External Affairs drafted the speech, the Viet Cong set off a car bomb outside the US embassy in Saigon. Twenty-two people were killed, including two Americans. In response, DEA officials moderated Pearson's language, but Secretary of State for External Affairs Paul Martin pleaded with Pearson not to make the speech at all: "If you publicly criticize the United States like this, you're going to discount our influence in Washington and your own forever. And you must not do that."[60] Martin suggested that the prime minister instead broach the subject with Johnson privately.

Pearson initially agreed, but ultimately he and Canada's ambassador to the United States decided to further modify the text.[61] This decision may have been the result of Pearson's 30 March meeting with a Washington journalist and long-time acquaintance, Marquis Childs. Childs contended that the White House needed to hear a contrary view and that the speech "would not be resented" in Washington.[62] The fact that Johnson was scheduled to be in Texas at the time likely made Pearson's decision easier. Nonetheless, the Canadians deliberately held off providing an advance copy of the speech to anyone in Washington until it was too late for the Americans to react.[63]

As historian Robert Bothwell notes, "The speech, as delivered, was hardly a revolutionary document. It did not question Johnson's motivation or the larger themes of American policy. It went out of its way to applaud American sacrifice and leadership" in Vietnam and the broader Cold War.[64] But it did ultimately recommend a bombing pause and, by implication, breached an unstated diplomatic rule that foreign leaders did not criticize presidents of the United States on American soil.[65] Johnson, who had returned to Camp David, insisted on meeting with Pearson.

The US president was livid. For over an hour, he gave Pearson what the historian John English called "the famous 'Johnson treatment,' a combination of

Figure 5.1 Duncan Macpherson, "Hi, Mister President…" *Toronto Star*, 17 July 1966. On 2 April 1965, as Canadians began to grow weary of America's intervention in Vietnam, Prime Minister Lester Pearson travelled to Philadelphia to receive the Temple University Peace Award. In his acceptance speech, much to the chagrin of the Lyndon Johnson administration, Pearson called for a temporary cessation of hostilities in Indochina. Johnson, a brash and fiery politician at the best of times, was furious. No foreign politician had any business criticizing US policy on American soil. The following day, Johnson berated Pearson at the presidential country retreat at Camp David. As this political cartoon makes clear, there was little the Canadian could say to assuage the president at the time, but Pearson did later write a lengthy letter of apology. No matter, the relationship with Johnson was never the same.

relentless admonition and physical domination."[66] Johnson's staff made sure that the Canadian media were aware of how the president had "chewed out" Canada's leader.[67] Upon his return to Ottawa, Pearson wrote to Johnson, emphasizing his motivation for speaking out: "I was trying to make the kind of suggestion—carefully guarded—that might be of help to him in circumstances

Figure 5.2 Prime Minister Lester B. Pearson on Tractor Driven by President Lyndon B. Johnson.

This photograph captures the essence of the Pearson-Johnson confrontation. The two leaders could not be more different. Pearson is dressed formally, in a suit with a bow tie. Johnson is dressed significantly more casually as he drives the tractor. The US president's frustration with Pearson is obvious, just as Pearson's grimacing smile captures his diplomatic background and desire to keep relations with Johnson cordial. © Government of Canada. Reproduced with the permission of Library and Archives Canada (2022). Library and Archives Canada/Paul Joseph Martin fonds/PA-117604.

where the stepped-up bombing of North Vietnam had not achieved the desired result." He continued: "public opinion in my country was profoundly disturbed by the implications of certain aspects of US policy." As prime minister, he had an obligation to demonstrate that Canada did not blindly follow America's lead.[68] Johnson was hardly assuaged, yet he never retaliated and even saw the Auto Pact through to its completion. When Washington did institute a bombing pause later in 1965, it failed to produce a settlement with the North Vietnamese.

Evaluations of what historian Brendan Kelly has rightly called "one of the most significant events in the history of Canadian–American relations"[69] are mixed. To some, Johnson had been pushed too far by the hawks in his administration. The Canadian prime minister had to make Canada's position clear and couched his concerns in sufficiently diplomatic language so as to project an appropriate tone and message.[70] Others have criticized Pearson's approach as disingenuous, noting that Canadian companies were profiting from selling war supplies to the American military.[71] The most critical note that while Pearson urged a bombing pause, his Temple speech defended American intervention in Vietnam, a sign of Canadian complicity in the war.[72]

Canada's ambassador to the United States at the time, Charles Ritchie, saw both sides. While he claims to have told Pearson that he had "never been prouder of him"[73] than when he stood up to Johnson, his diary condemns Canadian Vietnam policy in harsh terms: "As anyone who lived through the last World War knows, a nation at war requires total support from its friends, not qualified approval, still less wise advice from the sidelines."[74]

There is no right answer to this debate. Pearson clearly did not follow his own advice on how to manage Canada–US relations. Domestic politics ruled, as they often do in the practice of foreign policy. The Temple speech was not the last time a prime minister would need to weigh relations with the United States against the need to appeal to voters at home. As for the Liberals, the result of the November 1965 election was another minority government.

Conclusion

When Lester Pearson became prime minister in 1963, observers of Canadian foreign policy were largely relieved. A pair of safe hands, Pearson could be trusted to restore calm and order in the aftermath of the tumultuous Diefenbaker years. Yet, much of Prime Minister Pearson's attention had to be devoted to domestic challenges amid revolutionary social change and minority parliaments. Foreign policy in the Pearson years proved unexpectedly complex. The Quiet Revolution, aided and abetted by Charles de Gaulle, transformed the province of Quebec's international posture. Canada–US relations were hardly more stable than they had been under Diefenbaker, and decolonization continued to affect the balance of global power.

Canadian foreign policy at the highest levels continued to stress the importance of the United Nations and multilateral institutions, the inevitability of close relations with the United States and other Cold War allies, and the obligation of governments in Ottawa to contribute actively to the world around them. For many, that continuity was comforting. For others, Pearson's refusal to forsake nuclear weapons, his unwillingness to explicitly condemn American conduct in Vietnam, and Ottawa's privileging of relations with traditional allies and alliances over the development of new relationships in

120 CANADA FIRST, NOT CANADA ALONE

the Global South reflected an approach to world affairs that was no longer relevant in a post-colonial world.

Readings

Internationally, the 1960s was a decade of profound change. Important works on myriad issues in US foreign relations include Diane B. Kunz, ed., *The Diplomacy of the Crucial Decade: American Foreign Relations During the 1960s* (New York: Columbia University Press, 1994) and Francis J. Gavin and Mark Atwood Lawrence, eds., *Beyond the Cold War: Lyndon Johnson and the New Global Challenges of the 1960s* (New York: Oxford University Press, 2014). Fredrik Logevall's *Choosing War: The Lost Chance for Peace and the Escalation of War in Vietnam* (Berkeley: University of California Press, 2002); Mark Philip Bradley and Marilyn Young, eds., *Making Sense of the Vietnam Wars: Local, National, and Transnational Perspectives* (New York: Oxford University Press, 2008); and Lien-Hang T. Nguyen's *Hanoi's War: An International History of the War for Peace in Vietnam* (Chapel Hill: University of North Carolina Press, 2012) are the seminal works on the Vietnam War. On developments in Europe, see Thomas Alan Schwartz, *Lyndon Johnson and Europe: In the Shadow of Vietnam* (Cambridge, MA: Harvard University Press, 2003) and Jeffrey Glen Giauque, *Grand Designs and Visions of Unity: The Atlantic Powers and the Reorganization of Western Europe, 1955–1963* (Chapel Hill: University of North Carolina Press, 2002). The sixties as an era of global protest is covered in Jeremi Suri, *Power and Protest: Global Revolution and the Rise of Détente* (Cambridge, MA: Harvard University Press, 2003). Important examinations of events in the Global South in the sixties and beyond include Adom Getachew, *Worldmaking after Empire: The Rise and Fall of Self-Determination* (Princeton: Princeton University Press, 2019); Robert J. McMahon, *The Cold War in the Third World* (New York: Oxford University Press, 2013); and Vijay Prashad, *The Darker Nations: A People's History of the Third World* (London: The New Press, 2007).

A good introduction to Canadian foreign policy in the Pearson years are the essays in Asa McKercher and Galen Perras, eds., *Mike's World: Lester B. Pearson and Canadian External Affairs* (Vancouver: UBC Press, 2017). For an essential study of Canada–US relations, see Greg Donaghy's *Tolerant Allies: Canada and the United States, 1963–1968* (Montreal: McGill-Queen's University Press, 2002). Several books examine Canadian protest movements in the sixties, including protests over foreign policy issues. See, for example, Lara A. Campbell, Dominique Clément, and Greg Kealey, eds., *Debating Dissent: Canada and the 1960s* (Toronto: University of Toronto Press, 2012) and Dimitry Anastakis, ed., *The Sixties: Passion, Politics, and Style* (Montreal and Kingston: McGill-Queen's

University Press, 2008). On Canada and Canadians' changing relationship with Britain, see Phillip Buckner, ed., *Canada and the End of Empire* (Vancouver: UBC Press, 2005).

The first comprehensive assessment of the Canada-Quebec-France relationship was Dale C. Thomson's *Vive Le Québec Libre* (Toronto: Deneau, 1988). Since then, scholars have uncovered significant additional archival evidence. The case presented in this chapter draws heavily from Brendan Kelly's "Pearson, France, and Quebec's international personality," in Asa McKercher and Galen Perras, eds., *Mike's World: Lester B. Pearson and Canadian External Affairs* (Vancouver: UBC Press, 2017), 297–319. Kelly has also produced an excellent biography of Marcel Cadieux, *The Good Fight: Marcel Cadieux and Canadian Diplomacy* (Vancouver: UBC Press, 2019). Robin Gendron has written extensively about Canada, Quebec, and French Africa. His most comprehensive work is *Towards a Francophone Community: Canada's Relations with France and French Africa, 1946–1968* (Montreal: McGill-Queen's University Press, 2006). For a Quebec insider's account, see Claude Morin and Richard Howard, *Quebec versus Ottawa: The Struggle for Self-Government, 1960–72* (Toronto: University of Toronto Press, 1973). The clearest Canadian government statement on the role of the provinces in foreign policy was published after this case ends: Paul Martin, *Federalism and International Relations* (Ottawa: Information Canada, 1968). See also the supplement, Mitchell Sharp, *Federalism and International Conferences of Education* (Ottawa: Queen's Printer, 1968). French language sources include Stéphane Roussel and Greg Donaghy, eds., *Mission Paris: Les ambassadeurs du Canada en France et le triangle Ottawa—Québec—Paris* (Montmagny, QC: Hurtubise, 2012) and Stéphane Paquin, ed., *Les relations internationales du Québec depuis la Doctrine Gérin-Lajoie (1965–2005)* (Lévis, QC: Les Presses de l'Université Laval, 2006).

The most thorough assessments of Lester Pearson's response to American conduct during the Vietnam War can be found in Brendan Kelly, "Lester B. Pearson's Temple University speech revisited: The origins and evolution of the proposal for a bombing pause," *American Review of Canadian Studies* 47, no. 4 (2017): 373–84, https://doi.org/10.1080/02722011.2017.1399281 and Greg Donaghy, "Minding the minister: Pearson, Martin and American policy in Asia, 1963–1967," in Norman Hillmer, ed., *Pearson: The Unlikely Gladiator* (Montreal: McGill-Queen's University Press, 1999), 131–49. Kelly and Donaghy draw on new archival evidence that further enriches John English's "Speaking out on Vietnam, 1965," in Don Munton and John Kirton, eds., *Canadian Foreign Policy: Selected Cases* (Scarborough: Prentice-Hall, 1992), 135–52. Douglas A. Ross, *In the Interests of Peace: Canada and Vietnam, 1954–1973* (Toronto: University of Toronto Press, 1984) emphasizes the international strategic context. For the text of Pearson's speech, see Roger Frank Swanson, *Canadian-American*

122   CANADA FIRST, NOT CANADA ALONE

Summit Diplomacy, 1923–1973: Selected Speeches and Documents (Toronto: McClelland and Stewart, 1975), 251–4. Lester B. Pearson, *The Memoirs of the Right Honourable Lester B. Pearson*, vol. 3, *1957–1968*, edited by John A. Munro and Alex I. Inglis (Toronto: University of Toronto Press, 1975), includes Pearson's letter to Johnson afterwards (142–3).

Beyond the Book

Managing the Impact of Split-Run Magazines in Canada, 1964–1965

In 1951, the Royal Commission on National Development in the Arts, Letters and Sciences (the Massey Commission) issued a landmark report on the state of the arts and culture in Canada. The commission recommended that Ottawa take an active role in promoting and preserving elements of Canadian culture that differentiated Canada from its international competitors. When Ottawa offered tax credits to businesses that advertised in Canadian magazines, two leading American publishers, *Time* and *Reader's Digest*, discovered a loophole. "Canadian" editions of their publications—essentially the American version with an additional Canadian story or two—could qualify for federal support. By 1954, the United States had captured 80 per cent of the Canadian magazine market, exactly what the Massey Commission had hoped to avoid.

In 1960, the Diefenbaker government established a Royal Commission on Publications (the O'Leary Commission). Its 1961 report concluded that "only a truly Canadian printing press, one with the 'feel' of Canada and directly responsible to Canada, can give us the critical analysis, the informal discourse and dialogue which are indispensable in a sovereign society." It recommended a series of policy changes that ultimately would have forced *Time* and *Reader's Digest* to end their Canadian editions, a move that would have damaged Canada–US relations. The Diefenbaker government's efforts to deal with the issue were hampered by the prime minister's indecision and then interrupted by the elections of 1962 and 1963, leaving the problem to its successor.

Questions

1. What are Canada's interests in this case?
2. At what point, if ever, does the level of foreign investment in Canada become a risk to national sovereignty?
3. Should the promotion and protection of Canadian cultural outputs and institutions be a foreign policy priority?

Readings

The sources for this case are limited, but also very good. Isaiah Litvak and Christopher Maule were the first to examine this case in detail in their *Cultural Sovereignty: The* Time *and* Reader's Digest *Case in Canada* (New York: Praeger, 1974), especially chapters 3 and 4. Their research drew primarily from public sources. More recent work draws from extensive archival research. See Stephen Azzi, "Magazines and the Canadian dream: The struggle to protect Canadian periodicals 1955–1965," *International Journal* 54, no. 3 (1999): 502–23, https://doi.org/10.1177/002070209905400310 and Greg Donaghy, *Tolerant Allies: Canada and the United States 1963–1968* (Montreal: McGill-Queen's University Press, 2002), 149–57. Lester Pearson provides a brief summary of the issue in his *Mike: The Memoirs of the Rt. Hon. Lester B. Pearson*, vol. 3, *1957–1968*, edited by John A. Munro and Alex I. Inglis (Toronto: University of Toronto Press, 1975), 133–4. The original Report of the O'Leary Commission can be found at Canada, Royal Commission on Publications, *Report* (Ottawa: Queen's Printer, 1961).

6

Pierre Elliott Trudeau and the Re-Imagination of "Canada First," 1968–1984

Trudeaumania

In 1968, Pierre Trudeau took Canada by storm. Handsome, youthful, and cerebral, the lawyer turned politician became prime minister amid a wave of media attention and popular enthusiasm dubbed "Trudeaumania."[1] As part of his promise to build a "just society," in 1969 Parliament approved legislation that decriminalized homosexuality, allowed easier access to abortion, and simplified the divorce process.[2] Two years later, Trudeau proclaimed that Canada was a multicultural country, staking out a distinctive civic nationalism. He also pushed back against growing Quebec separatism, the defining issue of his time.

Although he was hardly a foreign policy expert, the new prime minister was a cosmopolitan world traveller. He had even visited Communist China, a rare feat for a Westerner at the height of the Cold War. In 1963, prior to joining the Liberals, Trudeau had criticized Lester Pearson's commitment to accept nuclear weapons, denouncing the Nobel Prize–winner as the "defrocked priest of peace."[3] In a major statement on "Canada in the World" shortly after becoming Liberal leader and prime minister, Trudeau promised to take "a fresh look at the fundamentals of Canadian foreign policy to see whether there are ways in which we can serve more effectively Canada's current interests, objectives and priorities." This re-evaluation was "necessary," he explained, "not because of the inadequacies of the past but because of the changing nature of Canada and of the world around us."[4] Privately, he told British officials, "Canada had become involved in a great many things which were not really appropriate to her present relative position."[5]

The ethos of change was emphasized in *Foreign Policy for Canadians*, an official report released in 1970. In six multicoloured booklets that were widely circulated to non-governmental stakeholders, the "white paper" flagged five areas where Canada would focus its efforts: Europe, the Pacific, Latin America, the United Nations, and international development. In the last two areas Canada could play an outsized role, while the three geographical regions were

Canada First, Not Canada Alone: A History of Canadian Foreign Policy. Adam Chapnick and Asa McKercher,
Oxford University Press. © Oxford University Press 2024. DOI: 10.1093/oso/9780197653715.003.0007

Figure 6.1 Duncan Macpherson, "NATO" *Toronto Star*, 29 January 1969. Pierre Trudeau's doubts about the value of Canada's membership in the North Atlantic Treaty Organization were evident well before he became prime minister. Trudeau did not understand why Europeans needed Canadian troops on their soil for protection when it had been over 20 years since the Second World War. He also believed that the cooling of Western-Soviet tensions would persist. Finally, he objected to his foreign service officials' risk aversion and lack of creativity. This political cartoon, depicting an American NATO commander lecturing what should have been a Canadian soldier but appears instead to be empty body armour, was released during a series of reviews of Canada's foreign, defence, and European policies. By January 1969, it was clear that Ottawa would reduce its commitment to NATO in Europe; the only question was by how much. The lack of sympathy evident in the portrayal of the American suggests that not all Canadians were uncomfortable with Trudeau's decision.

places where Canada could expand its presence, particularly in economic terms. Curiously, no booklet was devoted to Canada's southern neighbour. Overall, the report asserted that external activities would be "directly related to national policies pursued within Canada, and serve the same objectives"[6]—a "Canada-first" foreign policy.

Canada and Détente

Prior to the release of *Foreign Policy for Canadians*, the Trudeau government had already undertaken two initiatives meant to transform Canada's international posture: rethinking the deployment of military forces to Western Europe to meet Canada's obligations to NATO and recognizing the People's Republic of China. Nineteen sixty-eight was part of a period of détente in Europe, during which relations across the East-West divide improved. This spirit briefly faded in August, when Soviet bloc forces crushed the Prague Spring, a liberal reform effort in Czechoslovakia. Canada responded to the subsequent refugee crisis by welcoming thousands of refugees. Despite the violence, détente continued, reducing the apparent need for large military deployments. In light of Western Europe's post-war recovery, some Canadians judged that the money spent on overseas forces would be better allocated to domestic programs. After a policy review and Cabinet fight, Canada reduced its NATO commitment.[7] In 1971, Trudeau paid an official visit to the USSR and hosted a reciprocal visit by Soviet Premier Alexei Kosygin. A series of economic, scientific, and cultural agreements followed. The capstone initiative was the 1972 eight-game "summit series" between the Soviet and Canadian men's hockey teams, which the Canadians won.[8] Other Western countries—including the United States—undertook similar initiatives, but Robert Ford, the Canadian ambassador in Moscow, saw Trudeau's outreach to the USSR as a "watershed in the evolution of Canada's position in the world."[9]

This same observation can be applied to Canadian policy with the People's Republic of China (PRC). Most Western countries had adopted a position of non-recognition in the wake of the communist seizure of power in 1949 but this looked increasingly outmoded given the PRC's stability and widespread recognition by much of the Global South. When France recognized the Beijing government in 1964, the Pearson government was ready to follow, but it backed away because of US opposition.[10] Trudeau showed no such reticence. After lengthy negotiations, Sino-Canadian diplomatic relations were established in 1970. Summing up the prevailing hopes of many Westerners, Trudeau and his foreign policy advisor Ivan Head later contended that "a China open to the world...could be expected over time to adjust its political, economic, and

Figure 6.2 Prime Minister Rt Hon. Pierre E. Trudeau walking in a street with officials. 1973.

This photo captures Pierre Trudeau during his 1973 trip to China, the first by a Canadian prime minister. His wife, Margaret Trudeau, is visible over his left shoulder. Chinese Vice Premier Deng Xiaoping is also present. © Library and Archives Canada. Reproduced with the permission of Library and Archives Canada. Library and Archives Canada/Duncan Cameron fonds/a136978.
Credit: Duncan Cameron.

social practices to bring them into harmony with international norms."[11] Three years later, the Canadian prime minister paid an official visit to Beijing.

Trudeau and Nixon

Trudeau made deliberate efforts to forge policies independent of the United States. During a visit to the White House in March 1969, he famously explained his view of Canada's neighbour: "Living next to you is in some ways like sleeping with an elephant. No matter how friendly and even-tempered the beast, one is affected by every twitch and grunt."[12] Recognizing China was a prime example of Canada escaping the elephant's shadow. So was Ottawa's confrontational approach to the voyage of the SS *Manhattan* through the Northwest Passage in 1968. Nonetheless, in what one official called a "textbook example of how governments should use their diplomats," Ottawa kept Washington apprised of the

128 CANADA FIRST, NOT CANADA ALONE

Sino-Canadian negotiations, and the conflict over the Northwest Passage did not upset the Canada–US relationship writ large.[13]

Though there was little love for Trudeau in Richard Nixon's White House, American officials took Canadian moves in stride. "Canada has its own right to its destiny," admitted Nixon, "and no Canadian politician could survive without that ideology." However, he added, "we have to look out for our own interests."[14] In 1971, to deter inflation, the White House implemented the so-called Nixon Shock, ending the international convertibility of the US dollar into gold and imposing a surcharge on imports. The latter measure alarmed Canadians, who were used to preferential economic treatment.[15] Washington ultimately withdrew the surcharge, but this brush with overt American unilateralism was worrying.[16]

In March 1970, Trudeau had asked Herb Gray, a minister without portfolio, to produce a study on foreign investment. Gray's report was completed in May 1971, several months before the Nixon Shock. Among its recommendations was the creation of what later became the Foreign Investment Review Agency (FIRA), which could impose conditions on foreign investment and even block foreign takeovers. In 1972, SSEA Mitchell Sharp issued a paper on Canada–US relations, which reiterated America's centrality to "virtually every aspect of the Canadian national interest, and thus [to] Canadian domestic concerns." Sharp proposed three options for managing the relationship: the status quo; closer integration via free trade or a customs union; or "a comprehensive, long-term strategy" to reduce national vulnerabilities "and develop a more confident sense of Canadian identity."[17] The government opted for what become known as the Third Option.

Diversification

Diversifying the Canadian economy was never going to be easy. An economic slowdown in the 1970s—high inflation and slow growth, dubbed stagflation—did not help. A trade and investment promotion blitz in 1976 produced economic agreements with Japan and with the European Community, of which Britain was a member. FIRA was an element of Third Option thinking, as was the 1975 formation of the Crown corporation Petro-Canada, ensuring greater Canadian ownership over petroleum resources. Ottawa also sponsored a variety of cultural and heritage initiatives. A Canadian Studies program launched in 1975 to support the academic study of Canada at foreign universities; new cultural centres opened in London, Brussels, and New York; and tours by ballet and orchestral companies and artists proliferated.[18]

Ottawa sought to expand commercial and cultural relations with thriving Asian economies, such as Japan, Indonesia, and India.[19] It established trade and ministerial missions to Latin America, highlighted by a 1976 prime ministerial visit to Mexico, Venezuela, and Cuba. Trudeau's bonhomie with the Cuban communist dictator Fidel Castro, with whom he dined, debated, and snorkelled, captured global headlines. At a public rally, the Canadian prime minister even proclaimed: *"Viva Cuba y el pueblo cubano! Viva el Primer Ministro Fidel Castro! Viva la amistad cubano-canadiense!"*[20] Although the optics of Trudeau meeting with an American Cold War nemesis were awkward, the trip marked an important effort to drum up business in a region of growing economic importance. Trudeau's conduct did not dissuade US President Gerald Ford from backing Canada's entry into the G-6 group of highly industrialized countries in 1976.

Canada and the Global South

Positioning Canada first was not always so well received. Links with the Global South generated criticism over issues of human rights, economic inequality, and environmental degradation. Academics and activists questioned the frugality of Canada's development assistance program, as well as the emergency policy of "tied" aid, which required recipient countries to spend donor dollars on Canadian goods and services, often at uncompetitive prices.[21] To its credit, the Trudeau government responded constructively. One of its first acts in 1968 had been to turn the External Aid Office, housed in the Department of External Affairs, into the Canadian International Development Agency (CIDA). Two years later, Canada founded the International Development Research Centre to encourage the study of economic and social challenges facing members of the Global South. CIDA expanded Canadian development programs to include Latin America, and overall spending reached its all-time peak in 1975 at 0.53 per cent of GDP. That same year, in London, Trudeau called for a concerted international effort aiming "for nothing less than an acceptable distribution of the world's wealth."[22] Over the next half decade he backed an ultimately failed effort to establish a New International Economic Order.[23] This effort aside, Canada remained a capitalist, developed country, often finding itself on the opposite side of international issues from the Global South. In 1975, Canada joined with other Western countries in voting against UN Resolution 3379, which declared that "Zionism is Racism." The proposal was widely supported in the Global South, and it signified to Canadian officials the increasing radicalism of this bloc of countries and their clout within the United Nations. As one Canadian diplomat recalled, the resolution did great harm to the UN's reputation in Canada, with enthusiasm for that organization ebbing considerably.[24]

Another aspect of Canadian–Global South interaction that drew activists' attention was the disappointing behaviour of Canadian multinational corporations abroad. Many were accused of labour exploitation and dealings with governments with little respect for human rights. New trade and investment opportunities also trumped concerns over repressive regimes in Indonesia, South Africa, and Brazil.[25] As the prime minister later recalled, many rights violations occurred in places "where Canada had only limited influence," so Ottawa did little to help, even while serving on the United Nations Security Council in 1977-8.[26] Another limiting factor was the Canadian government's respect for the principle of state sovereignty and a corresponding reluctance to be seen to be interfering in another country's domestic sphere. Facing Paris's encouragement of a rise in separatist sentiment in Quebec, Trudeau was keenly aware of the need to uphold this principle. In 1968, in responding to an effort by the region of Biafra to secede from Nigeria, Trudeau quipped to reporters, "Where's Biafra?"[27] Beyond providing food aid to combat a famine in the area, Ottawa ignored demands for more aggressive action that would have interfered in Nigerian internal politics.[28]

The Liberals' refugee policy was more accepting. In 1969, Canada ratified the 1951 Geneva Convention on Refugees, though it took until 1976 for Canadian immigration law to provide a regular, uniform process for accepting asylum seekers. In the interim, Ottawa instituted impromptu programs in response to Tibetans escaping China (1971); Ugandan Asians expelled from Uganda (1972); and Chileans fleeing a military coup (1973).[29] The 1973 program was less well received because the Canadian government continued to recognize the Chilean regime and refrained from imposing economic sanctions.

Indigenous Peoples in Canada as the World Looks On

In human rights terms, positioning Canada first meant focusing on implementing international agreements "to protect and safeguard the rights of Canadians, both individually and as disadvantaged minorities."[30] The minority group facing the greatest systemic discrimination within Canada was the Indigenous population. In 1969, Ottawa issued a white paper on First Nations policy that proposed to eliminate Indigenous peoples' special status within the federation and to grant them instead "full and equal participation in the cultural, social, economic and political life of Canada."[31]

Indigenous activists were furious with the proposal. Three years earlier, University of British Columbia professor Harry B. Hawthorn's commissioned study *A Survey of the Contemporary Indians of Canada: Economic, Political, and Educational Needs and Policies* had deplored the horrific treatment of Indigenous peoples across the country.[32] Harmful programs like residential schools had reduced their status in Canada to what he called "citizens minus."

Hawthorne had recommended that Ottawa recognize Indigenous peoples as what came to be known as "citizens plus," a term that was meant to take into consideration the treaty obligations owed to them by the Crown. In this context, the government proposal came across as another attempt at assimilation. "We will not trust the government with our futures any longer," wrote Harold Cardinal, one of the white paper's leading opponents. "Now they must listen to and learn from us."[33] The backlash caused Ottawa to withdraw the draft policy.

An Indigenous "awakening,"[34] in the words of George Manuel, Chief of the National Indian Brotherhood (now known as the Assembly of First Nations), followed. While some activists occupied illegally settled land at places like Anicinabe Park in Kenora, Ontario,[35] others took their land claims to court. In *Calder v. The Attorney General of British Columbia* (1973), the Supreme Court established that Indigenous land title existed prior to colonization, raising significant questions about land rights in areas like British Columbia, where few treaties had been signed. Two years later, following a court case challenging the construction of a hydroelectric project without consultation, the James Bay Cree forced Quebec's government to conclude the first modern land treaty, opening the door to further agreements. These domestic legal developments complemented an international effort to bring UN attention to the plight of Indigenous people. In 1981, the United Nations Human Rights Commission concluded that Canada's Indian Act violated the rights of Sandra Lovelace by denying her Indian status after she married a non-Indigenous man. (There were no such restrictions placed on Indigenous men who married non-Indigenous women.) Four years later, the Canadian Parliament removed the offending section of the legislation.[36]

Canada and Quebec under Trudeau

The Québécois were undoubtedly the minority group that dominated Trudeau's thinking. His staunch federalism and defence of Canadian unity against rising separatism had attracted voters to the Liberals in the 1968 election. As prime minister, Trudeau sought to make more room for Canada's francophone heritage. The 1969 Official Languages Act made French and English the country's official languages and required federal services to be available in both languages. In his first major speech on international affairs after becoming prime minister, Trudeau declared a "permanent interest" in ensuring "the political survival of Canada as a federal and bilingual sovereign state." That meant "reflecting in our foreign relations the cultural diversity and the bilingualism of Canada as faithfully as possible."[37] Ottawa boosted economic, cultural, and

132 CANADA FIRST, NOT CANADA ALONE

diplomatic engagement with French-speaking countries, notably in Africa, and supported the activities of La Francophonie, the multilateral organization representing former French colonies.[38]

These efforts were timely. Beginning in 1963, members of the Front de Libération de Québec (FLQ)—a collection of radicals inspired by Cuban and Algerian revolutionaries—began bombing federal property and buildings associated with Quebec's anglophone elite. The terror campaign accelerated in October 1970, when the FLQ kidnapped James Cross, a British diplomat, and Pierre Laporte, a provincial Cabinet minister. When the Quebec government appealed to Ottawa for help, Trudeau invoked the War Measures Act, which suspended civil liberties, and dispatched military forces to assist police efforts. Hundreds of suspected FLQ supporters were arrested and held without charges. Trudeau put the matter bluntly in an exchange with a reporter: "society must take every means at its disposal to defend itself."[39] The crisis ended in December when Cross was released and his captors were exiled to Cuba; Laporte was murdered by his kidnappers.

Quebec separatists responded by largely disavowing violence and pursuing independence via the ballot box. In 1976, René Lévesque, a former minister in Quebec's provincial Liberal government who had quit the party to found the (separatist) Parti Québécois (PQ), became the provincial premier. His promise to hold a referendum on the province's future shocked the business community. In January 1977, Lévesque reassured members of the Economic Club of New York that an independent Quebec would be open for business. In Ottawa, government officials viewed this speech as an effort to curry international legitimacy. Trudeau responded by securing an invitation to the White House, which arranged for him to become the first Canadian prime minister to address a joint session of the US Congress. In a press conference with the prime minister, President Jimmy Carter stressed his "preference" for a united Canada.[40]

In the May 1980 referendum, nearly 60 per cent of Quebecers voted to remain within Canada. During the campaign, Trudeau had promised a new constitutional arrangement and the patriation of Canada's constitution, still under British parliamentary control. Following the referendum, Trudeau secured British support for patriation and opened deliberations with provincial governments. Indigenous groups also pressed their positions. "We will be telling the people of the world of our rights," affirmed the Union of British Columbia Indian Chiefs, "and of the responsibilities which other nations have to us."[41] British parliamentarians ultimately supported passage of the Canada Act.[42] At a Parliament Hill ceremony on 17 April 1982, Queen Elizabeth II signed the patriated constitution. The document recognized Indigenous and treaty rights and established the Charter of Rights and Freedoms, which guaranteed constitutionally entrenched rights for every Canadian.

The Joe Clark Interlude

At the time, the Official Opposition was in turmoil. In May 1979, Joe Clark's Progressive Conservatives had won a minority government, only to fall in a confidence vote that December. At 39, Clark, an Albertan, was Canada's youngest-ever prime minister, and his interregnum was notable for several developments in the greater Middle East. The Tories' electoral promise to move Canada's embassy in Israel from Tel Aviv to Jerusalem was a thorny issue, showcasing connections between foreign and domestic policy. Far less controversial was the so-called Canadian Caper. Following the 1979 Iranian revolution, Iranian radicals, outraged over American support for their country's deposed dictator, seized the US embassy in Tehran, along with 52 US citizens. Amidst the chaos, Ken Taylor, Canadian ambassador in Tehran, sheltered six Americans. They were eventually smuggled out of the country, earning Canada high praise in the United States.[43] Foreign Minister Flora MacDonald, the first woman to hold the post, announced a crash program to admit over 60,000 Vietnamese, Cambodian, and Hmong refugees fleeing political violence in Vietnam and Cambodia.[44] When the Soviet Union invaded Afghanistan in December 1979, Clark and MacDonald joined with Canada's allies in denouncing this aggressive action and committed to boycotting the July 1980 Moscow Olympics, a decision Trudeau upheld when his Liberals formed a new majority government in February 1980.

Trudeau Returns

Although Trudeau's final four years in office were consumed by constitutional wrangling, there were other pressing issues with foreign policy implications. Ottawa introduced the National Energy Program (NEP)—an attempt to Canadianize the oil and gas industry, keep energy prices low at home, and share the profits from Canada's natural resources across the country—that outraged Washington, where arch-conservative Ronald Reagan had become president. Ideologically, Trudeau and Reagan were at odds. The leaders differed on a number of policy issues, too, chiefly the prime minister's "peace initiative." Fearful of a worsening Cold War climate and with rising nuclear disarmament activism at home, Trudeau sought to open communications among leading countries in order to settle major global disputes. Over several months in late 1983 he visited Washington, Beijing, Moscow, New Delhi, and capitals across Europe, but his powers of persuasion were lacking and the initiative fizzled with little to show for it.[45] The problem, reflected veteran diplomat Allan Gotlieb, was that by inserting Canada into great power politics, Trudeau was "playing with other people's marbles."[46] Ironically, the peace initiative was the

134 CANADA FIRST, NOT CANADA ALONE

sort of idealistic "honest broker," "helpful fixer" diplomacy that Trudeau had decried upon first becoming prime minister.[47] But by 1984 when Trudeau left office, the heady days of Trudeaumania were long gone.

Case Studies

The cases for this chapter highlight the Trudeau government's adamance that Canada foreign policy revert to a distinctly "Canada-first" posture. The first case examines the clash between Trudeau's vision of Canadian foreign and defence policy—which de-emphasized Canada's longstanding military commitment to NATO in Europe—and the preferences of his public service officials (not to mention their Cabinet ministers), nearly all of whom believed that Ottawa's post–Second World War commitment to multilateralism continued to serve the national interest. As prime minister, Trudeau eventually got his way, though external circumstances compelled Canada to reinvest in European defence just a few years later.

Ottawa's Canada-first policy was significantly more successful in the environmental realm, as the second case shows. When an American oil company sought to send a tanker through the Northwest Passage in the Canadian Arctic, the Trudeau government unilaterally declared Canadian control of the disputed waters and refused to allow Washington to challenge its declaration at the International Court of Justice. The move was bold and ultimately succeeded, in large part because Ottawa framed its decision as an effort to stimulate progress in international law rather than to ignore it.

Although Joe Clark was not prime minister for very long, he grappled with an issue of ongoing relevance: the question of whether the Canadian embassy in Israel should be moved from Tel Aviv to Jerusalem. This was crassly politicized, to ill effect, by the Progressive Conservatives in 1979, and 40 years later, it was revived by the opposition Conservative party during the government of Pierre Trudeau's son, Justin.

The fourth case looks at putting Canada first through an interprovincial lens. In 1980, a returning Trudeau Liberal government pledged to put the interests of Canadians as a whole ahead of those in a single province (Alberta) on an issue with national and international implications. The National Energy Program was popular at the time, but its success hinged on an ever-increasing price of oil. After the price plunged, Western Canadians in Alberta and Saskatchewan were livid. It has been over 40 years since the NEP was first introduced, and many Westerners still have not forgiven the Liberals.

The Beyond the Book case examines the Trudeau government's effort to recognize communist China from 1968–70. This was one of the few foreign policy

Reconsidering Canada's Military Role in NATO, 1968–1969

decisions of the period during which Trudeau's External Affairs officials supported his vision almost unconditionally.

Reconsidering Canada's Military Role in NATO, 1968–1969

Why do governments review foreign policy?

When Pierre Trudeau became Canada's fifteenth prime minister in April 1968, he inherited a just-finished confidential report on the future of Canadian foreign policy by Norman Robertson, the former undersecretary of state for external affairs. Among Robertson's recommendations was a call for all 10,000 Canadian troops stationed in West Germany on behalf of NATO to remain there for the time being. Trudeau was unimpressed and soon launched the most comprehensive, public review of Canadian foreign policy ever undertaken.[48] This case examines that review's implications.

Trudeau made his views on NATO clear during the 1968 election. "Canada's position in the world is now very different from that of the post-war years," he said. "Then we were probably the largest of the small powers...our economy was much stronger than the European economies. Ours were among the very strongest navy and air forces. But now Europe has regained its strength."[49] As a result, Canada would "take a hard look" at its military commitment in Europe to determine whether it was "still appropriate."[50] Rooted in a recognition of Western Europe's post-war recovery and a growing East-West détente, Trudeau's thinking was also "inspired by an emerging strategic counterculture that, by 1968, was spreading rapidly in the educated public."[51] Some academics, and even some Liberal ministers, advocated Canadian neutrality. Trudeau never went that far, but he did see value in discussing every possible option.[52] He wanted members of Cabinet to "think more for themselves and depend less on civil servants."[53] He was determined, recalls one minister, "to shake up the establishment."[54]

Immediately after the 1968 election, the Liberal government initiated a three-pronged review process. Secretary of State for External Affairs Mitchell Sharp tasked two senior diplomats to lead a Special Task Force on Europe (STAFFEUR), while he and Minister of National Defence Léo Cadieux reconsidered Robertson's findings more generally. Trudeau and others reached out to the academic community. And the House of Commons Standing Committee on External Affairs and National Defence (SCEAND) launched hearings on Canada's future in NATO.

Defence officials had initially been given a deadline of July 1968 for their review, but when Cadieux recommended maintaining the status quo, Trudeau

136 CANADA FIRST, NOT CANADA ALONE

ordered him to start over. The prime minister wanted "an in-depth analysis of all the available options, including complete withdrawal from NATO and neutrality."[55] Since NATO required all members to affirm their troop contributions every spring, the question of Canada's military presence in Europe became the reviewers' top priority.

STAFFEUR's 400-page report, submitted to the Cabinet Committee on External Policy and Defence in February 1969, recognized that Ottawa's appetite for defence spending outside of the country had decreased. Canada's military contribution to NATO would ultimately have to be scaled back. Still, such a reduction was inadvisable, especially in light of the Warsaw Pact's invasion of Czechoslovakia in August 1968.[56] The joint submission from the departments of External Affairs and National Defence concurred. According to Marcel Cadieux, the undersecretary of state for external affairs (no relation to Léo Cadieux), Norman Robertson had already identified the real problem: "though Canada's policy toward NATO was perfectly defensible, Canadians did not understand it."[57]

The overwhelming majority of academics disagreed. Trudeau initiated conversations with them through the Canadian Institute of International Affairs, and Ottawa separately sponsored four conferences on the future of Canadian foreign policy.[58] The discussions met the prime minister's request for "wider public debate," but they do not appear to have affected policy.[59] SCEAND also held twice-weekly meetings over the first three months of 1969.[60] According to one committee member, he and his colleagues were prone to dismissing testimony from the academics "because of their apparent self-righteousness, arrogance, and ivory-tower idealism."[61] A tour of Western Europe toward the end of the review had a more significant impact. As with STAFFEUR, External Affairs, and National Defence, SCEAND recommended that Canada's NATO troops remain in Europe.[62]

Seven inconclusive meetings of the Cabinet Committee on External Policy and Defence were held in March 1969. Members of the Priorities and Planning Committee were similarly divided. Ministers Sharp and Cadieux fought to retain as many NATO troops as possible. Trudeau and others remained unmoved, in part because of the costs of the deployment. As historian Robert Bothwell has explained: "Economically, the European Common Market excluded Canadian agriculture products and subsidized sales of European wheat in Canada's remaining markets. Canada spent much on NATO; NATO spent little on Canada."[63]

To break the deadlock, Trudeau asked his personal advisor on foreign policy, former diplomat Ivan Head, to form a "Non-Group" of staff from the Privy Council Office and the Treasury Board. The Non-Group's unofficial report, "A Study of Defence Policy," recommended a reduction in Canadian NATO troops in Europe from 10,000 to 3000 and an abandonment of Canada's nuclear role in the alliance.[64] The document was secretly added to the preparatory material for Cabinet with a note from Trudeau.[65] When Marcel Cadieux learned that neither his minister nor the minister of national defence had been informed of the prime minister's actions, he wrote in his diary: "There is something hypocritical, disgusting, secretive, malicious, and nasty in this way of proceeding that astonishes and shocks me deeply."[66]

Léo Cadieux interpreted the new study as a lack of confidence in his department and threatened to resign. The paper was withdrawn, but Trudeau's views were clear. Cabinet ultimately agreed that Canada would "remain a member of NATO *but* on different terms and with increased control over our contribution."[67] There would be fewer troops—ultimately 5000—and no nuclear strike role for them. Trudeau announced the phased reduction of Canadian forces in Europe on 3 April.[68] Ministers Cadieux and Sharp spent much of the next six months reassuring NATO members that Ottawa remained a committed partner. Still, according to Sharp, the failure to consult Canada's allies "had unfortunate repercussions for years."[69]

When he later reflected on the broader review process, Marcel Cadieux lamented the decline of morale within his department and the opportunity costs of such a resource-intensive activity that, to him, hardly altered the general thrust of Canadian foreign policy.[70] But what if the purpose of the review was not about policy? Ivan Head and Pierre Trudeau later celebrated "the necessary dominance of ministerial decisions over official advice."[71] By bringing popular attention to Canada's role in the world, Trudeau achieved what has come to be known as social licence to re-imagine international priorities, however limited Ottawa's capacity to effect change might be.[72]

The Voyages of the SS *Manhattan* through the Northwest Passage, 1968–1970

What role can, or should, support for an international legal regime play in Canadian foreign policy?

Although most Canadians have never travelled to the Arctic, many still feel a visceral attachment to the North and want their government to "stand up for our Arctic sovereignty,"[73] even if they do not know exactly what that might entail. Between 1968 and 1970, Ottawa faced what some experts have called "a litmus test for Canadian sovereignty" in the North.[74] The threat came from the United States, a rare instance where the two allies have maintained a stubborn and long-lasting dispute. The Canadian response to the American challenge forms the basis of this case.

138   CANADA FIRST, NOT CANADA ALONE

In July 1968, Humble Oil announced that its partner, Atlantic Richfield, had discovered oil beneath Prudhoe Bay, Alaska. The oil strike had the potential to increase North American energy security and create new employment throughout the North. Initially, the Trudeau government welcomed it as a means of advancing its own northern development agenda. More problematically, the discovery reinvigorated a Canadian–American governance dispute surrounding the navigation of Canada's Northwest Passage (water routes through the Arctic islands between the Chukchi Sea and the Atlantic Ocean).[75]

Canada considered the passage internal waters, travel through which was controlled by Ottawa. The United States viewed it as an international strait, which provided unabridged transit for any vessel by connecting two bodies of water within the high seas. Since the passage was coated with thick ice, Ottawa could argue that it did not qualify as an international strait as it failed to provide a consistent opportunity for Arctic shipping. Washington would ultimately respond that the potential for passage was sufficient. For the most part, Canadian claims focused on historic use—the route had always been managed by Canada, and no one had ever objected seriously.[76] The dispute had simmered for years, and since the most efficient way to bring the newly discovered Arctic oil to market would be by tanker, it required resolution.

The Canadian government had three objectives. Practically, it sought to confirm its right to control any new traffic through the region. Diplomatically, it aimed to reaffirm its support for international law without compromising relations with Washington. Bridging both concerns was a commitment to safeguard the northern environment consistent with Canada's adherence to the first International Convention for the Prevention of Pollution of the Seas by Oil (1958).[77] The United States rejected Canada's claim that the Northwest Passage was internal waters out of fear that Canadian control of the Arctic archipelago would set a precedent that might implicate more valuable straits like Malacca and Hormuz.[78] Humble Oil's only concern was getting its product to market.

Humble planned to test the feasibility of the Northwest Passage as a shipping route by sailing a tanker through it. While it retrofitted the SS *Manhattan* for the voyage, the Canadian government took a number of actions to demonstrate its charge over the region. The governor general toured the Arctic. Ottawa declared that the primary responsibility of the Canadian military consisted of "the surveillance of our own territory and coast lines."[79] And in a move that was poorly received in Washington and only tangentially related, the Cabinet announced its intent to amend the Territorial Sea and Fishing Zones Act to protect the Canadian fisheries industry without compromising Indigenous rights.[80]

On 26 August 1968, more than 100 people boarded the *Manhattan*, including Humble employees, scientists, and reporters.[81] A retired Canadian Coast Guard captain, T.C. Pullen, served as Canada's official observer. The ship would be guided through the water by a Canadian icebreaker, the *John A. Macdonald*, and the US Coast Guard's *Northwind*. The Department of External Affairs called on the *Northwind* to request formal permission to join the expedition, but its appeal was ignored. The *Manhattan*'s voyage was smooth until it reached the McClure Strait, at which point the *Macdonald* was needed to break up the ice. The vessels ultimately turned back and traversed the passage through an alternative route.

By the time the voyage ended in mid-September, and Humble began planning a second attempt, the political temperature in Canada had risen. A combination of visceral anti-Americanism—exacerbated by US refusals to recognize Canadian sovereignty—and genuine environmental concerns stemming from a series of headline-worthy oil spills put pressure on the Trudeau government to respond boldly. Washington's insistence that Ottawa refrain from unilateral action failed to deter members of the Cabinet, most of whom believed that they could assert Canadian sovereignty while concurrently reaffirming their support for international law.[82]

The problem, from Ottawa's point of view, was that the legal regime that governed the Law of the Sea had yet to incorporate environmental security. Canada, Foreign Minister Mitchell Sharp declared, would have to act alone first, in anticipation of the regime catching up in the future.[83] A series of announcements by the ministers of Northern Development, Transport, and Defence highlighted Canada's responsibility for the safety and security of the Arctic.[84] On 24 October 1969, Prime Minister Trudeau confirmed that his government's forthcoming Arctic waters pollution prevention legislation would reflect Canada's commitment to responsible custodianship of the northern ecology. As the Department of External Affairs' legal advisor, Alan Beesley, would later explain: "The unique environmental characteristics of the Arctic, with its minute rate of decomposition, its relatively low restorative capacity, and the hazards it presents for navigation, all ma[d]e it particularly susceptible to pollution."[85] On 11 November, Trudeau briefed the United Nations secretary general, making clear that Ottawa's refusal to allow the International Court of Justice to determine the legality of its approach was "a kind of interim measure pending the clarification and development of international environmental law."[86]

The Arctic Waters Pollution Prevention Act (1970) unilaterally extended Canada's territorial sea (the air, water, and seabed beyond the coast over which a country exercises sovereignty) from the international standard of 3 miles to 12 and imposed a series of measures to limit pollution and ensure that passage through the Arctic by large vessels would be undertaken safely and responsibly. Canada also pledged to legitimize its unilateral assertion of custodianship of the North under international law at scheduled Law of the Sea negotiations.[87]

140 CANADA FIRST, NOT CANADA ALONE

Predictably, Washington objected vehemently, but its efforts to portray the Canadians as having violated the spirit of multilateralism that served as the underpinning of a stable, international legal regime were unsuccessful. Canada's effort was received globally as reasonable and well meaning.[88] In April 1970, Humble Oil agreed to all of Ottawa's regulations and stipulations in advance of its second voyage.

Due to the costs associated with efforts to traverse the Northwest Passage, Washington ultimately authorized the construction of a Trans-Alaska pipeline to enable the transport of oil along the North American west coast. Canadians applauded their government's success at resisting US efforts to shape Canada's northern policy, and the spirit of Ottawa's legislation was enshrined in revisions to the United Nations Law of the Sea. In 1985, Canada accepted the jurisdiction of the International Court of Justice over its Arctic policies once more.[89] The effects of climate change have made the question of control over the Northwest Passage more pressing in the twenty-first century.

Joe Clark's Proposal to Move the Canadian Embassy in Israel from Tel Aviv to Jerusalem, 1979–1980

What role can, or should, discussions of Canadian foreign policy play in federal elections?

In his account of the rise and fall of Joe Clark's Progressive Conservative government, journalist Jeffrey Simpson wrote: "Of all the errors Joe Clark made as leader of the Conservative Party, none rivalled his promise to move the Canadian embassy in Israel from Tel Aviv to Jerusalem. Through a numbing mixture of unforgivable stupidity and crass politics, Clark stumbled into a promise that was to haunt him through all his days as Prime Minister."[90] Simpson was right about the extent of the error, but this case suggests that more than poor judgment and gross partisanship were at play.

When Israel was founded in 1948, its capital, Jerusalem, was divided. Israel controlled the western part; Jordan governed the east. Foreign states established embassies in Tel Aviv, which briefly served as a temporary government centre in 1948–9. During the 1967 Six-Day War, Israel captured, annexed, and unified Jerusalem. In an effort to institutionalize its gains, the Israeli government encouraged members of the international community to move their embassies from Tel Aviv.[91] Since doing so would have undermined UN Security Council Resolution 242, which called for an Israeli withdrawal from territories occupied during the war, Canada (and every other country) refused.[92]

RE-IMAGINATION OF "CANADA FIRST," 1968–1984   141

When Israeli Prime Minister Menachem Begin visited Canada in November 1978, the Trudeau government reiterated Canada's position on Jerusalem, so Begin urged the members of a prominent Jewish lobby group, the Canada-Israel Committee (CIC), to politicize the issue in the next election.[93] When the leader of the Progressive Conservative opposition, Joe Clark, visited the Middle East in January 1979, Begin made his case again. Perhaps he thought that Clark was vulnerable; some members of his caucus supported the move, and the Tory leader had recently been criticized for failing to prevent the candidacy of an alleged anti-Semite in a federal by-election.[94] In Israel, Clark was briefed by Canadian Ambassador Joseph Stanford. Since moving the embassy risked compromising Canada's growing economic relationship with the entire Arab world and undermining ongoing US peace efforts in the Middle East, Clark rejected Begin's entreaties.[95]

When the CIC scheduled a meeting with Clark during the 1979 election campaign, some of his advisors saw an opening. The Liberals had recently disappointed much of the Jewish community by failing to pass legislation confirming their opposition to an Arab League boycott of Israel.[96] Perhaps voters in Liberal-held ridings in Toronto with significant Jewish populations could be swayed by a commitment to move the embassy. Some of Clark's confidantes disagreed with the proposal, but they arrived late for the meeting during which it was considered.[97] Clark himself might have supported the idea in principle, but his final decision appears to have been based on electoral considerations. On 25 April, he announced that, if elected, a Progressive Conservative government would "be prepared to move the Canadian Embassy from Tel Aviv to the western part of Jerusalem, which has been part of Israel since the creation of the country in 1948."[98] Although Clark failed to say so explicitly, the move was not meant to happen immediately and was intended to be balanced by official Canadian recognition of the Palestinian Liberation Organization.[99]

An effort to micro-target a specific electoral constituency quickly morphed into a broader controversy. Clark's announcement was attacked as misguided by the national press, Canadian academics, and the business community. Making clear that their ire was directed at Canada, the Arab League called for sanctions against any country that moved their embassy to Jerusalem. Even among Conservatives, only the few candidates in implicated Toronto ridings were remotely pleased.[100] The Tories secured a minority government that May, and four of the six ridings with significant Jewish populations elected Progressive Conservatives, but it appears that the embassy proposal played little role in the outcome.[101]

It did, however, lead to a clear warning from officials in the Department of External Affairs that moving the Canadian embassy to Jerusalem would undermine Canada's credibility as an impartial player in Middle Eastern politics,

142   CANADA FIRST, NOT CANADA ALONE

compromise Washington's peace initiative, and risk significant economic and commercial repercussions for Canadian businesses. Even Clark's successful Toronto members of Parliament saw little reason to press the issue right away.[102]

On 5 June, after the Conservative campaign chair, Lowell Murray, watched Foreign Minister Flora MacDonald downplay the importance of the embassy promise on a morning television show, he suggested to Clark that she had been hoodwinked by her bureaucrats. Murray recommended that the prime minister remind officials of their obligation to implement the will of the new government.[103] Other advisors agreed on the importance of asserting prime ministerial authority but counselled against highlighting the Jerusalem promise. Clark appears to have initially accepted the advice, but at a press conference later that day, he reasserted the embassy commitment. As one analyst has put it: "The young and inexperienced prime minister was so consumed by the need to appear prime ministerial that he used the wrong issue to make the point."[104]

Representatives from the Arab world responded with vitriol. Iraq announced an oil embargo against Canada. State-owned oil companies threatened to cancel contracts with their Canadian partners.[105] Canada's business community revolted; both employers and unions criticized the government. When members of Clark's Cabinet expressed concern, they were advised to stay silent. National media covered the story for more than two consecutive weeks. A Gallup poll suggested that close to 70 per cent of Canadians opposed the policy. The Jewish community remained divided; even most supporters of the move were concerned by the politicization of Canada's Middle East posture over a relatively minor issue.[106]

Clark recognized the need for a strategic retreat. The Department of External Affairs recommended a fact-finding and face-saving mission to examine Canadian policy toward Middle Eastern countries. MacDonald appears to have suggested that Clark's still-popular predecessor as Progressive Conservative leader, Robert Stanfield, be appointed Canada's Special Representative. Clark announced that his plan to move the embassy would be postponed for at least a year pending the results of Stanfield's investigation.[107] Although he was not expected to present any findings until early 1980, Stanfield submitted an interim report in October. He would not be able to complete the rest of his mission successfully unless Ottawa immediately cancelled its plans to move the embassy. Clark's pledge had undermined Canada's credibility in the region as an impartial player. Stanfield's final report was released in February, two days after a general election that removed Clark from power.[108]

Although some critics have been inclined to blame the fiasco on Clark and his lack of foreign policy experience, others are more sympathetic to the structural difficulties faced by leaders of the opposition in the Canadian parliamentary system.[109] The House of Commons Standing Committee on External

Affairs and National Defence offered members of Parliament an opportunity to question Canadian diplomats in 1979, but leaders of the opposition did not have regular access to top secret security briefings. (They still don't.) The resultant ignorance can affect all aspects of public policy decision making, but it can be particularly damaging to politicians' thinking about international relations. This shortcoming is particularly problematic in Canada, where the official opposition is meant to be the government-in-waiting.

The National Energy Program, 1980–1984

How do issues with international and domestic implications fit within Canada's foreign policy framework?

The National Energy Program (NEP) might not have been Canada's first major public policy challenge with international and domestic policy implications (dubbed *intermestic* by political scientists), but it was likely the most controversial.[110] Its international implications form the basis of this case.

Canadian petroleum policy is inherently complex. The bulk of the natural resource is located in a single province, Alberta, yet it has typically been transported on a national pipeline infrastructure approved and sometimes even subsidized by the federal government. The management of natural resources is a provincial responsibility, but the regulation of trade and commerce falls under federal jurisdiction.[111]

For much of the early post-war era, federal policy supported the development of a vibrant oil and gas sector on the Prairies. Western Canada's energy needs were met by Albertan oil and gas, while a dearth of pipelines running east-west meant that Eastern Canada imported its fuel from abroad, mainly from Venezuela. Extending the domestic pipelines was not a priority because Albertans could earn more by selling their surplus energy to the United States. In 1973, a crisis in the Middle East exposed the vulnerability of this arrangement. When an Organization of Petroleum Exporting Countries (OPEC) oil embargo quadrupled the global price of energy, Eastern Canadians faced massive increases to their heating bills; conversely, Western Canadian oil companies anticipated extraordinary profits. To mitigate the economic disparity, the Liberal government fixed the domestic price of oil and gas, using profits from the West to subsidize the cost of fuel in the East.[112] Albertans were furious, but Trudeau was unmoved. In 1975, his government founded Petro-Canada, a Crown corporation meant to provide greater domestic ownership of the country's oil resources.

OPEC's aggression accelerated American energy prospecting in Canada. Despite federal (Petro-Canada) and provincial (the Alberta Energy Company) efforts, by 1980, nearly three-quarters of the Canadian oil and gas industry—including the six largest companies—was foreign owned, with Americans accounting for nearly 80 per cent of all foreign ownership. The Canadian energy industry, which already relied extensively on its US sales, became a net capital exporter, selling more abroad than Canadians consumed at home.[113]

When the world price of oil once again doubled in response to the 1979 Iranian Revolution, energy security re-emerged as a political issue. Campaigning in Halifax in January 1980, Trudeau pledged to re-establish Canadian control over the state's natural resources.[114] While the Liberals and their External Affairs officials disagreed over whether the DEA was kept appropriately informed of plans for what became the National Energy Program, it is clear that the department's views were never sought.[115] As a result, concerns about what the clerk of the Privy Council Office called "the twisting of the American tail," not to mention the implications for Canada's international commitments on trade and investment, were minimized throughout the planning process.[116]

The National Energy Program that was introduced to Canadians in October 1980 came directly from the Liberal platform. According to Marc Lalonde, the minister of energy, mines and resources, the NEP had three goals: "to provide Canadians with energy *security*, the *opportunity* to participate in energy development, and *fairness* in the manner in which the benefits of the nation's rich resources are shared."[117] More concretely, the government envisioned that by 1990, Canada would be energy self-sufficient; 50 per cent of the industry would be under Canadian ownership; and Ottawa would control a greater share of oil revenues.[118]

The program was deliberately aggressive, if not confrontational, based on the premises that the federal government, not the provinces, was the rightful custodian of Canadian national interests and that revenue generated from Canada's natural resources should be shared more equitably across the country.[119] Two initiatives—the establishment of fixed Canadian prices for oil and gas, and the promulgation of a series of new taxes that transferred revenue to Ottawa—infuriated Albertans.[120] After Premier Peter Lougheed coordinated with American multinationals to cut production and withdrew Alberta from a series of federal-provincial energy projects, Ottawa and Edmonton negotiated a Memorandum of Agreement that temporarily ameliorated relations.[121]

The international fallout was less easily assuaged. The NEP's Petroleum Incentives Program privileged domestically owned and controlled companies willing to pursue oil and gas exploration on Crown (rather than provincial) lands. Another policy—takeovers of foreign-owned energy companies by Canadian firms—facilitated Canadianization. Most controversially, Ottawa retroactively claimed a 25 per cent share of all oil developments on Crown land without promising compensation.[122] Over the next 18 months, domestic ownership in the industry rose from less than 7 per cent to over 34.[123]

The initial response from Washington was incredulous.[124] In December 1981, Canada's ambassador to the United States, Allan Gotlieb, wrote in his diary: "So bad has been the reaction to our investment and energy policies that retaliatory proposals are spewing out of the volcano on Capitol Hill. I count eleven initiatives in Congress aimed at Canada....The Americans want us to rescind the NEP. They hate it. They regard it as confiscation."[125] The Canadianization initiatives and the retroactive provision were especially problematic. The *Wall Street Journal* dubbed the NEP a "xenophobic" policy.[126]

The State Department launched complaints through the Organisation for Economic Co-operation and Development, the International Energy Agency, and the General Agreement on Tariffs and Trade, alleging that Ottawa had failed to live up to its international commitments to provide national treatment to foreign investors in the energy industry. US officials attacked Canadian policy in the popular media. Staff in the White House contemplated various methods of direct retaliation: at one point, Washington even considered limiting Canadian participation at a forthcoming G7 summit.[127]

The effects of these efforts were limited. The launch of the NEP just before the US election meant that the incoming Ronald Reagan administration was ill-prepared to coordinate an appropriate response until the Canadian initiatives were well under way. Reagan hoped to establish a cordial relationship with Canada and cautioned against overly aggressive reactions. In an early meeting with Trudeau, he stated that he understood the attraction of economic nationalism, joking of "recently seeing on a truck a bumper sticker reading 'Buy America', the only trouble was it was on a Toyota!"[128] Perhaps most important, it was difficult to identify an appropriate retaliatory strategy. "Anything we've come across so far would hurt us more than them," explained one senior official.[129]

Nonetheless, Washington did elicit concessions. Ottawa scaled back its commitment to Canadianization by amending legislation that provided for fairer competition across the energy industry, cancelling a plan to privilege Canadian-owned companies in gas exports, and committing to limit Canadianization efforts to the energy industry. Finally, American companies that had been forced to sell equity to the federal government were compensated with no admission of wrongdoing.[130]

Still, the Trudeau government refused to concede Ottawa's right to interfere in the market to promote and defend the national interest. The popularity of this stance—at the time, 84 per cent of Canadians agreed with efforts to increase

146 CANADA FIRST, NOT CANADA ALONE

national ownership in the energy sector—ultimately convinced Washington that further objections were futile.[131]

The NEP swiftly became one of the Trudeau government's greatest political and policy failures. As two contemporary ministers later conceded, its success hinged on a continued and sustained increase in the price of oil. Without the "perception of a huge windfall profit to oil and gas producers and producer provinces," Albertans would have recoiled at Ottawa's blatant power grab.[132] When a sharp recession led to a steep decline in oil prices, the Trudeau Liberals found themselves vilified in the West, disliked in Washington, and—ironically, thanks in part to the success of the Canadianization initiatives—guardians of a fast-growing federal deficit.

Conclusion

When Pierre Trudeau became prime minister, he promised to re-imagine foreign policy. No longer would Department of External Affairs staff monopolize the official and popular understandings of the national interest. It was time to position Canada first and worry less about the needs of the international community. After all, there was only so much that a declining middle power could be expected to do.

This sentiment was evident in the decision to reduce Canada's NATO troops in Europe, in Ottawa's initial disregard of international law during the early stages of the SS *Manhattan* affair, and in the introduction of the NEP. In each case, Canada's global posture eventually reverted. Defence spending increased, Ottawa accepted the jurisdiction of the International Court of Justice, and the NEP collapsed. The prime minister came to embrace some of the multilateral institutions that he had initially doubted and even embarked in 1983 on the type of global peace mission he would have abhorred 15 years earlier. While he might never have said so explicitly, Trudeau came to recognize that putting Canada first was easier when Ottawa used all of the diplomatic tools at its disposal, many of which required working multilaterally.

But there was more to the Trudeau era than just his creation of an illusion of change. Trudeau's Canada was at once both more generous and more hypocritical in its approach to international assistance; more concerned with, and yet more troubling in its selective support for, human rights; more committed to, yet also more criticized internationally for, its treatment of minority groups within Canada. The prime minister who preferred to stand separately from his American counterparts oversaw a period during which Canadians devoured American culture and came to support freer trade. He who championed a united Canada left office having alienated much of the Prairies.

Readings

The 1970s are receiving increasing attention from international historians, whose work has emphasized growing global interconnections during this period. Important examinations of early globalization in the 1970s are Thomas Borstelmann's *The 1970s: A New Global History from Civil Rights to Economic Inequality* (Princeton: Princeton University Press, 2012) and the essays in Niall Ferguson et al., eds., *The Shock of the Global: The 1970s in Perspective* (Cambridge, MA: Harvard University Press, 2010). Among the most significant issues to gain global prominence was the idea of human rights, which came to affect a wide array of political, economic, social, and cultural matters. On the "breakthrough" of human rights in the 1970s, see Jan Eckel and Samuel Moyn, eds., *The Breakthrough: Human Rights in the 1970s* (Philadelphia: University of Pennsylvania Press, 2014). The 1970s also saw important changes in American foreign policy and in the US economy—with important global ramifications— topics covered in Daniel J. Sargent's *A Superpower Transformed: The Remaking of American Foreign Relations in the 1970s* (New York: Oxford University Press, 2017) and Judith Stein's *Pivotal Decade: How the United States Traded Factories for Finance in the Seventies* (New Haven: Yale University Press, 2011).

Bruce Thordarson's *Trudeau and Foreign Policy: A Study in Decision-Making* (Toronto: Oxford University Press, 1972) is the only book-length treatment of a Canadian foreign policy review process and serves as the backbone of this chapter's first case. J.L. Granatstein and Robert Bothwell's *Pirouette: Pierre Trudeau and Canadian Foreign Policy* (Toronto: University of Toronto Press, 1990) remains the authoritative source on Trudeau and foreign affairs but should be read in conjunction with their *Trudeau's World: Insiders Reflect on Foreign Policy, Trade, and Defence, 1968–84* (Vancouver: UBC Press, 2017), which offers summaries of the extensive interviews they conducted to write it. Mitchell Sharp's *Which Reminds Me...A memoir* (Toronto: University of Toronto Press, 1994) provides an insider's view. For primary source evidence, see John Gellner, *Canada in NATO* (Toronto: Ryerson Press, 1970) and Arthur E. Blanchette, ed., *Canadian Foreign Policy 1966–1976: Selected Speeches and Documents* (Ottawa: Gage Publishing, 1980).

The most up-to-date, comprehensive account of the *Manhattan* voyages is Adam Lajeunesse's *Lock, Stock, and Icebergs: A History of Canada's Arctic Maritime Sovereignty* (Vancouver: UBC Press, 2016), chapter 7. John Kirton and Don Munton's "The *Manhattan* voyages and their aftermath," in Franklyn Griffiths, ed., *Politics of the Northwest Passage* (Montreal: McGill-Queen's University Press, 1987), 67–97 is also helpful, as is chapter 4 of Brian Bow's *The Politics of Linkage: Power, Interdependence, and Ideas in Canada-US Relations* (Vancouver: UBC Press, 2009). The account in chapter 2 of Ivan L. Head and

148 CANADA FIRST, NOT CANADA ALONE

Pierre Elliott Trudeau, *The Canadian Way: Shaping Canada's Foreign Policy, 1968–1984* (Toronto: McClelland and Stewart, 1995) is self-serving but exceptionally detailed. The primary source evidence available to support this case is outstanding. See, for example, P. Whitney Lackenbauer and Peter Kikkert, eds., *The Canadian Forces and Arctic Sovereignty: Debating Roles, Interests and Requirements, 1968–1974* (Waterloo: LCMSDS Press of Wilfrid Laurier University, 2010), chapter 2; Lajeunesse, *Documents on Canadian Arctic Maritime Sovereignty: 1950–1988* DCASS, no. 13 (2018), http://pubs.aina.ucalgary.ca/dcass/84387.pdf, docs 49–70; and Lackenbauer and Lajeunesse, eds., *In Manhattan's Wake: Lieutenant Commander E.B. Stolee's Accounts of the Canadian Arctic Voyages of CCGS* John A. Macdonald *and* Louis St. Laurent, *1969/70* [Arctic Operational History Series, no. 8] (Antigonish, NS: Brian Mulroney Institute of Government, 2019), http://operationalhistories.ca/wp-content/uploads/2019/10/In-Manhattans-Wake.pdf.

The most authoritative source on Joe Clark and the Israeli embassy is Charles Flicker, "Next year in Jerusalem: Joe Clark and the Jerusalem affair," *International Journal* 58, no. 1 (2003): 115–38, https://doi.org/10.1177/002070200305800106. See also George Steven Takach, "Clark and the Jerusalem Embassy affair: Initiative and constraint in Canadian foreign policy" (Carleton University, MA thesis, 1980). A summary of Takach's thesis is included in David Taras and David H. Goldberg, eds., *The Domestic Battleground: Canada and the Arab-Israeli Conflict* (Montreal: McGill-Queen's University Press, 1989), 144–66. The Stanfield report is included as an appendix to Tarek Y. Ismael, ed., *Canada and the Arab World* (Edmonton: University of Alberta Press, 1985), 179–206. Alan Bones's chapter, "Zionist interest groups and Canadian foreign policy," in the same book (151–71) is also helpful.

The most comprehensive source on the National Energy Program remains G. Bruce Doern and Glen Toner, *The Politics of Energy: The Development and Implementation of the NEP* (Toronto: Methuen, 1985). Chapter 5 of Brian Bow's *The Politics of Linkage: Power, Interdependence, and Ideas in Canada-US Relations* (Vancouver: UBC Press, 2009) is also excellent. Helpful personal accounts include Marc MacGuigan, *An Inside Look at External Affairs During the Trudeau Years: The Memoirs of Mark MacGuigan*, edited by P. Whitney Lackenbauer (Calgary: University of Calgary Press, 2002), 116–21 and Marc Lalonde, "Riding the storm: Energy policy, 1968–1984," in Thomas S. Axworthy and Pierre Elliott Trudeau, eds., *Towards a Just Society: The Trudeau Years* (Toronto: Penguin, 1990), 49–77. See also Edward Wonder, "The US government response to the Canadian National Energy Program," *Canadian Public Policy* 8, sl (1982): 480–93 and David Leyton-Brown, "Canadianizing oil and gas: The National Energy Program, 1980–83," in Don Munton and John Kirton, eds., *Canadian Foreign Policy: Selected Cases* (Scarborough: Prentice Hall,

1992), 299–310. The NEP itself can be found at Energy, Mines and Resources Canada, *The National Energy Program* (Ottawa: Minister of Supply and Services Canada, 1980).

Beyond the Book

Recognizing the People's Republic of China (PRC), 1968–1970

At the end of the Chinese civil war in 1949, the victorious communists controlled the mainland while the defeated nationalists retreated to the island of Formosa (now Taiwan). With the exception of Britain, Western governments refused to recognize the communists' People's Republic of China as the rightful government. Over the next two decades, the United States sought to ensure that its allies adhered to this non-recognition position. To Washington, the nationalists had never formally surrendered, and therefore remained entitled to the Chinese seat on the UN Security Council. Ottawa thought seriously of recognizing the PRC during this early period but chose not to in response to an urgent American appeal.

Even before he became prime minister, Pierre Trudeau had expressed a strong conviction that it was time for Canada to recognize the PRC. The proposal was risky—Washington did not approve; Canada's political and trade relationship with Taiwan could be compromised; and failed negotiations risked undermining Canada's growing exports to the Chinese mainland—but Trudeau had the support of his External Affairs officials. The negotiations began almost immediately after he became prime minister. The communists were more difficult to deal with than Ottawa had anticipated. They insisted that Canada not just recognize the PRC as the rightful government of all of China and support their claim to the Chinese seat on the Security Council, but that Ottawa also endorse the PRC's sovereignty over Taiwan—a move that would inevitably end Canadian-Taiwanese relations altogether. Negotiations stalled for over a year.

Questions

1. What are Canada's national interests in this case?
2. Are ending relations with Taiwan and risking a rift with Washington acceptable risks in efforts to achieve the prime minister's objective?
3. Might there be a way to recognize the PRC and still salvage relations with Taiwan?

150 CANADA FIRST, NOT CANADA ALONE

Readings

The key sources for this case can be found in section IV of Paul M. Evans and B. Michael Frolic, eds., *Reluctant Adversaries: Canada and the People's Republic of China, 1949–1970* (Toronto: University of Toronto Press, 1991). Frolic's "The Trudeau initiative," (189–216) outlines the case and its outcomes. Janet Lum's "Recognition and the Toronto Chinese community," (217–40) offers a glimpse into the reaction of Chinese Canadians. See also Evans's more recent *Engaging China: Myth, Aspiration, and Strategy in Canadian Policy from Trudeau to Harper* (Toronto: University of Toronto Press, 2014), 16–32. Diplomat Arthur Andrew's "'A reasonable period of time': Canada's de-recognition of Nationalist China," (241–52) examines the fallout in Canadian-Taiwanese relations. Andrew's memoir, *The Rise and Fall of a Middle Power: Canadian Diplomacy from King to Mulroney* (Toronto: James Lorimer, 1993), 88–93 adds further personal observations, as does a short autobiographical piece by diplomat Robert Edmonds, "Canada's recognition of the People's Republic of China: The Stockholm negotiations, 1968–1970," *Canadian Foreign Policy Journal* 5, no. 2 (1998): 201–17, https://doi.org/10.1080/11926422.1998.9673140. Mitchell Sharp also offers insider views in *Which Reminds Me...A Memoir* (Toronto: University of Toronto Press, 1994), 203–7. Sharp's speech explaining the establishment of relations with the PRC to the House of Commons on 13 October 1970 can be found in Canada, House of Commons, *Debates*, 28th Parliament, 3rd session, vol. 1, https://parl.canadiana.ca/view/oop.debates_HOC2803_01/51?r=0&s=1.

7

Brian Mulroney and the Transformation of Canadian International Affairs, 1984–1993

Liberals Out, Tories In

In 1984, Brian Mulroney became prime minister of a Progressive Conservative (PC) government with the largest majority in Parliament in Canadian history. Mulroney's background gives some insights into his party's electoral success. A corporate executive, he appealed to fiscal conservatives upset with decades of government expansion at the expense of free enterprise; hailing from a small, remote town, he related to rural Canadians, particularly from the West, where resentment toward Ottawa was significant; and as a Quebecer, he spoke to voters in his native province, a traditional bastion of Liberal support. After a decade-and-a-half of Pierre Trudeau, Canadians desired change. John Turner, Trudeau's successor, could not escape his predecessor's shadow; his government lasted from June to September 1984.[1]

The Tories ended the National Energy Program and sold off Petro-Canada. Other Crown corporations were also privatized, among them Air Canada in 1988. The Foreign Investment Review Agency, meant to limit American ownership of Canadian industry, became Investment Canada, with the objective of promoting foreign investment. Minister of Finance Michael Wilson favoured deregulation, tax reform, and austerity in his effort to limit government and promote free markets. This neoliberal policy mix complemented developments in Britain and the United States, where the Conservatives under Margaret Thatcher and the Republicans under Ronald Reagan were similarly recalibrating the state–free market relationship. Even so, the Mulroney government retained many of the social programs instituted in previous decades, a nod to the moderate conservatives, or Red Tories, who made up the party's support base in Central and Eastern Canada. "As Leader of the Progressive Conservatives," Margaret Thatcher wrote of Mulroney, "I thought he put too much emphasis on the adjective as opposed to the noun."[2]

In global affairs, Mulroney proved to be one of Canada's boldest prime ministers.[3] His activism fit an era of considerable drama, from the initial

Canada First, Not Canada Alone: A History of Canadian Foreign Policy. Adam Chapnick and Asa McKercher, Oxford University Press. © Oxford University Press 2024. DOI: 10.1093/oso/9780197653715.003.0008

152 CANADA FIRST, NOT CANADA ALONE

heightening of Cold War tensions, to the peaceful collapse of the Soviets' eastern European empire, to the demise of the USSR itself, and then the hopeful dawning of what US President George H.W. Bush called a new world order.[4] Ottawa's foreign policy posture was true to the consensus guiding Canadian policymakers since the late 1940s: support for a range of multilateral institutions and the alliance with the United States.[5] Roy McMurtry, a Red Tory, became high commissioner to London. Allan Gotlieb, a long-time civil servant, remained ambassador in Washington. Stephen Lewis, a New Democratic Party luminary, became ambassador to the United Nations. Mulroney appointed Joe Clark, the former prime minister and his defeated rival, as SSEA. The government's first test was responding to a famine in Ethiopia. Although Ottawa responded courageously, over the next nine years, Canadian engagement abroad was affected by budget cuts. The Department of External Affairs ultimately closed 18 of its 124 posts abroad.

Super Relations with the United States

The new government stuck to the main lines of Canadian external relations, but with an emphasis on Mulroney's personal priorities. Growing up in a company town and then working in the business world, the new prime minister had a fondness for the United States and deplored the economic nationalism prevailing in much of Canada. "Good relations, super relations, with the US will be the cornerstone of our foreign policy," he affirmed shortly after becoming prime minister.[6] Mulroney quickly established a friendly rapport with Reagan, whose arch-conservative administration had dreaded Trudeau's protectionist policies. The two held informal summits annually that continued after Reagan was succeeded by George H.W. Bush.

The Reagan-Mulroney camaraderie was on early display at the Shamrock Summit in Quebec City in March 1985, where the leaders and their wives sang on stage. Although some Canadians were embarrassed by the warm display of affection, it had a positive impact on the president. "I have to believe U.S.-Canadian relations have never been better & certainly not at the leader level," he confided to his diary.[7] The friendship gave Mulroney access and sympathy, key assets. In fact, US officials complained to Gotlieb about the prime minister's ability to influence the president, leading the Canadian ambassador to ask, "Who can reasonably say, in the light of this, that summitry is not useful or that good personal chemistry doesn't count?"[8]

There was easiness elsewhere in the Canada–US relationship. Clark continued a process—begun under his Liberal predecessor Allan MacEachen—of quarterly meetings with Secretary of State George Schultz. In Washington,

Figure 7.1 On 17 March 1985, Canadian Prime Minister Brian Mulroney and his wife, Mila, hosted US President Ronald Reagan and his wife, Nancy, along with 2000 other guests at a televised Gala Performance at the Grand Théâtre de Québec. The couples joined in a rendition of "When Irish Eyes are Smiling," a song that recalled both leaders' Irish roots. The highly unusual event garnered significant popular and critical attention, but it was hardly the most important part of Reagan's 24-hour visit. What came to be known as the Shamrock Summit secured the president's commitment to reduce trade barriers with Canada as well as the appointment of special envoys to study acid rain. Reagan left Quebec the following day under the impression that relations with Canada had never been better, and he and Mulroney met regularly over the rest of his presidency. Mulroney's diplomatic method might have been unusual, but it worked. NAID 75853989/National Archives and Records Administration/C27800-8A.

Gotlieb and his staff pioneered what they called "the new diplomacy," which encompassed outreach to government agencies and departments beyond State, members of Congress and their staffers, civil society organizations, and the press corps. Canada's embassy hosted black-tie galas, where Canadian celebrities were enlisted in the diplomatic campaign.[9] These efforts proved helpful in getting Canada a favourable hearing in the US Capitol and contributed to the successful conclusion of the Canada–US Free Trade Agreement in 1988.

The trade pact was controversial in Canada, where nationalist fears were high. The 1988 federal election, fought largely over free trade, was highly divisive. "The Mulroney trade agreement," the Liberal opposition complained, "sells out Canada's sovereign control over its own economic, social, cultural,

154 CANADA FIRST, NOT CANADA ALONE

and regional policies. It turns Canada into a colony of the United States."[10] Hyperbole aside, the concerns resonated with Canadians who were uncomfortable with the closeness between their prime minister and the Americans. Some commentators dubbed Mulroney a "Yankee Doodle Dandy" and "A Star-Spangled Tory."[11]

Contrary to his critics' assumptions, Mulroney's friendly relationship with Reagan did not preclude differences or disputes over policy. When the president launched the Strategic Defense Initiative, meant to protect North America from a nuclear attack, the prime minister opted to avoid the expensive and controversial program, though Canadian businesses or universities could take part if they wished.[12] A more pronounced dispute occurred over Arctic sovereignty after a US Coast Guard ship, the *Polar Sea*, traversed the Northwest Passage in 1985. Ottawa objected, claiming that the passage lay within Canadian waters; Washington saw it as an international strait. The impasse persisted through 1987 until, amid talks with Mulroney, Reagan encouraged his advisors to draft a new position respecting some of Canada's concerns. When Defense Secretary Frank Carlucci objected, the president snapped, "'You do it.'" As Carlucci reflected, "It was the only time I saw Ronald Reagan lose his temper."[13] The resulting January 1988 Arctic Cooperation Agreement was a compromise acceptable to both sides.

A thornier issue, the effort to combat acid rain, reflected Ottawa's wider international environmental agenda.[14] In 1989, Mulroney told President George Bush that "the environment was becoming a prominent foreign policy issue."[15] The following year, he warned fellow G7 leaders of the dangers of "global warming."[16] Under the Progressive Conservatives, Ottawa took a leading role in the conclusion of the 1987 Montreal Protocol on Substances that Deplete the Ozone Layer, a major international environmental accord. At the 1992 Earth Summit in Rio de Janeiro, Canada backed several environmental agreements, including the Rio Convention on Climate Change.

Multilateralism's Embrace

The Mulroney government's support for global solutions to environmental challenges is evidence that prioritizing the bilateral relationship with the United States did not come at the expense of a broader national embrace of multilateralism. As Clark boasted in 1988, "no other major power has Canada's institutional reach."[17] In 1986, Mulroney helped to regularize leaders' summits of La Francophonie and worked out an agreement allowing for provincial participation, paving the way for attendance by Quebec and New Brunswick. In 1989, Canada joined the newly formed Asia-Pacific Economic Cooperation (APEC).

In 1990, it took its place in the Organization of American States, and soon increased its democracy promotion efforts in the Western Hemisphere. In 1993, the Mulroney government supported, somewhat reluctantly, the creation of the North American Free Trade Agreement (NAFTA), which superseded the 1988 trade pact and included Mexico.[18] "Canada is not a big player in Mexico," Mulroney told George Bush, "but we hope to be."[19] These moves broadened the institutional and geographic bases of Canadian foreign policy.

Ottawa also championed the Commonwealth, which faced an existential crisis over South African apartheid. The issue was prominent internationally, with human rights activists and African countries advocating sanctions against Pretoria and the eventual end of white minority rule. While successive Canadian governments since John Diefenbaker had criticized apartheid, the Mulroney government took action. Throughout 1985, Joe Clark announced a range of voluntary and mandatory economic sanctions targeting Canadian business dealings with South Africa. These steps came as Commonwealth leaders met in October 1985 at Nassau, where Mulroney confronted Margaret Thatcher over British support for the apartheid regime, telling her that it had to be made clear to Pretoria that "effective reform can no longer be delayed."[20] Thatcher disagreed and blocked Commonwealth-wide sanctions. Mulroney broke not only with Britain, but also the United States, and took his case to the UN General Assembly. In a well-regarded speech, he threatened that if "there is no progress in dismantling apartheid, Canada's relations with South Africa may have to be severed absolutely."[21]

Given the British and American positions, as well as the indifference of other leading Western countries, Canada's open support for apartheid's opponents was notable. At the August 1986 Commonwealth summit, Mulroney and five other leaders challenged Thatcher by endorsing further economic sanctions. Ottawa expanded its range of contacts with anti-apartheid activists, invited prominent leaders of the movement to Canada, and provided moral and material support through the Canadian diplomatic mission in South Africa. In 1987, Mulroney visited the front-line states bordering South Africa in a show of solidarity.[22] Canada's official efforts were matched by a wave of activism on the part of everyday Canadians. Union members, student groups, and religious organizations were, as Clark acknowledged, Ottawa's "indispensable partners."[23] The South African government finally repealed its apartheid legislation in 1991.

The End of the Cold War

That same year, the Soviet Union collapsed. The Cold War had conditioned much of Canada's post–Second World War foreign policy, from military deployments to reactions to international events. On the campaign trail in 1984, Mulroney had pledged to boost military spending, declaring that Canada was "a first-class country and we're going to go first class in the area of conventional defence."[24] While some new weapons systems were purchased, the defence buildup was cut back amid later austerity measures. Moreover, the rationale for a larger military soon abated as the new Soviet leader, Mikhail Gorbachev, committed himself in 1985 to political and economic reform. Gorbachev sought warmer relations with the West and found willing partners, including Reagan, Thatcher, and Mulroney. Canada's prime minister visited Moscow in November 1989, just as Soviet control over Eastern Europe unravelled. The largely peaceful end of communist regimes in Poland, Czechoslovakia, East Germany, Hungary, and Romania, and Gorbachev's unwillingness to crack down on dissidents and activists, were momentous, as was the dissolution of the Soviet Union itself. When Ukraine became the first Soviet republic to declare independence from the USSR in December 1991, Canada was one of the first two states to recognize Ukrainian independence (Poland was the other), a testament to the hundreds of thousands of Ukrainian Canadians living across the country.[25] Over the next three decades, Ottawa would undertake efforts to support the establishment of democratic institutions throughout post-Soviet Europe.

The rapidly evolving global situation highlighted Canada's roles in NATO and the UN, two pillars of Canadian multilateralism. Having initially boosted the Canadian Forces' military deployment in West Germany, the Mulroney government began a withdrawal with the demise of the Soviet threat. Still, Ottawa remained committed to European security: when Yugoslavia splintered into rival states formed around ethnic and religious identity in 1992, Canada contributed troops to the UN Protection Force (UNPROFOR) in the new state of Croatia; when a second UNPROFOR was formed for neighbouring Bosnia-Herzegovina, Canada shifted military personnel from NATO to the UN mission. The Mulroney government deployed other peacekeepers to post-conflict reconstruction missions in Namibia, Cambodia, and Central America as well as to Somalia, where international efforts sought to distribute food supplies amid a crushing famine and the collapse of the central government. The missions in Somalia and the former Yugoslavia proved controversial, because Canadian peacekeepers found there was little peace to keep.[26]

The UN deployments gave Canada's military a post–Cold War purpose that was popular at home. Many Canadians saw their country as an international peacekeeper and contributor to the resolution of humanitarian crises. In July 1991, Mulroney had impressed upon his fellow G7 leaders the "need to strengthen the UN," an organization that seemed to take on new importance amid the decline of Cold War hostilities.[27] During the 1991 Gulf War, a US-led operation to liberate Kuwait from the forces of Iraqi dictator Saddam Hussein, the broad international coalition opposing Iraq, to which Canada contributed air and naval assets, was sanctioned by the UN. There was an expectation that the crisis served, as Joe Clark put it, as "a litmus test for what the United Nations can become. If we succeed here, the United Nations will send a clear and unambiguous signal to others that the world is now different; that it will not tolerate aggression and that international law is to be obeyed and not ignored."[28] The first conflict in which Canadian soldiers fought since the Korean War, the Gulf War was controversial at home, particularly given the leading role of the United States. "Canada," Clark assured worried Canadians, "will continue as a peacekeeper."[29]

Domestic Unrest

Internally, from July to September 1990 Canada faced its own unrest, a 78-day standoff pitting Quebec provincial police and over 2500 Canadian soldiers against Mohawk from the Kanesatake territory near Oka, Quebec. Stemming from Mohawk opposition to a local plan to build a golf course on disputed land (that included a burial ground), the Kanesatake Resistance, or Oka Crisis, highlighted Canada's unequal treatment of Indigenous people. Grand Chief Joseph Norton of the nearby Kahnawake reserve spoke for over 150 other chiefs in declaring that the Canadian government should be subjected to the same sanctions imposed on South Africa because "they are dealing with natives in the same way as the South African white government is dealing with its black people."[30] Despite deaths on both sides of the conflict, negotiation eventually defused the standoff, but not before reporters captured tense scenes of Canadian soldiers and Mohawk warriors squaring off. Once the crisis ended, Ottawa established the Royal Commission on Aboriginal Peoples, which recommended that Canada build "nation-to-nation relationships" with Indigenous groups.[31]

Indigenous activism was not the only source of internal tension in Canada in the early 1990s. A recession and skyrocketing debt plagued the economy, and with the Progressive Conservatives failing to balance the budget or reverse the downturn, some analysts warned that the federal government faced bankruptcy. In Quebec, Prime Minister Mulroney's failure to appease nationalists despite a proposed series of constitutional amendments led to increasing support for separatism. The Bloc Québécois, a new federal separatist party, counted among its members many disaffected Tories, including a former member of Mulroney's Cabinet. Another new party, Reform, formed in Western Canada as a right-wing alternative to the Progressive Conservatives and aimed

158   CANADA FIRST, NOT CANADA ALONE

to ensure better representation of Western interests. Together, these two parties splintered Mulroney's political coalition. When Mulroney stepped down in June 1993, his successor, Kim Campbell, faced a fractured conservative movement as well as the brunt of public anger over the struggling economy and nearly a decade of scandal-plagued PC rule. Campbell, Canada's first woman prime minister, served for less than five months. In the November 1993 federal election, the Tories fell from 156 seats to 2; Reform took 52 seats, while the Bloc took 54, becoming the official opposition. Meanwhile, Jean Chrétien became prime minister of a majority Liberal government and of a country whose future seemed in doubt.

Case Studies

What "Canada first" meant during the Mulroney era is open to debate. Between 1984 and 1993, Canada pursued a foreign policy that was at times internationalist and at others focused on North America. At times it was non-partisan; at others, it was overwhelmingly political. At times, it benefited from the enthusiastic support and engagement of a variety of non-state actors; at others, non-state actors were among Ottawa's most aggressive opponents. Perhaps the only consistent theme is the Progressive Conservative government's commitment to active engagement in the world.

The first case explores the national response to an overwhelming famine in Ethiopia. Like so many Canadians, members of the Mulroney government were personally moved after watching the devastation experienced by millions of Ethiopians play out on television. Ottawa immediately pledged to do whatever Canada could to help. The result was a comprehensive commitment that received staunch public support.

Whereas the parliamentary opposition played an active role in responding to the Ethiopian famine, negotiations to conclude a free trade agreement with the United States were highly divisive. As a Conservative leadership candidate, Mulroney had rejected free trade, and members of the Liberal opposition, which still held a majority in the Senate, used his prior position to justify their refusal to pass implementation legislation without an election. The Tories ultimately won a second majority government, but the issue caused lasting fractures in the national psyche.

The third case reflects the Mulroney government's interest in and commitment to environmental reform. Ottawa faced considerable difficulty in convincing Washington to respond to the increasing acidification of several lakes in central Canada's cottage country. Mulroney's insistence that Canada not call on Washington to tighten its environmental standards until changes had already been made at home is particularly notable.

The Beyond the Book case explores how the fallout from the free trade debate affected Canadian foreign policy in the aftermath of Iraq's invasion of Kuwait in 1990. Canada was a member of the UN Security Council at the time, and Ottawa used its position to shape the international response while facing domestic criticism for its alliance with the United States.

Responding to Famine in Ethiopia, 1984–1986

What role can, or should, the Canadian public play in the establishment and implementation of Canada's foreign policy priorities?

The international response to a tragic famine in Ethiopia in 1984 has been called "one of the greatest mobilizations of global empathy and humanitarian relief in the latter part of the 20th century."[32] It was also, according to one analyst, "one crisis where Canada truly made a difference."[33] This case reveals some of the complexities of an initiative that was shaped, for good and for ill, by the Mulroney government's conscious decision to mobilize the Canadian public in the face of an international emergency.

In 1974, a military junta led by Mengistu Haile Mariam established a one-party Marxist regime across Ethiopia. Ongoing civil strife and a series of droughts followed, along with destruction of much of the country's economic and agricultural infrastructure. The UN Food and Agriculture Organization identified the dangerous state of food insecurity across the country in 1982, but the initial global response was insufficient.[34] By the fall of 1984, six million Ethiopians were at risk of starvation.[35] Although the figures remain disputed, it appears that over 1,000,000 of them ultimately died, 200,000 children were orphaned, and millions of others were internally displaced.[36]

Despite Ethiopia's close ties to the Soviet Union, Ottawa was a major donor of food aid. In 1983, the Trudeau government had considered a $20 million emergency initiative, although that proposal was ultimately rejected by a Cabinet committee.[37] When the Progressive Conservatives took over in September 1984, there were no indications of a pending change in policy. Indeed, the Tories appeared to be more concerned by the Ethiopian government's communist sympathies than with the state of its people.[38]

The crisis came to global attention after a devastating exposé by the British Broadcasting Corporation's Michael Burek.[39] His 25 October 1984 report was ultimately rebroadcast by 425 media organizations and reached nearly half

160   CANADA FIRST, NOT CANADA ALONE

a billion people. The following week, the CBC's Brian Stewart produced a four-minute follow-up for Canada's flagship news program, *The National*. The accompanying video of starving children and piles of corpses unleashed what one scholar has called "a political tsunami" across the country.[40]

In his memoirs, Mulroney recalls being "shocked by what I saw coming from my television."[41] He immediately contacted Canada's ambassador to the United Nations, Stephen Lewis. When Lewis indicated that the international community had yet to mobilize, Mulroney authorized him to speak out boldly. Lewis's speech at the UN General Assembly was just that.[42]

Foreign Minister Joe Clark assumed the political lead for Ottawa's official response. He flew to Ethiopia, becoming the first international leader to witness the famine in person. When he returned, Clark rescinded planned cuts to Canada's foreign aid budget and pledged $7.5 million in immediate relief and an additional $50 million through a Special Fund for Africa.[43]

Perhaps most important, Clark courted widespread backing for this relief effort. As he told the Progressive Conservative Party caucus, "We will treat Ethiopia as an all-party matter....We want support from all Canadians....MPs should contact service clubs and local mayors and ask them to lend their efforts to provide aid."[44] Ottawa promised to match up to $15 million in personal contributions from individual Canadians through a fund to be known as African Emergency Aid. Clark then offered representatives from the non-governmental organization (NGO) community the majority of the seats on the fund's board.[45] African Emergency Aid was so successful that Ottawa soon doubled its contribution.

Clark also appointed the highly regarded former MP, United Church minister, and human rights activist David MacDonald as Emergency Coordinator/African Famine. MacDonald had authority to bypass both the Canadian International Development Agency (for which he technically worked) and the Department of External Affairs to manage Canada's operational response.[46] MacDonald's public profile also made him the "chief cheerleader" of the Canadian effort.[47] In addition to undertaking numerous trips to Ethiopia and its neighbouring countries on Canada's behalf, part of his job was to motivate individual Canadians and link public offers of support to existing needs.[48]

The public hardly needed encouragement.[49] More than two out of every three Canadian families ultimately contributed.[50] Some did so individually, others through their religious organizations, still more through their unions and service groups. Cities "twinned" with struggling Ethiopian communities, often working directly with NGOs. Famous musicians, calling themselves Northern Lights, recorded a song, "Tears are not enough," that dominated the Canadian music charts and raised over $3 million.[51] When momentum began to wane, MacDonald's office launched Forum Africa, a series of public symposia across the country with the goal of solidifying Canada's long-term commitment to African peace and security.[52]

The Canadian mobilization was not without its difficulties. Exaggerated public expectations of the Ethiopian state's capacity to receive and distribute food aid initially led to frustration and disappointment. As MacDonald later reflected, "Few understandably appreciated the complexities of transporting and distributing food to starving people in a hostile environment where temperatures at the Red Sea or in the Sahel reached 45°C; where there are no refrigerators; where transport is a problem; where storage is practically nonexistent; and where many products would have been unsuited for people on the point of starvation."[53] Further complicating the situation, the Ethiopian government manipulated the relief effort to suppress its political opposition, even if that meant starving its own people, relocating others by force, and banishing NGOs that spoke out against it. As reports of the state's corruption became increasingly difficult to ignore, MacDonald's justifications for Canada's continued collaboration with the Mengistu regime became harder to sustain.[54] There were clear differences between development assistance professionals, whose primary aim was to improve the long-term plight of the Ethiopian people, and the Canadian public, the majority of whom cared primarily about the immediate crisis.[55]

The ultimate results of the Canadian response were mixed. As MacDonald has noted, the global effort, of which Canada was undoubtedly a leading player, "saved millions of lives and relieved the suffering of millions more. The world *did* make a difference."[56] The famine did subside, and in 1986, Ambassador Lewis helped negotiate a $112 billion UN recovery plan for Africa. Ottawa also launched its own 15-year program, Africa 2000, and committed $150 million to its first five years.[57] The relationships developed between civil society and the Ethiopian people persisted. Yet when Ethiopia faced a new drought in 1989, the international community, sapped by donor fatigue, was less enthused about helping.[58]

The Origins of the Canada–United States Free Trade Agreement, 1983–1989

How does trade policy fit within Canada's foreign policy framework?

Canada is a "trading nation," disproportionately reliant (relative to its allies and associates) on the import and export of goods and services to fuel economic growth.[59] Trade policy is therefore a vital concern for any Canadian government, and Ottawa's room to manoeuvre, regardless of the party in

162 CANADA FIRST, NOT CANADA ALONE

power, is relatively limited. Nonetheless, in the mid-1980s, the Mulroney government's negotiation of a free trade agreement with the United States resulted in an extended outbreak of often-vicious partisanship.[60] This case seeks to explain why.

The Canadian economy was struggling when Brian Mulroney's Progressive Conservatives took power in 1984. Unemployment was over 11 per cent. International competition and the rise of regional trading blocs threatened Canada's industrial prospects. Even though over 75 per cent of Canadian exports already went south, further penetration of the US market was the best strategy for economic recovery, notwithstanding protectionist moves by Congress that threatened access.[61] The Trudeau Liberals had been aware of the situation. Between 1975 and 1982, the Standing Senate Committee on Foreign Affairs issued three reports calling for freer trade with the United States. A 1982 DEA task force identified consistent access to the US market as critical to Canada's future. In 1983, Ottawa even announced plans to pursue a limited bilateral free trade agreement.[62] Yet there had been no progress prior to the 1984 election.

Mulroney's position on free trade was complicated. In his campaign for leadership of the Progressive Conservatives in 1983, he had aggressively opposed the idea by paraphrasing Trudeau. "Free trade with the United States is like sleeping with an elephant," he told the *Globe and Mail*. "It's terrific until the elephant twitches, and if the elephant rolls over, you are a dead man."[63] But, as he later admitted in his memoirs, "it was a less than honest position for me to take."[64] He and his strategists had concluded (correctly) that any other policy might have compromised his path to victory.

As prime minister, Mulroney was forced to confront a rise in American protectionism that Foreign Minister Joe Clark described as "the single most immediate threat to Canadian prosperity."[65] The business community, particularly in the West and in Quebec, was calling for free trade, as did a major study by one of Canada's leading economic think tanks, the C.D. Howe Institute. Public opinion surveys suggested that three-quarters of Canadians were supportive. The Reagan Administration expressed openness to negotiations, not long after which Alberta's premier and close Mulroney confidant Peter Lougheed warned the prime minister that if Canada did not pursue an agreement immediately, "the opportunity [would] probably be lost for many years."[66] Finance Minister Michael Wilson's first economic statement largely concurred, as did Trade Minister Jim Kelleher.[67] Perhaps most important, in late 1984, Mulroney learned that the chair of the Trudeau-appointed Royal Commission on the Economic Union and Development Prospects for Canada, former Liberal Cabinet minister Donald Macdonald, was about to recommend that Canadians take "a leap of faith" and pursue free trade with the United States.[68]

Mulroney had promised to revitalize the Canadian economy, restore federal-provincial harmony (particularly in Quebec and Western Canada), and improve relations with the United States. Free trade could meet all three objectives. The endorsement from a highly regarded Liberal made it political gold. As two analysts have noted, "Free trade was not, therefore, a Conservative idea whose time had come; rather, it was a policy that had been thrust onto the agenda through a series of conjunctions of events and that was finally chosen as the result of cold political calculation."[69] At the March 1985 Shamrock Summit, Mulroney and Reagan pledged to investigate means of reducing trade barriers between their countries. In the aftermath of the release of the Macdonald Commission's report on 5 September, Mulroney told his ambassador in the United States, Allan Gotlieb, to prepare for negotiations. He informed the House of Commons later that month. Although it was more difficult than anticipated, Reagan obtained authority to fast track the bill through Congress so long as there was an agreement by 3 October 1987.[70]

Theoretically, free trade with the United States would transition the Canadian economy from its historical east-west orientation into the modern age by increasing competition and establishing a long-term basis for managing bilateral relations. Practically, Canadian businesses desperately needed more consistently reliable access to their most important market.[71] As one member of Canada's negotiating team recalled, it was critical that trade "be governed by a set of rules that would be equally binding on the U.S. and Canadian governments and certain procedures to ensure that these rules would actually be implemented."[72] America's strategic goals were less clear, but Washington's lead negotiator, Peter Murphy, came armed with a list of issues he hoped to resolve.

The difference in national outlooks was reflected in the size and composition of the negotiating teams. The soft-spoken Murphy was Washington's 36-year-old delegate to the General Agreement on Tariffs and Trade (GATT). He had a staff of three and was initially expected to maintain his commitments in Geneva. Murphy had only vague official instructions, limited access to the White House, and still less sway with Congress.

Canada's chief negotiator, Simon Reisman, was a former deputy minister of finance who had negotiated the Canada–US Auto Pact 20 years earlier. Reisman was knowledgeable, committed, and always exceptionally prepared but, as three former colleagues put it: "His were not the virtues of collegiality, hierarchy, and anonymity."[73] Pat Carney, Canada's minister of trade throughout the negotiations, recalled that Reisman "also disliked working with women. In fact, the PM had admonished him about his exclusively male negotiating team."[74] In sum, a Washington insider suggested aptly, the negotiations constituted "a set of talks between a man who can't talk and a man who won't listen."[75] A series of unexpected protectionist measures announced by Washington created further discord.[76]

164   CANADA FIRST, NOT CANADA ALONE

On 23 September 1987, with no agreement in sight, Reisman declared the negotiations over and returned to Ottawa. His abrupt departure finally spurred movement at the political level. US Treasury Secretary James Baker and Mulroney's chief of staff and former External Affairs official, Derek Burney, took over. A deal was completed just minutes before the fast-track deadline.[77] Mulroney and Reagan signed the agreement on 2 January 1988.

By then, Canadian opponents of free trade had mobilized. They saw the deal as a threat to Canada's independence and identity.[78] In April 1987, over 20 national, but primarily anglophone, organizations formed the Pro Canada Network (PCN) to advance their cause.[79] The political opposition joined them. On 26 October, Liberal leader John Turner—who supported free trade in principle, as did many members of his party—told the House of Commons: "I will fight that agreement. I will fight it to the point of running the next election on it....We did not negotiate the deal, we are not bound by the deal, we will not live with this deal."[80] The PCN produced a petition signed by 400,000 Canadians demanding an election. As his biographer notes, Turner sympathized: "the Mulroney government had not included free trade in its platform during the previous election, and the issue was too important to the future of the country to be adopted without a mandate from the Canadian public."[81] Turner instructed the Liberal-dominated Senate not to pass legislation providing for free trade without an election. Since the Progressive Conservatives had already considered consulting the electorate, they welcomed the move.[82]

The 1988 election was acrimonious and emotional. The PCN's initial efforts and the Liberal and New Democratic Party (NDP) campaigns produced significant momentum (largely outside of Quebec) by warning Canadians that the social fabric of the nation and their sovereignty were threatened.[83] The climax was undoubtedly the leaders' English language debate on 25 October. Turner accused a stunned Mulroney of selling Canada out to the United States, and the normally loquacious prime minister found himself tongue-tied.[84] Support for the Liberals skyrocketed. As one free trade negotiator recalled, "never in the history of polling had a single event caused such a dramatic swing during an election."[85]

The Conservatives' recovery was equally dramatic. Flanked by his most senior ministers, Mulroney mounted an aggressive cross-country response that was intensely negative and utterly effective.[86] The business community countered the PCN with its own Canadian Alliance for Trade and Job Opportunities, at one point taking out advertisements in over 40 popular newspapers. The Liberals had captured the leadership of the anti–free trade cause, but the NDP worked with sympathetic premiers like Saskatchewan's Roy Romanow to warn that the agreement would dismantle Canada's social security system. Still, a majority of Canada's provincial leaders, along with most Quebecers, maintained their support for Mulroney's effort.[87]

BRIAN MULRONEY AND THE TRANSFORMATION   165

The Progressive Conservatives won a reduced majority on 21 November 1988, with the anti–free trade Liberals and NDP together capturing more votes (and a majority of the popular vote). The Mulroney government quickly passed implementation legislation. The public reacted sharply to the initial economic displacement but both economies adjusted, Canadian culture flourished, and bilateral trade increased dramatically. Mexico ultimately sought a similar arrangement with Washington, and Ottawa joined what became the North American Free Trade Agreement in 1993.[88]

Negotiating the Canada-United States Air Quality Agreement, 1991

What role can, or should, public diplomacy play in an effective diplomatic posture?

In the 1970s, scientists from Ontario became alarmed by the acidification of several lakes in cottage country. The cause was nitrogen and sulphur oxides, typically released from power plants and vehicle exhausts, that would acidify in the atmosphere and travel through the air before landing. Much of the pollution could not be attributed to the Inco smelter in Sudbury. Rather, it was coming from coal-burning power plants in the American Midwest.[89] The situation posed an exceptional, transboundary foreign policy challenge. It was, on its surface, a domestic Canadian problem—but one Ottawa could not solve on its own.[90] This case examines the impact of over a decade of Canadian diplomatic efforts to effect changes to the US Clean Air Act and the complementary Canada-United States Air Quality Agreement.

Acid deposition became part of the Canadian foreign policy lexicon in 1977 when Minister of the Environment Romeo LeBlanc called it "an environmental time bomb."[91] At the time, few people even knew what acid rain was. Canada and the United States did form a Bilateral Research Consultation Group on Long-Range Transport of Air Pollutants, but friends of the coal lobby in the Reagan administration negated its impact.[92] The Trudeau government had worked with Norway and Sweden on an anti-pollution regime, but the outcome—the Convention on Long-Range Transboundary Air Pollution (1979)—had little immediate effect.[93] A Joint Statement on Transboundary Air Quality issued by the Department of External Affairs and the State Department was aspirational.[94]

In a profoundly unorthodox move, Ottawa turned to a non-governmental organization, the Canadian Coalition on Acid Rain (CCAR), to help advance its case across the border.[95] Canada's ambassador to the United States, Allan

166 CANADA FIRST, NOT CANADA ALONE

Gotlieb, explained the government's thinking in his diary: "As a private organization, the coalition can engage in some visible and direct lobbying on the Hill without triggering the kind of xenophobic reactions that can result from direct interventions by a foreign government."[96]

The Department of External Affairs' efforts focused on educating skeptical Americans about why acid rain was a problem. Canadian scientists testified before Congress. The Government of Ontario offered American politicians guided visits across the border to see the results of the pollution first hand. When US tourists came to Canada, customs officers handed them "Stop Acid Rain" pamphlets and buttons. In the end, over $1 million was spent on what political scientist Stephen Clarkson has called "the largest effort Canada has made to attempt to shape the policy of another country."[97]

Nothing worked. As a future Canadian ambassador to the United States explained in his memoirs, US President Ronald Reagan "was convinced that acid rain was a figment of someone's imagination. He had read an article somewhere (in the *Reader's Digest* perhaps) which convinced him on this point, and he would not be moved."[98] At one point, he even suggested that it "was caused by trees."[99] American representatives were also quick to counter—correctly— that Canada's environmental record was worse than theirs.[100]

The return of the Progressive Conservatives in 1984 prompted another shift in strategy. Brian Mulroney had embraced the importance of environmental protection even before he took office, but he also recognized that credible international advocacy required "clean hands."[101] As one official recalled, "This meant getting our own house in order before approaching the United States."[102] Canada pledged to match US automobile emissions standards, and Ottawa negotiated a formula with all of the provinces east of Saskatchewan to reduce sulphur dioxide emissions to 50 per cent of 1980 levels by 1994.[103]

Mulroney and his officials made clear to the White House that progress on acid rain would serve as "the litmus test of the new relationship" to which both governments had committed to improving.[104] Despite continued reticence from some American legislators, the two leaders agreed in 1985 to appoint special envoys to study the issue, a small concession from the White House.[105]

The January 1986 report of Bill Davis, the former Tory premier of Ontario, and Drew Lewis, Reagan's former transport secretary, marked the first time that someone in the Reagan administration had conceded that pollution from the United States was causing harmful acid deposition in Canada. Rather than advocating hard reduction targets, the envoys recommended that Washington invest in clean coal technology. Activists in both countries were disappointed. Gotlieb and Mulroney were initially more hopeful, only to discover later the envoys' recommendations were never funded.[106]

At his 1987 summit with Reagan, Mulroney demanded that Washington nego-tiate a bilateral acid rain agreement. The president was clearly taken aback by the Canadian prime minister's bellicosity and ordered his advisors to rewrite his planned address to Parliament to make mention of his willingness to consider such a deal.[107] When Washington stonewalled once more, Mulroney's Minister of the Environment Tom Macmillan called out an interim report from the US National Precipitation Assessment Program as "voodoo science" and labelled opponents of environmental reform as "Neanderthals."[108] Mulroney presented Reagan with the basis of a bilateral accord at their final summit in Washington in April 1988 and raised the acid rain issue at the G7 summit meeting in Toronto that summer. He then directed his attention to Vice President George H.W. Bush.[109]

Bush had promised to revise the Clean Air Act during the 1988 presidential primaries. Once elected, he was true to his word. On 9 February 1989, he com-mitted to new legislation that would include an emission reduction plan.[110] The following day, at a meeting with reporters in Ottawa, Bush reiterated: "I think the prime minister is aware of the political divisions and political waves there [are] in our country on this issue. But I assured him that the time for just pure study was over and that we've now approached time for legislative action."[111]

The Bush administration released its proposed changes to the Clean Air Act in June 1989. Included was a pledge to unilaterally reduce sulphur dioxide emis-sions by more than half. Consultations with Ottawa on a more comprehensive agreement began almost immediately.[112] Congress passed the amended act in October 1990. The following March, President Bush travelled to Ottawa to sign the Canada-United States Air Quality Agreement (AQA).[113]

Scholars are divided on the significance of Canadian public diplomacy efforts for the AQA. At the time, Bush praised staff at the Canadian embassy. "They were on us like ugly on an ape," he said at the signing ceremony.[114] Two recent books concur.[115] Critics are less certain, focusing instead on the impact of domestic politics and the science itself.[116] Political scientist Don Munton is also critical of the modest impact of the agreement writ large, noting that Ottawa quickly tired of its implementation.[117]

Ambassador Gotlieb offers a balanced assessment. To him, Ottawa's most significant contribution was its establishment, with both presidents, of what he calls "the Canadian factor—the importance of addressing acid rain as an ele-ment of good relations with Canada."[118] Washington acted on acid rain when a combination of scientific evidence, domestic political pressure, and a commit-ted president and members of Congress concluded that it was in America's interests to do so. That Washington agreed to the AQA not long after Congress passed the amendments to the Clean Air Act, however, might be viewed as a testament to Canadian persistence.

168 CANADA FIRST, NOT CANADA ALONE

Conclusion

The Mulroney era in Canadian foreign policy was chock full of national and international drama. The election of 1988 indicated that the Canadian electorate included a fierce strand of anti-Americanism but, at the executive level, relations were as "super" as Mulroney had promised. Although Ottawa continued to disagree with Washington on a variety of bilateral and multilateral issues—from missile defence, to South African apartheid, to environmental reform—it did so without being disagreeable. Few eras in the history of Canadian foreign policy saw greater transformation. The unprecedented impact of television reports on the Ethiopian famine was representative of the increasing role of national publics in strategic decision making. The fall of the Berlin Wall and the dissolution of the Soviet Union marked the end of the ironic stability of 45 years of Cold War politics. Climate change activism foreshadowed broader public understandings of national security and its implications.

Whether Canada was prepared to meet the challenges of the post–Cold War world was unclear. The rise of the Bloc Québécois was a warning that Quebec separatism had reached a feverish point; a second secession referendum was all but assured. The Reform Party's foreign policy platform—which called for restrictions to immigration and the end of multiculturalism—marked the beginning of the end of the national consensus on world affairs that had largely withstood successive transitions to and from Liberal and Progressive Conservative governments. The Mulroney government's inability to tame Canada's overwhelming national debt meant that cuts to diplomacy, defence, and development initiated under the Progressive Conservatives would inevitably accelerate under their successors.

Readings

A variety of issues in the international history of the 1980s are covered in Jonathan Davis, *The Global 1980s: People, Power and Profit* (Abingdon: Routledge, 2019). More focused studies on the end of the Cold War are Simon Miles, *Engaging the Evil Empire: Washington, Moscow and the Beginning of the End of the Cold War* (Ithaca: Cornell University Press, 2020) and James Wilson, *The Triumph of Improvisation: Gorbachev's Adaptability, Reagan's Engagement, and the End of the Cold War* (Ithaca: Cornell University Press, 2015). On Eastern European activism, see Sarah Snyder, *Human Rights Activism and the End of the Cold War: A Transnational History of the Helsinki Network* (Cambridge: Cambridge University Press, 2011) and Mary Sarotte, *1989: The Struggle to Create Post-Cold War Europe* (Princeton: Princeton University

Press, 2014). The demise of the USSR is the subject of Vladislav Zubok's *Collapse: The Fall of the Soviet Union* (New Haven: Yale University Press, 2021). On apartheid, see Saul Dubow's *Apartheid: 1948–1994* (Oxford: Oxford University Press, 2014).

The foreign policies of presidents Ronald Reagan and George H.W. Bush are examined in Jonathan Hunt and Simon Miles, eds., *The Reagan Moment: America and the World in the 1980s* (Ithaca: Cornell University Press, 2021) and Jeffrey Engel, *When the World Seemed New: George H.W. Bush and the End of the Cold War* (Boston: Houghton Mifflin, 2017). For studies of Reaganism and Thatcherism, consult Doug Rossinow, *The Reagan Era: A History of the 1980s* (New York: Columbia University Press, 2015) and Ben Jackson and Robert Saunders, *Making Thatcher's Britain* (Cambridge: Cambridge University Press, 2012). Important, too, is David Harvey's *A Brief History of Neoliberalism* (Oxford: Oxford University Press, 2005).

The most thorough summary of the Ethiopian famine case is Nassisse Solomon's "'Tears are not enough': Canadian political and social mobilization for famine relief in Ethiopia, 1984–1988," in Greg Donaghy and David Webster, eds., *A Samaritan State Revisited: Historical Perspectives on Canadian Foreign Aid* (Calgary: University of Calgary Press, 2019), 245–67, https://prism.ucal-gary.ca/bitstream/handle/1880/110848/9781773850412_chapter10.pdf. The best critical reading of the literature remains Mark W. Charlton, *The Making of Canadian Food Aid Policy* (Montreal: McGill-Queen's University Press, 1992), specifically 166–202. More broadly, see Tanja R. Müller, "'The Ethiopian famine' revisited: Band Aid and the antipolitics of celebrity humanitarian action," *Disasters* 37, no. 1 (2013): 61–79, https://doi.org/10.1111/j.1467-7717.2012.01293.x. For primary source evidence, see the MacDonald and Decima reports cited in the endnotes. They can be found online through the Jules Léger library https://www.international.gc.ca/gac-amc/programs-programmes/jll-bjl/index.aspx?lang=eng.

The three most important books on the free trade negotiations are G. Bruce Doern and Brian W. Tomlin, *Faith and Fear: The Free Trade Story* (Toronto: Stoddart, 1991); Michael Hart, with Bill Dymond and Colin Robertson, *Decision at Midnight: Inside the Canada-US Free Trade Negotiations* (Vancouver: UBC Press, 1994); and Gordon Ritchie, *Wrestling with the Elephant: The Inside Story of the Canada-US Free Trade Wars* (Toronto: Macfarlane, Walter & Ross, 1997). On opposition to free trade, see Jeffrey M. Ayres, *Defying Conventional Wisdom: Political Movements and Popular Contention against North American Free Trade* (Toronto: University of Toronto Press, 1998) and the relevant portions of Paul Litt, *Elusive Destiny: The Political Vocation of John Napier Turner* (Vancouver: UBC Press, 2011). On gender, see Pat Carney, *Trade Secrets* (Toronto: Key Porter, 2000). On the implications of the election for Canadian

170 CANADA FIRST, NOT CANADA ALONE

nationalism, see Raymond B. Blake, "The Canadian 1988 election: The nationalist posture of Prime Minister Brian Mulroney and the Progressive Conservatives," *Canadian Review of Studies in Nationalism* 30, nos. 1–2 (2003): 65–82.

Don Munton is the most prolific scholar on Canada and acid rain. See his "Acid rain politics in North America: Conflict to cooperation to collusion," in Gerald R. Visigilio and Diana M. Whitelaw, eds., *Acid in the Environment: Lessons Learned and Future Prospects* (New York: Springer 2007), 175–201, along with his other work cited in the endnotes. The memoirs of Brian Mulroney [*Memoirs, 1939–1993* (Toronto: McClelland and Stewart, 2007)] and Allan Gotlieb [*The Washington Diaries 1981–1989* (Toronto: McClelland and Stewart, 2006)] are also helpful. On the environmental context, see Fen Osler Hampson, "Pollution across borders: Canada's international environmental agenda," in Maureen Appel Molot and Fen Olser Hampson, eds., *Canada among Nations 1989: The Challenge of Change* (Ottawa: Carleton University Press, 1990), 175–92. For primary source evidence, see James McGrath and Arthur Milnes, eds., *Age of the Offered Hand: The Cross-Border Partnership between President George H.W. Bush and Prime Minister Brian Mulroney: A Documentary History* (Kingston: School of Policy Studies, 2009).

Beyond the Book

Responding to Iraq's Invasion of Kuwait, 1990–1991

On 2 August 1990 (1 August in Canada), President Saddam Hussein authorized 140,000 Iraqi troops to invade and annex neighbouring Kuwait. Iraq's economy was still recovering from a decade-long war with Iran, and oil-rich Kuwait's unwillingness to reduce production in order to raise global energy prices had made Hussein furious. Kuwait also refused to forgive Iraqi debts. The invasion and annexation marked one of the most blatant violations of the UN Charter since the Korean War. It also occurred at a time when the UN Security Council was functioning unusually co-operatively due to productive US–Soviet relations.

The United States had ample reasons to become engaged. Americans had economic interests in the region, and President George H.W. Bush was personally committed to maintaining the integrity of the United Nations as the world's centre for global governance. Not everyone in Washington shared Bush's faith in the UN. Canada had fewer direct interests in the Middle East, but the Mulroney government was a close US ally and a strong UN supporter. Canada was also, until the end of 1990, a non-permanent member of the Security Council. But Canadians saw their country as peacekeepers, and the challenge

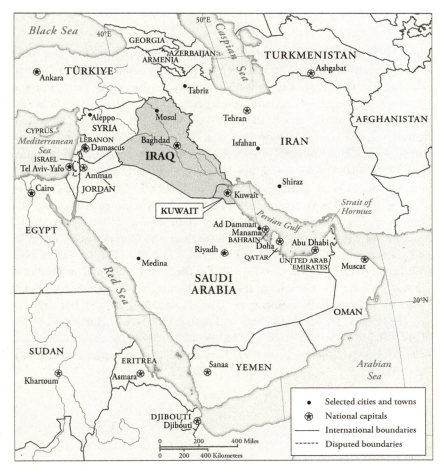

Figure 7.2 The Persian Gulf.

facing the UN was a war. In the aftermath of the free trade negotiations, many were also uncomfortable with American global leadership.

Questions

1. What are Canada's national interests in this case?
2. How, if at all, should membership on the Security Council affect the Canadian response to the Iraqi invasion?
3. What role should Parliament play in any government decision to become involved militarily?

172   CANADA FIRST, NOT CANADA ALONE

Readings

Much of the material that supports this case was produced prior to the opening of the relevant archives. The first comprehensive account is Martin Rudner, "Canada, the Gulf crisis and collective security," in Fen Osler Hampson and Christopher J. Maule, eds., *Canada among Nations 1990–91: After the Cold War* (Ottawa: Carleton University Press, 1991), 241–80. John Kirton, "Liberating Kuwait: Canada and the Persian Gulf War, 1990–91," in Don Munton and John Kirton, eds., *Canadian Foreign Policy: Selected Cases* (Scarborough: Prentice Hall, 1992), 382–93 adds detail, but its major arguments are challenged convincingly by the latter sections of Harald von Riekhoff, "Canada and collective security," in David B. Dewitt and David Leyton-Brown, *Canada's International Security Policy* (Scarborough: Prentice Hall, 1995), 240–50. On public opinion, see Kim R. Nossal, "Quantum leaping: The Gulf debate in Australia and Canada," in Michael McKinley, ed., *The Gulf War: Critical Perspectives* (Canberra: Allen & Unwin, 1994), 48–71. On the Security Council implications, see Adam Chapnick, *Canada on the United Nations Security Council: A Small Power on a Large Stage* (Vancouver: UBC Press, 2019), 149–51. For primary source evidence, see James McGrath and Arthur Milnes, eds., *Age of the Offered Hand* (Kingston: School of Policy Studies, 2009), 55–62, 66–8, and 75–8 and Brian Mulroney, *Memoirs 1939–1993* (Toronto: McClelland and Stewart, 2007), 799–802, 833–5.

8

Jean Chrétien, Frugality, and Boldness, 1993–2001

Jean Chrétien

In October 1993, Jean Chrétien became Canada's twentieth prime minister. A plain-spoken politician who evinced a small-town populism reflecting his roots in Shawinigan, Quebec, Chrétien was first elected as a Liberal MP in 1963 and had served in Cabinet under Pierre Trudeau and John Turner. Chrétien's Liberals won a sizeable majority, a victory made easier by ongoing divisions among the political right: the Progressive Conservatives bled support to the upstart, Western-based Reform Party as well as to the separatist Bloc Québécois (BQ). These ongoing fractures contributed to Liberal electoral successes in 1997 and 2000. Chrétien's hold on power was such that one veteran political journalist likened him to a "friendly dictator."[1]

When the Liberals took over, the Canadian economy was in free fall, unemployment was accelerating, and decades of profligate deficit spending meant that Ottawa risked default. In January 1995, the *Wall Street Journal* dubbed Canada "an honorary member of the Third World."[2] In response, Finance Minister Paul Martin reduced transfer payments to the provinces and instituted massive funding cuts across the government. Remaining public servants faced frozen wages and crimped operating budgets. "It's no pleasure at all," Chrétien said of the austerity measures. "I'm not doctrinaire, a right-winger. I'm a Liberal, and I feel like a Liberal, and it is painful. But it is needed."[3] In 1998, thanks to the combination of Martin's cuts and a booming US economy, Ottawa posted its first balanced budget since 1972. Over the remainder of Chrétien's time in office, the Liberals ran surpluses, paid down debt, and slowly restored program spending.

The state of the economy might not have been the Liberals' most pressing initial concern. Thanks to its 54 seats in Quebec, the BQ formed the official Opposition. Leader Lucien Bouchard leveraged his status and experience as a former Canadian ambassador to Paris to promote separatism among a series of high-profile visiting dignitaries, including US President Bill Clinton. Bouchard was further emboldened by the 1994 provincial election victory of the separatist Parti Québécois (PQ). In response, Chrétien personally lobbied foreign

Canada First, Not Canada Alone: A History of Canadian Foreign Policy. Adam Chapnick and Asa McKercher,
Oxford University Press. © Oxford University Press 2024. DOI: 10.1093/oso/9780197653715.003.0009

174 CANADA FIRST, NOT CANADA ALONE

leaders to support federalism and declared that Canadian embassy officials would accompany all travelling provincial representatives.[4] These moves proved successful. In 1995, French President Jacques Chirac softened his previous support for Quebec separatism.[5] That same year, Clinton reflected publicly on how "a strong and united Canada ha[d] been a wonderful partner for the United States and an incredibly important and constructive citizen throughout the entire world."[6]

The American president's comments anticipated a 30 October 1995 provincial referendum on Quebec's future within Canada. The campaign began well for the federalist side, but support for separatism grew amid the Martin funding cuts and a weak economy. Direct interventions by a chastened Chrétien and others culminated in a rally in Montreal just days before the referendum. Tens of thousands of Canadians voiced their support for federalism. The result was close: 50.6 per cent voted *non* to separation; 49.4 per cent voted *oui*. Just over 50,000 votes divided the two sides.[7]

NAFTA and Beyond

The state of the Canadian economy all but dictated that the Liberals' international agenda would have a strong commercial focus. Having served as minister of trade and commerce in 1976–7, Chrétien believed in free trade. Despite Liberal campaign rhetoric that sowed doubts over Canada's commitment to NAFTA, Ottawa quickly ratified the deal, much to the relief of the United States.[8]

With NAFTA affirmed, the newly renamed Department of Foreign Affairs and International Trade (DFAIT) sought to diversify Canada's trade and investment links. As Minister Roy MacLaren explained, NAFTA was a "nucleus for a more open, global trading endeavour."[9] Ottawa supported the advent of the World Trade Organization (WTO), formed in 1995 out of the old General Agreement on Tariffs and Trade, but its primary focus was bilateral. In 1994, Chrétien launched the first Team Canada mission to China. Federal, provincial, and municipal government officials, businesspeople, and university administrators travelled together to promote investment and trading prospects. "Team Canada was the prime minister's chosen instrument to compensate for generations of political neglect," recalled his foreign affairs advisor, "to blast awareness of the world outside North America into the consciousness of Canadians, and to expose Asians to Canada."[10] Subsequent missions went to South Asia (1996), South Korea, Thailand, and the Philippines (1997); Latin America (1998); Japan (1999); and again to China (2001). Team Canada also visited Los Angeles and Dallas in 2001.[11]

Figure 8.1 Canadian Prime Minister Jean Chrétien rides a bicycle down a street in Shanghai, 10 November 1994. Jean Chrétien was a small-town, populist prime minister who had a knack for exuding a common touch. In this picture from 10 November 1994, dressed in a business suit and a (Liberal) red tie, he climbed aboard a bicycle in Shanghai, China, all but compelling his Chinese-appointed military guard to run alongside. Chrétien's East Asia visit included over 400 provincial premiers, city mayors, and Canadian business elite—the largest peacetime Team Canada trade mission ever. It resulted in over $2.6 billion in signed contracts and the potential for several billion dollars more. Although most of the deals involved Chinese businesses, the Canadians said virtually nothing publicly about China's dismal human rights record. After a stop in Hong Kong as part of Remembrance Day and brief visits to the Asia-Pacific Economic Cooperation summit in Jakarta, Indonesia, and the new Canadian embassy in Hanoi, Vietnam, Chrétien returned to Canada overwhelmingly proud of his economic achievements. The Canadian Press/Tom Hanson/CP2670946.

176 CANADA FIRST, NOT CANADA ALONE

Emerging economies in Asia and Latin America were tempting targets for Canadian officials eager to promote new avenues of economic activity and to take advantage of rapid changes in transportation and communication together known as globalization. The speed of travel, ease of foreign investment, and changes wrought by the internet created an increasingly interconnected global economy, leading one proponent of the new dynamic to declare "The World Is Flat."[12]

But globalization had its downsides. Several Asian and Latin American countries targeted for Canadian economic expansion had poor labour and environmental standards and human rights records. Initially, the Chrétien government was unconcerned. As Foreign Minister André Ouellet explained in 1995, the Liberal government planned to diversify Canada's trading partners "irrespective of their human rights records."[13] Indonesia was one such country that received considerable focus even as its government repressed domestic dissidents and committed acts of ethnic cleansing in occupied East Timor.[14] When Indonesian dictator Suharto attended the 1997 Asia-Pacific Economic Cooperation (APEC) summit in Vancouver, a broad-based collection of thousands of opponents of globalization—human rights defenders, environmentalists, feminists, union members, Indigenous activists, cultural nationalists, and anti-capitalists—protested. Their Peoples' Summit coalesced around the theory that economic globalization was serving the exclusive interests of Western multinational corporations that plundered resources, exploited cheap labour, and ignored the interests of local citizens, particularly in the Global South. The World Bank and International Monetary Fund became particular targets for making poverty alleviation efforts contingent on recipient governments imposing austerity measures. Some of the criticism was prescient: financial deregulation ultimately led to economic crises in East Asia and Latin America.

Relations with the United States

The Liberals' support for open markets, deregulation, and austerity—what became known as neoliberalism—parallelled shifts within Tony Blair's Labour Party in the United Kingdom and Bill Clinton's Democratic Party in the United States. Indeed, the Liberal government and Clinton administration had much in common. Although Chrétien had campaigned on skepticism of the close personal relationships that Mulroney had established with Ronald Reagan and George H.W. Bush, he signalled to the White House that a lack of chumminess did not have to prevent constructive ties. "I don't want to get too close to you," he explained to Clinton at their first meeting in 1993. "Canada is your best friend, largest trading partner, and closest ally, but we are also an independent country. Keeping some distance will be good for both of us. If we look as though we're the 51st state of the United States, there's nothing we can do for you internationally." He then added, in an astonishing turn of phrase, "But if we look independent enough, we can do things for you that even the CIA cannot do."[15] Chrétien and Clinton ultimately became golfing buddies, though the prime minister sought to hide these visits from the press. Their personal relationship undoubtedly contributed to Clinton's willingness to speak out in favour of Canadian unity prior to the 1995 referendum.

Canada–US co-operation during the Chrétien-Clinton years (1993–2001) was evident in response to a crisis in Haiti. The Haitian military had overthrown the short-lived government of Jean-Bertrand Aristide in 1991, and the Clinton administration sought to restore his rule. An initial diplomatic effort failed, so in 1994 US forces formed an international coalition, the UN Mission in Haiti (UNMIH), to return Aristide to power. Since Washington had little interest in occupying the island, Clinton appealed to Canada to take over leadership of the mission in March 1996.[16] Chrétien was mindful of Canada's own Haitian community and of his country's interest in regional stability in the Caribbean. He was also intent on leveraging Haiti to press Washington for support on other matters. As he accidentally revealed over a hot microphone in 1997, "So he [President Clinton] calls me, okay, I send my soldiers. Thank you very much, but later I ask for something in return."[17] Clinton took the comment in stride, telling reporters that he would "get even" with the prime minister on the golf course.[18]

Chrétien's gaffe aside, Canada–US relations were generally smooth during this period. Two notable exceptions included split-run magazines and Cuba. The former issue, recalled one diplomat with 20 years' experience in the bilateral relationship, was the "most serious dispute I have witnessed, in both length and bitterness."[19] The popularity of American magazines in Canada was a decades-long concern for both Canadian nationalists and publishers. Split-run magazines, which kept American content but included Canadian advertisements, took advertising dollars away from Canadian publications. Nationalists, meanwhile, feared Canadians would consume too much American content. In 1965, the Canadian government had banned split-run magazines that were published abroad from entering the country. Three decades later, *Sports Illustrated* circumvented the ban by printing a split-run edition in Canada. The Chrétien government imposed a hefty tax on split-run advertising revenue, so the Clinton administration took Canada to the WTO. The organization decided in favour of the Americans and ruled against the 1965 ban. In 1999, the two countries finally reached a complex settlement that included a cap on the amount of advertising that could appear in a split-run magazine. Commenting on the dispute, one journalist observed a fundamental disconnect in that "the Americans said the magazine business was just that—business. The Canadians clung to the position that it was something more—culture."[20]

As for Cuba, Clinton's ambassador in Ottawa later wrote that this issue "was the focus of the only real, measurable difference between our foreign policies."[21] Since the early 1960s, the communist island had been subjected to a US economic embargo, one that Canada had refused to join. With the fall of the Soviet Union, Cuba's economy plunged into chaos. The Chrétien government offered economic assistance, increased trade and investment, and opened the way for an influx of tourists, while the US Congress strengthened the American embargo by adding a series of extraterritorial provisions that threatened Canadian sovereignty. Canada's diplomats protested, the White House relented, and Chrétien used the positive outcome to his political advantage. "I like to stand up to the Americans," he admitted. "It's popular...people like it, but you have to be careful because they're our friends."[22]

Human Rights and Human Security

Chrétien sought to use Canada's economic leverage in Cuba to promote market and political reforms and improve human rights. As his second foreign minister, Lloyd Axworthy, explained: "we share the end objective [with the Americans], which is to see a transition in Cuba into a democratic society. We have chosen different methods."[23] Dictator Fidel Castro resented this effort. After a stormy showdown with the Cuban leader in 1998, Chrétien declared that he was putting "northern ice" on the bilateral relationship.[24]

The Liberals were more willing to countenance Chinese misbehaviour. The communist regime's efforts to transform the country's economy in the 1990s led to an influx of Western officials keen to promote investment and tap into the billion-person market. Chrétien recognized the economic possibilities of a closer relationship with Beijing and found support from the Chinese diaspora and groups such as the Canada-China Business Council and the Canada-China Legislative Association. As for the regime's repression of dissidents and the lack of political rights, Chrétien offered the assurance, common among Western leaders at the time, "that opening of the market, the opening of these countries to outsiders coming with our values and traditions will help a bit."[25] Less convinced, Axworthy secured the prime minister's permission to engage in a human rights dialogue.[26] This effort and others achieved little. Sino-Canadian relations were limited in political terms, with Beijing's rights record "the principal obstacle."[27]

On paper, human rights promotion was a major goal for the Chrétien government. A 1995 white paper, *Canada in the World*, had listed three pillars of Canadian foreign policy: promoting prosperity and employment, protecting the country's security, and projecting its values and culture.[28] For the prime minister, the first objective clearly took precedence. For Axworthy, efforts to promote human rights in Cuba and China were more important. A former left-leaning student activist, Axworthy had studied international relations and held a PhD in politics. During his years as foreign minister (1996–2000), he put his own stamp on world affairs by recognizing Canada's "duty as a global citizen."[29] His human security agenda sought to capitalize on increasing global interconnectedness and the emergence of transnational non-governmental organizations (NGOs). It prioritized the rights and security of people and recognized, as he put it, "that sustained economic development, human rights and fundamental freedoms, the rule of law, good governance, sustainable development and social equity are as important to global peace as arms control and disarmament."[30]

The result was a flurry of Canadian diplomatic activity. Axworthy championed the process leading to the 1997 Ottawa Agreement to ban the production and sale of anti-personnel land mines. He also played a role in the negotiation of the Rome Statute of 1998, which established an International Criminal Court (ICC).[31] The ICC provided a means to prosecute individuals accused of war crimes, genocide, and crimes against humanity.[32] Canada's UN Ambassador Robert Fowler had Axworthy's support in spearheading an initiative at the Security Council that produced the Kimberley Process Certification Scheme on conflict diamonds. Canada was also a strong supporter of the Security Council's resolution 1325 on women, peace, and security. Finally, in September 2000, in Winnipeg, Axworthy hosted an International Conference on War-Affected Children, bringing together more than 50 governments and dozens of NGOs to address the tragedy of children caught in war zones, either as victims or child soldiers.

For its supporters, the focus on human security allowed Canada to play an outsized role in world affairs. It reflected a broader sense that "soft power"—a termed coined by political scientist Joseph Nye—was a potent tool of statecraft.[33] Proponents claimed that "negotiating, building coalitions and presenting diplomatic initiatives" could influence "the behaviour of other nations not through military intimidation, but through a variety of diplomatic tools."[34] For its detractors, the human security agenda was a distraction from the more serious business of advancing Canadian national interests along more traditional lines. To them, Axworthy was a practitioner of "pulpit diplomacy," full of stirring and self-aggrandizing rhetoric but devoid of meaningful results.[35]

National Defence and UN Peacekeeping

Critics particularly complained about the decline of the Canadian Forces. The Liberals cancelled a controversial contract to purchase new search-and-rescue helicopters, fulfilling an election pledge. Then, as the government pursued its austerity agenda, bases were shuttered, personnel made redundant, and further procurement efforts curtailed, leaving the Department of National Defence demoralized and with increasingly outdated equipment.

In spite of the cuts, Chrétien refused to decrease the military's operational tempo. The Mulroney government had committed Canada to over a dozen UN peacekeeping missions. In Somalia, the situation was complicated by the conduct of members of the Canadian Airborne Regiment, who tortured and killed a local teenager. The incident and its attempted cover-up by senior departmental officials exposed deep problems within the unit, leading to its disbandment and the end of Canada's mission.[36] In the former Yugoslavia, Canadian peacekeepers witnessed horrific ethnic cleansing but were unable to prevent atrocities or even adequately defend themselves because of the restrictive UN resolutions authorizing their presence. As Chrétien's foreign policy advisor put it, Canada was "in over its head."[37] NATO ultimately imposed a military solution that brought most of the regional fighting to an end, but not until the UN's shortcomings undermined the traditional idea of blue helmeted peacekeepers inserting themselves between warring sides.

The 1994 Rwandan genocide likely inflicted the greatest damage on the reputation of UN peacekeeping. Soldiers failed to prevent the mass slaughter of hundreds of thousands. Their commander, Canadian Major-General Roméo Dallaire, later wrote that "the international community, of which the UN is only a symbol, failed to move beyond self-interest for the sake of Rwanda."[38] Increasingly, it seemed that what was required to end conflicts was peacemaking—the use of concerted force by international coalitions.[39]

The crisis of peacekeeping in the early to mid-1990s challenged an important pillar of Canada's foreign policy, at least as far as the Canadian public was concerned. During the Cold War, Canada had participated in every UN peacekeeping mission and contributed 10 per cent of the UN's total forces. "Canada has an exemplary record in peacekeeping," a Senate report concluded in 1993. "In fact, it is the sole military activity which Canadians fully support."[40] To its champions, peacekeeping was an important way for Canada to play an active role in a multilateral setting, one apart from the United States. "They think it is a nice way for Canadians to be present around the world," Chrétien stated in regard to public backing of peacekeeping efforts. "We are always there, like the Boy Scouts."[41] Detractors criticized peacekeeping as a distraction from serious military matters, such as defending Canadian territory and sovereignty, and complained about the negative impact of budget cuts on increasingly overstretched forces.[42] In the aftermath of Rwanda, Somalia, and other failures, Canadian participation in UN peacekeeping missions declined precipitously.[43]

When the situation demanded it, the Chrétien government was still willing to use the Canadian Forces for more traditional purposes. In the 1995 Turbot "war," naval vessels were deployed to intercept Spanish trawlers fishing illegally in Canadian waters. The incident had a deleterious impact on Canadian relations with Europe as Spain blocked efforts to deepen Canada–European Union ties.[44] Four years later, the Canadian Forces contributed to NATO operations to stop acts of genocide in Kosovo. The Kosovo War, as senior Canadian diplomat Paul Heinbecker put it, was "a war of values, a war for Human Security."[45] It also reinforced Canada's commitment to NATO and to Europe. In 1997, the Chrétien government supported NATO expansion into Central and Eastern Europe to incorporate three former members of the Soviet bloc: Hungary, Poland, and the Czech Republic.[46]

Departmental Decline

Jean Chrétien's first seven years in power were marked by internal crises and by accelerating links to a more globalized, but still fractious, post–Cold War world. His foreign policy advisor lauded his integration of "foreign- and domestic-policy goals from the outset to lead Canada out of the recession of the early 1990s by export-led growth."[47] Other observers have been less kind. "Pinchpenny diplomacy" is how political scientist Kim Richard Nossal characterized this approach to foreign affairs.[48] Under the Liberals, DFAIT's budget was cut nearly every year.[49] International development spending plummeted to its lowest level in decades. On the positive side, the percentage of women foreign service officers more than doubled to 28.2 per cent between 1984 and 1998, although few women held senior management positions.[50] Administratively, leadership within DFAIT was exercised by a "confusing triumvirate" of ministers of foreign affairs, international trade, and international development, while decision-making authority shifted to the prime minister and the Privy Council Office. This centralization of power created internal tensions and further diminished the role of the professional diplomats.[51] The collective result was a sense of Canada losing its way in a world that was becoming increasingly globalized.

Case Studies

Between 1993 and 2000, members of the Chrétien government directed a Canadian foreign policy that might best be described as "Canada first!" The exclamation point is critical. The overwhelming assertiveness of policy practitioners was unusual, as was their willingness to take significant public diplomatic risks.

The first case explores Fisheries Minister Brian Tobin's brash defence of Canadian interests in the establishment of a global conservation regime for declining fish stocks in the North Atlantic. Tobin's aggressive posture nearly resulted in an armed conflict between the Canadian navy and Canada's European allies. Cooler heads prevailed in what has since become known as the Turbot War.

Foreign Minister Lloyd Axworthy was equally bold. His successful advocacy of an international treaty to ban anti-personnel landmines, the focus of the second case, risked the opprobrium of the American diplomatic establishment, not to mention members of Canada's own Department of National Defence. Axworthy's new emphasis on privileging human security was equally critical in the third case: Canada's involvement in NATO's intervention into Kosovo in 1999. Here, Ottawa engaged the Canadian Forces in a combat role without the explicit approval of the UN Security Council.

The Beyond the Book case examines yet another radical, and successful, Canadian initiative to increase the intensity of the UN sanctions regime to prevent rogue actors from profiting from the illegal diamond trade in Angola.

The Turbot War, 1994–1995

What constitutes a Canadian foreign policy victory?

Practitioners, journalists, and scholars rarely disagree over Canadian foreign policy as they did in the aftermath of a violent fishing dispute between Canada and Spain in 1995. In his memoirs, Canada's Minister of Fisheries and Oceans Brian Tobin reflected: "Did we gain anything from breaking the widely accepted character of Canada as a peace-loving, non-belligerent nation in defence of an ugly fish? Yes, yes and yes."[52] Journalist Michael Harris described the outcome as "Canada's victory."[53] International law professor Allen Springer called it a "major victory."[54] In the eyes of the foreign and defence policy advisor to the prime minister, James Bartleman, Canada's conduct was embarrassing: "We learned the dark arts quickly, and...some of us did not know when to stop...Lester Pearson must have turned over in his grave."[55] Historians Norman Hillmer and J.L. Granatstein saw this as "no victory, except perhaps for

JEAN CHRÉTIEN, FRUGALITY, AND BOLDNESS, 1993–2001   183

unbridled nationalism and adventurism."[56] This case examines the idea of success in Canadian foreign policy.

For much of the late twentieth century, one-quarter of employed Newfoundlanders worked in the fishing industry.[57] By the early 1990s, a combination of reckless overfishing (by Canadians and Europeans), scientific errors, and unanticipated climate change had caused a collapse of the fish stocks. When the Mulroney government imposed a moratorium on fishing to allow the resource to recover, tens of thousands lost their jobs, as did every Progressive Conservative MP from Newfoundland after the 1993 federal election.[58]

Liberal Prime Minister Jean Chrétien appointed his trusted Newfoundland lieutenant and former speechwriter, Brian Tobin, as his first minister of fisheries and oceans. Tobin's political and communications acumen, not to mention his "in your face"[59] approach to conflict management, were well-suited to the portfolio. In 1979, Ottawa had seized 19 US tuna boats. In 1987, the department's "armed-boarding" policy had resulted in warning shots being fired at American ships fishing illegally off the coast of Nova Scotia.[60]

Such aggressive unilateralism had traditionally been accompanied by efforts to strengthen the global conservation regime. The 1982 Law of the Sea convention had created a 200-mile exclusive economic zone (EEZ) for coastal states. Fish knew no borders, but the moment they moved beyond the EEZ, they became exempt from the coastal state's conservation efforts. The Northwest Atlantic Fisheries Organization (NAFO) and its predecessor, the International Commission of the Northwest Atlantic Fisheries, had, since the late 1940s, been tasked with providing a framework to effectively manage fishing in the North Atlantic so that the industry could remain sustainable. Without enforcement powers, it proved ineffective. In 1992, UN members pledged to establish what eventually became the UN Conference on Straddling Fish Stocks and Highly Migratory Fish Stocks, but progress was slow.[61]

On 2 April 1994, in the aftermath of a failed effort to have member states of NAFO enforce the quotas that were established for each species, the Department of Fisheries and Oceans (DFO) ordered the arrest of the Canadian owner of the *Kristina Logos* for illegal fishing in international waters.[62] The following month, Ottawa amended the Coastal Fisheries Protection Act. In Tobin's words, the legislation provided "the authority to enforce rules that would protect straddling stocks from commercial extinction, including taking action beyond our 200-mile limit."[63] The latter power was unprecedented and quite possibly illegal under international law. A European Union (EU) spokesperson compared it "to the actions of Saddam Hussein."[64] Tobin responded that overfishing was "a 'genuine desecration' of the world's food basket and... 'all of our best Boy Scout behaviour was yielding nothing.'"[65] Seizure of two US ships soon followed. Tobin also reduced Canada's own turbot quota by 75 per cent—the

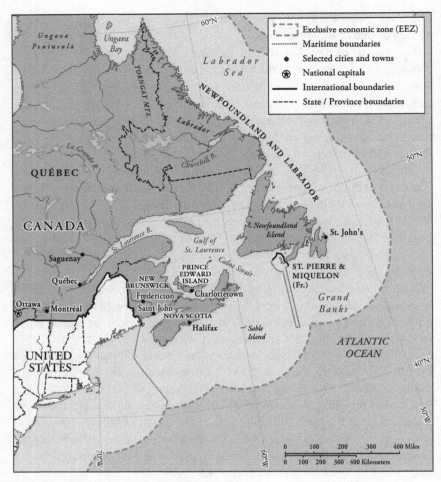

Figure 8.2 The Turbot War.

turbot, or Greenland halibut, had become the focus of the industry in light of the decline of the cod—and the DFO charged four Canadian shipmasters for overfishing later that summer.[66]

Canada's radical posture caught its traditional allies by surprise. Spain and Portugal had been harvesting turbot aggressively since 1991. Thousands of jobs depended on the industry, and the Spanish government's political opponents were capitalizing on its appearance of weakness.[67] When Tobin lobbied NAFO to dramatically reduce the total allowable catch of turbot for 1995, Spain's minister of fisheries and agriculture demanded 75 per cent of it for Spain alone. Ultimately, Tobin's superior negotiating skills meant that Canada was allocated 60 per cent, while the entire EU received just 12 per cent.[68]

The EU fisheries commissioner, Emma Bonino, rejected the NAFO ruling and announced that the union planned to harvest 69 per cent of the total allowable catch. By early March, EU vessels had already nearly doubled their NAFO quota.[69] In response, Ottawa included Spain and Portugal in its controversial regulations that restricted fishing outside of Canada's EEZ and threatened to seize any vessels that failed to comply. The Spanish ambassador objected vociferously, as did conflict-averse Canadian officials from the Departments of Justice, Foreign Affairs, and National Defence, as well as members of the Royal Canadian Mounted Police. Nonetheless, Prime Minister Chrétien and his Cabinet, who owed their electoral success in Newfoundland to their promise to protect the fisheries, backed Tobin.[70]

On 9 March 1995, the Canadian government ordered the arrest of the Spanish trawler *Estai* for repeated violations of the conservation regime. The ship's captain, Enrique Davila Gonzalez, cut his fishing nets and twice prevented Canadians from boarding, but after a series of warning shots from a ship-mounted machine gun aboard the Coast Guard's *Cape Roger*, he surrendered. Gonzalez was charged with "unlawful fishing, failing to stop when required, obstructing a fisheries officer, and throwing fishing equipment overboard."[71]

The Canadian public was ecstatic. According to one poll, 89 per cent backed Ottawa's actions and 58 per cent would have supported a further use of force if Spanish fishers persisted. Tobin received a standing ovation in the House of Commons and was embraced as a hero in his native Newfoundland. Nonetheless, the following day, Ottawa dispatched a high-level delegation to Brussels to negotiate a resolution to the crisis with the European Commission.[72]

It was a prudent move. The commission called the arrest "organized piracy."[73] Its Council of Ministers suspended negotiations with Ottawa on a series of collaborative scientific and technical initiatives and hinted at the possibility of economic sanctions. The government of Spain dispatched a warship, the *Vigia*, to the Grand Banks and authorized it "to use 'deadly force' by opening fire to protect its fishing vessels."[74]

As the negotiations sputtered, Canadian patrol vessels cut the nets of another Spanish ship, the *Pescamaro Uno*, outside of Canada's EEZ. Tobin and Bonino were in New York at the time, attending the UN Conference on Straddling and Highly Migratory Fish Stocks. When a flabbergasted Bonino accused Ottawa of fabricating evidence against the *Estai*, Tobin responded with what journalist Peter Jennings called "the best public relations stunt he had ever seen in politics."[75] Members of the media were invited to walk to a barge in New York's East River, where Canadian officials displayed the illegal nets that the ship's captain had cut during his attempted escape. As the minister recalls: "We had to get our message across powerfully, and displaying the net at that time and in that

186 CANADA FIRST, NOT CANADA ALONE

fashion did the job.... Bonino and the EU challenged us to put up or shut up, and we responded in a manner that left them, not us, speechless."[76]

While Spain took its case to the International Court of Justice, Canadian inspectors discovered that Gonzalez had kept two sets of books; had used nets with a mesh size that contravened European and NAFO regulations; and had hidden 25 tonnes of American plaice (a fish under moratorium) in a secret compartment aboard the ship.[77] When Spanish representatives rejected a final Canadian offer to resolve the dispute on 14 April, Chrétien ordered a frigate and a destroyer to join submarines already stationed off the east coast and promised action the following day. Just moments before what could have been a shooting war between two NATO allies, the Spanish agreed to the Canada-EU Control and Enforcement Agreement.[78]

The agreement set both Canada's and the EU's 1995 turbot quotas at 37 per cent of Total Allowable Catch. That summer, the UN Conference on Straddling Fish Stocks and Highly Migratory Fish Stocks finally established a functioning global regime.[79] Over the next five years, Canadian-EU conservation efforts improved, temporarily.[80] Bilateral relations recovered more slowly.[81]

When Prime Minister Chrétien reflected on the near war with Spain in his memoirs, he concluded: "We succeeded in putting a better international regime in place because of our forceful action."[82] The Canadian public was ecstatic, and Newfoundlanders made Tobin their premier shortly thereafter. Regrettably, noted one senior official, "Spain, bitter and humiliated, would make us pay a price by throwing roadblock after roadblock into Canada's efforts to forge closer ties with Europe for years to come."[83] Whether the outcome constitutes a foreign policy success story might never be entirely clear.

The International Campaign to Ban Anti-Personnel Landmines, 1994–1997

How do changes in communications technology shape the international negotiation environment?

Jean Chrétien called the international treaty to ban landmines "one of the greatest achievements in Canada's diplomatic history."[84] Thanks in part to aggressive Canadian leadership and a constructive partnership with a collection of NGOs, 122 states signed a binding agreement that prohibited the use, production, stockpiling, and transfer of anti-personnel landmines.[85] The implications of this success form the basis of this case.

Unlike other weapons of war, landmines disproportionately harm civilians. Militaries do not normally de-mine when they leave the battlefield, and the mines that remain are hard to identify and even harder to remove. The International Committee of the Red Cross (ICRC) first brought the issue to the world's attention in the 1970s. Nonetheless, the 1980 Convention on Certain Conventional Weapons (CCW) failed to end what was fast becoming a humanitarian catastrophe in parts of Africa, Central America, and Southeast Asia. By the early 1990s, landmines—too often carelessly spread by militaries and rebel groups—were annually killing or injuring 25,000 innocent civilians, many of them children.[86]

In 1991, representatives of the Women's Commission for Refugee Women and Children urged the US Congress to act. Asia Watch, Physicians for Human Rights, and the Vietnam Veterans of America Foundation (VVAF) soon added their voices. In 1992, Washington announced a one-year moratorium on landmine exports. France called for a review of the CCW the following year.[87] By then, the International Campaign to Ban Landmines (ICBL), initially a coalition of six NGOs coordinated by the VVAF's Jody Williams, had begun to assemble what ultimately became nearly 1000 organizations in almost fifty countries.[88] In 1994, US President Bill Clinton publicly endorsed their cause.[89]

Canada's initial engagement in the issue was hesitant and uneven. Chrétien took a personal interest after a meeting with ICRC President Cornelio Sommaruga in May 1994. He raised the topic at the G7 summit in Naples that June, to no avail.[90] Chrétien's concerns did not reach Canada's Department of Foreign Affairs and International Trade (DFAIT), where the incoming deputy director in the Non-Proliferation, Arms Control, and Disarmament Division was warned by his predecessor that "nobody here is interested in this file, and nobody else in the world will let it go anywhere."[91] The Department of National Defence maintained that landmines remained a necessary weapon of war.

As one analyst notes, the evolution of the official Canadian position was accidental.[92] After the UN mistakenly identified Canada as having already issued an export moratorium on landmines, DFAIT announced one, ostensibly to avoid public embarrassment. The move engaged the outgoing Foreign Minister André Ouellet, who had never understood how Ottawa could fund de-mining projects around the world and yet still tolerate landmines writ large. In January 1996, just weeks before his retirement, he announced Canadian support for a total ban. His successor, Lloyd Axworthy, arrived at the job to which he had long aspired in search of opportunities for activism. Landmines were an obvious choice.[93]

The timing was fortuitous. International momentum for a ban was growing, and activists were losing faith in the ability of the consensus-based CCW to effect change. In May, working alongside members of the ICBL, the Government of Canada invited interested state and non-state actors to a strategy conference. Attendees would self-select based on their explicit commitment

188   CANADA FIRST, NOT CANADA ALONE

to a total ban. Those unwilling to commit, including the leading military powers, could merely observe.[94] This unique, three-pronged approach—"(1) a partnership between states and NGOs in the conduct of international diplomacy; (2) the practice of bringing together small- and medium-sized, like-minded states into a coalition; and (3) a willingness to operate outside of the normal channels and fora"—became known as the Ottawa Process.[95] The Chrétien government would use it regularly over the next four years.

On 3 October, Axworthy welcomed 50 states and 24 observers to Ottawa. The conference plenaries and workshops were notable for the collaboration between diplomatic officials and NGO representatives.[96] As it became clear that the Belgians were aspiring to lead on the anti-landmine initiative, the Canadian delegation considered a radical move: Axworthy would conclude the event by inviting the delegates to return the following year to sign a ban treaty.[97] The foreign minister's announcement was greeted with cheers from the UN and NGO communities. US representatives, as well as much of the international diplomatic establishment, were furious that the Canadians were undermining the traditional negotiating process and depriving Washington of control.[98]

What followed was unprecedented. There would be just 15 months to draft a treaty to which sufficient signatories could agree. In his memoirs, Axworthy describes a three-track process: traditional diplomatic negotiations, a complementary global public relations campaign, and the solidification of political Ottawa's whole-hearted commitment to the cause.[99] A core group of middle-power countries coordinated the diplomatic effort. Austria had brought a draft treaty to the first Ottawa conference and agreed to serve as the "pen" going forward. Multiple consultation sessions among potential signatory states and members of the ICBL followed. They were informed and complemented by a series of regional meetings. The formal diplomatic work culminated at a conference in Oslo, Norway, in September 1997. Although Oslo failed to convince the Americans, newly elected governments in France and Britain proclaimed their support.[100]

To enable the success of the public campaign, the Canadian government kept the ICBL fully informed and championed its participation in the formal negotiation process.[101] NGOs were particularly effective in involving the Global South, whose importance was spotlighted when Britain's Princess Diana, one of the world's most famous ban proponents, travelled to Angola to meet with young landmine victims. The ICBL and its coordinator were ultimately awarded the Nobel Peace Prize for their innovative efforts.[102]

At home, members of Parliament from across the political spectrum embraced the cause. Chrétien lobbied on Canada's behalf at every multilateral meeting he attended, and his Cabinet approved the necessary financial support.[103]

The Ottawa Conference of December 1997 celebrated the completion of the Convention on the Prohibition of the Use, Stockpiling, Production, and

Transfer of Anti-Personnel Mines and on their Destruction. Over 2000 political, diplomatic, and UN officials, practitioners, landmine survivors, and NGO representatives witnessed the extraordinary event, which included a commitment to develop an "Agenda for Mine Action" to ensure the treaty's implementation.[104] A new NGO, Landmine Monitor, was formed to track compliance.[105] Within 15 months, the convention had achieved the 60 ratifications necessary to come into force. Although the leading users of landmines did not initially sign the treaty, within less than a decade, nearly every remaining landmine producer began to wind down its production and distribution processes.[106] The campaign had succeeded in creating a new international norm.[107]

To Axworthy, the success of the landmines campaign legitimized "a new way of looking at the very notion of security and its preservation."[108] The human dimensions of security, elements over which states did not hold a monopoly, had achieved a level of importance that could no longer be ignored. Others have reflected on "the emergence of new networks of decision-making and public deliberation, partnerships between states and non-state actors, and mechanisms of accountability"[109]—a "new multilateralism,"[110] so to speak.

Such assessments might undervalue the impact of an ongoing revolution in communications technology. In the aftermath of the second Ottawa conference, Axworthy wrote: "In a wired world, knowledge and information confer influence, and that influence is power."[111] He was right. As one analyst has argued: "The distinctive feature of the Ottawa Process was not greater representativeness but greater publicity.... Military bureaucrats, unaccustomed to providing public reasons for their weapons systems, found themselves inadequate to explain the need for mines and their arguments failed in the court of public opinion."[112] In contrast, the anti-landmine forces skilfully used fax machines, cellular phone call-in campaigns, electronic mail, websites, newsletters, and captivating videos, in addition to television and print media, to dominate the popular narrative.[113] Their technological superiority persisted just long enough to see the landmines campaign through. But it was never sustainable.

NATO's Military Intervention in Kosovo, 1998–1999

What role can, or should, the Canadian Forces play in Canadian foreign policy?

In theory, states maintain militaries as forces of last resort. When all else fails, soldiers, sailors, aviators, and members of the Special Forces put service before self and employ violence to defend the national interest. The need for a military deterrent was obvious during the Cold War. Canada and its allies faced a clear and threatening adversary: the Soviet Union. On the ground, militaries were useful as peacekeepers; by maintaining distance between opposing states, they prevented smaller conflicts from implicating the rival great powers. Once the Cold War ended, the role of national armed forces, particularly NATO's collective defence provisions, was less clear. This case examines how the Canadian military came to be used in pursuit of humanitarian objectives in the Balkans, or how the national interest evolved to include "the prevention of crimes against humanity."[114]

For over 700 years, Kosovo's Serbian and Albanian inhabitants have contested control of the southern province of what was known for much as the twentieth century as Yugoslavia. Between 1987 and 1989, an ambitious new nationalist ruler, Slobodan Milošević, began to consolidate Serbia's power. His chaotic and ruthless policy of ethnic cleansing led to Yugoslavia's collapse. Western military intervention limited Serbia's advances in Bosnia, but the 1995 Dayton peace talks that quelled the fighting made no mention of Milošević's efforts to subjugate the largely peaceful Kosovar Albanians. The latter felt abandoned, and some formed the Kosovo Liberation Army (KLA). As one Canadian official recalls, over the next two years, "On the ground in Kosovo, matters progressively worsened, with KLA gunmen killing Serbian policemen, and the

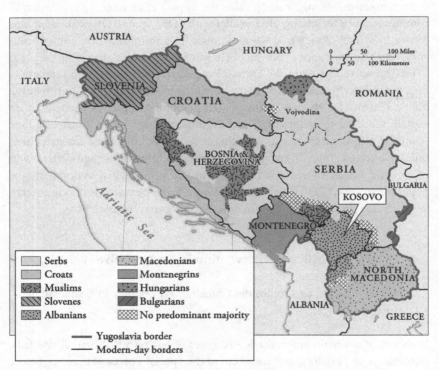

Figure 8.3 Map of the Former Yugoslavia and Surrounding Region in 1998.

Milosevic regime striking back savagely."[115] The displacement of tens of thousands of Kosovar Albanians soon made it impossible for Milošević to claim that their repression was an internal matter.[116]

The humanitarian crisis in Kosovo coincided with a shift in Canadian thinking about the relationship between state sovereignty and international security.[117] Independent, sovereign states were supposed to be the ultimate guardians of a just and peaceful world, but leaders of some of those states had begun to violate the human rights of their own citizens.[118] Human security became a national priority just as United Nations peacekeepers were proving incapable of protecting civilian lives in Bosnia prior to the Dayton meetings.[119] NATO, on the other hand, was effective in pushing back the Serbs in Bosnia, and public affinity for the organization among Canadians, the national media, and members of the armed forces was strong.[120]

By 1998, Milošević's ethnic cleansing had become intolerable. UN Security Council Resolution (SCR) 1160 (1998) of 31 March imposed a weapons embargo on the region.[121] At a ministerial meeting that May, Canadian representatives supported NATO's commitment to military action if diplomacy failed. In October, in anticipation of US special envoy Richard Holbrooke's direct negotiations with Milošević, NATO approved an activation order that committed its members to an air campaign. The threat seemed to work. Milošević agreed to the Kosovo Verification Mission—to be coordinated by the Organisation for Security and Co-operation in Europe—and to withdraw most of his paramilitary forces. The agreement was affirmed by SCR 1203 (1998).[122]

But Milošević was merely stalling.[123] On 15 January 1999, Serbian forces massacred and mutilated the bodies of 45 Albanian civilians at the village of Račak (Reçak). Shortly thereafter, the UN High Commissioner for Refugees estimated that the number of displaced Kosovar Albanians had reached 300,000, many of whom began fleeing into neighbouring Macedonia and Albania. While Canada's European allies negotiated unsuccessfully with the Russians (Serbia's proverbial ally), Ottawa used its recently acquired seat on the Security Council to lobby for UN involvement. Once Russian and Chinese intransigence made it clear that any resolution would be vetoed, the Canadians became full-fledged supporters of a NATO military intervention.[124]

Political scientist Michael Manulak offers the most compelling explanation for Ottawa's decision to proceed without the UN's legal authority: "Canadian and NATO policy makers believed that no [Security Council] resolution was better than proceeding in defiance of a vetoed one.... The perceived urgency of the crisis also contributed."[125] More broadly, Ottawa engaged the armed forces for a variety of complementary reasons. NATO's legitimacy was at stake and Canada would not be able to shape the peace to follow if it did not participate in the military intervention. At home, all of Canada's political parties supported the mission. Apart from the Serbian–Canadian community (many of whom were transfixed by Milošević's effective propaganda campaign), Canadians as a whole believed the mission to be just. Media reports were similarly sympathetic to the use of force to support a humanitarian imperative.[126] In his memoirs, Lloyd Axworthy explained: "It was evident that 'hard power' might have to be used to protect against the abuses and atrocities that had become so endemic in the Balkans and elsewhere. If you are going to have standards and laws to protect people, then there are times when such laws have to be enforced."[127]

NATO launched the first air strikes of Operation Allied Force on 24 March 1999. Four Canadian CF-18 Hornets participated. The goal, according to two Canadian diplomats, was to destroy "Milosevic's war machine, while (i) incurring minimal Allied losses; (ii) inflicting the least possible number of civilian casualties; and (iii) synchronizing the campaign with a multitrack diplomatic effort."[128] Two days later, Moscow introduced a Security Council resolution condemning the bombing. Its defeat, 12–3, was interpreted by proponents of the military engagement as tacit council approval.[129] When the initial bombing campaign failed to fully achieve its aims, NATO had little choice but to increase the intensity of its efforts. Canadian CF-18s ultimately flew nearly 700 combat sorties and led approximately 10 per cent of the alliance's air strikes. Had ground troops been needed, the Chrétien government was prepared to contribute.[130] Ottawa augmented its military contribution with $44 million in economic assistance, and Canada opened its doors to over 7000 Kosovar-Albanian refugees.[131] Senior Ottawa officials held daily press briefings on the status of the campaign. Ministers attended in person when required. This transparent approach appears to have worked.[132] Although the Serbian-Canadian protests continued, polls from the period indicate overwhelming public support.[133]

The Russians ultimately sought a diplomatic solution. A 6 May 1999 G-8 statement, shaped in significant part by Canadian negotiators, formed the basis of subsequent negotiations. Milošević signalled his willingness to surrender, and the Security Council was re-engaged through SCR 1244 (1999) in June.[134] Serbia was to withdraw its forces while the KLA demilitarized. There would be a United Nations Interim Administration Mission in Kosovo (UNMIK), and a NATO-led peacekeeping force, KFOR (Kosovo Force), would handle military and policing responsibilities. Canada served in KFOR for a year.[135] UNMIK was hardly perfect: returning Kosovar Albanians sought revenge against the minority Serbian population, often with brutal results. Nonetheless, according to one senior official, "the ethnic cleansing was stopped, the refugees and internally displaced did return, the economy was restarted, and the basis for a better future for Kosovars was laid."[136]

During the Cold War, Canadians tended to think of their military forces as peacekeepers. In Kosovo, there initially was no peace to keep, but the humanitarian imperative was deemed sufficiently grave so as to bypass the need for Security Council approval.[137] Minister Axworthy's later advocacy of the responsibility to protect would seek to avoid any future inconsistencies.

Conclusion

The Chrétien Liberals' approach to foreign policy in the immediate post–Cold War era defies any coherent explanation. Here was a government that promoted itself as a global exemplar even as members of its second-largest province very nearly voted to separate. It made extensive use of the Canadian Forces but also slashed the defence budget and eventually all but abandoned the national peacekeeping tradition. It diversified Canada's commercial ties but consciously overlooked the human rights atrocities committed by some of its new trading partners. It celebrated the work of its diplomats in ending the blood diamond trade in Namibia but ignored their advice completely during the Turbot War. It championed multilateralism through the United Nations but secured a landmine treaty outside of the UN negotiating process and contributed extensively to a military engagement in Kosovo without the Security Council's authorization.

Supporters of the government argue that the Liberals were bold risk-takers. They demonstrated international leadership and deserved credit for a series of practical achievements stemming from their human security agenda. Prime Minister Chrétien prevented Quebec from separating, managed the Canada–US relationship effectively, and directed the recovery of the Canadian economy. Critics counter that Ottawa's rhetorical flourish covered up a miserly, perhaps even irresponsible, approach to funding its defence, diplomacy, and development establishments. They deem the emphasis of Liberal foreign ministers on Canadian values naive and hypocritical, and they argue that working with non-state actors should never have come at the expense of vital national relationships and interests.

In sum, there was no agreement during this era as to what it meant to put Canada first. Nor was there consensus on the types of partnerships necessary to prevent Ottawa from ending up alone on the world stage. Less than a year after the Chrétien Liberals formed their third consecutive majority government in 2000, however, these disagreements appeared trivial and inconsequential.

Readings

Aspects of globalization and its history are explored in Jürgen Osterhammel and Niels P. Petersson's *Globalization: A Short History* (Princeton: Princeton University Press, 2009) and Gary Gerstle's *The Rise and Fall of the Neoliberal Order: America and the World in the Free Market Era* (New York: Oxford University Press, 2022). For perspectives on the crises of peacekeeping in the 1990s, see the essays in Joachim Koops et al., eds., *The Oxford Handbook of United Nations Peacekeeping Operations* (Oxford: Oxford University Press, 2017); Mary Kaldor's *New and Old Wars: Organized Violence in a Global Era*, 3rd ed. (Cambridge: Polity, 2012); the contemporaneous analyses in Samantha Power, *"A Problem from Hell": America and the Age of Genocide* (New York: Basic Books, 2002); and Michael Ignatieff, *Virtual War: Kosovo and Beyond* (Toronto: Penguin, 2000). A good introduction to human security is David Andersen-Rodgers and Kerry Crawford, *Human Security: Theory and Action* (Lanham, MD: Rowman and Littlefield, 2018). M.E. Sarotte's *Not One Inch: America, Russia, and the Making of Post-Cold War Stalemate* (New Haven: Yale University Press, 2021) is a vital work on the changing geopolitical situation in Europe, while Derek Chollet and James Goldgeier look at US foreign policy during the 1990s in *America Between the Wars: The Misunderstood Years Between the Fall of the Berlin Wall and the Start of the War on Terror* (New York: PublicAffairs, 2009).

The most comprehensive account of the Turbot War is Adam Gough's "The Turbot War: The arrest of the Spanish vessel *Estai* and its implications for Canada-EU relations" (University of Ottawa, MA thesis, 2009). See also chapter 3 of Donald Barry, Bob Applebaum, and Earl Wiseman, *Fishing for a Solution: Canada's Fisheries Relations with the European Union, 1977–2013* (Calgary: University of Calgary Press, 2014), 53–74, https://press.ucalgary.ca/books/9781552387788/; chapter 5 of Raymond B. Blake, *From Fishermen to Fish: The Evolution of Canadian Fishery Policy* (Toronto: Irwin, 2000), 91–111; and Brendan Howe and Matthew Kerby, "The Canada-EU Turbot War of 1995 and the cybernetic model of decision-making," *The Round Table* 98, no. 401 (2009): 161–79, https://doi.org/10.1080/00358530902757883. A number of relevant memoirs are mentioned in the endnotes. The most thorough summary of the current state of the international regime is Manuel Pacheco Coelho, Rui Junqueira Lopes, and André Estrela Pires, "Lessons from the 'turbot war': The future of high seas governance," *Aquatic Living Resources* 33, no. 6 (2020): 1–10, https://doi.org/10.1051/alr/2020009.

In addition to Lloyd Axworthy's personal scholarship, there are three key sources for the landmines case: Maxwell A. Cameron, Robert J. Lawson, and Brian W. Tomlin, eds., *To Walk without Fear: The Global Movement to Ban Landmines* (Toronto: Oxford University Press, 1998) and the collection of papers published in *Canadian Foreign Policy Journal* 5, no. 3 (1998): 1–165 provide a thorough account of the Canadian perspective. Richard A. Matthew, Bryan McDonald, and Kenneth R. Rutherford, eds., *Landmines and Human Security: International Politics and War's Hidden Legacy* (Albany: State University of New York Press, 2004) offers a global assessment. John English has updated his article cited in the notes to this chapter as "The Ottawa convention on anti-personnel landmines," in Andrew F. Cooper, Jorge Heine, and Ramesh Thakur, eds., *The Oxford Handbook on Modern Diplomacy* (Oxford: Oxford University Press, 2013), 797–809, https://doi.org/10.1093/oxfordhb/9780199588862.001.0001. For more critical views, see Maxwell A. Cameron, "Global civil society and the Ottawa Process: Lessons from the movement to ban anti-personnel landmines," *Canadian Foreign Policy Journal* 7, no. 1 (1999): 85–102, https://doi.org/10.1080/11926422.1999.9673202; Nicola Short, "The role of NGOs in the Ottawa Process to ban landmines," *International Negotiation* 4, no. 3 (1999): 481–500, https://doi.org/10.1163/15718069920848589; and Adam Chapnick, "The Ottawa Process revisited: Aggressive unilateralism in the post-Cold War world," *International Journal* 58, no. 3 (2003): 281–93, https://doi.org/10.2307/40203860.

The most straightforward summary of the Kosovo case is Hevina S. Dashwood, "Canada's participation in the NATO-led intervention in Kosovo," in Maureen Appel Molot and Fen Osler Hampson, eds., *Canada among Nations 2000: Vanishing Borders* (Don Mills, ON: Oxford University Press, 2000), 275–302. The most comprehensive (and theoretically informed) is Michael W. Manulak, "Canada and the Kosovo crisis: An agenda for intervention," *Martello Papers* 36 (Centre for International Relations, Queen's University, Kingston, 2011), 1–88. Also helpful are the relevant pages from Frank Chalk, Roméo Dallaire, Kyle Matthews, Carla Barqueiro, and Simon Doyle, *Mobilizing to Intervene: Leadership to Prevent Mass Atrocities* (Montreal: McGill-Queen's University Press, 2010), 61–9. For an intriguing analysis of the domestic politics of the period, see Krenare Recaj, "Sovereignty sensitivities and the Kosovo crisis: The impact of domestic considerations on Canada's foreign policy," *Canadian Journal of History* 56, no. 2 (2021): 136–65, https://doi.org/10.3138/cjh-56-2-2020-0076 and "Diaspora discontent: Canada and the Kosovo crisis," *Journal of Military and Strategic Studies* 20, no. 4 (2021): 66–103, https://jmss.org/article/view/73316. A more critical view can be found in Wayne Nelles, "Canada's human security agenda in Kosovo and beyond," *International Journal* 57, no. 3 (2002): 459–79, https://doi.org/10.1177/002070200205700310. For primary source evidence, see the work of Paul Heinbecker and Lloyd Axworthy cited in the notes as well as Canada, House of Commons, Standing Committee Foreign Affairs and International Trade, *FAIT Committee Report* no. 8 (36-2), June 2000, https://www.ourcommons.ca/DocumentViewer/en/36-2/FAIT/report-8/page-2.

196 CANADA FIRST, NOT CANADA ALONE

Beyond the Book

Conflict Diamonds in Angola and UN Security Council
Sanctions Reform, 1999–2000

For much of the 1990s, the National Union for the Total Independence of Angola (UNITA) used money obtained through the sale of illegally obtained diamonds ("conflict" or "blood" diamonds) to fund its efforts to displace the sitting government. The United Nations Security Council imposed sanctions to curb the practice, but to no avail.

When Canada joined the Security Council in 1999, its permanent representative to the UN, Bob Fowler, saw an opportunity to effect change. His plan was to co-operate with Angola's neighbouring states, the mining industry, and select NGOs to build the necessary momentum to reform the sanctions regime and starve UNITA of its primary source of funds. Such an effort was risky—the UN regime was long-established, as were the networks that profited from the illegal diamond trade. Armed security guards ultimately had to join Fowler and his staff as they travelled across Europe and Africa building support for their reforms. Even if they succeeded, it was unclear whether their efforts could be sustained beyond Canada's council term. Still, the Canadians persisted, the sanctions regime was reformed, violators were "named and shamed" for the first time in the UN's history, and UNITA ultimately collapsed. Whether those successes led to broader, lasting systemic change is less clear.

Questions

1. What are Canada's national interests in this case?
2. What role should sanctions play in Canadian foreign and security policy?
3. Why were Fowler and his staff able to shift international opinion on an issue that had until then appeared intractable?

Readings

Basic summaries of this case can be found in Adam Chapnick, *Canada on the United Nations Security Council: A Small Power on a Large Stage* (Vancouver: UBC Press, 2019), 167–9; and Chris Brown, "Africa in Canadian foreign policy 2000: The human security agenda," in Fen Osler Hampson, Norman Hillmer, and Maureen Appel Molot, eds., *Canada among Nations 2001: The Axworthy Legacy* (Don Mills, ON: Oxford University Press, 2001), specifically 198–202.

More detailed depictions of the Canadian contribution by practitioners who were involved include Robert Fowler and David Angell, "Angola sanctions," in Rob McRae and Don Hubert, eds., *Human Security and the New Diplomacy* (Montreal: McGill-Queen's University Press, 2001), 190–8, as well as the background in pp. 178–89 and David J.R. Angell, "The Angola sanctions committee," in David M. Malone, ed., *The UN Security Council: From Cold War to the 21st Century* (Boulder, CO: Lynne Rienner, 2004), 195–204. On Angola specifically, see Jake H. Sherman, "Profit vs. peace: The clandestine diamond economy of Angola," *Journal of International Affairs* 53, no. 2 (2000): 699–719 and Quint Hoekstra, "Conflict diamonds and the Angolan Civil War (1992–2002)," *Third World Quarterly* 40, no. 7 (2019): 1322–39, https://doi.org/10.1080/01436597.2019.1612740. On sanctions, see Joanna Weschler, "The evolution of Security Council innovations in sanctions," *International Journal* 65, no. 1 (2010): 31–43, https://doi.org/10.1177/002070201006500103. For a more pessimistic take on the Canadian experience, see chapter 5: "Angola: Another distracting side show" of Ian Smillie, *Blood on the Stone: Greed, Corruption and War in the Global Diamond Trade* (Ottawa: Anthem Press, 2010), 63–78, https://idl-bnc-idrc.dspacedirect.org/bitstream/handle/10625/44666/IDL-44666.pdf?sequence=1&isAllowed=y.

9

Jean Chrétien, Paul Martin, and the Aftermath of 9/11, 2001–2006

11 September 2001

Jean Chrétien's twilight years as prime minister were marked by several new initiatives intended to burnish his foreign policy record, including Ottawa's ambitious commitment to tackle poverty and the HIV/AIDS crisis in Africa, with the Canadian government pledging to double its overall foreign aid commitment by 2010. At the 2002 World Economic Forum, Chrétien quoted Mahatma Gandhi in declaring poverty "the worst form of violence."[1] As chair of the G8 meeting in Kananaskis, Alberta, later that year, he worked with British Prime Minister Tony Blair and French President Jacques Chirac to solidify the New Partnership for Africa's Development.

These achievements have been overshadowed by the defining moment of the early twenty-first century: the 11 September 2001 terrorist attacks on the United States in New York and Washington. Two Canadians, Major-General Eric Findley and Captain Mike Jellinek, were in decision-making positions at the North American Aerospace Defence Command (NORAD) command centre at the time and therefore coordinated the initial response. They deployed fighter jets, grounded hundreds of civilian aircraft, and diverted hundreds more to Canadian airports. The attacks killed 3000 people, including 27 Canadians, but the most significant damage might well have been psychological: 19 terrorists had levelled New York's World Trade Center and damaged the Pentagon, inflicting symbolic blows on American economic and military power. "The world just changed," Chrétien stated upon learning of the events. Later that day, he called US President George W. Bush and pledged Canada's full support. In an economically damaging step for both countries, the Canada–US border was tightened, preventing thousands of trucks from delivering their goods and upsetting the just-in-time supply chain relied on by businesses across North America. On 12 September, NATO invoked Article 5 of its treaty, the collective security clause, for the first time in its history.[2]

Canadians reacted to the 9/11 attacks with demonstrations of assistance and solidarity. Thousands of donors contributed to a blood donation drive, first responders travelled to New York to comb the rubble for survivors, and local

Canada First, Not Canada Alone: A History of Canadian Foreign Policy. Adam Chapnick and Asa McKercher, Oxford University Press. © Oxford University Press 2024. DOI: 10.1093/oso/9780197653715.003.0010

citizens sheltered more than 33,000 stranded travellers. On 14 September, 100,000 Canadians gathered for a vigil on Parliament Hill. Several weeks later, the leaders of Canada's political parties toured Ground Zero in New York City. Given this outpouring of support, many Canadians were upset that on 20 September, in a major address before Congress, President Bush failed to mention Canada among a list of various countries providing help. Meeting with Chrétien days later, Bush remarked to reporters that it had been unnecessary to praise a "brother." Privately, the president and other administration officials underscored that the snub had not been deliberate.[3] Unintentional or not, the incident foreshadowed tension in the bilateral relationship.[4] Americans, observed one political columnist, "know and care the square root of squat about Canada."[5]

American ignorance of Canada seemed magnified during the George W. Bush years. A Texan, the president had little first-hand knowledge of his country's northern neighbour and made his first foreign excursion to Mexico shortly after taking office. Chrétien replaced Lloyd Axworthy as foreign minister with John Manley, a politician with a more favourable view of the Americans. "It's sort of self-evident that the United States is our key bilateral relationship," Manley remarked soon after his appointment, "not by a small margin but by an enormous margin."[6] Following the 9/11 attacks, Manley negotiated a Smart Border Accord with Washington. The agreement boosted security at customs points and ensured that commerce could flow relatively unimpeded across the border.

Keeping the border open to trade and tourism was critical. That meant reassuring the Americans that Canada did not pose a terrorist threat at a time when, as Paul Cellucci, Bush's ambassador in Ottawa, put it, "security trumps trade."[7] Washington had cause for concern. In 1999, al-Qaeda operative Ahmed Ressam, who was living illegally in Montreal, had been arrested while trying to cross into the United States with a bomb he intended to plant at Los Angeles International Airport. In the wake of 9/11, the Canadian government's "worst nightmare," admitted Transportation Minister Jean Lapierre, was an attack on the United States planned in, or coming directly from, Canada.[8] Regrettably, the rumour persisted in the United States that the al-Qaeda terrorists who undertook the attacks had arrived from the north. "Well, everybody knows they came through Canada,"[9] stated New York Senator Hillary Clinton. Beyond correcting the record, Canadian officials had to crack down on terrorists, real and imagined.

The 9/11 attacks led to the creation of a new Department of Public Safety (2003), a new Canadian Border Services Agency (2004), and significant increases in funding to security agencies such as the RCMP, Canadian Security Intelligence Service (CSIS), and Financial Transactions and Reports Analysis

200   CANADA FIRST, NOT CANADA ALONE

Centre of Canada (FINTRAC). The funding was complemented by expanded powers: the October 2001 Anti-Terrorism Act allowed for increased surveillance of Canadian citizens, pre-emptive detention of suspects, and even secret trials. The legislation, one Liberal Cabinet minister later admitted, was "certainly done in haste. In the heat of the crisis, when fear and anger ran high, there wasn't enough time or will for reflection."[10] As a result, there were incidents in which authorities overstepped, violating Canadians' civil liberties. Members of the Muslim and Arab communities as well as other visible minorities were particularly affected by what was dubbed the Global War on Terror. In the most egregious incident, in September 2002 Syrian-born Canadian Maher Arar was detained in New York City en route to Canada. Arar was then deported to Syria, where he was held and tortured for a year before being released. As later investigations showed, Canadian officials had abetted Arar's detainment and deportation, prompting an official governmental apology and multi-million-dollar settlement.[11]

Wars in Afghanistan and Iraq

By the time Arar had reached Syria, the United States and its allies were at war in Afghanistan. The country was largely ruled by the Taliban, a theocratic militia force that had provided haven to al-Qaeda as it planned and launched the 9/11 attacks. The US intervention, Operation Enduring Freedom, quickly toppled the Taliban. American troops proceeded to hunt al-Qaeda across Afghanistan's mountainous landscape, while diplomats and other officials worked to set up a new Afghan government. Canada supported these efforts through Operation Apollo, as Special Forces and infantry joined the hunt for al-Qaeda and Taliban fighters, with naval and air assets providing support. Canadian military units also contributed to the UN-sanctioned, NATO-led International Security Assistance Force (ISAF). This mission, Operation Athena, aimed to secure Kabul, the Afghan capital, allowing the new, democratically elected government and UN agencies to operate. In February 2003, the Chrétien government deployed 2000 soldiers to ISAF on a rotating basis. By then, Washington's focus was elsewhere.

In his January 2002 State of the Union speech, President Bush had accused an "Axis of Evil"—Iraq, Iran, and North Korea—of threatening US interests. When asked about the rhetoric, John Manley, serving as deputy prime minister, worried it was "bellicose."[12] Over the next year, the Bush administration, along with Tony Blair's government, attempted to link Saddam Hussein's regime to al-Qaeda and to make the case that the Iraqis possessed weapons of mass destruction. To confront Iraq, the Americans and British built a so-called coalition of the willing, which Ottawa resisted the calls to join. "Iraq under Saddam Hussein is clearly always a threat," stated Foreign Minister Bill Graham in mid-2002, "but we have no evidence he is in possession of weapons of mass destruction or that he would intend to use them at this time."[13]

The Chrétien government's decision to formally sit out the Iraq War proved popular with Canadians and, given the disastrous effects of that conflict, highly prudent. But support for the decision was hardly unanimous. "Disarming Iraq is necessary for the long term security of the world, to the collective interests of our historic allies and, therefore, manifestly it is in the national interest of this country," argued Canadian Alliance leader Stephen Harper.[14] Progressive Conservative premiers in Ontario and Alberta agreed. Other Canadian supporters of the war—including Allan Gotlieb, ambassador to Washington in the 1980s—feared the impact of the Chrétien government's decision on Canada–US relations.[15] The business community, meanwhile, worried about the economic fallout of upsetting Canada's major trading partner. In his memoirs, Graham recalled a time as foreign minister waiting in an airport departure lounge when he "was set upon by every business executive in the room rushing over to scream at me for risking his exports to the United States or making his life uncomfortable in New York."[16] Apart from a cancelled presidential visit to Canada in May 2003, there was no significant retaliation from the American side. No doubt it helped that Canadian military units were indirectly involved in the conflict, even if Ottawa's political support was lacking.

Differences over Iraq were symptomatic of wider cultural divergences between Canada and the United States. The 1990s had witnessed increasing interaction among North Americans in terms of trade, tourism, and entertainment, leading writers to speculate about a growing continental identity.[17] A *Maclean's* cover story from 1999 had even predicted a "Vanishing Border."[18] Such talk was muted following the post-9/11 increase in border security. Meanwhile, American belligerence in the War on Terror and the Bush administration's conservative policy agenda stood in contrast to a more progressive Canadian outlook and support for peacekeeping. In his bestselling look at societal values on both sides of the border, pollster Michael Adams characterized the United States as fire and Canada as ice.[19] Ambassador Cellucci also observed a rise in anti-American sentiment among Canadians—though this development was a global one during the Bush years.[20]

Formally sitting out the Iraq war was Chrétien's last major foreign policy decision. Despite his belated efforts to leave a foreign policy legacy, as his time as prime minister came to an end in late 2003, there was growing concern that Canada had lost its way in the world. Over a decade of budget cuts to the military and foreign service had reduced Canadian capacity and sapped morale. "We are still trading on a reputation that was built two generations and more ago,"

202   CANADA FIRST, NOT CANADA ALONE

John Manley had said shortly after becoming foreign minister, "but that we haven't continued to live up to. You can't just sit at the G8 table and then, when the bill comes, go to the washroom."[21] A group of eminent foreign policy experts agreed. "Canada has slipped badly in international influence," they wrote.[22] Shortly thereafter, Canadians turned journalist Andrew Cohen's book, *While Canada Slept: How We Lost Our Place in the World*, into a national bestseller.[23]

Paul Martin and Foreign Policy Renewal

Chrétien's successor as Liberal leader and prime minister, Paul Martin, committed to reversing this alleged decline. The son of a former foreign minister, and Chrétien's finance minister from 1993 to 2002, Martin had been active with the International Monetary Fund and World Bank and had worked with US Treasury Secretary Lawrence Summers in 1999 to establish the G-20 meetings of finance ministers and central bank governors of the world's leading economies. As prime minister, he suggested that the G-20 heads of the government meet as an L(eaders)-20; his proposal ultimately became the G-20 leaders' summit in 2008.[24]

In early 2004, Martin committed to a foreign policy "concentrating on what we do best and on what the world needs most."[25] Increased military spending and outlays to foreign aid followed, along with 2005's international policy statement (IPS), *A Role of Pride and Influence in the World*. The report was largely written by political scientist Jennifer Welsh, author of a 2004 book in which she proposed "a simple but ambitious vision for Canada's global role: as Model Citizen."[26] The IPS was more grounded, calling for a bold reassertion of Canadian influence in a world that was "changing, quickly and radically" amid "a major rebalancing of global power." In his foreword, Martin stressed that words would not be enough. Canadians needed to "earn our way" through involvement in international issues and investment in the tools of statecraft— the military, the foreign service, and development programs.[27] As for process, the IPS called for a comprehensive approach to deal with issues as diverse as terrorism, epidemic disease, environmental disasters, and global poverty. After years of drift in foreign affairs, *A Role of Pride and Influence in the World* was a sensible blueprint for action, but its shelf life was cut short.

Martin's Liberals first faced Canadian voters in June 2004. The election introduced the country to the reunified and strengthened right-wing Conservative Party of Canada, formed in 2003 by a merger between the Progressive Conservatives and the Canadian Alliance. The Liberals were also damaged by revelations of corruption involving public funds meant to promote

Canadian unity in Quebec. The Sponsorship Scandal had occurred under Chrétien, but it was Martin who was tarnished by it. Amid the resulting media storm, the Liberals could form only a minority government. For the next 18 months, maintaining a narrow hold on power in the House of Commons preoccupied Martin, and critics increasingly castigated him for a lack of focus and follow-through. There were some notable achievements, such as the passage of the Civil Marriage Act in 2005—legalizing same-sex marriage—and increases in funding for health care, child care, and Indigenous programs. Nonetheless, the British magazine *The Economist* reported that Martin was being called "Mr. Dithers" in Ottawa and the epithet stuck.[28]

International Assistance

In foreign policy, the Martin government expanded upon Chrétien's commitment to poverty alleviation in Africa, focusing the G-8 and G-20 on debt relief for the world's poorest countries, and devoted considerable attention to the HIV/AIDS crisis. A new Canada Corps, created in 2004 and administered by the Canadian International Development Agency, encouraged young Canadians to travel abroad to promote good governance through election monitoring. Ottawa also became involved in a humanitarian crisis in Darfur, where a Sudanese government–backed militia sought to suppress an independence movement among indigenous Darfuris. "Never again after Rwanda struck me," Martin affirmed.[29] He visited the region in November 2004 and set up a special advisory team to focus Canada's contribution. Ottawa's capacity to effect change independently on the world stage limited further action. Martin may have pledged "whatever is required" to intervene in Darfur, but the international community, divided by the Iraq war, stood by in the face of the slaughter.[30]

Canada's impact was more notable in Haiti. In 2003, Canadian, US, and French officials had met in Ottawa to discuss the removal of Haitian president Jean-Bertrand Aristide.[31] The following year, Canadian soldiers joined a UN-authorized coalition that replaced him with a new Haitian leader. "This was not a coup d'état," Foreign Minister Bill Graham assured fellow MPs, despite appearances to the contrary. "This was the Security Council of the United Nations acting with the highest authority of the charter to restore order in the area."[32] Canadian troops and civilian officials subsequently participated in the UN Stabilization Mission in Haiti (MINUSTAH) and the country continued to receive large outlays of Canadian development funding.[33]

Many locals viewed MINUSTAH as a foreign occupation that did little to stabilize Haitian politics or improve the desperate economic situation. Graham defended the intervention in his memoirs, but later he was more candid: "there

Figure 9.1 International leaders look on as Canadian Prime Minister Paul Martin addresses the 10th Sommet de la Francophonie in Ouagadougou, Burkina Faso, 26 November 2004. On 26 November 2004, Prime Minister Paul Martin was in Ouagadougou, Burkina Faso, addressing the tenth Sommet de la Francophonie. His remarks stressed Canada's commitment to the international organization, security and development in Africa and beyond, as well as the need for La Francophonie to modernize and position itself as an influential international institution. Martin arrived in Burkina Faso from Khartoum, Sudan, where he had been critical of the Al Bashir government's failure to control Janjaweed rebel militias whose actions had displaced over one million Sudanese. Martin's efforts to restore what many had argued was a decline in Canada's international stature were promising but short-lived. Just over a year to the day of his Francophonie speech, his government fell after a vote of non-confidence in the House of Commons. Canadian Press/Adrian Wyld/CP2816396.

is a limit to how much we can constantly say no to the political masters in Washington...eventually we came on side on Haiti, so we got another arrow in our quiver."[34] In addition to concern over Aristide's corruption, Canadian support for regime change in Haiti appears to have been an effort to appease the Bush administration.

"Our most important relationship is with the United States," wrote Martin, and he aimed to keep it in good repair.[35] Washington appreciated that

Canadians led the International Mission for Iraqi Elections, which oversaw a series of votes in 2005. At home, economic issues were central, keeping the border open to trade and commerce while ensuring heightened security. In March 2005, Martin, Bush, and Mexican President Vicente Fox—dubbed by the media the "Three Amigos"—announced a Security and Prosperity Partnership (SPP).[36] Still, there were strains. A long-standing dispute over Canadian softwood lumber exports dragged on, while a single case of mad cow disease led the Americans to shut the border to Alberta beef between 2003 and 2005. Another divisive issue was the Martin government's decision to keep Canada out of the US Ballistic Missile Defense program.

The most momentous decision of Martin's brief tenure was the expansion of Canadian involvement in Afghanistan. "As members of NATO, which is after all a self-defence pact," he wrote in his memoir, "we had a moral if not legal duty to support them. We also had a self-interest in doing so."[37] Tim Murphy, Martin's chief of staff, put the matter somewhat differently: the prime minister and his team "viewed Afghanistan as something we *had* to do more than something we wanted to do."[38] The expanded role in Afghanistan complemented the Martin government's goal of rebuilding the Canadian Forces. But by the time Canada's military deployed to Kandahar in February 2006, the Liberals were out of power.

Case Studies

The cases for this chapter consider what it means, and does not mean, for Canada to be alone on the world stage. The first case examines the Chrétien government's decisions to sign and ratify the Kyoto Protocol. Ottawa played an active role in the negotiations to create the agreement and then chose not to follow the United States when Washington withdrew its support in 2001. By remaining a party to the protocol, Ottawa was able to negotiate better terms for itself while maintaining its reputation for good international citizenship. Efforts to fulfill Canada's Kyoto commitments were less impressive.

The Chrétien government diverges from the United States again in the second case, about Washington's decision to intervene in Iraq without the blessing of the United Nations. According to Prime Minister Chrétien, part of the reasoning behind his decision to largely stay out of the war was the importance of maintaining the integrity of the international order.

The third case sees Ottawa co-operating with all of its major NATO allies, including the United States, in a UN-sanctioned military engagement in Afghanistan. Here, Canada's interests can only be understood in the context of alliance politics.

206   CANADA FIRST, NOT CANADA ALONE

The Beyond the Book case considers another divergence from the United States, over ballistic missile defence. Part of the Martin government's reasoning includes a commitment to prevent the weaponization of space, a change that would have risked undermining a fragile international consensus on state behaviour beyond the earth's atmosphere.

The Kyoto Protocol, 1997–2002

Why does Canada sign and ratify international agreements?

In 1992, Canada and 153 other states signed the United Nations Framework Convention on Climate Change (UNFCCC). The treaty established a "global climate regime" to manage the international response to the threat of human-induced climate change as well as initial, non-binding emissions reductions targets for its wealthier members.[39] Five years later, having previously joined with Japan, the United States, Australia, and New Zealand in efforts to weaken the agreement's targets, the Chrétien government signed the Kyoto Protocol.[40] Upon ratification, Canada would face binding emissions reductions obligations that far exceeded those contemplated by even the most ambitious environmental advocates. A lengthy national negotiation process to develop a workable implementation strategy followed. By 2002, those negotiations had largely collapsed. Nonetheless, over significant opposition from the Canadian Alliance, industry, provincial governments, and even members of the Liberal Cabinet, Ottawa ratified the agreement. This case examines why.

In 1995, the Intergovernmental Panel on Climate Change's (IPCC's) second assessment report made clear that humankind was responsible for an increase in global greenhouse gas emissions that, if not deterred, would result in permanent damage to the earth's ecosystem.[41] The study's conclusions spurred members of the UNFCCC to negotiate deeper, binding emissions reductions targets (at first, only for developed countries) to replace those established in 1992.[42] A meeting to finalize those targets was set for December 1997 in Kyoto, Japan.

As analyst Paul Halucha has explained, in anticipation of Kyoto, "The Canadian negotiating position evolved from the interaction of two pressures, one rooted in the country's historic dependence on low-cost energy sources to offset the high energy costs of extracting, processing, and transporting raw materials, the other rooted in our growing trade dependence on the United States. The first pressure dictated that Canada be very cautious in its adoption of targets and timetables and placed it in opposition to Europe. The second pressure demanded that we closely harmonize our response with that adopted by the [also cautious] US."[43] A joint meeting of federal and provincial ministers of energy and the environment ultimately reached a general consensus (the Quebec government was the only dissenter) that Ottawa stabilize its emissions at 1990 levels by 2010.[44]

Although the evidence is not entirely clear, political scientist Kathryn Harrison has suggested convincingly that, shortly before Kyoto, President Clinton urged Prime Minister Chrétien to bridge the gap between the polarized US and EU positions.[45] Much to the chagrin of the oil-producing provinces of Alberta and Saskatchewan, Canada therefore announced a preliminary negotiating position of a 3 per cent reduction in emissions from 1990 levels by 2010. During the conference, apparently again at the behest of the White House, Chrétien instructed Canada's negotiating team to increase its ambition to 1 per cent less than any American pledge.

When Washington announced a 7 per cent reduction from 1990 levels by 2012, Ottawa committed to 6 per cent, with the (unspoken) caveat that Canada would benefit from a number of accounting "loopholes," that, taken together, would hardly change its initial proposal.[46] The Climate Action Network—a group of civil society organizations devoted to combatting climate change—found Ottawa's negotiating tactics so appalling that they gave Canada their Fossil Award: "a badge of shame presented to the country that argued for the most regressive policies and ideas."[47]

In Ottawa's defence, maintaining the original target in light of Washington's more significant ambitions would have resulted in national embarrassment and possible American retaliation.[48] Without a serious commitment, Canada also risked being excluded from a leadership role in future negotiations.[49] Optimistically, one analyst suggests that the government interpreted the national interest in more expansive terms, taking into consideration the strategic benefits of environmental protection and good international citizenship.[50]

Ottawa's commitment remained provisional until the protocol was ratified, and Prime Minister Chrétien was in no hurry to do so. As Kyoto was ending, he joined the premiers at a first ministers meeting and promised greater federal-provincial collaboration in generating an implementation plan that would not unduly burden any province or region.[51] A National Climate Change Secretariat, co-chaired by senior officials from Ottawa and Alberta, launched an ultimately futile consultation process that engaged hundreds of experts and stakeholders.[52] Three years later, Canada's emissions had actually increased by nearly 20 per cent over 1990 levels.[53]

Just as the IPCC's third report warned of the visible impacts of climate change, the new United States president, George W. Bush, announced that America was withdrawing from the treaty. Since the protocol would not enter into force without its ratification by two-thirds of the industrialized countries who together emitted 55 per cent of the world's greenhouse gases in 1990,

208 CANADA FIRST, NOT CANADA ALONE

there was real risk of its collapse.[54] Rather than following the American lead, Ottawa lobbied for additional concessions.[55] By remaining within the regime, Ottawa continued to shape its rules, presented itself as a team player internationally, and sent a message of environmental progressivism to a general public that largely supported the protocol.[56]

The success of Canadian negotiators in securing additional credit for actions Canada had already taken and Ottawa's decision to release a federal implementation plan in May 2002 made it increasingly likely that the Chrétien government would ratify the agreement.[57] Alberta therefore resigned as co-chair of the National Climate Change Secretariat, launched a national advertising campaign against ratification, and announced its own plan with overwhelmingly weaker reductions targets.[58] A coalition of business groups speculated that ratification would cost the Canadian economy over 450,000 jobs.[59] The leader of the Canadian Alliance, Stephen Harper, released a fundraising letter that referred to Kyoto as "a socialist scheme to suck money out of the wealth-producing nations."[60] Inside the government, the Liberals were divided.

On 2 September 2002 at the Conference on Environment and Development in Johannesburg, Prime Minister Chrétien announced that he planned to introduce a parliamentary resolution in support of ratification before the end of the year. It was a clever move. Parliament does not hold the power to ratify treaties; only the Cabinet does. Nonetheless, by introducing a resolution in the House of Commons, and then declaring it a matter of confidence, Chrétien all but compelled his entire caucus to vote in favour. Once they had done so, any hesitancy in Cabinet to support ratification that December became moot.[61] Ottawa quickly guaranteed the oil and gas sector that it would not be responsible for more than 15 per cent of Canada's emissions reductions, and that the federal government would pay all abatement costs beyond $15 per tonne of CO_2. That promise made it impossible for Canada to meet its obligations without significant and expensive government intervention.[62]

Chrétien has offered a number of reasons for his decision. In his 2007 memoirs, he explained: "ratifying Kyoto was both a statement of our values and a pledge to reduce greenhouse gas emissions. It was popular at home, especially among the young; it fit our image abroad as an environmentally conscious, socially progressive nation; and, just as with the government's fight against the deficit, I thought it was important first to establish an obtainable target and then to figure out how to meet it step by step, year by year. The fact is, if you have no set destination in mind, you'll never get anywhere."[63] A decade later, he argued differently: "I knew that it would be practically impossible for Canada to reach 100 percent of the objectives; at best we might reach 80 percent. On the other hand, if I said yes to ratification of the Protocol, and we made it to 80 percent, that was much better than zero. Not perfect, but to do nothing at all seemed to me totally irresponsible."[64] His chief of staff, Eddie Goldenberg, agreed that Canada ratified the agreement without a plan to meet its objectives, but added that doing so was "absolutely necessary to prepare public opinion for the actions that would have to come in the future to address climate change."[65] Ministers and senior officials confirmed that Chrétien believed "it was the right thing to do," but added that ratification also affirmed the prime minister's commitment to multilateralism.[66] Others have suggested that Chrétien's desire to establish his own environmental legacy came into play.[67] If the latter was indeed the case, it is hard to say that he succeeded. By 2006, Canada's emissions levels relative to 1990 had increased by nearly 27 per cent.[68]

Canada's Response to the American Decision to Invade Iraq, 2002–2003

Who speaks for Canada on the world stage?

According to Prime Minister Jean Chrétien's long-serving Chief of Staff Eddie Goldenberg, "the decision of the Canadian government not to participate in Iraq was a seminal event in Canadian foreign policy."[69] Chrétien himself called it "one of the most important moments in our history."[70] Critics of the move accused the prime minister of failing to take a "clear position" prior to his policy announcement in the House of Commons in March 2003. To them, Chrétien had misled Canada's most significant ally and damaged the country's most important bilateral relationship.[71] George W. Bush's chief of staff, Andrew Card, disagreed. "You told us right from the beginning what you intended to do," he said to Chrétien in the summer of 2003, "and it was our mistake that we did not take you seriously.... That was our fault. We should have believed you. Others may have double-crossed us, but not you."[72] This case examines the reasons behind Washington's mistake.

In February 2002, Canada's Intelligence Assessment Secretariat (IAS) concluded that "there was a high probability" that the US military would pursue regime change in Iraq. In April, a further IAS report indicated that Washington intended to justify the intervention by linking Iraqi leader Saddam Hussein to the 9/11 attackers. If that failed, Saddam would be accused of retaining the weapons of mass destruction that he had promised to destroy after the American-led UN intervention in 1991. Canadian analysts were not initially convinced by either argument.[73]

Their thinking was prescient. Thanks in part to early military success in Afghanistan, the White House shifted its focus to Iraq in mid-2002. When accusations of Saddam's ties to al-Qaeda rang hollow, Washington, with the support of Tony Blair, negotiated the passage of United Nations Security Council

210   CANADA FIRST, NOT CANADA ALONE

Resolution 1441 (2002), calling on Iraq to disarm or face "serious conse-quences."[74] UN inspectors were tasked with verifying Saddam's compliance, and America and Britain embarked on a diplomatic campaign to convince their allies that evidence of non-compliance would justify a military intervention. More specifically, they aimed to establish international legitimacy for a pre-emptive strike.[75] Their efforts failed in large part because they consistently over-stated the certainty of US intelligence analysts.[76]

Bush personally reached out to Chrétien multiple times. On 9 September 2002, the two spoke in Detroit. Chrétien pledged his support if the president could secure UN Security Council approval for an intervention but warned: "I've been reading my briefings about the weapons of mass destruction and I'm not convinced. I think the evidence is very shaky."[77] Bush offered a private meeting with his top intelligence officers, but Chrétien declined. "Canadians will not accept that I've been briefed by American officials," he explained. "If you have proof, send it to my analysts under normal channels. They will look at it, and I will decide."[78] When the two leaders spoke in January 2003, Chrétien merely left the definition of Security Council "approval" sufficiently vague to enable Ottawa to support an invasion if a council resolution was vetoed by a small minority.[79] His continued refusal to commit vexed both the American and British governments.[80]

Some US officials remained optimistic. For one, Canada's leading opposition party, the Canadian Alliance, was on their side, and the party's criticism of the Liberals focused on the opaqueness of their position.[81] If the opposition was not certain of where Canada stood, surely there was room for hope.

The Canadian media also offered mixed messages. As historian Stephen Azzi has noted, in late January 2003, in the aftermath of a single leader-to-leader meeting, the *Globe and Mail* ran a headline: "PM to Bush: Hold Off on War," while the *Toronto Star* announced: "Chrétien Supports U.S. Push for War."[82] Indeed, Canada's prime minister was not always clear in public. At one point, when asked what might constitute proof that Saddam Hussein possessed weap-ons of mass destruction, Chrétien replied: "I don't know. A proof is a proof. What kind of proof? It's a proof. A proof is a proof, and when you have a good proof, it's because it's proven."[83] While Foreign Minister Bill Graham consist-ently reiterated Chrétien's skepticism of the American case to US Secretary of State Colin Powell, significant numbers of officials from Canada's Department of National Defence and the Canadian Forces, along with select members of CSIS, sent their US colleagues different messages.[84] Indeed, many military officers were stunned when Chrétien formally rejected calls to join the US-led coalition.[85]

In February 2003, Powell addressed the UN Security Council in a last-ditch attempt to convince critics of the US plan that Iraq continued to hide weapons of mass destruction.[86] Although he spoke authoritatively, within days, intelligence experts had demonstrated the flimsiness of the American evidence.[87] As Chrétien quipped in his memoirs, "I wouldn't have been able to convince a judge of the municipal court in Shawinigan with the evidence I was given."[88]

On 12 February, Ottawa, sensing that nothing would stop Washington, increased its military commitment to Afghanistan. Even if Canada had wanted to send troops to Iraq, it would no longer have any to offer. Moreover, a commitment to take command of the International Security Assistance Force would free up American military personnel to deploy to the Middle East. The White House welcomed the move, but it did nothing to negate the Pentagon's desire for diplomatic support in Iraq.[89] Chrétien also empowered his ambassador to the United Nations, Paul Heinbecker, to seek a compromise at the Security Council. As Heinbecker recalls, "We were fully conscious at the time that we had about a 5 percent chance of success...but we gave it a 100 percent effort, because we were sure the consequences of war were going to be disastrous."[90] To no one's surprise, the initiative failed.

On 17 March the British government demanded immediate clarity from Canada's Department of Foreign Affairs and International Trade on Ottawa's position on Iraq. The tight deadline infuriated Chrétien and his staff and might well have contributed to their decision to respond via Parliament without warning.[91] That afternoon, Chrétien announced that "If military action [against Iraq] proceeds without a new resolution of the Security Council, Canada will not participate."[92] An apparent internal miscommunication prevented the inclusion of additional words recognizing the sincere efforts of Canada's American and British allies to avoid war and reiterating Ottawa's continued commitment to Afghanistan.[93]

The Canadian public, which was divided on the merits of the war, generally supported the prime minister.[94] The over 200,000 who had protested US policy in Canada's largest cities just days earlier were particularly ecstatic.[95] The Americans were disappointed. Part of the problem was the prime minister's unwillingness to sufficiently condemn a series of inexcusable public and personal criticisms of President Bush by senior ministers and members of his own staff. More important were US Ambassador Paul Cellucci's prior assurances to the White House that the Canadians would eventually come around.[96] In Graham's words, Cellucci "had gotten shit from Washington because he misled them about our intentions."[97] Put more tactfully in the foreign minister's memoirs, Cellucci's "overreliance on the hawks in our Defence Department, his contacts in the business community, and the right-wing press," led him to the wrong conclusion, one that he conveyed to Bush's staff with grave overconfidence.[98]

Cellucci's response at the time, and later in his own memoirs, rivalled the pettiness of the senior Liberals' anti-American outbursts.[99] President Bush

CANADA FIRST, NOT CANADA ALONE

cancelled a planned visit to Canada, and Canadian defence and security officials briefly lost access to Five Eyes and Department of Defense intelligence reports. The recriminations did not last. Chrétien did not ask the 31 Canadian Forces officers on exchange with the US and UK militaries to leave Iraq, Ottawa remained committed to Afghanistan, and bilateral trade continued to increase. In the end, however unclear he might have been in public, Chrétien was true to his word to the US president, and his was the only word that mattered.

Deploying to Kandahar Province, 2003–2005

What role does, or should, the chief of the defence staff play in the formulation of Canadian foreign policy?

When Paul Martin became prime minister in December 2003, he promised a more activist, engaged Canadian foreign policy. Martin was conscious of the impact of Liberal budget cuts in the mid-1990s on Ottawa's international posture, and he resolved to rebuild his country's capacity to effect global change. The Canadian Forces' ongoing 2000-troop commitment in Afghanistan was part of that posture, but he had no interest in making Central Asia his focus. As one senior Liberal staff member recalled, Martin viewed Afghanistan "as an inheritance from the previous government....as a member of NATO, [Canada] had an obligation to stand with the alliance in Afghanistan, but his interest in Afghanistan ended there."[100] Just 18 months later, Martin's hand-picked Chief of the Defence Staff (CDS) Rick Hillier was travelling the country to promote Ottawa's decision to dispatch a provincial reconstruction team (PRT) and battle group to Kandahar province, a move that all but guaranteed an extended commitment of thousands of Canadian civilian and military personnel, not to mention significant casualties. This case seeks to explain how and why the prime minister appears to have approved a far more ambitious mission than he had initially envisaged.

The aftermath of 9/11 led to two military interventions in Afghanistan: America's anti-terrorism mission (Operation Enduring Freedom [OEF]) and a UN-sanctioned reconstruction effort (the International Security Assistance Force [ISAF]). Canada was implicated in both. Its Special Forces joined OEF almost immediately, while its ambassador to NATO, David Wright, urged that organization to take responsibility for ISAF.[101] Wright's advocacy was well-received; without active American leadership, the UN mission was rudderless. Canada agreed to take command of ISAF for a year beginning in early 2004 under NATO's auspices, while the alliance assumed greater control of the operation writ large, with a plan to progressively expand ISAF's security and reconstruction footprint from the capital, Kabul, throughout the rest of the country. PRTs were to be the main vehicle for this effort.[102]

Ottawa's willingness to make a significant commitment to Afghanistan from 2002 onwards was broadly supported. As Martin concedes in his memoirs, "we were in Afghanistan for the right reasons and, having been part of displacing the Taliban regime, we continued to have a duty to help construct something sturdy to replace it."[103] He also wanted to toughen Canada's image without compromising public support for the military mission.[104] Martin's inclination was shared by members of the Canadian Forces (CF), officials in the Departments of National Defence (DND) and Foreign Affairs and International Trade (DFAIT), and even some of the leading figures in the Canadian International Development Agency responsible for Afghanistan.[105]

Martin was unwilling to extend the CF's engagement in Kabul, but he understood that more would be asked of Canada going forward and was adamant that any commitment be recognized and rewarded.[106] A request to establish a Canadian PRT in Chaghcharan district in Ghor province was poorly received. It was too low profile, and the distance from both a major airport and a US military base meant that the Canadians would be operating largely unseen.[107] Herat's geography was similarly problematic, and sharing command with Italy was not ideal. The chief of the defence staff at the time, General Ray Henault, considered Herat briefly, but the CF wanted partners they had worked with before and trusted.[108] The Canadian officer commanding ISAF, Lieutenant-General Rick Hillier, favoured taking over responsibility for Kabul International Airport, but his idea did not find popular favour either.[109]

By late 2004, talks with the Dutch and British about a coordinated deployment into the restive south of Afghanistan prompted discussion of a more ambitious mission: battle groups would be needed to protect the PRTs. Kandahar province quickly emerged as Canada's favoured site, and senior CF officials eventually secured it in a series of meetings with the Netherlands and UK. As political scientist Stephen Saideman has explained, "It was going to be one of the most important provinces in the country given its history as the homeland of the Taliban, its proximity to Pakistan, the size of its population, and its location in between the British, Dutch, and American sectors of Helmand, Uruzgan, and Zabul."[110] Kandahar was appealing for several practical reasons as well: the opportunities to provide international assistance were better; it was logistically friendly (near a major airbase); and both the Afghan and American governments were supportive.[111] Equally important, the larger commitment Kandahar entailed suited the armed forces. In the 1990s, CF members had engaged intensely in the Balkans without gaining any political or diplomatic capital, a problem they attributed to having served primarily under other countries' commands. Ever since then, planners insisted that any Canadian

Figure 9.2 Afghanistan.

engagement be able to demonstrate impact.[112] The deployment to the south—a PRT, a battle group, and shared leadership of the regional effort with the Netherlands and UK—ticked essential boxes.

When Rick Hillier became chief of the defence staff in February 2005, the Kandahar consensus had already been reached, but the implications had yet to be fully worked out. According to Defence Minister Bill Graham, General Hillier presented him a detailed plan

> that included sending our PRT from August 2005 to February 2007, along with Joint Task Force 2 (JTF2) special forces and a fifteen-person Strategic Advisory Team (SAT) to help with governance issues in Kabul. In addition, he was eager for Canada to assume the "region lead" in Kandahar by fielding a brigade headquarters of 320 personnel to oversee operations under the American-led Operation Enduring Freedom and later under ISAF. Finally, he wanted to deploy approximately one thousand combat troops for one year, starting in February 2006, who would fight the Taliban side-by-side with the Americans until NATO took over command, as expected, in 2006.[113]

It was ambitious, but Martin and Graham had selected Hillier because of their shared view about the need for Canadian interventions to make a difference.[114] Hillier easily gained the support of his defence minister. Martin's backing was secured after reassurances that the commitment would include a fixed end-date and would not preclude Ottawa's pursuit of additional defence and security priorities.[115]

There was never any question that a Kandahar mission would incur casualties. The location was significant to the Taliban and largely insecure. Minister Graham and General Hillier therefore launched cross-country speaking tours—referred to by some in the media as "body bag tours"—to prepare the Canadian public. Graham focused on the purpose and the value of the mission, both for Canada's national interests and the people of Afghanistan, noting the physical and safety risks that would be borne by the Canadian Forces in bringing about the security necessary to support reconstruction.[116] Hillier's speeches were devoid of such nuance. He called the Taliban "detestable murderers and scumbags." The job of Canadian soldiers was "to go out and bayonet somebody" and "to be able to kill people."[117] As political scientist Joseph Jockel put it, "by the time the new Kandahar mission began...any Canadian who thought it would be a binoculars and blue helmets operation without combat was just not paying attention."[118]

Clearly, many were not.[119] Not only were Canadians shocked by the casualties, but Ottawa had also profoundly underestimated the precarity of the security situation, as well as the hesitancy of Canada's NATO partners to replace the CF at the end of the year.[120] By that time, Martin's government had been defeated.

Conclusion

Prior to 9/11, the Chrétien government's efforts to restore the country's financial position had precluded significant investments in defence, development, or diplomacy. At the time, the idea of putting Canada first had a profoundly inward orientation, despite the efforts of Foreign Minister Lloyd Axworthy and others. The combination of Canada's improved fiscal health, Chrétien's desire to leave behind a foreign policy legacy, and the events of 9/11 reshaped Ottawa's priorities. The prime minister's newfound boldness was evident in Canada's acceptance of an all-but-impossible target to reduce its greenhouse gas emissions, a commitment to double Canadian aid in less than ten years, and Canada's most significant and deadly military commitment since the Korean War. When Paul Martin took over for Chrétien in late 2003, Ottawa increased its financial commitments to international affairs even more aggressively. The larger budget meant more opportunities to engage with other countries at the highest levels. Even though he was not in power when it was finally established, the leaders' G20 will likely be recalled as Martin's most significant foreign policy achievement.

216   CANADA FIRST, NOT CANADA ALONE

The election of US President George W. Bush and the post-9/11 Global War on Terror created tensions in the Canada–US relationship that neither Chrétien nor Martin could resolve. Ottawa's refusal to support Washington's controversial intervention in Iraq left hard feelings in the Bush White House, made significantly worse by Martin's refusal to contribute to the American Ballistic Missile Defense Program. Although the continent's economic integration continued, by 2006, the Bush administration could not help but look forward to the arrival of a new Conservative government in Ottawa.

Readings

Works examining the 9/11 attacks and the War on Terror include Lawrence Wright, *The Looming Tower: al-Qaeda and the Road to 9/11* (New York: Vintage, 2007); National Commission on Terrorist Attacks, *The 9/11 Commission Report* (New York: W.W. Norton, 2004); and Samuel Moyn, *Humane: How the United States Abandoned Peace and Reinvented War* (New York: Farrar, Straus and Giroux, 2021). Steve Coll's *Ghost Wars: The Secret History of the CIA, Afghanistan, and Bin Laden, from the Soviet Invasion to September 10, 2011* (New York: Penguin, 2004) is an essential work on the roots of the American war in Afghanistan. Spencer Ackerman traces the domestic impact of the War on Terror within the United States in *Reign of Terror: How the 9/11 Era Destabilized America and Produced Trump* (New York: Penguin, 2021). On the Bush administration's march to war in Iraq, see Robert Draper, *To Start a War: How the Bush Administration Took America into Iraq* (New York: Penguin, 2020). For an accessible introduction to the science of climate change, consult Kerry Emanuel, *What We Know About Climate Change* (Cambridge, MA: MIT Press, 2018). Nathaniel Rich explores the political aspects of the climate crisis in *Losing Earth: A Recent History* (New York: Farrar, Straus and Giroux, 2019).

The best literature on Canada's ratification of the Kyoto Protocol begins with Kathryn Harrison, "The struggle of ideas and self-interest in Canadian climate policy," in Harrison and Lisa McIntosh Sundstrom, eds., *Global Commons, Domestic Decisions: The Comparative Politics of Climate Change* (Cambridge, MA: MIT Press, 2010), 169–200. See also the relevant sections of Douglas Macdonald's *Carbon Province, Hydro Province: The Challenge of Canadian Energy and Climate Federalism* (Toronto: University of Toronto Press, 2020); Robert MacNeil's *Thirty Years of Failure: Understanding Canadian Climate Policy* (Halifax: Fernwood Publishing, 2019); and Frederic Hanusch's *Democracy and Climate Change* (London and New York: Routledge, 2018);

along with James P. Bruce and Doug Russell, "A Canadian policy chronicle," in Harold Coward and Andrew J. Weaver, eds., *Hard Choices: Climate Change in Canada* (Waterloo: Wilfrid Laurier University Press, 2004), 201–13 and Heather A. Smith, "Canada and Kyoto: Independence or indifference?" in Brian Bow and Patrick Lennox, eds., *An Independent Foreign Policy for Canada? Challenges and Choices for the Future* (Toronto: University of Toronto Press, 2008), 207–21. Jean Chrétien and Elizabeth May's personal accounts, both cited in the notes, should be also be considered, albeit skeptically.

The most comprehensive scholarship on Chrétien's decision not to actively support America's intervention in Iraq can be found in Ramesh Thakur and Jack Cunningham, eds., *Australia, Canada, and Iraq: Perspectives on an Invasion* (Toronto: Dundurn, 2015). See, in particular, the chapters by Cunningham (247–74) and Timothy Andrews Sayle (210–27). Alan Barnes, "Getting it right: Canadian intelligence assessments on Iraq, 2002–2003," *Intelligence and National Security* 35, no. 7 (2020): 925–53, https://doi.org/10.1080/02684527.2020.1771934 draws extensively from previously classified material. Sayle has made much of that material accessible through his *Canada Declassified* website, https://declassified.library.utoronto.ca/exhibits/show/canada-and-the-iraq-war/canada-and-the-iraq-war. Brian Bow's *The Politics of Linkage: Power, Interdependence, and Ideas in Canada-US Relations* (Vancouver: UBC Press, 2009) offers a theoretically sophisticated yet accessible explanation of the limitations of Washington's ability to compel Ottawa's support. Jean Chrétien, Eddie Goldenberg, Bill Graham, and Paul Cellucci all deal with this case extensively in their memoirs (cited in the notes).

The key article from which the Afghanistan case is derived is Matthew Willis's excellent "An unexpected war, a not unexpected mission: The origins of Kandahar 2005," *International Journal* 67, no. 4 (2012): 979–1000, https://doi.org/10.1177/002070201206700408. Janice Gross Stein and Eugene Lang's *The Unexpected War: Canada in Kandahar* (Toronto: Viking Canada, 2007) provides a number of helpful insights, but its overall interpretation is questionable. The memoirs cited throughout the notes to this case should also be read judiciously. For a provocative interpretation on why Kandahar went wrong, see M.L. Roi and Gregory Smolynec, "Canadian civil-military relations: International leadership, military capacity, and overreach," *International Journal* 65, no. 3 (2010): 705–24, https://doi.org/10.1177/002070201006500311. For a broader examination of the power of the defence establishment in the formulation of Canadian foreign policy, see Danford W. Middlemiss and Denis Stairs, "Is the defence establishment driving Canada's foreign policy?" in Jean Daudelin and Daniel Schwanen, eds., *Canada among Nations, 2007: What Room for Manoeuvre?* (Montreal: McGill-Queen's University Press, 2008), 66–90.

Beyond the Book

Participating in the United States Ballistic Missile Defense Program, 2003–2006

In the aftermath of 9/11, long-standing American efforts to develop an effective ballistic missile defence (BMD) system accelerated. Since BMD would protect all of upper North America from attack, Washington sought Canada's co-operation. Canadian involvement would enable BMD to be integrated into NORAD's responsibilities and provide Ottawa with a degree of input into America's continental defence strategy. The Chrétien government initially hesitated, based on fears that a commitment to BMD would indicate implicit support to American officials who subscribed to the inevitability of the weaponization of space.

As a candidate for the Liberal leadership, Paul Martin supported Canadian involvement in BMD. If decisions were going to be made about intercepting missiles flying over Canadian territory, he wanted Ottawa to be involved. At the time, a majority of Canadians agreed. When Martin became prime minister, his Defence Minister David Pratt wrote his American counterpart to that effect. Over time, Martin's enthusiasm waned. Unplanned and unwelcomed public comments by President Bush urging Canada to join the program during a visit to Halifax in late 2004 made the prime minister even less comfortable. By then, his government had been reduced to a minority, and the program had lost its appeal among an increasing number of Liberal caucus members, especially in Quebec. Martin sought more detailed information about the tactical implications of BMD from the foreign and defence ministries and was disappointed in their vague responses. Even though Ottawa had yet to be officially invited by Washington to join BMD, the Martin government announced in February 2005 that it would not be taking part. The Americans were incredulous and disappointed. Washington continued to develop the BMD technology without Canadian input.

Questions

1. What are Canada's national interests in this case?
2. What role might personality have played in Martin's final decision?
3. Why couldn't the national security community explain the case for BMD to the Canadian public convincingly?

Readings

A basic summary of the case can be found in Stephen Azzi, *Reconcilable Differences: A History of Canada-US Relations* (Don Mills, ON: Oxford University Press, 2015), 251–4. The most authoritative book on the history of Canada and BMD is James G. Fergusson, *Canada and Ballistic Missile Defence, 1954–2009: Déjà Vu All Over Again* (Vancouver: UBC Press, 2010), see specifically Act (chapter) 5, 206–55. The political side of the issue is dealt with tangentially in Janice Gross Stein and Eugene Lang, *The Unexpected War: Canada in Kandahar* (Toronto: Viking 2007), 121–7, 159–77. It is also covered in the memoirs of Paul Martin, Bill Graham, and US Ambassador to Canada Paul Cellucci. See Martin, *Hell or High Water: My Life In and Out of Politics* (Toronto: McClelland and Stewart, 2008), 384–90; Graham, *Call of the World: A Political Memoir* (Vancouver: UBC Press, 2016), 361–6; and Cellucci, *Unquiet Diplomat* (Toronto: Key Porter, 2005), 147–66. Finally, for a sanctimonious, yet still relevant, outsider's account of public efforts to derail Canada's accession to BMD, see Steven Staples, *Missile Defence: Round One: An Insider's Account of How and Why Canada Said No to George W. Bush—and Why this Issue Won't Die* (Toronto: James Lorimer, 2006).

10

Stephen Harper's Conservative Values on the World Stage, 2006–2015

Stephen Harper's New Conservative Government

The Conservative Party of Canada that formed a minority government in January 2006 was not an obvious successor to Brian Mulroney's Progressive Conservatives. Prime Minister Stephen Harper's public pledge "to pull the centre of the political spectrum toward conservatism" indicated a much more ideological orientation.[1] Observers generally agree that Harper had given little thought to Canadian foreign policy before becoming prime minister.[2] Shortly after his party formed a majority government in 2011, he reflected candidly: "the thing that's probably struck me the most in terms of my previous expectations…is not just how important foreign affairs/foreign relations is, but in fact that it's become almost everything."[3]

Nonetheless, Harper quickly put his stamp on Canada's global outlook. In the 2006 campaign, the Conservatives had promised to make "decisions that are not only independent, but are actually noticed by other powers around the world."[4] As John Baird, foreign minister from 2011 to 2015, explained,[5] Ottawa's new "values-based foreign policy" would reflect that Canada had "a side. The side is freedom. The side is human rights. The side is open economies."[6] Despite the often-complicated nature of international politics, the Conservatives adopted a single-minded, partisan approach to foreign affairs that narrowed the field of activity.[7]

The government encountered resistance—some real, some imagined—from the public service. "All the leaders I've talked to," the new prime minister told supporters in 2007, "complain to me that their foreign service wants to do what [it] believes is foreign policy, not what the government-of-the-day's foreign policy is."[8] Previous Conservative leaders R.B. Bennett, John Diefenbaker, and Brian Mulroney had also initially viewed members of the foreign service as opponents, but they largely came to recognize their diplomats' value. Less so Harper. The Conservatives' years in power were marked by tension between the Prime Ministers' Office and the Department of Foreign Affairs and International Trade (DFAIT), part of a wider clash between political staff and public officials.[9]

Canada First, Not Canada Alone: A History of Canadian Foreign Policy. Adam Chapnick and Asa McKercher, Oxford University Press. © Oxford University Press 2024. DOI: 10.1093/oso/9780197653715.003.0011

The government typically prevailed. In 2009, Ottawa ended funding to several development NGOs undertaking advocacy work. Instead, Harper stated, his government would "fund aid that actually makes a difference."[10] Three years later, the Conservatives cancelled the Understanding Canada program, a cultural diplomacy initiative funding Canadian studies abroad. An Office of Religious Freedom was established within DFAIT in 2013, and shortly thereafter the Canadian International Development Agency (CIDA) was folded into a new Department of Foreign Affairs, Trade, and Development (DFATD). In order to balance the federal budget, the Conservatives also subjected DFAIT and then DFATD to deep cuts, going so far as to sell off a number of diplomatic properties. Tensions culminated in a foreign service strike in 2013.

The Warrior Nation

As part of his effort to present a harder-edged image of Canada in the world, Prime Minister Harper paid his first foreign visit to Canadian troops in theatre in Afghanistan. "Your work," he told the gathered personnel, "is important because it is in our national interest to see Afghanistan become a free, democratic, and peaceful country."[11] The Kandahar mission fit with the government's emphasis on rebuilding the military, contributing to the war against terrorism, and supporting Canada's allies, particularly the United States. In the spring of 2006, the Conservatives and a majority of Liberal MPs supported a House of Commons motion to extend the Kandahar mission until February 2009.[12] An independent panel chaired by the former Liberal Foreign Minister John Manley later recommended a second extension, having concluded that "Canadian interests and values, and Canadian lives" were now invested in Afghanistan.[13]

Liberal backing of the war effort was important not only because the Conservatives lacked a majority in the House of Commons prior to 2011, but also because the Afghan mission rarely commanded majority public support. Mounting casualties and a lack of tangible progress in the battle against the Taliban made matters worse. Even though the Afghan war was a NATO mission, few alliance members (save the Americans, the British, the Dutch, and non-member Australia) would commit soldiers to combat operations. Harper himself appears to have written off the conflict by 2009. That March, he told an interviewer that "we're not ever going to defeat the insurgency."[14] The Canadian Forces remained beyond 2011 only thanks to a direct American appeal. Ottawa agreed to a final three-year training initiative focused on the Afghan military and police even though, the prime minister admitted, "my preference would be, would have been, to see a complete end to the military mission."[15]

222 CANADA FIRST, NOT CANADA ALONE

Between 2001 and 2014, roughly 100,000 Canadian military personnel were deployed to Afghanistan; 2071 were wounded and 159 were killed, along with a diplomat and two aid workers.[16] The war, observed two historians, was nothing like the traditional UN peacekeeping that Canadians seemed to prefer.[17] Combined with the Tory government's championing of Canadian military history, some commentators portrayed Harper as bent on transforming Canada into a "warrior nation." "I'm not dismissing peacekeeping," the prime minister stated in 2011, "but the real defining moments for the country and for the world are those big conflicts where everything's at stake and where you take a side and show you can contribute to the right side."[18] Indeed, the turn away from traditional peacekeeping had begun under the Chrétien Liberals, with NATO's war in Kosovo.[19]

As Canada's mission in Kandahar came to an end, Canadian military forces were deploying to Libya on a NATO mission in support of Libyans protesting the decades-long rule of Muammar Gadhafi as part of the Arab Spring (2010–12)—the revolt of common people in the Middle East against their authoritarian governments. When Gadhafi's security forces attacked the demonstrators, Western powers pushed for a UN intervention. Eventually, Russia and China agreed to two Security Council resolutions authorizing NATO's Operation Unified Protector. The initiative was commanded by Canadian Lieutenant-General Charles Bouchard. Ottawa also contributed fighter aircraft and a naval vessel with the express purpose of protecting Libyan civilians. The intervention resulted in the takeover of most of the country by anti-Gadhafi forces and the dictator's summary execution. "A handful of soldiers is better than a mouthful of arguments," Harper boasted at the time, "for the Gadhafis of this world pay no attention to the force of argument. The only thing they get is the argument of force."[20] Once Gadhafi was gone, the NATO mission ended and Libya descended into chaos.

A similar situation unfolded in Syria, where the Bashar al-Assad regime's brutal crackdown against protestors in 2011 morphed into a full-fledged civil war. The fighting spilled over into Iraq, and by mid-2014, a group of extremist Islamist insurgents—opponents of both the Iraqi government and the al-Assad regime—had seized parts of Iraq and Syria, forming a so-called Islamic State of the Levant (ISIL). ISIL (also known as ISIS—the Islamic State in Iraq and Syria—or Daesh) imposed a brutal form of theocratic rule while using social media to solicit support from around the world. Canada was not spared ISIL's violence. In October 2014, an armed attacker, after murdering a soldier on ceremonial sentry duty at the National War Memorial, was shot dead inside the Parliament buildings where he had intended to continue his rampage.

Western forces ultimately intervened to assist the Baghdad government in northern Iraq. Canada committed several combat and support aircraft as well as Special Forces troops to train the local military. In 2015, the Harper government expanded the mission into Syria and pledged Canadian involvement for "the long haul."[21] By then, Ottawa was able to draw on members of the Canadian Armed Forces (CAF) who had returned from Ukraine, part of an international response to Russian aggression.[22]

Despite the Conservatives' strong rhetoric in support of the Canadian military and an initial surge in defence spending largely connected to the Afghan war, efforts to rearm the CAF soon petered out. A much-touted Canada First Defence Strategy announced in 2008 was declared unaffordable in 2011 as austerity measures swept the government. By 2015, defence spending had plummeted to 1 per cent of GDP, the lowest ratio in 80 years and well short of the 2 per cent figure pledged by all NATO members.[23]

Figure 10.1 Canadian Prime Minister Stephen Harper speaks to sailors aboard the HMCS *Fredericton* in Gydnia, Poland, 10 June 2015. On 10 June 2015, Prime Minister Stephen Harper boarded the Halifax-class frigate, HMCS *Fredericton*, amid its deployment to the Baltic Sea as part of a NATO training exercise. Two Russian vessels tracked the ship from afar. In addition to spending the night on the ship with his wife, Laureen, Harper spoke to crew members and presented one with a special service medal. He also gave a speech critical of Russia and its president, Vladimir Putin, whom he charged with seeking to disrupt and undermine the stable world order that NATO would continue to proudly defend. The photo reflects several themes from the Harper era. The military backdrop is consistent with the Conservatives' valorization of Canada as a "warrior nation." The colour blue, not coincidentally the colour of the Conservative Party, is predominant throughout. The prime minister's position at the podium on his own (his Minister of Defence Jason Kenney was also aboard the ship) reflects the personification of the government in his image. Canadian Press/Adrian Wyld/CP13384519.

224 CANADA FIRST, NOT CANADA ALONE

A Northern Foreign Policy

The government's fiscal agenda compromised other international priorities as well. When he announced the purchase of new Arctic patrol ships in 2007, Harper spoke at length about the need to defend "our nation's sovereignty" in the North. "More and more," he added, "as global commerce routes chart a path to Canada's North and as the oil, gas and minerals of this frontier become more valuable, northern resource development will grow ever more critical to our country."[24] In 2009, the government released a Northern Strategy.[25] The follow-up Statement on Canada's Arctic Foreign Policy (2010) included pledges to promote resource development and respect for territorial and maritime boundaries through the Arctic Council as well as plans for a maritime refuelling facility at Nanisivik; an all-weather road between Tuktoyaktuk and Inuvik; a Canadian High Arctic Research Station at Cambridge Bay; and a fleet of heavy icebreakers.[26] The entire agenda—which already paid limited attention to the individual and collective needs of members of the northern communities—was ultimately scaled back in the face of budget cuts.[27]

Climate Change and the UN

The Arctic's renewed relevance was a direct result of climate change. The Conservatives proved recalcitrant to act in the face of increasing scientific evidence that human activity was responsible for warming temperatures and altered weather patterns. Prime Minister Harper was particularly concerned that meeting national commitments under the Kyoto Protocol would undermine Canada's position as what he called an "energy superpower"[28] and compromise economic growth in the Conservative heartland of Alberta and Saskatchewan. At the 2007 UN Climate Change Conference in Bali, Indonesia, Environment Minister John Baird conceded the obvious: Canada would not meet its emissions reduction targets. More surprising was Ottawa's outright withdrawal from the protocol in 2011. The move outraged environmentalists, who consistently awarded Canada "Fossil Awards."[29]

The withdrawal from Kyoto suggested a more unilateralist approach to defending Canadian interests on the world stage. As Foreign Minister Baird remarked at the UN in 2013, Canada's government no longer cared "to have our own values or own principled foreign policy validated by elites who would rather 'go along to get along.'"[30] In truth, the Conservative approach might be termed selective multilateralism. Stephen Harper had no problem engaging in the activities of the G-8 and G-20. Indeed, while hosting the 2010 G-8 in Huntsville, the prime minister launched the Muskoka Initiative on Maternal,

Newborn, and Child Health. Pushed by Baird, Canada also became an outspoken advocate of LGBTQ+ rights and a critic of child marriage.

Ottawa was less interested in Latin America and the Caribbean. The Conservatives initially committed to a "re-engagement in our hemisphere" and even issued an Americas Strategy in 2009.[31] Apart from select trade and investment initiatives and slightly expanded development programs, there was little serious interaction with Canada's southern neighbours and limited involvement with multilateral organizations such as the Organization of the American States or the Summits of the Americas.[32]

The government's interest in the UN was similarly limited. In 2007, Canada opposed the UN Declaration on the Rights of Indigenous Peoples (UNDRIP). As part of a shift toward a more pro-Israel position in the Middle East, in 2009 the Conservatives ceased funding the UN Relief and Works Agency for Palestinian Refugees. Differences with members of the Arab League likely contributed to Canada's failure to secure a non-permanent seat on the UN Security Council in 2010. A lack of attention to climate change and a shrinking aid budget also undermined the Canadian campaign.[33]

China and Economic Diplomacy

The assertiveness evident on Kyoto and Israel also characterized the Conservatives' early dealings with China. "I think Canadians want us to promote our trade relations worldwide," Harper remarked to reporters en route to the Asia-Pacific Economic Cooperation summit in 2006, "and we do that, but I don't think Canadians want us to sell out important Canadian values. They don't want us to sell out to the almighty dollar."[34] In 2006, Ottawa bestowed honorary Canadian citizenship on the Dalai Lama. In 2007, Harper upset the Chinese again by meeting with the leader of Tibetan Buddhism. The Conservative government declined Beijing's invitation to the opening and closing ceremonies of the 2008 summer Olympics, a showcase event for the communist regime.

Members of the Canadian business community struggled to access the booming Chinese economy, and they grew more vocal following the Great Recession of 2008–9.[35] The result was a sea change in Conservative policy. Harper finally visited Beijing in December 2009. He hosted Chinese president Hu Jintao the following year. Additional prime ministerial visits followed in 2012 and 2014. The government's rhetoric also softened. On his first official trip to China as foreign minister in 2011, Baird declared that bilateral economic engagement was "a clear priority."[36] In 2012, the Harper government approved a controversial sale of Calgary-based Nexen Energy to China's state-owned oil

226 CANADA FIRST, NOT CANADA ALONE

company, and Ottawa and Beijing agreed to a Foreign Investment Promotion and Protection Agreement (FIPA) to encourage investment. The FIPA raised the prospects of a free trade agreement. Canadian officials prepared a study and recommended against it. "Canada," Harper later wrote, "is simply not in a position to get a good deal bargaining one-on-one with the People's Republic."[37] Other factors were at also play: China's lacklustre human rights record, its espionage activities, and its aggressive actions toward its neighbours. As David Mulroney, ambassador in Beijing from 2009 to 2012, put it, efforts to deepen relations with China were "beyond the comfort zone of many Canadians."[38]

China's newfound importance reflected the Conservatives' growing emphasis on what they called "economic diplomacy."[39] Ottawa concluded bilateral free trade deals with the European Free Trade Association (2009), Peru (2009), Colombia (2011), Jordan (2012), Panama (2013), Honduras (2014), South Korea (2014), and Ukraine (2015), and updated an existing agreement with Israel. This trade offensive's centrepiece was the Comprehensive Economic and Trade Agreement (CETA) with the European Union. Harper later recalled the signing ceremony for CETA in 2014 as "one of my best days in office."[40] Canada also joined talks for a Trans-Pacific Partnership (TPP) that would secure access to over a dozen Asia-Pacific countries, an outcome that the prime minister deemed "essential."[41] The negotiations continued right through the 2015 election.

Relations with the United States

The emphasis on trade sought in part to expand Canadian commercial linkages beyond the United States, though it was not inflected with anti-American undertones. In 2011, Harper reaffirmed that "having good relations, first and foremost, with our most critical ally, the United States, is essential to Canada's well-being."[42] However, in 2008 the Canadian prime minister had already foreseen problems with the Americans. US environmental policy was hampering Canadian exports of oil and gas and there was "an increasing thickening of the border for security reasons or justified by security criteria, sometimes, not always, disguising protectionist sentiment that we think is very worrisome."[43]

These concerns emerged toward the end of George W. Bush's presidency. Although Harper and Bush were ideologically aligned, the latter's unpopularity among Canadians hampered the Tories' public embrace of the United States.[44] Still, Harper and Bush renewed the NORAD agreement and resolved, at least temporarily, a long-standing softwood lumber dispute. The Canadian government also sought to work with Washington and Mexico City on the Security and Prosperity Partnership (SPP), the 2005 trilateral agreement meant to harmonize border security and cross-boundary trade. The SPP failed. In 2009, US Homeland Security Secretary Janet Napolitano decried the "fiction that there's no longer a border between Canada and the United States."[45] In 2011 Ottawa and Washington concluded the Beyond the Border initiative, a bilateral border and trade scheme. The agreement excluded Mexico, reflecting the Harper government's preference to keep relationships with its two continental partners separate. In 2009, Ottawa imposed a visa requirement on Mexican travellers. The following year, Harper suspended the North American Leaders Summit process. His focus was on the United States alone.

The relationship between Harper and US President Barack Obama began positively. The new president paid his first foreign visit to Ottawa in February 2009 amid a financial crisis that saw the Canadian and US governments coordinate a multi-billion-dollar bailout of North American automakers. Disagreements soon emerged, partly over policy differences rooted in the leaders' divergent political beliefs. The White House's efforts to pursue a middle ground on the Israeli–Palestinian conflict at the 2011 G8 Summit clashed with Ottawa's unabashedly pro-Israel stance.[46] That same year, Washington temporarily blocked Canadian participation in the TPP talks over Canada's protection of its dairy industry.

The most significant bilateral dispute concerned the proposed extension of the Keystone XL pipeline, a project that would transport Albertan oil to refineries on the Gulf Coast of Texas. There was no room for middle ground on this issue—the pipeline would either be extended, or it would not—and the final decision was in the hands of the American president. In the view of the Canadian government, Keystone would provide US consumers with energy from a friendly, secure source. Approval, Prime Minister Harper stated bluntly, was a "complete no-brainer."[47] In Washington, Keystone became a proxy for the Obama administration's position on climate change as well as a source of local opposition from environmentalists and farmers worried about any resulting pollution. Canadian diplomats and political officials lobbied extensively in Washington, with the prime minister telling a New York business audience that Ottawa "won't take no for an answer."[48] The White House resented such interference with what had become a sensitive political issue, and Ottawa grew increasingly impatient with the president's indecision. As US Ambassador Bruce Heyman later recalled, this "political frost" put an "icy chill" over Canadian–American relations.[49] Obama rejected Keystone after Canada's 2015 election.

The 2015 Election

The election served as a referendum on nearly a decade of Conservative rule. Foreign policy was part of the debate, with critics decrying the prime minister for moving Canada away from what they saw as its traditional role in the world, and supporters of the government praising the new Conservative emphasis on

228 CANADA FIRST, NOT CANADA ALONE

foreign affairs.[50] Polling data released in the midst of the campaign found 41 per cent of respondents agreed that Canada's global reputation had worsened since 2006, 30 per cent believed that it has stayed the same, and 21 per cent stated that it had improved, views that seemed to align with party affiliation among the populace.[51]

During the first-ever election debate devoted entirely to Canadian foreign affairs, the party leaders addressed a host of challenges, from Keystone and climate change to Russian aggression toward Ukraine and the Western campaign against ISIS. The issue that likely affected the election the most was the government's response to the Syrian refugee crisis. Amid the ongoing and brutal civil war, millions of Syrians fled their homes. The Harper government committed to resettling 10,000 Syrian refugees over three years, a paltry figure that reinforced a perception among voters of Conservative indifference. In contrast, the opposition parties promised to bring tens of thousands of refugees into Canada by year end, to reverse a ban on wearing the niqab at citizenship ceremonies, and to eliminate the Conservatives' plans for a "barbaric cultural practices hotline," which would enable Canadians to inform on practices of their neighbours of which they did not approve.[52] The public chose a change in political direction, and in 2015 the Liberals formed their first majority government since 2003.

Case Studies

The cases for this chapter add a layer of complexity to the most common explanations of the Harper government's approach to foreign policy. Together, they suggest that the Conservatives ascribed to the mantra of "Canada first, but not Canada alone" more than some critics have suggested.

The first case examines the government's decision to vote against the United Nations Declaration on the Rights of Indigenous Peoples in 2007 and subsequent reversal in 2010. Based on conversations with political insiders, it suggests that being alone on the world stage was hardly the government's preference.

The second case considers what was arguably the government's most successful foreign policy achievement: the Muskoka Initiative on Maternal, Newborn, and Child Health. From the evidence available, it appears that Stephen Harper's Ottawa was open to proposals from civil society when they were framed appropriately. Whether such "framing" constituted a betrayal of best practices in international development assistance is debatable.

The third case focuses on the Conservatives' response to Russia's 2014 invasion of Crimea and the impact of a well-established diaspora lobby group, the Ukrainian Canadian Congress, on the government's thinking. Again, it is possible to see Ottawa as less insular and inflexible than some have contended.

The Beyond the Book case highlights the role of public administration in foreign policy. Aligned with an international trend, the Harper government amalgamated the Department of Foreign Affairs and International Trade with the Canadian International Development Agency in 2013. Although the scholarship surrounding the merger is still in its early stages, the role of bureaucratic organization in the shaping of Canadian foreign policy and strategic decision making deserves greater scrutiny.

All four issues share a common theme: the direct impact of Prime Minister Stephen Harper. Unlike earlier periods covered in this book, by the twenty-first century, the role of Canada's foreign minister in international affairs had become secondary, at best.

Affirming Support for the United Nations Declaration on the Rights of Indigenous Peoples (UNDRIP), 2007–2010

What role do close allies play in Canadian foreign policy decision making?

In 2007, Canada and three of its "Anglosphere" allies—Australia, New Zealand, and the United States—stood alone in opposition to the United Nations Declaration on the Rights of Indigenous Peoples at the UN General Assembly. Within three years, all four states had changed their positions. This case explores the degree to which the views of Canada's allies might have affected Ottawa's policy shift.

The United Nations began investigating discrimination against Indigenous peoples in 1971.[53] In 1982, a Working Group on Indigenous Peoples (WGIP) was formed. According to political scientist and Anishinaabe scholar Sheryl Lightfoot, by 1985 the WGIP had committed to drafting an official statement on Indigenous peoples' rights.[54] After nearly 10 years of negotiations, the Sub-Commission on Prevention of Discrimination and Protection of Minorities created an Inter-sessional Working Group to prepare the draft declaration for broader consideration.

Canadian engagement in reconciliation efforts has a similarly lengthy history. The World Council on Indigenous Peoples—an advocacy-based, non-governmental organization with standing at the UN—was founded at a conference in British Columbia in 1975. Its first leader was the chief of the National Indian Brotherhood, George Manuel.[55] Successive Canadian governments participated actively in the WGIP, even if the two implicated departments viewed the process differently. According to what was then Indian and Northern Affairs Canada (INAC), "the experts were crafting a Declaration by

230   CANADA FIRST, NOT CANADA ALONE

and for indigenous peoples, and…the concerns of States were not given adequate consideration in this process."[56] INAC viewed the negotiations through a legal lens and was most concerned with the practical implications of any emergent declaration. Members of DFAIT understood the exercise as an aspirational process. They were most concerned with maintaining Canada's global reputation as a reliable multilateral partner.[57] In spite of INAC's reservations, Ottawa continued to negotiate through 2005.

Late that year, the chairperson-rapporteur of the working group introduced a compromise proposal. Members considered his suggestions in good faith, but disputes over self-determination and land rights persisted. In an effort to bring two decades of discussions to a positive conclusion, the chair made additional, unilateral changes and submitted a revised text to the United Nations Human Rights Council for consideration.[58]

Canada was a member of the council at the time, and its representatives were uncomfortable with the chair's revisions. Ottawa lobbied extensively for further changes and a longer negotiating process. Its efforts failed, and Canada was one of two countries (along with the Russian Federation) to vote against sending the draft declaration to the UN General Assembly in June 2006.[59] Outside of the council, close allies and fellow settler states Australia, New Zealand, and the United States also had concerns, as did a number of African countries that had not been involved in the working groups. The Africans successfully insisted on further amendments—specifically around the language defining self-determination and "Indigenous" peoples—which delayed the General Assembly debate until September 2007. Ottawa and its allies continued to lobby—unsuccessfully—for more radical modifications.[60]

On 13 September 2007, members of the General Assembly adopted what the UN called "a landmark declaration that brought to an end nearly 25 years of contentious negotiations over the rights of native people to protect their lands and resources, and to maintain their unique cultures and traditions."[61] Canada joined Australia, New Zealand, and the United States as the only countries to vote against the declaration. One hundred and forty-three states voted in favour; 11 abstained; and 31 did not appear for the vote. Every country that abstained was home to Indigenous peoples, as were 28 of the 31 states that absented themselves.[62]

In explaining his country's vote, Canada's permanent representative to the UN, John McNee, indicated that, "unfortunately, the provisions in the Declaration on lands, territories and resources were overly broad, unclear, and capable of a wide variety of interpretations, discounting the need to recognize a range of rights over land and possibly putting into question matters that have been settled by treaty."[63] His comments were consistent with INAC's 5000-word explanation of Canada's negative vote at the Human Rights Council, as well as with those of INAC's minister, Jim Prentice, in the House of Commons.[64]

STEPHEN HARPER'S CONSERVATIVE VALUES ON THE WORLD STAGE   231

Two academic explanations for the Canadian decision prevail. The first suggests that had Paul Martin's Liberals won the January 2006 election, Ottawa would have supported the declaration. The Harper government's failure to consult with Indigenous groups upon taking power and its more general "ideological bias" were to blame.[65] Others emphasize Ottawa's insistence on a state-centric model of reconciliation that is incompatible with the vision of many Indigenous groups.[66]

Political insiders suggest a third possibility that highlights what diplomats call the importance of being "in good company."[67] They point specifically to a meeting between Australian Prime Minister John Howard and Canadian Prime Minister Stephen Harper in May 2006.[68] At the time, Ottawa was faced with contradictory recommendations from DFAIT—which suggested that Canada had to support the declaration because its allies planned to—and INAC, which made a case more consistent with the latter academic explanation. Apparently, just as Harper had been advised that Australia would back the declaration, Howard had been advised that Canada would. Once the two leaders realized that they were not bound to support a statement that had elicited significant concerns from other parts of their bureaucracies, at Howard's suggestion, they chose restraint.

INAC made specific reference to a joint statement issued by Australia, New Zealand, and the United States condemning the "fundamentally flawed" draft declaration in the aftermath of the vote at the Human Rights Council in June 2006.[69] McNee alluded to "a number of other States with large indigenous populations" in his explanation of the September 2007 vote.[70] In the aftermath of the General Assembly meeting, all four countries explained their negative votes similarly.[71]

The international outcry against the dissenters was overwhelming. Criticism came from the Special Rapporteur on the Rights of Indigenous Peoples, the UN Committee on the Elimination of Racial Discrimination, the UN Human Rights Council, participants at the UN Permanent Forum on Indigenous Issues, and a plethora of NGOs.[72] At home, the Conservatives ignored a parliamentary resolution calling on them to endorse the declaration.[73] Neither the Harper government's residential schools apology nor its establishment of a Truth and Reconciliation Commission (which ultimately recommended supporting UNDRIP) could staunch the public criticism.[74]

Without documentary evidence, it is difficult to determine exactly what caused the Government of Canada to change its position. By 2010, there were new elected and unelected officials at INAC and DFAIT. The Harper government was angling to transform its minority standing in the House of Commons into a majority. The international pressure on Ottawa was relentless. In time, all four Anglosphere states reconsidered their positions. In April 2009, a new Australian Labour government announced that it planned to support the declaration as an aspirational document. New Zealand—led by a new government that relied on an agreement with the Māori Party to stay in power—followed, with similar caveats, in April 2010, by which point the now Democrat-led White House was also hinting at a change.[75]

Ottawa indicated that it planned to follow a similar path in its 3 March 2010 throne speech: "A growing number of states have given qualified recognition to the United Nations Declaration on the Rights of Indigenous Peoples. Our Government will take steps to endorse this aspirational document in a manner fully consistent with Canada's Constitution and laws."[76] The official change took place quietly, on 12 November, and came with qualifiers similar to those expressed by Canadian allies. The declaration was "an aspirational document" that did not "reflect customary international law nor change Canadian laws."[77] Lightfoot described the move as "seemingly intended to reduce the significance of the declaration for Canada, domesticate Indigenous issues, [and] maintain the status quo in terms of policy, law and institutional structures."[78]

Neither it, nor Prime Minister Harper's subsequent invitation to the Assembly of First Nations to negotiate a transformation of Ottawa's strategic approach to Indigenous affairs, satisfied the government's most ardent domestic critics.[79] It did, however, relieve some of the international pressure that would have been felt had Canada been left standing alone in opposition.

The Muskoka Initiative on Maternal, Newborn, and Child Health, 2009–2010

> What role can, or should, civil society play in the shaping of Canada's foreign policy agenda?

In 2015, the United Nations Children's Fund (UNICEF) referred to Canada as "an established global leader on child and maternal health."[80] It was high praise for a country led by a government that was often accused of militarizing the national approach to world affairs.[81] It also validated a multi-year campaign by a coalition of civil society organizations (CSOs) to shape Canadian foreign policy.[82] This case examines the extent to which they succeeded.

In 1987, the Conference on Safe Motherhood brought together representatives from 37 countries, civil society organizations, and UN institutions in Nairobi, Kenya, to discuss the high rates of women dying during pregnancy and childbirth.[83] The issue of maternal health was revisited at the UN's Cairo International Conference on Population and Development in 1994 and was included in the Millennium Development Goals (MDGs)—targets to reduce extreme poverty and other hardships around the world—announced by the UN in 2000.[84]

The MDGs' 15-year timeline was ambitious. By the late 2000s it had become clear that goals of reducing child mortality and improving maternal health would be the most difficult to reach.[85] Canada was scheduled to host the G8 leaders' summit in June 2010. Ottawa needed a signature initiative to shape the agenda and reaffirm the importance of the G8. The combination of the Conservative government's limited summitry experience and lack of a comprehensive development assistance plan left it open to external advocacy.[86]

World Vision, a well-established CSO focused on children in need, had begun to coordinate advocacy efforts on child mortality and maternal health in 2006. Save the Children, one of World Vision's partner organizations in what became known as the Canadian Coalition for Maternal, Newborn, and Child Health, met with senior government officials to discuss Canada's G8 plans in the summer of 2008. By November, the coalition had developed a template for a Canadian maternal, newborn, and child health initiative. The plan was presented to senior officials in the Prime Minister's Office in March 2009. Recognizing the Harper government's concerns about aid transparency, accountability, and measurable results, the meeting focused on practical interventions that Ottawa could champion that would produce immediate, life-saving effects. The presentation was well-received, as were further outreach efforts to the Canadian International Development Agency (CIDA), the Department of Foreign Affairs and International Trade, the Privy Council Office, and ultimately to the prime minister's G8 personal representative and health advisor.[87]

The CSOs were not the only advocates. CIDA had sponsored UNICEF's Accelerated Child Survival and Development project in the early 2000s and had begun funding the Catalytic Initiative to Save a Million Lives in 2007, both programs that emphasized high-impact, inexpensive interventions targeting women and children.[88] Health was therefore already a CIDA priority, and its officials had also identified an opportunity for Canadian leadership.[89] Few members of the agency were confident that the Harper government would agree.[90]

In retrospect, there was reason for greater optimism.[91] After much internal debate, the CSOs and CIDA had deliberately framed the initiative in practical, rather than sociologically transformative, terms: "By focusing on interventions such as training healthcare workers, providing supplies and infrastructure, improving managerial capacity and data collection," they presented Ottawa with "a technical problem that [could] be solved through provision of relatively straightforward interventions."[92] It was, as the former director of policy in the Prime Minister's Office reflected, an ideal Conservative initiative: "simple, straightforward, easily communicated, and had the ability to have a huge impact on a large number of people, fairly quickly. It wasn't big government . . . it could be pushed out at the local level. . . . Of course, it was politically beneficial, too."[93] Most important, it resonated with the prime minister, who embraced it wholeheartedly.[94]

234 CANADA FIRST, NOT CANADA ALONE

Still, it almost did not happen. The Harper government announced a vague plan to launch a maternal, newborn, and child health program shortly after taking over the presidency of the G8 in January 2010. By March, questions were being asked about whether the Muskoka Initiative, named after the Central Ontario district where the summit took place, would fund women's reproductive health, including legal abortions, something that many Conservatives opposed. The government appears to have assumed that the good coming from the Muskoka Initiative would make it widely politically acceptable, even if access to abortion was not part of the services provided.[95] It was wrong.[96]

When Foreign Minister Lawrence Cannon mistakenly suggested in early March that the undertaking excluded all family planning services, the domestic and international fallout was overwhelming. Harper ultimately clarified that contraception would be included, but not abortion. "We want to make sure our funds are used to save the lives of women and children and are used on the many, many things that are available to us that frankly do not divide the Canadian population," he explained.[97] The Conservative position led to a raucous debate in the House of Commons and to public rebukes from US Secretary of State Hillary Clinton, British Foreign Secretary David Miliband, and the British medical journal The Lancet.[98] In May, an article indicating that CIDA had advocated including abortion revived the controversy, but the government held firm.[99]

On 26 June 2010, G8 leaders committed US$5 billion to the Muskoka Initiative. Ottawa pledged $1.1 billion over five years in new money, along with the $1.75 billion it had previously set aside.[100] The Canadian government swiftly established 10 partner countries and launched or enhanced programs meant to strengthen domestic health-care systems, combat disease, and improve nutrition.[101] The UN held a special, high-level meeting on maternal and child health in September, where Secretary-General Ban Ki-moon announced a Global Strategy for Women's and Children's Health that raised an additional US$40 billion. Before year's end, Prime Minister Harper and Tanzanian President Jakaya Kikwete had accepted Ban's invitation to co-chair a UN Commission on Information and Accountability for Women's and Children's Health.[102] In May 2014, Harper hosted the Saving Every Woman, Every Child summit in Toronto and pledged an additional $3.5 billion to extend Canada's commitment through 2020.[103] That September, he lobbied at the UN General Assembly for further support.[104]

In spite of the abortion controversy, the Muskoka Initiative was well received abroad.[105] The reception at home was mixed. Supporters emphasized Ottawa's successful organizational efforts and the prime minister's sustained personal commitment to resolving a clear international problem.[106] Critics, largely from civil society and the academic community, raised three main points.

The Canadian commitments coincided with a freeze to the international assistance budget, which meant that funding for the Muskoka Initiative came at the expense of other CIDA priorities. Despite efforts to hold Canada's G8 partners accountable for their pledges, several states failed to meet them.[107] Finally, gender equality experts noted that the government's emphasis on short-term, practical interventions failed to address the underlying causes of inequality.[108]

After the Conservatives were defeated in 2015, the Trudeau government recast the Muskoka Initiative with a new focus on sexual and reproductive health and rights, explicitly including support for "the right to choose safe and legal abortion; and increase[d] access to post-abortion care."[109] How important civil society was to that decision remains unclear.

Canada's Response to the Euromaidan, 2013–2015

> What role do, or should, organized diaspora groups play in the development and implementation of Canadian foreign policy?

Canadian multiculturalism encourages all citizens, but particularly immigrants, to celebrate their multiple identities.[110] Few immigrant communities have embraced that political element as enthusiastically as Ukrainian Canadians. This case examines the impact of this "diaspora" community on Canadian foreign policy toward Ukraine.[111]

Ukraine became an independent, sovereign state in the aftermath of the collapse of the Soviet Union. Over the next 20 years, successive Ukrainian governments struggled to maximize the economic and security benefits that would result from closer integration with either the European Union to the west or Russia to the east. By 2013, the pressure to choose between the two orientations had become overwhelming.[112]

At the time, Canada was home to approximately 1.3 million Ukrainian Canadians, the largest Ukrainian diaspora apart from Russia. Advocacy was coordinated in large part by the Ukrainian Canadian Congress (UCC), a well-established and politically sophisticated umbrella organization. In the early 1990s, the UCC called for investment in Ukraine's social and economic development through Canada's international assistance program. In 1994, a Joint Canada-Ukraine Declaration of a Special Partnership affirmed Ottawa's commitment.[113] The partnership could have been anticipated. The Canada-Ukraine "special relationship"[114] has enjoyed cross-partisan support ever since Canada recognized the state's independence in December 1991.[115]

Nonetheless, when the Conservatives formed a government in 2006, they found the failure of Ukraine's President Viktor Yushchenko to fully embrace

236 CANADA FIRST, NOT CANADA ALONE

democratic reform disconcerting. At the 2006 G8 summit in Moscow, Finance Minister Jim Flaherty dismissed a gas dispute between Russia and Ukraine as part of Russia's "internal affairs."[116] Ottawa also briefly contemplated reducing its diplomatic presence in Kyiv. Russian aggression against Georgia in 2008 gradually changed the government's political and diplomatic calculus. By 2013, Foreign Minister John Baird had developed a trusted relationship with UCC president Paul Grod, and officials were speaking out more regularly, albeit still cautiously, against Russian influence in the region.[117]

In November 2013, after private consultations with Moscow, Ukraine's new pro-Russian President Viktor Yanukovych abruptly abandoned negotiations for an association agreement with the European Union in favour of a customs agreement with Russia. Almost immediately, protestors gathered on the Maidan Square in Kyiv. Yanukovych responded with deadly force that triggered greater civil unrest and resistance. At the peak of the brutality in February 2014, 77 people were shot dead in a single day. Leaders of the Maidan called for Yanukovych's resignation. Eventually, the disgraced president fled the country.[118] Looking to secure advantage in the chaos and uncertainty, Russia dismissed the new government in Kyiv as putchist and illegitimate. Russian forces invaded and annexed Crimea, while Moscow encouraged, armed, and then supported pro-Russian insurgents in the Donbas region of southeastern Ukraine. These actions violated the Budapest Memorandum on Security Assurances that Russia had signed with Britain and the United States in 1994 as well as the Treaty of Friendship, Co-operation, and Partnership it had signed with Ukraine three years later.[119] Although a ceasefire was reached in September 2014, the violence never fully abated.

In response to the crisis, the Ukrainian Canadian Congress organized 20 peaceful protests across Canada; facilitated humanitarian assistance and relief efforts; and maintained regular contact with the Harper government. Grod accompanied Canada's foreign minister, and later the prime minister, on visits to Ukraine, while pressing Ottawa to increase its support for the country and its aspirations.[120]

The Conservatives hardly needed prompting.[121] The extensive Ukrainian diaspora in the Prairies—where Conservative support was strong—partially explains their sense of urgency. But Ukraine garnered significant cross-partisan backing. Canada's House of Commons held an emergency debate on the crisis during which all sides agreed that Ukrainians deserved Canada's help.[122]

Still, there was no denying the Harper government's unusually firm position. At a pivotal moment in the crisis, Foreign Minister Baird stood in solidarity with the Euromaidan protestors in Kyiv's Independence Square. Ukraine's national flag was flown over Parliament Hill as a symbol of support. Once Russia invaded Crimea, Ottawa advocated Russia's expulsion from the G8,

Figure 10.2 Ukraine and Russia.

withdrew the Canadian ambassador from Moscow, imposed a series of economic sanctions on Russian and Ukrainian pro-Russian institutions and officials, and restarted free trade negotiations with Ukraine. Canada also contributed to a mission of the Organisation for Economic Co-operation and Development (OECD) to eastern Ukraine, sent 20 Canadian Armed Forces (CAF) personnel and six CF-188 Hornet aircraft to the Baltics as part of NATO's Operation REASSURANCE, and deployed a frigate to the Black Sea. The CAF participated in a series of military training exercises with their Ukrainian counterparts as part of Operation UNIFIER.

In June 2014, Stephen Harper personally attended the installation ceremony of the new Ukrainian president, Petro Poroshenko. Shortly thereafter, Canada sent Kyiv large quantities of non-lethal military supplies and gave it select access to geospatial intelligence.[123] As Harper explained, a bilateral free trade agreement, signed in July, did not just promise economic benefits for both

238 CANADA FIRST, NOT CANADA ALONE

countries but was "a step towards helping Ukrainians realize the future that they want," that is "a Western future, a future of prosperity."[124] The following month, Canada's mission at NATO made international headlines with a clever tweet of a map that "was meant to aid Russian soldiers who occasionally get 'lost' and end up 'accidentally entering' Ukrainian territory."[125]

Harper's rhetoric was direct and unapologetic. At a speech at the United for Ukraine Gala in September, he declared: "The only truth we can be certain of in any statement coming out of the Putin regime is that the truth must be something else entirely."[126] When he saw Putin at the November meeting of the G20, he said: "I guess I'll shake your hand but I have only one thing to say to you: You need to get out of Ukraine."[127] When Putin replied, "That's impossible, because we are not there," Harper answered: "That's why I don't want to have a meeting with you. You'll just lie to me."[128] He appears never to have spoken with Putin again.

Analysts have offered four explanations for Ottawa's posture. Some focus on partisanship and diaspora politics. The Conservative government was courting the Ukrainian-Canadian vote while signalling to other immigrants that Ottawa would be there for them as well.[129] Journalist Mike Blanchfield points more specifically to the refusal of the Prime Minister's Office to allow members of the opposition to join Minister Baird during a 2014 visit to Ukraine as well as the politicization of Canada's contribution to election-monitoring in the country.[130] Others credit the sophisticated mobilizing and advocacy strategies of a mature and sophisticated Ukrainian-Canadian community for shaping the government's agenda.[131] A third view emphasizes the pressure Russia had brought to bear on the liberal-democratic international order upon which Canadian interests depended. Ottawa paid close attention to Ukraine only once Russia attacked. Even then, it refused to ship lethal weapons to Ukraine—despite the UCC's urging—unless Washington did so first.[132] There is general agreement that what Minister Baird lauded as Prime Minister Harper's "moral clarity" also played a role.[133]

When the Liberals formed government in 2015, they initially offered toned-down rhetoric on Ukraine, but retained the general thrust of the Canadian position.[134] Only time will tell whether the new government's posture was evidence of the continuing politicization of Canadian foreign policy (in accordance with party preferences) or an indication of de-politicization.

Conclusion

Under Stephen Harper's leadership, the Conservative government's approach to positioning Canada first in world affairs might be explained most simply by paraphrasing former Prime Minister William Lyon Mackenzie King's attitude toward conscription: "Canada alone if necessary, but not necessarily Canada alone." On issues such as the Israeli-Palestinian conflict, LGBTQ+ rights, Ukraine, or extending the Keystone XL pipeline, Ottawa expressed its thinking publicly and unreservedly. Canada's values-based foreign policy meant taking clear stands, regardless of their impact on a bid for a seat on the UN Security Council or relations with the United States. The Harper government had no time for UN treaties it found unrealistic and unhelpful, as well as diminishing interest in Afghanistan once the prime minister determined that the war was unwinnable. It did not hesitate to upset its own public officials by amalgamating its foreign service with its development agency, or civil society in its broader approach to development assistance.

Yet, there is significant evidence that the Conservatives recognized the value of working with partners and allies and even taking the advice of experts. It made sense to share a position on the UN Declaration on the Rights of Indigenous Peoples with other members of the Anglosphere. There was value in launching a maternal, child, and newborn health initiative through the G-7, and civil society's advice on how and why to do so was largely well taken. In its support for Ukraine, there were limits on what Canada could commit to the cause without the backing of its Western allies.

The government's approach toward what it called "economic diplomacy" became more predictable over time. Ottawa prioritized bilateral and multilateral trade agreements with already prosperous countries. This resulted in a series of successful bilateral and multilateral free trade agreements, but also meant selling arms to Saudi Arabia and increasing trade with China despite the two regimes' deplorable human rights records.

In the end, the Harper government's global posture improved Canada's international economic prospects. Its impact on the country's wider role in the world and the legacy of its increasing tendency to frame foreign policy in partisan terms were much less positive.

Readings

Key studies of the Afghanistan war are Carter Malkasian, *The American War in Afghanistan: A History* (New York: Oxford University Press, 2021) and Craig Whitlock, *The Afghanistan Papers: A Secret History of the War* (New York: Simon & Schuster, 2021). Fawaz Gerges looks at ISIS in *ISIS: A History*, 2nd ed. (Princeton: Princeton University Press, 2021). On the Great Recession, see Adam Tooze's *Crashed: How a Decade of Financial Crises Changed the World* (New York: Viking, 2018). Important examinations of Ukraine and its relations

240 CANADA FIRST, NOT CANADA ALONE

with Russia are Anna Reid's *Borderland: A Journey Through the History of Ukraine* (New York: Basic Books, 2015) and Serhii Plokhy's *The Gates of Europe: A History of Ukraine* (New York: Basic Books, 2021). Introductions to international politics and environmental issues in the Arctic are provided in Wilfrid Greaves and P. Whitney Lackenbauer, eds., *Breaking Through: Understanding Sovereignty and Security in the Circumpolar Arctic* (Toronto: University of Toronto Press, 2021) and Klaus Dodds and Mark Nuttall, *The Arctic: What Everyone Needs to Know* (New York: Oxford University Press, 2019). For a look at international relations and its connection to energy and climate change, see Daniel Yergin, *The New Map: Energy, Climate, and the Clash of Nations* (New York: Penguin, 2021).

The best Canadian scholarship on the UN Declaration on the Rights of Indigenous Peoples comes from Sheryl R. Lightfoot. Start with her *Global Indigenous Politics: A Subtle Revolution* (New York: Routledge, 2016), but also see her other work cited in the notes. Ken S. Coates's work is generally more sympathetic to the government. See, for example, Blain Favel and Ken S. Coates, "Understanding UNDRIP: Choosing action on priorities over sweeping claims about the United Nations *Declaration on the Rights of Indigenous Peoples*," (Ottawa: Macdonald-Laurier Institute, May 2016), 1–40, https://www.macdonaldlaurier.ca/files/pdf/MLI-10-UNDRIPCoates-Flavel05-16-WebReadyV4.pdf. The government's own thinking is best explained in the INAC documents cited in the notes. For a broader sense of the Harper government's policy toward Indigenous peoples, see Cynthia Wesley-Esquimaux, "Stephen Harper and Indigenous peoples," in Jennifer Ditchburn and Graham Fox, eds., *The Harper Factor: Assessing a Prime Minister's Political Legacy* (Montreal: McGill-Queen's University Press, 2016), 220–32.

The article that forms the basis of the maternal and child heath case is John Kirton, Julia Kulik, and Caroline Bracht, "The political process in global health and nutrition governance: The G8's 2010 Muskoka Initiative on Maternal, Child, and Newborn Health," *Annals of the New York Academy of Sciences* no. 1331 (2014): 186–200, https://doi.org/10.1111/nyas.12494. For a civil society perspective, see Elly Vandenberg, "How an NGO coalition helped score the Muskoka Initiative," *Policy Options*, 7 February 2017, https://policyoptions.irpp. org/magazines/february-2017/how-an-ngo-coalition-helped-score-the-muskoka-initiative/. On the abortion issue, see Melissa Haussman and Lisa Mills, "Doing the North American two-step on a global stage: Canada, its G8 Muskoka Initiative, and safe abortion funding," in G. Bruce Doern and Christopher Stoney, eds., *How Ottawa Spends 2012–2013: The Majority, Budget Cuts, and the New Opposition* (Montreal: McGill-Queen's University Press, 2012), 242–60. For critiques of the initiative, see work written or edited by Rebecca Tiessen cited in the notes. For a more balanced view, see David R. Black,

"The Muskoka Initiative and the politics of fence-mending with Africa," in Rohinton Medora and Yiagadeesen Samy, eds., *Canada among Nations 2013: Canada-Africa Relations, Looking Back, Looking Ahead* (Waterloo: CIGI and Carleton University, 2013), 239–51.

The most comprehensive and theoretically informed source for the Ukraine case is Bohdan S. Kordan and Mitchell C.G. Dowie, *Canada and the Ukrainian Crisis* (Montreal: McGill-Queen's University Press, 2020). See also chapter 4 of Kordan's *Strategic Friends: Canada-Ukraine Relations from Independence to the Euromaidan* (Montreal: McGill-Queen's University Press, 2018). On diaspora engagement in foreign policy, see David Carment, Milana Nikolko, and Sam MacIsaac, "Mobilizing diaspora during crisis: Ukrainian diaspora in Canada and the intergenerational sweet spot," *Diaspora Studies* 14, no. 1 (2021): 22–44, https://doi.org/10.1080/09739572.2020.1827667 and Klavdia Tatar, "Helping the homeland in troubled times: Advocacy by Canada's Ukrainian diaspora in the context of regime change and war in Ukraine," *Central and Eastern European Migration Review* 9, no. 2 (2020): 35–51, https://doi.org/10.17467/ceemr.2020.01. On the Euromaidan and civil society, see David R. Marples and Frederick V. Mills, eds., *Ukraine's Euromaidan: Analyses of a Civil Revolution* (Stuttgart: ibidem Press, 2015).

Beyond the Book

Creating the Department of Foreign Affairs, Trade, and Development, 2013

The Harper government announced its plan to amalgamate the Department of Foreign Affairs and International Trade (DFAIT) with the Canadian International Development Agency (CIDA) in the March 2013 budget. Although speculation about a merger was hardly new, the announcement of the new Department of Foreign Affairs, Trade, and Development (DFATD) came as a shock to Canadian public servants and to foreign policy analysts. A few months later, Australia unveiled a similar merger. Ottawa framed its decision as an effort to bring greater coherence to Canada's international posture. It also hoped for administrative efficiencies. Initial reactions to the announcement were mixed. Some analysts looked forward to a more streamlined Canadian approach to world affairs in which limited resources could be maximized in support of the national interest. Others were stunned by the lack of consultation and worried about the implications of the move on the institutions' two distinct cultures. Still more feared that the merger was less an amalgamation than a takeover of CIDA that would see diplomatic and trade objectives prioritized over

242 CANADA FIRST, NOT CANADA ALONE

development assistance aims. In 2015, the new Liberal government maintained the department as a single administrative unit.

Questions

1. What Canadian national interests informed the government's decision to merge the Department of Foreign Affairs and International Trade with the Canadian International Development Agency?
2. How do institutional cultures affect the conception, development, and implementation of Canadian foreign policy?
3. Must Canadian foreign, trade, and aid policies always be coherent?

Readings

The most comprehensive reading on this case is a commissioned Masters of Public Administration thesis by Janice L. Harley, "Appraising the CIDA-DFAIT amalgamation: From consolidating organizations to building a collaborative culture" (University of Victoria, MPA thesis, 2016), https://dspace.library.uvic.ca/handle/1828/7644. Jamey Essex and Joshua Bowman, "Striped pants and Birkenstocks: Work culture, gender, and clothing at Global Affairs Canada," *International Feminist Journal of Politics* 23, no. 2 (2021): 309–29, https://doi.org/10.1080/14616742.2020.1724814 examines the case through a sociological lens. On the labour-relations implications, see Jamey Essex and Logan Carmichael, "Restructuring development expertise and labour in the CIDA-DFAIT merger," *The Canadian Geographer* 61, no. 2 (2017): 266–78, https://doi.org/10.1111/cag.12328. On the impact of organizational design on aid effectiveness, see Nilima Gulrajani, "Dilemmas in donor design: Organisational reform and the future of foreign aid agencies," *Public Administration and Development* 35 (2015): 152–64, https://doi.org/10.1002/pad.1713. For the global context, see Joe Devanny and Philip A. Berry, "The Conservative Party and DFID: Party statecraft and development policy since 2017," *Contemporary British History* 36, no. 1 (2022): 86–123, https://doi.org/10.1080/13619462.2021.1969232.

11

Justin Trudeau and an Increasingly Dangerous World, 2015–

Sunny Ways

The October 2015 general election was what political strategists often call a "change election." After nearly ten years of Conservative rule, Justin Trudeau led the Liberal party from third place in the House of Commons to a strong majority. With his charming personality and good looks the new prime minister promised "sunny ways"—a sharp contrast to the dour, reserved, and seemingly mean-spirited Stephen Harper. In his first post-election press conference, Trudeau reiterated his campaign's positive message in foreign policy terms: "I want to say this to this country's friends around the world: Many of you have worried that Canada has lost its compassionate and constructive voice in the world over the past 10 years. Well, I have a simple message for you on behalf of 35 million Canadians. We're back."[1]

This statement reflected a sense among the Liberals that Harper had taken Canada away from its foreign policy traditions, positioning Canada first, but also alone.[2] Trudeau pledged to reverse course. In a letter to Canadian envoys overseas, he assured the high commissioners and ambassadors that his government was eager for their advice. "Today begins a new era in Canadian international engagement," he wrote. "You are experienced, skilled professionals, and some of Canada's best assets internationally. Under my leadership, you will have a government that believes in you and will support you in your work around the world."[3] At a time when Britain was contemplating an exit from the European Union, and the Republican Party was seriously considering the protectionist, xenophobic businessperson Donald Trump as its presidential candidate, the *Economist* praised Trudeau as the exception to the proliferation of "wall-builders, door-slammers, and draw bridge-raisers."[4]

Initially, Ottawa seemed to live up to its self-aggrandizing "Canada's back" rhetoric, at least in terms of staking out new positions. The Liberals tackled the pressing issue of Syrian refugees and their election promise to take in 25,000 by year end. A crash program was implemented, and although the government missed its deadline by two months, the difference from the Tories was apparent. What had been the Department of Foreign Affairs, Trade, and Development

---

Canada First, Not Canada Alone: A History of Canadian Foreign Policy. Adam Chapnick and Asa McKercher,
Oxford University Press. © Oxford University Press 2024. DOI: 10.1093/oso/9780197653715.003.0012

became Global Affairs Canada (GAC), emphasizing a broader scope of responsibility. Trudeau appointed the former Liberal leader and environmental advocate Stéphane Dion his first minister of foreign affairs and pledged to make climate change a major focus of his brief. At the end of November, Trudeau, Dion, and Environment Minister Catherine McKenna travelled to the UN Climate Change Conference in Paris where they re-committed Canada to the global effort to limit emissions and curb rising temperatures. The new prime minister also pulled Canadian aircraft out of combat operations against the Islamic State, while boosting troop levels for the training mission of Iraqi forces. Although pundits had warned that the move would upset Washington, President Barack Obama seemed unfazed.

Relations with the Obama Administration

The Trudeau-Obama rapport was excellent. When the president finally cancelled the Keystone XL pipeline, Canada offered little protest. Relations with US Ambassador Bruce Heyman were also positive. Like many liberal and progressive Americans, Heyman was captivated by Trudeau, praising his "warm, invigorating, and youthful" style. In a saccharine passage in his memoir, he characterized the friendly overlap between the Obama administration and the Trudeau government as "a Camelot moment: eighteen months during which two leaders were actually learning from each other, and two countries were learning from each other, too."[5]

In March 2016, Obama hosted Trudeau in Washington for a state visit, an honour the Canadians repaid in June. The latter coincided with the North American Leaders Summit, which Trudeau had revived. That December, Ottawa cancelled the Harper-era visa requirement for Mexican entry into Canada (only to reinstate it in 2024). Meanwhile, the new prime minister garnered positive international press coverage in publications ranging from the *New York Times* to *Vogue*.[6] Still, warm relations with the White House went only so far. Efforts to secure a deal with the Obama administration over the expiring softwood lumber agreement, a longstanding source of bilateral tension, were unsuccessful.

A Progressive and Feminist Agenda

Whereas the Trudeau Liberals differed from their Conservative predecessors in their initial attitude toward Syrian refugees, the UN, and relations with Washington, they approached international trade with similar objectives, albeit through an explicitly progressive lens. Chrystia Freeland, the new minister of international trade, was a journalist with degrees from Harvard and Oxford and a critic of economic inequality. Her background made her an ideal champion of a trade agenda that respected labour and environmental standards. Freeland's skills as a negotiator were tested following efforts by various EU members to block ratification of the Canada-European Union Comprehensive Economic and Trade Agreement (CETA). The European Parliament eventually approved the deal in February 2017, with Canada following that September. At a speech in Toronto shortly thereafter, Freeland noted that similarities between Canada and EU member states had been important to the deal's passage. "We were able to make the case, based on who we are," she told her audience, "a progressive country with progressive values."[7]

The emphasis on progressive trade foreshadowed the announcement in June 2017 of Canada's new Feminist International Assistance Policy (FIAP). Minister of International Development Marie-Claude Bibeau declared FIAP "the most ambitious and progressive in the history of Canada's diplomacy. It will make Canada a global leader in promoting gender equality and the empowerment of women and girls."[8] The new policy was embedded within what Ottawa would soon describe as Canada's feminist foreign policy. "It is important, and historic," as Freeland put it in a major speech to Parliament, "that we have a prime minister and a government proud to proclaim ourselves feminists. Women's rights are human rights. That includes sexual reproductive rights and the right to safe and accessible abortions. These rights are at the core of our foreign policy."[9] Ottawa's feminist bona fides were tested by the government's determination to proceed with a $15-billion sale of light armoured vehicles to Saudi Arabia, a country where women have few rights. This controversial decision highlights one of the central criticisms of the Trudeau government: its policies, both foreign and domestic, rarely matched its rhetoric.[10]

Policy Disappointments

Speaking at the UN shortly after becoming prime minister, Trudeau had proclaimed a goal of "re-engaging in global affairs through institutions like the United Nations." "We're Canadians," he said, "And we're here to help."[11] While the early acceptance of Syrian refugees was admirable, Ottawa offered a mixed response to an influx of asylum-seekers fleeing the United States for Canada in the wake of Donald J. Trump's election as president and subsequent immigration crackdown. This and the slow uptake of Afghan refugees fleeing the country after its takeover by the Taliban in August 2021 undermined Canada's reputation as a refugee haven. The Liberals had promised to prioritize relations with

246 CANADA FIRST, NOT CANADA ALONE

Indigenous peoples and abide by the UN Declaration on the Rights of Indigenous Peoples, but made only slow, cautious progress.[12] Similarly, they had pledged to recommit Canada to UN peacekeeping. Apart from the 2017 launch of the Elsie Initiative for Women in Peace Operations, an effort to increase women's participation in the peace support arena, Canada's actions fell short. In 2018, the government offered a small contingent of troops and helicopters to a UN mission in Mali for a year, but nothing more. The international community was unimpressed. In 2020, Ottawa's late effort to secure a nonpermanent seat on the UN Security Council for the 2021–2 term ended in failure.[13] By then, a series of domestic ethics scandals and the prime minister's exposure for having repeatedly dressed up in racist make-up prior to entering politics had resulted in the Liberals being reduced to a minority in the House of Commons. In the 2021 election, they again failed to secure a majority.

Trudeau and the Trump White House

Much of the government's struggles in foreign policy can be attributed to the degree of attention Ottawa was forced to pay to the unpredictable moves and tweets of President Trump. A serial bankruptee and alleged billionaire, Trump built his political career on a mix of xenophobia and economic grievance, complaining that foreigners were "making billions screwing" the United States.[14] For Canada, these sentiments were worrying on two counts: they jeopardized the North American Free Trade Agreement (NAFTA), and they called into question the American role as guardian of the liberal democratic world order. Over the first months of the Trump presidency, Canadian public servants, Cabinet ministers, and political staffers sought to build links with the new administration, even employing what came to be known as "daughter diplomacy" to make allies of trusted members of Trump's family.[15] An early meeting between president and prime minister at the White House in February 2017 proved positive, with Trudeau shrugging off calls from some Canadians for confrontation. "It is the job of the Canadian prime minster to have a constructive working relationship with the president of the United States," he affirmed prudently, "and that is exactly what I intend to do."[16]

Relations quickly soured. In April, the president attacked NAFTA, recanted his criticism, and then savaged the deal once more in a chaotic display typical of his presidency.[17] In August, the United States formally announced its intent to renegotiate the agreement. Ottawa faced a difficult negotiation process given the free trade deal's trilateral nature. There were plenty of commentators— Stephen Harper among them—who urged the government to abandon Mexico and pursue a bilateral agreement with the United States instead.[18] Addressing the threat of the loss of preferential trade access to the American market became the full-time job for Chrystia Freeland, who replaced Stéphane Dion as foreign minister but retained NAFTA as part of her portfolio. As the political leader of a wily negotiating team, Freeland had her effectiveness validated when Trump decried her as a "nasty woman" at a 2018 rally.[19]

These comments came amid the president's repeated attacks on a liberal international order that had prevailed since the end of the Second World War. Trump regularly questioned the value of NATO—in 2018 he reportedly considered pulling out of the pact—and actively courted the leaders of Russia, North Korea, and other authoritarian regimes while routinely disparaging purported American allies.[20] Particularly galling for Canada was the White House's imposition of steel and aluminium tariffs in 2018 through a loophole in American trade law that declared Canada a threat to US national security.

Matters reached a tipping point at the June 2018 G7 summit in Charlevoix, Quebec. The Americans and other G7 members clashed over Trump's desire to readmit Russia (it had been expelled following its invasion of Ukraine in 2014) as well as language in the communiqué. Upset, the president left early. When host Justin Trudeau responded to a reporter's question by declaring the US steel and aluminium tariffs "insulting" to Canadians, and then adding "we're polite, we're reasonable, but we also will not be pushed around," Trump took to Twitter (now X) to denounce the prime minister as "dishonest and weak."[21] Ottawa ultimately imposed its own countervailing duties on various US imports, while everyday Canadians boycotted American goods.[22]

As the NAFTA talks dragged on, relations with the White House remained awkward. At one point, Trump even threatened Canada with "ruination" by imposing new automobile tariffs.[23] To its credit, the Trudeau government largely ignored the bluster, and the three North American governments reached a draft Canada-United States-Mexico-Agreement (CUSMA). It was signed in November 2018 at a ceremony with little fanfare. The overall experience showcased both the strength and skill of Canadian trade negotiators as well as Canada's economic vulnerability to the United States. Shortly after the Charlevoix summit, the Cabinet Committee on Canada–United States Relations became the Cabinet Committee on Canada–United States Relations, Trade Diversification, and Internal Trade, a sign of the government's intent to diversify Canada's economic linkages.

Efforts to expand Canadian trading partnerships outside of North America were hardly new. The Trudeau government had inherited two nearly complete agreements doing just that from its predecessor: CETA and the Trans-Pacific Partnership, a pact that sought to bring together a dozen countries in the Asia-Pacific that accounted for 40 per cent of global economic output. The latter agreement seemed in doubt after the Trump administration withdrew the United States from it in January 2017. But the remaining 11 signatories persisted,

248 CANADA FIRST, NOT CANADA ALONE

dropping some of the provisions meant to appeal to the United States. As the negotiations proceeded, Canada proved to be a source of intransigence, insisting that the final draft reflect elements of the Liberals' progressive trade agenda. The situation reached a breaking point at the November 2017 Asia-Pacific Economic Cooperation summit where Trudeau temporarily withheld Canada's signature, leading the other 10 parties to threaten to sign a deal without him.[24] The parties finally announced the new Comprehensive and Progressive Agreement for Trans-Pacific Partnership (CPTPP) in March 2018.

Conflict with China and Russia

China was deliberately excluded from the CPTPP, but for many Canadian businesses China continued to offer the greatest potential opportunities for economic expansion. Initially, the Trudeau Liberals sought closer relations with Beijing despite its geopolitical ambitions and poor human rights record. Indeed, as an opposition MP, Trudeau himself had courted controversy by stating his "admiration" for China's "basic dictatorship," which had allowed the communist regime "to turn their economy around on a dime."[25] In September 2016, Trudeau exchanged back-to-back state visits with Chinese Premier Li Keqiang.[26] Ottawa and Beijing soon launched talks on a free trade agreement as well as a possible extradition treaty. Skeptics of closer ties with China criticized these moves. One former ambassador characterized Trudeau as being "smitten with the dynamic, entrepreneurial, and innovative China that dominated the business pages, whilst remaining largely silent about the China that tramples human rights at home and intimidates rivals abroad."[27]

This skepticism was ultimately vindicated. Canada was targeted by Chinese intimidation following Canadian authorities' arrest of senior executive Meng Wanzhou from telecommunications giant Huawei in December 2018 on fraud charges. Beijing detained two Canadian expatriates and embargoed Canadian agricultural goods. Because Meng's arrest followed an extradition request from the United States, many observers concluded that Canada had become collateral damage in the Trump administration's trade war against China.[28] However, there were other sources of discontent with the Chinese: the regime's crackdown on civil liberties in Hong Kong, state-directed espionage against Chinese immigrants to Canada, unauthorized surveillance on Canadian businesses and government agencies, expansive ambitions in the South China Sea, and cultural genocide of the Uyghur population in China's Xinjiang province.[29] Revelations of Chinese interference in Canadian elections further damaged China's reputation in Canada.

Remarkably, tensions with China paled in comparison to those with Russia. Since the 2014 Russian invasion of eastern Ukraine, relations between Ottawa and Moscow had been strained. The Trudeau government maintained its predecessor's position that Russia be excluded from the G7 and continued to support Operation UNIFIER, the Canadian Armed Forces' training mission in Ukraine. As part of NATO's effort to reassure the Baltic member states of the alliance's commitment, in 2016 Canada agreed to lead a multilateral battle group in Latvia, dubbed Operation REASSURANCE. Ottawa's engagement, accompanied by a new defence policy that pledged to increase the defence budget by 70 per cent over the next decade, was not simply meant to deter Russian aggression, but to signal the government's commitment to the rules-based international order.[30] When Russia launched a second invasion of Ukraine in 2022, Canada rushed matériel and aid to the besieged country and implemented an emergency program to accept refugees. Whatever its failure to live up to its other multilateral commitments, the Trudeau government's staunch defence of Ukraine through NATO and its pledge to defend long-standing institutions of global governance were notable.

COVID-19

While it is difficult to know what events of the Trudeau years will stand out as important to later generations, surely the COVID-19 pandemic will rank highly. The arrival of the virus in Canada in late February 2020 and the imposition of various quarantine measures in March collapsed the economy. The federal government implemented a range of temporary programs to cushion the damage caused by public health measures, while an agreement was worked out with Washington to keep the Canada–US border open to commercial travel, even as international passenger travel was restricted.

Co-operation at the highest levels was more difficult. The Trump administration's attempts to restrict exports of, first, personal protective equipment and, later, vaccines, increased calls for Canada to accelerate efforts to reduce its dependence on the United States.[31] The president's full-throated opposition to public health measures showcased the extent to which COVID responses came to reflect political and ideological fissures.

Canada was not immune from pandemic-fuelled unrest. The so-called Freedom Convoy's occupation of Ottawa in the winter of 2022 and anti-government demonstrations at border crossings and in city centres showcased growing right-wing populism that was occurring across the world, exacerbated by the COVID restrictions.

The pandemic created other stresses, from disruptions to global supply chains that fuelled inflation to strains on the health-care system and the deaths of tens of thousands of Canadians.[32] Clouding much of Trudeau's time as prime minister in a minority Parliament, the global health crisis demonstrated

250 CANADA FIRST, NOT CANADA ALONE

the limits of government capacity and public receptivity to experts' recommendations—perhaps the gravest threat to Canada's future given the environmental, economic, and societal upheaval expected to result from climate change.

Case Studies

The cases in this chapter share one thing in common: none were anticipated to be significant foreign policy challenges when Justin Trudeau's Liberals formed a government in 2015. In the first case, Ottawa realizes that a controversial arms sale to Saudi Arabia that was thought to have been completed by the Harper Conservatives was not. A self-described feminist government was left struggling to explain the compatibility of its ideological leanings with the sale of light armoured vehicles to a country with a reputation for violating its own people's human rights.

The three subsequent cases are drawn from the fallout of the 2016 US election. The second case examines the aftermath of President Donald Trump's demand to renegotiate NAFTA and whether Canadian interests were best served through negotiations with or without Mexico. The third case involves two Canadians who were arbitrarily arrested and imprisoned in China in response to Ottawa's detention of business leader Meng Wanzhou at the request of the United States via the Extradition Act. How to free the Canadians without compromising relations with the United States divided public policy commentators for over a year. The Beyond the Book case has its origins in President Trump's crackdown on legal and illegal immigration. After undocumented Americans discovered a loophole in the Canada-US Safe Third Country Agreement that requires asylum seekers to make their claim in their first country of arrival, Ottawa had to determine what to do with them.

With multiple national interests at stake, there is no clear guide to determine how one might put Canada first. What is clear is that working with other states tends to grant decision makers greater flexibility.

Selling Light Armoured Vehicles to Saudi Arabia, 2015–2019

What role does, or should, the Canadian defence industry play in shaping Canada's foreign policy agenda?

Few Canadians are aware of the size of the country's defence industry. Even before the Harper government negotiated a $15-billion sale of over 900 light

Figure 11.1 David Parkins, "No pressure…", *Globe and Mail*, May 2019. In August 2018, US President Donald Trump signed the Defense Authorization Act, which prevented the US government from using Huawei technology. Washington feared that the Chinese telecommunications company might share confidential America data with Beijing. A May 2019 executive order broadened the ban to all Americans. The White House pressured US allies to enact similar policies. Many did, but Prime Minister Justin Trudeau hesitated. China had taken two Canadians hostage (ironically, in response to an American request to extradite a senior Huawei executive), and Ottawa feared for their safety. The longer the Canadians delayed, the greater the risk to Ottawa's relationship with its Five Eyes allies, each of which had taken a harder line. Much to Washington's consternation, Trudeau would only commit to deciding in due course. The two Canadians were finally released in September 2021. Canada announced its intention to ban Huawei from its 5G networks in May 2022. By permission of David Parkins.

armoured vehicles (LAVs) to Saudi Arabia in 2014, defence production accounted for 63,000 high-paying, high-tech Canadian jobs and $10 billion in revenue, half of which came from exports.[33] The LAV deal briefly made Canada the second-largest arms exporter to the Middle East and left some 73 per cent of newly aware Canadians uncomfortable with the idea of supplying lethal weapons to a regime with a reputation for repressing its own people.[34] When the Trudeau Liberals were elected in 2015, they faced public pressure to cancel the contract. This case examines why they did not.

The arms deal was long in the making. Ottawa had been granting General Dynamics Land Systems Canada export permits to sell LAVs to the Saudis for 20 years, and Riyadh was already the largest importer of Canadian goods in the Middle East. Critics had had concerns about what Saudi Arabia might do with the LAVs, but the Conservatives were not deterred.[35] Saudi Arabia was a regional partner in the Middle East. The agreement was going to create 3000 unionized jobs for middle-class workers in London, Ontario, where Conservative support was tenuous. The sale would also support the independence of Canada's own defence establishment; the industry was unsustainable without international sales, and Ottawa was unwilling to give up the ability to procure LAVs for the Canadian Armed Forces independently. Because the Harper government had not joined the rest of Canada's G7 colleagues and NATO allies in signing the 2013 Arms Trade Treaty, international scrutiny of the agreement was limited.[36] A number of senior Liberal strategists were critical of the deal before the 2015 election, but the Conservatives were vulnerable in London, so neither Justin Trudeau nor the NDP's Thomas Mulcair would pledge to cancel it.[37]

Shortly after the Liberals formed a government, they learned that General Dynamics' export permits had yet to be approved. Normally, such approvals were handled by the public service on the minister's behalf; controversial cases required political sign-off. Minister of International Trade Chrystia Freeland was briefed in December 2015, and a memorandum recommending that Foreign Minister Stéphane Dion sign the permits followed three months later. The memo recalled Canada's history of arms sales to Saudi Arabia and stressed the jobs that would be created, American support for the program, and Saudi Arabia's contribution to Middle Eastern stability through its opposition to Iran and ISIS. No concerns were raised by the minister's own department; the Department of National Defence; Innovation, Science and Economic Development Canada; or the Assistant Deputy Minister Review Committee. Riyadh's human rights record was problematic, but there was no reason to "believe that the proposed exports would be used to violate human rights in Saudi Arabia."[38] Although Dion's signature is dated 10 August, it appears that he approved permits encompassing 70 per cent of the contract in April.[39]

Anticipating that this decision might be controversial, the minister explained his thinking in a public lecture at the University of Ottawa in March 2016. The Harper government had already completed the agreement, and his party had promised to respect it. Cancellation would result in a large financial penalty and significant job losses, not to mention harm to Canada's international reputation. Besides, Riyadh could always purchase similar vehicles elsewhere. To be "a responsible decision maker," Dion argued, his "peaceful conviction" had to "take the real world into account."[40] He promised that the deal would be examined rigorously to ensure that it was consistent with the national interest, international law, and Canada's human rights obligations.

The "responsible conviction" speech did not quell the controversy in part because Dion made a series of inconsistent public remarks before and afterwards. Having initially implied that the deal was already complete, he later conceded that it was not. He also failed to explain convincingly why he refused to reveal details about the penalties for cancellation (the contract prevented him from doing so) and only released a redacted version of his department's human rights assessment after significant public pressure.[41]

That pressure escalated when the CBC and the *Globe and Mail* alleged that Canadian-made weapons were being used against Saudi citizens in the country's eastern province. Riyadh claimed to be fighting terrorism, but Canadians were skeptical, as were members of Parliament. A Saudi-led intervention into Yemen to roll back the influence of Iranian-backed Houthi rebels that seemed to worsen the humanitarian disaster added to their doubts.[42] After Freeland took over as foreign minister, she suspended the export of one particular vehicle so that her department could investigate allegations that were ultimately deemed inaccurate.[43] She also introduced legislation to enable the Liberals to join the Arms Trade Treaty.[44] During this period, it appears that the Saudis scaled the contract back by about 20 per cent, although the details are unclear.[45]

Canadian-Saudi tensions increased in August 2018 when Freeland demanded, in a tweet in Arabic, that Riyadh immediately release a women's rights activist. The Saudis responded by expelling the Canadian ambassador, recalling their own, and announcing a series of additional punitive measures.[46] Two months later, as it became clear that Crown Prince Mohammed bin Salman had ordered the murder of journalist Jamal Khashoggi in Turkey, and with the situation in Yemen deteriorating, Prime Minister Trudeau suspended the LAV deal to allow for a review of all export permits to Saudi Arabia while the government sought a means of cancelling the agreement.[47]

In September 2019, the deputy ministers of foreign affairs and international trade advised Minister Freeland that, despite Saudi Arabia's problematic human rights record, they "found no credible evidence linking Canadian

254 CANADA FIRST, NOT CANADA ALONE

exports of military equipment or other controlled items to any human rights or humanitarian law violations."[48] A redacted version of Global Affairs Canada's final report, which found "no substantial risk" that military exports to Saudi Arabia would compromise the national interest, was released shortly thereafter.[49] In April 2020, Freeland's successor, François-Philippe Champagne, announced a revised arms sales agreement that promised greater transparency. When asked why Ottawa did not just cancel the deal, he noted that "the Saudis would have been able to sue for the full value of the agreement."[50]

Scholars have differed over Ottawa's conduct. In July 2016, political scientist Thomas Juneau endorsed the agreement, with reluctance. To him, the short- and long-term economic benefits of the arms sales and Riyadh's strategic significance as a partner in the Middle East justified the moral awkwardness that came with the deal.[51] Three years later, Mohammed bin Salman's reckless disregard for human rights led Juneau to call for a suspension of the LAV sale. If Saudi behaviour did not change, he advocated cancellation, no matter the economic and political costs.[52]

Political scientists Ellen Gutterman and Andrea Lane have questioned the Canadian arms trade in its entirety. To them, it is wrong to privilege commercial and political interests over Canada's long-term strategic concerns: "Weapons sales exacerbate kleptocracy, grand corruption and anti-democratic practices in areas already affected by chronic political instability, sluggish economic growth, human rights abuses and widespread corruption. This corruption in turn feeds political instability, sustains poverty and inequality, undermines public trust in society's institutions of governance, leads to social unrest, and supports the proliferation of transnational crime and terrorism."[53] Although they are hardly alone in this view, there is little evidence to suggest that a change in government policy is forthcoming.[54]

Renegotiating the North American Free Trade Agreement, 2017–2018

What role does, or should, trilateralism play in the development and implementation of Canadian foreign policy in North America?

The 1994 North American Free Trade Agreement (NAFTA) created the largest free trade area in the world at the time and marked the first significant trilateral partnership among Canada, the United States, and Mexico. According to Global Affairs Canada, over the next two decades, "total merchandise trade between Canada and the United States tripled and total merchandise trade between Canada and Mexico grew almost 10-fold."[55] Nonetheless, both countries continued to do significantly more business with the United States than they did with one another.[56]

When US presidential candidate Donald Trump threatened to withdraw from NAFTA during the 2016 election campaign, the Trudeau government had two choices. It could maintain its predecessor's view of Mexico as "an unfortunate drag on Canadian progress with Washington,"[57] or it could consider Mexico and Canada "two weary travellers seeking shelter from the same storm," who would "be able to withstand that storm if they [stood] together."[58] During the negotiations that followed, Ottawa used both approaches. This case examines why.

The Trudeau government took Trump's threats seriously. In early 2017, Canadian and US officials held a series of confidential meetings to resolve the president-elect's criticisms of the agreement.[59] Even though the negotiations failed, and Washington seemed more concerned about Mexico, some analysts called for Canada to continue its independent, behind-the-scenes efforts. Others saw Trump's rhetoric as an attempt to "divide and conquer" and urged the two less powerful countries to stick together.[60] The failure of the initial meetings, as well as the good relations between the Trudeau government and President Enrique Peña Nieto's administration, seems to have led to Ottawa's public announcement on 21 February that it had "no intention of sacrificing Mexico to improve its relations with US President Donald Trump."[61] As International Trade Minister François-Philippe Champagne later explained, "NAFTA is a three-nation agreement. So the way to renegotiate a three-nation agreement is on a trilateral basis."[62] Mexico City appeared to agree, as did a variety of trade experts from both sides.[63] Formal efforts to modernize the agreement officially began on 16 August 2017, and Canada's chief negotiator, Steve Verheul, was reiterating his country's commitment to Mexico as late as that December.[64]

There were benefits and drawbacks to the strength-in-numbers strategy. The Americans failed to secure all of their desired concessions, but Washington also grew disappointed with Ottawa. A Canadian decision to challenge American trade practices over softwood lumber at the World Trade Organization in January 2018, and the president's personal disdain for Canada's foreign minister and lead political negotiator, Chrystia Freeland, also did not help.[65]

Ottawa interpreted Washington's frustration as weakness.[66] President Trump desperately wanted a deal ratified by a Republican-dominated Congress well before the 2019 mid-term elections. Mexico's presidential election was in the spring; because Peña Nieto was not running, his leverage was also limited. Canadian negotiators seemed to establish a breakthrough in negotiations over the future of the automotive industry. NAFTA required that 62.5 per cent of vehicle parts be made in North America to escape tariffs. Washington wanted to increase that percentage to 85 and require that 50 per cent of each vehicle be made in the United States. Ottawa suggested instead that 40 per cent of the content of each vehicle come from factories that paid their employees at least US$16 per hour. Both proposals would increase protectionism and limit the expansion of the auto industry in Mexico, where workers were typically paid much less. But because the Canadian auto industry was unionized and Canada's workers were well paid, Ottawa's version protected Canadian jobs. Mexico City objected to its lack of inclusion in the talks, but in mid-May 2018, when the Trudeau government thought it saw an opportunity for a quick agreement, Canadian negotiators nonetheless attempted to make a separate deal.[67]

Perhaps the prime minister and his advisors underestimated Washington's frustration with Ottawa's boldness, because they seemed surprised when US Trade Representative Robert Lighthizer rejected their offer. Mexico City was hardly pleased that Ottawa had acted alone. Days later, President Trump announced tariffs against Canadian (and Mexican) steel and aluminum that caused Ottawa to retaliate in kind. The bilateral dispute escalated at the June 2018 G7 summit when Trudeau's suggestion that Canada would not be pushed around offended the US president and his team.[68]

On 1 July, Andrés Manuel López Obrador overwhelmingly defeated Peña Nieto's preferred candidate in the Mexican presidential election. The next day, President Trump called López Obrador—ostensibly to congratulate him on his victory—and asked whether he was interested in a bilateral trade agreement. Mexico's president-elect did not object, in part because he wanted the deal finalized before he took power in December.[69] Shortly thereafter, Lighthizer invited the Mexicans to Washington for talks that were allegedly meant to resolve smaller, bilateral issues that were of no interest to Canada. López Obrador's representative, Jesús Seade, joined them. As the *Globe and Mail* notes: "When U.S.-Mexico talks ended Aug. 27, the charade was exposed: The two countries emerged with a complete deal to overhaul nearly every aspect of NAFTA....Mexico joined the U.S. in warning that, if Canada did not accept the revamped pact, it would be cut out of NAFTA."[70]

This time, it was the Canadians' turn to be disappointed.[71] On 28 August, Freeland calmly, yet forcefully, confronted her Mexican colleagues. Mexico's Secretary of the Economy Ildefonso Guajardo, who maintained a good professional relationship with the Canadian foreign minister, suggested that his country's actions were no different from what Ottawa had tried a few months earlier. Mexico, he claimed, had kept Canada's negotiating team informed throughout the discussions.[72]

Ottawa did not panic. Congress had not granted the US president permission to replace NAFTA with a bilateral agreement, and both US big business and labour lobbyists opposed such an arrangement.[73] The Liberal government had achieved overwhelming domestic support for its approach to the negotiations from across the political spectrum. Ottawa believed that if NAFTA ultimately failed, the old Canada–US free trade agreement would still apply. Prime Minister Trudeau was sufficiently confident to announce a series of Canadian "red lines"—including an insistence on maintaining a dispute resolution mechanism and a rejection of Lighthizer's proposed "sunset clause" on the agreement as a whole—on an Edmonton radio show in early September.[74]

Canada delivered a final offer to Washington later that month. After a series of frantic negotiations facilitated on the American side primarily by the president's son-in-law, Jared Kushner, it was accepted on 30 September.[75] Trudeau, Trump, and Peña Nieto held a signing ceremony on 30 November, the Mexican president's final day in power. The White House announced a plan to drop its steel and aluminum tariffs in May 2019. Having apparently resolved their differences, Canada and Mexico reciprocated. The Mexican Senate ratified what Trump named the US-Mexico-Canada Agreement on 19 June. In December, all three parties agreed to a Protocol of Amendment called for by the US Congress.[76] That amendment enabled Trump to sign Congressional legislation approving the deal on 29 January 2020. Canada completed its approval process three months later.

Although it will be difficult to fully appreciate the nuances of this case until all of the relevant documentation has been made public, it appears that, even as Ottawa and Mexico City recognized the benefits of leveraging their mutual interests through co-operation, both deemed bilateral relations with the United States so critical as to justify, to paraphrase a former Mexican deputy foreign minister, throwing one another under the bus.[77] What lessons Ottawa has learned from the process will become clearer over time.

China's Arbitrary Imprisonment of Michael Kovrig and Michael Spavor, 2018–2021

How should the Canadian government respond to "hostage diplomacy"?

In June 2014, Canadian officials arrested Chinese national Su Bin on a US extradition warrant. Beijing soon charged two Canadians living in northern China, Kevin and Julia Garratt, with espionage. While the American charges were legitimate—Su later confessed and pleaded guilty—China's response was a form of "hostage diplomacy," or "the taking of hostages under the guise of national law for diplomatic purposes."[78] The Garratts were ultimately released,

Figure 11.2 Canadian Prime Minister Justin Trudeau, with Foreign Affairs Minister Chrystia Freeland, 20 June 2019. Prime Minister Justin Trudeau and Foreign Affairs Minister Chrystia Freeland took questions from reporters on the roof of the Canadian Embassy in Washington. The press conference followed another day of intense negotiations to replace the North American Free Trade Agreement. On paper, the agreement had served Canada, the United States, and Mexico well, but US President Donald Trump did not believe in win-win negotiations. During the negotiations, Trump imposed significant steel and aluminum tariffs against Canada and Mexico, alleging incredibly that US national security was threatened by such imports. Those tariffs were finally lifted in May 2019, nearly six months after the basis for a new trade agreement had been confirmed. This photo depicts Prime Minister Trudeau's perpetual frustration with the Trump administration as well as Freeland's calm and determined posture throughout the negotiations. Associated Press/J. Scott Applewhite/CP13615146.

but only after Prime Minister Trudeau's personal visit to China in 2016, commitment to reset Canadian-Chinese relations, and pledge to launch free trade negotiations.[79] Barely two years later, another American extradition request led to the arbitrary arrest and lengthy imprisonment of Canadians Michael Kovrig and Michael Spavor. This case examines Ottawa's response in the face of significant popular pressure.

The detention of the "Two Michaels" can be traced back to an effort by the Chinese communications company Huawei to evade sanctions imposed on Iran by successive American administrations. According to the US Department of Justice, Huawei was also stealing technology and trade secrets from a competitor, T-Mobile USA, while its chief financial officer Meng Wanzhou—the daughter of Huawei's billionaire founder, Ren Zhengfei—had lied about her companies' business practices to convince the bank HSBC USA to clear a series of illegal transactions. Meng had also allegedly committed bank and wire fraud.[80]

Washington issued an arrest warrant for Meng in August 2018. When it learned that she would be flying into Vancouver on 1 December, it liaised with the Royal Canadian Mounted Police to arrange for her arrest. Meng's bail was set at $10 million and she was largely confined to one of her Vancouver mansions for the duration of the extradition hearing.[81]

Since Ren Zhengfei had close ties to China's Communist Party, Beijing was infuriated by Meng's arrest. The Chinese Embassy in Ottawa demanded that Canada "immediately correct the wrongdoing,"[82] and they rejected Prime Minister Trudeau's claim that he could not interfere in the proceedings because Canada was "a country of an independent judiciary."[83] Canada's Ambassador John McCallum was informed that Meng's detention was "unreasonable, unconscionable, and vile" and warned of "grave consequences" to come.[84]

On 10 December, China arrested former Canadian diplomat Michael Kovrig, then working for the International Crisis Group, in Beijing. At about the same time, Canadian entrepreneur Michael Spavor was detained in the Chinese northeast. Both men were imprisoned—initially without explanation—under cruel and inhumane conditions. They were eventually charged with endangering national security.[85] A few weeks later, Robert Schellenberg, a Canadian serving a 15-year sentence in China for drug trafficking, was suddenly retried and sentenced to death. Beijing would arbitrarily deny a number of Canadian firms export permits over the months that followed.[86]

The moment the Two Michaels were arrested, their release became a critical priority across Ottawa.[87] The government's approach was three-pronged. In Beijing, the Canadian Embassy secured monthly consular access to each prisoner. Those visits were suspended for 10 months due to the COVID-19 pandemic, but later restored in virtual form. In Ottawa, the government encouraged Canada's allies to speak out against Beijing, reminding them that their citizens were also at risk.[88] The US State Department, Great Britain, and the European Union were among the first to voice full-fledged support. Australia, France, the Netherlands, and others followed.[89] Although the Chinese dismissed the pressure as ineffective, as one magazine observed, "hollering that someone should stop doing something is an odd way to demonstrate that you don't care about it."[90] When François-Philippe Champagne took over as foreign minister in November 2019, he launched a complementary, discrete campaign to establish a global Declaration against Arbitrary Detention in State-to-State Relations.[91] The declaration was made public in February 2021 with over 50 founding endorsers. The third prong of the Canadian strategy focused on minimizing the risk of

260   CANADA FIRST, NOT CANADA ALONE

unnecessarily antagonizing the Chinese. Ottawa indefinitely delayed a decision on whether to permit Huawei to develop 5G mobile networks in Canada, and later deliberately framed the Declaration against Arbitrary Detention in terms that never referred to Beijing explicitly.[92]

Back in Vancouver, Meng's lawyers offered a series of defences against her extradition to the United States. They suggested that, since Canada was not sanctioning Iran, the allegations against their client did not constitute a crime for which she could be extradited. They claimed that the RCMP, CSIS, and the Canadian Border Services Agency had violated Meng's rights when they arrested her. Finally, they argued that Donald Trump's public expressions of a willingness to intervene in the case if doing so resulted in a better trade agreement with China was evidence that Meng's arrest had been politicized from the outset. None of the arguments appeared likely to result in a dismissal.[93]

In November 2019, former Liberal Cabinet Minister Allan Rock led an unofficial diplomatic mission to Chengdu, China, to meet with the president of the Chinese People's Institute of Foreign Affairs, Wang Chao. Wang demanded Meng's release and refused to concede a linkage between her arrest and the Two Michaels. Rock replied that Canada had extradition obligations under international law and that the Michaels had been treated inhumanely. Wang referred to section 23(3) of Canada's Extradition Act, which allowed the minister of justice to end an extradition proceeding at any time. Rock replied that the section was not intended to apply to a case like Meng's. Although the conversations were less heated on the second day, the Canadians emerged from the trip convinced that it was time for Ottawa to pursue a suggestion made months earlier by former Prime Minister Jean Chrétien: an exchange of Meng for the Michaels.[94]

In May 2020, Rock and former Supreme Court Justice Louise Arbour secured a legal opinion affirming the minister of justice's right to intervene in the Meng case and recruited 17 academics, retired public servants, and ex-politicians to sign a letter to the prime minister advocating a prisoner exchange.[95] The authors cited the health of the Michaels, the compromises that had been made to Canadian foreign policy to protect them, and the continued risk of Chinese escalation among their motivations. "Although the American President will no doubt object if we act in our interest instead of his," they added, "fear of his retribution cannot be a sound reason for continuing the present, unwise course."[96]

On 25 June, Trudeau turned them down. Canada did not "want China or other countries to get the message that all they have to do to get leverage over the Canadian government is randomly arrest a couple of Canadians," he explained.[97] The following day, a group of over 50 academics and practitioners released an open letter supporting the prime minister's position: "This would be no 'prisoner exchange,'" they argued. "That assumes a false equivalence between Canada's legitimate arrest of Meng in accordance with our legal obligations and China's kidnapping of Kovrig and Spavor....Such an exchange would be nothing less than the abandonment of the rule of law *and* acceding to the demands of hostage-takers."[98] Polls by Angus Reid and Nanos Research indicated that over 70 per cent of Canadians supported the government as well.[99]

As President-elect Joe Biden began his transition to the White House in the fall of 2020, the US Department of Justice revisited its position.[100] Although the case against Meng was compelling, Huawei was hardly the only organization in violation of the Iran sanctions regime. In December, Washington launched negotiations with Meng's lawyers over a deferred prosecution agreement (DPA). In exchange for Meng admitting to the facts of Washington's case and not committing any further offences through 1 December 2022, the Department of Justice would drop the charges against her and withdraw the request for her extradition. According to both Washington and Ottawa, negotiation of the Michaels' release was undertaken separately. Meng's team finally agreed to the DPA early on 24 September 2021. She was released three hours later and boarded a plane to China that afternoon. The moment Meng was in the air, both Michaels— allegedly for medical reasons—were returned home by Beijing.[101]

Washington viewed the result positively. Meng's admission would be useful in a broader case against Huawei. Canadians were relieved, but relations with China remained strained.[102] The two countries' foreign ministers did not speak directly again until 5 April 2022.[103]

Conclusion

The Trudeau Liberals took power on a wave of political optimism and promises to refresh and renew Canada's global posture. Within months, they faced the harsh realities of a world that was not nearly so optimistic. In that sense, the controversy over selling arms to Saudi Arabia was a preview of the challenges to come, and the election of Donald Trump was symptomatic of trends emerging on the international landscape.

In a 2017 policy address, Chrystia Freeland took note of the growing sense that the United States was deliberately retrenching from the world stage. "The fact that our friend and ally has come to question the very worth of its mantle of global leadership," she explained, "puts into sharper focus the need for the rest of us to set our own clear and sovereign course."[104] The following year, shortly after the G7 fiasco at Charlevoix, she spoke to a Washington audience on the themes of the changing international order and "the threat that resurgent authoritarianism poses to liberal democracy itself." Freeland rejected a "Metternichian world defined...by a ruthless struggle between great powers governed solely by the narrow, short-term and mercantilist pursuit of self-interest" and called for the protection and preservation of a multilateral, rules-based system.[105]

The onset of the COVID-19 pandemic might have brought the world closer together, but instead both China and the United States turned inward, and the World Health Organization was left all but impotent to respond. Add to that Russian aggression in Ukraine, ongoing tensions with China in the aftermath of the imprisonment of the Two Michaels, and the frostiness of Canadian–US relations made clear by a refugee crisis along the Quebec border, and Ottawa's foreign policy vulnerabilities had become abundantly clear. By the early 2020s, positioning Canada alone was no longer even an option.

Readings

On the Trump presidency and US foreign policy, see the essays in Robert Jervis, Francis J. Gavin, Joshua Rovner, and Diane Labrosse's *Chaos in the Liberal Order: The Trump Presidency and International Politics in the Twenty-First Century* (New York: Columbia University Press, 2018). Trumpism in the United States is explored in David Frum's *Trumpocracy: The Corruption of the American Republic* (New York: Harper, 2018) and Julian E. Zelizer's *The Presidency of Donald J. Trump: A First Historical Assessment* (Princeton: Princeton University Press, 2022). On the emergence of global right-wing populism, see the essays in Boris Vormann and Michael D. Weinman, eds., *The Emergence of Illiberalism: Understanding a Global Phenomenon* (New York: Routledge, 2020). Various perspectives on the rise of China are explored in David Shambaugh, ed., *China and the World* (New York: Oxford University Press, 2020). Early assessments of the COVID-19 pandemic include Jaclyn Duffin, *COVID-19: A History* (Montreal: McGill-Queen's University Press, 2022); Adam Tooze, *Shutdown: How COVID Shook the World's Economy* (New York: Penguin, 2021); and Hal Brands and Francis J. Gavin, eds., *COVID-19 and World Order: The Future of Conflict, Competition, and Cooperation* (Baltimore: Johns Hopkins University Press, 2020).

The case on selling LAVs to Saudi Arabia is based largely on the contrast between Ellen Gutterman and Andrea Lane, "Beyond LAVs: Corruption, commercialization, and the Canadian defence industry," *Canadian Foreign Policy Journal* 23, no. 1 (2017): 77–92, https://doi.org/10.1080/11926422.2016.1254663 and Thomas Juneau, "Canada and Saudi Arabia: A deeply flawed but necessary partnership," Canadian Global Affairs Institute *Policy Paper* (July 2016): 1–6, https://www.cgai.ca/canada_and_saudi_arabia. See also Thomas Juneau, "A surprising spat: The causes and consequences of the Saudi-Canadian dispute," *International Journal* 74, no. 2 (2019): 313–23, https://doi.org/10.1177/0020702019855347; Jennifer Pederson, "'We will honour our good name': The Trudeau government, arms exports, and human rights," in Norman Hillmer and Philippe Lagassé, eds., *Canada among Nations 2017: Justin Trudeau and Canadian Foreign Policy* (Cham: Palgrave Macmillan, 2018), 207–32; and Peterson, "Selling weapons: Saudi Arabia and the Trudeau government's feminist foreign policy," in Thomas Juneau and Bessma Momani, eds., *Power in the Middle East: Canada's Foreign and Defence Policies in a Changing Region* (Toronto: University of Toronto Press, 2022), 169–87. The primary source evidence is exceptional. See Daniel Jean to Stéphane Dion [DM to Minister], Memorandum for Action, "Export of light armoured vehicles and weapons systems to Saudi Arabia," 21 March 2016, BPTS: 00013-2016, https://www.international.gc.ca/controls-controles/assets/pdfs/documents/Memorandum_for_Action-eng.pdf; John Hannaford and Marta Morgan, "Memorandum for Information," BPTS: 03575-2019, 17 September 2019, https://www.international.gc.ca/trade-commerce/assets/pdfs/controls-controles/arms-export-saudi-arabia_exportations-armes-arabie-saoudite_eng.pdf; and Global Affairs Canada, "Final Report: Review of Export Permits to Saudi Arabia," n.d., 2019, https://www.international.gc.ca/trade-commerce/assets/pdfs/memo/saudi-arabia-export-permits-exportation-licences-arabie-saoudite-EN.pdf.

The most helpful academic article that informs the NAFTA case is Laura Macdonald's "Stronger together? Canada-Mexico relations and the NAFTA renegotiations," *Canadian Foreign Policy Journal* 26, no. 2 (2020): 152–66, https://doi.org/10.1080/11926422.2019.1698442. Aaron Wherry's *Promise and Peril: Justin Trudeau in Power* (Toronto: HarperCollins, 2019), chapters 5 and 6 offers a significant amount of detail on the negotiations, as do Adrian Morrow's *Globe and Mail* articles. During the negotiations, former Canadian diplomat Colin Robertson published a series of helpful commentaries. They can be found in the archive section of https://www.colinrobertson.ca/. For technical details on the agreement, see Global Affairs Canada, "The Canada-United States-Mexico Agreement: Economic Impact Assessment," 26 February 2020, https://www.international.gc.ca/trade-commerce/assets/pdfs/agreements-accords/cusma-aceum/CUSMA-impact-repercussion-en.pdf. For a US perspective, see Robert Lighthizer, *No Trade Is Free: Changing Course, Taking on China, and Helping America's Workers* (New York: HarperCollins, 2023), chapter 13.

The only comprehensive account of the Two Michaels saga is Mike Blanchfield and Fen Osler Hampson, *The Two Michaels* (Toronto: Sutherland House, 2021). Note that Hampson was an active participant in the affair

264   CANADA FIRST, NOT CANADA ALONE

(working with Allan Rock). The next most detailed Canadian account only reaches January 2019: Shannon Proudfoot, John Geddes, Paul Wells, Claire Brownell, Aaron Hutchins, and Jason Markusoff, "Huawei's Meng Wanzhou: The world's most wanted woman," *Macleans.ca*, 4 February 2019, https://www.macleans.ca/news/canada/huaweis-meng-wanzhou-the-worlds-most-wanted-woman/. The best American source is Drew Hinshaw, Joe Parkinson, and Aruna Viswanatha, "Inside the secret prisoner swap that splintered the U.S. and China," *Wall Street Journal* (online), 27 October 2022, https://www.wsj.com/articles/huawei-china-meng-kovrig-spavor-prisoner-swap-11666877779. The case itself is best summarized by contrasting Louise Arbour et al., "A Letter to the Prime Minister of Canada," 23 June 2020, s3.documentcloud.org/documents/6956527/Letter-to-Prime-Minister.pdf and Eugene Lang, "Can the national interest be served through a prisoner exchange?" Canadian Global Affairs Institute *Policy Perspective* (July 2020): 1–3, https://www.cgai.ca/can_the_national_interest_be_served_through_a_prisoner_exchange with Patricia Adams et al., "Canada must reject calls to release Meng Wanzhou," 26 June 2000, https://macdonaldlaurier.ca/canada-must-reject-calls-release-meng-wanzhou-open-letter-prime-minister-trudeau/ and David Mulroney, "The stakes just went up in Canada's conflict with China—so what is the end game?" *Globe and Mail*, 5 March 2019, https://www.theglobeandmail.com/opinion/article-the-stakes-just-went-up-in-our-conflict-with-china-so-what-is-the/.

Beyond the Book

Responding to a Dramatic Increase in Irregular Migration, 2017–2020

In 2002, Canada and the United States signed the Safe Third Country Agreement (STCA). As of 29 December 2004, refugee claimants would be "required to request refugee protection in the first safe country they arrive[d] in."[106] Since Canada and the United States recognized one another as safe countries, Ottawa would be obligated to automatically reject refugee claimants arriving from the United States and presenting themselves at designated border crossings. The goal of the policy was to reduce what was known as "asylum shopping" without compromising the safety of the endangered.

President Donald Trump's 2017 immigration reforms caused thousands of undocumented Americans to flee north to Canada. To avoid the STCA, many presented themselves at non-designated points of entry, primarily at the Roxham Road crossing in Lacolle, Quebec. Between January 2017 and March 2020, nearly 60,000 refugee claims were made, overwhelming the Canadian immigration system, not to mention the cities and towns faced with an unanticipated surge of newcomers. Members of Canada's Conservative opposition criticized the Trudeau government for enabling and indeed facilitating the influx of what they deemed to be illegal immigrants in violation of the STCA. Members of the New Democratic Party argued that the United States under President Trump was no longer a safe third country, making the STCA moot. The government described the new arrivals as "irregular": one could not determine the legality of their claims without a proper hearing.

The issue implicated local, provincial, and federal administrators. It risked further damaging Canada–US relations, dividing Canadians, and undermining Ottawa's claims of having one of the most welcoming immigration policies in the world.

Questions

1. What are Canada's national interests in this case?
2. To what degree should local and provincial capacity shape federal immigration and refugee policy?
3. What constitutes a safe third country?

Readings

The key sources for this case are Monica Boyd and Nathan T.B. Ly, "Unwanted and uninvited: Canadian exceptionalism in migration and the 2017–2020 irregular border crossings," *American Review of Canadian Studies* 51, no. 1 (2021): 95–121, https://doi.org/10.1080/02722011.2021.1899743; Mireille Paquet and Robert Schertzer, *Irregular Border Crossings and Asylum Seekers in Canada: A Complex Intergovernmental Problem*, IRPP Study 80 (Montreal: Institute for Research on Public Policy, 2020): 1–40, https://centre.irpp.org/research-studies/irregular-border-crossings-and-asylum-seekers-in-canada-a-complex-intergovernmental-problem/; and Aaron Wherry, *Promise and Peril: Justin Trudeau in Power* (Toronto: HarperCollins, 2019), 236–45. For a concise summary, see Monica Romero, *Irregular Migration to Canada: Addressing Current Policy Responses that Impact Refugee Claimants' Arrival and Settlement in the Country*, Policy Points 16 (Waterloo: International Migration Research Centre, 2019): 1–7. Craig Damian Smith and Stephanie Hofmann's "Will Canada Suspend Its Safe Third Country Agreement With the United States," *Foreign Policy*, 6 November 2019, https://foreignpolicy.com/2019/11/06/

canada-suspend-safe-third-country-immigration-united-states/ draws from interviews with over 300 asylum-seekers. For a critical view, see Sean Rehaag, Janet Song, and Alexander Toope, "Never letting a good crisis go to waste: Canadian interdiction of asylum seekers," *Frontiers in Human Dynamics* 2, no. 588961 (2020): 1–6, https://doi.org/10.3389/fhumd.2020.588961. On the politicization of the issue, see Megan Gaucher, "Keeping your friends close and your enemies closer: Affective constructions of 'good' and 'bad' immigrants in Canadian Conservative discourse," *Canadian Ethnic Studies* 52, no. 2 (2020): 79–98, https://doi.org/10.1353/ces.2020.0014. Canada and the United States updated the Safe Third Country agreement in 2023. The most thorough summary of that story thus far is Alexander Panetta and Philip Ling, "How—and why—Canada and the U.S. kept their border deal secret for a year," *CBC News*, 28 March 2023, https://www.cbc.ca/news/politics/safe-third-country-migrants-roxham-trudeau-biden-1.6792676.

Conclusion

Canada First in the Future

What was Canada to do? A global pandemic had ravaged the state's finances and scarred the national psyche. Russia's illegal invasion of Ukraine threatened the basis of the liberal international order that had served Canadians and their Western allies so well for nearly 80 years. China and other state and non-state actors were deliberately interfering in democratic elections to an unprecedented extent, taking advantage of advances in communication technologies and unregulated artificial intelligence to sow popular and cultural divisions. The United States, so often relied upon to ensure international peace and stability, was mired in political deadlock brought about by increasing polarization and a decline in public trust. Despite desperate pleas for action from environmental scientists, the world continued to warm too quickly, transforming the hypothetical notion of the climate refugee into an all-too-common reality in the face of extreme weather phenomena.

Some of the challenges confronting Canadian foreign policy practitioners in recent times have much in common with those faced by the King government in 1935. Canada was not responsible for the COVID-19 pandemic or the Great Depression, but both had transformative effects at home. Russia's attack on Ukraine recalls Italy's invasion of Ethiopia. Populist movements inspired by outside forces that risk undermining liberal democracy are hardly new. America's commitment to invest disproportionately in the maintenance of the international order has waxed and waned for decades. Scientists have often been ahead of the general public in calling for environmental reform. In these and other ways, many of the factors that frame Canada's foreign policy posture are enduring. Apart from the addition of Newfoundland and Labrador and the establishment of Nunavut, Canada's basic geography has not changed since the early twentieth century. Demographically, the Canadian population has increased, but not sufficiently to mitigate the national reliance on foreign trade and the importance of good relations with the United States. Thanks to Canada's liberal democratic tradition, politics continues to play a role in foreign policy formulation and action, and federalism has compelled the government in Ottawa to take the perspectives of provincial and now also Indigenous governments into consideration on global issues.

Canada First, Not Canada Alone: A History of Canadian Foreign Policy. Adam Chapnick and Asa McKercher, Oxford University Press. © Oxford University Press 2024. DOI: 10.1093/oso/9780197653715.003.0013

268 CANADA FIRST, NOT CANADA ALONE

There are still changes worth noting. The difference between the meaning of national unity in King's foreign policy calculus and contemporary strategic thought is striking. In 1935, in the midst of an economic depression, unforeseen aggression abroad, and an isolationist United States, King dismissed the internationalist instincts of Canada's representatives at the League of Nations because he feared alienating francophone Catholic Quebecers, whose support he deemed critical to the maintenance of a united Canada, not to mention his own political success. King's parochial vision excluded Indigenous peoples, individuals who did not identify as men, and non-Christians, among others. More recently, a still-evolving national commitment to equity, diversity, inclusion, and Indigeneity; the opening up of Canada to global immigration; and successive governmental efforts to reduce economic dependence on the United States have created a body politic that is more difficult to reconcile. Global Affairs Canada uses Gender-Based Analysis Plus (GBA+) "to assess how different women, men and gender diverse people may experience policies, programs and initiatives" in advance of every major policy choice to temper this challenge, but the implementation of GBA+ across the Government of Canada is a work in progress.[1]

Recent technological advances have enabled individual Canadians and civil society organizations to participate in Canadian foreign policy in both official languages to an unprecedented extent. Cooperation Canada (previously the Canadian Council for International Cooperation) brings together and supports nearly 100 civil society organizations committed to poverty alleviation and sustainable development around the world.[2] In collaboration with the Canadian Partnership for Women and Children's Health and Global Canada, in 2021 the Canadian International Council (formerly the Canadian Institute of International Affairs) hosted a representative sample of over 400 Canadians for a series of online conversations and discussions with experts about Canada's worldwide engagement. The reports they produced, *Foreign Policy by Canadians*, were disseminated and discussed across the country.[3] Civil society is equally active in the defence and immigration fields.[4] In crafting foreign policy, King never had to deal with so many stakeholders.

The global threats to Canada's national interests have also multiplied. Election interference is just one element of a suite of cyber-security and disinformation challenges that Global Affairs Canada and other departments deal with every day.[5] Threats to research security, defined by Public Safety Canada as "the measures that protect knowledge, technologies, and data that could assist in the advancement of a foreign threat actor's geopolitical, economic, and security interests to the detriment of Canada's," have complicated Canadian post-secondary institutions' efforts to increase their international student cohort in line with Canada's International Education Strategy.[6] Environmental

CONCLUSION   269

degradation has made water security a growing threat. An increasing number of states, not all of which share Canada's global outlook, are showing significant interest in the Arctic.[7] Money laundering fuels the success of rogue state and non-state actors, and the Canadian government has only recently begun to address the problem.[8] There is growing interest in Canada and abroad in the responsible use of artificial intelligence.[9]

Taken together, these new threats reflect the increased complexity of international relations as well as the diffusion of responsibility for foreign policy away from Global Affairs Canada. The prime minister remains the ultimate arbiter of Canada's engagement in the world, but King would not recognize the complicated bureaucracy that supports the head of government today. In 1935, the Department of External Affairs (DEA) had a virtual monopoly on foreign policy advice—and King served a dual role as foreign minister. Today, a separate minister for foreign affairs leads a three-minister super-department that includes colleagues responsible for international trade and international development assistance. They are supported by four parliamentary secretaries, three deputy ministers, and one associate deputy minister.[10] Their reports must be cleared by the prime minister's own public service department, the Privy Council Office, and political staff in the Prime Minister's Office. The former includes the prime minister's personal national security and intelligence advisor and personal foreign and defence policy advisor. The latter includes additional partisan foreign policy aides. Other government departments, such as Public Safety, National Defence, Finance, Immigration, Industry, Fisheries, and Health, also play distinct roles in setting and implementing Canada's global agenda.

The diplomatic experience has also evolved. In King's time, bilingualism among DEA officers was a bonus. Today, fluency in two languages is an absolute minimum. External Affairs traditionally preferred foreign policy generalists. Recently, a lack of sufficient regional, linguistic, and issue-area specialists has risked compromising Canada's ability to advance its interests.[11] Perhaps most important, King-era diplomats were either single or partnered with individuals who gave up their careers to follow them from posting to posting. So-called diplomatic spouses today have their own career aspirations that have made the recruitment and retention of career foreign service officials more difficult.[12] Recruitment and retention have also suffered in the wake of budget cuts, interference in diplomatic processes by political staff in Ottawa, and the de-prioritization of international policy by successive Canadian governments.

In 1935, Canadians differed over the meaning of positioning Canada first in international affairs. Many—King included—were focused on Europe and the United States to the exclusion of other areas of the world. Canada belonged to just a handful of international organizations. Today, Canadians are all but unanimous in recognizing that the contemporary challenges that threaten their

270 CANADA FIRST, NOT CANADA ALONE

country's security, political autonomy, and economic prosperity require active engagement around the world, and that such engagement is best achieved in collaboration with others. Although Canadians debate the benefits and drawbacks of different partners and groups, governments since the Second World War have committed to building and sustaining an international order consistent with liberal-democratic traditions. Canada was among the strongest initial supporters of new institutions of global governance such as the UN, the World Bank, and the International Monetary Fund. Ottawa was active in the Commonwealth and, later, la Francophonie, a co-founder of NATO, and a partner to the United States in NORAD. Its diplomatic footprint gradually expanded across Asia, Africa, and Latin America, as did its commercial relationships and its immigration ties.

There was a conservative humility to Canada's initial embrace of liberal internationalism. Ottawa's commitment to be a helpful fixer at the UN was genuine, grounded in a mixture of national interests and values. Over time, that humility was overtaken by a level of self-assurance that, at its worst, veered dangerously into national chauvinism. By the late 1960s, during a period of détente, the Liberal government of Pierre Trudeau was wondering aloud whether Canada spent too much political and diplomatic capital on its American and European allies and not enough on itself and perhaps also the poorest countries. New initiatives were launched to broaden ties with other regions of the world. But the intensity of the Cold War returned, as did economic regionalization. By the 1980s, Canada had reaffirmed its commitment to defending the international system through NATO and the Five Eyes intelligence alliance with the United States, the United Kingdom, Australia, and New Zealand, and tied itself more closely to Washington economically. The activist impulse, at times admirable, but too often driven by the arrogant belief that the world needed more Canada, persisted.

The end of the Cold War and an unsustainable financial situation at home led successive governments in Ottawa to reduce spending on Canada's foreign policy tool kit but it did not temper the national penchant to wax poetically in global affairs. Critics lamented Ottawa's tendency "to speak loudly and carry a bent twig,"[13] but not all of that diplomacy was for naught. The focus on effecting change in international norms, or altering the so-called rules of the game, made sense for a foreign ministry that lacked the resources to do much more. Some financial support returned in the early twenty-first century, but much of it was spent on a decade-long largely unsuccessful venture in Afghanistan. That conflict also necessitated an increase in defence spending, which dropped precipitously once Canada's military role came to an end.

The efforts of Stephen Harper's Conservative government to reimagine a "Canada-first" approach to world affairs met the same fate as Pierre Trudeau's.

In the contemporary international operating environment, going it alone was not an option for a relatively small power like Canada. Justin Trudeau's Liberal government recognized as much but was more interested in domestic policy than world affairs. Politically, such a focus was understandable. Although Canadian immigrants might arrive having experienced the horrors of war on their soil, Canada itself has not been attacked militarily in any significant manner since before Confederation, leaving most Canadians feeling safe in their homes and their country.[14] Such good fortune is, paradoxically, also an inhibitor of strategic planning in a liberal democracy. Governments respond to urgent situations, and the need to fund an effective international diplomatic apparatus does not feel like a high priority. Long protected by three oceans and a friendly giant to the south, successive generations of Canadians have been able to ignore problems that bedevil less geographically fortunate countries. More recent global challenges—climate change, a pandemic, supply chain disruption, election interference, American political polarization—serve as a stark reminder that the world is changing in ways that necessitate a more active Canadian posture.

However ad hoc it might be, Canadian foreign policy is likely to remain a delicate balancing act among practical, idealistic, and political international priorities. The cases faced by future governments will be new, but the factors that strategic decision makers must take into consideration in managing them are likely to resemble those discussed throughout this book. Despite the stark challenges ahead, Canada's fortunate geographic position and long history of managing its interests prudently provide reason for optimism—so long as decision makers have the humility to recognize that standing alone on the world stage is no way to protect and promote the national interest.

Endnotes

Introduction

1. Robert Bothwell and John English, "'Dirty work at the crossroads': New perspectives on the Riddell incident," *Historical Papers* 7, no. 1 (1972): 266–8.
2. Richard Veatch, *Canada and the League of Nations* (Toronto: University of Toronto Press, 1975), 148–50.
3. Lapointe, quoted in Veatch, *Canada and the League of Nations*, 145.
4. Secretary of State for External Affairs to Advisory Officer, 29 October 1935, in Alex I. Inglis, ed., *Documents on Canadian External Relations* (*DCER*), vol. 13, *1931–1935* (Ottawa: Information Canada, 1973), 403.
5. Walter Alexander Riddell, *World Security by Conference* (Toronto: Ryerson Press, 1947), 113–26.
6. Secretary of State for External Affairs to Advisory Officer, 6 November 1935, in Inglis, *DCER*, vol. 13, 406–7.
7. Acting Secretary of State for External Affairs to Advisory Officer, 1 December 1935, in Inglis, *DCER*, vol. 13, 415.
8. William Lyon Mackenzie King, 23 March 1936, cited in C.P. Stacey, *Canada and the Age of Conflict*, vol. 2 (Toronto: University of Toronto Press, 1981), 195. See also Norman Hillmer, *O.D. Skelton: A Portrait of Canadian Ambition* (Toronto: University of Toronto Press, 2015), 227, and John Hilliker, *Canada's Department of External Affairs*, vol. 1, *The Early Years, 1909–1946* (Montreal and Kingston: McGill-Queen's University Press, 1990), 180.
9. Lester B. Pearson, *Mike: The Memoirs of the Right Honourable Lester B. Pearson*, vol. 1, *1897–1948* (Toronto: University of Toronto Press, 1972), 101. See also Veatch, *Canada and the League of Nations*, 159.
10. King, cited in Bothwell and English, "Dirty work," 273.
11. John Wendell Holmes, "Canadian foreign policy," John Holmes Papers, 002–0001/060 (2), Papers Collected for the Shaping of Peace (General). Trinity College Archives, Toronto.
12. Holmes, "Canadian foreign policy."
13. On Canada's national interests, see Adam Chapnick, "Much ado about very little: Canada's national interests in history and practice," *International Journal* 77, no. 3 (2022): 515–28, https://doi.org/10.1177/00207020221143279 and Norman Hillmer, "O.D. Skelton: Innovating for independence," in Greg Donaghy and Kim Richard Nossal, eds., *Architects and Innovators: Building the Department of Foreign Affairs and International Trade, 1909–2009* (Montreal: McGill-Queen's University Press, 2009), especially 70.
14. R.J. Sutherland, "Canada's long term strategic situation," *International Journal* 17, no. 3 (1962): 201, https://doi.org/10.1177/002070206201700301; See also Kim Richard Nossal, Stéphane Roussel, and Stéphane Paquin, *The Politics of Canadian Foreign Policy*, 4th ed. (Kingston: McGill-Queen's University Press, 2015). The public intellectual F.R. Scott called them "The permanent bases of Canadian foreign policy." See Scott, "The permanent bases of Canadian foreign policy," *Foreign Affairs* 10, no. 1 (1931): 617–31, https://doi.org/10.2307/20030465.
15. Scott, "Permanent bases," 27.
16. Sutherland, "Canada's long term strategic situation," 202.
17. F.R. Scott, *Canada Today: A Study of National Interest and National Policy*, 2nd ed. (London: Oxford University Press, 1939), 149–50. See also James Eayrs, *The Art of the Possible: Government and Foreign Policy in Canada* (Toronto: University of Toronto Press, 1961), 153–4.
18. Denis Stairs, David J. Bercuson, Mark Entwistle, J.L. Granatstein, Kim Richard Nossal, and Gordon S. Smith, *In the National Interest: Canadian Foreign Policy in an Insecure World* (Calgary: Canadian Defence and Foreign Affairs Institute, 2003), 10.
19. Adapted from Nossal, *Politics of Canadian Foreign Policy*, xv.
20. For core examples of more recent approaches to Canadian foreign policy, see Adam Chapnick and Jean-Christophe Boucher, "Canadian foreign policy," in Sandy Maisel, ed., *Oxford*

274 NOTES TO PAGES 5–13

Bibliographies in Political Science (New York: Oxford University Press, 2021), https://doi.org/10.1093/OBO/9780199756223-0175, as well as Catherine Tsalikas, "The making of a gender-balanced foreign service," *opencanada.org*, 3 April 2018, https://opencanada.org/making-gender-balanced-foreign-service/; David Webster, "Rethinking religion's role in international relations," CIH/HIC, 12 June 2018, https://cihhic.ca/2018/06/12/rethinking-religions-role-in-international-relations/; and Hayden King, "The erasure of Indigenous thought in foreign policy," *opencanada.org*, 31 July 2017, https://opencanada.org/erasure-indigenous-thought-foreign-policy/. On the current state of the field, see also Brian Bow and Andrea Lane, eds., *Canadian Foreign Policy: Reflections on a Field in Transition* (Vancouver: UBC Press, 2020) and Asa McKercher and Philip van Huizen, eds., *Undiplomatic History: Rethinking Canada in the World* (Montreal: McGill-Queen's University Press, 2019).

21. John W. Holmes, cited in Kim Richard Nossal, ed., *An Acceptance of Paradox: Essays on Canadian Diplomacy in Honour of John W. Holmes* (Toronto: Canadian Institute of International Affairs, 1982), v.

22. Eayrs, *Art of the Possible*, 3.

23. Kaya Yilmaz, "Historical empathy and its implications for classroom practices in schools," *The History Teacher* 40, no. 3 (2007): 331, https://doi.org/10.2307/30036827.

Chapter 1

1. On the Seven Years' War and its aftermath, see Fred Anderson, *Crucible of War: The Seven Years' War and the Fate of Empire in British North America, 1754–1766* (New York: Knopf, 2000); Colin Calloway, *The Scratch of a Pen: 1763 and the Transformation of North America* (New York: Oxford University Press, 2006); Phillip Buckner and John G. Reid, *Revisiting 1759: The Conquest of Canada in Historical Perspective* (Toronto: University of Toronto Press, 2012).

2. On Pontiac, see David Dixon, *Never Come to Peace Again: Pontiac's Uprising and the Fate of the British Empire in North America* (Norman: University of Oklahoma Press, 2005).

3. J.R. Miller, *Compact, Contract, Covenant: Aboriginal Treaty Making in Canada* (Toronto: University of Toronto Press, 2009), 70.

4. Francis M. Carroll, *A Good and Wise Measure: The Search for the Canadian-American Boundary, 1783–1842* (Toronto: University of Toronto Press, 2001); C.P. Stacey, *The Undefended Border: The Myth and the Reality* (Ottawa: Canadian Historical Association, 1953), https://cha-shc.ca/_uploads/5c38a87c593f8.pdf.

5. Robin Winks, *The Civil War Years: Canada and the United States*, 2nd ed. (Montreal: McGill-Queen's University Press, 1998); Adam Mayers, *Dixie & the Dominion: Canada, the Confederacy, and the War for the Union* (Toronto: Dundurn Press, 2003); John Boyko, *Blood and Daring: How Canada Fought the American Civil War and Forged a Nation* (Toronto: Penguin, 2013).

6. Jacqueline Krikorian and David Cameron, "The 1867 Union of the British North American colonies: A view from the United States," in Jacqueline Krikorian, Marcel Martel, and Adrian Shubert, eds., *Globalizing Confederation: Canada and the World in 1867* (Toronto: University of Toronto Press, 2017), 47–60.

7. Peter Vronsky, *Ridgeway: The American Fenian Invasion and the 1866 Battle That Made Canada* (Toronto: Penguin, 2012); Patrick Steward and Bryon McGovern, *The Fenians: Irish Rebellion in the North Atlantic World* (Knoxville: University of Tennessee Press, 2013).

8. Quoted in Christopher Moore, *1867: How the Fathers Made a Deal* (Toronto: McClelland & Stewart, 1997), 43.

9. Quoted in John Hilliker, *Canada's Department of External Affairs: The Early Years, 1909–1946* (Montreal: McGill-Queen's University Press, 1990), 7.

10. Quoted in Stéphane Kelly, "Canada and its aims, according to Macdonald, Laurier, Mackenzie King, and Trudeau," in Jacqueline Krikorian, David Cameron, Marcel Martel, Andrew McDougall, and Robert Vipond, eds., *Roads to Confederation: The Making of Canada, 1867*, vol. 2 (Toronto: University of Toronto Press, 2017), 77.

11. Joseph Pope, *Memoirs of the Right Honourable Sir John Alexander Macdonald* (Ottawa: J. Durie, 1894), 464. Macdonald's anger aside, the Treaty of Washington did benefit Canada by reducing Anglo-American tension and confirming American recognition of Canada. See Barbara Messamore, "Diplomacy or duplicity? Lord Lisgar, John A. Macdonald, and the Treaty of Washington, 1871," *Journal of Imperial and Commonwealth History* 32, no. 2 (2004): 29–53, https://doi.org/10.1080/03086530410001700390.

NOTES TO PAGES 15–19   275

12. "The future of Canada," *Globe*, 10 July 1867.
13. David Shi, "Seward's Attempt to Annex British Columbia, 1865–1869," *Pacific Historical Review* 47, no. 2 (1978): 217–38, https://doi.org/10.2307/3637972.
14. Quoted in P.B. Waite, *Life and Times of Confederation: Politics, Newspapers, and the Union of British North America* (Toronto: University of Toronto Press, 1962), 329.
15. Sarah Carter, *Lost Harvests: Prairie Indian Reserve Farmers and Government Policy* (Montreal: McGill-Queen's University Press, 1990); James Daschuk, *Clearing the Plains: Disease, Politics of Starvation, and the Loss of Aboriginal Life* (Winnipeg: University of Manitoba Press, 2013).
16. Tony Rees, *Arc of the Medicine Line: Mapping the World's Longest Undefended Border across the Western Plains* (Vancouver: Douglas & McIntyre, 2007); Benjamin Hoy, *A Line of Blood and Dirt* (New York: Oxford University Press, 2021).
17. Tony McCulloch, "Theodore Roosevelt and Canada: Alaska, the 'big stick' and the North Atlantic triangle, 1901–1909," in Serge Ricard, ed., *The Blackwell Companion to Theodore Roosevelt* (New York: Wiley-Blackwell, 2011), 293–313.
18. Norman Penlington, *The Alaska Boundary Dispute: A Critical Reappraisal* (Toronto: McGraw-Hill, 1972).
19. Canada, House of Commons, *Debates*, 9th Parliament, 3rd session, vol. 6, 23 October 1903, 14817, https://parl.canadiana.ca/view/oop.debates_HOC0903_06/1109?r=0&s=2; O.D. Skelton, *Life and Letters of Sir Wilfrid Laurier*, vol. 2 (Toronto: McClelland & Stewart, 1965), 298.
20. Penlington, *Alaska Boundary Dispute*, 86.
21. Quoted in D.J. Hall, *Clifford Sifton: A Lonely Eminence, 1901–1929*, vol. 2 (Vancouver: UBC Press, 1985), 111.
22. Canada, House of Commons, *Debates*, 4th Parliament, 4th session, vol. 1, 21 April 1882, 1078, https://parl.canadiana.ca/view/oop.debates_HOC0404_04/1086?r=0&s=1.
23. Canada, House of Commons, *Debates*, 4th Parliament, 2nd session, vol. 2, 29 April 1880, 1859, https://parl.canadiana.ca/view/oop.debates_HOC0402_02/764?r=0&s=1.
24. Bernard Pénisson, "Le commissariat canadien à Paris (1882–1928)," *Revue d'histoire de l'Amérique française* 34, no. 3 (1980): 357–76, https://doi.org/10.7202/303878ar.
25. Quoted in C.P. Stacey, *Canada and the Age of Conflict*, vol. 1: *1867–1921* (Toronto: University of Toronto Press, 1984), 47.
26. Kurkpatrick Dorsey, *The Dawn of Conservation Diplomacy: US-Canadian Wildlife Protection Treaties in the Progressive Era* (Seattle: University of Washington Press, 1998); Daniel Macfarlane and Murray Clamen, eds., *The First Century of the International Joint Commission* (Calgary: University of Calgary Press, 2020), https://press.ucalgary.ca/books/9781773851075/.
27. Robert Bothwell, "Canadian representation at Washington: A case study in colonial responsibility," *Canadian Historical Review* 53, no. 2 (1972): 126, https://doi.org/10.3138/CHR-053-02-01; Peter Neary, "Grey, Bryce and the settlement of Canadian-American differences, 1905–1911," *Canadian Historical Review* 49, no. 4 (1968): 357–80, https://doi.org/10.3138/CHR-049-04-02.
28. Canada, House of Commons, *Debates*, 11th Parliament, 1st session, vol. 1, 4 March 1909, 1983, 1978, https://parl.canadiana.ca/view/oop.debates_HOC1101_01/1001?r=0&s=1.
29. Hilliker, *Canada's Department of External Affairs*, 32.
30. Robert Bothwell, *Your Country, My Country: A Unified History of the United States and Canada* (New York: Oxford University Press, 2016), 121–2.
31. Ninette Kelley and Michael Trebilcock, *The Making of the Mosaic: A History of Canadian Immigration Policy*, 2nd ed. (Toronto: University of Toronto Press, 2010), 113.
32. David Goutor, "Constructing the 'Great Menace': Canadian labour opposition to Asian migration, 1880–1914," *Canadian Historical Review* 88, no. 4 (2007): 549–76, https://doi.org/10.3138/chr.88.4.549.
33. Canada, House of Commons, *Debates*, 4th Parliament, 4th session, vol. 1, 12 May 1882, 1477, https://parl.canadiana.ca/view/oop.debates_HOC0404_04/1485?r=0&s=1.
34. W. Peter Ward, *White Canada Forever: Popular Attitudes and Public Policy Towards Orientals in British Columbia* (Montreal: McGill-Queen's University Press, 1978).
35. Adam McKeown, *Melancholy Order: Asian Immigration and the Globalization of Borders* (New York: Columbia University Press, 2008); Marilyn Lake and Henry Reynolds, *Drawing the Global Colour Line: White Men's Countries and the International Challenge of Racial Equality* (Cambridge: Cambridge University Press, 2008); Kornel Chang, *Pacific Community: The Making of the U.S.-Canadian Borderlands* (Berkeley: University of California Press, 2012);

276 NOTES TO PAGES 19-25

David Atkinson, *The Burden of White Supremacy: Containing Asian Migration in the British Empire and the United States* (Chapel Hill: University of North Carolina Press, 2016).

36. Patricia Roy, *A White Man's Province: British Columbia Politicians and Chinese and Japanese Immigrants, 1858-1914* (Vancouver: UBC Press, 1989).

37. Quoted in Kirt Niergarth, "'This continent must belong to the white races': William Lyon Mackenzie King, Canadian diplomacy and immigration law, 1908," *International History Review* 32, no. 4 (2010): 606, https://doi.org/10.1080/07075332.2010.535344.

38. Julie Gilmour, *Trouble on Main Street: Mackenzie King, Reason, Race and the 1907 Vancouver Riots* (Toronto: Penguin, 2014).

39. John Price, *Orienting Canada: Race, Empire, and the Transpacific* (Vancouver: UBC Press, 2011), 20-1.

40. Canada, House of Commons, *Debates*, 10th Parliament, 4th session, vol. 1, 21 January 1908, 1614, https://parl.canadiana.ca/view/oop.debates_HOC1004_01/815?r=0&s=1.

41. Quoted in P.B. Waite, *Canada 1874-1896: Arduous Destiny* (Toronto: McClelland & Stewart, 1971), 91.

42. Christopher Pennington, *The Destiny of Canada: Macdonald, Laurier, and the Election of 1891* (Toronto: Penguin, 2011).

43. "Like the life of rose is the policy of Mr. Borden," Toronto *Globe*, 15 October 1904.

44. *Congressional Record*, 61st Congress, 3rd session, 14 February 1911, 2520.

45. Quoted in W.M. Baker, "A case study of anti-Americanism in English-speaking Canada: The election campaign of 1911," *Canadian Historical Review* 51, no. 4 (1970): 438, 435, https://doi.org/10.3138/CHR-051-04-04.

46. Quoted in Paul Stevens, *The 1911 General Election: A Study in Canadian Politics* (Toronto: Copp Clark, 1970), 2. On the election, see Patrice Dutil and David MacKenzie, *Canada 1911: The Decisive Election That Shaped the Country* (Toronto: Dundurn, 2011).

47. Ian Miller, *Our Glory and Our Grief: Torontonians and the Great War* (Toronto: University of Toronto Press, 2002), 16.

48. O.D. Skelton, *Life and Letters of Sir Wilfrid Laurier*, vol. 2 (Toronto: McClelland & Stewart, 1965), 163-4.

49. Patrice Dutil and David MacKenzie, *Embattled Nation: Canada's Wartime Election of 1917* (Toronto: Dundurn Press, 2017).

50. On Vimy Ridge, see Geoffrey Hayes, Andrew Iarocci, and Mike Bechthold, eds., *Vimy Ridge: A Canadian Reassessment* (Waterloo: Wilfrid Laurier University Press, 2007); Ian McKay and Jamie Swift, *The Vimy Trap* (Toronto: Between the Lines, 2016); and Tim Cook, *Vimy: The Battle and the Legend* (Toronto: Penguin, 2017).

51. Robert Bothwell, *Loring Christie: The Failure of Bureaucratic Imperialism* (New York: Garland Publishing, 1988), 102.

52. Quoted in Stacey, *Canada and the Age of Conflict*, vol. 1, 213.

53. Canada, House of Commons, *Debates*, 12th Parliament, 7th session, vol. 2, 18 May 1917, 1539, https://parl.canadiana.ca/view/oop.debates_HOC1207_02/417?r=0&s=1.

54. Quoted in Margaret Macmillan, "Sibling rivalry: Australia and Canada from the Boer War to the Great War," in Margaret Macmillan and Francine McKenzie, eds., *Parties Long Estranged: Canada and Australia in the Twentieth Century* (Vancouver: UBC Press, 2003), 20.

55. Quoted in Margaret MacMillan, "Canada and the peace settlements," in David MacKenzie, ed., *Canada and the First World War: Essays in Honour of Robert Craig Brown* (Toronto: University of Toronto Press, 2005), 394.

56. Mark McGowan, *The Waning of the Green: Catholics, the Irish, and Identity in Toronto, 1887-1922* (Montreal: McGill-Queen's University Press, 1999).

57. James W. St G. Walker, "Race or recruitment in World War I: Enlistment of visible minorities in the Canadian Expeditionary Force," *Canadian Historical Review* 70, no. 1 (1989): 5, https://doi.org/10.3138/CHR-070-01-01.

58. Timothy Winegard, *For King and Kanata: Canadian Indians and the First World War* (Winnipeg: University of Manitoba Press, 2012), 8.

59. For competing views on the meaning of Vimy, see Ian McKay and Jamie Swift, *The Vimy Trap* (Toronto: Between the Lines, 2016) and Tim Cook, *Vimy: The Battle and the Legend* (Toronto: Penguin, 2017).

60. Erez Manela, *The Wilsonian Moment: Self-Determination and the International Origins of Anticolonial Nationalism* (New York: Oxford University Press, 2007).

NOTES TO PAGES 25–9   277

61. Six Nations, *The Redman's Appeal for Justice* (Brantford: D. Wilson Moore, 1924).

62. Yale D. Belanger, "The Six Nations of Grand River Territory's attempts at renewing international political relationships, 1921–1924," *Canadian Foreign Policy Journal* 13, no. 3 (2007): 29–43, https://doi.org/10.1080/11926422.2007.9673441.

63. Susan Pedersen, *The Guardians: The League of Nations and the Crisis of Empire* (New York: Oxford University Press, 2015); David Webster, "'Red Indians' in Geneva, 'Papuan Headhunters' in New York: Race, mental maps, and two global appeals in the 1920s and 1960s," in Laura Madokoro, Francine McKenzie, and David Meren, eds., *Dominion of Race: Rethinking Canada's International History* (Vancouver: UBC Press, 2017), 254–83.

64. Murray Donnelly, *Dafoe of the Free Press* (Toronto: Macmillan, 1968), 99.

65. Margaret Prang, *N.W. Rowell: Ontario Nationalist* (Toronto: University of Toronto Press, 1975), 361.

66. Richard Veatch, *Canada and the League of Nations* (Toronto: University of Toronto Press, 1975), 72–81.

67. King, diary entry, 17 September 1922, https://www.bac-lac.gc.ca/eng/discover/politics-government/prime-ministers/william-lyon-mackenzie-king/Pages/item.aspx?IdNumber=8228&.

68. Norman Hillmer, *O.D. Skelton: A Portrait of Canadian Ambition* (Toronto: University of Toronto Press, 2015), 105.

69. John MacFarlane, *Ernest Lapointe and Quebec's Influence on Canadian Foreign Policy* (Toronto: University of Toronto Press, 1999); Robert J. Talbot, "Francophone-Anglophone accommodation in practice: Liberal foreign policy and national unity between the wars," in Steve Marti and William John Pratt, eds., *Fighting with the Empire: Canada, Britain, and Global Conflict, 1867–1947* (Vancouver: UBC Press, 2019), 86–104.

70. Lorna Lloyd, "'Another National Milestone': Canada's 1927 Election to the Council of the League of Nations," *Diplomacy & Statecraft* 21, no. 4 (2010): 656, https://doi.org/10.1080/09592296.2010.529349.

71. Douglas Irwin, *Peddling Protectionism: Smoot-Hawley and the Great Depression* (Princeton: Princeton University Press, 2011), 154.

72. John Herd Thompson with Allen Seager, *Canada 1922–1939: Decades of Discord* (Toronto: McClelland & Stewart, 1985), 213.

73. P.B. Waite, *In Search of R.B. Bennett* (Montreal and Kingston: McGill-Queen's University Press, 2012), 83.

74. John Manley, "'Starve, be damned!' Communists and Canada's urban unemployed, 1929–39," *Canadian Historical Review* 79, no. 3 (1998): 489, https://www.muse.jhu.edu/article/590316.

75. "Parable of talents is cited by Bennett as economic truth," Toronto *Globe*, 10 November 1932, 10.

76. "Parable of talents is cited by Bennett as economic truth," Toronto *Globe*, 10 November 1932, 10.

77. "Parable of talents is cited by Bennett as economic truth," Toronto *Globe*, 10 November 1932, 10. See also Lita-Rose Betcherman, *The Little Band: The Clashes between the Communists and the Political and Legal Establishment in Canada, 1928–32* (Ottawa: Deneau, 1982).

78. Canada, House of Commons, *Debates*, 16th Parliament, 2nd session, vol. 3, 28 May 1928, 3477–8, https://parl.canadiana.ca/view/oop.debates_HOC1602_03/807.

79. Donald C. Story, "Canada, the League of Nations and the Far East, 1931–33: The Cahan incident," *International History Review* 3, no. 2 (1981): 236–55, http://www.jstor.org/stable/40105126; "Japan represents order," *Saturday Night*, 28 November 1931.

80. Roy MacLaren, *Mackenzie King in the Age of the Dictators: Canada's Imperial and Foreign Policies* (Montreal: McGill-Queen's University Press, 2019), 68–81.

81. Cecelia Lynch, *Beyond Appeasement: Interpreting Interwar Peace Movements in World Politics* (Ithaca: Cornell University Press, 1999); Priscilla Roberts, "Tweaking the lion's tail: Edgar J. Tarr, the Canadian Institute of International Affairs, and the British Empire, 1931–1950," *Diplomacy & Statecraft* 23, no. 4 (2012): 636–59, https://doi.org/10.1080/09592296.2012.736329; Lawrence Woods, "Canada and the Institute of Pacific Relations: Lessons from an earlier voyage," *Canadian Foreign Policy Journal* 6, no. 2 (1999): 119–38, https://doi.org/10.1080/11926422.1999.9673177; Donald Page, "The Institute's 'popular arm': The League of Nations Society in Canada," *International Journal* 33, no. 1 (1977/78): 28–65, https://doi.org/10.1177/002070207803300103.

82. Doris Pennington, *Agnes Macphail: Reformer* (Toronto: Simon and Pierre, 1989), 99.

278   NOTES TO PAGES 29–37

83. Quoted in Robert Bothwell and Norman Hillmer, eds., *The In-Between Time: Canadian External Policy in the 1930s* (Vancouver: Copp Clark, 1975), 111–2.

Chapter 2

1. King, diary entry, 9 September 1936, https://www.bac-lac.gc.ca/eng/discover/politics-government/prime-ministers/william-lyon-mackenzie-king/Pages/item.aspx?IdNumber=17185&.

2. Hughes Théorêt, *The Blue Shirts: Adrien Arcand and Fascist Anti-Semitism in Canada* (Ottawa: University of Ottawa Press, 2017); Luigi G. Pennacchio, "Exporting fascism to Canada: Toronto's Little Italy," in Franca Iacovetta, Roberto Perin, and Angelo Principe, eds., *Enemies Within: Italian and Other Internees in Canada and Abroad* (Toronto: University of Toronto Press, 2000), 52–75; Jonathan Wagner, *Brothers Beyond the Sea: National Socialism in Canada* (Waterloo: Wilfrid Laurier University Press, 1981); Esther Delisle, *The Traitor and the Jew: Anti-Semitism and the Delirium of Extremist Right-Wing Nationalism in French Canada from 1929 to 1939* (Toronto: Robert Davies Publishing, 1993); Esther Delisle, *Myths, Memory and Lies: Quebec's Intelligentsia and the Fascist Temptation, 1939–1960* (Toronto: Robert Davies Publishing, 1998).

3. Michael Petrou, *Renegades: Canadians in the Spanish Civil War* (Vancouver: UBC Press, 2008); David Goutor, *A Chance to Fight Hitler: A Canadian Volunteer in the Spanish Civil War* (Toronto: Between the Lines, 2019).

4. Roy MacLaren, *Mackenzie King in the Age of the Dictators: Canada's Imperial and Foreign Policies* (Montreal: McGill-Queen's University Press, 2019); Robert Teigrob, *Four Days in Hitler's Germany: Mackenzie King's Mission to Avert a Second World War* (Toronto: University of Toronto Press, 2019).

5. L. Ruth Klein, ed., *Nazi Germany, Canadian Responses: Confronting Antisemitism in the Shadow of War* (Montreal: McGill-Queen's University Press, 2012); Richard Menkis and Harold Troper, *More Than Just Games: Canada and the 1938 Olympics* (Toronto: University of Toronto Press, 2015).

6. King, diary entry, 29 June 1937, https://www.bac-lac.gc.ca/eng/discover/politics-government/prime-ministers/william-lyon-mackenzie-king/Pages/item.aspx?IdNumber=18112&.

7. King, diary entry, 26 August 1937, https://www.bac-lac.gc.ca/eng/discover/politics-government/prime-ministers/william-lyon-mackenzie-king/Pages/item.aspx?IdNumber=18292&. On Canada's Tokyo Legation, see John Meehan, *The Dominion and the Rising Sun: Canada Encounters Japan, 1929–41* (Vancouver: UBC Press, 2004).

8. Canada, House of Commons, *Debates*, 18th Parliament, 3rd session, vol. 1, 11 February 1938, 381, https://parl.canadiana.ca/view/oop.debates_HOC1803_01/383.

9. King diary entry, 19 October 1937, https://www.bac-lac.gc.ca/eng/discover/politics-government/prime-ministers/william-lyon-mackenzie-king/Pages/item.aspx?IdNumber=18414&. And see John Meehan, "Steering clear of Great Britain: Canada's debate over collective security in the Far Eastern Crisis of 1937," *International History Review* 25, no. 2 (2003): 253–81, https://doi.org/10.1080/07075332.2003.9640996.

10. Armour to Hull, 25 October 1935, and attached Memorandum, RG 59, Decimal File 1930–1939, 611.4231/1286, US National Archives and Records Administration.

11. Norman Hillmer, "O.D. Skelton and the North American mind," *International Journal* 60, no. 1 (2004–5): 93–110, https://doi.org/10.1177/002070200506000108.

12. King, diary entry, 13 September 1938, https://www.bac-lac.gc.ca/eng/discover/politics-government/prime-ministers/william-lyon-mackenzie-king/Pages/item.aspx?IdNumber=19388; J.L. Granatstein and Robert Bothwell, "'A self-evident national duty': Canadian foreign policy, 1935–1939," *Journal of Imperial and Commonwealth History* 3, no. 2 (1975): 212–33.

13. Stephen Leacock, "The Canadian monarchy," in Alan Bowker, ed., *On the Front Line of Life: Stephen Leacock: Memories and Reflections, 1935–1944* (Toronto: Dundurn Press, 2004), 185.

14. John Bartlet Brebner, *North Atlantic Triangle: The Interplay of Canada, the United States, and Great Britain* (New Haven, CT: Yale University Press, 1945).

15. For an overview of the literature on the triangle, see Tony McCulloch, "The North Atlantic Triangle: A Canadian myth," *International Journal* 66, no. 1 (2010–11): 197–207, https://doi.org/10.1177/002070201106600113.

16. Quoted in C.P. Stacey, *Canada and the Age of Conflict*, vol. 2, *1921–1948* (Toronto: University of Toronto Press, 1981), 226.

NOTES TO PAGES 37–44   279

17. King, diary entry, 24 October 1938, https://www.bac-lac.gc.ca/eng/discover/politics-government/prime-ministers/william-lyon-mackenzie-king/Pages/item.aspx?IdNumber=19511&.
18. Galen Roger Perras, "The myth of Obsequious Rex: Mackenzie King, Franklin D. Roosevelt, and Canada-US security, 1935–1940," in Michael Behiels and Reginald Stuart, eds., *Transnationalism: Canada-United States History into the Twenty-first Century* (Montreal: McGill-Queen's University Press, 2010), 203–23.
19. King, 20 March 1939, in Canada, House of Commons, *Debates*, 18th Parliament, 4th session, vol. 2, 2042–3, https://parl.canadiana.ca/view/oop.debates_HOC1804_02/894.
20. King, diary entry, 3 September 1939, https://www.bac-lac.gc.ca/eng/discover/politics-government/prime-ministers/william-lyon-mackenzie-king/Pages/item.aspx?IdNumber=20684&.
21. William Lyon Mackenzie King, *Canada and the War: Canada's Contribution to Freedom* (Ottawa: E. Cloutier, 1941), 4.
22. Skelton, "Canada and the Polish War, A Personal Note," 25 August 1939, in John A. Munro, ed., *Documents on Canadian External Relations*, vol. 6, *1936–1939* (Ottawa: Information Canada, 1972), 1247–9.
23. Quoted in C.P. Stacey, *Arms, Men and Governments: The War Policies of Canada, 1939–1945* (Ottawa: Information Canada, 1970), 339.
24. John English and Norman Hillmer, "Canada's alliances," *Revue internationale d'histoire militaire*, Edition Canadienne 51 (1982): 31–52.
25. American and Far Eastern Division to USSEA, Report on Canadian Representation with the United States of America, 31 March 1942, RG 25, vol. 6786, file 1415–40, Library and Archives Canada (LAC).
26. Kenneth Coates and William Morrison, *The Alaska Highway in World War II: The US Army of Occupation in Canada's Northwest* (Toronto: University of Toronto Press, 1992).
27. King, quoted in Lord Moran, *Churchill: Taken from the Diaries of Lord Moran* (Boston: Houghton Mifflin, 1966), 117, note 3.
28. Wrong to Robertson, 20 January 1942, RG 25, file 3265-A-40, LAC; Adam Chapnick, "Principle for profit: The functional principle and the development of Canadian foreign policy, 1943–1947," *Journal of Canadian Studies* 37, no. 2 (2002): 68–85, https://doi.org/10.3138/jcs.37.2.68.
29. Maurice Pope, *Soldiers and Politicians: The Memoirs of Lt-General Maurice Pope* (Toronto: University of Toronto Press, 1962), 209.
30. Brian Buckley, *Canada's Early Nuclear Policy: Fate, Chance, and Character* (Montreal: McGill-Queen's University Press, 2000), 10.
31. Vivien Hughes, "Women, gender, and Canadian foreign policy, 1909–2009," *British Journal of Canadian Studies* 23, no. 2 (2010): 159–178, https://doi.org/10.3828/bjcs.2010.9; Margaret Weiers, *Envoys Extraordinary: Women of the Canadian Foreign Service* (Toronto: Dundurn Press, 1995).
32. Jeffrey Keshen, *Saints, Sinners, and Soldiers: Canada's Second World War* (Vancouver: UBC Press, 2007); Ruth Roach Pierson, *"They're Still Women After All": The Second World War and Canadian Womanhood* (Toronto: McClelland & Stewart, 1986); Jennifer Stephen, *Pick One Intelligent Girl: Employability, Domesticity, and the Gendering of Canada's Welfare State, 1939–1947* (Toronto: University of Toronto Press, 2007).
33. Quoted in Desmond Morton, *A Military History of Canada*, 5th ed. (Toronto: McClelland & Stewart, 2007), 192.
34. Francine McKenzie, "In the national interest: Dominions' support for Britain and the Commonwealth after the Second World War," *Journal of Imperial and Commonwealth History* 34, no. 4 (2006): 553–76, https://doi.org/10.1080/03086530600991472; Hector Mackenzie, "Sinews of war and peace: The politics of economic aid to Britain, 1939–1945," *International Journal* 54, no. 4 (1999): 648–70, https://doi.org/10.1177/002070209905400406.
35. "A foreign idea?" *The Economist*, 29 May 1943.
36. Lionel Gelber, "Canada's new stature," *Foreign Affairs* 24, no. 2 (1946): 277.
37. Adam Chapnick, "The Canadian middle power myth," *International Journal* 55, no. 2 (2000): 188–206, https://doi.org/10.1177/002070200005500202.
38. Robertson, quoted in John Holmes, *The Shaping of Peace: Canada and the Search for World Order, 1943–1957*, vol. 1 (Toronto: University of Toronto Press, 1979), 235. See also Adam Chapnick, *The Middle Power Project: Canada and the Founding of the United Nations* (Vancouver: UBC Press, 2005).

280 NOTES TO PAGES 44-8

39. On Canada and the UNSC, see Adam Chapnick, *Canada on the United Nations Security Council: A Small Power on a Large Stage* (Vancouver: UBC Press, 2019).
40. Tarah Brookfield, "Save the children / Save the world: Canadian women embrace the United Nations, 1940s–1970s," in Colin McCullough and Robert Teigrob, eds., *Canada and the United Nations: Legacies, Limits, Prospects* (Montreal: McGill-Queen's University Press, 2016), 104–36.
41. Memorandum from Under-Secretary of State for External Affairs to Prime Minister, "Defence Discussions," 12 November 1946, in Donald M. Page, ed., *Documents on Canadian External Relations*, vol. 12, *1946*, (Ottawa: Minister of Supply and Services Canada, 1977), 1670–2.
42. Hector Mackenzie, "Canada's international relations in the early Cold War: The impact and implications of the Gouzenko affair," in J.L. Black and Martin Rudner, eds., *The Gouzenko Affair: Canada and the Beginnings of Cold War Counter-Espionage* (Manotick: Penumbra Press, 2006), 15–37; Amy Knight, *How the Cold War Began: The Gouzenko Affair and the Hunt for Soviet Spies* (Toronto: McClelland & Stewart, 2005).
43. Louis St Laurent, 29 April 1948, quoted in Canada, House of Commons, *Debates*, 20th Parliament, 4th session, vol. 4, 3448, https://parl.canadiana.ca/view/oop.debates_HOC2004_04/324.
44. Chaim Weizmann, quoted in Irving Abella and Harold Troper, "'The line must be drawn somewhere': Canada and Jewish refugees, 1933–9," *Canadian Historical Review* 60, no. 2 (1979): 181, https://doi.org/10.3138/CHR-060-02-04.
45. Ninette Kelley and Michael Trebilcock, *The Making of the Mosaic: A History of Canadian Immigration Policy*, 2nd ed. (Toronto: University of Toronto Press [2000] 2010), 260.
46. Abella and Troper, "The line," 182.
47. Abella and Troper, "The line," 182–7.
48. King, diary entry, 29 March 1938, https://www.bac-lac.gc.ca/eng/discover/politics-government/prime-ministers/william-lyon-mackenzie-king/Pages/item.aspx?IdNumber=18924.
49. Abella and Troper, "The line," 189. See also Lita-Rose Betcherman, *The Swastika and the Maple Leaf: Fascist Movements in Canada in the Thirties* (Toronto: Fitzhenry & Whiteside, 1975). On the situation in Quebec, see Gerald E. Dirks, *Canada's Refugee Policy: Indifference or Opportunism?* (Montreal: McGill-Queen's University Press, 1977), 53–4.
50. Irving Abella and Harold Troper, *None Is Too Many: Canada and the Jews of Europe, 1933–1948* (Toronto: Lester & Orpen Dennys, 1982), 39.
51. King, diary entry, 13 November 1938, https://www.bac-lac.gc.ca/eng/discover/politics-government/prime-ministers/william-lyon-mackenzie-king/Pages/item.aspx?IdNumber=19558. See also Erna Paris, *Jews: An Account of Their Experience in Canada* (Toronto: Macmillan, 1980), 88–92.
52. "Manion policy of closed door divides M.P.'s," *Globe and Mail*, 16 December 1938, 5; Abella and Troper, *None Is Too Many*. 60.
53. On the voyage itself, see Richard Wood, "Prime Minister Mackenzie King turns away Jewish refugees on board the SS St. Louis," *The Beaver* 87, no. 3 (June/July 2007): 12–13; Robin Long Mullins, "The SS St. Louis and the importance of reconciliation," *Peace and Conflict: Journal of Peace Psychology* 19, no. 4 (2013): 393–8, https://doi.org/10.1037/a0034610; Abella and Troper, "The line," 178–80.
54. Abella and Troper, "The line," 180.
55. A more detailed account of the efforts to increase Jewish immigration can be found in Simon Belkin, *Through Narrow Gates: A Review of Jewish Immigration, Colonization and Immigrant Aid Work in Canada (1890–1940)* (Montreal: Eagle Publishing, 1966), 168–81, especially 176–80.
56. On the Wheel of Conscience, see https://libeskind.com/work/the-wheel-of-conscience/.
57. The apology can be watched at https://www.youtube.com/watch?v=WTQGr4OBEGE. For the text, see "Statement of apology on behalf of the Government of Canada to the passengers of the MS St. Louis," Ottawa, 7 November 2018, https://pm.gc.ca/en/news/speeches/2018/11/07/statement-apology-behalf-government-canada-passengers-ms-st-louis.
58. For evidence of disappointment in the King government's policy at the time, see Valerie Knowles, *Strangers at Our Gates: Canadian Immigration and Immigration Policy, 1540–2015*, 4th ed. (Toronto: Dundurn Press, 2016), chapter 7 and Escott Reid, "The conscience of the diplomat: A personal testament," *Queen's Quarterly* 74, no. 4 (1976): 586.
59. Kelley and Trebilcock, *Making of the Mosaic*, 258.
60. John Bartlet Brebner, *North Atlantic Triangle: The Interplay of Canada, the United States, and Great Britain* (New Haven, CT: Yale University Press, 1945).

NOTES TO PAGES 48–53   281

61. On these issues, see Robert B. Bryce, *Canada and the Cost of World War II: The International Operations of Canada's Department of Finance, 1939–1947* (Montreal: McGill-Queen's University Press, 2005), 98 and Hector Mackenzie, "Sinews of war and peace: The politics of economic aid to Britain, 1939–1945," *International Journal* 54, no. 4 (1999): 653, https://doi.org/10.1177/002070209905400406.

62. Robert Bothwell and William Kilbourn, *C.D. Howe: A Biography* (Toronto: McClelland and Stewart, 1979), 151.

63. J.L. Granatstein and R.D. Cuff, "The Hyde Park Declaration 1941: Origins and significance," *Canadian Historical Review* 55, no. 1 (1974): 59, https://doi.org/10.3138/CHR-055-01-03.

64. King, quoted in J.W. Pickersgill, *The Mackenzie King Record*, vol. 1, *1939–1944* (Toronto: University of Toronto Press, 1960), 191.

65. Stacey, *Canada in the Age of Conflict*, vol. 2, 135.

66. Cited in Pickersgill, *Mackenzie King Record*, vol. 1, 200.

67. Bothwell and Kilbourn, *C.D. Howe*, 152.

68. Kathleen Britt Rasmussen, "Canada and the reconstruction of the international economy, 1941–1947" (University of Toronto, PhD thesis, 2001), 23.

69. On Roosevelt's conception of a "good neighbour," see Warren F. Kimball, *The Juggler: Franklin Roosevelt as Wartime Statesman* (Princeton: Princeton University Press, 1991), 109–15.

70. Granatstein and Cuff suggest that, regardless of Hyde Park, the Americans would have soon increased their defence orders in Canada in response to the Japanese attack at Pearl Harbor. Granatstein and Cuff, "Hyde Park Declaration," 75.

71. Director of Public Information, Ottawa, *The Hyde Park Declaration*, Statement by Right Hon. W.L. Mackenzie King, M.P., House of Commons, April 28, 1941 (Ottawa: King's Printer, 1941), 9.

72. Director of Public Information, *Hyde Park Declaration*, 13.

73. Director of Public Information, *Hyde Park Declaration*, 15.

74. Escott Reid, *Time of Fear and Hope: The Making of the North Atlantic Treaty 1947–1949* (Toronto: McClelland and Stewart, 1977).

75. Lester B. Pearson, *The Memoirs of the Right Honourable Lester B. Pearson*, vol. 2, *1948–1957*, edited by John A. Munro and Alex I. Inglis (Toronto: University of Toronto Press, 1973), 39.

76. John Hilliker and Donald Barry, *Canada's Department of External Affairs*, vol. 2, *Coming of Age, 1946–1968* (Montreal: McGill-Queen's University Press, 1995), 34.

77. The North Atlantic Treaty, Article 2, https://www.nato.int/cps/en/natolive/official_texts_17120.htm.

78. John W. Holmes, *The Shaping of Peace: Canada and the Search for World Order, 1943–1957*, vol. 2 (Toronto: University of Toronto Press, 1982), 113; John C. Milloy, *The North Atlantic Treaty Organization 1948–1957: Community or Alliance?* (Montreal: McGill-Queen's University Press, 2006), 4.

79. Pearson, *Memoirs*, 44.

80. For a summary, see Reid, *Time of Fear and Hope*, 138–142.

81. Geoffrey A.H. Pearson, *Seize the Day: Lester B. Pearson and Crisis Diplomacy* (Ottawa: Carleton University Press, 1993), 40.

82. H.H. Wrong to Acting Under-Secretary of State for External Affairs, 17 June 1948, in Hector Mackenzie, ed., *Documents on Canadian External Relations*, vol. 14, document 348, http://epe.lac-bac.gc.ca/100/206/301/faitc-aecic/history/2013-05-03/www.international.gc.ca/department/history-histoire/dcer/details-en.asp@intRefid=10036.

83. Reid to Under-Secretary of State for External Affairs, 26 June 1948, in Mackenzie, *DCER*, vol. 14, document 353, http://epe.lac-bac.gc.ca/100/206/301/faitc-aecic/history/2013-05-03/www.international.gc.ca/department/history-histoire/dcer/details-en.asp@intRefid=10040.

84. On this issue, see Adam Chapnick, "Making Wrong right: The North Atlantic Treaty negotiations and the coming of age of Canadian diplomacy, 1947–1949," in Serge Bernier and John MacFarlane, eds., *Canada, 1900–1950: Un pays prend sa place, A Country Comes of Age* (Quebec: AGMV Marquis, 2003), 171, 174.

85. Among the more balanced depictions of the negotiations are James Eayrs, *In Defence of Canada*, vol. 4, *Growing Up Allied* (Toronto: University of Toronto Press, 1980), chapter 2 and Hector Mackenzie, "Canada, the Cold War and the negotiation of the North Atlantic Treaty," in John Hilliker and Mary Halloran, eds., *Diplomatic Documents and Their Users* (Ottawa: Department of Foreign Affairs and International Trade, 1995), 145–73.

282   NOTES TO PAGES 53–62

86. As Acheson sniffed in his memoirs, "Article 2 has continued to bedevil NATO. Lester Pearson has continually urged the Council to set up committees of 'wise men' to find a use for it, which the 'wise men' have continually failed to do." Acheson, *Present at the Creation: My Years at the State Department* (New York: W.W. Norton, 1987), 277.
87. Pearson, *Seize the Day*, 45.

Chapter 3

1. George Ignatieff, *The Making of a Peacemonger: The Memoirs of George Ignatieff* (Toronto: University of Toronto Press, 1985), 109.
2. Adam Chapnick, "The golden age: A Canadian foreign policy paradox," *International Journal* 64, no. 1 (2008/2009): 205–21, https://doi.org/10.1177/002070200906400118.
3. John Farley, *Brock Chisholm, The World Health Organization, and the Cold War* (Vancouver: UBC Press, 2009); David Mackenzie, *ICAO: A History of the International Civil Aviation Organization* (Toronto: University of Toronto Press, 2010).
4. Susan Armstrong-Reid and David Murray, *Arms for Peace: Canada and the UNRRA Years* (Toronto: University of Toronto Press, 2008); David Webster, "Modern missionaries: Canadian postwar technical assistance advisors in Southeast Asia," *Journal of the Canadian Historical Association* 20, no. 2 (2009): 86–111, https://doi.org/10.7202/044400ar.
5. Hector Mackenzie, "Knight errant, cold warrior or cautious ally? Canada on the United Nations Security Council, 1948–1949," *Journal of Transatlantic Studies* 7, no. 4 (2009): 453–75, https://doi.org/10.1080/14794010903286300.
6. Margaret Weiers, *Envoys Extraordinary: Women of the Canadian Foreign Service* (Toronto: Dundurn Press, 1995).
7. Quoted in William Schabas, "Canada and the adoption of the Universal Declaration of Human Rights," *McGill Law Journal* 43, no. 3 (1998): 424, https://canlii.ca/t/2bfj; Jennifer Tunnicliffe, *Resisting Rights: Canada and the International Bill of Rights, 1947–76* (Vancouver: UBC Press, 2019), chapter 1.
8. DEA to UN Delegation, tel. 117, 8 October 1948; and UN Delegation to DEA, tel. 461, 23 November 1948, both in RG 25, vol. 3701, file 5475-DP-40-pt. 1, LAC.
9. King, diary entry, 13 February 1947, https://www.bac-lac.gc.ca/eng/discover/politics-government/prime-ministers/william-lyon-mackenzie-king/Pages/item.aspx?IdNumber= 30503&.
10. Denis Stairs, *The Diplomacy of Constraint: Canada, the Korean War, and the United States* (Toronto: University of Toronto Press, 1974), 10–18.
11. John Price, "The 'cat's paw': Canada and the United Nations Temporary Commission on Korea," *Canadian Historical Review* 85, no. 2 (2004): 1–16, https://doi.org/10.3138/CHR. 85.2.297.
12. Canada, House of Commons, *Debates*, 21st Parliament, 2nd session, vol. 2, 28 June 1950, 4251, http://parl.canadiana.ca/view/oop.debates_HOC2102_04/955?r=0&s=1.
13. Cabinet Conclusions, 27 June 1950, RG 2, series A-5-a, vol. 2645, https://www.bac-lac.gc.ca/eng/discover/politics-government/cabinet-conclusions/Pages/image.aspx?Image=e000826910&URLjpg=http%3a%2f%2fcentral.bac-lac.gc.ca%2f.item%3fop%3dimg%26app%3dcabinet conclusions%26id%3de000826910&Ecopy=e000826910.
14. The Secretary of State to All Diplomatic Missions and Certain Consular Offices, 29 June 1950, *Foreign Relations of the United States* 1950, vol. VII, 232, doc. #153, https://history.state.gov/historicaldocuments/frus1950v07/d153.
15. Canada, DEA, *Statements & Speeches*, 50/26, "Canada and the Korean Situation," 14 July 1950.
16. Pearson to St Laurent, 3 August 1950, MG 26 N1, vol. 35, LAC.
17. William Johnston, *A War of Patrols: Canadian Army Operations in Korea* (Vancouver: UBC Press, 2004), 373.
18. R.D. Cuff and J.L. Granatstein, *American Dollars—Canadian Prosperity* (Toronto: Samuel-Stevens, 1978), 224.
19. SSEA to Ambassador in the United States, 4 December 1950, in Greg Donaghy, ed., *DCER*, vol. 16, *1950*, 253–5, doc. #175, http://epe.lac-bac.gc.ca/100/206/301/faitc-aecic/history/2013-05-03/www.international.gc.ca/department/history-histoire/dcer/details-en.asp@intRefid= 7195; George Egerton, "Lester B. Pearson and the Korean War: Dilemmas of collective security and international enforcement in Canadian foreign policy, 1950–1953," *International Peacekeeping* 4, no 1 (1997): 51–74, https://doi.org/10.1080/13533319708413651.

NOTES TO PAGES 62–5 283

20. Greg Donaghy, "Pacific diplomacy: Canadian statecraft and the Korean War, 1950–53," in Rick Guisso and Yong-Sik Yoo, eds., *Canada and Korea: Perspectives 2000* (Toronto: University of Toronto Press, 2002), 81–100; Donaghy, "Blessed are the peacemakers: Canada, the United Nations, and the search for a Korean armistice, 1952–53," *War & Society* 30, no. 2 (2011): 134–46, https://doi.org/10.1179/204243411X13026863176583.

21. Canada, DEA, *Statements & Speeches* 51/13, "The Role of the United Nations in a Two Power World," 31 March 1951.

22. They couldn't have been more wrong. In fact, US Secretary of State Dean Acheson dismissed the Canadian as an "empty glass of water." See Evelyn Shuckburgh, *Descent to Suez: Foreign Office Diaries, 1951–1956* (New York: Norton, 1987), 54.

23. Canada, DEA, *Statements & Speeches* 51/14, "Canadian Foreign Policy in a Two-Power World," 10 April 1951.

24. Ronning to Pearson, 15 August 1949, in Mackenzie, *DCER*, vol. 15, *1949*, 1175.

25. John Meehan, *Chasing the Dragon in Shanghai: Canada's Early Relations with China, 1858–1952* (Vancouver: UBC Press, 2011), 176.

26. Chester Ronning, *A Memoir of China in Revolution: From the Boxer Rebellion to the People's Republic* (New York: Pantheon, 1974), 178.

27. Memorandum of a Conversation with Mr. John Foster Dulles, 16 Mar. 1954, MG 26 N1, vol. 65, LAC; Greg Donaghy, "Canadian diplomacy and the Offshore Islands crisis, 1954–1955: A limited national interest," *International Journal* 68, no. 2 (2013): 242–54, https://doi.org/10.1177/0020702013492535.

28. Claxton, 26 November 1953, in Canada, House of Commons, *Debates*, 22nd Parliament, 1st session, 362–3, http://parl.canadiana.ca/view/oop.debates_HOC2201_01/364?r=0&s=1; http://parl.canadiana.ca/view/oop.debates_HOC2201_01/365?r=0&s=1.

29. "Genies out of the bottle," *Saturday Night*, 11 August 1945.

30. Andrew Burtch, *Give Me Shelter: The Failure of Canada's Cold War Civil Defence* (Vancouver: UBC Press, 2012).

31. Adam Chapnick, *Canada's Voice: The Public Life of John Wendell Holmes* (Vancouver: UBC Press, 2009), chapter 6.

32. The Great Unsolved Canadian Mysteries series includes a case study of the Herbert Norman affair. https://www.canadianmysteries.ca/sites/norman/home/indexen.html.

33. In 1947, amid the fallout over the Gouzenko affair, Canada's ambassador to the USSR had been withdrawn in protest.

34. Washington to DEA, tel. 601, 28 March 1956, in Greg Donaghy, ed., *DCER*, vol. 23, *1956–57*, pt II, 4–7, doc #4, http://epe.lac-bac.gc.ca/100/206/301/faitc-aecic/history/2013-05-03/www.international.gc.ca/department/history-histoire/dcer/details-en.asp?intRefid=4551

35. David MacKenzie, *Inside the Atlantic Triangle: Canada and the Entrance of Newfoundland into Confederation, 1939–1949* (Toronto: University of Toronto Press, 1986).

36. Robin S. Gendron, *Towards a Francophone Community: Canada's Relations with France and French Africa, 1945–1968* (Montreal: McGill-Queen's University Press, 2006), 6–44.

37. Notes for Mr. Pearson's Broadcast for CBC, 12 January 1950, MG 31 E46, vol. 7, LAC.

38. Greg Donaghy, "A Voyage of Discovery: St. Laurent's World Tour of 1954," in Patrice Dutil, ed., *The Unexpected Louis St. Laurent: Politics and Policies for a Modern Canada* (Vancouver: UBC Press, 2020), 466–82.

39. Cabinet Conclusions, 17 Mar. 1949, RG 2, series A-5-a, vol. 2643, https://www.bac-lac.gc.ca/eng/discover/politics-government/cabinet-conclusions/Pages/image.aspx?Image=e000825582&URLjpg=http%3a%2f%2fcentral.bac-lac.gc.ca%2f.item%3fop%3dimg%26app%3dcabinetconclusions%26id%3de000825582&Ecopy=e000825582; Hector Mackenzie, "An old dominion and the new Commonwealth: Canadian policy on the question of India's membership, 1947–49," *Journal of Imperial and Commonwealth History* 27, no. 3 (1999): 82–112, https://doi.org/10.1080/03086539908583074.

40. SSEA to Canadian High Commission in New Delhi, 12 April 1955, in Greg Donaghy, ed., *DCER*, vol. 21, *1955*, 1615–16, doc. #779, http://epe.lac-bac.gc.ca/100/206/301/faitc-aecic/history/2013-05-03/www.international.gc.ca/department/history-histoire/dcer/details-en.asp@intRefId=1308.

41. SSEA to Minister of Finance, 17 January 1951, in Donaghy, *DCER*, vol. 17, *1951*, 1042, doc. # 543, http://epe.lac-bac.gc.ca/100/206/301/faitc-aecic/history/2013-05-03/www.international.gc.ca/department/history-histoire/dcer/details-en.asp@intRefId=5921.

284   NOTES TO PAGES 65–72

42. Pearson to Robertson, 28 July 1956, MG 26 N 1 vol. 37, LAC.
43. Paul Martin, *A Very Public Life. Volume II: So Many Worlds* (Toronto: Deneau, 1985), 178–217.
44. Green, 27 November 1956, in Canada, House of Commons, *Debates*, 22nd Parliament, 4th session, vol. 1, 49, http://parl.canadiana.ca/view/oop.debates_HOC2204_20/67?r=0&s=1; and Pearson, 27 November 1956, in Canada, House of Commons, *Debates*, 22nd Parliament, 4th session, vol. 1, 51, http://parl.canadiana.ca/view/oop.debates_HOC2204_20/69?r=0&s=1.
45. José Igartua, *The Other Quiet Revolution: National Identity in English Canada, 1945–1971* (Vancouver: UBC Press, 2005).
46. Blair Fraser, "The Pipeline Uproar," *Maclean's*, 5 July 1958; Janice Cavell, "The spirit of '56: The Suez crisis, anti-Americanism, and Diefenbaker's 1957 and 1958 election victories," in Janice Cavell and Ryan Touhey, eds., *Reassessing the Rogue Tory: Canadian Foreign Policy in the Diefenbaker Era* (Vancouver: UBC Press, 2018), 67–84.
47. Jill Campbell-Miller, "The mind of modernity: Canadian bilateral foreign assistance to India, 1950–1960," (University of Waterloo, PhD dissertation, 2014), 50. On Canada and UNRRA, see Susan Armstrong-Reid and David Murray, *Arms for Peace: Canada and the UNRRA Years* (Toronto: University of Toronto Press, 2008).
48. David Morrison, *Aid and Ebb Tide: A History of CIDA and Canadian Development Assistance* (Waterloo: Wilfrid Laurier University Press, 1998), 30.
49. Ademola Adeleke, "Ties without strings? The Colombo Plan and the geopolitics of international aid, 1950–1980," (University of Toronto, PhD dissertation, 1996), 3. See also David McGee and Rian Manson, "Canada, communism, and the Colombo Plan," in Nina Mollers and Bryan Dewalt, eds., *Objects in Motion: Globalizing Technology* (Washington, DC: Smithsonian Institution Scholarly Press, 2016), 46 and David Webster, *Fire and the Full Moon: Canada and Indonesia in a Decolonizing World* (Vancouver: UBC Press, 2009), 50.
50. Campbell-Miller, "Mind of modernity," 56–64; Webster, *Fire and the Full Moon*, 49–50; McGee and Manson, "Canada, communism and the Colombo Plan," in Mollers and Dewalt, *Objects in Motion*, 49.
51. Ryan M. Touhey, *Conflicting Visions: Canada and India in the Cold War World, 1946–76* (Vancouver: UBC Press, 2015), 47–8.
52. Lester B. Pearson, *The Memoirs of the Right Honourable Lester B. Pearson*, vol. 2, *1948–1957*, edited by John A. Munro and Alex I. Inglis (Toronto: University of Toronto Press, 1973), 107; Geoffrey A. H. Pearson, *Seize the Day: Lester B. Pearson and Crisis Diplomacy* (Ottawa: Carleton University Press, 1993), 51–3.
53. Webster, *Fire and Full Moon*, 49; Campbell-Miller, "Mind of Modernity," 65.
54. Instructions for the Canadian delegation to the meeting of the Commonwealth Consultative Committee on South and South-East Asia to be held at Sydney, Australia, the 15th of May, 1950, 2 May 1950, in Greg Donaghy, ed., *Documents on Canadian External Relations*, vol. 16, *1950* (Ottawa: Minister of Supply and Services Canada, 1996), 1206, document #659, http://epe.lac-bac.gc.ca/100/206/301/faitc-aecic/history/2013-05-03/www.international.gc.ca/department/history-histoire/dcer/details-en.asp@intRefid=7679. Italics in the original.
55. John W. Holmes, *The Shaping of Peace: Canada and the Search for World Order 1943–1957*, vol. 2 (Toronto: University of Toronto Press, 1982), 174.
56. Morrison, *Aid and Ebb Tide*, 30.
57. G. Pearson, *Seize the Day*, 57–60; L. Pearson, *Memoirs*, vol. 2, 111.
58. David Webster and Greg Donaghy, "Introduction," in Donaghy and Webster, eds., *A Samaritan State Revisited: Historical Perspectives on Canadian Foreign Aid* (Calgary: University of Calgary Press, 2019), 2–3.
59. Donald C. Masters, *Canada in World Affairs 1953 to 1955* (Toronto: Oxford University Press, 1959), 61.
60. James Louis Isemann, "To detect, to deter, to defend: The Distant Early Warning (DEW) Line and early Cold War defense policy, 1953–1957," (Kansas State University, PhD dissertation, 2009), 260; Matthew Trudgen, "Coping with fallout: The influence of radioactive fallout on Canadian decision-making on the Distant Early Warning (DEW) Line," *International Journal* 70, no. 2 (2015): 233, 236, https://doi.org/10.1177/0020702015573521.
61. Isemann, "To detect, to deter, to defend," 119–21; James Eayrs, *Canada in World Affairs: October 1955 to June 1957* (Toronto: Oxford University Press, 1959), 141.
62. Joseph T. Jockel, *No Boundaries Upstairs: Canada, the United States, and the Origins of North American Air Defence, 1945–1958* (Vancouver: UBC Press, 1987), 60–70; Alexander W.G. Herd, "A practicable project: Canada, the United States, and the construction of the DEW Line," in

P. Whitney Lackenbauer, ed., *Canadian Arctic Sovereignty and Security: Historical Perspectives* (Calgary: Centre for Military and Security Studies, 2011), 174–5; Draft Memorandum from the Secretary of State for External Affairs to Cabinet, 21 January 1953, in Donald Barry, ed., *Documents on Canadian External Relations*, vol. 19, *1953* (Ottawa: Minister of Supply and Services Canada, 1991), 1047–8, document #694, https://epe.lac-bac.gc.ca/100/206/301/faitc-aecic/history/2013-05-03/www.international.gc.ca/department/history-histoire/dcer/details-en.asp@intRefId=2325.

63. Eayrs, *Canada in World Affairs*, 143–4.

64. Adam Lajeunesse, "The Distant Early Warning Line and the Canadian battle for public perception," *Canadian Military Journal* 8, no. 2 (2007): 55, http://www.journal.forces.gc.ca/vo8/no2/lajeunes-eng.asp.

65. Isemann, "To detect," 260.

66. Trudgen, "Coping with fallout," 232–49; W.H.S. Maklin, "The costly folly of our defense policy," *Maclean's*, 18 February 1956, 20–1, 50–6.

67. Jockel, *No Boundaries*, 84; David Jay Bercuson, *True Patriot: The Life of Brooke Claxton, 1898–1960* (Toronto: University of Toronto Press, 1993), 262–3. See also Claxton to St Laurent, 21 October 1953, in Barry, *DCER 1953*, 1092–3, document #718, https://epe.lac-bac.gc.ca/100/206/301/faitc-aecic/history/2013-05-03/www.international.gc.ca/department/history-histoire/dcer/details-en.asp@intRefid=2349.

68. Draft conditions to govern participation by the United States in the establishment of a distant early warning system in Canadian territory, dated 15 November 1954, attached to M.H. Wershof to Canadian Ambassador in the United States, 16 November 1954, in Greg Donaghy, ed., *Documents on Canadian External Relations*, vol. 20, *1954* (Ottawa: Minister of Public Works and Government Services, 1997), 1047–52, document #483, https://epe.lac-bac.gc.ca/100/206/301/faitc-aecic/history/2013-05-03/www.international.gc.ca/department/history-histoire/dcer/details-en.asp@intRefid=657. See also Jockel, *No Boundaries*, 83; Herd, "Practicable project," 182; Lajeunesse, "Distant Early Warning Line," 54.

69. A copy of the exchange can be found in Whitney Lackenbauer, Matthew J. Farish, and Jennifer Arthur-Lackenbauer, "The Distant Early Warning (DEW) Line: A bibliography and documentary resource list," paper prepared for the Arctic Institute of North America (2005), http://pubs.aina.ucalgary.ca/aina/DEWLineBib.pdf, 3–8.

70. Jockel, *No Boundaries*, 84.

71. Herd, "Practicable project," 192.

72. Antony Anderson, *The Diplomat: Lester Pearson and the Suez Crisis* (Fredericton: Goose Lane, 2015), 293.

73. Lester B. Pearson, *Mike: The Memoirs of the Rt. Hon. Lester B. Pearson*, vol. 2, *1948–1957*, edited by John A. Munro and Alex I. Inglis (Toronto: University of Toronto Press, 1973), 243. See also Antony Anderson, *The Diplomat: Lester Pearson and the Suez Crisis* (Fredericton: Goose Lane, 2015), 293.

74. Holmes, *Shaping of Peace*, vol. 2, 375.

75. The best summary is in Anderson, *The Diplomat*, chapters 8–12. See also Robert W. Reford, *Canada and Three Crises* (Toronto: CIIA, 1968), 75–133.

76. Escott Reid, *Hungary and Suez 1956: A View from New Delhi* (Oakville: Mosaic Press, 1986), 31–4; Peter C. Boyle, "The Hungarian Revolution and the Suez Crisis," *History* 90, no. 4 (2005): 551–3, https://doi.org/10.1111/j.1468-229X.2005.00350.x; John C. Campbell, "The Soviet Union, the United States, and the twin crises of Hungary and Suez," in W. Roger Louis and Roger Owen, eds., *Suez 1956: The Crisis and its Consequences* (Oxford: Clarendon Press, [1989] 2003), 236–9.

77. Anderson, *The Diplomat*, 266–7.

78. Pearson, *Memoirs*, 250–4.

79. Boyle, "Hungarian Revolution," 555.

80. Reid, *Hungary and Suez*, 40–55.

81. Gerald E. Dirks, *Canada's Refugee Policy: Indifference or Opportunism?* (Montreal: McGill-Queen's University Press, 1977), 192–202.

82. Reid, *Hungary and Suez*, 136. See also Escott Reid, "The conscience of the diplomat: A personal testament," *Queen's Quarterly* 74, no. 4 (1967): 582–3.

83. Pearson, *Mike*, 254. For a defence of Pearson's conduct, see Holmes, *Shaping of Peace*, vol. 2, 375–6.

84. Reford, *Canada and Three Crises*, 112; Colin McCullough, *Creating Canada's Peacekeeping Past* (Vancouver: UBC Press, 2016).

286 NOTES TO PAGES 84-9

Chapter 4

1. Quoted in Asa McKercher, "Dealing with Diefenbaker: Canada-US Relations in 1958," *International Journal* 66, 4 (2011): 1045, https://doi.org/10.1177/002070201106600403.

2. H. Basil Robinson, *Diefenbaker's World: A Populist in Foreign Affairs* (Toronto: University of Toronto Press, 1989), 103.

3. Arthur Andrew, *The Rise and Fall of a Middle Power* (Toronto: Lorimer, 1993), 48; Ken Rasmussen, "Bureaucrats and politicians in the Diefenbaker era: A legacy of mistrust," in D.C. Story and R.B. Shepard, eds., *The Diefenbaker Legacy: Politics, Law and Society Since 1957* (Regina: Canadian Plains Research Centre, 1998), 155–68; John Hilliker, "The politicians and the 'Pearsonalities': The Diefenbaker government and the conduct of Canadian external relations," *Historical Papers* 19, no. 1 (1984): 151–67, https://doi.org/10.7202/030922ar; Asa McKercher, "No, Prime Minister: Revisiting Diefenbaker and the 'Pearsonalities'," *Canadian Journal of History* 52, no. 2 (2017): 264–89, https://doi.org/10.3138/cjh.ach.52.2.003.

4. Michael D. Stevenson, "Sidney Smith, Howard Green, and the conduct of Canadian foreign policy during the Diefenbaker Government, 1957–63," in Janice Cavell and Ryan M. Touhey, eds., *Reassessing the Rogue Tory: Canadian Foreign Relations in the Diefenbaker Era* (Vancouver: UBC Press, 2018), 249–70.

5. H. Basil Robinson served as the liaison for most of the Diefenbaker era, and his memoirs are a vital source on this period. See Robinson, *Diefenbaker's World.*

6. Francine McKenzie, "A new vision for the Commonwealth: Diefenbaker's Commonwealth tour of 1958," in Cavell and Touhey, *Reassessing the Rogue Tory*, 25–44.

7. Ruth Compton Brouwer, *Canada's Global Villagers: CUSO in Development, 1961–86* (Vancouver: UBC Press, 2013).

8. Note of a discussion with Mr. Bryce and Mr. Kenneth Taylor, 10 September 1957, DO 35/8731, The National Archives [United Kingdom]; Tim Rooth, "Britain, Europe, and Diefenbaker's trade diversion proposals, 1957–58," in Phillip Buckner, ed., *Canada and the End of Empire* (Vancouver: UBC Press, 2004), 117–32.

9. Harold Macmillan, diary entry, 12 September 1962, in Macmillan, *The Macmillan Diaries*, vol. 2, *Prime Minister and After, 1957–66*, edited by Peter Catterall (London: Macmillan, 2011), 496.

10. Kildare Dobbs, "The case for kicking Canada out of the Commonwealth," *Maclean's*, 6 May 1961, https://archive.macleans.ca/article/1961/5/6/kildare-dobbs-makes-the-case-for-kicking-canada-out-of-the-commonwealth.

11. Quoted in Asa McKercher, "Sound and fury: Diefenbaker, human rights, and Canadian foreign policy," *Canadian Historical Review* 97, no. 2 (2016): 173, https://doi.org/10.3138/chr.3241.

12. Quoted in Robert Vineberg, "The winds of change: Ellen Fairclough and the removal of discriminatory immigration barriers," in Cavell and Touhey, *Reassessing the Rogue Tory*, 242.

13. Robertson to Green, 13 July 1960, RG 25, file 6386-C-40-pt. 6, LAC; Kevin Spooner, *Canada, the Congo Crisis, and UN Peacekeeping, 1960–1964* (Vancouver: UBC Press, 2009).

14. Telephone Conversation with the President, 8 April 1960, Christian Herter Papers, box 10, folder Presidential Phone Calls 1–6/60, Dwight D. Eisenhower Library.

15. Heeney to file, "Memorandum of Conversations with the Prime Minister in Ottawa, Tuesday, August 30, 1960, and Wednesday, August 31, 1960," n.d, MG 30 E144, vol. 1.15, LAC.

16. Quoted in Asa McKercher, "The trouble with self-determination: Canada, Soviet colonialism and the United Nations," *International Journal of Human Rights* 20, no. 3 (2015): 347, https://doi.org/10.1080/13642987.2015.1090431.

17. Thérèse Casgrain, *A Woman in a Man's World* (Toronto: McClelland & Stewart, 1972), 157; Tarah Brookfield, *Cold War Comforts: Canadian Women, Child Safety, and Global Insecurity* (Waterloo: Wilfrid Laurier University Press, 2012), chapter 3.

18. Eric Bergbusch and Michael D. Stevenson, "Howard Green, public opinion, and the politics of disarmament," in Greg Donaghy and Kim Richard Nossal, eds., *Architects and Innovators: Building the Department of Foreign Affairs and International Trade, 1909–2009* (Montreal: McGill-Queen's University Press, 2010), 118–31; Daniel Heidt, "'I think that would be the end of Canada': Howard Green, the nuclear test ban, and interest-based foreign policy, 1946–1963," *American Review of Canadian Studies* 42, no. 3 (2012): 343–69, https://doi.org/10.1080/02722011.2012.705865.

NOTES TO PAGES 89–93   287

19. Nicole Marion, "'I would rather be right': Diefenbaker and Canadian disarmament movements," in Cavell and Touhey, *Reassessing the Rogue Tory*, 143–66.
20. Charles Ritchie, *Storm Signals: More Undiplomatic Diaries, 1962–1971* (Toronto: Macmillan, 1983), 47.
21. Robert Bothwell, *Alliance and Illusion: Canada and the World, 1945–1984* (Vancouver: UBC Press, 2007), 136; Janice Cavell, "Introduction," in Cavell and Touhey, *Reassessing the Rogue Tory*, 3–24.
22. Jon B. McLin, *Canada's Changing Defense Policy, 1957–1963: The Problems of a Middle Power in Alliance* (Baltimore: Johns Hopkins Press, 1967), 38.
23. John G. Diefenbaker, *One Canada: Memoirs of the Right Honourable John G. Diefenbaker*, vol. 3, *The Tumultuous Years 1962–1967* (Toronto: Macmillan, 1977), 18.
24. Joseph T. Jockel, *No Boundaries Upstairs: Canada, the United States and the Origins of North American Air Defence, 1945–1958* (Vancouver: UBC Press, 1987), 95–6; Joseph T. Jockel, *Canada in NORAD, 1957–2007: A History* (Montreal: McGill-Queen's University Press, 2007), 23–31.
25. "Integration of operational control of the continental air defences of Canada and the United States in peacetime(s)," appended to Eighth Report of the Canada-U.S. Military Study Group, 19 December 1956, in Greg Donaghy, ed., *Documents on Canadian External Relations*, vol. 23, *1956–1957*, pt. 2 (Ottawa: Minister of Public Works and Government Services, 2002), 60, document #41, https://epe.lac-bac.gc.ca/100/206/301/faitc-aecic/history/2013-05-03/www.international.gc.ca/department/history-histoire/dcer/details-en.asp@intRefid=4588.
26. Memorandum from Defence Liaison (1) Division to Deputy Under-Secretary of State for External Affairs, 13 February 1957; and Jules Léger, Memorandum from Under-Secretary of State for External Affairs to Secretary of State for External Affairs, 12 June 1957, both in Donaghy, *DCER*, vol. 23, *1956–1957*, pt. 2, 71–3; 81–2, docs #46; 50, https://epe.lac-bac.gc.ca/100/206/301/faitc-aecic/history/2013-05-03/www.international.gc.ca/department/history-histoire/dcer/details-en.asp@intRefid=4593; https://epe.lac-bac.gc.ca/100/206/301/faitc-aecic/history/2013-05-03/www.international.gc.ca/department/history-histoire/dcer/details-en.asp@intRefid=4597.
27. Extract from Cabinet Conclusions, 13 June 1957, in Donaghy, *DCER*, vol. 23, *1956–1957*, pt. 2, 82–3, doc. #51, https://epe.lac-bac.gc.ca/100/206/301/faitc-aecic/history/2013-05-03/www.international.gc.ca/department/history-histoire/dcer/details-en.asp@intRefid=4598. See also Jockel, *No Boundaries*, 103; McLin, *Canada's Changing Defense Policy*, 39–41; Robinson, *Diefenbaker's World*, 17; John Hilliker and Donald Barry, *Canada's Department of External Affairs*, vol. 2, *Coming of Age, 1946–1968* (Montreal: McGill-Queen's University Press, 1995), 109–10.
28. General Charles Foulkes, 22 October 1963, in Canada, House of Commons, *Committees*, 26th Parliament, 1st session: *Special Committee on Defence*, vol. 1, 510, https://parl.canadiana.ca/view/oop.com_HOC_2601_4_1/558; Jockel, *No Boundaries*, 105; Robinson, *Diefenbaker's World*, 18.
29. J.L. Granatstein, *A Man of Influence: Norman A. Robertson and Canadian Statecraft 1929–68* (Toronto: Deneau Publishers, 1981), 317.
30. Hilliker and Barry, *Canada's Department of External Affairs*, vol. 2, 236; Robinson, *Diefenbaker's World*, 19.
31. Acting Under-Secretary of State for External Affairs to Deputy Minister of National Defence, 2 August 1957, in Michael D. Stevenson, ed., *DCER*, vol. 25, *1957–1958*, pt. 2 (Ottawa: Minister of Public Works and Government Services, 2004), 33–34, doc. #15, https://epe.lac-bac.gc.ca/100/206/301/faitc-aecic/history/2013-05-03/www.international.gc.ca/department/history-histoire/dcer/details-en.asp@intRefid=8104.
32. Chairman, Chiefs of Staff Committee to Acting Under-Secretary of State for External Affairs, 7 August 1957, in Stephenson, *DCER*, vol. 25, *1957–1958*, pt. 2, 37, doc. #16, https://epe.lac-bac.gc.ca/100/206/301/faitc-aecic/history/2013-05-03/www.international.gc.ca/department/history-histoire/dcer/details-en.asp@intRefid=8105.
33. Robinson, *Diefenbaker's World*, 21.
34. On the debates, see McLin, *Canada's Changing Defense Policy*, 47–56; Jockel, *No Boundaries*, 110–7; Jockel, *Canada in NORAD*, 33–5.
35. Jockel, *Canada in NORAD*, 33. See also Jockel, *No Boundaries*, 33, 108, 125–6; Bothwell, *Alliance and Illusion*, 153; McLin, *Canada's Changing Defense Policy*, 51, 58; Denis Smith,

288   NOTES TO PAGES 94-8

Rogue Tory: The Life and Legend of John G. Diefenbaker (Toronto: Macfarlane Walter & Ross, 1995), 296.

36. Diefenbaker, *One Canada*, vol. 3, 23. See also Patricia I. McMahon, *Essence of Indecision: Diefenbaker's Nuclear Policy, 1957-1963* (Montreal: McGill-Queen's University Press, 2009), 13.

37. Adam Chapnick, *Canada's Voice: The Public Life of John Wendell Holmes* (Vancouver: UBC Press, 2009), 94-8.

38. Linda Freeman, *The Ambiguous Champion: Canada and South Africa in the Trudeau and Mulroney Years* (Toronto: University of Toronto Press, 1997), 19.

39. Daniel Manulak, "Blood brothers: Moral emotion, the Afro-Asian-Canadian bloc, and South Africa's expulsion from the Commonwealth, 1960-1," *Canadian Historical Review* 103, no. 2 (2022): 256, https://doi.org/10.3138/chr-2020-0041.

40. Freeman, *Ambiguous Champion*, 16; Frank Hayes, "South Africa's departure from the Commonwealth, 1960-1961," *International History Review* 2, no. 3 (1980): 457-9, https://doi.org/10.1080/07075332.1980.9640222; Peter Henshaw, "Canada and the 'South African disputes' at the United Nations, 1946-1961," *Canadian Journal of African Studies* 33, 1 (1999): 5-8, 27, https://doi.org/10.1080/00083968.1999.10751154.

41. Brian Douglas Tennyson, *Canada Relations with South Africa: A Diplomatic History* (Washington, DC: University Press of America, 1982), 140.

42. Asa McKercher, "Sound and fury: Diefenbaker, human rights, and Canadian foreign policy," *Canadian Historical Review* 97, no. 2 (2016): 174-5, https://doi.org/10.3138/chr.3241.

43. Hayes, "South Africa's departure," 461; Tennyson, *Canadian Relations with South Africa*, 158.

44. Robinson, *Diefenbaker's World*, 123, 178-9; Freeman, *Ambiguous Champion*, 23.

45. Harold Macmillan: The Wind of Change Speech, 3 February 1960, Address by Harold Macmillan to Members of both Houses of the Parliament of the Union Of South Africa, Cape Town, https://www.thoughtco.com/harold-macmillans-wind-of-change-speech-43760; Tennyson, *Canadian Relations with South Africa*, 158-63; Ronald Hyam, "The parting of ways: Britain and South Africa's departure from the Commonwealth, 1951-61," *Journal of Imperial and Commonwealth History* 26, no. 2 (1998): 164-5, https://doi.org/10.1080/03086539808583030.

46. Richard Preston, *Canada in World Affairs 1959 to 1961* (Toronto: Oxford University Press, 1965), 201-2; Hayes, "South Africa's departure," 463.

47. John G. Diefenbaker, *One Canada: Memoirs of the Right Honourable John G. Diefenbaker*, vol. 2, *The Years of Achievement, 1957-1962* (Toronto: Macmillan, 1976), 210.

48. Ironically, Pretoria itself had sponsored the motion that produced this policy in 1955. See J.R.T. Wood, "The roles of Diefenbaker, Macmillan, and Verwoerd in the withdrawal of South Africa from the Commonwealth," *Journal of Contemporary African Studies* 6, nos. 1-2 (1987): 167, https://doi.org/10.1080/02589008708729471.

49. Wood, "Roles," 157-61.

50. Diefenbaker, *One Canada*, vol. 2, 216-7.

51. Manulak, "Blood brothers," 268.

52. Hilliker and Barry, *Canada's Department of External Affairs*, vol. 2, 164-5; Robinson, *Diefenbaker's World*, 180-6.

53. Wood, "Roles," 165-76; Hayes, "South Africa's departure," 473-6; Hyam, "The parting of ways," 166-72.

54. McKercher, "Sound and fury," 168.

55. Charles Ritchie, diary entry, 30 September 1962, in Ritchie, *Undiplomatic Diaries 1937-1971* (Toronto: McClelland and Stewart, 2008), 449-50.

56. On the historiography, see Jocelyn Maynard Ghent, "Did he fall or was he pushed? The Kennedy Administration and the collapse of the Diefenbaker government," *International History Review* 1, no. 2 (1979): 246-70, https://doi.org/10.1080/07075332.1979.9640184; McMahon, *Essence of Indecision*; Michael D. Stevenson, "'Tossing a match into dry hay': Nuclear weapons and the crisis in U.S.-Canadian relations, 1962-1963," *Journal of Cold War Studies* 16, no. 4 (2014): 5-34, https://doi.org/10.1162/JCWS_a_00514.

57. Sean Maloney, "The missing essential part emergency provision of nuclear weapons for RCAF Air Defence Command, 1961-1964," *Canadian Military History*, 23, no. 1 (2015): 35, http://scholars.wlu.ca/cmh/vol23/iss1/3.

NOTES TO PAGES 98–108   289

58. Isabel Campbell, "The defence dilemma, 1957–1963: Reconsidering the strategic, technological, and operational contexts," in Cavell and Touhey, *Reassessing the Rogue Tory*, 123–5; McMahon, *Essence of Indecision*, 41.
59. Andrew Richter, *Avoiding Armageddon: Canadian Military Strategy and Nuclear Weapons 1950–1963* (Vancouver: UBC Press, 2002), 81.
60. Ghent, "Did he fall," 251; Stevenson, "Tossing a match," 9; McMahon, *Essence of Indecision*, 87.
61. McMahon, *Essence of Indecision*, 106, 122.
62. Nicole Marion, "'I would rather be right': Diefenbaker and Canadian disarmament movements," in Cavell and Touhey, *Reassessing the Rogue Tory*, 152; McMahon, *Essence of Indecision*, 130.
63. Norstad, quoted in Mark Andrew Eaton, "The liberal and conservative internationalist divide: societal responses to Canada's transatlantic nuclear commitments," *Journal of Transatlantic Studies* 15, no. 3 (2017): 210, https://doi.org/10.1080/14794012.2017.1337669.
64. The reiteration undermines the suggestion elsewhere that Norstad regretted what he said. See Robinson, *Diefenbaker's World*, 304.
65. Stevenson, "Tossing a match," 19.
66. Asa McKercher, *Camelot and Canada: Canadian-American Relations in the Kennedy Era* (New York: Oxford University Press, 2016), 184; McMahon, *Essence of Indecision*, 166; Stevenson, "Tossing a match," 21; Eaton, "The liberal and conservative internationalist divide," 211.
67. Canada, House of Commons, *Debates*, 25th Parliament, 1st session, vol. 3, 3125–37, http://parl.canadiana.ca/view/oop.debates_HOC2501_03/907?r=0&s=1.
68. US Department of State, cited in Robinson, *Diefenbaker's World*, 306–7; Eaton, "The liberal and conservative internationalist divide," 212; Stevenson, "Tossing a match," 25–7. The release is reprinted in Smith, *Rogue Tory*, 473–4. See also McKercher, *Camelot and Canada*, 189–90; Ghent, "Did he fall," 256–60; Stevenson, "Tossing a match," 24.
69. Patrick Brennan, *Reporting the Nation's Business: Press-Government Relations during the Liberal Years 1935–1957* (Toronto: University of Toronto Press, 1994).

Chapter 5

1. Joey Smallwood, *The Time Has Come to Tell* (St. John's: Newfoundland Book Publishers, 1979), 137.
2. Peter Newman, *The Distemper of Our Times: Canadian Politics in Transition 1963–1968* (Toronto: McClelland and Stewart, 1968), xiii.
3. Penny Bryden, *Planners and Politicians: Liberal Politics and Social Policy, 1957–1968* (Montreal: McGill-Queen's University Press, 1998).
4. Stephen Azzi, "Lester Pearson and the substance of the sixties," in Asa McKercher and Galen Perras, eds., *Mike's World: Lester B. Pearson and Canadian External Affairs* (Vancouver: UBC Press, 2017), 117–9.
5. Paul A. Evans, *The Least Possible Fuss and Publicity: The Politics of Immigration in Postwar Canada, 1945–1967* (Montreal: McGill-Queen's University Press, 2021).
6. House of Commons, *Debates*, 25th Parliament, 1st session, vol. 3, 17 December 1962, 2722, https://parl.canadiana.ca/view/oop.debates_HOC2501_03/504?r=0&s=1.
7. Robert Bothwell, Ian Drummond, and John English, *Canada since 1945: Power, Politics, and Provincialism* (Toronto: University of Toronto Press, 1981), 285.
8. George Grant, *Lament for a Nation: The Defeat of Canadian Nationalism* (Montreal: McGill-Queen's University Press, 2000 [1965]).
9. Asa McKercher, "Neutralism, nationalism, and nukes, Oh my! Revisiting *Peacemaker or Powdermonkey?* and Canadian strategy in the missile age," in Susan Colbourn and Timothy Andrews Sayle, eds., *The Nuclear North: Histories of Canada in the Atomic Age* (Vancouver: UBC Press, 2020), 88–108.
10. Stephen Azzi, *Walter Gordon and the Rise of Canadian Nationalism* (Montreal: McGill-Queen's University Press, 1999).
11. Asa McKercher, *Camelot and Canada: Canadian-American Relations in the Kennedy Era* (New York: Oxford University Press, 2016).
12. Norman Hillmer, Daniel Macfarlane, and Michael Manulak, "The Pearson government and the diplomacy of the environment," in McKercher and Perras, *Mike's World*, 320–41.

290 NOTES TO PAGES 109–12

13. George Ball, Speech to the Canadian and Empire Clubs, Royal York Hotel, 22 March 1965, MG 30 E144, vol. 3, file Canada-US relations 1964–1967, miscellaneous, LAC.
14. Greg Donaghy, *Tolerant Allies: Canada and the United States, 1963–1968* (Montreal: McGill-Queen's University Press, 2002), 130. On the Auto Pact, see Dimitry Anastakis, *Auto Pact: Creating a Borderless North American Auto Industry, 1960–1971* (Toronto: University of Toronto Press, 2005).
15. Telcon, Johnson and Bayh, 15 June 1965, 1:20 p.m., Recordings and Transcripts of Telephone Conversations and Meetings, White House Series, box 7, folder June 1965, Lyndon Baines Johnson Presidential Library.
16. Telcon, Johnson and Bayh, 15 June 1965, 1:20 p.m., Recordings and Transcripts of Telephone Conversations and Meetings, White House Series, box 7, folder June 1965, Lyndon Baines Johnson Presidential Library.
17. Victor Levant, *Quiet Complicity: Canadian Involvement in the Vietnam War* (Toronto: Between the Lines, 1986).
18. Andrew Preston, "Missions impossible: Canadian secret diplomacy and the quest for peace in Vietnam," in Lloyd Gardner and Ted Gittinger, eds., *The Search for Peace in Vietnam, 1964–1968* (College Station: Texas A&M University Press, 2004), 117–43.
19. Michael Carroll, "Pragmatic peacekeeping: The Pearson years," in McKercher and Perras, *Mike's World*, 48–69.
20. Adam Chapnick, *Canada on the United Nations Security Council: A Small Power on a Large Stage* (Vancouver: UBC Press, 2019), 80–7. On UNEF, see Michael K. Carroll, *Pearson's Peacekeepers: Canada and the United Nations Emergency Force, 1956–1967* (Vancouver: UBC Press, 2009).
21. Robert Carty, "Going for gain: Foreign aid and CIDA," in Richard Swift and Robert Clarke, eds., *Ties That Bind: Canada and the Third World* (Toronto: Between the Lines, 1982), 155. In retirement, Pearson chaired the World Bank's Commission on International Development, which proposed that donor countries dedicate 0.7 per cent of their GDP (now GNI) to international assistance, which has since become the global standard. See Kevin Brushett, "Robert McNamara, Lester Pearson and the Commission on International Development 1967–1973," *Diplomacy and Statecraft* 26, no. 1 (2015): 84–102, https://doi.org/10.1080/09592296.2015. 999626.
22. José Igartua, *The Other Quiet Revolution: National Identity in English Canada, 1945–1971* (Vancouver: UBC Press, 2005).
23. Lester B. Pearson, *Words and Occasions* (Toronto: University of Toronto Press, 1970), 228.
24. Lester B. Pearson, *Mike: The Memoirs of the Right Honourable Lester B. Pearson*, vol. 3, *1957–1968*, edited by John A. Munro and Alex I. Inglis (Toronto: University of Toronto Press, 1975), 301.
25. Pearson, *Words and Occasions*, 275; Helen Davies, "Canada's centennial experience," in Raymond B. Blake and Matthew Hayday, eds., *Celebrating Canada: Commemorations, Anniversaries, and National Symbols* (Toronto: University of Toronto Press, 2018), 174–206.
26. Pierre Berton, *1967: The Last Good Year* (Toronto: Doubleday, 1997).
27. British North American Act, 1867, Section 132, https://laws-lois.justice.gc.ca/eng/const/page-7.html#h-28.
28. Claude Morin and Richard Howard, *Quebec versus Ottawa: The Struggle for Self-Government, 1960–72* (Toronto: University of Toronto Press, 1973), 5. On the impact of decolonization in Quebec, see David Meren, *With Friends Like These: Entangled Nationalisms and the Canada-Quebec-France Triangle, 1944–1970* (Vancouver: UBC Press, 2013), 110; Magali Deleuze, *L'une et l'autre indépendance 1954–1964: Les medias au Québec et la guerre d'Algérie* (Outremont: Les Éditions Point de Fuite, 2001).
29. Robin S. Gendron, *Towards a Francophone Community: Canada's Relations with France and French Africa, 1946–1968* (Montreal: McGill-Queen's University Press, 2006), 100–1.
30. John English, *The Worldly Years: The Life of Lester Pearson*, vol. II: *1949–1972* (Toronto: Alfred A. Knopf Canada, 1992), 276–7.
31. Pearson, *Memoirs*, vol. 3, 237.
32. Brendan Kelly, "Pearson, France, and Quebec's international personality," in McKercher and Perras, *Mike's World*, 297.

NOTES TO PAGES 112–17 291

33. Kelly, "Pearson, France, and Quebec's international personality," in McKercher and Perras, *Mike's World*, 301.
34. In historian David Meren's words, "Gaullism, with its early-nineteenth century conceptualization of nation, considered Canada, with its marginalized francophone population, an anachronism." Meren, *With Friends Like These*, 97.
35. Gendron, *Towards a Francophone Community*, 90; Robert Bothwell, *Alliance and Illusion: Canada and the World, 1945–1984* (Vancouver: UBC Press, 2007), 246.
36. Kelly, "Pearson, France, and Quebec's international personality," in McKercher and Perras, *Mike's World*, 304.
37. Gendron, *Towards a Francophone Community*, 105.
38. Gendron, *Towards a Francophone Community*, 106; Meren, *With Friends Like These*, 155–6.
39. Morin and Howard, *Quebec versus Ottawa*, 35.
40. Pearson, *Memoirs*, vol. 3, 263; Gendron, *Towards a Francophone Community*, 106.
41. Brendan Kelly, *The Good Fight: Marcel Cadieux and Canadian Diplomacy* (Vancouver: UBC Press, 2019), 205.
42. Gendron, *Towards a Francophone Community*, 110–4; Gendron, "Educational aid for French Africa and the Canada-Quebec dispute over foreign policy in the 1960s," *International Journal* 56, no. 1 (2000–1): 31–4, https://doi.org/10.1177/002070200105600102.
43. Gendron, *Towards a Francophone Community*, 126.
44. Robin S. Gendron, "Education and the origins of Quebec's international engagement," *American Review of Canadian Studies* 46, no. 2 (2016): 228, https://doi.org/10.1080/0272201 1.2016.1187971; Kelly, "Pearson, France, and Quebec's international personality," in McKercher and Perras, *Mike's World*, 310.
45. Morin and Howard, *Quebec versus Ottawa*, 37.
46. Kelly, "Pearson, France, and Quebec's international personality," in McKercher and Perras, *Mike's World*, 315.
47. Morin and Howard, *Quebec versus Ottawa*, 52.
48. Stephen Azzi, *Reconcilable Differences: A History of Canada-US Relations* (Don Mills, ON: Oxford University Press, 2015), 170.
49. Brendan Kelly, "Lester B. Pearson's Temple University speech revisited: The origins and evolution of the proposal for a bombing pause," *American Review of Canadian Studies* 47, no. 4 (2017): 373, https://doi.org/10.1080/02722011.2017.1399281; Douglas A. Ross, *In the Interests of Peace: Canada and Vietnam, 1954–1973* (Toronto: University of Toronto Press, 1984), 265; Bothwell, *Alliance and Illusion*, 227.
50. Kelly, *Good Fight*, 165.
51. Pearson, quoted in Bothwell, *Alliance and Illusion*, 223.
52. Norman Hillmer and J.L. Granatstein, *Empire to Umpire: Canada and the World into the Twenty-First Century*, 2nd ed. (Toronto: Thomson Nelson, 2008), 238.
53. Greg Donaghy, "Minding the minister: Pearson, Martin and American policy in Asia, 1963–1967," in Norman Hillmer, ed., *Pearson: The Unlikely Gladiator* (Montreal: McGill-Queen's University Press, 1999), 136.
54. Donaghy, "Minding the minister," in Hillmer, *Pearson*, 133.
55. Pearson, quoted in English, *Worldly Years*, 361.
56. Kelly, "Lester B. Pearson's Temple University speech," 373.
57. Kelly, "Lester B. Pearson's Temple University speech," 374.
58. Cadieux, diary entry, 6 April 1965, cited in Kelly, "Lester B. Pearson's Temple University speech," 382, note 26.
59. Donaghy, *Tolerant Allies*, 130.
60. Martin, quoted in Greg Donaghy, *Grit: The Life and Politics of Paul Martin Sr.* (Vancouver: UBC Press, 2015), 233–4.
61. Kelly, "Lester B. Pearson's Temple University speech," 379.
62. Childs, quoted in Donaghy, "Minding the minister," in Hillmer, *Pearson*, 137.
63. Kelly, "Lester B. Pearson's Temple University speech," 377.
64. Bothwell, *Alliance and Illusion*, 225.
65. Peter Stursberg, *Lester Pearson and the American Dilemma* (Toronto: Doubleday, 1980), 223; English, *Worldly Years*, 365. Johnson called this "pissing on your neighbour's rug."
66. Hillmer and Granatstein, *Empire to Umpire*, 240.
67. John English, *Worldly Years*, 364.

292 NOTES TO PAGES 118–29

68. Pearson, *Memoirs*, vol. 3, 140.
69. Kelly, "Lester B. Pearson's Temple University Speech," 380.
70. Ross, *In the Interests of Peace*, 257, 269.
71. Hillmer and Granatstein, *Empire to Umpire*, 240. On Pearson's own hypocrisy, see English, *Worldly Years*, 365.
72. Ian McKay and Jamie Swift, *Warrior Nation: Rebranding Canada in an Age of Anxiety* (Toronto: Between the Lines, 2012), 157.
73. Charles Ritchie, *Undiplomatic Diaries, 1937–1971* (Toronto: McClelland and Stewart, 2008), 500.
74. Ritchie, *Undiplomatic Diaries*, 495.

Chapter 6

1. Paul Litt, *Trudeaumania* (Vancouver: UBC Press, 2016).
2. Christopher Dummitt and Christabelle Sethna, eds., *No Place for the State: The Origins and Legacies of the 1969 Omnibus Bill* (Vancouver: UBC Press, 2020).
3. Pierre Trudeau, "Pearson ou l'abdication de l'esprit," *Cité Libre*, avril 1963.
4. Pierre Trudeau, "Canada and the World," *Statements and Speeches* no. 68/17, 29 May 1968.
5. Lintott to Morrice James, 29 April 1968, Foreign and Commonwealth Office Papers, FCO 49/107, The National Archives, United Kingdom.
6. Canada, Department of External Affairs, *Foreign Policy for Canadians* (Ottawa: Information Canada, 1970), 9, https://gac.canadiana.ca/view/ooe.b1603784E/15?r=0&s=1; Mary Halloran, John Hilliker, and Greg Donaghy, "The white paper impulse: Reviewing foreign policy under Trudeau and Clark," *International Journal* 70, no. 2 (2015): 309–21, https://doi.org/10.1177/0020702015577920.
7. Mary Halloran, "'A planned and phased reduction': The Trudeau government and the NATO compromise, 1968–1969," in Christian Nuenlist and Anna Locher, eds., *Transatlantic Relations at Stake: Aspects of NATO, 1956–1972* (Zurich: Center for Security Studies and Conflict Research, 2006), 125–43.
8. John Soares, "Cold War, hot ice: International ice hockey, 1947–1980," *Journal of Sport History* 34, no. 2 (2007): 207–30, https://www.jstor.org/stable/43610017; James Hershberg, "Breaking the ice: Alexei Kosygin and the secret background of the 1972 Hockey Summit Series," in Robert Edelman and Christopher Young, eds., *The Whole World Was Watching: Sport in the Cold War*, (Palo Alto: Stanford University Press, 2019), 59–72.
9. Robert Ford, *Our Man in Moscow: A Diplomat's Reflections on the Soviet Union* (Toronto: University of Toronto Press, 1989), 123.
10. Greg Donaghy, "Red China blues: Paul Martin, Lester B. Pearson, and the China conundrum, 1963–1967," *Journal of American-East Asian Relations* 20, no. 2–3 (2013): 190–202, https://doi.org/10.1163/18765610-02003006.
11. Ivan Head and Pierre Trudeau, *The Canadian Way: Shaping Canada's Foreign Policy, 1968–1984* (Toronto: McClelland & Stewart, 1995), 227.
12. Pierre Trudeau, *Conversations with Canadians* (Toronto: University of Toronto Press, 1972), 174.
13. Arthur Andrew, *The Rise and Fall of a Middle Power* (Toronto: James Lorimer, 1993), 93.
14. John English, *Just Watch Me: The Life of Pierre Elliott Trudeau, 1968–2000* (Toronto: Knopf Canada, 2009), 171.
15. Canada, Senate Committee on Foreign Affairs, *Proceedings*, 30th Parliament, 1st session, (25 March 1975), 11: 18, https://parl.canadiana.ca/view/oop.com_SOC_3001_4_1/306?r=0&s=1.
16. Washington to DEA, tel. 344, 27 January 1972, RG 25, vol. 8678, file 20-USA-1-3 pt. 24, LAC.
17. Mitchell Sharp, "Canada-U.S. relations: Options for the future," *International Perspectives* (Autumn 1972): 1, 13, 17.
18. John Hilliker, Mary Halloran, and Greg Donaghy, *Canada's Department of External Affairs*, vol. 3, *Innovation and Adaptation, 1968–1984* (Toronto: University of Toronto Press, 2017), 194–8.
19. Greg Donaghy, "Pierre Trudeau and Canada's pacific tilt," *International Journal* 74, no. 1 (2019): 135–50, https://doi.org/10.1177/0020702019834883.
20. Greg Donaghy and Mary Halloran, "*Viva el pueblo cubano*: Pierre Trudeau's distant Cuba, 1968–1978," in Robert A. Wright and Lana Wylie, eds., *Our Place in the Sun: Canada and Cuba in the Castro Era* (Toronto: University of Toronto Press, 2009), 143–62.
21. Keith Spicer, *A Samaritan State? External Aid in Canada's Foreign Policy* (Toronto: University of Toronto Press, 1966); Clyde Sanger, *Half a Loaf: Canada's Semi-Role Among Developing Countries* (Toronto: Ryerson Press, 1969).

NOTES TO PAGES 129–33 293

22. Pierre Trudeau, Speech at Mansion House, London, *Statements & Speeches* 75/6, 13 March 1975.
23. Greg Donaghy, "A wasted opportunity: Canada and the New International Economic Order, 1974–82," in Colin McCullough and Robert Teigrob, eds., *Canada and the United Nations: Legacies, Limits, Prospects* (Montreal: McGill-Queen's University Press, 2017), 183–207.
24. William Barton Interview in Robert Bothwell and J.L. Granatstein, eds., *Trudeau's World: Insiders Reflect on Foreign Policy, Trade, and Defence, 1968–84* (Vancouver: UBC Press, 2017), 100–101.
25. David Webster, *Challenge the Strong Wind: Canada and East Timor, 1975–99* (Vancouver: UBC Press, 2020); Stephanie Bangarth, "'Vocal but not particularly strong?' Air Canada's ill-fated vacation package to Rhodesia and South Africa and the anti-apartheid movement in Canada," *International Journal* 71, no. 3 (2016): 488–97, https://doi.org/10.1177/0020702016661184.
26. Head and Trudeau, *The Canadian Way*, 161.
27. Asa McKercher, "Reason over passion: Pierre Trudeau, human rights, and Canadian foreign policy," *International Journal* 73, no. 1 (2018): 133, https://doi.org/10.1177/0020702018765079.
28. George Ignatieff, *The Making of a Peacemonger: The Memoirs of George Ignatieff* (Toronto: University of Toronto Press, 1985), 237–8.
29. Jan Raska, "Humanitarian gesture: Canada and the Tibetan Resettlement Program, 1971–75," *Canadian Historical Review* 97, no. 4 (2016): 546–75, https://doi.org/10.3138/chr.Raska; Shezan Muhammedi, *Gifts from Amin: Ugandan Asian Refugees in Canada* (Winnipeg: University of Manitoba Press, 2022); Francis Peddie, *Young, Well-Educated and Adaptable: Chilean Exiles in Ontario and Quebec, 1973–2010* (Winnipeg: University of Manitoba Press, 2014).
30. Canada, Department of External Affairs, *Foreign Policy for Canadians: United Nations* (Ottawa: Information Canada, 1970), 27, https://gac.canadiana.ca/view/ooe.b1603784E/183?r=0&s=1.
31. Department of Indian Affairs and Northern Development, *Statement of the Government of Canada on Indian Policy* (Ottawa: Queen's Printer, 1969), https://oneca.com/1969_White_Paper.pdf.
32. The *Hawthorn Report* (2 vols., 1967) can be found at https://www.sac-isc.gc.ca/eng/1293033391108/1618944624384 and https://www.sac-isc.gc.ca/eng/1293034224686/1618944528155.
33. Harold Cardinal, *The Unjust Society* (Vancouver: Douglas & McIntyre, 1969), 17.
34. George Manuel and Michael Posluns, *The Fourth World: An Indian Reality* (Don Mills: Collier-Macmillan, 1974), 70.
35. Scott Rutherford, "Canada's other red scare: Indigenous anti-colonialism and the Anicinabe Park occupation," in Dan Berger, ed., *The Hidden 1970s: Histories of Radicalism* (New Brunswick: Rutgers University Press, 2010), 77–96.
36. Andrew S. Thompson, *On the Side of the Angels: Canada and the United Nations Commission on Human Rights* (Vancouver: UBC Press, 2017), 77–87.
37. Trudeau, "Canada and the World," *Statements & Speeches* 68/17, 29 May 1968.
38. Robin S. Gendron, "Advancing the national interest: Marcel Cadieux, Jules Léger, and Canadian participation in the Francophone community, 1964–1972," in Greg Donaghy and Michael Carroll, eds., *In the National Interest: Canada's Department of Foreign Affairs and International Trade, 1909–2009* (Calgary: University of Calgary Press, 2011), 121–36.
39. Quoted in English, *Just Watch Me*, 85.
40. Washington to DEA, tel. 882, 9 March 1977, RG 25, vol. 9246 file 20-CDA-9-TRUDEAU-USA-pt.5, LAC; "Trudeau says Canada may amend charter," *The New York Times*, 23 February 1977.
41. "Union of British Columbia Indian Chiefs Constitution Express #2," October 1981, http://constitution.ubcic.bc.ca/node/158.
42. Frédéric Bastien, *The Battle of London: Trudeau, Thatcher, and the Fight for Canada's Constitution* (Toronto: Dundurn, 2014).
43. Robert Wright, *Our Man in Tehran: Ken Taylor, the CIA, and the Iran Hostage Crisis* (Toronto: HarperCollins, 2010).
44. Michael Molloy, Peter Duschinsky, Kurt Jensen, and Robert Shalka, *Running on Empty: Canada and the Indochinese Refugees, 1975–1980* (Montreal: McGill-Queen's University Press, 2017). The Hmong are an Indigenous group from East and Southeast Asia.
45. Greg Donaghy, "The 'ghost of peace': Pierre Trudeau's search for peace, 1982–84," *Peace Research* 39, no. 1/2 (2007): 38–57, http://www.peaceresearch.ca/pdf/39/Donaghy.pdf; Susan

294 NOTES TO PAGES 133–7

Colbourn, "'Cruising toward nuclear danger': Canadian anti-nuclear activism, Pierre Trudeau's peace mission, and the transatlantic partnership," *Cold War History* 18, no. 1 (2018): 19–36, https://doi.org/10.1080/14682745.2017.1370456.

46. Allan Gotlieb, *The Washington Diaries* (Toronto: McClelland and Stewart, 2006), 180.
47. J.L. Granatstein and Robert Bothwell, *Pirouette: Pierre Trudeau and Canadian Foreign Policy* (Toronto: University of Toronto Press, 1990), xiv.
48. Bruce Thordarson, *Trudeau and Foreign Policy: A Study in Decision-Making* (Toronto: Oxford University Press, 1972), 27, 122; Edna Keeble, "Rethinking the 1971 white paper and Trudeau's impact on Canadian defence policy," *American Review of Canadian Studies* 27, no. 4 (1997): 553, https://doi.org/10.1080/02722019709481141; Head and Trudeau, *Canadian Way*, 66.
49. Policy Statement by Prime Minister Pierre Elliott Trudeau, 29 May 1968, in John Gellner, *Canada in NATO* (Toronto: Ryerson Press, 1970), 97.
50. Policy Statement by Prime Minister Pierre Elliott Trudeau, 29 May 1968, in Gellner, *Canada in NATO*, 98.
51. Michel Fortmann and Martin Larose, "An emerging strategic counterculture? Pierre Elliott Trudeau, Canadian intellectuals and the revision of Liberal defence policy concerning NATO (1968–1969)," *International Journal* 59, no. 3 (2004): 541, https://doi.org/10.1177/002070200405900305. For a summary of such thinking, see Stephen Clarkson, ed., *An Independent Foreign Policy for Canada?* (Toronto: McClelland and Stewart, 1968), in particular, section III: Togetherness in Atlantic Patterns, 132–83.
52. J.L. Granatstein and Robert Bothwell, "Pierre Trudeau on his foreign policy," *International Journal* 66, no. 1 (2010–11): 174, https://doi.org/10.1177/002070201106600111.
53. Brendan Kelly, *The Good Fight: Marcel Cadieux and Canadian Diplomacy* (Vancouver: UBC Press, 2019), 264.
54. Mitchell Sharp, *Which Reminds Me... A Memoir* (Toronto: University of Toronto Press, 1994), 174.
55. Hilliker, Halloran, and Donaghy, *Canada's Department of External Affairs*, vol. 3, 55.
56. Kelly, *Good Fight*, 266; Thordarson, *Trudeau and Foreign Policy*, 136, 147; Fortmann and Larose, "An emerging strategic counterculture?" 55; Granatstein and Bothwell, *Pirouette*, 19.
57. Kelly, *Good Fight*, 271–2.
58. Denis Stairs, "Pierre Trudeau and the politics of the Canadian foreign policy review," *Australian Outlook* 26, no. 3 (1972): 274–5, https://doi.org/10.1080/10357717208444447; Hilliker, Halloran, and Donaghy, *Canada's Department of External Affairs*, vol. 3, 55.
59. Hilliker, Halloran, and Donaghy, *Canada's Department of External Affairs*, vol. 3, 55.
60. The minutes of SCEAND's consultations can be found at House of Commons, *Committees*, 28th Parliament, 1st session: Standing Committee on External Affairs and National Defence, 2 vols, https://parl.canadiana.ca/view/oop.com_HOC_2801_3_1/1 and https://parl.canadiana.ca/view/oop.com_HOC_2801_3_2/1.
61. Thordarson, *Trudeau and Foreign Policy*, 129. The member was Douglas Harkness.
62. Thordarson, *Trudeau and Foreign Policy*, 135; Stairs, "Pierre Trudeau and the politics of the Canadian foreign policy review," 283.
63. Robert Bothwell, *Alliance and Illusion: Canada and the World, 1945–1984* (Vancouver: UBC Press, 2007), 286.
64. Granatstein and Bothwell, *Pirouette*, 20–1; Fortmann and Larose, "An emerging strategic counterculture?" 552.
65. Interview with Michael Shenstone, 2 February 1989, in Robert Bothwell and J.L. Granatstein, eds., *Trudeau's World: Insiders Reflect on Foreign Policy, Trade, and Defence, 1968–84* (Vancouver: UBC Press, 2017), 154.
66. Quoted in Kelly, *Good Fight*, 283.
67. Granatstein and Bothwell, *Pirouette*, 24. Italics in the original.
68. Statement to the Press by Prime Minister Pierre Elliott Trudeau, Ottawa, 3 April 1969, in Gellner, *Canada in NATO*, 101.
69. Sharp, *Which Reminds Me*, 176.
70. Kelly, *Good Fight*, 280. Scholars like Michel Fortmann, Edna Keeble, and Denis Stairs agree. See Fortmann and Larose, "An emerging strategic counterculture?" 556; Keeble, "Rethinking the 1971 white paper," 546–7; Stairs, "Pierre Trudeau and the politics of the Canadian foreign policy review," 289–90.
71. Head and Trudeau, *The Canadian Way*, 83.
72. Thordarson, *Trudeau and Foreign Policy*, 214–6.

NOTES TO PAGES 137–41   295

73. "Harper stands up for Arctic sovereignty," Address by the Hon. Stephen Harper, P.C., M.P. Leader of the Conservative Party of Canada, 22 December 2005, in P. Whitney Lackenbauer and Ryan Dean, eds., *Canada's Northern Strategy under Prime Minister Stephen Harper: Key Speeches and Documents, 2005–15* (Calgary: Centre for Military, Security, and Strategic Studies, 2016), 1, http://pubs.aina.ucalgary.ca/dcass/82783.pdf; J. Alan Beesley, "The Arctic Pollution Prevention Act: Canada's perspective," *Syracuse Journal of Law and Commerce* 1, no. 2 (1973): 229.

74. Ken S. Coates et al., *Arctic Front: Defending Canada in the Far North* (Toronto: Dundurn, 2008), chapter 3, e-book.

75. For the background to this case, see Adam Lajeunesse, *Lock, Stock, and Icebergs: A History of Canada's Maritime Sovereignty* (Vancouver: UBC Press, 2016), chapter 7.

76. Lajeunesse, *Lock, Stock, and Icebergs*, 154.

77. David Meren and Bora Plumptre, "Rights of passage: The intersecting of environmentalism, Arctic sovereignty, and the Law of the Sea, 1968–1982," *Journal of Canadian Studies* 47, no. 1 (2013): 179, https://doi.org/10.3138/jcs.47.1.167; John Kirton and Don Munton, "The *Manhattan* Voyages and their aftermath," in Franklyn Griffiths, ed., *Politics of the Northwest Passage* (Montreal: McGill-Queen's University Press, 1987), 96–7.

78. Christopher Kirkey, "The Arctic Waters Pollution Prevention initiatives: Canada's response to an American challenge," *International Journal of Canadian Studies* 13 (1996): 45.

79. Kirkey, "Arctic Waters," 43.

80. Kirton and Munton, "*Manhattan* Voyages," 73; Lajeunesse, *Lock, Stock, and Icebergs*, 150.

81. The following description is drawn primarily from Lajeunesse, *Lock, Stock, and Icebergs*, 145–50.

82. Head and Trudeau, *Canadian Way*, 52–3. On the debate within Cabinet, see Kirton and Munton, "*Manhattan* voyages," 78–9, and Lajeunesse, *Lock, Stock, and Icebergs*, 158–61.

83. Mitchell Sharp, "A ship and sovereignty in the north," *Globe and Mail*, 18 September 1969, 7; Lajeunesse, *Lock, Stock, and Icebergs*, 164; Kirkey, "Arctic Waters," 46.

84. Kirton and Munton, "*Manhattan* voyages," 76.

85. J.A. Beesley, "Rights and responsibilities of Arctic coastal states: The Canadian view," *Journal of Marine and Maritime Law and Commerce* 3, no. 1 (1971): 4; Meren and Plumptre, "Rights of passage," 182.

86. Beesley, "Arctic Pollution Prevention Act," 232; Lajeunesse, *Lock, Stock, and Icebergs*, 164.

87. Government of Canada, *Arctic Waters Pollution Prevention Act*, https://laws-lois.justice.gc.ca/eng/acts/a-12/.

88. Lajeunesse, *Lock, Stock, and Icebergs*, 164.

89. Head and Trudeau, *Canadian Way*, 63–4; Meren and Plumptre, "Rights of passage," 174; Lajeunesse, *Lock, Stock, and Icebergs*, 172–6.

90. Jeffrey Simpson, *Discipline of Power: The Conservative Interlude and the Liberal Restoration* (Toronto: Pearson Library, 1980), 146. For an equally damning condemnation, see Howard Adelman, "Clark and the Canadian Embassy in Israel," *Middle East Focus* 3 (1980): 18.

91. Alan Bones, "Zionist interest groups and Canadian foreign policy," in Tarek Y. Ismael, ed., *Canada and the Arab World* (Edmonton: University of Alberta Press, 1985), 163.

92. Charles Flicker, "Next year in Jerusalem: Joe Clark and the Jerusalem affair," *International Journal* 58, no. 1 (2003): 117, https://doi.org/10.1177/002070200305800106; Adelman, "Clark and the Canadian Embassy," 7. Even Washington, which did propose to move the US embassy in 1976, never followed through.

93. Flicker, "Next year," 117; Bones, "Zionist interest groups," in Ismael, *Canada and the Arab World*, 165. Some members of the committee preferred that all Jewish advocacy be strictly non-partisan. See also Adelman, "Clark and the Canadian Embassy," 12–14.

94. Simpson, *Discipline of Power*, 158.

95. Flicker, "Next year," 118; Simpson, *Discipline of Power*, 149. The following month, Conservative foreign policy critic Douglas Roche indicated that his party might be open to a move in the aftermath of an Egyptian-Israeli peace treaty, but his comments were not taken as a fundamental shift in Clark's position. See George Steven Takach, "Clark and the Jerusalem Embassy affair: Initiative and constraint in Canadian foreign policy," (Carleton University, MA thesis, 1980), 25; Adelman, "Clark and the Canadian Embassy," 9.

96. Takach, "Canada and the Jerusalem Embassy affair," 17; Robert Stanfield, "Final Report of the Special Representative of the Government of Canada Respecting the Middle East and North Africa," in Ismael, *Canada and the Arab World*, 197–9.

296 NOTES TO PAGES 141–4

97. Flicker, "Next year in Jerusalem," 121–3; J.L. Granatstein and Bothwell, *Pirouette*, 214.
98. Quoted in Takach, "Canada and the Jerusalem Embassy affair," 32.
99. Takach, "Canada and the Jerusalem Embassy affair," 32.
100. Simpson, *Discipline of Power*, 153–4; Takach, "Canada and the Jerusalem Embassy affair," 50–1.
101. Takach, "Canada and the Jerusalem Embassy affair," 43; Simpson, *Discipline of Power*, 153; Adelman, "Clark and the Canadian Embassy," 6. Other Toronto ridings, where the embassy issue would not have been salient, also flipped to the Conservatives.
102. Flicker, "Next year in Jerusalem," 123–5.
103. Hilliker, Halloran, and Donaghy, *Canada's Department of External Affairs*, vol. 3, 307–8.
104. Flicker, "Next year in Jerusalem," 128.
105. On Arab sanctions, see Norrin M. Ripsman and Jean-Marc F. Blanchard, "Lightning rods rather than light switches: Arab economic sanctions against Canada in 1979," *Canadian Journal of Political Science* 35, no. 1 (2002): 151–74, http://www.jstor.org/stable/3233173.
106. Flicker, "Next year in Jerusalem," 131–5. On the Cabinet's reaction, see the Cabinet conclusions from 7 and 19 June 1979, RG2, Series A-5-a, vol. 26847, https://www.bac-lac.gc. ca/eng/discover/politics-government/cabinet-conclusions/Pages/list.aspx?k=jerusalem& MeetingDate=1979&, items 46664 and 46697.
107. Hilliker, Halloran, and Donaghy, *Canada's Department of External Affairs*, vol. 3, 308; Flicker, "Next year in Jerusalem," 135–6; Takach, "Clark and the Jerusalem affair," 84; Ripsman and Blanchard, "Lightning rods," 164–5; Cabinet conclusions, 21 June 1979, RG2 Privy Council Office Papers, Series A-5-a, vol. 26847, https://www.bac-lac.gc.ca/eng/discover/politics-government/cabinet-conclusions/Pages/list.aspx?k=jerusalem&MeetingDate=1979&, item 46716.
108. Ripsman and Blanchard, "Lightning rods," 163–4; Simpson, *Discipline of Power*, 156–7; Robert Stanfield, "Final Report of the Special Representative of the Government of Canada Respecting the Middle East and North Africa," 20 February 1980, in Ismael, *Canada and the Arab World*, 179–206.
109. Takach, "Clark and the Jerusalem Embassy affair," 112. See also Adelman, "Clark and the Canadian Embassy," 8.
110. Stephen Clarkson, *Canada and the Reagan Challenge: Crisis and Adjustment, 1981–85* (Toronto: James Lorimer, 1985), 55.
111. Charles Getman, "Canada's National Energy Program: An analysis," *Houston Journal of International Law* 3, no. 1 (1981): 164, http://hjil.org/articles/hjil-3-1-getman.pdf.
112. G. Bruce Doern and Glen Toner, *The Politics of Energy: The Development and Implementation of the NEP* (Toronto: Methuen, 1985), 160; Mark MacGuigan, *An Inside Look at External Affairs During the Trudeau Years: The Memoirs of Mark MacGuigan*, edited by P. Whitney Lackenbauer (Calgary: University of Calgary Press, 2002), 117.
113. Charles F. Doran, *Forgotten Partnership: U.S.-Canada Relations Today* (Baltimore: Johns Hopkins University Press, 1984), 230; Getman, "Canada's National Energy Program," 162; David Leyton-Brown, "Canadianizing oil and gas: The National Energy Program, 1980–83," in Don Munton and John Kirton, eds., *Canadian Foreign Policy: Selected Cases* (Scarborough: Prentice Hall, 1992), 300; Brian Bow, *The Politics of Linkage: Power, Interdependence, and Ideas in Canada-US Relations* (Vancouver: UBC Press, 2009), 104–6.
114. Larry Pratt, "Energy: The roots of national policy," *Studies in Political Economy* 7, no. 1 (1982): 30, https://doi.org/10.1080/19187033.1982.11675694; English, *Just Watch Me*, 482–3.
115. Interview with Hon. Mark MacGuigan, 18 January 1988, in Bothwell and Granatstein, *Trudeau's World*, 227; Gotlieb, *Washington Diaries*, 29; Tammy Nemeth, "Conflicting visions: Pierre Trudeau, External Affairs, and energy policy," in Donaghy and Carroll, *In the National Interest*, 173.
116. Interview with Hon. Michael Pitfield, 25 February 1988, in Bothwell and Granatstein, *Trudeau's World*, 42.
117. Marc Lalonde, quoted in Energy, Mines and Resources Canada, *The National Energy Program* (Ottawa: Minister of Supply and Services Canada, 1980), 22.
118. Doern and Toner, *Politics of Energy*, 4.
119. English, *Just Watch Me*, 483; Doern and Toner, *Politics of Energy*, 2; Clarkson, *Canada and the Reagan Challenge*, 82.
120. The NEP also established grants for oil exploration on Crown lands and incentives to develop alternative energy.

NOTES TO PAGES 144–54   297

121. Granatstein and Bothwell, *Pirouette*, 319; MacGuigan, *Inside Look*, 117–8; Doern and Toner, *Politics of Energy*, 112.
122. MacGuigan, *Inside Look*, 117–8; Stephen Azzi, *Reconcilable Differences: A History of Canada-US Relations* (Don Mills, ON: Oxford University Press, 2015), 205; Marc Lalonde, "Riding the storm: Energy policy, 1968–1984," in Thomas S. Axworthy and Pierre Elliott Trudeau, eds., *Towards a Just Society: The Trudeau Years* (Toronto: Penguin, 1990), 66; Getman, "Canada's National Energy Program," 165–6.
123. Clarkson, *Canada and the Reagan Challenge*, 82.
124. Nemeth, "Conflicting visions," in Donaghy and Carroll, *In the National Interest*, 171.
125. Gotlieb, diary entry, 4 December 1981, in Gotlieb, *Washington Diaries*, 16.
126. Edward Wonder, "The US government response to the Canadian National Energy Program," *Canadian Public Policy* 8, s1 (1982): 480–1; "Welcoming Mr. Trudeau," *Wall Street Journal*, 9 July 1981.
127. Leyton-Brown, "Canadianizing oil and gas," in Munton and Kirton, *Canadian Foreign Policy*, 304–6; Roy MacLaren, "Canadian views on the US government reaction to the National Energy Program," *Canadian Public Policy* 8, s1 (1982): 495; Christina McCall and Stephen Clarkson, *Trudeau and Our Times*, vol. 2, *The Heroic Delusion* (Toronto: McClelland and Stewart, 1994), 191–205; Doern and Toner, *Politics of Energy*, 106–7; Interview with Paul H. Robertson, Jr, Chicago, 1986, in Bothwell and Granatstein, *Trudeau's World*, 229.
128. DEA to Washington, EGL-0057, 11 Mar. 1981, RG 25, vol. 16815, file 20-1-2-USA-pt. 62, LAC.
129. Granatstein and Bothwell, *Pirouette*, 324. See also Wonder, "The US government response," 484–6; Hilliker, Halloran, and Donaghy, *Canada's Department of External Affairs*, vol. 3, 377–8.
130. Leyton-Brown, "Canadianizing oil and gas," in Munton and Kirton, *Canadian Foreign Policy*, 307; Doern and Toner, *Politics of Energy*, 111; MacGuigan, *Inside Look*, 119–20.
131. Doern and Toner, *Politics of Energy*, 107; Clarkson, *Canada and the Reagan Challenge*, 79.
132. MacGuigan, *Inside Look*, 120. See also Lalonde, "Riding the storm," in Axworthy and Trudeau, *Towards a Just Society*, 70; English, *Just Watch Me*, 493.

Chapter 7

1. Paul Litt, *Elusive Destiny: The Political Vocation of John Napier Turner* (Vancouver: UBC Press, 2011).
2. Margaret Thatcher, *The Downing Street Years, 1979–1990* (New York: HarperCollins, 1993), 321.
3. Nelson Michaud and Kim Richard Nossal, "Out of the blue: The Mulroney legacy in foreign policy," in Raymond B. Blake, ed., *Transforming the Nation: Canada and Brian Mulroney* (Montreal: McGill-Queen's University Press, 2007), 113. For a thorough, albeit hagiographical, look at Mulroney's foreign policy, see Fen Osler Hampson, *Master of Persuasion: Brian Mulroney's Global Legacy* (Toronto: Signal, 2018).
4. Jeffrey Engel, *When the World Seemed New: George H.W. Bush and the End of the Cold War* (Boston: Houghton Mifflin, 2017).
5. Joe Clark, "Foreword," *Competitiveness and Security: Directions for Canada's International Relations* (Ottawa: Minister of Supply and Services, 1985), https://gac.canadiana.ca/view/ooe.b1955366E/1.
6. "An outspoken US friend in Ottawa," *Wall Street Journal*, 24 September 1984.
7. Douglas Brinkley, *The Reagan Diaries* (New York: Harper, 2007), 309.
8. Allan Gotlieb, *The Washington Diaries, 1981–1989* (Toronto: McClelland & Stewart, 2006), 558.
9. Allan Gotlieb, *I'll Be With You in a Minute, Mr. Ambassador: The Education of a Canadian Diplomat in Washington* (Toronto: University of Toronto Press, 1991); Colin Robertson, "Changing conditions and actors, but the game remains the same: Revisiting Gotlieb's 'New Diplomacy'," in Janice Gross Stein, ed., *Diplomacy in the Digital Age: Essays in Honour of Ambassador Allan Gotlieb* (Toronto: McClelland & Stewart, 2011), 51–69.
10. "Liberal blueprint for Canada," *Toronto Star*, 29 September 1988.
11. Marci McDonald, *Yankee Doodle Dandy: Brian Mulroney and the American Agenda* (Toronto: Stoddart, 1995); Lawrence Martin, *Pledge of Allegiance: The Americanization of Canada in the Mulroney Years* (Toronto: McClelland & Stewart, 1993), 11.
12. Brinkley, *Reagan Diaries*, 351.

298   NOTES TO PAGES 154-9

13. Stephen Knott and Jeffrey Chidester, *At Reagan's Side: Insiders' Recollections from Sacramento to the White House* (Lanham: Rowman and Littlefield, 2009), 170–1.
14. Heather Smith, "Shades of grey in Canada's greening during the Mulroney era," in Nelson Michaud and Kim Richard Nossal, eds., *Diplomatic Departures: The Conservative Era in Canadian Foreign Policy, 1984–93* (Vancouver: UBC Press, 2002), 71–83.
15. Memorandum of Conversation, "Meeting with Prime Minister Brian Mulroney of Canada," 4 May 1989, George H.W. Bush Library, Memoranda of Conversations and Telephone Conversations, https://bush41library.tamu.edu/archives/memcons-telcons.
16. Memorandum of Conversation, "Opening Session of the 16th Economic Summit of Industrialized Nations," 9 July 1990, George H.W. Bush Library, Memoranda of Conversations and Telephone Conversations, https://bush41library.tamu.edu/archives/memcons-telcons.
17. Joe Clark, "Canada's new internationalism," in John Holmes and John Kirton, eds., *Canada and the New Internationalism* (Toronto: CIIA, 1988), 4. Shortly after, an overwhelming majority of UN members elected Canada to a non-permanent seat on the Security Council.
18. Maxwell Cameron and Brian Tomlin, *The Making of NAFTA: How the Deal Was Done* (Ithaca: Cornell University Press, 2000).
19. Memorandum of Telephone Conversation with Prime Minister Mulroney of Canada, 12 August 1992, George H.W. Bush Library, Memoranda of Conversations and Telephone Conversations, https://bush41library.tamu.edu/archives/memcons-telcons.
20. Mulroney to Thatcher, 2 October 1985, PREM 19/1644 f320, The National Archives of the United Kingdom.
21. Mulroney, "Principles of UN Charter signposts to peace," *Statements and Speeches* 85/14, 23 October 1985.
22. Daniel Manulak, "'A marathon, not a sprint': Canada and South African apartheid, 1987–1990," *International Journal* 75, no. 1 (2020): 90, https://doi.org/10.1177/0020702020917179; Daniel Manulak, "'An African representative': Canada, the Third World, and South African apartheid, 1984–1990," *Journal of Imperial and Commonwealth History* 49, no. 2 (2021): 368–99, https://doi.org/10.1080/03086534.2020.1783474; For a critical view, see Linda Freeman, *The Ambiguous Champion: Canada and South Africa in the Trudeau and Mulroney Years* (Toronto: University of Toronto Press, 1997).
23. Joe Clark, *How We Lead: Canada in a Century of Change* (Toronto: Random House, 2013), 65. Renate Pratt, *In Good Faith: Canadian Churches Against Apartheid* (Waterloo: Wilfrid Laurier University Press, 1997); John Saul, *On Building a Social Movement: The North American Campaign for South African Liberation* (Halifax: Fernwood, 2016).
24. Joseph Jockel and Joel Sokolsky, *Canada in NATO, 1949–2019* (Montreal and Kingston: McGill-Queen's University Press, 2021), 148.
25. Bohdan Kordan, *Strategic Friends: Canada-Ukraine Relations from Independence to Euromaidan* (Montreal: McGill-Queen's University Press, 2019).
26. Nicholas Gammer, *From Peacekeeping to Peacemaking: Canada's Response to the Yugoslav Crisis* (Montreal: McGill-Queen's University Press, 2001); Grant Dawson, *"Here Is Hell": Canada's Engagement in Somalia* (Vancouver: UBC Press, 2007).
27. Memorandum of Conversation. "Opening Session of the London Economic Summit," 15 July 1991, George H.W. Bush Library, Memoranda of Conversations and Telephone Conversations, https://bush41library.tamu.edu/archives/memcons-telcons.
28. "Canada urging no unilateral move," *Globe and Mail*, 27 September 1990.
29. Joe Clark, "Peacekeeping and peacemaking: The Persian Gulf crisis and its consequences," *Statements & Speeches* 91/6, 24 January 1991.
30. "Chiefs urge swift recall of Parliament," *Globe and Mail*, 21 July 1990.
31. Royal Commission on Aboriginal Peoples, *Report*, vol. 1: *Looking Forward, Looking Back* (Ottawa: Minister of Supply and Services, 1996), 610, http://data2.archives.ca/e/e448/e011188230-01.pdf.
32. Brian Stewart, "When Brian Mulroney was great," *CBC News*, 14 May 2009, https://www.cbc.ca/news/canada/when-brian-mulroney-was-great-1.859343.
33. Hampson, *Master of Persuasion*, 55. See also Nassisse Soloman, "'Tears are not enough': Canadian political and social mobilization for famine relief in Ethiopia, 1984–88," in Greg Donaghy and David Webster, eds., *A Samaritan State Revisited: Historical Perspectives on Canadian Foreign Aid, 1950–2016* (Calgary: University of Calgary Press, 2019), 245–67, https://prism.ucalgary.ca/bitstream/handle/1880/110848/9781773850412_chapter10.pdf.

NOTES TO PAGES 159–61   299

34. David R. Morrison, *Aid and Ebb Tide: A History of CIDA and Canadian Development Assistance* (Waterloo: Wilfrid Laurier University Press, 1998), 234; Hampson, *Master of Persuasion*, 42.
35. Bello, "The international politics of famine relief," 32. David MacDonald, "The Africa famine and Canada's response," Report by the Honourable David MacDonald, Canadian Emergency Coordinator/African Famine for the period from November 1984 to March 1985 (Hull, QC: Canadian Emergency Coordinator/African Famine, 1985), 5–13. According to one analyst, "at the peak of the emergency 6000 people were dying daily and an estimated 1,000,000 people were being treated in 43 emergency shelters." See Ghaji Ismailia Bello, "The international politics of famine relief operations in Ethiopia: A case study of the 1984–86 famine relief operations," (London School of Economics, PhD thesis, 1990), 35.
36. Bello, "International politics," 36.
37. Hampson, *Master of Persuasion*, 47; Bello, "International politics," 119–20, 124.
38. Solomon, "'Tears are not enough'," in Donaghy and Webster, *Samaritan State*, 255.
39. Tanja R. Müller, "'The Ethiopian famine' revisited: Band Aid and the antipolitics of celebrity humanitarian action," *Disasters* 37, no. 1 (2013): 66, https://doi.org/10.1111/j.1467-7717.2012. 01293.x. The report can be seen at http://news.bbc.co.uk/2/hi/8315248.stm.
40. Hampson, *Master of Persuasion*, 43. For the report, see Brian Stewart, "Alerting the world to the famine in Ethiopia," CBC Archives, https://www.cbc.ca/archives/entry/alerting-the-world-to-famine-in-ethiopia.
41. Brian Mulroney, *Memoirs 1939–1993* (Toronto: McClelland and Stewart, 2007), 331; Bello, "International politics," 121.
42. Hampson, *Master of Persuasion*, 45.
43. Hampson, *Master of Persuasion*, 49; Mulroney, *Memoirs*, 332; Nelson Michaud and Kim Richard Nossal, "Out of the blue: The Mulroney legacy in foreign policy," in Blake, *Transforming the Nation*, 118–9.
44. Clark, quoted in Solomon, "'Tears are not enough'," in Donaghy and Webster, *Samaritan State*, 247.
45. David MacDonald, "No more famine: A decade for Africa," Report by the Honourable David MacDonald, Canada Emergency Coordinator/African Famine, for the period ending March 31, 1986 (Hull, QC: Canadian Emergency Coordinator, 1986), 16.
46. Solomon, "'Tears are not enough'," in Donaghy and Webster, *Samaritan State*, 250; Mark W. Charlton, *The Making of Canadian Food Aid Policy* (Montreal: McGill-Queen's University Press, 1992), 168–9. On the mandate of MacDonald's office, see David MacDonald, "The African famine and Canada's response," Report by the Honourable David MacDonald, Canadian Emergency Coordinator/African Famine, for the period from November 1984 to March 1985 (Hull, QC: Canadian Emergency Coordinator/African Famine, 1985), 41.
47. Quoted in Charlton, *Making of Canadian Food Aid Policy*, 169.
48. MacDonald, "African famine," 39.
49. On Canadian public opinion, see Decima Research, "Canadians and Africans: What was said," A report for the Honourable David MacDonald, Canadian Emergency Coordinator/African Famine, of a nation-wide survey by Decima Research Ltd conducted in February 1986 (Hull, QC: Canadian Emergency Coordinator, 1986), 1–46; Solomon, "'Tears are not enough'," in Donaghy and Webster, *Samaritan State*, 245.
50. Hampson, *Master of Persuasion*, 50.
51. Solomon, "'Tears are not enough'," in Donaghy and Webster, *Samaritan State*, 246–51; MacDonald, "African famine," 23–4; Elizabeth Smythe, "Don't you know that tears are not enough? Transnational campaigns, Canadian foreign aid and the politics of shame," Paper presented at the annual meeting of the Canadian Political Science Association, Saskatoon, 30 May 2007, https://www.cpsa-acsp.ca/papers-2007/Smythe.pdf. A video of "Tears are not enough" can be found at https://www.youtube.com/watch?v=VJN3u1wAWIk.
52. Michaud and Nossal, "Out of the blue," in Blake, *Transforming the Nation*, 119.
53. MacDonald, "African famine," 29. See also MacDonald, "No more famine," 15; Decima Research, "Canadians and Africans," 20; Charlton, *Making of Canadian Food Aid Policy*, 168.
54. Solomon, "'Tears are not enough'," in Donaghy and Webster, *Samaritan State*, 256; Morrison, *Aid and Ebb Tide*, 235; Charlton, *Making of Canadian Food Aid Policy*, 170–1; Müller, "'The Ethiopian famine' revisited," 70.
55. Decima Research, "Canadians and Africans," 15, 24, 33; Charlton, *Making of Canadian Food Aid Policy*, 181–5.

300 NOTES TO PAGES 161–5

56. MacDonald, "No more famine," 9.
57. Hampson, *Master of Persuasion*, 53; Morrison, *Aid and Ebb Tide*, 237; Müller, "'The Ethiopian famine' revisited," 74.
58. Solomon, "'Tears are not enough," in Donaghy and Webster, *Samaritan State*, 261.
59. Michael Hart, *A Trading Nation: Canadian Trade Policy from Colonialism to Globalization* (Vancouver: UBC Press, 2002).
60. Derek Burney, *Getting It Done: A Memoir* (Montreal: McGill-Queen's University Press, 2005), 109, 129; G. Bruce Doern and Brian W. Tomlin, *Faith and Fear: The Free Trade Story* (Toronto: Stoddart, 1991), 206, 305; Hart, *Trading Nation*, 371.
61. Michael Hart, "Free trade and Brian Mulroney's economic legacy," in Blake, *Transforming the Nation*, 64; Hampson, *Master of Persuasion*, 15–6; Michael Hart, with Bill Dymond and Colin Robertson, *Decision at Midnight: Inside the Canada-US Free Trade Negotiations* (Vancouver: UBC Press, 1994), 21, 50.
62. Hart, *Decision at Midnight*, 13; Brian W. Tomlin, "Leaving the past behind: The free trade initiative assessed," in Michaud and Nossal, *Diplomatic Departures*, 49–50.
63. Mulroney, quoted in his *Memoirs*, 230. See also Gordon Ritchie, *Wrestling with the Elephant: The Inside Story of the Canada-US Trade Wars* (Toronto: Macfarlane, Walter & Ross, 1997), 43.
64. Mulroney, *Memoirs*, 231.
65. Mulroney, *Memoirs*, 384.
66. Lougheed, quoted in Mulroney, *Memoirs*, 386; Doern and Tomlin, *Faith and Fear*, 23; Tomlin, "Leaving the past behind," in Michaud and Nossal, *Diplomatic Departures*, 49–54.
67. Hart, *Trading Nation*, 373; Hampson, *Master of Persuasion*, 19.
68. Doern and Tomlin, *Faith and Fear*, 24.
69. Tomlin, "Leaving the past behind," in Michaud and Nossal, *Diplomatic Departures*, 57.
70. "In essence, the Congress delegates its authority to permit the administration to conduct negotiations, but only within the parameters set by the Congress and subject to congressional approval. In return, if the administration meets these conditions, the legislation to give effect to this executive agreement will be put on a fast track through the legislature, which will be limited to voting approval or rejection, without amendments." Ritchie, *Wrestling with the Elephant*, 67. See also Gotlieb, *Washington Diaries*, 319; Gotlieb, *I'll be with you in a minute*, 103–12; Tomlin, "Leaving the past behind," in Michaud and Nossal, *Diplomatic Departures*, 55.
71. Burney, *Getting It Done*, 113.
72. Hart, "Free trade," in Blake, *Transforming the Nation*, 67.
73. Hart, *Decision at Midnight*, 126.
74. Pat Carney, *Trade Secrets* (Toronto: Key Porter, 2000), 228.
75. Hart, *Decision at Midnight*, 315.
76. Mulroney, *Memoirs*, 448–9.
77. Gotlieb, *Washington Diaries*, 493–4.
78. Hart, *Trading Nation*, 371.
79. Doern and Tomlin, *Faith and Fear*, 207; Jeffrey M. Ayres, *Defying Conventional Wisdom: Political Movements and Popular Contention against North American Free Trade* (Toronto: University of Toronto Press, 1998), 76.
80. Turner, quoted in Ritchie, *Wrestling with the Elephant*, 127; Litt, *Elusive Destiny*, 302.
81. Litt, *Elusive Destiny*, 364; Ayres, *Defying Conventional Wisdom*, 80.
82. Mulroney, *Memoirs*, 613–4.
83. For details, see Ayres, *Defying Conventional Wisdom*, 94.
84. The heart of the debate can be found in the CBC Archives, "Betting on free trade 1988," https://www.youtube.com/watch?v=gyYjRmM7RDY. See also Litt, *Elusive Destiny*, 379; Mulroney, *Memoirs*, 628–9.
85. Ritchie, *Wrestling with the Elephant*, 172.
86. John C. Crosbie, with Geoffrey Stevens, *No Holds Barred: My Life in Politics* (Toronto: McClelland and Stewart, 1997), 316; Mulroney, *Memoirs*, 629.
87. Ayres, *Defying Conventional Wisdom*, 102–13; Ritchie, *Wrestling with the Elephant*, 172.
88. Robert Bothwell, *Your Country, My Country: A Unified History of the United States and Canada* (New York: Oxford University Press, 2015), 289–90; Hart, *Decision at Midnight*, 389; Doern and Tomlin, *Faith and Fear*, 305; Hampson, *Master of Persuasion*, 33–5.
89. Jurgen Schmandt, Hilliard Roderick, and Andrew Moss, "Acid rain is different," in Schmandt, Judith Clarkson, and Roderick, eds., *Acid Rain and Friendly Neighbors: The Policy Dispute*

NOTES TO PAGES 165–7 301

between Canada and the United States, rev. ed. (Durham, NC: Duke University Press, 1990), 8; Don Munton and Geoffrey Castle, "Reducing acid rain, 1980s," in Munton and John Kirton, eds., *Canadian Foreign Policy: Selected Cases* (Scarborough: Prentice Hall, 1992), 367; Munton, "Acid rain politics in North America: Conflict to cooperation to collusion," in Gerald R. Visigilio and Diana M. Whitelaw, eds., *Acid in the Environment: Lessons Learned and Future Prospects* (New York: Springer, 2007), 175–7.

90. Political scientist Don Munton describes the Canadian predicament as "environmental dependence." See his "Transboundary air pollution: Dependence and interdependence," in Philippe le Prestre and Peter Stoett, eds., *Bilateral Ecopolitics: Continuity and Change in Canadian-American Environmental Relations* (Aldershot, Hampshire, UK: Ashgate, 2006), 74 and Charles F. Doran with Puay Tang, "Canada: Unity in diversity," Foreign Policy Association *Headline Series* 291 (1989–90): 58.

91. LeBlanc, quoted in Munton and Castle, "Reducing acid rain," in Munton and Kirton, *Canadian Foreign Policy*, 367.

92. Munton and Castle, "Reducing acid rain," in Munton and Kirton, *Canadian Foreign Policy*, 368; Stephen Clarkson, *Canada and the Reagan Challenge: Crisis and Adjustment, 1981–85* (Toronto: James Lorimer, 1985), 187.

93. Smith, "Shades of grey," in Michaud and Nossal, *Diplomatic Departures*, 74; Munton, "Acid rain politics," in Visigilio and Whitelaw, *Acid in the Environment*, 177.

94. Clarkson, *Canada and the Reagan Challenge*, 187; Munton and Castle, "Reducing acid rain," in Munton and Kirton, *Canadian Foreign Policy*, 369.

95. Canadians had begun to refer to the long-range transport of acid precipitation as acid rain in 1979. See Elizabeth May, "Brian Mulroney and the environment," in Blake, *Transforming the Nation*, 385.

96. Allan Gotlieb, diary entry, 18 June 1982, in Gotlieb, *Washington Diaries*, 69.

97. Clarkson, *Canada and the Reagan Challenge*, 193; Munton and Castle, "Reducing acid rain," in Munton and Kirton, *Canadian Foreign Policy*, 372–3; Munton, "Acid rain politics," in Visigilio and Whitelaw, *Acid in the Environment*, 178.

98. Burney, *Getting It Done*, 103.

99. Mulroney, *Memoirs*, 496.

100. Gotlieb, *Washington Diaries*, 209.

101. Smith, "Shades of grey," in Michaud and Nossal, *Diplomatic Departures*, 71; Hampson, *Master of Persuasion*, 122. Gotlieb, *Washington Diaries*, 226.

102. May, "Mulroney and the environment," in Blake, *Transforming the Nation*, 385.

103. Hampson, *Master of Persuasion*, 122; Gotlieb, *Washington Diaries*, 278; Schmandt, Roderick, and Moss, "Acid rain is different," in Schmandt, Clarkson, and Roderick, *Acid Rain and Friendly Neighbors*, 18.

104. Mulroney, *Memoirs*, 405, 430; Gotlieb, *I'll be with you in a minute*, 74.

105. Burney, *Getting It Done*, 103–4; Munton and Castle, "Reducing acid rain," in Munton and Kirton, *Canadian Foreign Policy*, 374; Gotlieb, *Washington Diaries*, 275.

106. Gotlieb, *I'll be with you in a minute*, 70; Mulroney, *Memoirs*, 429.

107. Mulroney, *Memoirs*, 498–500; May, "Brian Mulroney and the environment," in Blake, *Transforming the Nation*, 386.

108. Munton, "Acid rain politics," in Visigilio and Whitelaw, *Acid in the Environment*, 179.

109. Hampson, *Master of Persuasion*, 131–3.

110. Bush, quoted in Mulroney, *Memoirs*, 650; Munton, "Transboundary air pollution," in le Prestre and Stoett, *Bilateral Ecopolitics*, 79–80.

111. Bush, in Remarks and a Question-and-Answer Session with Reporters, Ottawa, Canada, 24 Sussex Drive, 10 February 1989, in James McGrath and Arthur Milnes, eds., *Age of the Offered Hand: The Cross-Border Partnership between President George H.W. Bush and Prime Minister Brian Mulroney, A Documentary History* (Kingston: School of Policy Studies, 2009), 5.

112. Hampson, *Master of Persuasion*, 137–8; Hampson, "Pollution across borders," in Molot and Hampson, *Canada among Nations 1989*, 189–90; Munton and Castle, "Reducing acid rain," in Munton and Kirton, *Canadian Foreign Policy*, 376.

113. Munton and Castle, "Reducing acid rain," in Munton and Kirton, *Canadian Foreign Policy*, 377; Mulroney, *Memoirs*, 84. See also Agreement between the Government of the United States of American and the Government of Canada on Air Quality (1991), https://www.ijc. org/sites/default/files/2018-07/Agreement%20Between%20the%20Government%20of%20

302 NOTES TO PAGES 167–78

the%20United%20States%20of%20America%20and%20the%20Government%20of%20
Canada%20on%20Air%20Quality.pdf.

114. Bush, in Remarks by the President and the Prime Minister at the Air Quality Agreement Signing Ceremony, Ottawa, 3 March 1991, in McGrath and Milnes, *Age of the Offered Hand*, 71.

115. Stephen Azzi, *Irreconcilable Differences: A History of Canada-US Relations* (Don Mills, ON: Oxford University Press, 2015), 222–3; Hampson, *Master of Persuasion*, 144.

116. Smith, "Shades of grey," in Michaud and Nossal, *Diplomatic Departures*, 75; Munton and Castle, "Reducing acid rain," in Munton and Kirton, *Canadian Foreign Policy*, 377.

117. Don Munton, "Dispelling the myths of the acid rain story," *Environment* 40, no. 6 (1998): 4–7; 27–34, https://doi.org/10.1080/00139159809604593; Munton, "Transboundary air pollution," in le Prestre and Stoett, *Bilateral Ecopolitics*, 80–2; Munton, "Acid rain politics," in Visigilio and Whitelaw, *Acid in the Environment*, 183–8.

118. Gotlieb, *I'll be with you in a minute*, 73. See also 99–101.

Chapter 8

1. Jeffrey Simpson, *The Friendly Dictatorship* (Toronto: McClelland & Stewart, 2001).

2. "Bankrupt Canada?" *Wall Street Journal*, 12 January 1995, A14.

3. Quoted in Susan Delacourt, "Chrétien strains to balance views on party's direction." *Globe and Mail*, 2 March 1995.

4. James Bartleman, *Rollercoaster: My Hectic Years as Jean Chrétien's Diplomatic Advisor, 1994–1998* (Toronto: McClelland & Stewart, 2005), 168.

5. Quoted in Frédéric Bastien, *Le poids de le cooperation: Le rapport France-Quebec* (Montréal: Québec Amérique, 2006), 328.

6. Quoted in James Blanchard, *Behind the Embassy Door: Canada, Clinton, and Quebec* (Toronto: McClelland & Stewart, 1998), 248.

7. On the referendum, see Chantal Hébert and Jean Lapierre, *The Morning After: The 1995 Quebec Referendum and the Day that Almost Was* (Toronto: Random House, 2014).

8. Blanchard, *Behind the Embassy Door*, 81.

9. "Notes for an Address by the Hon. Roy MacLaren," *Statements and Speeches* 94/23, 24 May 1994.

10. Bartleman, *Rollercoaster*, 200.

11. Michael Hart, *Fifty Years of Canadian Tradecraft: Canada at the GATT 1947–1997* (Ottawa: Centre for Trade Policy and Law, 1998), 190–1.

12. Thomas Friedman, *The World Is Flat: A Brief History of the Twenty-First Century* (New York: Farrar, Straus and Giroux, 2005).

13. Quoted in Kenneth Bush, "NGOs and the international system: Building peace in a world at war," in Fen Osler Hampson and Maureen Appel Molot, eds., *Big Enough to be Heard: Canada among Nations 1996.* (Ottawa: Carleton University Press, 1996), 263.

14. David Webster, *Challenge the Strong Wind: Canada and East Timor, 1975–99* (Vancouver: UBC Press, 2020).

15. Jean Chrétien, *My Years as Prime Minister* (Toronto: Alfred A. Knopf Canada, 2007), 87.

16. Andrew Thompson, "Entangled: Canadian engagement in Haiti, 1968–2010," in Michael K. Carroll and Greg Donaghy, eds., *From Kinshasa to Kandahar: Canada and Fragile States in Historical Perspective*, (Calgary: University of Calgary Press, 2016), 97–119, https://press.ucalgary.ca/books/9781552388440/.

17. Alan Freeman, "Chrétien's wisecracks overheard," *Globe and Mail*, 10 July 1997, A1.

18. "Clinton shrugs off comments," *Globe and Mail*, 12 July 1997, A5.

19. John Stewart, "Magazines, ministers and 'monoculture': The Canada-United States dispute over 'split run' magazines in the 1990s," *Canadian Foreign Policy* 16, no. 1 (2010): 35, https://doi.org/10.1080/11926422.2010.9687292.

20. John Geddes, "Magazine deal between Canada, US," *Maclean's*, 7 June 1999.

21. Blanchard, *Behind the Embassy Door*, 146.

22. Tim Harper, "PM's private jabs at Clinton go public: Didn't know mike was live," *Toronto Star*, 10 July 1997, A1; Heather Nicol, ed., *Canada, the US and Cuba: Helms-Burton and Its Aftermath* (Kingston: Centre for International Relations, Queen's University, 1999).

23. Quoted in Lana Wylie, *Perceptions of Cuba: Canadian and American Policies in Comparative Perspective* (Toronto: University of Toronto Press, 2010), 58.

NOTES TO PAGES 178–81   303

24. Robert Wright, "'Northern ice': Jean Chrétien and the failure of constructive engagement in Cuba," in Robert Wright and Lana Wylie, eds., *Our Place in the Sun: Canada and Cuba in the Castro Era* (Toronto: University of Toronto Press, 2009), 213.

25. Carol Goar, "PM confident Asia tour will help human rights," *Toronto Star*, 18 November 1994, A16.

26. Lloyd Axworthy, *Navigating a New World: Canada's Global Future* (Toronto: Alfred A. Knopf Canada, 2003), 57.

27. Bartleman, *Rollercoaster*, 224.

28. Department of Foreign Affairs and International Trade, *Canada in the World* (Ottawa: Public Works and Government Services, 1995), i.

29. Axworthy, *Navigating a New World*, 7.

30. Lloyd Axworthy, "Canada and human security: The need for leadership," *International Journal* 52, no. 2 (1997): 184, https://doi.org/10.1177/002070209705200201.

31. Greg Donaghy, "All God's children: Lloyd Axworthy, human security and Canadian foreign policy, 1996–2000," *Canadian Foreign Policy* 10, no. 2 (2003): 39–59, https://doi.org/10.1080/11926422.2003.9673326.

32. Lloyd Axworthy, "Human security: An opening for UN reform," in Richard Price and Mark Zacher, eds., *The United Nations and Global Security* (New York: Palgrave, 2004), 252.

33. Joseph S. Nye, *Soft Power: The Means to Success in World Politics* (New York: PublicAffairs, 2004).

34. Lloyd Axworthy, "Why 'soft power' is the right policy for Canada," *Ottawa Citizen*, 25 April 1998, B6.

35. Dean Oliver and Fen Hampson, "Pulpit diplomacy: A critical assessment of the Axworthy doctrine," *International Journal* 53, no. 3 (1997–8): 379–406, https://doi.org/10.1177/002070209805300301.

36. Grant Dawson, *"Here Is Hell": Canada's Engagement in Somalia* (Vancouver: UBC Press, 2007).

37. Bartleman, *Rollercoaster*, 114; Carol Off, *The Lion, the Fox & the Eagle: A Story of Generals and Justice in Rwanda and Yugoslavia* (Toronto: Random House, 2000); Carol Off, *The Ghosts of Medak Pocket: The Story of Canada's Secret War* (Toronto: Random House, 2004).

38. Lt. General Roméo Dallaire with Major Brent Beardsley, *Shake Hands with the Devil: The Failure of Humanity in Rwanda* (Toronto: Viking, 2004), 516.

39. Nicholas Gammer, *From Peacekeeping to Peacemaking: Canada's Response to the Yugoslav Crisis* (Montreal: McGill-Queen's University Press, 2001).

40. Senate, Standing Committee on Foreign Affairs, *Meeting New Challenges: Canada's Response to a New Generation of Peacekeeping* (Ottawa: Government of Canada, 1993).

41. Steven Pearlstein, "Peacekeepers: Military budget puts constraints on Canadians," *Washington Post*, 26 September 1999, A25. On Canadian support for peacekeeping, see Colin McCullough, *Creating Canada's Peacekeeping Past* (Vancouver: UBC Press, 2016).

42. J.L. Granatstein, *Who Killed the Canadian Military?* (Toronto: HarperCollins, 2004).

43. Kevin Spooner, "Legacies and realities: UN peacekeeping and Canada, past and present," in Colin McCullough and Robert Teigrob, eds., *Canada and the United Nations: Legacies, Limits, Prospects* (Montreal: McGill-Queen's University Press, 2017), 208–20; Michael K. Carroll, "Canada and peacekeeping: Past, but not present and future?" *International Journal* 71, no. 1 (2016): 167–76, https://doi.org/10.1177/0020702015619857.

44. Jacques Roy, *Diplomatic Odyssey: From Gaspésie to Paris* (Ottawa: Jacques Roy, 2020), 255–9.

45. Paul Heinbecker, "Human security," *Canadian Foreign Policy* 7, no. 1 (1999): 21, https://doi.org/10.1080/11926422.1999.9673197.

46. Joseph T. Jockel and Joel J. Sokolsky, *Canada in NATO, 1949–2019* (Montreal: McGill-Queen's University Press, 2021), 172–7.

47. Bartleman, *Rollercoaster*, 324.

48. Kim Richard Nossal, "Pinchpenny diplomacy: The decline of 'good international citizenship' in Canadian foreign policy," *International Journal* 54, no. 1 (1998–9): 88–105, https://doi.org/10.1177/002070209905400107.

49. Stephen Clarkson, *Uncle Sam and Us: Globalization, Neoconservatism and the Canadian State* (Toronto: University of Toronto Press, 2002), 393.

50. Vivien Hughes, "Women, gender, and Canadian foreign policy, 1909–2009," *British Journal of Canadian Studies* 23, no. 2 (2010): 165, https://doi.org/10.3828/bjcs.2010.9.

304   NOTES TO PAGES 181–6

51. James Bartleman, *On Six Continents: A Life in Canada's Foreign Service, 1966–2002* (Toronto: McClelland & Stewart, 2004), 233.
52. Brian Tobin, with John Lawrence Reynolds, *All in Good Time* (Toronto: Penguin Canada, 2002), 136.
53. Michael Harris, *Lament for an Ocean: The Collapse of the Atlantic Cod Fishery: A True Crime Story* (Toronto: McClelland & Stewart, 1998), 34.
54. Allen L. Springer, "The Canadian turbot war with Spain: Unilateral state action in defense of environmental interests," *Journal of Environment & Development* 6, no. 1 (1997): 36, https://www.jstor.org/stable/44319249. His colleagues, Christopher C. Joyner and Alejandro Alvarez von Gustedt describe Canadian conduct as "highly satisfactory and effective" in "The turbot war of 1995: Lessons for the Law of the Sea," *International Journal of Marine and Coastal Law* 11, no. 4 (1996): 454, https://doi-org.cfc.idm.oclc.org/10.1163/157180896X00267.
55. Bartleman, *Rollercoaster*, 85. See also Brendan Howe and Matthew Kerby, "The Canada-EU Turbot War of 1995 and the cybernetic model of decision-making," *The Round Table* 98, no. 401 (2009): 162, https://doi.org/10.1080/00358530902757883.
56. Norman Hillmer and J.L. Granatstein, *Empire to Umpire: Canada and the World into the Twenty-First Century*, 2nd ed. (Toronto: Thomson Nelson, 2008), 325.
57. Donald Barry, "The Canada-European Union turbot war: Internal politics and transatlantic bargaining," *International Journal* 53, no. 2 (1998): 254, https://doi.org/10.101177/002070209805300205.
58. Barry, "The Canada-European Union turbot war," 256; Raymond B. Blake, *From Fishermen to Fish: The Evolution of Canadian Fishery Policy* (Toronto: Irwin, 2000), 91; Joyner and von Gustedt, "The turbot war," 436.
59. Edward Greenspon and Anthony Wilson-Smith, *Double Vision: The Inside Story of the Liberals in Power* (Toronto: Doubleday, 1996), 298.
60. Adam Gough, "The turbot war: The arrest of the Spanish vessel *Estai* and its implications for Canada-EU relations," (University of Ottawa, MA thesis, 2009), 29–35, quotation from 34; Howe and Kerby, "The Canada-EU turbot war," 172–3; Harris, *Lament for an Ocean*, 9.
61. Joyner and von Gustedt, "The turbot war," 427–35; Springer, "The Canadian turbot war," 33; Gough, "The Turbot War," 31–5.
62. Michael Keiver, "The turbot war: Gunboat diplomacy or refinement of the Law of the Sea?" *Les Cahiers de Droit* 37, no. 2 (1996): 555, https://doi.org/10.7202/043395ar.
63. Tobin, *All in Good Time*, 83; Blake, *From Fishermen to Fish*, 97.
64. Springer, "The Canadian turbot war," 39.
65. Tobin, Quoted in Gough, "The Turbot War," 38.
66. Springer, "The Canadian turbot war," 35. The Americans later acknowledged that their ships were in the wrong. See also Tobin, *All in Good Time*, 89–95.
67. Donald Barry, Bob Applebaum, and Earl Wiseman, *Fishing for a Solution: Canada's Fisheries Relations with the European Union, 1977–2013* (Calgary: University of Calgary Press, 2014), 120, https://press.ucalgary.ca/books/9781552387788/. See also Blake, *From Fishermen to Fish*, 93.
68. Blake, *From Fishermen to Fish*, 92–4.
69. Barry, "The Canadian-European turbot war," 263–4; Gough, "The Turbot War," 54; Blake, *From Fishermen to Fish*, 95–6.
70. Bartelman, *Rollercoaster*, 85, 94–6; Barry, "The Canada-European turbot war," 264–5; Harris, *Lament for an Ocean*, 2–3.
71. Blake, *From Fishermen to Fish*, 99–102, quotation from 102; Gough, "The Turbot War," 56–62.
72. Harris, *Lament for an Ocean*, 7, 20; Barry, "The Canada-European turbot war," 279–80; Howe and Kerby, "The Canada-EU turbot war," 163.
73. Joyner and von Gustedt, "The turbot war," 441.
74. Bartleman, *Rollercoaster*, 103; Joyner and von Gustedt, "The turbot war," 441; Harris, *Lament for an Ocean*, 10, 28.
75. Jennings, cited in Chrétien, *My Years as Prime Minister*, 111.
76. Tobin, *All in Good Time*, 132. See also Joyner and Gustedt, "The turbot war," 443; Barry, "The Canada-European turbot war," 271–3; Blake, *From Fishermen to Fish*, 104–5; Bartleman, *Rollercoaster*, 106. According to two journalists, Tobin "so outshone his European opponent in presenting his case that a British journalist working for a Portuguese paper stood up and applauded...You don't necessarily have to agree with him to recognize a great performance, the reporter explained." Cited in Greenspon and Wilson-Smith, *Double Vision*, 281.

NOTES TO PAGES 186-8 305

77. Gough, "The Turbot War," 77; Blake, *From Fishermen to Fish*, 103; Joyner and von Gustedt, "The turbot war," 442.
78. Barry et al., *Fishing for a Solution*, 71-2; Blake, *From Fishermen to Fish*, 107; Keiver, "The turbot war," 561; Nicholas Tracy, *A Two-Edged Sword: The Navy as an Instrument of Canadian Foreign Policy* (Montreal: McGill-Queen's University Press, 2012), 250.
79. Joyner and von Gustedt, "The turbot war," 446-53; Keiver, "The turbot war," 561-2, 580.
80. Gough, "The Turbot War," 96-9; Barry, Applebaum, and Wiseman, *Fishing for a Solution*, 74-5, 122; Tobin, *All in Good Time*, 137-8.
81. Bartleman, *Rollercoaster*, 113; Roy MacLaren, *The Fundamental Things Apply: A Memoir* (Montreal: McGill-Queen's University Press, 2011), 204-5; Barry, "The Canadian-European Union turbot war," 277-8; Howe and Kerby, "The Canada-EU turbot war," 162.
82. Chrétien, *My Years as Prime Minister*, 112.
83. Bartleman, *Rollercoaster*, 113.
84. Chrétien, *My Years as Prime Minister*, 337.
85. For the treaty text, see http://www.icbl.org/en-gb/the-treaty/treaty-in-detail/treaty-text.aspx.
86. John English, "The Ottawa Process: Paths followed, paths ahead," *Australian Journal of International Affairs* 5, no. 2 (1998): 121-32, https://doi.org/10.1080/10357719808445245; Robert Lawson, "The Ottawa Process: Fast-track diplomacy and the international movement to ban anti-personnel mines," in Fen Osler Hampson and Maureen Molot, eds., *Canada among Nations 1998: Leadership and Dialogue* (Toronto: Oxford University Press, 1998), 82-3. On the problems with the CCW, see Christopher Kirkey, "Washington's response to the Ottawa land mines process," *Canadian-American Public Policy* 46 (2001): 4, https://journals.uvic.ca/index.php/capp/article/view/16464.
87. Bryan McDonald, "The global landmine crisis in the 1990s," in Richard A. Matthew, Bryan McDonald, and Kenneth R. Rutherford, eds., *Landmines and Human Security: International Politics and War's Hidden Legacy* (Albany: State University of New York Press, 2004), 25; Veronica Kitchen, "The rhetoric to reality: Canada, the United States, and the Ottawa Process to ban landmines," *International Journal* 57, no. 1 (2002): 39-40, https://doi.org/10.1177/002070200205700103; David Long and Laird Hindle, "Europe and the Ottawa Process: An overview," *Canadian Foreign Policy* 5, no. 3 (1998): 69, https://doi.org/10.1080/11926422.1998.9673150.
88. Jody Williams and Stephen Goose, "The international campaign to ban landmines," in Maxwell A. Cameron, Robert J. Lawson, and Brian W. Tomlin, eds., *To Walk without Fear: The Global Movement to Ban Landmines* (Toronto: Oxford University Press, 1998), 22-3; Nicola Short, "The role of NGOs in the Ottawa Process to ban landmines," *International Negotiation* 4, no. 3 (1999): 483, https://doi.org/10.1163/15718069920848589.
89. Fen Osler Hampson and Holly Reid, "Coalition diversity and normative legitimacy in human security negotiations," *International Negotiation* 8, no. 1 (2003): 13, https://doi.org/10.1163/138234003769590659; Kitchen, "From rhetoric to reality," 40.
90. Bartleman, *Rollercoaster*, 44-5, 149. See also Axworthy, *Navigating a New World*, 141.
91. Brian W. Tomlin, "On a fast track to a ban: The Canadian policy process," in Cameron, Lawson, and Tomlin, *To Walk without Fear*, 186.
92. Kitchen, "From rhetoric to reality," 41.
93. Tomlin, "On a fast track," in Cameron, Lawson, and Tomlin, *To Walk without Fear*, 191-4.
94. Williams and Goose, "The international campaign," in Cameron, Lawson, and Tomlin, *To Walk without Fear*, 33; Kitchen, "From rhetoric to reality," 43-4; English, "The Ottawa Process," 123.
95. Maxwell A. Cameron, "Global civil society and the Ottawa Process: Lessons from the movement to ban anti-personnel mines," *Canadian Foreign Policy* 7, no. 1 (1999): 91, https://doi.org/10.1080/11926422.1999.9673202.
96. Robert J. Lawson, Mark Gwozdecky, Jill Sinclair, and Ralph Lysyshyn, "The Ottawa Process and the international movement to ban anti-personnel mines," in Cameron, Lawson, and Tomlin, *To Walk without Fear*, 162.
97. Tomlin, "On a fast track," in Cameron, Lawson, and Tomlin, *To Walk without Fear*, 203.
98. Kirkey, "Washington's response," 8.
99. Axworthy, *Navigating a New World*, 138-9.
100. Lawson et al., "The Ottawa Process," in Cameron, Lawson, and Tomlin, *To Walk without Fear*, 167-79; Lawson, "The Ottawa Process," in Hampson and Molot, *Canada among Nations 1998*, 86-7.

306 NOTES TO PAGES 188–91

101. Short, "The role of NGOs," 492.
102. English, "The Ottawa Process," 123–4; Short, "The role of NGOs," 488–92; Hampson and Reid, "Coalition diversity," 20; Lawson et al., "The Ottawa Process," in Cameron, Lawson, and Tomlin, *To Walk without Fear*, 179
103. Bartleman, *Rollercoaster*, 150–2; Axworthy, *Navigating a New World*, 141
104. Lloyd Axworthy and Sarah Taylor, "A ban for all seasons: The landmines convention and its implications for Canadian diplomacy," *International Journal* 53, no. 2 (1998): 197, https://doi.org/10.1177/002070209805300201; Lawson, "The Ottawa Process," in Hampson and Molot, *Canada among Nations 1998*, 82.
105. Landmine and Cluster Munition Monitor, "History," http://www.the-monitor.org/en-gb/our-expertise/history.aspx.
106. Richard A. Matthew, "Human security and the mine ban movement I: Introduction," in Matthew, McDonald, and Rutherford, *Landmines and Human Security*, 9.
107. Cameron, "Global civil society," 88.
108. Lloyd Axworthy, "Towards a new multilateralism," in Cameron, Lawson, and Tomlin, *To Walk without Fear*, 450.
109. Cameron, "Global civil society," 87; English, "The Ottawa Process," 131.
110. Axworthy, "Towards a new multilateralism," in Cameron, Lawson, and Tomlin, *To Walk without Fear*, 453; Stephen Goose and Jody Williams, "The campaign to ban antipersonnel landmines: Potential lessons," in Matthew et al., *Landmines and Human Security*, 241, 246.
111. Axworthy, "Towards a new multilateralism," in Cameron, Lawson, and Tomlin, *To Walk without Fear*, 452.
112. Cameron, "Global civil society," 99.
113. Williams and Goose, "The international campaign to ban landmines," in Cameron, Lawson, and Tomlin, *To Walk without Fear*, 23–4; Lawson, "The Ottawa Process," in Hampson and Molot, *Canada among Nations 1998*, 89, 93, 96; Axworthy, *Navigating a New World*, 132; Mark Gwozdecky and Jill Sinclair, "Landmines and human security," in Rob McRae and Don Huebert, eds., *Human Security and the New Diplomacy: Protecting People, Promoting Peace* (Montreal: McGill-Queen's University Press, 2001), 32, 36–7; Axworthy and Taylor, "A ban for all seasons," 197.
114. Frank Chalk, Roméo Dallaire, Kyle Matthews, Carla Barqueiro, and Simon Doyle, *Mobilizing to Intervene: Leadership to Prevent Mass Atrocities* (Montreal: McGill-Queen's University Press, 2010), 72.
115. Paul Heinbecker, "Kosovo," in David Malone, ed., *The UN Security Council: From the Cold War to the 21st Century* (Boulder, CO: Lynne Reiner, 2004), 539; Krenare Recaj, "Sovereignty sensitivity and diaspora discontent: Domestic influences on Canadian foreign policy decision making in the Kosovo war," (University of Waterloo, MA thesis, 2021), 28–39; Michael W. Manulak, "Canada and the Kosovo crisis: A 'golden moment' in Canadian foreign policy?" *International Journal* 64, no. 2 (2009): 566–7, https://doi.org/10.1177/002070200906400215.
116. Kofi Annan, *Interventions: A Life in War and Peace* (New York: Penguin, 2012), 89–90.
117. Address by Lloyd Axworthy at the G-8 Foreign Ministers' Meeting, Cologne, Germany, 9 June 1999, cited in Don Hubert and Michael Bosner, "Humanitarian military intervention," in McRae and Hubert, *Human Security and the New Diplomacy*, 113.
118. Mendes, cited in Marketa Geislerova, "Report from the roundtable on Canada, NATO and the UN: Lessons learned from the Kosovo crisis," *Canadian Foreign Policy* 7, no. 1 (1999): 16, https://doi.org/10.1080/11926422.1999.9673196.
119. Hevina S. Dashwood, "Canada's participation in the NATO-led intervention in Kosovo," in Maureen Appel Molot and Fen Osler Hampson, eds., *Canada among Nations 2000: Vanishing Borders* (Don Mills, ON: Oxford University Press, 2000), 282.
120. Michael W. Manulak, "Canada and the Kosovo crisis: An agenda for intervention," *Martello Papers* 36 (Centre for International Relations, Queen's University, Kingston, 2011), 46–7; Chalk et al., *Mobilizing to Intervene*, 63; Kim Richard Nossal and Stéphane Roussel, "Canada and the Kosovo war: The happy follower," in Pierre Martin and Mark R. Browley, eds., *Alliance Politics, Kosovo, and NATO's War: Allied Force or Forced Allies* (New York: Palgrave, 2000), 194, available at https://nossalk.files.wordpress.com/2021/10/nossal-roussel_2000_canada-and-kosovo.pdf.
121. UNSCR 1160 (1998), 31 March 1998, http://unscr.com/en/resolutions/1160.

NOTES TO PAGES 191–200   307

122. UNSCR 1203 (1998), 24 October 1998, http://unscr.com/en/resolutions/1203; Manulak, "Canada and the Kosovo crisis," 12–3; Heinbecker, "Kosovo," in Malone, *UN Security Council*, 539; Dashwood, "Canada's participation," in Molot and Hampson, *Canada among Nations 2000*, 285; Recaj, "Sovereignty sensitivity," 41.
123. Michael Manulak, "Forceful persuasion or half-hearted diplomacy: Lessons from the Kosovo crisis," *International Journal* 66, no. 2 (2011): 360, https://www.jstor.org/stable/i27976089.
124. Manulak, "Canada and the Kosovo crisis," *Martello*, 19, 23.
125. Manulak, "Canada and the Kosovo crisis," *Martello*, 60.
126. Recaj, "Sovereignty sensitivity," 24; 83–4; Manulak, "Canada and the Kosovo crisis," 570–2; Sean M. Maloney, *Operation Kinetic: Stabilizing Kosovo* (Lincoln, NE: Potomac Books, 2018), e-book, 25, 63, 92; Dashwood, "Canada's participation," in Molot and Hampson, *Canada among Nations 2000*, 295–6; Chalk et al., *Mobilizing to Intervene*, 67.
127. Axworthy, *Navigating a New World*, 183.
128. Paul Heinbecker and Rob McRae, "The Kosovo air campaign," in McRae and Hubert, *Human Security and the New Diplomacy*, 122.
129. Heinbecker, "Kosovo," in Malone, *UN Security Council*, 542.
130. Manulak, "Canada and the Kosovo crisis," 576.
131. Centre for Refugee Studies and Joint Centre of Excellence for Research on Immigration and Settlement, York University, "A report on the settlement experiences of Kosovar refugees in Ontario," November 2001, 9, https://yorkspace.library.yorku.ca/xmlui/bitstream/handle/10315/2673/Lawrence+Lam+-+A+Report+on+the+Settlement+Experiences+of+Kosovar+Refugees+in+Ontario.pdf?sequence=1.
132. Recaj, "Sovereignty sensitivity," 78.
133. Recaj, "Sovereignty sensitivity," 83.
134. UNSCR 1244 (1999), 10 June 1999, http://unscr.com/en/resolutions/1244.
135. Recaj, "Sovereignty sensitivity," 47.
136. Heinbecker, "Kosovo," in Malone, *UN Security Council*, 547. See also Bob Bergen, *Scattering Chaff: Canadian Air Power and Censorship during the Kosovo War* (Calgary: University of Calgary Press, 2019), 265.
137. Marketa Geislerova, "Report from the roundtable," 13–8.

Chapter 9

1. William Orme, "At talks, much of it ducks behind doors," *Los Angeles Times*, 2 February 2002, https://www.latimes.com/archives/la-xpm-2002-feb-02-mn-26041-story.html.
2. Paul Wells, "How our leader reacted," *National Post*, 20 September 2001.
3. Linda Debel, "Not important to praise 'brother,'" *Toronto Star*, 25 September 2001; Paul Cellucci, *Unquiet Diplomacy* (Toronto: Key Porter, 2007), 91; Eddie Goldenberg, *The Way It Works: Inside Ottawa* (Toronto: McClelland & Stewart, 2006), 280.
4. David Frum, a conservative expatriate Canadian serving as Bush's speechwriter, wrote that "Canada was omitted because it is easy to forget friends whose governments give you no cause to remember them." David Frum, *The Right Man: The Surprise Presidency of George W. Bush* (New York: Random House, 2003), 150.
5. Jeffrey Simpson, "And nary a mention of Canada," *Globe and Mail*, 22 September 2001.
6. Quoted in Allan Thompson, "Canada's new face," *Toronto Star*, 20 January 2001.
7. Policy Options staff, "When security trumps trade," *Policy Options*, 1 May 2003, https://policyoptions.irpp.org/magazines/canada-and-the-iraq-war/when-security-trumps-trade-keeping-americas-doors-open-to-canada/.
8. Quoted in Graham Allison, "Is nuclear terrorism a threat to Canada's national security?" *International Journal* 60, no. 3 (2005): 717, https://doi.org/10.1177/002070200506000308.
9. Quoted in Hugh Winsor, "Dispelling myth about Canada as terrorist portal," *Globe and Mail*, 4 December 2001.
10. Bill Graham, *The Call of the World: A Political Memoir* (Vancouver: UBC Press, 2016), 223.
11. Daniel Livermore, *Detained: Islamic Fundamentalist Extremism and the War on Terror in Canada* (Montreal: McGill-Queen's University Press, 2018); Kerry Pither, *Dark Days: The Story of Four Canadians Tortured in the Name of Fighting Terror* (Toronto: Viking, 2008).

308 NOTES TO PAGES 200–5

12. "Deputy PM calls 'Axis of Evil' remark too harsh as Canada discusses joint defence plan," *Ottawa Citizen*, 9 February 2002.
13. "Graham critical of US stance," *Calgary Herald*, 7 August 2002.
14. "War isn't justified, PM says," *Globe and Mail*, 19 March 2003.
15. Allan Gotlieb, "Ottawa led down two nations," *National Post*, 26 March 2003; "Business groups warn of big Canada-US rift," *Globe and Mail*, 26 March 2003.
16. Graham, *Call of the World*, 312.
17. Ronald Inglehart, Neil Nevitte, and Miguel Basañez, *The North American Trajectory: Cultural, Economic, and Political Ties among the United States, Canada, and Mexico* (New York: Aldine De Gruyter, 1996); Anthony DePalma, *Here: A Biography of the New North American Continent* (New York: PublicAffairs, 2001).
18. "The vanishing border," *Maclean's*, 20 December 1999, https://archive.macleans.ca/issue/19991220.
19. Michael Adams, *Fire and Ice: The United States, Canada and the Myth of Converging Values* (Toronto: Penguin Canada, 2003).
20. Ottawa Embassy Cable 723, 14 March 2003, Wikileaks, http://wikileaks.org/plusd/cables/03OTTAWA723_a.html.
21. Paul Wells, "We don't pull our weight: Manley," *National Post*, 5 October 2001.
22. Denis Stairs et al., *In the National Interest: Canadian Foreign Policy in an Insecure World* (Calgary: Canadian Defence and Foreign Affairs Institute, 2003), viii.
23. Andrew Cohen, *While Canada Slept: How We Lost Our Place in the World* (Toronto: McClelland & Stewart, 2003).
24. Paul Martin, "A global answer to global problems," *Foreign Affairs* 84, no.3 (2005): 2–6, https://www.foreignaffairs.com/articles/2005-05-01/global-answer-global-problems.
25. Quoted in Norman Hillmer, Fen Osler Hampson, and David Carment, "Smart power in Canadian foreign policy," in Hillmer, Hampson, and Carment, eds., *Setting Priorities Straight: Canada among Nations 2004* (Montreal: McGill-Queen's University Press, 2005), 3.
26. Jennifer Welsh, *At Home in the World: Canada's Global Vision for the 21st Century* (Toronto: HarperCollins, 2004), 189.
27. Paul Martin, "Foreword," in DFAIT, *A Role of Pride and Influence in the World—Overview* (Ottawa: DFAIT, 2005).
28. "'Mr Dithers' and his distracting 'fiscal cafeteria'," *The Economist*, 17 February 2005, https://www.economist.com/the-americas/2005/02/17/mr-dithers-and-his-distracting-fiscal-cafeteria.
29. Peter Pigott, *Canada in Sudan: War Without Borders* (Toronto: Dundurn Press, 2009), 28.
30. "Martin vows to ease Darfur's suffering," *Globe and Mail*, 23 February 2005.
31. Michel Vastel, "Haïti mise en tutelle par l'ONU?" *L'actualité*, 15 March 2003, https://lactualite.com/monde/haiti-mise-en-tutelle-par-lonu/.
32. Canada, House of Commons, *Debates*, 37th Parliament, 3rd session, 10 March 2004, https://openparliament.ca/debates/2004/3/10/bill-graham-1/.
33. Gaëlle Rivard Piché, "Securing the pearl of the Caribbean: The Canadian contribution to Haiti's security and stability, 2004–2014," in Fen Osler Hampson and Stephen Saideman, eds., *Canada among Nations 2015: Elusive Pursuits: Lessons from Canada's Interventions Abroad* (Waterloo: CIGI, 2015), 117–38; Andrew S. Thompson, "Entangled: Canadian engagement in Haiti, 1968–2010," in Michael Carroll and Greg Donaghy, eds., *From Kinshasa to Kandahar: Canada and Fragile States in Historical Perspective* (Calgary: University of Calgary Press, 2016), 97–119, https://prism.ucalgary.ca/bitstream/handle/1880/51199/From_Kinshasa_to_Kandahar_2016_chapter05.pdf.
34. Martin Lukacs, "Welcoming Haitian refugees to Canada isn't about generosity but justice," *The Guardian*, 29 August 2017, https://www.theguardian.com/environment/true-north/2017/aug/29/welcoming-haitian-refugees-to-canada-isnt-about-generosity-but-justice; Graham, *Call of the World*, 346.
35. Martin, "Foreword," in DFAIT, *A Role of Pride and Influence*.
36. On these developments, see the essays in Jonathan Paquin and Patrick James, eds., *Gamechanger: The Impact of 9/11 on North American Security* (Vancouver: UBC Press, 2014).
37. Paul Martin, *Hell or High Water: My Life In and Out of Politics* (Toronto: McClelland & Stewart, 2008), 391.
38. Quoted in Janice Gross Stein and Eugene Lang, *The Unexpected War: Canada in Kandahar* (Toronto: Viking, 2007), 114. Italics in the original.

NOTES TO PAGES 206–8   309

39. Robert MacNeil, *Thirty Years of Failure: Understanding Canadian Climate Policy* (Halifax: Fernwood Publishing, 2019), 15.
40. MacNeil, *Thirty Years of Failure*, 13–6.
41. Intergovernmental Panel on Climate Change, *IPCC Second Assessment: Climate Change 1995* (New York: WMO and UNEP, 1995), https://www.ipcc.ch/site/assets/uploads/2018/05/2nd-assessment-en-1.pdf.
42. James Murton, *Canadians and Their Natural Environment: A History* (Don Mills, ON: Oxford University Press, 2021), 266.
43. Paul Halucha, "Climate change politics and the pursuit of national interests," in Fen Osler Hampson and Maureen Appel Molot, eds., *Canada among Nations 1998: Leadership and Dialogue* (Don Mills, ON: Oxford University Press, 1998), 298.
44. Douglas Macdonald, *Carbon Province, Hydro Province: The Challenge of Canadian Energy and Climate Federalism* (Toronto: University of Toronto Press, 2020), 146; MacNeil, *Thirty Years of Failure*, 16.
45. Kathryn Harrison, "The road not taken: Climate change policy in Canada and the United States," *Global Environmental Politics* 7, no. 4 (2007): 101, https://doi.org/10.1162/glep.2007.7.4.92. See also Elizabeth E. May, "The Kyoto debate: Separating rhetoric from reality," *Sierra Club*, December 2002, https://www.sierraclub.ca/national/programs/atmosphere-energy/climate-change/kyoto-debate-12-2002.html.
46. May, "The Kyoto debate"; MacNeil, *Thirty Years of Failure*, 16–7. The loopholes included credits for Canada's forests, which held carbon out of the atmosphere, as well as for the export of green technology.
47. MacNeil, *Thirty Years of Failure*, 17.
48. Heinbecker, quoted in Macdonald, *Carbon Province*, 147; Kathryn Harrison, "The struggle of ideas and self-interest in Canadian climate policy," in Harrison and Lisa McIntosh Sundstrom, eds., *Global Commons, Domestic Decisions: The Comparative Politics of Climate Change* (Cambridge, MA: MIT Press, 2010), 178–9.
49. Douglas Macdonald and Heather A. Smith, "Promises made, promises broken: Questioning Canada's commitment to climate change," *International Journal* 55, no. 1 (2000): 124, https://doi.org/10.1177/002070200005500108.
50. Ingrid Barnsley, "Dealing with change: Australia, Canada and the Kyoto Protocol to the Framework Convention on climate change," *The Round Table* 95, no. 385 (2006): 400, https://doi.org/10.1080/00358530600748358.
51. MacNeil, *Thirty Years of Failure*, 17–8; Harrison, "The struggle of ideas," in Harrison and Sundstrom, *Global Commons*, 179; Douglas Macdonald, Benjamin Donato-Woodger, and Stefan Hostetter, "The challenge of Canadian climate an energy federalism: Explaining the collapse of the Canadian national climate change process, 1998–2002," Paper presented at the annual meeting of the Canadian Political Science Association, Ottawa, 4 June 2015, 11, https://tspace.library.utoronto.ca/bitstream/1807/77152/1/Macdonald-CPSA-2015May22.pdf.
52. Macdonald, *Carbon Province*, 157–65; Harrison, "The road not taken," 106; Heather A. Smith, "Canada and Kyoto: Independence or indifference?" in Brian Bow and Patrick Lennox, eds., *An Independent Foreign Policy for Canada? Challenges and Choices for the Future* (Toronto: University of Toronto Press, 2008), 215.
53. Keith Brownsey, "Alberta's oil and gas industry in the era of the Kyoto Protocol," in G. Bruce Doern, ed., *Canadian Energy Policy and the Struggle for Sustainable Development* (Toronto: University of Toronto Press, 2005), 215; James P. Bruce and Doug Russell, "A Canadian policy chronicle," in Harold Coward and Andrew J. Weaver, eds., *Hard Choices: Climate Change in Canada* (Waterloo: Wilfrid Laurier University Press, 2004), 207.
54. May, "The Kyoto debate"; McNeil, *Thirty Years of Failure*, 19.
55. See, for example, Chrétien, *My Years as Prime Minister*, 385–6.
56. Smith, "Canada and Kyoto," in Bow and Lennox, *Independent Foreign Policy*, 211.
57. Since the provinces share responsibility for the environment, Ottawa's unilateral plan indicated that the Chrétien Liberals believed they could somehow achieve the necessary reductions without provincial co-operation. No provincial government was impressed.
58. Brownsey, "Alberta's oil and gas industry," in Doern, *Canadian Energy Policy*, 215.
59. Harrison, "The struggle of ideas," in Harrison and Sundstrom, *Global Commons*, 180.
60. Robert C. Paehlke, *Some Like It Cold: The Politics of Climate Change in Canada* (Toronto: Between the Lines, 2008), 87.
61. Harrison, "The road not taken," 107–8; MacNeil, *Thirty Years of Failure*, 21–2.

310   NOTES TO PAGES 208–11

62. Harrison, "The struggle of ideas," in Harrison and Sundstrom, *Global Commons*, 182.
63. Chrétien, *My Years as Prime Minister*, 388.
64. Jean Chrétien, *My Stories, My Times*, translated by Sheila Fischman and Donald Winkler (Toronto: Random House, 2018), 234.
65. "Not ready for Kyoto, Chretien adviser says," *Toronto Star*, 22 February 2007, https://www.thestar.com/news/2007/02/22/not_ready_for_kyoto_chretien_adviser_says.html?rf.
66. Harrison, "The struggle of ideas," in Harrison and Sundstrom, *Global Commons*, 192.
67. Barnsley, "Dealing with change," 407.
68. MacNeil, *Thirty Years of Failure*, 25.
69. Goldenberg, *The Way It Works*, 298.
70. Chrétien, *My Years as Prime Minister*, 318.
71. Rick Fawn, "No consensus with the Commonwealth, no consensus with itself? Canada and the Iraq war," *The Round Table* 97, no. 397 (2008): 521, https://doi.org/10.1080/00358530802207229. The most critical assessment is Frank P. Harvey, *Smoke and Mirrors: Globalized Terrorism and the Illusion of Multilateral Security* (Toronto: University of Toronto Press, 2004), specifically 193–215.
72. Card, quoted in Chrétien, *My Years as Prime Minister*, 315.
73. Alan Barnes, "Getting it right: Canadian intelligence assessments on Iraq, 2002–2003," *Intelligence and National Security* 35, no. 7 (2020): 928, https://doi.org/10.1080/02684527.2020.1771934; Timothy Andrews Sayle, "Taking the off-ramp: Canadian diplomacy, intelligence, and decision-making before the Iraq war," in Ramesh Thakur and Jack Cunningham, eds., *Australia, Canada, and Iraq: Perspectives on an Invasion* (Toronto: Dundurn, 2015), 211.
74. United Nations Security Council Resolution 1441 (2002), 8 September 2002, https://www.un.org/Depts/unmovic/documents/1441.pdf.
75. Brian Bow, *The Politics of Linkage: Interdependence and Ideas in Canada-US Relations* (Vancouver: UBC Press, 2009), 134; Donald Barry, "Chrétien, Bush, and the war in Iraq," *American Review of Canadian Studies* 35, no. 2 (2005): 217, https://doi.org/10.1080/02722010509481371.
76. Sayle, "Taking the off-ramp," in Thakur and Cunningham, *Australia, Canada, and Iraq*, 217; Barnes, "Getting it right," 932.
77. Chrétien, *My Years as Prime Minister*, 309; Goldenberg, *The Way It Works*, 287; Donald Barry, "Chrétien, Bush, and the war in Iraq," *American Review of Canadian Studies* 35, no. 2 (2005): 215, https://doi.org/10.1080/02722010509481371.
78. Chrétien, *My Years as Prime Minister*, 309.
79. Goldenberg, *The Way It Works*, 296. Sayle, "Taking the off-ramp," in Thakur and Cunningham, *Australia, Canada, and Iraq*, 214.
80. Barnes, "Getting it right," 941.
81. Fawn, "No consensus," 521; Barry, "Chrétien, Bush, and the war in Iraq," 219.
82. Stephen Azzi, *Reconcilable Differences: A History of Canada-US Relations* (Don Mills, ON: Oxford University Press, 2015), 247.
83. Quoted in Azzi, *Reconcilable Differences*, 247.
84. Barnes, "Getting it right," 934, 937, 940; Bow, *Politics of Linkage*, 135, 148; Barry, "Chrétien, Bush, and the war in Iraq," 221; Graham, *Call of the World*, 274, 304.
85. Bow, *Politics of Linkage*, 135.
86. Briefing Security Council, US Secretary of State Powell presents evidence of Iraq's failure to disarm, 5 February 2003, SC/7658, https://www.un.org/press/en/2003/sc7658.doc.htm.
87. Graham, *Call of the World*, 293; Barry, "Chrétien, Bush, and the war in Iraq," 223.
88. Chrétien, *My Years as Prime Minister*, 312.
89. Barry, "Chrétien, Bush, and the war in Iraq," 224; Sayle, "Taking the off-ramp," in Thakur and Cunningham, *Australia, Canada, and Iraq*, 213–14.
90. Paul Heinbecker, *Getting Back in the Game: A Foreign Policy Handbook for Canada* (Toronto: Key Porter, 2010), 88.
91. Chrétien, *My Years as Prime Minister*, 314–5; Goldenberg, *The Way It Works*, 1–7; Graham, *Call of the World*, 307; confidential sources.
92. Chrétien, House of Commons, *Debates*, 37th Parliament, 2nd session, 17 March 2003, at 1415, Oral Question Period, https://www.ourcommons.ca/DocumentViewer/en/37-2/house/sitting-71/hansard#Int-452528.
93. Jack Cunningham, "The politics of disarmament: Canada and the invasion of Iraq, 2002-03," in Thakur and Cunningham, *Australia, Canada, and Iraq*, 262.

NOTES TO PAGES 211–20   311

94. Barry, "Chrétien, Bush, and the war in Iraq," 229, 235; Cunningham, "The politics of disarmament," in Thakur and Cunningham, *Australia, Canada, and Iraq*, 267–8.
95. Sayle, "Taking the off-ramp," in Thakur and Cunningham, *Australia, Canada, and Iraq*, 220.
96. John Stewart, *Strangers with Memories: The United States and Canada from Free Trade to Baghdad* (Montreal: McGill-Queen's University Press, 2017), 120–2; Barry, "Chrétien, Bush, and the war in Iraq," 235; Bow, *Politics of Linkage*, 140–1, 148–9.
97. Graham, quoted in Cunningham, "The politics of disarmament," in Thakur and Cunningham, *Australia, Canada, and Iraq*, 265.
98. Graham, *Call of the World*, 310; Stephen Azzi and Norman Hillmer, "Intolerant allies: Canada and the George W. Bush administration," *Diplomacy and Statecraft* 27, no. 4 (2015): 733, https://doi.org/10.1080/09592296.2016.1238704; Sayle, "Taking the off-ramp," in Thakur and Cunningham, *Australia, Canada, and Iraq*, 222.
99. Chrétien, *My Years as Prime Minister*, 314–5; Goldenberg, *The Way It Works*, 1–7; Graham, *Call of the World*, 307; confidential sources.
100. Stein and Lang, *Unexpected War*, 192; Martin, *Hell or High Water*, 391–3; Graham, *Call of the World*, 378.
101. Matthew Willis, "An unexpected war, a not unexpected mission: The origins of Kandahar 2005," *International Journal* 67, no. 4 (2012): 982, https://doi.org/10.1177/002070201206700408.
102. Willis, "An unexpected war," 985–9; Stephen M. Saideman, *Adapting in the Dust: Lessons Learned from Canada's War in Afghanistan* (Toronto: University of Toronto Press, 2016), 37; Graham, *Call of the World*, 379.
103. Martin, *Hell or High Water*, 391–2.
104. Kimberly Marten, "From Kabul to Kandahar: The Canadian Forces and change," *American Review of Canadian Studies* 40, no. 2 (2010): 218, https://doi.org/10.1080/0272201100373720; Saideman, *Adapting in the Dust*, 37.
105. David Bercuson and J.L. Granatstein, with Nancy Pearson Mackie, *Lessons Learned? What Canada Should Learn from Afghanistan* (Calgary: Canadian Defence & Foreign Affairs Institute, October 2011), 22, https://d3n8a8pro7vhmx.cloudfront.net/cdfai/pages/41/attachments/original/1413662111/Lessons_Learned.pdf?1413662111; Saideman, *Adapting in the Dust*, 30, 37.
106. Graham, *Call of the World*, 379.
107. Marten, "From Kabul to Kandahar," 219.
108. Willis, "An unexpected war," 992; Saideman, *Adapting in the Dust*, 38; Hillier, *A Soldier First*, 343.
109. Hillier, *A Soldier First*, 342–3. Although Hillier does not explain why, it is clear that Canada's development assistance professionals would have opposed his plan to "paint a huge maple leaf on the middle of the runway" (343), as it represented the antithesis of recipient-centric (and therefore best practice in) international development assistance.
110. Saideman, *Adapting in the Dust*, 37.
111. Graham, *Call of the World*, 380–1; Marten, "From Kabul to Kandahar," 219–20; Bercuson and Granatstein, *Lessons Learned?*, 21–2; Saideman, *Adapting in the Dust*, 37.
112. Willis, "An unexpected war," 990.
113. Graham, *Call of the World*, 382.
114. Martin, *Hell or High Water*, 392; Saideman, *Adapting in the Dust*, 39. On Hillier's suitability, see Marten, "From Kabul to Kandahar," 217–8.
115. Stein and Lang, *Unexpected War*, 191; Graham, *Call of the World*, 382–3; Martin, *Hell or High Water*, 394–5.
116. Stein and Lang, *Unexpected War*, 198–9.
117. Hillier, quoted in Graham, *Call of the World*, 384.
118. Joseph T. Jockel, "Canada and the Netherlands in Afghanistan," *Martello Papers* 38 (Kingston: Queen's University, Centre for International and Defence Policy, 2014): 56, https://www.queensu.ca/cidp/sites/webpublish.queensu.ca.cidpwww/files/files/publications/Martellos/Martello38.pdf.
119. Willis, "An unexpected war," 996.
120. Saideman, *Adapting in the Dust*, 33.

Chapter 10

1. Paul Wells, "Harper's Canadian revolution," *Maclean's*, 17 September 2008.

312   NOTES TO PAGES 220–4

2. For instance, Mike Blanchfield, *Swingback: Getting Along in the World with Harper and Trudeau* (Montreal: McGill-Queen's University Press, 2017), 31.
3. Kenneth Whyte, "In conversation: Stephen Harper," *Maclean's*, 5 July 2011.
4. Quoted in Paul Wells, "Lost in a crowd," *Maclean's*, 18 June 2007.
5. L. Ian MacDonald, "A conversation with John Baird," *Policy Options*, April 2012.
6. Lee Berthiaume, "Canada takes sides, not a world referee, Baird says," *Ottawa Citizen*, 22 December 2012, https://www.pressreader.com/canada/ottawa-citizen/20121222/281659662369212.
7. Kim Richard Nossal, "Old habits and new directions indeed," *International Journal* 69, no. 2 (2014): 257; Adam Chapnick, "A diplomatic counter-revolution: Conservative foreign policy, 2006–2011," *International Journal* 67, no. 1 (2011–12): 137–54.
8. Allan Woods, "PM, public servants at odds over policy," *Toronto Star*, 25 June 2007, A1.
9. Mark Bourrie, *Kill the Messengers: Stephen Harper's Assault on Your Right to Know* (Toronto: HarperCollins, 2005); Peter McKenna, "Bullies, busy-work and bureaucrats: Inside 'Fort Pearson' during the Harper years," in Peter McKenna, ed., *Harper's World: The Politicization of Canadian Foreign Policy, 2006–2015* (Toronto: University of Toronto Press, 2022), 41–74.
10. Whyte, "In conversation." See also Stephen Brown, Molly den Heyer, and David R. Black, eds., *Rethinking Canadian Aid* (Ottawa: University of Ottawa Press, 2014).
11. Stephen Harper, "Address by the Prime Minister to the Canadian Armed Forces in Afghanistan," 13 March 2006, https://www.canada.ca/en/news/archive/2006/03/address-prime-minister-canadian-armed-forces-afghanistan.html.
12. Technically, the motion was unnecessary—Cabinet can dispatch the military without consulting the House of Commons—but the vote divided the Liberals, as was Harper's intent. See Justin Massie, "'Stephen Harper's war in Afghanistan' eagerly in, cautiously out," in McKenna, *Harper's World*, 145.
13. Independent Panel on Canada's Future Role in Afghanistan, *Final Report* (Ottawa: Government of Canada, 2008), 22, 32.
14. Jean-Christophe Boucher and Kim Richard Nossal, *The Politics of War: Canada's Afghanistan Mission, 2001–14* (Vancouver: UBC Press, 2017), 79.
15. Campbell Clark, "Harper's turnaround: PM says he felt he had to extend Afghan mission," *Globe and Mail*, 11 November 2010, https://www.theglobeandmail.com/news/politics/harpers-turnaround-pm-says-he-felt-he-had-to-extend-afghan-mission/article1259532/.
16. On the war, see Saideman, *Adapting in the Dust*.
17. Bercuson and Granatstein, *Lessons Learned?*, 21.
18. Whyte, "In conversation."
19. Michael K. Carroll, "Peacekeeping: Canada's past, but not its present and future," *International Journal* 71, no. 1 (2016): 167–76, https://doi.org/10.1177/0020702015619857.
20. Quoted in Aaron Wherry, "The argument of force," *Maclean's*, 1 September 2011.
21. Mark Kennedy, "Canada is facing 'long haul' mission: Harper," *Ottawa Citizen*, 8 September 2015, A5.
22. The government began referring to what had been the Canadian Forces as the Canadian Armed Forces (both names are included in the National Defence Act) in 2013. See Postmedia News, "Canada's military is getting a new name – again," *National Post*, 12 March 2013, https://nationalpost.com/news/canada/canadas-military-is-getting-a-new-name-again/. With thanks to Charlotte Duval-Lantoine for the reference.
23. Paul Chapin, J.L. Granatstein, Don Macnamara, and Hugh Segal, "A roadmap to a stronger military," *National Post*, 28 September 2015, A11.
24. Prime Minister Stephen Harper Announces new Arctic Offshore Patrol Ships, 9 July 2007, https://www.canada.ca/en/news/archive/2007/07/prime-minister-stephen-harper-announces-new-arctic-offshore-patrol-ships.html.
25. Government of Canada, *Northern Strategy: Our North, Our Heritage, Our Future* (Ottawa: Minister of Public Works and Government Services, 2009), 1.
26. Government of Canada, *Statement on Canada's Arctic Foreign Policy: Exercising Sovereignty and Promoting Canada's Northern Strategy* (Ottawa: Government of Canada, 2010); Heather Exner-Pirot, "Canada's Arctic Council chairmanship (2013–2015): A post-mortem," *Canadian Foreign Policy Journal* 22, no. 1 (2016): 84–96.
27. Andrea Charron, "The recasting of the Arctic sovereignty theme: Assessing Harper's Arctic foreign policy," in McKenna, *Harper's World*, 226.

28. Jane Taber, "PM brands Canada an 'Energy Superpower'," *Globe and Mail*, 15 July 2006, https://www.theglobeandmail.com/news/national/pm-brands-canada-an-energy-superpower/article18167474/.
29. "Kent says Fossil Awards are 'worn with honour'," *CTV News*, 7 May 2013, http://www.ctvnews.capolitics/kent-says-fossil-awards-are-worn-with-honour-1.1271877.
30. "John Baird's speech to the United Nations General Assembly," *Maclean's*, 30 September 2013, https://www.macleans.ca/general/john-bairds-speech-to-the-united-nations-general-assembly/.
31. Prime Minister Harper Signals Canada's Renewed Engagement in the Americas, 17 July 2007, https://www.canada.ca/en/news/archive/2007/07/prime-minister-harper-signals-canada-renewed-engagement-americas.html.
32. Peter McKenna, ed., *Canada Looks South: In Search of an Americas Policy* (Toronto: University of Toronto Press, 2012).
33. On the 2010 Security Council election, see Adam Chapnick, *Canada on the United Nations Security Council: A Small Power on a Large Stage* (Vancouver: UBC Press, 2019), chapter 10.
34. "Won't 'sell out' on rights despite China snub: PM," *CBC News*, 15 November 2006, http://www.cbc.ca/news/world/won-t-sell-out-on-rights-despite-china-snub-pm-1.570708.
35. Kim Richard Nossal and Leah Sarson, "About face: explaining changes in Canada's China policy, 2006–2012," *Canadian Foreign Policy Journal* 20, no. 2 (2014): 146–62.
36. "Canada-China relationship improving, Baird says," *CBC News*, 20 July 2011, https://www.cbc.ca/news/politics/canada-china-relationship-improving-baird-says-1.983751.
37. Stephen J. Harper, *Right Here Right Now: Politics and Leadership in the Age of Disruption* (Toronto: McClelland & Stewart, 2018), 109.
38. David Mulroney, *Middle Power, Middle Kingdom: What Canadians Need to Know about China in the 21st Century* (Toronto: Penguin, 2015), 284.
39. Address by Minister Fast to the Economic Club of Canada, 27 November 2013, http://www.international.gc.ca/media/comm/speeches-discours/2013/12/11a.aspx.
40. Harper, *Right Here*, 107.
41. "Canada can pursue trade deal while protecting supply management: Harper," *CBC News*, 25 June 2015, http://www.cbc.ca/news/politics/canada-can-pursue-trade-deal-while-protecting-supply-management-harper-1.3127674.
42. Whyte, "In conversation."
43. "A conversation with the prime minister," *Policy Options*, February 2008, https://policyoptions.irpp.org/magazines/the-dollar/a-conversation-with-the-prime-minister-interview/.
44. Ian Brodie, *At the Centre of Government: The PM and the Limits on Political Power* (Montreal: McGill-Queen's University Press, 2018), 34.
45. Neil Macdonald, "Interview with U.S. Homeland Security Secretary Janet Napolitano," *CBC News*, 20 April 2009, http://www.cbc.ca/m/touch/news/story/1.780829.
46. Barak Ravid, "Netanyahu asked Canada PM to thwart G8 support for 1967 borders," *Haaretz*, 29 May 2011, https://www.haaretz.com/2011-05-29/ty-article/netanyahu-asked-canada-pm-to-thwart-g8-support-for-1967-borders/0000017f-e807-da9b-a1ff-ec6f78d20000.
47. Shawn McCarty, "Keystone Pipeline approval 'Complete No-Brainer', Harper says," *Globe and Mail*, 21 September 2011.
48. Joanna Slater, "Harper 'won't take no for an answer' from US on Keystone XL," *Globe and Mail*, 27 September 2013, https://www.theglobeandmail.com/report-on-business/harper-wont-take-no-for-an-answer-from-us-on-keystone-xl/article14547474/.
49. Bruce Heyman and Vicki Heyman, *The Art of Diplomacy: Strengthening the Canada-US Relationship in Times of Uncertainty* (Toronto: Simon & Schuster, 2019), 79; Campbell Clark, "How Ottawa left U.S. Ambassador Bruce Heyman out in the cold," *Globe and Mail*, 18 March 2015.
50. For competing perspectives, see Mark MacKinnon, "Harper's world: Canada's new role on the global stage," *Globe and Mail*, 25 September 2015; and "The choices before us, Part 2: Defending Canada and its interests," *National Post*, 13 October 2015.
51. "Voters more concerned with trade than aid," *Globe and Mail*, 28 September 2015.
52. Campbell Strategies, Inc., "Barbaric cultural practices hotline," *Dictionary of Canadian Politics*, https://parli.ca/barbaric-cultural-practices-hotline/.
53. Ravi de Costa, "Implementing UNDRIP: Developments and possibilities," *Prairie Forum* no. 36 (2011): 57.

314   NOTES TO PAGES 229–32

54. Sheryl Lightfoot, *Global Indigenous Politics: A Subtle Revolution* (London: Taylor and Francis e-books, 2016), ProQuest Ebook Central, http://ebookcentral.proquest.com/lib/cfvlibrary-ebooks/detail.action?docID=4530723, chapter 2.

55. Lightfoot, *Global Indigenous Politics*, e-book, chapter 2.

56. Indian and Northern Affairs Canada, "Canada's Position: United Nations Draft Declaration on the Rights of Indigenous Peoples," 29 June 2006, https://web.archive.org/web/20061001214741/http://www.ainc-inac.gc.ca/nr/spch/unp/06/ddr_e.html.

57. Confidential interview.

58. INAC, "Canada's Position" 29 June 2006.

59. Lightfoot, *Global Indigenous Politics*, e-book, chapter 2.

60. Kenneth Deer, "Reflections on the development, adoption, and implementation of the UN Declaration on the Rights of Indigenous Peoples," in Jackie Hartley, Paul Joffe, and Jennifer Preston, eds., *Realizing the UN Declaration on the Rights of Indigenous Peoples: Triumph, Hope, and Action* (Saskatoon: Purich Publishing, 2010), 24–5.

61. United Nations Press Release GA 10612, 13 September 2007, "General Assembly adopts Declaration on Rights of Indigenous Peoples," https://www.un.org/press/en/2007/ga10612.doc.htm.

62. Data from Thomas Isaac, as cited in Blain Favel and Ken S. Coates, "Understanding UNDRIP: Choosing action on priorities over sweeping claims about the United Nations *Declaration on the Rights of Indigenous Peoples*," (Ottawa: Macdonald-Laurier Institute, May 2016), 7, https://www.macdonaldlaurier.ca/files/pdf/MLI-10-UNDRIPCoates-Flavel05-16-WebReadyV4.pdf.

63. UN Press Release GA 10612.

64. INAC, "Canada's Position," 29 June 2006; Prentice's view is cited in Favel and Coates, "Understanding UNDRIP," 17, https://www.macdonaldlaurier.ca/files/pdf/MLI-10-UNDRIPCoates-Flavel05-16-WebReadyV4.pdf.

65. Paul Joffe, "Canada's opposition to the *UN Declaration*: Legitimate concern or ideological bias?" in Hartley, Joffe, and Preston, *Realizing the UN Declaration*, 71; Deer, "Reflections," in Hartley, *Realizing the UN Declaration*, 24, 26; Joyce Green, "Canada the bully: Indigenous human rights in Canada and the United Nations Declaration on the Rights of Indigenous Peoples," *Prairie Forum* no. 36 (2011): 11.

66. Yale D. Belanger, "The United Nations Declaration on the Rights of Indigenous Peoples and urban Aboriginal self-determination in Canada: A preliminary assessment," *Aboriginal Policy Studies* 1, no. 1 (2011): 137, https://doi.org/10.5663/aps.v1i1.10134; Lightfoot, *Global Indigenous Politics*, e-book, chapter 7.

67. Confidential interview.

68. Media Advisory, "Official visit to Canada of the Honourable John Howard, Prime Minister of Australia," 18 May 2006, https://www.canada.ca/en/news/archive/2006/05/official-visit-canada-honourable-john-howard-prime-minister-australia.html.

69. INAC, "Canada's Position" 29 June 2006.

70. UN Press Release GA 10612.

71. Sheryl R. Lightfoot, "Selective endorsement without intent to implement: Indigenous rights and the Anglosphere," *International Journal of Human Rights* 16, no. 1 (2012): 103, https://doi.org/10.1080/13642987.2012.622139.

72. Lightfoot, "Selective endorsement," 103; Joffe, "Canada's opposition to the *UN Declaration*," in Hartley, Joffe, and Preston, *Realizing the UN Declaration*, 75.

73. Lightfoot, *Global Indigenous Politics*, e-book, chapter 7. For Ottawa's response to the House of Commons resolution, see Canada, House of Commons, *Debates*, 39th Parliament, 2nd session, 7 April 2008, https://www.ourcommons.ca/DocumentViewer/en/39-2/house/sitting-73/hansard.

74. Heather Exner-Pirot, "Friend or faux? Trudeau, Indigenous issues and Canada's brand," *Canadian Foreign Policy Journal* 24, no. 2 (2018): 165–81, https:///doi.org/10.1080/1192642 2.2018.1461667.

75. Sheryl Lightfoot, "A promise too far? The Justin Trudeau government and Indigenous rights," in Norman Hillmer and Philippe Lagassé, eds., *Justin Trudeau and Canadian Foreign Policy: Canada among Nations 2017* (Cham: Palgrave Macmillan, 2018), 169–70; Favel and Coates, "Understanding UNDRIP," 18; Belanger, "The United Nations Declaration," 134; Exner-Pirot, "Friend or faux?" 175.

NOTES TO PAGES 232–3   315

76. Governor General of Canada, Speech from the Throne, 40th Parliament, 3rd session, 3 March 2010, https://lop.parl.ca/sites/ParlInfo/default/en_CA/Parliament/throneSpeech/speech403.

77. INAC, "Canada's Statement of Support on the United Nations Declaration on the Rights of Indigenous Peoples," 12 November 2010, https://www.rcaanc-cirnac.gc.ca/eng/1309374239861/1621701138904.

78. Lightfoot, "Selective endorsement," 112–3.

79. De Costa, "Implementing UNDRIP," 63; Alex Neve and Craig Benjamin, "Canada and the UN Declaration on the Rights of Indigenous Peoples: Opposition must give way to implementation," *Prairie Forum* no. 36 (2011): 1–8; Amnesty International et al., "Joint Statement in Response to Canada's Endorsement of the UN Declaration on the Rights of Indigenous Peoples," 16 November 2010, https://www.culturalsurvival.org/news/joint-statement-response-canadas-endorsement-un-declaration-rights-indigenous-peoples; Ken Coates and Carin Holroyd, "Indigenous internationalism and the emerging impact of UNDRIP in Aboriginal affairs in Canada," in Terry Mitchell, ed., *The Internationalization of Indigenous Rights: UNDRIP in the Canadian Context* (Waterloo: CIGI, 2014), 8, https://www.cigionline.org/documents/855/indigenous_rights_special_report_web_1.pdf.

80. Cited in Kristina R. Proulx, Arne Ruckert, and Ronald Labonté, "Canada's flagship development priority: Maternal, newborn and child health (MNCH) and the Sustainable Development Goals (SDGs)," *Canadian Journal of Development Studies* 38, no. 1 (2017): 48, https://doi.org/10.1080/02255189.2016.1202103.

81. Jerome Klassen, "Joining empire: Canadian foreign policy under Harper," *Canadian Dimension*, 7 October 2015, https://canadiandimension.com/articles/view/joining-empire-canadian-foreign-policy-under-harper.

82. Elly Vandenberg, "How an NGO coalition helped score the Muskoka Initiative," *Policy Options*, 7 February 2017, https://policyoptions.irpp.org/magazines/february-2017/how-an-ngo-coalition-helped-score-the-muskoka-initiative/.

83. Jacqueline Potvin, "Biopolitics, risk, and reproductive justice: The governing of maternal health in Canada's Muskoka Initiative," (University of Western Ontario, PhD dissertation, 2018), 18, https://ir.lib.uwo.ca/etd/5956.

84. Melissa Haussman and Lisa Mills, "Doing the North American two-step on a global stage: Canada, its G8 Muskoka Initiative, and safe abortion funding," in G. Bruce Doern and Christopher Stoney, eds., *How Ottawa Spends 2012–2013: The Majority, Budget Cuts, and the New Opposition* (Montreal and Kingston: MQUP, 2012), 243–5; UN Department of Information, "The Millennium Development Goals," n.d., https://www.ndi.org/sites/default/files/Handout%207%20-%20Millennium%20Development%20Goals.pdf.

85. Krystel Carrier and Rebecca Tiessen, "Women and children first: Maternal health and the silencing of gender in Canadian foreign policy," in Heather A. Smith and Claire Turenne Sjolander, eds., *Canada in the World: Internationalism in Canadian Foreign Policy* (Don Mills, ON: Oxford University Press, 2013), 184–5.

86. Confidential interview.

87. John Kirton, Julia Kulik, and Caroline Bracht, "The political process in global health and nutrition governance: The G8's 2010 Muskoka Initiative on Maternal, Child, and Newborn Health," *Annals of the New York Academy of Sciences* no. 1331 (2014): 189–92, https://doi.org/10.1111/nyas.12494; Julia Keast, "Missed opportunity: A discursive analysis of Canada's commitments to maternal health under the Muskoka Initiative," in Rebecca Tiessen and Stephen Baranyi, eds., *Obligations and Omissions: Canada's Ambiguous Actions on Gender Inequality* (Montreal and Kingston: McGill-Queen's University Press, 2017), 61; confidential interviews.

88. Canadian Coalition for Maternal, Newborn and Child Health, "The 2010 Muskoka Summit: An Opportunity for Canada to Lead on Preventing the Deaths of Women and Children," 19 January 2010, http://www.g7.utoronto.ca/conferences/2010/ghdp/ccmnch.pdf. Descriptions of both interventions can be found at the Johns Hopkins Bloomberg School of Public Health's Institute for International Programs website: https://www.jhsph.edu/research/centers-and-institutes/institute-for-international-programs/completed-projects/.

89. Kirton et al., "The political process," 190; confidential interviews.

90. John Ibbitson, *Stephen Harper* (Toronto: McClelland and Stewart, 2015), 340; confidential interview.

316 NOTES TO PAGES 233-5

91. John Richards, "Can aid work? Thinking about development strategy," *C.D. Howe Institute Commentary* no. 231 (April 2006): 22, https://www.cdhowe.org/sites/default/files/attachments/research_papers/mixed/commentary_231.pdf. For empirical validation, see Emmanuel Banchani and Liam Swiss, "The impact of foreign aid on maternal mortality," *Politics and Governance* 7, no. 2 (2019): 53–67, https://doi.org/10.17645/pag.v7i2.1835.

92. Potvin, "Biopolitics, risk, and reproductive justice," 124; Rebecca Tiessen, "Gender equality and the 'Two CIDAs': Successes and setbacks, 1976–2015," in Stephen Brown, Molly den Heyer, and David R. Black, eds., *Rethinking Canadian Aid*, 2nd ed. (Ottawa: University of Ottawa Press, 2016), 197; Haussman and Mills, "Doing the North American two-step," in Doern and Stoney, *How Ottawa Spends 2012–2013*, 247–9.

93. Email exchange with Paul Wilson, 9 February 2022.

94. Blanchfield, *Swingback*, 118; confidential interviews.

95. David R. Black, "The Muskoka Initiative and the politics of fence-mending with Africa," in Rohinton Medora and Yiagadeesen Samy, eds., *Canada among Nations 2013: Canada-Africa Relations, Looking Back, Looking Ahead* (Waterloo: CIGI and Carleton University, 2013), 245.

96. Black, "The Muskoka Initiative," in Medora and Samy, *Canada among Nations 2013*, 245; confidential interviews.

97. Harper, quoted in Haussman and Mills, "Doing the North American two-step," in Doern and Stoney, *How Ottawa Spends 2012–2013*, 252.

98. Canada, House of Commons, *Debates*, 40th Parliament, 3rd session, 23 March 2010, https://www.ourcommons.ca/DocumentViewer/en/40-3/house/sitting-15/hansard, at 10:06; Blanchfield, *Swingback*, 107, 119; Carrier and Tiessen, "Women and children first," in Smith and Sjolander, *Canada in the World*, 185; Keast, "Missed opportunity," in Tiessen and Baranyi, *Obligations and Omissions*, 52–3.

99. Marie Vastel and Fannie Oliver, "Document suggests Harper government ignored its own advice on abortion," cp24.com, 24 May 2010, https://www.cp24.com/document-suggests-harper-government-ignored-its-own-advice-on-abortion-1.515397?cache=ngyhfzxv%3FclipId%3D64268.

100. "Muskoka Declaration: Recovery and New Beginnings," Muskoka, Ontario, 26 June 2010, http://www.g7.utoronto.ca/summit/2010muskoka/communique.html; Blanchfield, *Swingback*, 106–7; Kirton et al., "The political process," 193.

101. Rebecca Tiessen, "'Walking wombs': Making sense of the Muskoka Initiative and the emphasis on motherhood in Canadian foreign policy," *Global Justice: Theory Practice Rhetoric* 8, no. 1 (2015): 78–9.

102. Kirton et al., "The political process," 194–5; Kristina R. Proulx, Arne Ruckert, and Ronald Labonté, "Canada's flagship development priority: Maternal, newborn and child health (MNCH) and the Sustainable Development Goals (SDGs)," *Canadian Journal of Development Studies* 38, no. 1 (2017): 40–1, https://doi.org/10.1080/02255189.2016.1202103.

103. World Health Organization, Partnership for Maternal, Newborn & Child Health, "Saving Every Woman, Every Child: Within Arm's Reach," 29 May 2014, https://www.who.int/pmnch/media/events/2014/canada/en/.

104. United Nations News, "Peace will succeed only when people have a chance at a better life, Canada's leader tells UN Assembly," 26 September 2014, https://news.un.org/en/story/2014/09/479022-peace-will-succeed-only-when-people-have-chance-better-life-canadas-leader.

105. Proulx et al., "Canada's flagship development priority," 42, 47; Blanchfield, *Swingback*, 124.

106. Kirton et al., "The political process," 196; confidential interviews.

107. Black, "The Muskoka Initiative," in Medora and Samy, *Canada among Nations 2013*, 243; Blanchfield, *Swingback*, 107.

108. Carrier and Tiessen, "Women and children first," in Smith and Sjolander, *Canada in the World*, 187. See also Black, "The Muskoka Initiative," in Medora and Samy, *Canada among Nations 2013*, 246.

109. Global Affairs Canada, News Release: "Canada announces support for sexual and reproductive health and rights," 8 March 2017, https://www.canada.ca/en/global-affairs/news/2017/03/canada_announcessupportforsexualandreproductivehealthandrights.html.

110. Will Kymlicka, "The precarious resilience of multiculturalism in Canada," *American Review of Canadian Studies* 51, no. 1 (2021): 126, https://doi.org/10/1080/02722011.2021.1878544.

111. "The term 'Diaspora' here comprises a wide range of individuals who identify themselves as Ukrainian, either by national or ethnic origin, who reside outside of Ukraine." Svitlana

NOTES TO PAGES 235–8 317

Krasynska, "Digital civil society: Euromaidan, the Ukrainian Diaspora, and social media," in David R. Marples and Frederick V. Mills, eds., *Ukraine's Euromaidan: Analyses of a Civil Revolution* (Stuttgart: ibidem Press, 2015), 178.

112. Marko Bojcun, "Origins of the Ukrainian crisis," *Critique: Journal of Socialist Theory* 43, no. 3–4 (2015): 399–405, https://doi.org/10.1080/03017605.2015.1089085.

113. David Carment, Milana Nikolko, and Sam MacIsaac, "Mobilizing diaspora during crisis: Ukrainian diaspora in Canada and the intergenerational sweet spot," *Diaspora Studies* 14, no. 1 (2021): 26–7, https://doi.org/10.1080/09739572.2020.1827667.

114. Bohdan S. Kordan and Mitchell C.G. Dowie, *Canada and the Ukrainian Crisis* (Montreal: McGill-Queen's University Press, 2020), 3.

115. Bohdan S. Kordan, "'No better friend: Assessing the 'special' nature of the Canada-Ukraine relationship," *Cicero Foundation Great Debate Paper* 20, no. 4 (2020): 1–10, https://www.cicerofoundation.org/wp-content/uploads/Bohdan_S_Kordan_No_Better_Friend-1.pdf.

116. Quoted in Bohdan S. Kordan, *Strategic Friends: Canada-Ukraine Relations from Independence to the Euromaidan* (Montreal: McGill-Queen's University Press, 2018), 83.

117. John Ibbitson, *Stephen Harper* (Toronto: McClelland and Stewart, 2015), 330; Blanchfield, *Swingback*, 165; Kordan, *Strategic Friends*, 87–96; Aya Fujiwara, "Canada's response to Euromaidan," in Marples and Mills, *Ukraine's Euromaidan*, 200.

118. Kordan, *Strategic Friends*, 99–100; Bojcun, "Origins of the Ukrainian crisis," 408–10.

119. Bojcun, "Origins of the Ukrainian crisis," 413; Kordan and Dowie, *Canada and the Ukrainian Crisis*, 6; Fujiwara, "Canada's response to Euromaidan," in Marples and Mills, *Ukraine's Euromaidan*, 212.

120. Carment, Mikolko, and MacIsaac, "Mobilizing diaspora," 34–6; Kordan and Dowie, *Canada and the Ukrainian Crisis*, 62.

121. Mitchell C.G. Dowie, "A dangerous world: Stephen Harper's post-Maidan Ukraine policy," (University of Saskatchewan, MA thesis, 2017), 9, https://harvest.usask.ca/handle/10388/8441.

122. Ibbitson, *Stephen Harper*, 330; Fujiwara, "Canada's response to Euromaidan," in Marples and Mills, *Ukraine's Euromaidan*, 201; confidential sources.

123. For a complete list of Canadian government actions, see the chronology in Kordan and Dowie, *Canada and the Ukrainian Crisis*, 97–109.

124. Terry Pedwell, "Canada and Ukraine sign free trade deal," *Windsor Star*, 15 July 2014.

125. Alex Boutilier, "Russia, Canada engage in passive-aggressive cartography," *Toronto Star*, 28 August 2014, https://www.thestar.com/news/canada/2014/08/28/russia_canada_engage_in_passiveaggressive_cartography.html. See also Andrew Burtch, "Russia, not Russia: The Tweet heard round the world," *Canadian Eyes Only* blog, 2 February 2018, https://cihhic.ca/2018/02/02/russia-not-russia-the-tweet-heard-round-the-world/.

126. Quoted in Dowie, "A dangerous world," 36.

127. Blanchfield, *Swingback*, 177.

128. Blanchfield, *Swingback*, 177–8; Ibbitson, *Stephen Harper*, 330; Francis Elliott, "Canadian PM calls Putin a liar over Ukraine at summit," *The Times*, 16 November 2014, https://www.thetimes.co.uk/article/canadian-pm-calls-putin-a-liar-over-ukraine-at-summit-qkq6tmg7bc7.

129. Fujiwara, "Canada's response to Euromaidan," in Marples and Mills, *Ukraine's Euromaidan*, 199.

130. Blanchfield, *Swingback*, quotation from 165; examples from 168–9, 178–9. See also Roland Paris, "Harper's heroic Ukraine message does not reflect reality," *Globe and Mail*, 3 June 2014, https://www.theglobeandmail.com/opinion/harpers-heroic-ukraine-message-does-not-reflect-reality/article18959539/.

131. Klavdia Tatar, "Helping the homeland in troubled times: Advocacy by Canada's Ukrainian diaspora in the context of regime change and war in Ukraine," *Central and Eastern European Migration Review* 9, no. 2 (2020): 35–51, https://doi.org/10.17467/ceemr.2020.01.

132. Kordan and Dowie, *Canada and the Ukrainian Crisis*, 29, 37–9, 85; Kordan, *Strategic Friends*, 123.

133. John Baird, "Russia's aggression is against its own best interest," *Toronto Star*, 21 November 2014, https://www.thestar.com/opinion/commentary/2014/11/21/john_baird_russias_aggression_is_against_its_own_best_interest.html; Dowie, "A dangerous world," 70; Blanchfield, *Swingback*, 178, 165–6; Kordan and Dowie, *Canada and the Ukrainian Crisis*, 51; Kordan, *Strategic Friends*, 105.

134. Canada, Department of National Defence, Operation Unifier, updated 15 February 2022, https://www.canada.ca/en/department-national-defence/services/operations/military-operations/current-operations/operation-unifier.html.

318   NOTES TO PAGES 243–6

Chapter 11

1. Trudeau, cited in Pioneer Press, "Canada returns to Liberal roots under Trudeau," Twincities. com, 19 October 2015, https://www.twincities.com/2015/10/19/canada-returns-to-liberal-roots-under-trudeau/.

2. Roland Paris, "Are Canadians still liberal internationalists? Foreign policy and public opinion in the Harper era," *International Journal* 69, no. 3 (2014): 274–307: https://doi.org/10.1177/0020702014540282.

3. Trudeau, cited in Mike Blanchfield, "Trudeau reverses strict message control over diplomats," *CTV News*, 5 November 2015, https://www.ctvnews.ca/politics/trudeau-reverses-strict-message-control-over-diplomats-1.2643715.

4. "Liberty moves north," *The Economist*, 29 October 2016, https://www.economist.com/leaders/2016/10/29/liberty-moves-north; Ishaan Tharoor, "The many ways Canada's Trudeau is the anti-Trump," *Washington Post*, 29 February 2016, https://www.washingtonpost.com/news/worldviews/wp/2016/02/29/the-many-ways-canadas-trudeau-is-the-anti-trump/.

5. Bruce Heyman and Vicki Heyman, *The Art of Diplomacy: Strengthening the Canada-US Relationship in Times of Uncertainty* (Toronto: Simon & Schuster, 2019), 165, 110.

6. Michael D. Shear and Coral Davenport, "Justin Trudeau, Canadian prime minister, making rare official visit," *The New York Times*, 10 March 2016, https://www.nytimes.com/2016/03/10/us/politics/canada-leader-justin-tredeau-obama-visit.html; John Powers, "Justin Trudeau is the new young face of Canadian politics," *Vogue*, 9 December 2015, https://www.vogue.com/article/justin-trudeau-prime-minister-canada.

7. Quoted in Meredith Lilly, "International trade: The rhetoric and reality of the Trudeau government's progressive trade agenda," in Norman Hillmer and Philippe Lagassé, eds., *Justin Trudeau and Canadian Foreign Policy: Canada among Nations 2017* (Cham: Palgrave Macmillan, 2018), 129.

8. Quoted in Michelle Carbert, "Ottawa unveils new feminist foreign aid policy," *Globe and Mail*, 9 June 2017, https://www.theglobeandmail.com/news/politics/ottawa-unveils-new-feminism-focused-foreign-aid-policy/article35260311/.

9. Quoted in "Is the future of foreign policy feminist?" *Opencanada.org*, n.d., https://opencanada.org/indepth/future-foreign-policy-feminist/. See also Adam Chapnick, "The origins of Canada's feminist foreign policy," *International Journal* 74, no. 2 (2019): 191–205, https://doi.org/10.1177/0020702019850827.

10. Jocelyn Coulon, *Canada Is Not Back: How Justin Trudeau Is in Over His Head on Foreign Policy* (Toronto: Lorimer, 2019); Alex Marland, "The brand image of Canadian Prime Minister Justin Trudeau in international context," *Canadian Foreign Policy Journal* 24, no. 2 (2018): 139–44, https://doi.org/10.1080/11926422.2018.1461665; Marland and Richard Nimijean, "Rebranding brand Trudeau," in David Carment and Richard Nimijean, eds., *Political Turmoil in a Tumultuous World: Canada among Nations 2020* (Cham: Springer International Publishing, 2021), 55–76.

11. "Justin Trudeau at UN: 'We're Canadian. And we're here to help'," *Maclean's*, 20 September 2016, https://www.macleans.ca/news/canada/justin-trudeau-at-the-un-were-canadian-and-were-here-to-help/.

12. Sheryl Lightfoot, "A promise too far?" in Hillmer and Lagassé, *Justin Trudeau and Canadian Foreign Policy*, 165–86.

13. Adam Chapnick, "Canada's ill-fated quest for a UN Security Council seat," *Policy Options*, 19 June 2020, https://policyoptions.irpp.org/magazines/june-2020/ottawas-ill-fated-quest-for-a-un-security-council-seat/.

14. Quoted in Micah Zenko and Rebecca Friedman Lissner, "Trump is going to regret not having a grand strategy," *Foreign Policy*, 13 January 2017, https://foreignpolicy.com/2017/01/13/trump-is-going-to-regret-not-having-a-grand-strategy/.

15. Daniel Dale, "Daughter diplomacy: Trudeau's unorthodox play for Donald Trump's approval," *Toronto Star*, 16 March 2017, https://www.thestar.com/news/world/2017/03/16/daughter-diplomacy-trudeaus-unorthodox-play-for-donald-trumps-approval.html.

16. Ian Austin, "Justin Trudeau facing pressure to oppose Donald Trump, opts to get along," *The New York Times*, 3 February 2017, https://www.nytimes.com/2017/02/03/world/canada/canada-trudeau-trump.html.

17. Jacob Schlesinger and Peter Nicholas, "Trump drops NAFTA pullout threat," *Wall Street Journal*, 27 April 2017, https://www.wsj.com/articles/white-house-weighs-nafta-withdrawal-threat-1493240396.

NOTES TO PAGES 246–52   319

18. Alex Panetta, "Harper to Trudeau: Canada is 'napping on NAFTA,'" *Maclean's*, 27 October 2017, https://www.macleans.ca/politics/harper-to-trudeau-canada-is-napping-on-nafta/.
19. Aaron Wherry, *Promise and Peril: Justin Trudeau in Power* (Toronto: HarperCollins, 2019), 154–55.
20. Julian E. Barnes and Helene Cooper, "Trump discussed pulling US from NATO, aides say amid new concerns over Russia," *The New York Times*, 14 January 2019, https://www.nytimes.com/2019/01/14/us/politics/nato-president-trump.html.
21. Mary Papenfuss, "Justin Trudeau to Trump: Canada 'will not be pushed around,'" *Huffington Post*, 9 June 2018, https://www.huffpost.com/entry/justin-trudeau-vows-canada-wont-be-pushed-around-by-trump_n_5b1c49f0e4b0adfb826a02b4.
22. John Geddes and Shannon Proudfoot, "Don't mess with Canada," *Maclean's*, 1 August 2018, https://archive.macleans.ca/article/2018/8/1/dont-mess-with-canada
23. Ted Mellnik and Aaron Williams, "Is Canada 'ripping us off'? Or is it the best U.S. trade partner?" *Washington Post*, 21 September 2018, https://www.washingtonpost.com/graphics/2018/business/us-canada-trade-balance/.
24. Stuart Thomson, "Justin Trudeau accused of 'sabotaging' trade deal with meeting no-show," *National Post*, 10 November 2017, https://nationalpost.com/news/politics/justin-trudeau-accused-of-sabotaging-trade-deal-and-infuriating-world-leaders-with-meeting-no-show.
25. David Akin, "Trudeau admires China's 'basic dictatorship',", *Toronto Sun*, 8 November 2013, https://torontosun.com/2013/11/08/trudeau-admires-chinas-basic-dictatorship.
26. Giuseppe Valiante, "Chinese premier calls for 'new golden decade' with Canada," *Toronto Star*, 23 September 2016, https://www.thestar.com/news/canada/2016/09/23/chinese-premier-calls-for-new-golden-decade-with-canada.html.
27. David Mulroney, "Trudeau's embrace of China exposes his naïveté," *Globe and Mail*, 14 January 2017, https://www.theglobeandmail.com/opinion/trudeaus-embrace-of-china-exposes-his-naivete/article33619462/.
28. Meredith Lilly, "Hewers of wood and drawers of water 2.0: How American and Chinese economic nationalism influence Canadian trade policy in the twenty-first century," *Canadian Foreign Policy Journal*, 26, no. 2 (2020): 167–81, https://doi.org/10.1080/11926422.2020.1750444.
29. Joanna Chiu, *China Unbound: A New World Disorder* (Toronto: House of Anansi Press, 2021).
30. Canada, Department of National Defence, *Strong, Secure, Engaged: Canada's Defence Policy* (Ottawa: Minister of National Defence, 2017, https://www.canada.ca/en/department-national-defence/corporate/reports-publications/canada-defence-policy.html; Canada, House of Commons, *Debates*, 42nd Parliament, 1st session, 6 June 2017, https://www.ourcommons.ca/Document Viewer/en/42-1/house/sitting-188/hansard.
31. Philippe Lagassé and Srdjan Vucetic, "Coronavirus shows why Canada must reduce its dependence on the US," *The Conversation*, 4 May 2020, https://theconversation.com/coronavirus-shows-why-canada-must-reduce-its-dependence-on-the-u-s-136357.
32. Leah West, Thomas Juneau, and Amarnath Amarasingam, *Stress Tested: The COVID-19 Pandemic and Canadian National Security* (Calgary: University of Calgary Press, 2021), https://press.ucalgary.ca/books/9781773852430/.
33. Ellen Gutterman and Andrea Lane, "Beyond LAVs: Corruption, commercialization, and the Canadian defence industry," *Canadian Foreign Policy Journal* 23, no. 1 (2017): 81–2, https://doi.org/10.1080/11926422.2016.1254663; Canadian Association of Defence and Security Industries, "Study of Canada's Defence Industry, 2014," n.d., http://www.defenceandsecurity.ca/UserFiles/File/Presentations/StateOfDefenceIndustry/State%20of%20Canada's%20Defence%20Industry%202014.pdf, 1, 10, 11.
34. Gutterman and Lane, "Beyond LAVs," 78.
35. Thomas Juneau, "Canada and Saudi Arabia: A deeply flawed but necessary partnership," Canadian Global Affairs Institute *Policy Paper* (July 2016): 2, https://www.cgai.ca/canada_and_saudi_arabia; Jennifer Pederson, "'We will honour our good name': The Trudeau government, arms exports, and human rights," in Hillmer and Lagassé, *Justin Trudeau and Canadian Foreign Policy*, 209.
36. Sonal Marwah, "Arms and forced displacement: The case of the Canada-Saudi Arabia arms deal," *Ploughshares Monitor* 38, no. 2 (2017): 9–10, https://ploughshares.ca/wp-content/uploads/2017/06/ProjectPloughsharesMonitorSummer2017FINALweb.pdf.
37. Pederson, "'We will honour our good name',", in Hillmer and Lagassé, *Justin Trudeau and Canadian Foreign Policy*, 209–10; Gutterman and Lane, "Beyond LAVs," 80–1.
38. Daniel Jean to Stéphane Dion [DM to Minister], Memorandum for Action, "Export of light armoured vehicles and weapons systems to Saudi Arabia," 21 March 2016, BPTS:

320 NOTES TO PAGES 252–5

00013–2016, https://www.international.gc.ca/controls-controles/assets/pdfs/documents/Memorandum_for_Action-eng.pdf. Quotation from p. 4.

39. Mike Blanchfield, *Swingback: Getting Along in the World with Harper and Trudeau* (Montreal: McGill-Queen's University Press, 2017), 237.

40. Maclean's, "Stéphane Dion: On 'responsible conviction' and Liberal foreign policy," *Macleans*, 29 March 2016, https://www.macleans.ca/politics/ottawa/stephane-dion-how-ethics-inspires-liberal-foreign-policy/.

41. Pederson, "'We will honour our good name,'" in Hillmer and Lagassé, *Justin Trudeau and Canadian Foreign Policy*, 211–3; Blanchfield, *Swingback*, 237–8.

42. Cesar Jaramillo, "Canada and Saudi Arabia: An arms deal no matter what," *Ploughshares Monitor* 39, no. 1 (2018): 3, https://ploughshares.ca/wp-content/uploads/2019/04/PloughsharesMonitorSpring2018WEB2.pdf; Pederson, "'We will honour our good name,'" in Hillmer and Lagassé, *Justin Trudeau and Canadian Foreign Policy*, 214–20; confidential interviews. On the House debate, see Canada, House of Commons, *Debates*, 42nd Parliament, 1st session, vol. 148, no. 84, 29 September 2016, 5250–5317, https://www.ourcommons.ca/DocumentViewer/en/41/house/sitting-84/hansard.

43. Global Affairs Canada, "Final Report: Review of Export Permits to Saudi Arabia," n.d., 2019, 21, https://www.international.gc.ca/trade-commerce/assets/pdfs/memo/saudi-arabia-export-permits-exportation-licences-arabie-saoudite-EN.pdf; Jaramillo, "Canada and Saudi Arabia," 3.

44. Srdjan Vucetic, "A nation of feminist arms dealers? Canada and military exports," *International Journal* 72, no. 4 (2017): 518, https://doi.org/10.1177/0020702017740156; Srdjan Vucetic, "What joining the Arms Trade Treaty means for Canada," *Open Canada*, 19 April 2017, https://opencanada.org/what-joining-arms-trade-treaty-means-canada/; Jaramillo, "Canada and Saudi Arabia," 4. On the debate over the legislation, see Openparliament.ca, "Bill C-47 (historical)," https://openparliament.ca/bills/42-1/C-47/?tab=major-speeches&singlepage=1.

45. Thomas Juneau, "A surprising spat: The causes and consequences of the Saudi-Canadian dispute," *International Journal* 74, no. 2 (2019): 315–6, https://doi.org/10.1177/0020702019855347; confidential sources.

46. Grant Dawson, "Classical realism, status, and emotions: Understanding the Canada / Saudi Arabia dispute and its implications for global politics," *Global Studies Quarterly* 1, no. 4 (2021): 1–11, https://doi.org/10.1093/isagsq/ksab027; Juneau, "A surprising spat," 316.

47. Steven Chase, "Trudeau says Canada trying to end arms contract with Saudi Arabia," *Globe and Mail*, 16 December 2018, https://www.theglobeandmail.com/politics/article-trudeau-says-canada-trying-to-end-arms-export-deal-to-saudi-arabia/.

48. John Hannaford and Marta Morgan, "Memorandum for Information," BPTS: 03575–2019, 17 September 2019, 1, https://www.international.gc.ca/trade-commerce/assets/pdfs/controls-controles/arms-export-saudi-arabia_exportations-armes-arabie-saoudite_eng.pdf.

49. Global Affairs Canada, "Final Report," 5, 8, 18, 22.

50. Murray Brewster, "Canada strikes new deal with Saudi Arabia, clearing way for armoured vehicle sales," *CBC News*, 9 April 2020, https://www.cbc.ca/news/politics/canada-saudi-arabia-lav-1.5528460.

51. Juneau, "Canada and Saudi Arabia," 4–5.

52. Juneau, "A surprising spat," 321–2.

53. Gutterman and Lane, "Beyond LAVs," 84.

54. Steven Chase, "Advocates push for independent review into use of Canadian-made armoured vehicles in Saudi Arabia," *Globeand Mail*, 5 July 2018, https://www.theglobeandmail.com/politics/article-advocates-push-for-independent-review-into-use-of-canadian-made/; Jeremy Wildeman and Anthony Fenton, "Trading values to sell weapons: The Canada-Saudi relationship," *The Conversation* 17 October 2019, https://theconversation.com/trading-values-to-sell-weapons-the-canada-saudi-relationship-124961.

55. Global Affairs Canada, "The Canada-United States-Mexico Agreement: Economic Impact Assessment," 26 February 2020, 2, https://www.international.gc.ca/trade-commerce/assets/pdfs/agreements-accords/cusma-aceum/CUSMA-impact-repercussion-en.pdf.

56. Gilbert Gagné and Michèle Rioux, "Introduction," in Gilbert Gagné and Michèle Rioux, eds., *NAFTA 2.0* (Cham: Palgrave Macmillan, 2021), 5.

57. Greg Anderson, "Canada and the United States in the Harper years," in Adam Chapnick and Christopher J. Kukucha, eds., *The Harper Era in Canadian Foreign Policy: Parliament, Politics, and Canada's Global Posture* (Vancouver and Toronto: UBC Press, 2016), 144.

NOTES TO PAGES 255–9 321

58. Mike Blanchfield, "Will Canada and Mexico stick together on NAFTA?" *Maclean's*, 10 May 2017, https://www.macleans.ca/politics/will-canada-and-mexico-stick-together-on-nafta/. See also Colin Robertson, "In NAFTA talks, Canada and Mexico need to stick together," *Globe and Mail*, 23 May 2018, https://www.theglobeandmail.com/opinion/article-in-nafta-talks-canada-and-mexico-need-to-stick-together/.

59. Wherry, *Promise and Peril*, 124.

60. Laura Macdonald, "Stronger together? Canada-Mexico relations and the NAFTA re-negotiations," *Canadian Foreign Policy Journal* 26, no. 2 (2020): 159, https://doi.org/10.1080/11926422.2019.1698442.

61. EFE News Service, Madrid, "Canada: We will not sacrifice Mexico in NAFTA renegotiation," 22 February 2017.

62. Champagne, quoted in Macdonald, "Stronger together?" 160.

63. Dave Graham, "How Trump split Mexico and Canada in NAFTA talks," *Reuters*, 25 September 2018, https://www.reuters.com/article/us-trade-nafta-mexico-insight-idUSKCN1M51F6; Macdonald, "Stronger together?" 163.

64. Alex Brinkley, "Canada, Mexico ponder a NAFTA without the US," *Ontario Farmer*, 19 December 2017, A22.

65. John Geddes, "How NAFTA was saved: The bitter fight and the final breakthrough," *Maclean's*, 1 October 2018, https://www.macleans.ca/news/canada/how-nafta-was-saved-the-bitter-fight-and-last-minute-recovery/; John Ivison, *Trudeau: The Education of a Prime Minister* (Toronto: Penguin, 2019), 246; Adrian Morrow, Barrie McKenna, and Stephanie Nolen, "From NAFTA to USMCA: Inside the tense negotiations that saved North American trade," *Globe and Mail*, 5 October 2018, https://www.theglobeandmail.com/business/article-from-nafta-to-usmca-inside-the-tense-negotiations-that-saved-north/

66. Morrow, McKenna, and Nolen, "From NAFTA to USMCA."

67. Adrian Morrow and Stephanie Nolen, "Why Mexico stabbed Canada in the back in NAFTA negotiations," *Globe and Mail*, 8 September 2018, https://www.theglobeandmail.com/business/article-why-mexico-stabbed-canada-in-the-back-in-nafta-negotiations/; Morrow, McKenna, and Nolen, "From NAFTA to USMCA"; Wherry, *Promise and Peril*, 138–9.

68. Morrow and Nolen, "Why Mexico stabbed Canada in the back"; Morrow, McKenna, and Nolen, "From NAFTA to USMCA"; Wherry, *Promise and Peril*, 146.

69. Graham, "How Trump split Mexico and Canada."

70. Morrow and Nolen, "Why Mexico stabbed Canada in the back"; MacDonald, "Stronger together?" 161; Wherry, *Promise and Peril*, 147.

71. It wasn't just the Canadians. See Andrés Rozental, "Mexico and Canada must stand together on NAFTA," *Globe and Mail*, 29 August 2018, https://www.theglobeandmail.com/opinion/article-mexico-and-canada-must-stand-together-on-nafta/.

72. Morrow, McKenna, and Nolen, "From NAFTA to USMCA"; Wherry, *Promise and Peril*, 148.

73. Geddes, "How NAFTA was saved"; MacDonald, "Stronger together?" 162.

74. Wherry, *Promise and Peril*, 160–1.

75. Josh Wingrove, Jennifer Jacobs, and Eric Martin, "How the U.S. and Canada ended their feud and clinched a NAFTA deal," *Fortune*, 3 October 2018, https://fortune.com/2018/10/03/nafta-usmca-trump-kushner-canada-mexico/.

76. M. Angeles Villarreal and Ian F. Fergusson, "NAFTA and the United States-Mexico-Canada Agreement (USMCA)," Congressional Research Service, *CRS Report* R44981 (updated 2 March 2020), 13.

77. Rozental, "Mexico and Canada must stand together."

78. Danielle Gilbert and Gaëlle Rivard Piché, "Caught between giants: Hostage diplomacy and negotiation strategy for middle powers," *Texas National Security Review* 5, no. 1 (2021–22): 13, 22, https://doi.org/10.15781/4n39-ja85.

79. Jeremy Paltiel, "Facing China: Canada between fear and hope," *International Journal* 73, no. 3 (2018): 352, https://doi.org/10.1177/0020702018792908.

80. Shannon Proudfoot, John Geddes, Paul Wells, Claire Brownell, Aaron Hutchins, and Jason Markusoff, "Huawei's Meng Wanzhou: The world's most wanted woman," *Maclean's*, 4 February 2019, https://www.macleans.ca/news/canada/huaweis-meng-wanzhou-the-worlds-most-wanted-woman/; Mike Blanchfield and Fen Osler Hampson, *The Two Michaels* (Toronto: Sutherland House, 2021), 2–3, 121.

81. Proudfoot, "Huawei's Meng Wanzhou,"; Blanchfield, *Two Michaels*, 2–3, 14–8.

322 NOTES TO PAGES 259–68

82. Quoted in Proudfoot, "Huawei's Meng Wanzhou."
83. Quoted in Blanchfield, *Two Michaels*, 21.
84. Le Yucheng, quoted in Proudfoot, "Huawei's Meng Wanzhou."
85. Peter Humphrey, "The cruel fate of Michael Kovrig and Michael Spavor in China," *The Diplomat*, 10 December 2019, https://thediplomat.com/2019/12/the-cruel-fate-of-michael-kovrig-and-michael-spavor-in-china/.
86. Blanchfield, *Two Michaels*, 160; Roland Paris, "Alone in the world? Making sense of Canada's disputes with Saudi Arabia and China," *International Journal* 74, no. 1 (2019): 155–6, https://doi.org/10.1177/0020702019834652.
87. Marta Morgan to Christine Holke, 5 February 2020, Annex 1: Canada's approach to China, https://www.ourcommons.ca/content/Committee/431/CACN/WebDoc/WD10653524/431_CACN_reldoc_PDF/DepartmentOfForeignAffairsTradeAndDevelopment-1-e.pdf, 2.
88. Paris, "Alone in the world?" 156.
89. Proudfoot, "Huawei's Meng Wanzhou"; Blanchfield, *Two Michaels*, 82.
90. Proudfoot, "Huawei's Meng Wanzhou."
91. Global Affairs Canada, *Declaration against Arbitrary Detention in State-to-State Relations*, https://www.international.gc.ca/news-nouvelles/assets/pdfs/arbitrary_detention-detention_arbitraire-declaration-en.pdf; Blanchfield, *Two Michaels*, 210.
92. Blanchfield, *Two Michaels*, 110, 211–2; Proudfoot, "Huawei's Meng Wanzhou."
93. Blanchfield, *Two Michaels*, 123–6, 133; Proudfoot, "Huawei's Meng Wanzhou."
94. Blanchfield, *Two Michaels*, 165, 174–83.
95. Blanchfield, *Two Michaels*, 183–8, 193–5.
96. Louise Arbour et al., "A Letter to the Prime Minister of Canada," 23 June 2020, s3.documentcloud.org/documents/6956527/Letter-to-Prime-Minister.pdf, 4.
97. Trudeau, quoted in Blanchfield, *Two Michaels*, 195; Christopher W. Bishop, "Dealing with China: Lessons learned from three case studies," Canadian Global Affairs Institute *Policy Paper* (September 2020): 3, https://www.cgai.ca/dealing_with_china_lessons_learned_from_three_case_studies. His comments were consistent with his earlier refusal to negotiate the release of two Canadian hostages abducted in the Philippines.
98. Patricia Adams et al., "Canada must reject calls to release Meng Wanzhou," 26 June 2000, https://macdonaldlaurier.ca/canada-must-reject-calls-release-meng-wanzhou-open-letter-prime-minister-trudeau/. Italics in the original.
99. Bishop, "Dealing with China," 4.
100. Blanchfield, *Two Michaels*, 139, 248.
101. Blanchfield, *Two Michaels*, 244–5, 250.
102. Blanchfield, *Two Michaels*, 250–2; Gilbert, "Caught between giants," 21.
103. Global Affairs Canada, "Minister Joly speaks with China's Foreign Minister Wang Yi," *Readout*, 5 April 2022, https://www.canada.ca/en/global-affairs/news/2022/04/minister-joly-speaks-with-chinas-foreign-minister-wang-yi.html.
104. Global Affairs Canada, "Address by Minister Freeland on Canada's foreign policy priorities," 6 June 2017, https://www.canada.ca/en/global-affairs/news/2017/06/address_by_minister freelandoncanadas foreignpolicypriorities.html.
105. Global Affairs Canada, "Address by Minister Freeland when receiving *Foreign Policy*'s Diplomat of the Year Award," 13 June 2018, https://www.canada.ca/en/global-affairs/news/2018/06/address-by-minister-freeland-when-receiving-foreign-policys-diplomat-of-the-year-award.html.
106. Government of Canada, "Canada-U.S. Safe Third Country Agreement," last updated 23 July 2020, https://www.canada.ca/en/immigration-refugees-citizenship/corporate/mandate/policies-operational-instructions-agreements/agreements/safe-third-country-agreement.html.

Conclusion

1. Women and Gender Equality Canada, "Gender-based Analysis Plus (GBA+)," last modified 13 October 2022, https://women-gender-equality.canada.ca/en/gender-based-analysis-plus.html.; Office of the Auditor General of Canada, *2022 Reports of the Auditor General of Canada to the Parliament of Canada*, Report 3 – Follow-up on Gender-based Analysis Plus (Ottawa: Auditor General of Canada, 2022), https://www.oag-bvg.gc.ca/internet/English/parl_oag_202205_03_e_44035.html.

NOTES TO PAGES 268–71   323

2. Cooperation Canada, "About Cooperation Canada," accessed 26 May 2023, https://cooperation.ca/about/.

3. Canadian International Council, *Foreign Policy by Canadians*, accessed 26 May 2023, https://thecic.org/research/foreign-policy-by-canadians/.

4. On defence, see, for example, The Canadian Defence and Security Network, accessed 26 May 2023, https://www.cdsn-rcds.com/ and the Conference of Defence Associations (CDA) Institute, "About us," accessed 26 May 2023, https://cdainstitute.ca/about-us/. On citizenship and immigration, see the Institute for Canadian Citizenship, "Our approach," accessed 26 May 2023, https://inclusion.ca/about/ and the Canadian Council for Refugees, "About the Canadian Council for Refugees," accessed 26 May 2023, https://ccrweb.ca/en/about-ccr.

5. Public Safety Canada, *National Cyber Security Strategy: Canada's Vision for Security and Prosperity in the Digital Age* (Ottawa: Public Safety Canada, 2018).

6. Public Safety Canada, "Research security information update," May 2021, https://www.publicsafety.gc.ca/cnt/rsrcs/pblctns/2021-rsi-psr-ma/index-en.aspx. On Canada's International Education Strategy, see Global Affairs Canada, *Building on Success: International Education Strategy 2019–2024* (Ottawa: Global Affairs Canada, 2019), https://www.international.gc.ca/education/strategy-2019-2024-strategie.aspx?lang=eng.

7. Government of Saskatchewan, *Water Security Agency*, "Overview," accessed 26 May 2023, https://www.wsask.ca/about/overview/; Water Canada, "Canada Water Agency: Keeping our waters clean, now and into the future," 25 May 2023, https://www.watercanada.net/canada-water-agency-water-clean/; John McKay, *A Secure and Sovereign Arctic: Report of the Standing Committee on National Defence*, 44th Parliament, 1st session, April 2023, https://www.ourcommons.ca/DocumentViewer/en/44-1/NDDN/report-3/.

8. Department of Finance Canada, *Canada's Anti-Money Laundering and Anti-Terrorist Financing Regime Strategy 2023–2026* (Ottawa: Department of Finance Canada, 2023), https://www.canada.ca/en/department-finance/programs/financial-sector-policy/canadas-anti-money-laundering-and-anti-terrorist-financing-regime-strategy-2023-2026.html.

9. Government of Canada, "Responsible use of artificial intelligence (AI)," last modified 25 April 2023, https://www.canada.ca/en/government/system/digital-government/digital-government-innovations/responsible-use-ai.html.

10. For a summary of the state of the department, see Global Affairs Canada, *Deputy Minister of Foreign Affairs Briefing Book*, October 2022, https://www.international.gc.ca/transparency-transparence/briefing-documents-information/briefing-books-cahiers-breffage/2022-10-uss.aspx?lang=eng#6.

11. Ulric Shannon, "Competitive expertise and future diplomacy: Subject-matter specialization in generalist foreign ministries," *CIPS Policy Report*, August 2022, https://www.cips-cepi.ca/competitive-expertise-and-future-diplomacy-subject-matter-specialization-in-generalist-foreign-ministries/.

12. Annabel Hendry, "From parallel to dual careers: Diplomatic spouses," *Diplo*, 1988, https://www.diplomacy.edu/resource/from-parallel-to-dual-careers-diplomatic-spouses/.

13. Denis Stairs, "Canada in the 1990s: Speak loudly and carry a bent twig," *Policy Options*, 1 January 2001, https://policyoptions.irpp.org/magazines/2001-odyssee-espace/canada-in-the-1990s-speak-loudly-and-carry-a-bent-twig/.

14. John Monahan, Rima Berns-McGown, and Michael Morden, "The perception & reality of 'imported conflict' in Canada" The Mosaic Institute's *Kanishka Project*, March 2014, https://old.mosaicinstitute.ca/research/perceptions--realities-of-imported-conflict-1.

Index

Since the index has been created to work across multiple formats, indexed terms for which a page range is given (e.g., 52–53, 66–70, etc.) may occasionally appear only on some, but not all of the pages within the range.

9/11, *see* September 11 terrorist attacks

Abbott, Douglas 65
Abella, Irving 55–6
Aberhart, William 28
abortion 106, 124, 234, 245
Abyssinia (Ethiopia), invasion of 1–3, 6, 35–6
Acheson, Dean 51–3
acid rain 153–4, 165–7, 170
Ackerman, Spencer 216
Adam, Christopher 80–1
Adams, Michael 201
Adams, Patricia 263–4
Adeleke, Ademola 78–9
advertising 122
Afghanistan
   Canada's role in 205, 212–15, 221–4
   readings on 217, 239–40
   refugees 245–6
   war in 133, 200–2
African Emergency Aid 160
Akita, Shigeru 78–9
Alaska 14–16
   Canadian claim on 15–16
al-Assad, Bashar 222
Albania 191
Alberta 134
   and Kyoto Protocol 208
   oil 143–6, 227
   political priorities 4–5
Alberta Energy Company 143–4
al-Qaeda 199–200
American Jewish Joint Distribution Committee 47
Anastakis, Dimitry 120–1
Andersen-Rodgers, David 194
Anderson, Antony 80–1
Andrew, Arthur 81, 84–5, 150
Angell, David 196–7
Anglin, Douglas G. 83
Anglo-Japanese Treaty of Commerce and Navigation (1894) 19–20
Anglo-Russian Treaty of St Petersburg (1825) 15–16

Angola 182, 188, 196
anti-nuclear activism 88–9
anti-semitism 46–8
Anti-Terrorism Act 199–200
anti-war movement 109–10
apartheid in South Africa 86–7, 91, 94–7, 155, 168–9
Applebaum, Bob 194
Arab League 141, 225
Arab Spring 222
Arar, Maher 199–200
Arbour, Louise 260, 263–4
Arcand, Adrien 35
Archambault, Peter 105
Arctic
   and climate change 224
   DEW line 67–8, 71–4, 79–80
   Northwest Passage 127–8, 134, 137–40, 154
   readings on 239–40
   security 224, 268–9
   sovereignty 137, 154
Arctic Cooperation Agreement 154
Arctic Waters Pollution Prevention Act 139
Argentina 42
Aristide, Jean-Bertrand 177, 203
Aronsen, Lawrence 54–5
Arthur-Lackenbauer, Jennifer 79–80
artificial intelligence 268–9
Asia Watch 187
Asia-Pacific Economic Cooperation (APEC) 154–5
Asiatic Exclusion League 19–20
Assembly of First Nations 131
Atlantic Richfield 138
Australia
   Canadian mission in 17, 42
   and China 259–60
   Five Eyes Intelligence alliance 270
   foreign aid programs 65
   Kyoto Protocol 206
   UNDRIP 229–32
   United Nations 57
Austria 37, 188
Auto Pact 109, 116–18

326 INDEX

Automotive Products Trade Agreement 109, 116–18
automotive tariffs 109, 247, 255–6
Avro Arrow 88
Axis of Evil 200–1
Axworthy, Lloyd 178–9, 182, 187–9, 191–2, 195
Axworthy, Thomas S. 148–9
Ayres, Jeffrey M. 169–70
Azzi, Stephen 123, 210, 219

Baird, John 220, 224–6, 235–7
Baker, James 164
Balewa, Abubakar Tafawa 95–6
Balfour, Arthur 27
Ball, George 109
ballistic missile defence (BMD) 218
Bangarth, Stephanie 80–1
barbaric cultural practices hotline 228
Barnes, Alan 217
Barqueiro, Carla 195
Barros, James 82
Barry, Donald 6–7, 194
Bartleman, James 182–3
Bay of Pigs 89
Bechthold, Mike 32–3
Beesley, Alan 139
Begin, Menachem 141
Belgium 42, 113–14, 188
Bennett, R.B. 1, 3
    and communist threat 27–8
    and Department of External
        Affairs 29
    economic policy 27–8
    at Imperial Conference 27
    view on foreign service 220
Bennett, W.A.C. 108
Bercuson, David J. 81
Berger, Carl 32
Bernard, Montague 14
Berry, Philip A. 242
Berton, Pierre 111
Betcherman, Lita-Rose 6
Bevin, Ernest 51
Bialystok, Franklin 55–6
Bibeau, Marie-Claude 245
Biden, Joe 261
bilingualism 107, 131–2, 269
bin Salman, Mohammed 253–4
Bin, Su 257–8
Black, David R. 240–1
Blair, Doug 47–8
Blair, Frederick 45–7
Blair, Tony 176–7, 198, 200–1, 209–10

Blake, Raymond B. 169–70
Blanchette, Arthur E. 147
Blanchfield, Mike 238, 263–4
Bloc Québécois 157–8, 168, 173–4
Bones, Alan 148
Bonino, Emma 185–6
Borden, Robert
    1911 election campaign 20
    conscription 22
    First World War 21–4
    trade with US 21
    Paris peace talks 26
    reorganization of Department of External
        Affairs 18
borders 9–10
    and trade 11
    Canada-United States 4, 11–12, 15, 199, 226–7, 249
    with Alaska 15–16
Borstelmann, Thomas 147
Bosnia-Herzegovina 156, 190–1
Bothwell, Robert 6–7, 33–4, 56, 78, 81, 116, 136, 147
Bouchard, Charles 222
Bouchard, Lucien 173–4
Boucher, Jean-Christophe 7–8
Boundary Waters Treaty
    (1909) 17–18
Bourassa, Henri 22
Bow, Brian 7–8, 147–9, 217
Bowell, Mackenzie 17
Bowman, Joshua 242
Boyd, Monica 265–6
Boyle, Peter C. 80–1
Bracht, Caroline 240–1
Bradley, Mark Philip 120
Bradley, Omar 92
Brands, Hal 262
Brazil 42
Brexit 243
Britain, see United Kingdom
British Columbia 4–5, 14–16, 19–20, 108
British Commonwealth Air Training
    Plan 38
British North America Act 13, 112
Brown, Chris 196–7
Brown, J.C. Gordon 81
Brownell, Claire 263–4
Bryce, James 18, 216–17
Bryce, Robert 56, 95, 97
Buckner, Phillip 30–2, 120–1
Burek, Michael 159–60
Burney, Derek 164

INDEX 327

Bush, George H.W. 151–2
  environment 154, 167
  Iraq-Kuwait conflict 170–1
  readings on 169
Bush, George W. 198–9, 216
  invasion of Iraq 209–12
  and Kyoto Protocol 207–8
  readings on 216
  and Stephen Harper 226–7
  War on Terror 200–1, 216

Cadieux, Léo 135–7
Cadieux, Marcel 113–14, 116, 136–7
Callan, Les 66
Cambodia 133, 156
Cameron, Maxwell A. 194–5
Campbell, Isabel 103
Campbell, John C. 80–1
Campbell, Kim 157–8
Campbell, Lara A. 120–1
Campbell-Miller, Jill 78–9
Canada Assistance Plan 106
Canada Corps 203
Canada Pension Plan 106
Canada
  academic study of 128
  autonomy from Britain 23, 26–7,
    29–30, 110–11
  citizenship 65–7
  confederation 9, 12, 31
  demographics 4
  establishment of foreign service 16–18
  flag 110
  future of 267–71
  geography 4
  identity 23–5, 32, 53–4
  as middle power 74–7
Canada-China Business Council 178
Canada-China Legislative Association 178
Canada-European Union Comprehensive
  Economic and Trade Agreement
  (CETA) 244–5, 247–8
Canada-Israel Committee (CIC) 141
Canada-United States Air Quality
  Agreement 165–7
Canada-United States-Mexico Agreement
  (CUSMA) 247
Canadian Alliance for Trade and Job
  Opportunities 164
Canadian Alliance (Party) 201–3, 210
Canadian Association for Adult Education 29
Canadian Border Services Agency 199–200
Canadian Coalition on Acid Rain
  (CCAR) 165–6

Canadian Committee for the Control of
  Radiation Hazards 88–9
Canadian Commonwealth Federation 36
Canadian Institute of International Affairs 29,
  136, 268
Canadian International Council 268
Canadian International Development Agency
  (CIDA) 129, 160, 203, 213, 233
  amalgamation with DFAIT 221,
    229, 241–2
Canadian Jewish Congress 47
Canadian Meteorological Service 71
Canadian Security Intelligence Service
  (CSIS) 199–200
Canadian University Service Overseas
  (CUSO) 85
Canadian Youth Congress 29
Cannon, Lawrence 234
capital punishment 106
Card, Andrew 201, 209
Cardinal, Harold 130–1
Carlucci, Frank 154
Carment, David 7–8, 241
Carmichael, Logan 242
Carney, Pat 163, 169–70
Carroll, Francis M. 30–1
Carroll, Michael K. 80–1
Carter, Sarah 31–2
cartoons, political 3, 24, 40, 66, 90, 117, 251
Castro, Fidel 88, 128–9, 178
Cavell, Janice 102–3
Cavell, Richard 82
Cellucci, Paul 199, 201, 211–12, 217, 219
Ceylon 59–60, 95
Chalk, Frank 195
Chamberlain, Neville 37
Champagne, François-Philippe 253–5, 259–60
Chapnick, Adam 7–8, 57–8, 78, 172, 194–7
Charlton, Mark W. 169
Charter of Rights and Freedoms 132
child health 224–5, 228, 232–5, 240–1
Childs, Marquis 116
Chile 42
Chilton, Lisa 32
China 149
China
  Canadian mission in 42, 174–5
  civil war 62
  elections interference 267
  human rights 174–5, 178
  immigration to Canada 18–19
  invasion by Japan 28, 36
  Korean War 61–4
  readings on 262

328 INDEX

China (*Continued*)
  recognizing People's Republic of China
    (PRC) 126–7, 134, 149
  and Taiwan 61, 149
  tensions with 248–51, 257–61
  Tibet 130
  as trade partner 225–6, 239, 248–9
  and United Nations 57
Chinese Head Tax 18–19
Chirac, Jacques 173–4, 198
Chollet, Derek 194
Chrétien, Jean
  anti-landmine work 188
  ballistic missile defence (BMD) 218
  China 260
  free trade 174–6
  human rights 178–9
  Kyoto Protocol 207–9
  national defence 180–1
  on poverty 198
  as prime minister 157–8, 173–8, 181, 193,
    198, 215
  readings on 217
  September 11 attacks 198–200
  Turbot War 185–6
  war in Iraq 209–12
  writings of 216–17
Christie, Loring 22–3
Churchill, Winston 39, 41, 48
Civil Marriage Act 202–3
Clark, Clifford 49, 56
Clark, James "Champ" 21
Clark, Joe
  and apartheid 155
  as foreign minister 160, 162
  Gulf War 156–7
  and Israel 134, 140–3
  as prime minister 133
  readings on 148
  as secretary of state for external affairs
    151–2
Clarkson, Stephen 166
Clavin, Patricia 33
Clean Air Act 167
Clément, Dominique 120–1
Climate Action Network 207
climate crisis 154, 224–5, 243–4, 267
  Kyoto Protocol 205–9, 216–17, 224–5
  readings on 216, 239–40
Clinton, Bill 173–4, 176–8, 187, 207
Clinton, Hillary 199, 234
Coastal Fisheries Protection Act 183
Coates, Ken S. 240

Coelho, Manuel Pacheco 194
Cohen, Andrew 78
Cold War 44, 60–4, 87–91, 189–90
  DEW line 67–8, 71–4, 79–80
  end of 155–7
  and foreign aid programs 68
  readings on 54–5, 78, 100–3
Coll, Steve 216
Colombia 226
Colombo Plan 65, 68–71, 78–9
colonial expansion 9–10, 14–15
Combined Food Board 39–41
Combined Production and Resources Board
    39–41
Combined Universities Campaign for Nuclear
    Disarmament 88–9
Commonwealth
  Canada's role 110, 155, 269–70
  economic ties 86–7
  and foreign aid programs 68–9
  response to South African apartheid 91, 94–7
  see also United Kingdom
communism
  as global issue 61, 63–4, 68–9
  readings on 82
  threat to Canada 27–8, 78–9, 86–7
  see also Cold War
Compagnie Universelle du Canal Maritime de
    Suez 74–5
Comprehensive and Progressive Agreement for
    Trans-Pacific Partnership
    (CPTPP) 247–8
confederation 9, 12, 31
conflict diamonds 179, 182, 196
Congo 87
conscription 4–5, 22
Conservative Party of Canada 202–3, 220
constitution, patriation of 132
contraception 234
Convention of 1818 11–12
Convention on Long-Range Transboundary
    Air Pollution 165
Cook, Tim 32–3, 54–5
Cooper, Andrew F. 6–7
Cooperation Canada 268
Co-operative Commonwealth Federation
    28, 51–2
Cotton, James 57–8
Courville, Serge 32
COVID-19 249–50, 259–60, 262, 267
Crawford, Kerry 194
Crerar, Thomas 46–7
Crimea, invasion of 228, 236–7

INDEX 329

Croatia 156
Cross, James 132
Cuba
  Canadian mission in 42
  Cold War 89
  Cuban missile crisis 89, 91, 99, 103–4
  human rights 178
  and Jewish refugees 47
  post-Cold War 177–8
  revolution 88
  as trade partner 88
Cuff, R.D. 56
Cunningham, Jack 217
cyber-security 268–9
Czech Republic 181
Czechoslovakia 37–8
  invasion of 44, 136
  Prague Spring 126

Dafoe, J.W. 26
Daladier, Édouard 37
Dalai Lama 225
Dallaire, Roméo 180, 195
Dallek, Robert 54
Darfur 203
Daschuk, James 31–2
Dashwood, Hevina S. 195
Davis, Bill 166
Davis, Jonathan 168–9
de Gaulle, Charles 107, 112
debt relief 203
Declaration against Arbitrary
  Detention 259–60
decolonization 64–5, 78, 112
Defence Production Sharing Agreement 109
demographics 4
Deng Xiaoping 127
Department of External Affairs
  (DEA) 8, 18, 269
Department of Foreign Affairs and
  International Trade (DFAIT),
  amalgamation with CIDA 221,
  229, 241–2
Department of Foreign Affairs, Trade, and
  Development (DFATD) 221, 241–2
Depression, see Great Depression
Deskaheh 25
Devanny, Joe 242
DEW line, see Distant Early Warning
  (DEW) line
Dewalt, Bryan 78–9
diamonds, conflict 179, 182, 196
Diana, Princess 188

Diefenbaker, John
  Cold War 87–91
  Cuban Missile Crisis 103–4
  defeat of 97
  memoirs 101–2
  and NORAD 92–4
  and nuclear weapons 90, 97–100
  as prime minister 84–6, 89–91, 100
  readings on 100–3, 105
  and South Africa 94–7
  view on foreign service 220
Dion, Stéphane 243–4, 246–7, 252–3,
  262–3
Dirks, Gerald E. 55–6, 80–1
disinformation 268–9
Distant Early Warning (DEW) line 67–8,
  71–4, 79–80
Dixon, David 30–1
Doctrine, Gérin-Lajoie 112–14
Dodds, Klaus 239–40
Doern, G. Bruce 148–9, 169–70, 240–1
Donaghy, Greg 6–7, 78–82, 101–2, 109,
  120–3
Dowie, Mitchell C.G. 241
Doyle, Simon 195
Draper, Robert 216
Drummond, Ian M. 54–5
Dubinsky, Karen 7–8
Dubow, Saul 168–9
Duffin, Jaclyn 262
Dulles, John Foster 62, 93
Dumbarton Oaks proposals (1944) 57
Duplessis, Maurice 107
Dutil, Patrice 6–7, 31
Dymond, Bill 169–70

Eaton, Mark Andrew 103
Eayrs, James 6–7, 57–8
Eckel, Jan 147
economic diplomacy 225–6, 239
Eden, Anthony 75
Edmonds, Robert 150
Education
  international students 268–9
  as provincial jurisdiction 113
  Quebec context 113
  student loans 106
Egervari, Tibor 80–1
Egypt 59–60, 65–7, 74–7
Eisenhower, Dwight 63–4
  and nuclear weapons 99
  DEW line 73–4
  relationship with Diefenbaker 87–8

330 INDEX

elections
  (1878) 20–1
  (1911) 20–1
  (1917) 22
  (1930) 27
  (1940) 38
  (1945) 43
  (1957) 77, 84
  (1958) 85
  (1963) 89–90, 99–100, 106, 122
  (1965) 119
  (1968) 131–2, 135
  (1979) 140–3
  (1984) 162
  (1988) 153–4, 164, 168–70
  (1993) 157–8, 183
  (1994, Quebec) 173–4
  (2004) 202–3
  (2006) 231
  (2015) 226–8, 243
  (2021) 245–6
  interference in 267–9
  monitoring 60–1, 203–5, 238
  South Africa 94–5
  United States 145, 216, 245–6, 250
Elizabeth II, Queen 132
Emanuel, Kerry 216
Embargoes
  against Canada 142, 248
  against Cuba 88, 178
  oil 142–3
  against Soviet Union 27–8, 35
  weapons 191
employment insurance 43
Engel, Jeffrey 169
English, John 6, 81, 116–18, 121–2, 194–5
environmental protection 158–9,
  165–7, 267
acid rain 153–4, 165–7, 170
climate crisis 154, 224–5, 243–4, 267
  fisheries 182–6
  Kyoto Protocol 205–9, 216–17, 224–5
  ozone layer 154
  and oil shipping 137–40
  treaties with US 17–18
Errington, Jane 30–1
espionage 44, 225–6, 248, 257–8
Essex, Jamey 242
Ethiopia
  famine 151–2, 158–61, 169
  invasion of 1–3, 6, 35–6
Euler, William 35
Euromaidan 235–8

European Economic Community (EEC) 86
European Free Trade Association 226
European Union
  Brexit 243
  and China 259–60
  as trade partner 181, 226, 244–5
  and Turbot War 181, 183–4
  and Ukraine 235–6
Evans, Paul M. 150
Evatt, Herbert 57
Expo '67 111
External Aid Office 85, 129
extradition 248, 250–1, 257–8, 260

Fabre, Hector 17
fascism 28, 35–6; *see also* Second World War
Fairclough, Ellen 86–7
Farish, Matthew J. 79–80
Farmers
  and conscription 22
  as desired immigrants 45
Farrell, R. Barry 6–7
Favel, Blain 240
federalism 112, 114
  and jurisdiction 4–5, 143
  and Quebec nationalism 173–4
feminism 244–5
Feminist International Assistance Policy
  (FIAP) 245
Fenian Brotherhood 12–14
Ferdinand, Franz 21–2
Ferguson, Niall 147
Fergusson, James G. 219
Financial Transactions and Reports Analysis
  Centre of Canada (FINTRAC)
  199–200
Findley, Eric 198
First World War 21–5, 32–3
fishing
  agreements with US 26
  commercial fisheries 182–6
  illegal 181–6
  Inland Fisheries Treaty (1908) 17–18
  rights 13
Five Eyes intelligence alliance 211–12, 251, 270
flag 110
Flaherty, Jim 235–6
Flicker, Charles 148
Ford, Gerald 128–9
Ford, Robert 126
Foreign Investment Review Agency
  (FIRA) 128
Forum Africa 160–1

Foulkes, Charles 92–4
Fowler, Robert 179, 196–7
Fox, Vicente 204–5
France
  anti-landmine treaty 188
  Canada's relationship with 107, 112–13
  Canadian representation in 17, 42
  and China 259–60
  and Indochina 114–15
  decolonization 64
  educational agreements 113
  and NATO 107
  North American colonies 9–10
  and Quebec 112, 129–30
  Suez Crisis 65–7, 74–7
France-Quebec Permanent Commission on
    Cooperation 114
Francis, R. Douglas 32
Franco-Canadian Cultural Agreement 113–14
francophone culture 112
Francophonie 131–2, 154–5, 204, 269–70
free trade 36–7
  readings on 169–70
  with United States 20–1, 152–4, 158–9
Freedman, Lawrence 100–1
Freedom Convoy 249
Freeland, Chrystia
  as foreign minister 246–7, 253–6, 258
  foreign policy priorities 8, 261–2
  as minister of international trade 244–5,
    252
  and NAFTA 255–6, 258
Freeman, Linda 102–3
Frolic, B. Michael 150
Front de Libération de Québec (FLQ) 132
Frum, David 262
Fry, Michael G. 56, 80–1
functional principle 39–42
fur
  fur traders 9
  North Pacific Fur Seal Convention (1911)
    17–18
Fursenko, Aleksandr 100–1
future, Canada's 267–71

G-20 202
Gadhafi, Muammar 222
Galt, Alexander 16–17
Garratt, Julia 257–8
Garratt, Kevin 257–8
Gaucher, Megan 265–6
Gavin, Francis J. 100–1, 120, 262
Geddes, John 263–4

Gelber, Lionel 43
Gellner, John 147
Gender-Based Analysis Plus (GBA+) 268
Gendron, Robin S. 82, 121
General Agreement on Tariffs and Trade
    (GATT) 145, 163
General Dynamics Land Systems Canada 252
General, Levi 25
Geneva Accords 64
Geneva Convention on Refugees 130
Gentile, Patrizia 82
geography of Canada 4
George III, King 10
Georgia 235–6
Gerges, Fawaz 239–40
Gérin-Lajoie, Paul 113
Gerö, Ernö 75
Gerstle, Gary 194
Getachew, Adom 100–1, 120
Ghana 59–60, 95–7
Ghent-Mallet, Jocelyn 105
Giauque, Jeffrey Glen 100–1, 120
Gilmour, Julie 32
Gladman, Brad 101–2, 105
Glassford, Sarah 32–3
Glazebrook, G.P. de T. 6–7
Global Affairs Canada (GAC) 243–4, 269
Global South
  aid 67–9, 85, 129–30
  Canada's role 129–30
  communism 126–7
  human rights 77
  immigration 106
globalization, readings on 147, 194
gold rush 15–16
Goldberg, David H. 148
Goldenberg, Eddie 208–9, 217
Goldgeier, James 194
Gonzalez, Enrique Davila 185–6
Gorbachev, Mikhail 155–6
Gordon, Walter 108
Gotlieb, Allan 133–4, 151–3, 163, 165–7,
    201
  memoirs 170
Gough, Adam 194
Gouzenko, Igor 44
governor general, role of 65–7
Graham, Bill 200–1, 203–4, 210, 214–15
  memoirs 217, 219
Granatstein, J.L. 6–7, 32–4, 54–8,
    147, 182–3
Grant, George 108
Grant, Ulysses S. 20–1

332 INDEX

Gray, Herb 128
Great Depression 27, 42–3, 267
Great Recession 239–40
Great War, *see* First World War
Greaves, Wilfrid 239–40
Greece 42
Green, Howard 65–7, 85, 88–9
Grey & Ripon, Earl de 14
Grey, Lord 21
Griffiths, Franklyn 147–8
Grod, Paul 235–6
Grzyb, Amanda 55–6
Guajardo, Ildefonso 256
Guaranteed Income Supplement 106
Guisso, Rick 82
Gulf War 156–7, 159, 170–1
Gulrajani, Nilima 242
Gutterman, Ellen 254, 262–3

Haiti 177, 203–4
Halloran, Mary 6–7
Halucha, Paul 206–7
Hampson, Fen Osler 6–7, 170, 263–4
Hannaford, John 262–3
Hanusch, Frederic 216–17
Harley, Janice L. 242
Harper, Stephen
  2015 election 227–8
  Afghanistan 221–3
  Arctic sovereignty 224
  Canadian Alliance 201, 208
  China 225–6
  Department of Foreign Affairs, Trade, and
    Development 241–2
  climate change 224–5
  and George W. Bush 226–7
  Keystone pipeline 227
  Muskoka Initiative on Maternal, Newborn,
    and Child Health 228, 232–5
  NAFTA 246–7
  as prime minister 220–1, 223, 238–9,
    243, 270–1
  readings on 240
  Ukraine 237–8
  UNDRIP 231
Harris, Michael 182–3
Harrison, Kathryn 207, 216–17
Hart, Michael 33–4, 169–70
Harvey, David 169
Haudenosaunee 25
Haussman, Melissa 240–1
Hawthorn, Harry B. 130–1
Hayashi-Lemieux Agreement 19–20

Hayes, Frank 102–3
Hayes, Geoffrey 32–3
Head, Ivan 126, 136–7, 147–8
healthcare, national insurance
  program 106
Heeney, A.D.P. 81, 87–8
Heidt, Daniel 31
Heinbecker, Paul 181, 195, 211
Henault, Ray 213
Hennessy, Michael A. 80–1
Henshaw, Peter 102–3
Herd, Alexander W.G. 79–80
Heyman, Bruce 227, 244
Hill, O. Mary 33–4
Hillier, Rick 212–15
Hilliker, John 6–7, 33–4, 57–8
Hillmer, Norman 6–7, 33–4, 54–5, 80–1,
  121–2, 182–3
Hinshaw, Drew 263–4
Hiroshima 41–2
Hitchcock, William 100–1
Hitler, Adolf 28, 35–8
HIV/AIDS crisis 198, 203
hockey, summit series 126
Hoekstra, Quint 196–7
Hofmann, Stephanie 265–6
Holbrooke, Richard 191
Holmes, John 2, 5, 57–8, 78, 83, 93–4
homosexuality, decriminalization 124;
  see also LGBTQ+
Honduras 226
hostage diplomacy 257–61
Howard, John 231
Howard, Richard 121
Howe, Brendan 194
Howe, C.D. 49–50, 56
Huawei 248, 250–1, 258–60
Hudson's Bay Company, Rupert's Land 10, 15
Hughes, Billy 23
Hull, Cordell 49
human rights
  in Canada 130–1, 230–1, 250
  China 175, 178, 225–6, 239, 248
  Colombo Plan 65, 68–71, 78–9
  Global South 129–30
  as political priority 178–9, 191, 220
  readings on 147
  Saudi Arabia 252–4
  South Africa 86–7, 94–7, 155
  and trade partners 176, 193
  Universal Declaration of Human Rights
    (UDHR) 60
  women's rights 245

Humble Oil 138–40
Humphrey, John 60
Hungary 67–8, 74–7, 80–1, 181
Hunt, Jonathan 169
Hussein, Saddam 156–7, 170, 200–1, 209
Hutchins, Aaron 263–4
Hyam, Ronald 102–3
Hyde Park Declaration 39, 48–50, 56
Hydro-Québec 107

Iarocci, Andrew 32–3
identity, Canadian 23–5, 32
Ignatieff, George 59, 81
Ignatieff, Michael 194
immigration 4
  British Columbia 4–5
  incentives for 18
  "irregular" 264–5
  and multiculturalism 235–8
  points system 106
  race 4–5, 18–19, 60, 95, 106
  readings on 32, 55–6
  restrictions 18–19
  in United States 250
  see also refugees
Imperial War Cabinet 22–3
India
  Cold War 76
  decolonization 64
  immigration 18–19
  and Korean War 61–2
  nuclear program 64–5
  role in Commonwealth 64–5, 75, 97
  Second World War 68–9
  and Suez crisis 76
  as trade partner 128–9
Indian Act 15, 60, 131
Indian and Northern Affairs Canada
  (INAC) 229–30
Indigenous peoples 4
  activism 130–1
  as British allies 11
  Canadian policy 130–1
  and DEW line 73–4
  diplomacy 9
  displacement of 15
  and early settlers 9–10
  governance 267
  Indian Act 15, 60, 131
  and Justin Trudeau 245–6
  land claims 10
  military service 23–5, 43
  Oka Crisis 157

and patriation of the constitution 132
readings on 31–2, 240
reservations 10
rights 86–7
sovereignty 10
treaty system 10, 15
Truth and Reconcilliation Commission 231
United Nations Declaration on the Rights of
  Indigenous Peoples (UNDRIP)
  228–32, 240
and US border 15–16
veterans 43
voting rights 60, 95
Indochina, decolonization 64, 114–15
Indonesia 59–60, 64–5
Inglis, Alex I. 33–4, 78–9
Inland Fisheries Treaty (1908) 17–18
Institute of Economic and International
  Relations 29
Intelligence Assessment Secretariat (IAS) 209
Intergovernmental Panel on Climate Change
  (IPCC) 206–8
International Bank for Reconstruction and
  Development 59–60
International Civil Aviation Organization 59–60
International Commission for Supervision
  and Control
  Indochina 64
  Vietnam 59–60, 114–15
International Committee of the Red Cross
  (ICRC) 186–7
International Convention for the Prevention of
  Pollution of the Seas by Oil 138
International Court of Justice 59–60, 134
International Criminal Court 179
International Crisis Group 259
International Energy Agency 145
International Labour Organization 23
International Monetary Fund 59–60, 202
International Security Assistance Force 200
interwar period, readings on 33
Iran 133, 144, 200–1
Iraq 156–7, 159, 222–3
  elections 204–5
  invasion of Kuwait 156–7, 159, 170–1
  war in 200–2, 205, 209–12
Irish Republican Brotherhood 12–14
Isemann, James Louis 79–80
ISIS, see Islamic State of Iraq and the
  Levant (ISIL)
Islamic State of Iraq and the Levant (ISIL) 222,
  239–40, 252
Ismael, Tarek Y. 148

334 INDEX

Israel 140, 225
Canadian mission in 59–60, 133–4, 140–3
embassy 148
Six-Day War 109–10, 140
Suez Crisis 65–7, 74–7
as trade partner 226
Italy
in Afghanistan 213
fascism 28, 35
invasion of Abyssinia 1–3, 35–6

Jackson, Ben 169
James, Patrick 7–8
Jamieson, Brandon 7–8
Jansen, Jan C. 78
Japan
attack on Pearl Harbor 39
immigration 19–20
invasion of Manchuria 28, 36
and Kyoto Protocol 206
as trade partner 19, 85–6, 128
Japanese Canadians 19–20
Jay's Treaty (1794–5) 11
Jean, Daniel 262–3
Jellinek, Mike 198
Jennings, Peter 185
Jervis, Robert 262
Jintao, Hu 225–6
Jockel, Joseph 79–80, 101–2, 215
Johnson, Lyndon B. 109–10, 115–18
Johnston-White, Iain 54–5
Jordan 140, 226
Juneau, Thomas 254, 262–3
Jurisdiction, provincial vs federal 4–5, 143

Kaldor, Mary 194
Kanesatake Resistance 157
Kealey, Greg 120–1
Keating, Tom 6–7
Keelan, Geoff 32–3
Kelleher, Jim 162
Kelley, Ninette 32, 55–6
Kelly, Brendan 118–19, 121–2
Kennedy, John F. 89, 99, 103–4
Kenney, Jason 223
Keqiang, Li 248
Kerby, Matthew 194
Keystone XL pipeline 227, 244
Khashoggi, Jamal 253
Kikkert, Peter 147–8
Kikwete, Jakaya 234
Kilbourn, William 56, 81
Kimball, Warren F. 54

Ki-moon, Ban 234
King, William Lyon Mackenzie
and American trade 36–7
and communist threat 27–8
departure from politics 53–4
election of 1
Ethiopian crisis 1–3, 35–6
foreign policy 2
and the Hyde Park Declaration 48–50
and Jewish refugees 45–8
North Atlantic Treaty 50–3
readings on 54–6
relationship with Franklin Roosevelt 50
resistance to British imperialism 26
response to Japanese invasion of China 36
response to Nazism 28, 36–7
and Second World War 38–42
and social welfare 43
Kinsman, Gary 82
Kirkwood, Kenneth P. 81
Kirton, John 6–7, 105, 147–8, 172, 240–1
Klein, L. Ruth 55–6
Klondike gold rush 15–16
Knowles, Valerie 55–6
Koops, Joachim 194
Kordan, Bohdan S. 241
Korea 200–1, 226
Korean War 60–4, 82
Kosovo 181–2, 189–93, 195
Kosovo Liberation Army (KLA) 190–1
Kosygin, Alexei 126
Kovrig, Michael 257–61
Krikorian, Jacqueline 31
Kristallnacht 46
Krozewski, Gerold 78–9
Kulik, Julia 240–1
Kunz, Diane 100–1, 120
Kushner, Jared 257
Kuwait 156–7, 159, 170–1
Kyoto Protocol 205–9
Canada's withdrawal 224–5
readings on 216–17

Labrosse, Diane 262
Lackenbauer, P. Whitney 79–80, 147–9,
239–40
Lacombe, Sylvie 32
Laczko, Leslie 80–1
Lajeunesse, Adam 79–80, 147–8
Lalonde, Marc 144, 148–9
Landmine Monitor 188–9
landmines 182, 186–9
Lane, Andrea 7–8, 254, 262–3

INDEX 335

Lang, Eugene 217, 219, 263–4
Languages
  bilingualism 107, 131–2, 269
  diversity in Canada 4
Lapierre, Jean 199
Lapointe, Ernest 1–2, 47
Laporte, Pierre 132
Latin America, relations with 82–3, *see also* Global South
Laurier, Wilfrid
  1911 election campaign 20
  and Alaska claim 16
  and Department of External Affairs 18
  First World War 22
  National Policy 21
Lawrence, Mark Atwood 120
Lawson, Robert J. 194–5
Leacock, Stephen 37
League for Social Reconstruction 29
League of Nations 1, 29
  creation of 23, 26
  and Indigenous nations 25
  and Japanese invasion of Manchuria 28
  response to Italian invasion of Abyssinia 1–3, 35–6
Lebanon 59–60
LeBlanc, Romeo 165
Lee, David 57–8
Leffler, Melvyn P. 54
Léger, Jules 93–4
Lemieux, Rodolphe 19–20
Lenarcic, David A. 80–1
Lend-Lease Act 48–9
LePan, Douglas 70
Lesage, Jean 107, 112
Lévesque, René 132
Lewis, Drew 166
Lewis, Stephen 151–2, 160–1
Leyton-Brown, David 148–9
LGBTQ+
  decriminalization of homosexuality 124
  discrimination in civil service 63
  rights 224–5
Liberal Party of Canada 77, 84–5, 89–91, 108, 111, 164, 243
Libya 222
Lightfoot, Sheryl 229, 232, 240
Lighthizer, Robert 256, 263
Ling, Philip 265–6
Litt, Paul 169–70
Litvak, Isaiah 123
Lloyd George, David 22–4
Lodge, Henry Cabot 16

Logevall, Fredrik 120
Lopes, Rui Junqueira 194
López Obrador, Andrés Manuel 256
Lougheed, Peter 144, 162
Louis, William Roger 80–1
Louw, Eric 96
Lovelace, Sandra 131
Lower Canada rebellion 12
Lum, Janet 150
lumber 204–5, 226–7, 244, 255
Ly, Nathan T.B. 265–6
Lynch, Cecelia 33
Lyon, Peyton V. 82

MacArthur, Douglas 62
MacCallum, Elizabeth 42, 59–60
MacDonald, David 160–1
Macdonald, Donald 162
Macdonald, Douglas 216–17
MacDonald, Flora 133, 142
Macdonald, John A. 13–21
Macdonald, Laura 263
MacEachen, Allan 152–3
Macedonia 191
MacFarlane, John 6, 33–4
MacGuigan, Marc 148–9
MacIsaac, Sam 241
MacKay, R.A. 6–7
Mackenzie, Alexander 20–1
MacKenzie, David 31–3
Mackenzie, Hector 57–8, 78
Mackenzie-Papineau Brigade 35
MacLaren, Roy 6, 54–5, 174
Macmillan, Harold 86, 95–6
Macmillan, Tom 167
Macphail, Agnes 29
Macpherson, Duncan 117, 125
Macpherson, Marion 59–60
magazines 111, 122, 177–8
Maisel, Sandy 7–8
Malaya 95–7
Malaysia 59–60
Mali 245–6
Malkasian, Carter 239–40
Maloney, Sean 103
Manhattan Project 41–2
Manion, R.J. 46–7
Manitoba, founding of 15
Manley, John 199–202, 221
Manson, Rian 78–9
Manuel, George 131, 229–30
Manulak, Daniel 102–3
Manulak, Michael 191–2, 195

336 INDEX

Marcuse, Gary 82
Mariam, Mengistu Haile 159
Markusoff, Jason 263–4
Marples, David R. 241
Martel, Marcel 31
Martin, Ged 13
Martin, Paul
  Afghanistan 212–15
  and ballistic missile defence (BMD) 218
  as finance minister 173
  as prime minister 202–5, 215
  memoirs 219
Martin, Paul (Sr) 109, 113–14, 116, 121
Massey Commission 122
Massie, Justin 54–5
maternal health 240–1
  Muskoka Initiative on Maternal, Newborn,
    and Child Health 224–5, 228,
    232–5
Matthew, Richard A. 194–5
Matthews, Kyle 195
Maule, Christopher 123
May, Elizabeth 216–17
McCallum, John 259
McCullough, Colin 80–1
McDonald, Bryan 194–5
McGee, David 78–9
McGill Fence 72–3
McGrath, James 170, 172
McKay, Ian 32–3
McKenna, Catherine 243–4
McKenna, Peter 83
McKenzie, Francine 56
McKercher, Asa 6–8, 80–1, 102–3, 105,
    120–1
McKercher, B.J.C. 54–5, 80–1
McLin, Jon B. 101–2
McMahon, Patricia I. 101–2, 105
McMahon, Robert J. 78, 120
McMurtry, Roy 151–2
McNee, John 230–1
Meagher, Margaret 59–60
Meaney, Neville 57–8
Meng Wanzhou 248, 250–1, 258–61
Métis 15
Mexico
  Canadian mission in 42
  NAFTA 250, 254–7
  Security and Prosperity Partnership
    (SPP) 226–7
  as trade partner 204–5
  visa requirements 244
Mid-Canada Line 72–3

Middlemiss, Danford W. 217
middle power 74–7
Migratory Bird Treaty (1916) 17–18
Miles, Simon 168–9
Miliband, David 234
military service
  conscription 4–5, 22
  Indigenous peoples 23–5, 43
  volunteer-based 21–5
  and race 23–5
Millennium Development Goals
    (MDGs) 232–3
Miller, J.R. 31–2
Milloy, John C. 56
Milloy, John S. 31–2
Mills, Frederick V. 241
Mills, Lisa 240–1
Mills, Sean 7–8
Milnes, Arthur 170, 172
Milošević, Slobodan 190–2
Miscamble, Wilson D. 54
Mollers, Nina 78–9
Molot, Maureen Appel 170
Montreal Protocol on Substances that Deplete
    the Ozone Layer 154
Montreal Women's Anti-Reciprocity League 21
Moore, Christopher 31
Morgan, Marta 262–3
Morgenthau, Henry, Jr. 49
Morin, Claude 121
Morrow, Adrian 263
Moscow Olympics 133
Moyn, Samuel 147, 216
MS St Louis 45–8, 55–6
Mulcair, Thomas 252
Müller, Tanja R. 169
Mullins, Robin Long 55–6
Mulroney, Brian
  and apartheid 155
  environmental protection 154, 158–9
  Ethiopian famine 158–61
  free trade 161–5
  and Gorbachev 155–6
  Iraq-Kuwait conflict 170–1
  memoirs 170, 172
  multilateralism 154–5
  Oka Crisis 157
  as prime minister 151–2, 158–68
  recession 157–8
  and Ronald Reagan 152–4, 163
  view on foreign service 220
Mulroney, David 225–6, 263–4
Mulroney, Mila 153

INDEX 337

Munro, John A. 78–9
Munton, Don 6–7, 105, 147–8, 167, 170
Murphy, Charles 18
Murphy, Peter 163
Murphy, Tim 205
Murray, David R. 56
Murray, Lowell 142
Muskoka Initiative on Maternal, Newborn, and
    Child Health 224–5, 228, 232–5
Mussolini, Benito 1, 10
mutually assured destruction (MAD) 72–3

Naftali, Timothy 100–1
Nagasaki 41–2
Nagy, Imre 75
Namibia 156
Namikas, Lise 100–1
Napolitano, Janet 226–7
Nasser, Gamal Abdel 74–5
National Climate Change Secretariat 207–8
National Energy Program (NEP) 133–4, 143–6,
    148–9, 151
National Policy 20–1
National Resources Mobilization Act 38
National Union for the Total Independence of
    Angola (UNITA) 196
national unity 10, 48, 106–7, 112, 268
National Unity Party of Canada (NUP) 35
nationalism
    Canadian 23–5, 108–9
    Quebec 107, 111–14, 129–32, 173–4
Nazism 10, 37, 46
Nehru, Jawaharlal 76, 97
Nelles, Wayne 195
Netherlands 25, 42, 259–60
New Brunswick 154–5
New France 9–10
New Zealand
    Canadian high commission 42
    Five Eyes intelligence alliance 270
    Kyoto Protocol 206
    UNDRIP 229–32
    and United Nations 57
Newfoundland 64, 183, 267
Newman, Peter C. 101, 106
Nexen Energy 225–6
Nguyen, Lien-Hang T. 120
Nigeria 95–7, 129–30
Nikolko, Milana 241
Nixon, Richard 127–8
Nobel Peace Prize 67–8, 85, 188
non-governmental organizations (NGOs)
    29, 179

Norman, E. Herbert 63, 82
Norman, Herbert 94
Norstad, Lauris 99
North American Aerospace Defence Command
    (NORAD) 87–8, 91–4, 198, 269–70
    Cuban Missile Crisis 103–4
    readings on 101–2
North American Free Trade Agreement
    (NAFTA) 154–5, 165, 174–6, 246–7,
    250, 254–7
    readings on 263
North Atlantic Treaty Organization (NATO)
    50–3, 108
    and Afghanistan 221
    Canada's role 135–7, 156, 269–70
    creation of 44
    establishment of 2
    in Kosovo 189–93
    and Libya 222
    readings on 56
North Atlantic Triangle 36–7, 48–50
North Korea 200–1
North Pacific Fur Seal Convention (1911) 17–18
North Warning System 73–4
North, see Arctic
Northcote, Sir Stafford 14
Northwest Atlantic Fisheries Organization
    (NAFO) 183
Northwest Passage 127–8, 134, 137–40, 154
Norton, Joseph 157
Norway 42
Nossal, Kim Richard 6–7, 172, 181
nuclear disarmament 90
nuclear technology 64–5
nuclear weapons 41–2, 90, 97–100
    anti-nuclear activism 88–9
    Cuban missile crisis 89, 91, 99, 103–4
    fear of attack 63
    India 64–5
    readings on 103
    Soviet 63, 71
numbered treaties 15
Nunavut 267
Nuremburg Laws 45
Nuttall, Mark 239–40
Nye, Joseph 179

O'Leary Commission 122
Oakman, Daniel 78–9
Obama, Barack 227, 244
Obwandiyag (Pontiac) 10
October Crisis 132
Office of Religious Freedom 221

338 INDEX

Official Languages Act 131–2
Ogdensburg Agreement 39–40
oil 134, 137–40
  National Energy Program 133–4, 143–6, 148–9, 151
  pipelines 39, 67, 140, 143, 227, 238–9, 244
Oka Crisis 157
Olympics
  Beijing 225
  Moscow 35, 133
Operation Apollo 200
Operation Athena 200
Operation Enduring Freedom 200, 212–13
Oregon Treaty (1846) 11–12
Organisation for Economic Co-operation and Development 145
Organization of American States (OAS) 67–8, 82–3, 89, 154–5
Organization of Petroleum Exporting Countries (OPEC) 143
Osterhammel, Jürgen 78, 194
Ottawa Process 187–9
Ouellet, André 176, 187
Owen, Roger 80–1
ozone layer 154

Pakistan 59–60, 64–5
Palestine 64
  Palestinian Liberation Organization 141
Panama 226
Panetta, Alexander 265–6
Paquet, Mireille 265–6
Paquin, Stéphane 6–7, 121
Paris Peace Conference (1919) 23
Parkinson, Joe 263–4
Parti Québécois (PQ) 132, 173–4
patriation of the constitution 132
peace movement 109–10
peacekeeping 77, 109–10, 156–7, 180–1, 245–6
Pearkes, George 92–3
Pearl Harbor 39
Pearson, Lester B.
  and decolonization 64
  as DEA undersecretary 44
  election of 89
  on foreign aid 65
  as foreign minister 66
  foreign policy statements 8
  Korean War 61–2
  memoirs 6, 78–9, 121–2
  NATO 50–2
  Nobel Peace Prize 67–8, 85

NORAD 93
  nuclear weapons 99–100
  on O'Leary Commission 123
  P.E. Trudeau's view on 124
  as prime minister 106, 119–20
  and Quebec nationalism 107, 111–14
  readings on 120–2
  and relation with Britain 110–11
  Second World War 2
  as secretary of state for external affairs 59, 69
  Suez Crisis 65–7, 74–7
  United Nations 74
  Vietnam War 114–19
Pedersen, Susan 33
Pederson, Jennifer 262–3
Peña Nieto, Enrique 255–7
Pennington, Christopher 31
People's Republic of China (PRC), see China
Peoples' Summit 176
Permanent Joint Board on Defence 39–40
Perras, Galen Roger 54–6, 80–1, 120–1
Peru 42, 226
Petersson, Niels P. 194
Petro-Canada 128, 143–4, 151
Pharand, Donat 83
Phillips, Norman 96
Physicians for Human Rights 187
Pickersgill, J.W. 56
Pickles, Katie 32
Pinetree Line 71, 73
pipelines 39, 143
  Keystone XL 227, 238–9, 244
  Trans-Alaska 140
  TransCanada 67
Pires, André Estrela 194
Poland 38, 44, 181
political cartoons 3, 24, 40, 66, 90, 117, 251
Pontiac (Obwandiyag) 10
Pope, Maurice 41–2, 81
Pope, Sir Joseph 16, 19–20
populism 28, 100, 173, 249, 267
Poroshenko, Petro 237–8
Powell, Colin 210–11
Power, Samantha 194
Prague Spring 126
Prashad, Vijay 78, 100–1, 120
Pratt, David 218
Prentice, Jim 230
Price, John 82
Prince, Robert 82
Privy Council Office 269
Pro Canada Network (PCN) 164

Progressive Conservative Party 84–5, 95, 101,
    151, 157–8, 160, 173
  merger with Canadian Alliance 202–3
protectionism 20–1, 27, 152, 162–3, 255–6
Proudfoot, Shannon 263–4
provincial jurisdiction 4–5, 143
Public Safety Canada 268–9
publishers 122
Pullen, T.C. 138–9
Putin, Vladimir 223, 238

Quadrant Conference (1943) 41
Quebec
  and conscription 4–5
  Francophonie 154–5
  nationalism 107, 111–14, 129–32, 173–4
  Quebec Act (1774) 10–11
  Quiet Revolution 107, 112, 119
  readings on 121
  and refugees 46–7
  representation abroad 17
Quiet Revolution 107, 112, 119

race
  anti-Asian violence 19–20
  anti-semitism 46–8
  and immigration 4–5, 18–19, 60, 95, 106
  and imperialism 87
  and military service 23–5
  South African apartheid 86–7, 91, 94–7,
    155
railroad 18–19
Rasmussen, Kathleen Britt 56
Readers Digest 122
Reagan, Nancy 153
Reagan, Ronald 133–4, 151
  and acid rain 166
  and Brian Mulroney 152–4, 163
  and Gorbachev 155–6
  readings on 169
  relationship with Canada 145
rebellion, 1837–8 12
Recaj, Krenare 195
recession 146, 157–8, 181, 225–6
Reciprocity Treaty (1854) 12, 20–1
Reford, Robert 105
Reform Party 157–8, 168, 173
refugees 133, 245–6, 264–5
  Cambodia 133
  climate 267
  Geneva Convention 130
  Jewish 35, 45–8
  Kosovar-Albanian 192

Palestinian 225
  Quebec 46–7
  Syrian 228, 243–4
Regina Manifesto 28
Rehaag, Sean 265–6
Reid, Anna 239–40
Reid, Escott 56–8, 76–7, 80–1
  and NATO 50–3
  memoirs 81
Reid, John G. 30–1
Reisman, Simon 163
religion 10
reproductive rights 106, 124, 234, 245
residential schools 31–2, 130–1
Ressam, Ahmed 199
Reynolds, David 54
Rhineland, invasion of 10
Rich, Nathaniel 216
Richter, Andrew 103
Riddell, Walter Alexander 1, 3, 6
Rideau Canal 12
Riel, Louis 15
Rio Convention on Climate Change 154
Ritchie, Charles 81, 89, 97, 119
Ritchie, Gordon 169–70
Robertson, Colin 169–70, 263
Robertson, Norman 43–4, 51–4, 87, 135–6
Robinson, H. Basil 93, 101–2
Rock, Allan 260, 263–4
Rogers, E.B. 6–7
Roi, M.L. 217
Romania 44
Romanow, Roy 164
Romero, Monica 265–6
Ronning, Chester 62
Roosevelt, Franklin
  European refugee crisis 46
  free trade 36–7
  Hyde Park Declaration 49–50
  readings on 54
  relationship with Mackenzie King 50
  Second World War 39, 41
  trade policy 37
Roosevelt, Theodore 16
Root, Elihu 16
Ross, Douglas A. 121–2
Rossinow, Doug 169
Roussel, Stéphane 6–7, 57–8, 81, 121
Rovner, Joshua 262
Rowell, Newton 26
Roy, Patricia 32
Royal Canadian Mounted Police (RCMP)
    199–200, 259

340 INDEX

Royal Commission on Aboriginal Peoples 157
Royal Commission on Bilingualism and
    Biculturalism 107
Royal Commission on Canada's Economic
    Prospects 108
Royal Commission on National Development
    in the Arts, Letters and Sciences 122
Royal Commission on Publications 122
Royal Commission on the Status of
    Women 106
Royal Proclamation of 1763 10
Rudner, Martin 172
Rupert's Land 10, 15
Rush-Bagot Treaty (1817) 11–12
Russell, Doug 216–17
Russell, Ruth B. 57–8
Russia
    and Crimea 228, 236–7
    conflict with 248–9
    and G7 247–9
    and Georgia 235–6
    and Kosovo 191–2
    and Ukraine 235–8, 248–9, 267
    UNDRIP 230
    readings on 239–40
    see also Union of Soviet Socialist
      Republics (USSR)
Rutherford, Kenneth R. 194–5
Rutherford, Scott 7–8
Rwanda 180

Safe Third Country Agreement 250, 264–5
Saideman, Stephen 213–14
same-sex marriage 202–3
Sargent, Daniel J. 147
Sarotte, M.E. 194
Sarotte, Mary 168–9
Saudi Arabia 239, 250–4, 262–3
Saunders, Robert 169
Save the Children 233
Sayle, Timothy Andrews 56, 217
Schellenberg, Robert 259
Schertzer, Robert 265–6
Schultz, George 152–3
Schwartz, Thomas Alan 120
Scott, F.R. 6–7
Seade, Jesús 256
seals, North Pacific Fur Seal Convention
    (1911) 17–18
Second World War 2, 35, 38–9
    economic impact 48–50
    humanitarian crisis 45–8
    impact on Canadian identity 53–4

readings on 54–6
rebuilding liberated countries 68
Security and Prosperity Partnership (SPP)
    226–7
September 11 terrorist attacks 198–200,
    212–13, 216
Serbia 190–2
Seven Years' War 9, 30–1
Seward, William 14–15
Shambaugh, David 262
Shamrock Summit 152–3, 163
Sharp, Mitchell 121, 128, 135–7, 139, 147, 150
Shaw, Amy 32–3
Shepard, R. Bruce 101
Sherman, Jake H. 196–7
shipping, Northwest Passage 127–8, 134,
    137–40, 154
Short, Nicola 194–5
Shubert, Adrian 31
Simpson, Jeffrey 140
Six Nations of Grand River Territory 25
Six-Day War 109–10, 140
Skelton, O.D. 1, 3, 6, 36–8
Skilling, H. Gordon 6–7
slavery 9, 12
Smillie, Ian 196–7
Smith, Craig Damian 265–6
Smith, Denis 101
Smith, Heather A. 216–17
Smith, Sidney 85
Smolynec, Gregory 217
Smuts, Jan 22–3
Snyder, Sarah 168–9
Social Credit Party 28
social welfare programs 43
softwood lumber 204–5, 226–7, 244, 255
Solomon, Nassisse 169
Somalia 156, 180
Sommaruga, Cornelio 187
Song, Janet 265–6
South Africa
    apartheid 86–7, 91, 94–7, 155
    Canadian high commission 42
    readings on 102–3
    role in Commonwealth 94–7
sovereignty
    Canadian 12–14, 16–18
    Indigenous nations 25
Spain 35, 181–6
Spavor, Michael 257–61
Special Task Force on Europe
    (STAFFEUR) 135–6
Spencer, Diana 188

split-run magazines 122, 177–8
Sponsorship Scandal 202–3
Springer, Allen 182–3
Sri Lanka, *see* Ceylon
SS Manhattan 127–8, 137–40
St Jean Baptiste Society 46
St Laurent, Louis
  Cold War 60–4
  DEW line 73–4
  as foreign minister 53
  foreign policy statements 8
  Korean War 60–4
  and NATO 44, 50–1
  as prime minister 52–4, 59–60
  resignation 77
St Lawrence Seaway 87–8
Stacey, C.P. 6–7, 33–4, 54–5
Stairs, Denis 82, 217
Stalin, Joseph 27–8, 39, 63–4
Standing Committee on External Affairs and
    National Defence (SCEAND) 135–6
Stanfield, Robert 142
Stanford, Joseph 141
Staples, Steven 219
steel and aluminium tariffs 247, 256–8
Stein, Janice Gross 217, 219
Stein, Judith 147
Steiner, Zara 33, 54
Stevenson, Michael D. 101–3
Stewart, Brian 159–60
Stewart, Gordon T. 33–4
Stoney, Christopher 240–1
Story, Donald C. 101
Strategic Defense Initiative 154
student loans 106
Stursberg, Peter 101
Sudan 203–4
Sudetenland 37
Suez Crisis 65–7, 74–7, 80–1
Suharto 176
Summers, Lawrence 202
Summit series 126
Supreme Court of Canada,
    establishment of 65–7
Suri, Jeremi 120
Swanson, Roger Frank 121–2
Swift, Jamie 32–3
Syria 199–200, 222–3, 228, 243–4

Tadasu, Hayashi 19–20
Taft, William Howard 21
Taiwan 61, 149
Takach, George Steven 148

Taliban 200, 213, 215, 245–6
Taras, David 148
tariffs 20–1, 27
  automotive 109, 247, 255–6
  steel and aluminium 247, 256–8
Tatar, Klavdia 241
taxes
  on advertising 177–8
  British 10
  Chinese Head Tax 18–19
  on foreign takeovers 108
  on oil and gas 144
Taylor, Alan 30–1
Taylor, Ken 133
Team Canada trade missions 174–5
Tecumseh 11
Teigrob, Robert 54–5, 78
Teillet, Jean 31–2
Tennyson, Brian Douglas 102–3
Tenterden, Lord 14
terrorism, September 11 attacks 198–200,
    212–13, 216
Thakur, Ramesh 217
Thant, U 109–10
Thatcher, Margaret 127, 151, 155–6, 169
Thomas, Gordon 55–6
Thompson, Andrew 80–1
Thomson, Dale C. 81, 121
Thordarson, Bruce 147
Thornton, Sir Edward 14
Tibet 130
Tiessen, Rebecca 240–1
Time Magazine 122
Tobin, Brian 182–6
Tomlin, Brian W. 6–7, 169–70, 194–5
Toner, Glen 148–9
Toope, Alexander 265–6
Tooze, Adam 239–40, 262
Toronto Eighteen 21
Touhey, Ryan 78–9, 82, 103
Trans-Alaska pipeline 140
Trans-Canada Airlines 112
TransCanada Pipeline 67
Trans-Pacific Partnership 247–8
Treaty of Brussels 51
Treaty of Ghent 11
Treaty of Paris (1763) 9
Treaty of Paris (1783) 11
Treaty of Versailles 23
Treaty of Washington 13–14
treaty system 10, 15
Trebilcock, Michael 32, 55–6
Tremblay, Paul 94

342 INDEX

Troper, Harold 55–6
Trudeau, Justin
  China 248, 251, 257–61
  and Donald Trump 246–8
  feminism 244–5
  on Indigenous peoples 245–6
  Israel 134
  Muskoka Initiative 235
  NAFTA 254–7
  as prime minister 243–4, 250, 261–2,
    270–1
  refugees 47–8, 264–5
  relationship with Obama 244
  Saudi Arabia 250–4
Trudeau, Pierre Elliott
  and China 149
  Israel 141
  National Energy Program 143–6
  and NATO 124, 126, 135–7
  Northwest Passage 137–40
  nuclear weapons 124
  as prime minister 124–6, 270
  and Quebec nationalism 131–2
  readings on 147
  Trudeaumania 124
  writings of 147–9
Trudgen, Matthew 79–80
Truman, Harry 52–3, 61–2
Trump, Donald J. 243, 245–9, 261
  immigration reform 264–5
  NAFTA 250, 255–7
  readings on 262
Truth and Reconciliation Commission 231
Tupper, Sir Charles 17
Turbot War 181–6, 194
Turner, John 151, 164

Uganda 130
Ukraine 155–6, 222–3, 235
Ukraine
  diaspora 235–8
  readings on 239–41
  and Russia 235–8, 248–9, 267
  as trade partner 226, 237–8
Ukrainian Canadian Congress
  (UCC) 228, 235–6
Understanding Canada program 221
unemployment 28, 43, 46–7, 162, 173
Union of Soviet Socialist Republics (USSR)
  Canada's relationship with 42, 63–4, 126
  collapse of 155–6
  communist threat 27–8
  embargo of 35

espionage 44
Hungarian Revolution 75
readings on 168–9
trade agreements 63–4
and United Nations 57
see also Cold War
United Kingdom
  anti-landmine treaty 188
  Brexit 243
  Canada's autonomy from 23, 26–7,
    29–30, 110–11
  Canadian relationship with 43, 110–11
  Canadian representation in 16–17
  and China 259–60
  decolonization 64
  economy 48, 68–9
  Five Eyes Intelligence alliance 270
  foreign aid programs 65
  North American colonies 9–10
  rule over Canada 10–11
  Second World War 38–9
  Suez Crisis 65–7, 74–7
  as trade partner 85–91
  and United Nations 57
  war loans 43, 48
United Nations (UN)
  Canada's participation 43–4, 57, 59–60, 68,
    74, 76, 156
  Children's Fund (UNICEF) 232–3
  and climate change 224–5
  Cold War 60–1
  Conference on International Organization
    (1945) 57
  Declaration on the Rights of Indigenous
    Peoples (UNDRIP) 225, 228–32, 240
  Emergency Force (UNEF) 109–10
  founding of 2, 43–4
  Human Rights Commission 131
  Hungarian Revolution 74–7
  and Iraq-Kuwait conflict 170–1
  Korean conflict 60–1
  and Kosovo 191
  membership 65
  Relief and Rehabilitation Administration 68
  sanctions against Angola 196
  Security Council 57, 196
  Suez Crisis 67–8
  Temporary Commission on Korea
    (UNTCOK) 60–1
  veto power 43–4, 57
United States 267
  and Arctic sovereignty 137–40
  as ally 4

Ballistic Missile Defense Program 218
border with 4, 11–12, 199, 226–7, 249
Canadian embassy in 42
and China 251, 259–60
Civil War 12–13
Coast Guard 154
Cold War 60–4
conflict with Canada 12
cultural domination 111
as defence partner 92–4
DEW line 67–8, 71–4, 79–80
economic reliance on 85–6
environmental issues 17–18, 165–7
Five Eyes intelligence alliance 270
foreign aid programs 65, 70–1
free trade 20–1, 152–4, 158–9, 161–5, 174–6
immigration 250
independence 11
influence on Canadian foreign policy 11–12
invasion of Iraq 209–12
in Iraq-Kuwait conflict 170
Korean War 60–4
and Kyoto Protocol 206
NAFTA 154–5, 165, 174–6, 246–7, 250, 254–7
NORAD 87–8, 91–4, 103–4, 198, 269–70
and Northwest Passage 127–8, 134, 137–40, 154
nuclear weapons 97–100
oil interests 143–6
purchase of Alaska 14–16
reducing dependence on 128–9
refugees 264–5
relationship with 61–4, 77, 87–91, 108, 152–4, 176–8, 201, 226–7, 246–8
revolution 11
Second World War 39
Security and Prosperity Partnership (SPP) 226–7
slavery 9
Suez Crisis 75
as trade partner 4, 109, 153, 162, 206–7
UNDRIP 229–32
and United Nations 57
Vietnam War 109–11, 114–19
Weather Bureau 71
Universal Declaration of Human Rights 60
Universal Family Allowances 43
Upper Canada rebellion 12

van Huizen, Philip 7–8
Vandenberg, Elly 240–1

Venezuela 143
Verheul, Steve 255
Verwoerd, Hendrik 96–7
veterans benefits 43
Vietnam
    American military presence 89
    International Commission for Supervision and Control 59–60
    refugees 133
    War 109–11, 114–22
Vietnam Veterans of America Foundation (VVAF) 187
Vimy Ridge 25, 32–3
Visigilio, Gerald R. 170
Viswanatha, Aruna 263–4
Voice of Women 88–9
von Riekhoff, Harald 172
Vormann, Boris 262
voting rights
    immigrants 22
    Indigenous peoples 60, 95
    soldiers 22
    women 22

Waite, P.B. 31, 33–4
Wang Chao 260
War Measures Act 132
War on Terror 200–1, 216
War Supplies Limited 49–50
Watanabe, Shoichi 78–9
Watchmen for the Nations 47–8
water security 268–9
Webster, David 78–9, 169
Webster-Ashburton Treaty (1842) 11–12
Weiers, Margaret 81
Weinman, Michael D. 262
Welch, David A. 105
Wells, Paul 263–4
Welsh, Jennifer 202
Weschler, Joanna 196–7
Wesley-Esquimaux, Cynthia 240
Westad, Odd Arne 54, 78, 100–1
Western Union 51
Wherry, Aaron 263, 265–6
Whitaker, Reg 82
Whitelaw, Diana M. 170
Whitlock, Craig 239–40
wildlife 17–18
Williams, Jody 187
Willis, Matthew 217
Wilson, James 168–9
Wilson, Michael 151, 162
Wilson, Woodrow 25

INDEX

Winegard, Timothy 32–3
Winks, Robin 30–1
Wiseman, Earl 194
Witts, Max Morgan 55–6
Wolfe, James 9
women
  feminist policies 244–5
  in foreign service 42, 59–60, 81, 181
  maternal health 224–5, 228, 232–5, 240–1
  in non-governmental organizations 29
  in peacekeeping 245–6
  Royal Commission on the Status of Women 106
  voting rights 22, 29
  in the workforce 42–3
Women's Commission for Refugee Women and Children 187
Women's International League for Peace and Freedom (WILPF) 29
Wonder, Edward 148–9
Wood, J.R.T. 102–3
Woodsworth, J.S. 36, 38
World Bank 202

World Council on Indigenous Peoples 229–30
World Economic Forum 198
World Health Organization 59–60, 262
World Trade Organization (WTO) 174, 255
World Vision 233
World War I, *see* First World War
World War II, *see* Second World War
Wright, David 212–13
Wright, Lawrence 216
Wrong, Hume 39–41, 51–3

Yanukovych, Viktor 236
Yemen 253
Yergin, Daniel 239–40
Yoo, Yong-Sik 82
Young, Judy 80–1
Young, Marilyn 120
Yugoslavia 156, 180, 190–1
Yukon 15–16
Yushchenko, Viktor 235–6

Zelizer, Julian E. 262
Zhengfei, Ren 258–9
Zubok, Vladislav 168–9